3,000 years of
HEBREW LITERATURE

3,000 years of

HEBREW LITERATURE

from the earliest time through the 20th century

by NATHANIEL KRAVITZ

THE **SWALLOW PRESS** INC.

CHICAGO

First Edition
First Printing

Published by
The Swallow Press Incorporated
1139 South Wabash Avenue
Chicago, Illinois 60605

This book is printed on recycled paper

ISBN 0-8040-0505-2
LIBRARY OF CONGRESS CATALOG CARD NUMBER 73-150752

To my beloved wife
Anna

our children
Maurice and Mona

and our grandchildren
Sheryl and Franie

Contents

Introduction   **xiii**
  Literature • History • Translations

I

1. **Early Biblical Poetry and Traditions**   **3**
     Early Poetry • Biblical Prose • Moses •
     From Moses to Amos

2. **The Prophetic Age**   **21**
     The Prophets • The Two Kingdoms • Amos • Hosea •
     Isaiah • Micah • Jeremiah • Book of the Law •
     Babylonia • Ezekiel • Isaiah II • Other Prophets

3. **Poetic Works**   **66**
     Hebrew Poetry • The Psalms • Job • Song of Songs •
     Proverbs • Ecclesiastes

4. **Historical Works**   **84**
     Folklore and History • Twelve Books • Sample Stories

5. **The Second Commonwealth**   **94**
     From Bible to Talmud • The Chain of Tradition •
     Various Sects • The Dead Sea Scrolls • Apocrypha,
     Pseudepigrapha, Apocalypse, Apology • Ecclesiasticus •
     The Septuagint • Philo Judaeus • Flavius Josephus

II

6. The Talmudic Period 143

Torah and Talmud • Rome and the Jews • Two
Talmuds • The Talmud • Sample Mishnah Verdict •
Sample Talmudic Argumentation • Sample Mishnah
with Dual Solution • Talmudic Teachings on God,
Man, and the World • Talmudic and Midrashic
Proverbs and Parables • Sayings of the Fathers •
Short Life Stories of Sages • Personal Prayers by
Talmudic Sages • The Title "Rabbi"

7. The Geonic Period 189

Babylonia and the Jews • Responsa Literature •
Sample Responsa • Geonim • Early Liturgical
Poetry • Karaites • Saadia ben Joseph • Esoteric,
Mystical, and Fantastic Works • Sefer Yetzirah •
Hekalot Rabbati • Shi'ur Komah • Other Mystical
Books • The Book of Yosippon • Eldad Ha-Dani •
The River Sambation • Land of the Chazars •
Vocalization and Accentuation

III

8. The Golden Age 231

From Babylonia to Spain • Renaissance Beginnings •
Samuel ibn Nagdela • Isaac Alfasi • Solomon ibn
Gabirol • Bahaya ben Joseph ibn Pakuda • Moses
ibn Ezra • Judah ben Samuel Halevi • Abraham
ben Meir ibn Ezra • Joseph ben Jacob ibn Zaddik •
Abraham Bar Hiyya Hanasi • Abraham ibn Daud
Halevi • Moses ben Maimon (Maimonides) • Judah
al-Harizi • Parables, Fables, Humor • The Tibbon
and Kimhi Families • Moses ben Nahman • Solomon
ben Abraham Adret • Isaac Albalag • Immanuel
ben Solomon • Levi ben Gershon • Hasdai Crescas •
Joseph Albo • Don Isaac Abravanel • Abraham
ben Samuel Zacuto

9. The Franco-German Lands 309

Age of Darkness • Gershom ben Judah • Solomon
ben Isaac (Rashi) • Jacob ben Meir Tam • Abraham
ben David • Tosafists • Joseph ben Isaac Bekor
Shor • Judah ben Samuel Ha-Hasid • Eleazar ben

Judah ben Kalonymus • Moses ben Jacob • Meir
ben Baruch • Asher ben Jehiel • Behya ben
Asher • Jedaiah ben Abraham Bedersi

10. Cabala   **340**

What Is Cabala? • Sefer Ha-Bahir • Abraham ben
Solomon Abulafia • Moses de Leon • Sefer Zohar •
Cabala Center at Safed • David Re'ubeni and
Solomon Molko • Joseph Caro • Moses Alshech •
Solomon Alkabiz • Moses Cordovero • Isaac Luria
Ashkenazi • Hayyim Vital Calabrese • Israel ben
Moses Najara

11. Liturgical Poetry   **369**

IV

12. Period of Transition   **389**

Questions and Reevaluations • Obadiah Bertinoro •
Obadiah Sforno • Elija Levita • Azariah ben
Moses dei Rossi • Leon de Modena • Joseph
Solomon Delmedigo • Deborah Ascarelli • Sarah
Copia Sullam • Uriel da Costa • Manasseh ben
Israel • Baruch Spinoza • David ben Solomon Gans •
Judah Löw ben Bezalel • Moses Germanus • Glueckel
of Hameln • Israel Baal Shem Tov • Elijah ben
Solomon • Shneor Zalman of Liady

13. Enlightenment and Emancipation   **425**

From Darkness Into Light • Haskala • Modern
Hebrew Literature • Moses Hayyim Luzzatto •
Moses Mendelssohn • Naphtali Hirz Wessely •
Solomon Maimon • Manasseh ben Joseph of Ilye •
Nahman Krochmal • Isaac Baer Levinsohn • Abraham
Lebensohn • Isaac Erter • Joseph Perl • Solomon
Ludwig Steinheim • Rahel Luzzatto Morpurgo •
Solomon Rapoport • Leopold Zunz • Heinrich
Heine • Samuel David Luzzatto • Meir Halevi
Letteris • Simhah Pinsker • Abraham Mapu •
Abraham Geiger • Samson Rephael Hirsch •
Hayyim Selig Slonimski • Abraham Baer Gottlober •
Kalman Schulman • Micah Joseph Lebensohn •
Leon Gordon • Christian David Ginsburg •
Constantin Shapiro • Peretz Smolenskin • Moses

Lob Lilienblum • Mordecai David Branstadter
Nahum Meir Schaikewitz • Reuben Asher Braudes

14. Modern Hebrew Literature   **481**
Hebrew Language Revival • Sholem Jacob
Abramovich • Isaac Loeb Peretz • Sholem Rabinovitz
(Sholem Aleichem) • Minor Poets • David Frishman •
Hayyim Nahman Bialik • Saul Tchernihowsky •
Jacob Cohen • Zalman Schnaiur • Other Writers •
Hebrew Literature in Israel • Samuel Joseph Agnon •
Other Prose Writers • Poets

15. Modern Sages   **528**
Moses Hess • Isaac Hirsch Weiss • Moritz
Steinschneider • Heinrich Graetz • Hermann
Cohen • Asher Ginzberg • Aaron David Gordon •
Simon Dubnow • Micah Joseph Berdyczewski •
Israel Zinberg • Joseph Klausner • Leo Baeck •
Martin Buber • Franz Rosenzweig • Mordecai
M. Kaplan • Hebrew Writers in America

Appendix A: Important Dates in Jewish History   **553**

Appendix B: Other Hebrew Writers and Scholars   **555**

Notes   **560**

Bibliography   **567**

Index   **574**

Maps and Illustration

Near East c. 1800 B.C.E. 2

Land of Canaan 8

Palestine in the Prophetic Age 20

Early Talmudic Centers 142

Geonic Period 188

Golden Age 230

Franco-German Lands 308

Europe: Period of Transition 388

Europe: Enlightenment and Emancipation 424

Sample Talmud page 155

INTRODUCTION

LITERATURE

The history of the Jews presents the struggles for light and life of a people small in numbers and negligible in political power but great in achievement and unparalleled in endurance. This people, whom the historians and geographers of ancient Hellas hardly deigned to notice as a strange Syrian tribe, had already then produced one of the most remarkable literatures of all time as well as a body of men who were later on acclaimed as the ethical and religious teachers of mankind.

Paul Goodman (1875-1949)

Ancient Israel's artistic creation was literature. She produced no sculpture, no paintings, no plays as her heritage to the world. She is not renowned for her science, her philosophy, her sports. We do not remember her as a political giant or an economic innovator. Rather, she taught us religion. And we find it in the lives and the literature of the Jews. For the past 3,000 years they have continued to be "ethical and religious teachers of mankind." Further, significant contributions have occurred in *all* areas of life. When the light of knowledge flickered in Europe during the Middle Ages, the Jews preserved science and philosophy and fed the flame. They later gave to the world Sigmund Freud and Albert Einstein and hundreds of other original thinkers. But to catalog names and events and ideas is to satiate. We should simply bear in mind that undergirding the Jews' long history, expressing their agony and their jubilance, is a literature. They are a people of the word.

There is no lack of books on the Jews—histories of the people, of their trials and their triumphs; studies of their religion and their scripture; works on specific men or periods; and libraries more. But there is little which concentrates on the literature and sees it as a continuous stream flowing from hoary antiquity to our own day. This present book intends to be a story of that literature, an overview of Hebrew literary activity during the centuries, with pauses here and there for particulars. But with an emphasis on continuity.

The Jews have not appreciated Arnold Toynbee's conclusion that they "represent an extinct society which only survives as a fossil."[1] Inert, residual continuity they are not. The historic highroad the Jewish people have walked for over 3,000 years has been essentially the same, despite slight and casual digressions forced upon them by time and place. The pulsating core of Judaism, its creativeness, its innermost striving, its life—these have not changed. Abraham and Moses, Isaiah and Akiba, Judah the Prince and Saadia, Philo and Maimonides, Ashkenazic Jew and Sephardic Jew, the Gaon of Wilna and Martin Buber, a Babylonian exile returning to Zion in 538 B.C.E. and a Russian Jew joining an Aliyah to Israel in 1972 C.E.—all would readily understand one another if they came together, just as we understand them all when we read Hebrew literature. A dramatic illustration of this truth can be seen in Israel today. Whoever visits Israel and studies firsthand the Gathering of the Exiles can notice the historic continuity. Various types of Jews from all over the world, reared under the egis of many cultures, have merged into one. The world has been astonished at this latest Jewish renaissance: the cohesive power and the heroic persistence of a people who has never given up its right to exist and whose indomitable will has never been broken. Their very existence is still one of the greatest riddles of history. Their story is so overwhelmingly tragic but so profoundly human.

It is one of the strangest and most distressing ironies of history that both Christianity and Islam, two great world religions, whose very origins root in Judaism, whose loftiest ideals derived from the minds and hearts of Jews, should have been the mortal enemies of the Jewish people. How could it have happened that these people, major contributors to world culture and religion, were driven like lepers of old from land to land, homeless and destitute, scattered among the nations, robbed, burned at the stake, and slaughtered like sheep? How could it have happened in this enlightened century of ours, in the very heartland of Protestantism, in the home of Kant and Hegel, of Goethe and Schiller, that six million Jews were systematically murdered?

But they live on. The land of Israel and the people of Israel, soil and soul, united again. The Jews everywhere and their literature, united still. The written word, handed down from century to century and enriched by the best sons and daughters of Israel; a literature that instructed and inspired, preserved and protected, wiped away the tears and warmed the heart, registered the tragedies and maintained hope for redemption and restoration—such a literature is worth studying deeply.

HISTORY

It will aid our overview if we divide the long history of the Jewish people into major periods:

The Biblical period. From about 1800 before the Common Era to about 1300 B.C.E., or from the time of the first Patriarch of the Hebrews, Abraham, to the time of Moses. This period is covered in the Book of Genesis, where we find the life stories of the Patriarchs, including some stories of the pre-Patriarchal ages, back to the first man, Adam. Traditionally, the history of the Hebrews starts with Abraham, who was allegedly the first to proclaim One God. Genesis ends with the death of Joseph. From the 13th century B.C.E., the time of Moses, to the destruction of the First Commonwealth in the year 586 B.C.E. are 700 years which included: the Exodus and the wandering in the wilderness; the conquest of Canaan and the period of the judges; the monarchy; the split into two kingdoms, Israel and Judah; the destruction of Israel in 721 B.C.E.; and the fall of Judah in 586 B.C.E.

The post-Biblical period or *the period of the Second Commonwealth.* From the second half of the 6th century B.C.E. to the year 70 of the Common Era, when Jerusalem was destroyed by the Romans, were the following events: the return to Zion; the restoration of Jerusalem and the Second Temple; the religious autonomy under Persian rule; the surrender of Judah to Alexander the Great; the Maccabean struggle; the spread of Hellenism in the Diaspora, particularly in Egypt; the Septuagint, the first translation of the scriptures into Greek; the war against Rome.

The Talmudic period. From the 1st century to about 500 C.E. During this period the Mishnah was compiled and edited by Judah the Prince (c. 140). The Jerusalemite Talmud was closed about the 4th century; the Babylonian Talmud was completed in the year 499 by Rabina. The Talmud was a record of the intellectual and religious life of the Jews for a period of one thousand years, from the Babylonian captivity until 500 C.E. Other homiletic works were composed during this period.

The post-Talmudic period or *the Geonic period.* From the closing of the two Talmuds until about 1040. During this period the centers of Jewish learning were in Babylonia and in Tiberia, Palestine. Jewish life in the countries outside Palestine was directed by an Exilarch, a scion of the Davidic dynasty, who was recognized by the secular government as the leader of Diaspora Jewry. The Masoretes (preservers of tradition) introduced the system of vowel points and accentuation into Hebrew, which had heretofore been a consonantal language. Hebrew philology and grammar were developed to a high degree. Liturgical poetry flourished at that time. Works on religious philosophy appeared. The first Arabic translation of the scriptures was published.

The Spanish-Arabic period or *the Golden Age of Hebrew literature.* From about 1040, when the great Talmudic academies in Babylonia were closed and the center of learning shifted from East to West, to Spain; until well into the 15th century. Hebrew poetry and Jewish religious philosophy grew to a height never before attained.

The Jews in medieval Europe. Culturally, the Sephardic Jews, or the Jews of the Iberian peninsula, overshadowed the Ashkenazic Jews of northern and eastern Europe during the 10th-15th centuries. The story of these European Jews is one of being victimized by discrimination, persecution, banishment, and massacre.

Cabala and *liturgical poetry.* Beginning in the 13th century, Jewish mysticism, known as theoretical Cabala, flourished. Liturgical poetry in the form of supplications and prayers of repentance grew enormously. Many works on homiletics and morals as well as the final Code of Jewish Law, known as the Shulhan Aruk (The Prepared Table) by Joseph Caro, appeared.

The modern period. From the 16th century, we note a period of transition which culminated in the 18th century Enlightenment movement, a symbol and reality of the modern period. This movement was initiated among Judaism, on the one hand, by Moses Mendelssohn and his circle of adherents in Berlin, and, on the other hand, with the Hasidic movement in southern Russia led by Israel Baal Shem. The latter movement, which accentuated "joy of the heart" and prayer as against sheer learning of Torah, was fiercely opposed by circles of rabbis and learned Jews, who called themselves Mitnaggedim. This struggle continued into the 19th century. During the 19th century, there emerged two modern literatures: the new Hebrew literature and the Yiddish literature. The walls of the ghetto eventually collapsed. With the appearance of Zionism and some secular movements, the hold of traditional Judaism upon the Jewish masses was loosened.

In most instances, these historical periods match the periods of literary history chosen for this volume, but these latter periods are slightly more refined, taking into combined account such factors as time, geography, and type of literature.

TRANSLATIONS

Most Bible quotations in this volume are from the Masoretic text of the Jewish scriptures. The author has occasionally made his own translations, and in a few instances used passages from the Jerusalem Bible, Isaac Leeser's translation, and the King

James Version and the Revised Standard Version of the Old Testament. Talmudic excerpts are basically the author's translations. For other material (e.g., poems, secondary sources, etc.), translators are noted; where not indicated, renderings are by this author.

I

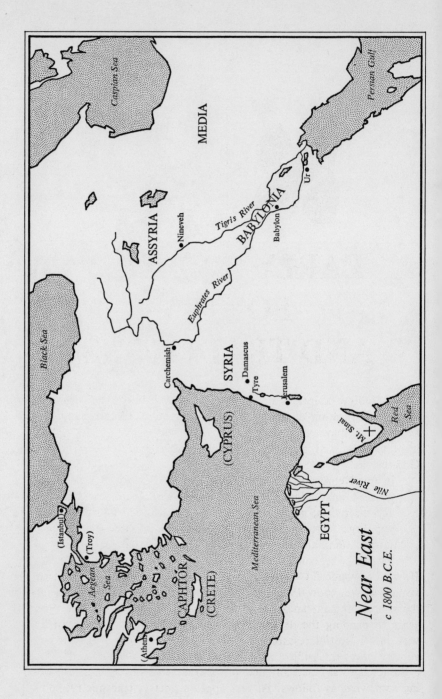

Near East

c 1800 B.C.E.

א | 1

EARLY BIBLICAL
POETRY
AND TRADITIONS

The Hebrew scriptures do not constitute one book. We have before us a collection of works, a compilation of various writings reflecting the emotional and intellectual life of many generations of men: teachers and moralists, dreamers and visionaries, critics and God-seekers.

> In the Hebrew Bible, without doubt, are history and tale;
> proverb and enigma; correction and wisdom; knowledge
> and discretion; poetry and word-play; conviction and coun-
> sel; dirge, entreaty, and prayer; praise, and every kind of
> supplication; and all this in a divine way superior to all
> the prolix benedictions in human books.[1]

How this wonderful collection came into being is very difficult to visualize. We know the finished product, though many phases of the process remain unexplained even today. Scholars have devoted years to probing the details of this process; they have provided us with much fruitful research and conclusions. However, this present volume leaves this subject for other books and for other scholars.

Suffice it to say that any people's literature usually comes into being somewhat as follows. At first appears poetry, epic poetry, com-

3

memorating great events: heroic deeds of mighty men, conflicts and battles, disasters and triumphs. This kind of poetry, reflecting joy or grief, is frequently accompanied by music and dancing. It is a tribe's poetry, a people's poetry, because it is collective in character: folk poetry, folk music. It belongs to no individual creator; it is the property of all. Later in the life of a people appear short tales, unusual experiences, legends, witty proverbs, fables. With maturity come chronicles, historical writings, and, finally, codes of law. It is at this stage that the individual writer is more likely to come to the fore. He is often the representative thinker of his generation.[2]

We begin our look at the scriptures with early poetry and stories of early traditions. That the Hebrew people had more ancient books than those which have been preserved for us in the scriptures is certain. In Numbers 21:14 a source called the Book of the Wars of the Lord is named and quoted. In Joshua 10:13 and in 2 Samuel 1:18 the Book of the Righteous is cited. The Chronicles of the Kings of Israel and the Chronicles of the Kings of Judah are mentioned various times in the Biblical books of Samuel, Kings, and Chronicles. Finally, of course, only a portion of the oral tradition survived into written form. We may regret the loss of many old, old accounts, oral and written, but what we have provides us with ample resources for thought—and for life.

EARLY POETRY

There are short passages, especially in the book of Genesis, that are recognized by scholars as belonging to the oldest strata of Biblical poetry, that is to say, to the earliest period, perhaps pre-Biblical. As they have all the earmarks of primitive expressions of either favor or disfavor, they must have come down from the hoary past in the form of oral traditions handed down from generation to generation. Though attributed to certain individuals or to God, their authorship, as in the case of folklore generally, is by no means known.

God Almighty Himself is the speaker in the first two poetic passages in the Bible. He addressed his command to Adam in simple prose: "Of the tree of the knowledge of good and evil, thou shalt not eat." (Gen. 2:17) However, after Adam and Eve violated the command, God's pronouncement of judgment was uttered in strong language—two- and three-word units of measured stanzas, paralleling prophetic poetry. Thus His curse against the serpent and His verdict against Eve carried, with this rhythmic nature, a powerful emotional impact; only Adam escaped with a prose-like judgment. Of course, the poetry and rhythm of the Hebrew is almost lost in translation.

The second passage is Genesis 4:6-7. Following his and his brother's offerings made to God, Cain is angry and jealous that Abel's gifts pleased God and his did not. God addressed Cain:

> Why art thou wroth?
> And why is thy countenance fallen?
> If thou doest well, shall it not be lifted up?
> And if thou doest not well,
> Sin croucheth at the door;
> And unto thee is its desire,
> But thou mayest rule over it.

This utterance is riddle-like, mysterious, obscure—both in the original Hebrew and in the English translation. It seems to echo, however, a theme prominent in Biblical literature: Virtue is rewarded. If one is good, it is well with him; if one does evil, it is not well with him. Had Cain hearkened to that voice, he would not have murdered his brother.

Lamech

We would fail to do justice to the early poets were we to ignore Lamech, son of Methushael and descendant of Cain, even though Lamech left us only six lines and we know little about him. He had two wives, Adah and Zillah; a beautiful daughter, Naamah; and three remarkable sons. Jabal was "the father of such as dwell in tents and have cattle" (Gen. 4:20): the first cattleman and tent-dweller. His brother, Jubal, was "the father of all such as handle the harp and the pipe": musician, perhaps poet. Lamech's third son, Tubal-cain was a forger of iron and brass instruments. Lamech's song (Gen. 4:23-24):

> Adah and Zillah, hear my voice,
> ye wives of Lamech, hearken unto my speech;
> for I have slain a man for wounding me;
> and a young man for bruising me;
> if Cain shall be avenged sevenfold,
> truly Lamech seventy and sevenfold.

It has been suggested that in his song Lamech seeks the aid of his wives: their consolation, their love, their embraces. This may be part of the motif. More likely the emphasis is one of hearty boast by a warrior. Lamech's song of revenge could have been for centuries the song of men who lived by the law of blood revenge. Perhaps the exceptional rhythm and rhyme of the song were accompanied by a dance; perhaps the scant six lines were part of a larger poem, a tribal hymn to a hero of revenge.

Noah

Following the incident of his drunkenness and nakedness, Noah issued a curse and blessing among his three sons (Gen. 9:25-27):

> Cursed be Canaan;
> a servant of servants shall he be unto his brethren.
> Blessed be the Lord, the God of Shem;
> and let Canaan be their servant.
> God enlarge Japheth,
> and He shall dwell in the tents of Shem;
> and let Canaan be their servant.

Note the repetitious use of "servant" in this poem; it appears to have been a refrain. These few lines might have been the climax of a larger poem, a kind of Song of Victory by Semitic and Japhethite tribes over the defeated Hamitic tribes who were known under the general name of "Canaan."

Miriam's Song

Another victory song, written in a different vein, is the one that Miriam, Moses' sister, sang after Pharaoh's army had been drowned in the Red Sea (Exodus 15:21):

> Sing ye to the Lord,
> for He hath triumphed gloriously;
> the horse and his rider
> hath He thrown into the sea.

This short poem follows a long ode, a hymn of praise to God known as the Song of the Sea, which is marked as the one that "Moses sang together with the children of Israel." This long ode, however, contains certain expressions which, according to most scholars, could not have been uttered at the time of Moses. They therefore think that the real song composed at that time was Miriam's song, which begins with almost the same words as the larger one. The text describes that "Miriam the prophetess. . . took a timbrel in her hand; and all the women went out after her with timbrels and with dances"—the earmarks of a real public demonstration in the form of dancing and singing. Miriam's song might have been composed on the spur of the moment at a spontaneous celebration. The words are simple and the tune could have been repeated many times.

Place-Name Song

A brief song segment appears in Numbers 21:14-15:

> What He did in the Red Sea
> and in the brooks of Arnon.
> And at the stream of the brooks
> that goeth down to the dwelling of Ar,
> and lieth upon the border of Moab.

This is from the lost Book of the Wars of the Lord. What does it tell about? Does it refer to where two mighty armies fought? Does it refer to some of the places through which Israel passed in the Exodus journey from Egypt to Canaan?

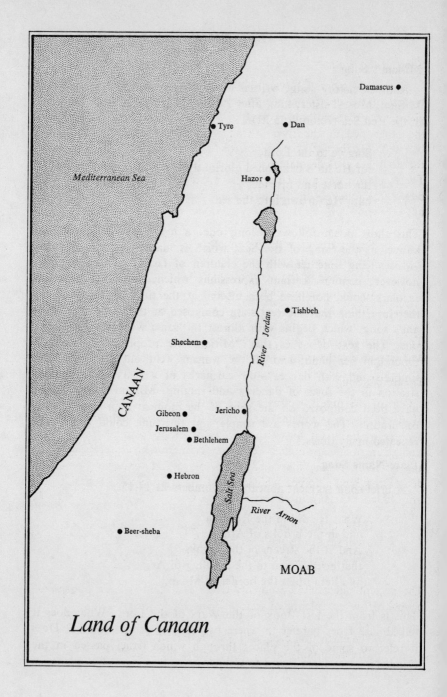

Land of Canaan

Song of the Well

Also in Numbers 21 (vs. 17-18) we have a song of thankfulness typical of the desert peoples. Very succinctly we see a picturesque view of a great national moment. The people at that time were on the other side of the river Arnon, "which is in the wilderness. . . between Moab and the Amorites." (Num. 21:13) They pitched their tents in that desolate place after a long series of bloody battles. There was no water and the desert was a furnace. The people were desperate. Suddenly, in the unbearable heat of the day, a song went up:

> Spring up, O well; sing ye unto it:
> the princes digged the well,
> the nobles of the people digged it,
> by the direction of the lawgiver,
> with their staves.

The "princes" and the "nobles" sought and discovered water, and Israel sang the song of life and of joy.

Deborah's Song

One of the oldest victory songs is the Song of Deborah (Judg. 5). Deborah, a prophetess and a judge in Israel, helped lead her people to throw off a twenty-year yoke of oppression. Under the leadership of Deborah and Barak, the children of Israel triumphed against King Jabin, the ruler of Hazor, and Sisera, the commander of the king's forces which included "nine hundred chariots of iron." Deborah sang in victory (vs. 3):

> Hear, O ye kings; give ear, O ye princes;
> I will sing unto the Lord;
> I will sing praise to the Lord God of Israel.

The ancient poem vividly portrayed the conditions of the oppressed people before the celebrated victory (vs. 4-6):

> The earth trembled, and the heavens dropped. . . .
> The mountains melted from before the Lord. . . .

The highways were unoccupied,
and the travellers walked through byways.

Praise is given the other key woman in the Israelite victory: Jael,
who drove a tent stake through the head of Sisera while he slept
(vs. 24):

Blessed above women shall Jael the wife of Heber be,
blessed shall she be above women in the tent.

For centuries this triumphal ode has been considered not only one
of the finest songs in Hebrew literature but in the literature of the
world as well.

BIBLICAL PROSE

Pentateuch

The first large division of the Scriptures is called the Torah or
the Law or the Pentateuch (Greek for "five books") or the Five
Books of Moses. Genesis, Exodus, Leviticus, Numbers, and Deuteronomy comprise the Torah.

Genesis, logically enough, begins with the story of creation. Then
come the Paradise story; the generations of men from Adam to
Noah, from Noah to Abraham, the Patriarch of the Hebrews; and
finally the death of Joseph in Egypt. It is a history composed of
stories handed down from generation to generation, from father
to son and from grandfather to grandson, for purposes of enter-
tainment, teaching, and morality. Thus history and story, literature
and philosophy, imagination and reason, legend and reality are
interwoven in this book; above all, the moral aspect is preeminent.

The Book of Exodus contains the colorful story of the liberation
of the children of Israel from Egyptian bondage; the Theophany,
or Revelation, on Mount Sinai, resulting in the Ten Commandments
as the basis of the Mosaic Law; the Covenant between Israel and
the One God—monotheism; and the establishment of the first national shrine, the Tabernacle, as the dwelling place of the living

God among men.

Leviticus deals primarily with the laws of ritual sacrifices, with social legislation, and with the code pertaining to Holiness.

In Numbers there are descriptions of the wanderings of the Hebrews in the wilderness, stories about conflicts among themselves, and accounts of the wars they waged until the Jordan was reached.

Deuteronomy is a summary of the Israelites' experiences on their way to Canaan. It is written in the first person in the form of addresses by Moses; it ends with his death. Deuteronomy is, as the English name we have for the book implies, a kind of "second lawgiving."

The question of authorship of the Five Books of Moses remains practically unanswerable. Traditionally, Moses is supposed to have been the author, despite contrary internal evidence (e.g., second person perspective, account of Moses' death, mention of post-Moses incidents, etc.). Talmudic sages held that God was the author: "God dictated and Moses wrote." Others suggested that the Torah existed long before the creation of the world. Equating it with the Mind and Wisdom of God, they declared it to contain the original design and aim of the Creator: "God looked into the Torah and created the world as an architect looks into his blueprints." Such suggestions, however, are better taken symbolically. The real answer lies probably in the fact that the Pentateuch is not a creation of one man but is rather a conglomerate work. It is a people's book, the authors of which lived during many centuries. It reminds one of a huge brick house built by bricklayers almost as numerous as the bricks. Most of the stories in these books must have been told and retold as oral traditions before they were finally written down. Later came the editors who assembled them and gave them their final form. Thus these books had lived in the minds and hearts and mouths of men as unwritten literature long before they became written scrolls. They were the tales relayed in the fields, around campfires, and in tents and homes. They reflected the regulations, customs, and traditions of centuries.

The One-God Idea

The Bible opens with a brief statement which proclaims: "In the beginning God created the heaven and the earth"—a handful of words purporting to declare the existence and the coming into being of the world as we know it. Heaven and earth—What does this mean? It means the cosmos, the universe, the whole, everything that exists. But this is not all. This simple and succinct statement implies more.[3] Where did the world come from? Is it eternal or did it have a beginning? If eternal, what does it mean? What is that which is changeable and what is that which is unchangeable? Who or what maintains the eternals? or initiates the changes? If the world had a beginning, who or what effected that beginning? What is more reasonable to accept in a world of change: the concept of a beginning or the concept of eternity?

Pondering deeply into the concepts of changeableness and unchangeableness, this early philosopher concluded that the world must have had a beginning, and because of that beginning, there must be a Creator who not only brought all this into being but maintains it in existence. That Creator is eternal, unchangeable, and One. The conclusion is clear-cut: "In the beginning God. . ." —one idea against all of humanity, one succinct statement against all cults and all religions and all cultures; the world as a Unity, now worshipping the whole instead of parts: trees, rivers, mountains, denizens of the sea, animals, demons, graven images, sun, moon, stars; Marduch, Ra-Amon, Sin, Moloch, Baal, and other gods with their temples and shrines must fall and be swept from the face of the earth. The One-God idea, monotheism, came to life!

Creation

The Genesis story of creation, therefore, rests upon the One-God idea. In this story we see that God neither needs nor wants any assistance. There are no angels at His side to help Him or advise Him; the author of this story seems not to have known anything about angels. What concerns him is nothing but the Creator and His handiwork. The act of creation emerges as the free will of the Creator. He wills a world and he makes it, and while making it demonstrates His capability to make *everything*.

The unity and uniqueness of the Creator still remain intact even after the world came into being. The Creator's power was not diminished thereby, because the world still depended upon Him. He created it and He could destroy it. No one could ever oppose Him or obviate His will.

The One-God idea gave birth to the idea of the unity of the world as the complete product of one Creator. The idea of the world as a unity, in its turn, gave birth to the idea of the unity of man. Mankind as a whole was given one father, Adam, who had been himself created by one Creator; Adam, the symbol for mankind as a unity. Further, man, who was created "in the image of god," was given the attribute of *one*; as God is one, so man is one: a personality, a conscious being capable of reflecting upon himself and aiming at something higher and greater than himself. It also means that under God man is a creator in his own right. Finally, under God every man is equal to another. Thus, a new understanding of order, peace, justice, love resulted.

Such declarations had no place in a polytheistic world. True, paganism also sought to strengthen morality by religious sanctions, but the essential nature of its gods militated against this. These gods warred with one another; they sinned, murdered, stole, fornicated. Therefore, pagan justice and morality could not derive from idolatry true justice as it was derived from the Unity of One God and could not equal the exalted concepts of righteousness we find in the Hebrew scriptures.

The Unity of God, the Unity of the World, the Unity of Man— that is, one God, one world, one man: This overall conception was given in the first three chapters of Genesis in the simplest terms possible, in the form of stories to be easily remembered by all who would hear, tell, and read them.

Disobedience

The first three chapters of Genesis also contain the story of the first disobedient man and the first disobedient woman: Adam and Eve. And the very next chapter tells of the first murderer, Cain, who slew his brother Abel. The idea in both of these stories is that God is the ultimate judge of man's deeds; man is responsible for his actions not only to himself and to others but also to a higher power, to the one who brought the world into being.

The equally familiar story of Noah and the flood enlarges man's disobedience against God, from individuals—Adam, Eve, Cain—to all men on the earth: "And God looked upon the earth, and, behold, it was corrupt. . . . And the Lord said, I will destroy man whom I have created." (Gen. 6:12,7) Only Noah—"a just man" —and his family were saved on the ark, to bring forth a new mankind after the flood. The idea here is clear: The earth belongs to the moral man. The wicked cannot rightfully claim it. Nay, more, if they do claim it, they eventually lose it, simply because it cannot be sustained by wickedness. Corruption results in destruction. Further, one good man is worth as much if not more than a whole world of wicked men. They perish but the righteous man lives.

"And it came to pass, as they journeyed eastward, that they found a plain in the land of Shinar; and they dwelt there." (Gen. 11:2) Who were "they"? No one knows; no one will ever know. "And they said, 'Come, let us build us a city and a tower, with its top in heaven; and let us make us a name, lest we be scattered abroad upon the face of the whole earth.' " (Gen. 11:4) God peacefully and quietly impaired their plan. He confounded their language, "that they may not understand one another's speech." Thus they were scattered upon the face of the earth. What is the meaning of this Tower of Babel story? Simply that there is one and only one absolute power—God. Let the man of pride and arrogance beware.

The First Hebrew

Abraham, of the city of Ur, was the first Hebrew, the Patriarch of the Hebrews. Commanded to leave his country, his kindred, his father's home, and go to a land which God would show him, he took his wife Sarah, his possessions, and a nephew named Lot, and wandered away from the Euphrates into Egypt. He observed the ways of many peoples and came into direct contact with the two greatest civilizations of ancient times: Babylonia and Egypt. He selected for permanent settlement, however, the land of Canaan, which served always as a bridge between Asia and Africa. We know nothing of Abraham's life before he appears as God's called, and his call itself is a mystery: Why Abraham? We are tempted to think that Abraham was chosen by God because the Patriarch himself had chosen the only living God. In any case, out of this relationship came God's great promise to Abraham:

I will make of thee a great nation, and I will bless thee,

and make thy name great; and thou shalt be a blessing.
And I will bless them that bless thee, and curse him that
curseth thee; and in thee shall all the families of the earth
be blessed. (Gen. 12:2-3)

Abraham was not faultless. We note a number of acts and attitudes which seem to us crude or dishonest; for example, passing
Sarah off as his sister to better secure his own life. Nevertheless, on
balance we can admit that in Abraham we see the character of a
great man, a visionary of immense power, a man of profound
sentiments, a prototype that marks off a standard of conduct to
which other men may aspire. He is hospitable, he is a loving and
faithful husband and family man, he refuses to take land from
anyone without paying fully for it, he is a man of obedience to
God's will, even ready to sacrifice his only son. The story, for instance, about the quarrel between Abraham's and Lot's shepherds
portrays Abraham as a man of peace; as a matter of fact, this is
the first time we hear of such a solution: giving way to the other
side for the sake of peace.

And Abraham said unto Lot, "Let there be no strife, I
pray thee, between me and thee, and between my herdmen
and thy herdmen; for we be brethren. Is not the whole land
before thee? Separate thyself, I pray thee, from me; if thou
wilt take the left hand, then I will go to the right; or if thou
depart to the right hand, then I will go to the left."

(Gen. 13:8-9)

The remainder of the Book of Genesis carries us through three
additional generations of the Hebrews: Isaac, the second Patriarch;
Jacob-Israel, the third Patriarch; and Joseph. Some of the best-
known and best-loved stories in Western literature come from this
portion of the Bible. There is the account of Esau's selling his
birthright to his brother Jacob for a bowl of pottage. There is
Jacob's dream-vision of the ladder whose top "reached to heaven;
and behold the angels of God ascending and descending on it."
(Gen. 28:12) There is Jacob's love and work for Rachel. There
is Jacob's wrestling with an angel. There is Joseph and his coat
and his brothers' jealousy, which drives them to sell him as a
slave into Egypt. And there is the denouement of the Joseph story
whereby he ends up ruling an empire as second only to the

Pharaoh, saving the land and his own people from famine. Down through the centuries these and other stories from the Hebrew's early history have found their way not only into Western prose literature, but also into art and music and poetry.

MOSES

It was in Egypt, under the egis of the mighty Pharaohs and in the shadows of the pyramids, that the small clan of Jacob's children had grown into a numerous people. At first received as invited guests and then as friendly settlers, in the course of centuries they were looked upon as dangerous to the state. The ruling Pharaoh, being suspicious of those strangers and their strange beliefs, decided to either get rid of them altogether or degrade them into slaves and thus break the spirit of this shepherd-people from Asia, who did not seem to fit into the Egyptian civilization.

While the Hebrews were laboring hard as slaves of Pharaoh, under the cruel rule of his taskmasters, there appeared a man, who, by the sheer force of his will and by the love of justice which animated him, stands out as one of the greatest leaders of antiquity, a mighty conquerer of the spirit, a hero of such dimensions that the world had never seen before. This man, Moses, towering above all great leaders, could have been an Egyptian prince, if not an heir to the throne; but, disdaining power and wealth, he went down to the lowest of the low, to the slaves in the lime pits, to the downtrodden Israelites, making their fate his own fate and sharing their misery and degradation. Nay, more, from the slime and the mud in which they had sunk, he picked up their ancestral ideas of God and man. Inspired and steeled by the vision of the freedom of man, Moses was destined to become not only the greatest lawgiver and ethical teacher but also the father of all the Biblical prophets. He just could not see justice trodden underfoot. In his consuming indignation and wrath at seeing a Hebrew slave beaten by a cruel taskmaster, he even committed murder. A fugitive from Pharaoh's police, Moses reached Midian and became a shepherd. Years later he came back to Egypt in order to free the slaves and lead them out of the country. The story of how he did this is given in bold strokes in the Book of Exodus. It is replete with miracles, and a miracle it indeed was, the greatest in fact in ancient history.

Again we come upon famous and familiar stories: Moses and the burning bush, the ten plagues, the Red Sea escape, manna, water from a rock. The task of liberating those who initially "hearkened not unto Moses for anguish of spirit and for cruel bondage" was one miracle. The task of making of these erstwhile slaves a united people was another equal or greater miracle. No small wonder that the exodus from Egypt has always been the central theme of the Torah, the most far-reaching event in the life of Israel, inspiring prophet, psalmist, scholar, and ordinary Jew. And Moses is at the center of the exodus event. This leader of men, this liberator and deliverer, was essentially a teacher, a prophet, who had been commissioned to bring to man a Torah, the universal teaching of divine law, a Decalogue (ten words), the Ten Commandments, which were destined to become not only the cornerstone of Judaism but the foundation upon which two other world religions would rest.

The laws of the Torah are Mosaic, whether all of them or only some of them were promulgated by Moses. Many of them could have developed later, just as the stalk sprouts forth from the seed. To the planter belongs the whole plant. Apart from the Torah's uncompromising monotheism, its principles and outstanding features were the sacredness of human life, the moral end of life, the equality of all men before God and before the Law, the combination of compassion and justice, the appeal to the divine in man, and the persistent demand of personal holiness in a kingdom of priests. The Torah also proclaimed the love of God and the love of man as the two basic principles of human life, something that had never been heard before. This was called the Sinaitic Revelation. It has never been duplicated since. At Mount Sinai, Israel was given a consciousness and a moral fiber as a base for a unique national existence, a spiritual aim that no other people has ever attempted or even aspired to attain. Thereby Moses caused the people of Israel to be different from others, a people created by a prophet of God. If there is a place where Israel's true spirit lives, it is certainly in the Torah of Moses.

FROM MOSES TO AMOS

Moses, liberator of slaves, lawgiver, organizer and founder of the Hebrews as a national entity, was proclaimed the greatest prophet.

And there hath not arisen a prophet since in Israel like
unto Moses, whom the Lord knew face to face. (Deut. 34:10)

Traditionally, Moses was also a poet. Three long poems were attributed to him: The Song of the Sea (Ex. 15:1-19) and the other two in the form of poetic orations before his death (Deut. 32:1-43; 33:1-29), although some scholars doubt their Mosaic authorship.

Next to Moses as a prophet stands Samuel (11th century), under whose guidance the tribes which hitherto were divided became again a united nation. Samuel was supreme leader, Judge, and teacher of Israel. He was both a seer and a prophet. Although Samuel did not leave any written prophecies, he is to be regarded as one of the great men of Israel. One of the psalmists placed him in line with Moses and Aaron. In 1 Samuel we find a lengthy address ascribed to him about the adverse effects of the monarchical system. It is one of the most forceful condemnations of kings. Some scholars doubt whether a man of so early a time in history could have arrived at such a radical denunciation. However, one would venture to say that precisely a prophet of Israel could arrive at such conclusions, conditions and time notwithstanding.

An old dictum of Samuel, written in poetic form, is still extant. It is to be found in 1 Samuel 15:22-23:

> Hath the Lord as great delight
> in burnt-offerings and sacrifices,
> as in obeying the voice
> of the Lord?
> Behold, to obey is better than sacrifice,
> and to hearken than the fat of rams.
> For rebellion is as the sin of witchcraft,
> and stubbornness is as iniquity and household gods.

Samuel's ideas as expressed here were carried further by the great prophets of Israel. It was a declaration of principles, which was probably inherent in pure monotheism.

Among the singers of Israel was King David. He was both a great warrior and a great poet. He was called the "sweet singer of Israel," and deservedly so. David is the author of many of the Psalms. David's lamentatation over the fallen King Saul and, particularly, over his dead friend Jonathan, is found in 2 Samuel 1:19-27. The friendship between Jonathan and David is classic, and David described it in the following words (2 Sam. 1:26):

> I am distressed for thee, my brother Jonathan;
> very pleasant hast thou been unto me;
> thy love to me was wonderful,
> passing the love of women.

During the reign of David and Solomon, two prophets, Nathan and Gad, were active. Nathan is known for his parable of "the poor man and the lamb." He was a man of God who dared tell the king the bitter truth: he called him a murderer deserving the death penalty for causing the death of Uriah and taking Bath-sheba for wife. Gad was probably a court prophet.

At the time of King Ahab (9th century), there appeared the prophet-fighter, Elijah of Tishbeh. He was a strange man, with long shaggy hair and a rough mantle of sheepskin fastened around his loins by a girdle of hide. No one knew of Elijah's whereabouts. He appeared and disappeared like lightning. When the rulers, exasperated at his audacity and fearlessness, wanted to lay hands on him, Elijah was already gone. He hid in the mountains, in caves, in the desert. He lived on fruit or vegetables. Elijah was not a man of words; he was a man of action. His fight against idolatry and for the worship of God never abated as long as he lived. His disciple, Elisha, who was more peaceful—more a teacher than a fighter—continued his work after his mysterious passing away. Neither Elijah nor Elisha left any written prophecies.

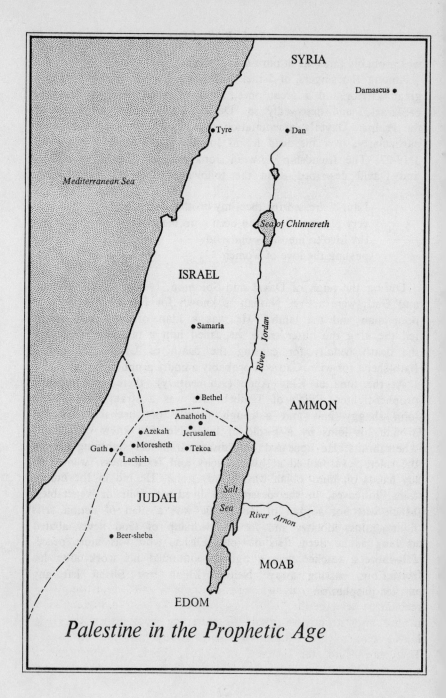

SYRIA

Damascus •

•Tyre   •Dan

Mediterranean Sea

Sea of Chinnereth

ISRAEL

•Samaria

                              River Jordan

•Bethel

Anathoth   AMMON

•Azekah   Jerusalem

Gath•   •Moresheth   •Tekoa

    •Lachish

                    Salt
JUDAH   Sea   *River Arnon*

•Beer-sheba

                              MOAB

EDOM

Palestine in the Prophetic Age

THE
PROPHETIC
AGE

THE PROPHETS

Amidst the great political events in eastern Asia, particularly between the 8th and 5th centuries B.C.E., amidst the rising and falling of powerful empires—Assyria, Babylonia, Egypt, Persia—there stood out a group of men known as prophets. At first regarded as mere visionaries to whom men turned with their petty problems, as Saul came to Samuel about his strayed asses, they became the mouthpieces of the God of Israel, the moral teachers of mankind.

The prophets whose writings have been preserved to us show an extraordinary zeal for justice and truth. One of the very first after Moses was Samuel, who led his people during a long and fruitful life; we hear soon of Elijah, a fierce champion of God and an uncompromising fighter against idolatry and injustice, who recognized God in the "still, small voice," instead of finding Him in fire and storm; we recall Nathan, the admonisher of King David, fearlessly pointing to the king as the murderer of Uriah. There are Amos, the shepherd of Tekoa, the first prophet-writer, who denounced the king of Israel and his minions for "selling

21

the poor for a pair of shoes"; Hosea, the prophet of love and
forgiveness; Micah, the peasant prophet, who engraved in human
hearts what God wanted man to do: "To act justly, love mercy,
and to walk humbly with thy God"; Isaiah, the prince-prophet,
the far-seeing statesman, the dreamer of world peace, the fiery de-
nouncer of luxury and licentiousness, the exponent of holiness
and purity; Jeremiah, the great patriot, who tried to save Judah
from downfall and doom, and who shared the fate of his people
in the hour of their greatest misery; Ezekiel, the priest-prophet, a
captive in a strange land, who proclaimed the responsibility of
the individual and foretold the restoration of Israel; the Prophet
of Redemption, the so-called Second Isaiah in whose heart burned
three consuming loves: the love of God, the love of Israel, and
the love of mankind; Joel, the prophet of divine judgment and
the future glory of Israel; Habakkuk, who, like Job and Jeremiah,
asked searching questions about God's justice; Zephaniah, a
prince-prophet like Isaiah, who was probably one of those who
brought about the reform of King Josiah; Haggai, Zechariah,
and Malachi, who stood by the returnees from the Babylonian
captivity in their efforts to rebuild Jerusalem and the Temple;
Nahum and Obadiah, who helped Israel bear the gloom and
terror of the time; Jonah, the fugitive from God, who taught a
great lesson by learning a great lesson; Daniel, who represents
unconquerable faith.

We are moved deeply by the prophets' matchless eloquence, their
conception of ethical monotheism, their unfathomable faith in a
God of justice, their passion for social righteousness, and their
courage to defend their ideals—fearlessly and unto death. These
exceptional men have indelibly stamped their teachings upon the
conscience of mankind.

THE TWO KINGDOMS

In order to understand the role the prophets played, we must
recall the historical background of their epoch. After the death
of Solomon (c. 937 B.C.E.), the United Kingdom established by

David came to an end. Ten tribes seceded and under the leadership of the rebel Jeroboam reorganized themselves as the Northern Kingdom, called Israel. Only two tribes, Judah and Benjamin, remained loyal to the Davidic dynasty, with Jerusalem as the capital. This was the Southern Kingdom, called Judah, with Rehoboam, Solomon's son, as the heir to the throne.

From the very beginning Israel turned away from monotheism and reinstituted idolatry in Bethel and Dan, in the form of golden calves, imitating the worship of the Egyptian god Apis and reflecting the Canaanite worship of Baal. This move was not only religious but political in intent, for Jeroboam, who proclaimed himself king of Israel, wanted thereby to wean the Israelites from visiting the national shrine in Jerusalem. The Kingdom of Israel existed 225 years, but apart from short periods of relative peace and prosperity its history was replete with turmoil, massacres, and wars with Judah. The frequent rebellions of army officers, for example, weakened the country internally and left it vulnerable to external threats. Between Assyria in Asia and Egypt in Africa, the two great powers then in that part of the world, Israel was a pawn on the political chessboard. She paid tribute to Assyria, but at the same time conspired with other small countries to throw off the oppressor's yoke. In the 730s, the Assyrians invaded Israel and occupied much of the country. A few years later another conquering effort was launched and in 721 B.C.E., after a three-year siege, the major city of Samaria fell to Sargon II, who razed it. King Sargon then carried most of the population away into distant regions of Asia and settled other peoples in their place. Israel was no more.

During the most tragic years of the Kingdom of Israel, two great prophets appeared: Amos and Hosea. Both left their writings as testimony to their work.

There were two factors that contributed to the ability of the Southern Kingdom to resist longer the cataclysms of the time. One was the Davidic dynasty which continued to rule Judah in an uninterrupted line, unimpeded by rebellions. The other factor was the religious cohesion and national unity symbolized by the Temple of Solomon. Yet, even in Judah the process of inner disintegration took its toll. Further, by the beginning of the 7th century Assyria

had conquered much of Judah, but not Jerusalem. For most of
the 7th century, however, Judah continued as a vassal of Assyria,
paying regular tribute. When Assyria fell at the end of the 7th century and Babylonia became the ruling power in western Asia,
Judah found herself still between two contending great powers:
Egypt and Babylonia. The prophets of Judah made valiant attempts at reform, as, for instance, Isaiah at the time of Hezekiah
and Jeremiah at the time of Josiah. But their work was invalidated
by succeeding kings. Judah's loyalty to Babylonia was more than
once in question. Finally, Nebuchadnezzar invaded the country
and in 586 B.C.E. captured and razed Jerusalem and the Temple,
destroyed most important Judean towns, and carried away into
exile all but some poor peasants. The Southern Kingdom had
fallen.

AMOS

We note with astonishment Amos' literary style. All his
addresses are in clear rhythmic lines, usually grouped
in strophes. This is characteristic of all the great
prophets, not only of Amos. In the exaltation of
the prophet's spirit the words flow from his lips in
rhythmic regularity. It is a well-recognized experience
not confined to the Hebrews, which makes the prophet and
the poet akin. In Amos poetic power was combined with
rhetorical skill. In his great address against the foreign
nations he used grave and impressive refrains at the
beginning and the end of each strophe. With consummate
skill he began with the hostile neighbors, scored their sins,
and predicted punishment to one after another, when suddenly, after intoning the same terrible opening refrain, he turned
on Israel, denounced her social corruption, and foretold her
certain doom.[1]

Who was this figure who appeared in the mid-8th century
B.C.E., bringing a new religious emphasis to the world? He was
"an herdman and a gatherer of sycamore fruit" (7:14)—a shep-

herd from Tekoa, a village near Jerusalem. Amos was neither of the priestly class nor a professional prophet. He simply felt deeply the call of God, an inner voice, driving him to speak and write.

> The lion hath roared,
> who will not fear?
> The Lord God hath spoken,
> who can but prophesy?
>
> (3:8)

Amos' prophecy was of the downfall of Israel. He rooted it in God's universality and in God's demand for social justice, a dual cry which not only shook Amos' contemporaries but also has inspired man for centuries. God will punish Damascus, Amos says, "because they have threshed Gilead with sledges of iron." God will punish the Philistines for delivering captives to Edom, Tyre for its slave trade, Edom for "casting off all pity," Ammon for its cruelty to women, Judah for rejecting the Law of the Lord, and Israel for selling "the righteous for silver" and "turning aside the way of the poor." God is Justice; He demands of all peoples that they be just and righteous. The law of justice has no national boundaries. Justice is One as God is One. The test of a people is not whether they have been delivered from bondage as has Israel; the real test is whether the people walk in the ways of God.

> Are ye not as children of the Ethiopians unto me, O children of Israel? saith the Lord. Have not I brought up Israel out of the land of Egypt? and the Philistines from Caphtor, and the Syrians from Kir? (9:7)

Israel's God is not a household god. He is not a national god. He is the God of the Universe. And he is a God of righteousness and a God of judgment.

Thus the first writing prophet speaks and writes, leaving us a small but powerful book. Suddenly, like lightning in a heavily laden sky before a storm, did Amos appear. A lonely man emerging from the hill country of Judah, he predicted the doom of a kingdom at a time when the country as a whole was outwardly prosperous under the reign of the Northern Kingdom's most successful king, Jeroboam II. The man from Tekoa, however, saw what others could not, and would not, see. He came from the south to preach God's judgment upon the north. He thundered his message at Bethel, a center of Israel's religious life—a national shrine, "the king's sanctuary." He demanded, in God's name, more spirit and less form, more justice and less luxury, more truth and less pretense and falsehood, more moral purity and less sacrifice or ceremony. What he demanded he did not get. And the Kingdom of the North came to its end.

The uniqueness of Amos and his 8th-century prophetic colleagues must not be overemphasized. The prophets did not speak and write in a vacuum and without a history. Their cries for justice and the social changes they demanded were not in themselves new. The prophets did not originate moral righteousness for the Hebrews; they were not the creators of Israel's religion. Rather, they were products of it. Their uniqueness lay in carrying to fullness the morality and the judgment which were in the teachings of old.

Amos may justly be called the prophet of righteousness, for that expresses his great contribution to religion. The moral character of Yahweh [God] had, of course, been recognized before. Amos himself did not believe that he had said anything new. He assumed the knowledge of the moral law in all men, and its implications as well. But nobody had ever seen so clearly what it involved or dared to be so thoroughgoing in the application of this truth. Significantly enough, it is this moral principle on which Amos' practical monotheism was based. Not because Yahweh is almighty, nor because He is the one great Cause behind the phenomena of the world, but because He is righteous and visits unrighteousness everywhere, did He come to be regarded as the one God. This is the so-called ethical monotheism of the prophets, of which Amos was the first exponent.[2]

HOSEA

Hosea, unlike Amos, was a citizen of the Kingdom of Israel. An old tradition has it that his father, Beeri, was the leader of a tribe, thus giving Hosea a higher social rank than Amos, his older contemporary. They differ also in style. We remember Amos for his impassioned pronouncements of God's righteousness and God's judgment; we recall especially his dramatic visions of judgment: a locust plague, a drought fire, the plumb line test, etc. Power, majesty, wisdom, righteousness, judgment—these are the attributes of God seen in Amos and other prophets. In Hosea we see God as love. There is a kind of quiet, warm-heartedness about Hosea. Judgment and punishment are not lacking in Hosea's work. Hosea portrays an uncompromising picture of Israel's unfaithfulness to God. He even names his children as living symbols of warning to Israel: Lo-ruhamah (Not having obtained mercy), Lo-ammi (Not my people). Yet the dominant metaphor of Hosea's book is that of a wife's (Hosea's wife) infidelity to her husband but her husband's continued love and forgiveness. The parallel is, of course, with God and his people. Does not God's sustaining love continue to seek out his bride, Israel, even in the midst of Israel's unfaithfulness and God's righteous indignation?

Hosea called the people to return to the God of their ancestors; but sunk as they were in idolatry they could hardly hear him (6:1):

> Come, and let us return unto the Lord;
> for He hath torn, and He will heal us.
> He hath smitten, and He will bind us up.

The people's return to God would be met immediately, because God loves Israel. He does not want to abandon His people; He only waits for them (11:8):

> How shall I give thee up, Ephraim?
> How shall I surrender thee, Israel?

No other prophet, excepting perhaps Jeremiah, displayed such touching tenderness, such heart-felt loyalty to his people. His conception of a loving God, pleading with his people to return to him, is graceful and profoundly human. He reproves and admonishes like any other prophet, but simultaneously he displays his compassion and love.

Hosea did not by any means neglect the social evils which Amos dwelt heavily upon. Justice meant as much to Hosea as to Amos. As a prophet it could not be otherwise. He was an opponent of the priestly caste, because as a man of truth he could not stand their formalism, their narrowness. He opposed the royal power and the nobility, because they were a source of evil and oppression. Indeed, the kings of Israel, especially those who loved pleasure and were lax of duty, regarded prophets like Amos and Hosea as enemies of the state.

ISAIAH

Isaiah, son of Amoz, perhaps the greatest of the classical prophets, came from an aristocratic and wealthy family in Jerusalem. According to an old Talmudic tradition, his father was King Amaziah's brother, which means that Isaiah was a member of the Davidic family, a prince of royal blood.

In his book, one of the longest in the Old Testament though only about half of it is by him, Isaiah indicates the year when he started on his prophetic mission: the year "that king Uzziah died" (c. 744 B.C.E.). Isaiah was probably a young man then. A great change must have taken place in the soul of the young prince, though we do not know what brought it about. It is colorfully portrayed in his vision of God sitting on a throne, with angels and seraphim all round. Isaiah there offers himself to be God's messenger to the people of Judah. This vision is unique in two ways. First, no other prophet offered himself willingly; they in fact argued against it, as Moses and Jeremiah did, and accepted the mission reluctantly. Second, no other prophet reported the actual "seeing" of God in such concrete terms. The entire vision as described in chapter 6 is breath-taking; it is a poetic confrontation of man and God. Standing there and glancing at the throne (no figure of God is given), Isaiah deplores the fact that he is "a man of unclean lips" dwelling among a people "with unclean lips." Then one of the seraphim flew unto him and "touched his mouth" with a glowing stone or coal from off the altar, saying, "Lo, this hath touched thy lips; and thine iniquity is taken away, and thy sin expiated." Thus Isaiah's soul was cleansed, purified.

The period of Isaiah's initial mission is well known, historically. The Kingdom of Judah, under the long reign of Uzziah and Jotham, enjoyed a temporary prosperity. Uzziah equipped an army of over 300,000 men "with shields, and spears, and helmets, and coats of mail, and bows, and stones for slinging." Jerusalem was fortified with towers and special "engines" invented by "skillful men" for throwing arrows and stones. As protection against invaders, he built fortifications in the wilderness. Soon enough this army dashed out against the surrounding enemies: the Philistine cities of Gath and Ashdod were conquered, the Arabians were driven back into the desert, and the Ammonites paid tribute. Uzziah's name, we are told by the chroniclers of the time (2 Chron. 26:6-10), "spread abroad even to the entrance of Egypt; for he waxed exceeding great."

But both the glory of conquests and the prosperity of the upper classes did not blind Isaiah. He saw through them. Isaiah was a prophet with rare qualities: a diplomat and statesman of great acumen, a scribe in the palace (2 Chron. 26:22), a royal counselor. He observed colossal empires rapidly forming and as rapidly falling apart in the struggle for supremacy in the world. No, Judah could not even dream of such imperialistic schemes, and if she did, she would surely meet her doom, as the Kingdom of Israel had met her doom before his very eyes. Isaiah looked deep into the internal life of Judah and saw corruption and degeneration. The wealthy obtained all the profits of trade, and some grew luxurious. But the peasants and the artisans were crushed under the weight of exorbitant taxes. The women of Jerusalem cared only for finery. In chapter 3 Isaiah denounces the women of Jerusalem in horrible terms. He describes their anklets and bracelets, their mufflers and perfume boxes, their amulets and their nose rings, their shawls and their turbans.

> Because the daughters of Zion are haughty
> and walk with outstretched necks,
> glancing wantonly with their eyes,
> mincing along as they go,
> tinkling with their feet;
> the Lord will smite with a scab
> the heads of the daughters of Zion,
> and the Lord will lay bare their secret parts . . . .
> Instead of perfume there will be rottenness;
> and instead of a girdle, a rope;
> and instead of well-set hair, baldness;
> and instead of a rich robe, a girding of sackcloth;
> instead of beauty, shame.
>
> (3:16, 17, 24)

Judah seemed to be going the sinful way of Israel. Would she not see? Would she not learn from her neighbor, from the past? Isaiah shouted out into the corruption rampant around him (1:21-23):

> How is the faithful city
> become a harlot!
> She that was full of justice,
> righteousness lodged in her,
> but now murderers.
> Thy silver is become dross,
> thy wine mixed with water.
> Thy princes are rebellious,
> and companions of thieves;
> every one loveth bribes,
> and followeth after rewards;
> they judge not the fatherless,
> neither does the cause
> of the widow come unto them.

Isaiah was unquestionably the most cultivated man of all Israel's prophets. His addresses are masterpieces both in form and content. As a master of style he has no peer. His phrases are laden with poetic figures. He was a literary genius aside from

having been a forceful prophet. Amos and Hosea could probably
meet him in the love of justice and truth, but not in style and in
form. Isaiah used the language of the Hebrews to his will, shaped
and molded it to his needs. In his hands every expression became
granite-like. Amos descends sometimes from the height of his
imagery into simple prose. Hosea, on the other hand, is sometimes
vague. Isaiah is always strong, always ready with words and
phrases; he is never short of breath, for he has always more and
more to say. Though an idealist of the highest calibre and an inspired prophet, he is still the practical man, the farsighted statesman; though the guide of kings, he is still the bold defender of the
oppressed and downtrodden. He knows man and he knows woman:
man in his overbearing pride and arrogance and woman in her
vanity and ostentation. He knows the false judges, the over-fed
priests, the arrogant nobles, and the shallow-minded teachers. He
knows the insolent youth who stand up against the elders and he
knows the "base" who oppose the "honorable."

Isaiah could speak harsh words to his generation, inflammable
words, but he could also speak lightly, in idyllic terms. A fine
parable of his is presented in chapter 5, known as the Song of the
Vineyard.

> let me sing for my beloved
> a love song concerning his vineyard . . . .

Of course we do not know immediately who that beloved is, but
we are bound soon to know. Isaiah's "beloved" owned a piece of
land in a corner which was fertile and "fat," ideal for planting a
vineyard. There were a few stones, but his friend cleared them
away. He dug and planted there the choicest vine. In order to be
able to watch it against marauders, he built a tower in the midst
of it. Then he fenced it around, and hewed out a vat therein.
Having taken care of everything, the good planter waited for
juicy grapes to grow and ripen. But when the time came for his
friend to taste the fruit of his efforts, there was nothing but frustration. The vineyard produced wild grapes—"rotten grapes."

> And now, O inhabitants of Jerusalem

> and men of Judah, judge, I pray you,
> between me and my vineyard.

And Isaiah goes on to say what his "well beloved" had decided
to do in his predicament. He, in fact, told distinctly:

> I will remove its hedge,
> and it shall be devoured;
> I will break down its wall,
> and it shall be trampled down.
> I will make it a waste;
> it shall not be pruned or hoed,
> and briers and thorns shall grow up;
> I will also command the clouds
> that they rain no rain upon it.

A tragic end indeed of a great hope is this. But what else should
his friend do? He could have tolerated some bad vine in his vineyard, but a whole vineyard growing bitter and poisonous grapes
he would not countenance. Isaiah's beloved, who had done everything possible, would not suffer it to exist. And now the prophet
divulges his secret:

> For the vineyard of the Lord of hosts
> is the house of Israel,
> and the men of Judah are his pleasant planting;
> and he looked for Justice, but behold, bloodshed;
> for righteousness, but behold a cry!

The prophecy that follows consists of six parts, each starting
with "Woe." Woe unto them that "join house to house," till there be
no room in the land for anyone besides themselves; woe unto them
that drink away their lives from early morning until late at night;
woe unto them that "draw iniquity with cords of vanity, and sin
as it were with a cart rope"; woe unto them that call evil good,
and good evil, that change darkness into light and light into
darkness; woe unto them that are wise in their own eyes; woe unto
them that "are mighty to drink wine."

Therefore as the tongue of fire
devoureth the stubble,
and as the chaff is
consumed in the flame,
so their root shall be
as rottenness,
and their blossom
shall go up as dust.

In the fateful year 721, the Kingdom of Israel came to its end after more than 225 years in existence. Samaria, its luxurious capital, was razed by the Assyrians (2 Kings 18:9) and most of the natives were exiled deep into Asia. Isaiah's heart trembled for the fate of little Judah lest her end would be as Israel's. He hoped there was still time to save Judah from destruction, that God would not let the last remnant of his people perish from the face of the earth. But the people themselves must do something, and he, Isaiah, having undertaken to be God's messenger, must warn and teach them. To him Assyria was only an instrument that God used to punish sinful nations. In fact, Isaiah predicted the downfall of Assyria in due time. Meanwhile, he called upon the people of Judah not to despair. Thus Isaiah made Israel's tragedy the opportunity of saving Judah through an inner spiritual regeneration under the young prince, Hezekiah, who became his disciple.

King Hezekiah, under the guidance of his great teacher, did effect a reformation. The idols were removed and destroyed, the images were broken, the anointed pillars for idol worshipping were overthrown, and the holy trees were cut down. Above all, the serpent-god worshipped since the days of Moses, in imitation of Egyptian idolatry, was broken to pieces. The High Places, on the top of which stone pillars were erected with cone-shaped wooden altars used for sacrificing, were torn down. The masses were so accustomed to these places that they looked at their overthrow as sacrilege. Besides, these were places where orgies and popular celebrations often took place, and the simple people were drawn by the hilarity, eating, drinking, and lewdness that accompanied such celebrations. Yet the reform went on. But this was an outward reform; the true worship of God had to be planted anew and that was not easy.

This was probably the time when the great visions of Isaiah—the vision of the King of Justice and the vision of World Peace—came to fruition. Never had another prophet overstepped the narrow limits of Judah to look at the world as a whole. Isaiah's view encompassed all of humanity. All peoples and nations constituted one world family and all men became brothers to each other. They recognized the one living God and came up to Jerusalem to learn His ways and "to walk in His paths." God will become their teacher and all of mankind will become His disciples. And what will they learn in the House of the God of Jacob? They will learn the great teaching of how to live in peace (2:4):

> And they shall beat their swords into plowshares,
> and their spears into pruning hooks;
> nation shall not lift up sword against nation,
> neither shall they learn war any more.

These words were penned by Isaiah almost 300 years before the great Plato composed his Republic. While trying to envisage the establishment of a new Great Society, Plato failed to see humanity. The Greeks lived within his utopia, a republic ruled by philosophers; barbarians lived elsewhere. The Platonic republic, of course, had to be defended against the encroachment of the barbarians. Consequently, an army had to be set up. Indeed, a third part of the citizens were to be professional soldiers well versed in the art of warfare. Such a republic did not mean anything to Isaiah. The "ruler" in his world would be a man upon whom "the spirit of the Lord shall rest" (ll:2-4):

> The spirit of wisdom and understanding,
> the spirit of counsel and might,
> the spirit of knowledge and the fear of the Lord.
> And his delight shall be in the fear of the Lord.
> He shall not judge by what his eyes see,
> or decide by what his ears hear;
> but with righteousness he shall judge the poor,
> and decide with equity for the meek of the earth.

The tribulations of the present were only steppingstones toward the future. Even the destruction of Judah, his beloved country, if it ever comes through the sinfulness of her inhabitants, would not be the end. The righteous few, the remnant, the prophet's party, would still continue. Revival would come, as indeed it came in due time. For the world, the handiwork of the Eternal God is not a chaotic mass. Great events do not happen by themselves; there is a divine plan and purpose. For God is not only the Creator of the world, but He is also the God of history. As a prophet of God, Isaiah regarded himself as a moral interpreter of history. To be dismayed, and to fall into the abyss of despair at seeing the great changes of history, was almost tantamount to being ignorant of the facts of life.

Thus Isaiah looked into the future instead of into the present. While all other nations placed the Golden Age in the past, at the very dawn of civilization, the Hebrew prophets realized that the future, near or remote, must hold within itself the greater possibilities. In this they saw God's participation in history.

MICAH

Micah was a contemporary of Isaiah, possibly a member of his circle (cf. Isaiah's world peace lyric of "swords into plowshares" is also to be found in Micah 4:3). That Isaiah was the older prophet may be learned from the fact that he started on his mission at the time of King Uzziah, whereas Micah's prophecies date from the reign of Jotham. He came to Jerusalem from the town of Moresheth, located not far from the Philistine city of Gath. Nothing about Micah's origin is mentioned. The fact that his father's name remained unknown is taken as an indication that he was the son of simple folk, possibly peasants.

The plain where Micah grew up was fertile and rich in vegetation, abounding with springs and bathed in sunshine, but nevertheless the peasant folk must have toiled long to eke out a living from the soil. Agricultural work in those parts of the world was hard and exacting. One had to do his work from early morning until nightfall while conditions were congenial. Since rainfall was scarce at the time when it was needed, and a scorching sun would not wait for the peasant to gather the fruit of his labor, man had to stand guard not to be late and to do his utmost at the proper time.

There was, however, another side to the picture. The plain here and there was studded with castles or houses of pleasure for the big city visitors. There were also a number of resort places. Micah enumerates such towns, satirizing the pleasure-seekers (1:10-15). The peasant boy must have seen how the poor were dispossessed of their land for either failing to pay their debts or their taxes, and how later a palace was erected on the land. At first, perhaps, Micah thought that such wanton actions were few and far between, and even when informed of their frequency he might have believed that these were events characteristic of the outlying districts only. Surely the king and his judges did not know what was going on outside the Holy City of Jerusalem.

When Micah, therefore, went to Jerusalem, he must have believed that the situation was by no means hopeless; the Elders, the learned priests, the leaders would rectify the situation in no time, if one would call their attention to it. But, to his great cha grin, what he saw in Jerusalem was indeed worse. Jerusalem was a city of sin and crime, a "harlot city," as Isaiah called her. In the midst of it was Solomon's Temple, dedicated to the only living God; but all around iniquity and deception reigned supreme. We do not know whether Micah joined a circle of "Sons of Prophets," as the close disciples of prophets called themselves. Perhaps he came in direct contact with Isaiah's disciples. What we do know is that Micah himself became a prophet. How this innermost change occurred, and where this peasant learned the art of writing, or who guided him on his new path, will perhaps remain a mystery forever. There is not the slightest hint in his small book as to these points. Suddenly the peasant from Moresha became a master of style, at times overreaching in forcefulness even the great Isaiah.

Indeed the older prophet, born in high station—his sympathies for the oppressed notwithstanding—could not feel so deeply the woes of the suffering masses as Micah did, who himself came from among them. Micah was a little different in yet another aspect: to Isaiah the Temple was God's House and Jerusalem was the capital of Judah; to him it was probably unthinkable that God would destroy His own House. Isaiah never predicted the destruction of the Temple and Jerusalem. Not so Micah: God would not spare the City of Jerusalem nor even the Temple (3:12):

> Therefore shall Zion for your sake
> be plowed as a field,
> and Jerusalem shall become heaps,
> and the mountain of the house
> as the high places of a forest.

Micah's greatness lies precisely in his being a "man of the people," in his simple idiom. When he speaks of fields that were seized, they are the fields of his native province. The flocks he mentions are scattered over the native pastures; the shining dew drops in the early morning are those that came down from the Lord, and "the showers upon the grass" are blessings from heaven. Micah knows about the serpent that licks the dust and the crawling things that fill the earth. When he turns towards the world, he sees the earth and her peoples instead of, like Isaiah, "heaven and earth."

> Hear, ye peoples, all of you;
> hearken, O earth, and all that therein is.

When the "day of God" would come "the mountains shall be molten" and "the valleys shall be cleft" as wax before the fire, as waters that are poured down a steep place.

In denouncing injustice, Micah is as forceful as Isaiah and Amos, but he can also be as gentle as Hosea. Twice in his little book, Micah bewails his fate. While speaking of Samaria and her doom, his eyes fill with tears, and he tells us (1:8-9):

> For this will I wail and howl,
> I will go stripped and naked,
> I will make a wailing like the jackals,
> and a mourning like the ostriches.
> For the wound is incurable;
> for it is come even unto Judah;

it reacheth unto the gate of my people,
even to Jerusalem.

Also, when he looks closely at the men of his generation and at
their doings, he breaks out in bewailing his fate (7:1-2);

Woe is me! for I am as the last of the summer fruit,
as the grape gleanings of the vintage;
there is no cluster to eat;
nor first-ripe fig which my soul desireth.
The godly man is perished out of the earth,
and the upright among man is no more;
they all lie in wait for blood.

The highest point of emotional impact that the peasant-prophet
reaches is when he speaks of God and his people, of God and
man (6:4):

O my people, what have I done unto thee?
And wherein have I wearied thee?
Testify against Me.
For I brought thee up out from the land of Egypt,
and redeemed thee out of the house of bondage,
and I sent before thee Moses, Aaron, and Miriam.

And having ascertained the loving-kindness of God to his people
(6:6-8):

Wherewith shall I come before the Lord,
and bow myself before God on high?
Shall I come before him with burnt offerings,
with calves of a year old?
Will the Lord be pleased with thousands of rams,
with ten thousands of rivers of oil?
Shall I give my firstborn for my transgression,
the fruit of my body for the sin of my soul?
It hath been told thee, O man, what is good,
and what the Lord doth require of thee:

only to do justly, and to love mercy,
and to walk humbly with thy God.

No wonder that moral teachers during the ages have found in these words of the peasant-prophet the sum-total of moral life.

JEREMIAH

Jeremiah has been called "the man of woe," and rightly so. A prophet of sorrow and grief, he seems to have borne all alone the weight of Judah's oncoming national catastrophe, which he had not only foreseen and forecast but also lived through to the very end. He drank the cup of bitterness to the last drop.

Because the Book of Jeremiah contains a variety of biographical and social details, personal as well as historical material, reflecting the conditions of the time, this prophet of woe is better known and understood than any other of his predecessors. His despair, his loneliness, the animosity he aroused, the tragic situation of a man who, having stood above his generation, saw the dark shadows of doomsday creeping all around, are close to our hearts because they are truly human and so deep-rooted in the emotional life of man.

Woe is me, my mother, that thou hast borne me—a man of strife and a man of contention to the whole earth! I have not lent, neither have men lent to me; yet every one of them doth curse me. (15:10)

Jeremiah was born into a priestly family in Anathoth, a small village not far from Jerusalem. Some scholars think that his family originated from the court priest Abiathar at the time of David. When Solomon became king he banished Abiathar into Anathoth for taking the side of Adonijah as the heir to the throne (1 Kings 1:7). Anathoth was in the province of the tribe of Benjamin, and the priests there must have been opponents of the Davidic dynasty. The mother of the tribe was Rachel, Jacob's beloved wife, whereas the tribe of Judah descended from the second wife—Leah. Yet Judah dominated all the tribes under David and Solomon. Did

Jeremiah share with his family the traditional animosity towards
Judah? There is no indication in his book as to such a hostile
attitude. For Jeremiah did not consider himself a priest at all; he
was a prophet, a rebel against the priestly caste, a severe critic,
"a man of strife and contention" as he called himself.

Though it is probable that he had first preached in Anathoth,
his native village, he soon found himself in the capital, only one
hour's walk away. The big city where life was intense tempted him.
Here political, social, and economic life was at its height; here was
the very source of concentrated power, influence, and wealth. It
was a great challenge to a young man who regarded himself as
a seeker of truth and as God's messenger of righteousness and
justice. No one but Jeremiah himself could explain what occurred
inside of his mind. So we have no other choice but turn to him;
let Jeremiah explain Jeremiah (1:4-19):

Then the word of the Lord came unto me saying, Before
thy birth I sanctified thee, and I ordained thee a prophet
unto the nations. Then said I, Ah, Lord God! behold I
cannot speak for I am a child. But the Lord said unto
me, Say not, I am a child: for thou shalt go to all that
I shall send thee, and whatsoever I command thee thou
shalt speak. Be not afraid of their faces: for I am with
thee to deliver thee, said the Lord. Then the Lord put
forth his hand, and touched my mouth. And the Lord
said unto me, Behold, I have put my words in thy mouth.
See, I have this day set thee over the nations and over
the kingdoms, to root out, and to pull down, and to destroy, and to throw down, to build, and to plant. Lo, I
will call all the families of the kingdoms of the north,
saith the Lord; and they shall come, and they shall set
every one his throne at the entering of the gates of Jerusalem, and against all the walls thereof round about, and
against all the cities of Judah. And I will utter my judgments against them touching all their wickedness, who
have forsaken me, and have burned incense unto other
gods, and worshiped the works of their own hands. Thou,
therefore, gird up thy loins, and arise, and speak unto

them all that I command thee: be not dismayed at their
faces, lest I confound thee before them. For, behold, I
have made thee this day a fortified city, and an iron pillar, and brazen walls against the whole land, against
the kings of Judah, against the princes thereof, against
the priests thereof, and against the people of the land.
And they shall fight against thee; but they shall not prevail against thee: for I am with thee, saith the Lord, to
deliver thee.

What we learn from this rather lengthy and self-revealing passage
is very difficult to convey in rational terms. The prophet, while
speaking of his great mission, stands too high above us. We do
not know, nor shall we ever, it seems, be able to comprehend
how a man might be placed under the stress of such overall responsibility. Such situations could never be realized under usual
circumstances. A mental as well as an emotional explosion must
have occurred in Jeremiah, an explosion that by its sheer force
removed everything tinted with the material—a state of being that
could have no other name but Divine. Thus Jeremiah became a
prophet.

BOOK OF THE LAW

About the year 621, under the reign of King Josiah, the High
Priest Hilkiah found a book that was hidden away in one of the
secluded parts of the Temple. This book was brought to the king
and Shaphan the Scribe read it to him. Its contents were so star-
tling that Josiah rent his clothes. He appointed a special royal
delegation and ordered them thus (2 Kings 22:13):

Go ye, inquire of the Lord for me, and for the people, and
for all Judah concerning the words of this book that is
found; for great is the wrath of the Lord that is kindled
against us, because our fathers have not hearkened to
the words of this book, to do according unto all that
which is written concerning us.

There lived at that time a prophetess by the name of Huldah, about whom we know very little. One thing, however, is certain: Huldah wielded some influence upon the king and the people and her words had to be listened to. The chronicler has this to say about her (2 Kings 22:14-17);

> So [they] went unto Huldah the prophetess . . . and they communed with her. And she said unto them: "Thus saith the Lord God of Israel, Tell the man that sent you to me, Thus saith the Lord, Behold I will bring evil upon this place, and upon the inhabitants thereof, even all the words of the book which the king of Judah hath read. Because they have forsaken me and have burned incense unto other gods, therefore my wrath shall be kindled against this place, and shall not be quenched."

The king received Huldah's orders and fully executed them. A spiritual revolution, much stronger and more basic than at the time of Hezekiah, several generations before, took place. Josiah went up to the House of the Lord, and with him the priests and prophets, and all the people both small and great; and he read all the words of the book of the covenant (2 Kings 23:2). Thus a renewed covenant between God and the people was entered upon, resulting in the following reformation described so vividly in 2 Kings 23:4, 24, 21, 25:

> And the king commanded Hilkiah the high priest, and the priests of the second order, and the keepers of the door, to bring forth out of the temple of the Lord all the vessels that were made for Baal, and for the grove, and for all the host of heaven; and he burned them outside Jerusalem in the fields of Kidron, and carried the ashes of them unto Beth-el. . . . And the idols, and all the abominations that were found in the land of Judah and in Jerusalem, did Josiah put away, that he might fulfil the words of the Law. . . . And the king commanded all the people, saying, Keep the Passover unto the Lord your God, as it is written in this book of this covenant . . . . And like unto him was there no king before him, that turned to the Lord with all his heart, and with all his soul, and with all his might.

What kind of a book was it that caused a spiritual revolution in the life of a people? Who composed and hid it? And what happened to it afterward? The chroniclers call it the Book of the Law and the Book of the Covenant. As to the rest we are in the dark. Yet we know that this book marked a turning point in the life of Judah.

Jeremiah started prophesying in the thirteenth year of King Josiah, five years before the discovery of the book. During the long reign of King Manasseh when terrible persecutions had been instituted against prophets and their adherents, and idolatry had been restored throughout the land to such an extent that even the king sacrificed his own son to Moloch, all anti-government activities seemed to have halted. Tradition has it that even Isaiah was executed, though we hear about it in much later times. A total change, however, occurred when young Josiah (a lad of only eight years) was put on the throne. The prophetic circles came to life again and strong efforts were made by way of restoring the pre-Manasseh days. The young king was under the influence of the prophets and Torah-true priests and needed only a rallying point.

The consensus of opinion among modern scholars is that the mysterious book which served as a rallying point was the last book of the Pentateuch, Deuteronomy. Written in a popular style in the form of exhortations and speeches by Moses before his death, this book speaks both to the mind and to the heart. Moses appears as the kind-hearted teacher, the truthful shepherd, and the wise leader who not only lays down the laws of life but also forecasts what would happen to the people if they disobey them. As a father loves his children, so Moses loves his people; but this flaming love does not blind him from seeing clearly the outcome of their straying from the right path. He warns and admonishes. He curses and blesses. No small wonder that such a book, discovered at the right time, was used to advantage.

Just at the time when Josiah was needed in the consolidation of his reform, he lost his life on the battlefield at Megiddo, on the plain of Jezreel. He led his army against Necho, king of Egypt. Fatally wounded in his chariot, he was brought home dead just at the dawn of a great career. The whole nation mourned him. Jeremiah, in a bitter lamentation characteristic of his mighty pen, bewailed the national loss. Judah became a vassal of Egypt. Necho appointed a new king, Jehoiakim, who was not only a sub-

servient slave to Egypt but actually nullified his father's great
work. Here is how Jeremiah describes the conditions under which
the people lived at that time. It is a sad picture indeed (Jer. 22:
13-17):

> Woe unto him that buildeth his house by unrighteousness,
> and his chambers by injustice; that useth his neighbor's
> service without wages, and giveth him not for his work;
> that saith, I will build me a spacious house and large
> chambers, and cutteth him out windows; and it is ceiled
> with cedar, and painted with vermillion. Shalt thou reign,
> because thou strivest to excel in cedar? Did not thy father
> eat and drink, and do judgment and justice, and then it
> was well with him? He judged the cause of the poor and
> needy; then it was well: was not this to know me saith the
> Lord? But thine eyes and thine heart are not but for thy
> covetousness, and for to shed innocent blood, and for op-
> pression, and for violence, to do it.

Jeremiah was justified in denouncing the king's apostasy. For
he had led the people back to idolatry. But was he the only cause
of the religious relapse? Jeremiah certainly did not think so. He
addressed himself not to one man but to the people as a whole.
Of course, The Sanctuary of the Lord, the Temple of Solomon,
was a holy place, but only when the people, the priests, the judges,
the rulers are God-fearing and righteous. Observing the forms
of worship, the religious ritual, without a change of heart was
nothing better than idolatry. In this respect he was not the first
one—other prophets proclaimed the same truth. But Jeremiah's
words were simpler, more heart-warming, and more human (Jer.
7:3-7, 9-10):

> Amend your ways and doings. . . . Trust not in lying
> words shouting 'the Sanctuary of the Lord!' 'the Sanctu-
> ary of the Lord!' 'the Sanctuary of the Lord!' Nay, but if
> you thoroughly amend your ways and your doings, if ye
> thoroughly execute justice between man and his neighbor,
> oppress not the stranger, the fatherless and the widow, and
> shed not innocent blood; then will I cause you to dwell in
> this place, in the land I gave to your fathers forever.
> Think you, you can steal, murder, commit adultery,
> swear falsely, and burn incense to Baal—and that then

you can come and stand before me in this House and say, 'We are delivered'? That you may forsooth do all these abominations?

BABYLONIA

At the end of the 7th century B.C.E., the Babylonians became the greatest power in the world. At first, Assyria fell. In the year 605, Nineveh, the capital city, was completely destroyed by the Babylonians and Medes, so much so that almost no trace of it was left. In the year 604, Pharaoh-Necho was defeated in the great battle of Carchemish, on the Euphrates, and having fled into Egypt, retracted completely from Asia Minor. The Kingdom of Judah and the meager remnant of the Northern Kingdom of Israel were bound to fall like ripe fruit into the hands of the Babylonians.

What was Jeremiah's stand about submission to Babylon? Like Isaiah a century before, Jeremiah regarded Babylon as the instrument of God. To Isaiah, Assyria was "the rod of God"; to Jeremiah, Babylonia. Little Judah could not stand up against the colossus of the Euphrates, nor could she afford to play the political games of the Pharaohs. The prophetic insight, however, dictated that the nation must clean its own house first in order to be able to live through any storm that might break out from either side. It so happened that when Nebuchadnezzar approached the borders of Judah, Jehoiakim at once submitted, as all other countries did. The Babylonians, this time, were not hostile: Judah remained semi-independent and paid tribute to the overlord. But this situation did not last long. The king and his advisers conspired with Egypt and finally Judah revolted and declared herself independent of Babylon. Soon enough, the other vassals of Nebuchadnezzar were ordered to attack Judah. The Ammonites and Moabites from the other side of the Jordan, and the Syrians from the north, quickly invaded the country. An expeditionary force from Babylonia then arrived and Jerusalem was surrounded. The awful siege began which lasted three years. Judah stood all alone at the very brink of the precipice.

Jeremiah was inside the city walls during that long siege, carry-

ing his message of woe. This most tender-hearted man, whose outcry of anguish and pain is even now being heard from across the
centuries, seemed to act most cruelly when truth and justice were
at stake. He would dramatize his oracle and demonstrate his
gloomy predictions in action. Once he hid a linen girdle in muddy
water, and showing it to the people, said: "So will the pride of
Jerusalem be soiled." On another occasion he took an earthen
vessel, and throwing it down, shattered it to pieces, saying: "The
people of this city will be shattered like this vessel that cannot be
pieced together again." He carried a yoke around his neck in order to demonstrate that Judah must submit for the time being to
Babylonia. One wonders how he was permitted to do such things
in a besieged city which was fighting for its survival. As a matter
of fact, Jeremiah lived through terrible moments. Here is a passage which gives us a picture of that time. Jeremiah stood at the
entrance of the Temple and addressed the people (Jer. 26:4,6):

> Thus saith the Lord: If ye will not hearken to me, to walk
> in my law, which I have set before you, . . . then will I
> make this house like Shiloh, and will make this city a
> curse to all the nations of the earth.

A throng of priests and Temple worshippers gathered around him.
They were all angry and threatened him with death. He was arrested and brought before the princes and the judges (Jer. 26:
12-19):

> Then spake Jeremiah unto all the princes and to all the
> people, saying, The Lord sent me to prophesy against
> this house and against this city all the words that ye have
> heard. Therefore now amend your ways and your doings,
> and obey the voice of the Lord your God; and the Lord
> will repent of the evil that he hath pronounced against
> you. As for me, behold, I am in your hand; do with me
> as seemeth good and meet unto you. But know ye for
> certain, that if ye put me to death, ye shall surely bring
> innocent blood upon yourselves, and upon this city and
> upon the inhabitants thereof: for of a truth the Lord hath
> sent me unto you to speak all these words in your ears.
> Then said the princes and all the people unto the priests
> and to the prophets: This man is not worthy to die; for

he hath spoken to us in the name of the Lord our God.
Then rose up certain of the elders of the land, and spake
to all the assembly of the people, saying, Micah prophesied, and spake to all the people of Judah, saying, Thus
said the Lord of hosts: Zion shall be ploughed like a
field, and Jerusalem shall become heaps, and the mountain of the House as the high places of a forest. Did Hezi-
kiah king of Judah and all Judah put him at all to death?
did he not fear the Lord, and besought the Lord, and the
Lord repented of the evil which he had pronounced against
them? Thus might we procure great evil against our
souls."

Nothing could stop Jeremiah from pursuing Truth. Anything
and everything that hinted of falsehood was so abominable to him
that he had to denounce it. He denounced the king, the princes, the
leaders, the government officials, the judges, the learners of Torah,
and the false prophets who catered to the mighty. Once he asked
his faithful disciple and secretary Baruch to write down a prophecy on a scroll and bring it personally to the king. Jehoiakim
was so enraged on hearing it that he tore it apart and cast it into
the burning furnance. But Jeremiah wrote out a severer warning
on another scroll.

Finally, Jerusalem fell. It was in the year 597 B.C.E. This time
both the city and the temple remained intact. The Babylonians
banished some forty thousand people from their native country,
among them the royal family, the nobles, the leading citizens,
and many of the priests. Jeremiah bemoaned the misfortunes of
the exiles in the following heart-rending passage (Jer. 8:18-9:1):

Oh, that I could comfort myself against sorrow. My heart
is faint within me. Behold the cry of my people from a
land that is far off. Is not the Lord in Zion? Is not her
King within her? The harvest is past, the summer is
ended, and we are not saved. For the hurt of my people
am I hurt. . . . Is there no balm in Gilead? Is there no
physician there? . . . Oh that my head were waters and
mine eyes a fountain of tears, then might I weep night
and day for the slain of my people.

But this was not the worst. And old Jeremiah lived to see it with his own eyes.

From 597 to 586, a period of eleven years, Judah found herself again on the brink of the precipice. Nebuchadnezzar had left Judah intact for the time being, because he wanted a bulwark against Egypt. But King Zedekiah, a weak-willed man, conspired in the name of national independence against Babylonia. He entered into an alliance with the surrounding peoples to throw off the yoke of being vassals. Egypt, of course, encouraged the rebellion. Nebuchadnezzar then sent a powerful army against Zedekiah, who had sworn allegiance to him. The alliance collapsed and Judah found herself alone in the field. In despair he sent for counsel to Jeremiah, who advised to surrender to Babylonia and save the country from a final catastrophe. This seemed unpatriotic and even bordering on treason. At about this time, when the destiny of Judah was hanging in the balance, Jeremiah's call for a return to God was heeded. He demanded that the slaves be freed in accordance with the Law of Moses, viewing it as an act of justice in a critical time. At a solemn ceremony they swore to obey the Law. This reform, however, did not last long. Soon enough the news reached Jerusalem that Egypt had mustered an army and had gone all out to meet the Babylonians on the battlefield. The nobles in Jerusalem, confident that Egypt would win, changed their course of action. Jeremiah appeared to them as a false prophet, a traitor to the national interests. All internal reforms were abandoned. Jerusalem waited for the outcome of the war between the two empires.

At that critical moment, the voice of the Prophet of Woe reverberated in the streets of Jerusalem (Jer. 34:13-17, 37:9-10):

> Thus saith the Lord, the God of Israel: I made a covenant with your fathers in the day that I brought them forth out of the land of Egypt, out of the house of bondage, saying: At the end of seven years let ye go every man his brother a Hebrew, which hath been sold unto thee; and when he hath served thee six years, thou shalt let him go free from thee. . . . And ye were now turned, and had done right in my sight, in proclaiming liberty every man to his neighbor; and ye had made a covenant before me in the house which is called by my name: But ye turned and polluted my name, and caused every man his servant,

and every man his handmaid, whom he had set at liberty
at their pleasure, to return, and brought them into sub-
jection, to be unto you for servants and for handmaids.
Therefore thus saith the Lord: Ye have not hearkened
unto me, in proclaiming liberty, every one to his brother,
and every man to his neighbor: behold, I proclaim a liberty for you, said the Lord, to the sword, to the pestilence,
and to the famine; and I will make you to be removed
into all the kingdoms of the earth. . . .

Deceive not yourselves, saying the Chaldeans will surely
depart from us; for they will not depart. Though you had
smitten the whole army of the Chaldeans and there remained only their wounded, yet would they rise up and
burn this city with fire.

The encounter between Egypt and the Chaldean army did not go
the way the nobles in Jerusalem anticipated. Egypt's first attacks
were repulsed, and a peace pact was somehow patched up. The
Babylonian army invaded Judah. The cities of Lachish and Azekah fell and Jerusalem was besieged. Jeremiah, who saw the end
rapidly approaching, warned and admonished the people and the
leaders. They were all infuriated against him. He was thrown into
a pit, a loathsome dungeon. They charged him with treason and
condemned him as an enemy of the state.

The siege continued month after month—eighteen terrible months
in all. Nothing could be brought in from the outside, for the enemy barred all roads. Food was so scarce that mothers resorted
to unimaginable means to satisfy the pangs of hunger, eating the
flesh of their own children. The Babylonians struck the walls with
their powerful battering rams in order to breach them. But their
most powerful weapon was starvation. On the tenth of Tebeth the
first breach was made, and on the ninth of Ab the lower city was
taken. The king and nobles escaped and fled at night. The Babylonian army entered the city. Solomon's Temple was completely
destroyed. All the treasures of the Temple and the palaces were
seized. The soldiers plundered Jerusalem and murdered thousands
of its inhabitants. The most prominent priests, nobles, officials were
taken captive. They were brought to Riblah, in Syria, where Nebuchadnezzar stopped at that time. They were all summarily put to

death. King Zedekiah and his entourage were caught in the plains of Jericho. His sons were slain while he was looking on. Then his eyes were put out. A blind man, broken physically and mentally, he was sent away to Babylonia where he languished in a dungeon until he died. The rebels who had hid in caves or on high cliffs were sought out and caught. Most of them were either sold as slaves on the markets of Asia, or hanged. Those who happened to survive the holocaust were exiled into the distant regions of Babylonia.

Jeremiah, who witnessed the total destruction of his beloved Judah, mourned its fate. Tradition has it that the Book of Lamentations was written by him. For almost 2,500 years this collection of eulogies has been read in the synagogues throughout the world, commemorating the day of Jerusalem's destruction. Remarkably enough, the Babylonians treated the old prophet with respect. Not only was he set at liberty, but he was offered refuge in Babylonia. Jeremiah refused. He could not desert his own people. He consoled the remainder, the poor people, peaceful peasants and artisans, who were left alone by the new rulers. At this tragic time, Jeremiah tried to heal the old wounds. He predicted national restoration. Later, however, Jeremiah decided to leave the ruined country together with many other Judeans. He escaped into Egypt where he soon afterward died.

Despite all the tribulations and endless suffering that Jeremiah experienced in his life, he had never given up his hope for his people's survival. His faith in God, his confidence in the future, his belief in Israel's mission never faltered, as the following prophecy clearly indicates (Jer. 32:37):

> Behold, I will gather them out of all countries, whither I
> I have driven them in great wrath; and I will bring them
> again unto this place, and I will cause them to dwell
> safely.

How was this to happen? And when would it take place? Jeremiah determined the time for the return to Zion: seventy years! And he continued (Jer. 32:38,39,42; 33:10,11,14,16):

> And they shall be my people, and I will be their God;
> And I will give them one heart, and one way, that they
> may fear me forever, for the good of them, and of their

children after them. For thus saith the Lord: Like as I brought all this great evil upon this people, so will I bring upon them all the good that I have promised them. Again there shall be heard in this place, which ye say shall be desolate without man and without beast, even in the cities of Judah, and in the streets of Jerusalem: the voice of joy, and the voice of gladness, the voice of the bridegroom and the voice of the bride, the voice of them that shall say, Praise the Lord of Hosts; for the Lord is good; for his mercy endureth forever. . . . For I will cause to return the captivity of the land, as at the first, saith the Lord. Behold the days come, saith the Lord, that I will perform that good thing which I have promised unto the house of Israel and to the house of Judah. In those days shall Judah be saved, and Jerusalem shall dwell safely; and this is the name wherewith she shall be called, The Lord is our Righteousness.

EZEKIEL

Among the thousands of exiles carried away into Babylonia after the 597 fall of Jerusalem was Ezekiel, a priest destined to become a major and unique prophet of Israel.

> Now it came to pass . . . in the fourth month, in the fifth day of the month, as I was among the captives by the river of Chebar, that the heavens were opened, and I saw visions of God (1:1)

Thus in 593 Ezekiel declared himself a prophet. He was apparently living with captives who had established a community in exile, on a tributary of the Euphrates. In Ezekiel's book, as it has come down to us, he is a moral teacher, a preacher, a "watchman," an interpreter of the Law, issuing verdicts in conjunction with the demands of the times. A visionary of great power and an original parable teller, Ezekiel excels in apocalyptic prophecies and mystical descriptions. His style varies from prose to poetry. He forecasts Israel's restoration and glorifies her future; his faith in redemption is so powerful that he gives, in his final chapters, a complete plan of the second Temple.

During the prophetic period, perhaps long before, there was a simple folk proverb which both Jeremiah and Ezekiel mention (Ez. 18:2):

> The fathers have eaten sour grapes, and the children's teeth are set on edge.

At the time of Ezekiel's exile, this simple proverb must have been used by the recalcitrants in ridiculing the prophets. There probably were many who seriously felt that they had been unjustly penalized for the sins of their forefathers. They questioned God's justice. By blaming their fathers they wanted to exonerate themselves. They doubted the connection between sin and punishment. A clarification was needed. The prophets of old concentrated their messages less on the individual and more on the community as a whole. The individual loomed larger in Ezekiel's consideration. Note, for example, his interpretation of his task as a prophet (3:17-18):

> Son of man, I have appointed thee a watchman unto the house of Israel; and when thou shalt hear a word at My mouth, thou shalt give them warning from Me. When I say unto the wicked: Thou shalt surely die; and thou givest him not warning, nor speakest to warn the wicked from his wicked way, to save his life; the same wicked man shall die in his iniquity, but his blood will I require at thy hand.

What a perilous task! To be personally responsible for each individual was really something new in prophecy. Both in this instance and his evaluation of the "sour grapes" proverb, Ezekiel proclaimed the responsibility of the individual, perhaps his most important teaching.

> As I live saith the Lord God, ye shall not have occasion any more to use this proverb in Israel. (18:3)

God is concerned not only with peoples and nations, but also with individuals. He is a personal God as well as the God of history.

What did this mean to the exiles? It meant that the burden of the past could be thrown off completely; it meant that they should be concerned only with themselves and not with the sins of their forefathers; it meant that the punishment of being exiles was the end of a process and a new beginning was soon to emerge; it meant that the humiliation of exile was not to last too long, because God was eager to accept them. What they had to do was to be worthy of this acceptance. Then they would all be gathered from the countries where they were scattered. Their country would be restored as of old and a King of the House of David would lead them on to even greater glory.

The great faith of Ezekiel in the restoration of his people and his hope for the glorious future of Israel are vividly illustrated in his vision of the "dry bones" (37:1-6):

> The hand of the Lord was upon me, and the Lord carried me out in a spirit, and set me down in the midst of the valley, and it was full of bones; and He caused me to pass by them round about, and, behold, there were very many in the open valley; and, lo, they were very dry. And He said unto me: Son of man, can these bones live? And I answered: O Lord God, Thou knowest. Then He said unto me: Prophesy over these bones, and say unto them: O ye dry bones, hear the word of the Lord: Thus said the Lord God unto these bones: Behold, I will cause breath to enter into you, and ye shall live. And I will lay sinews upon you, and will bring up flesh upon you, and cover you with skin, and put breath in you, and ye shall live; and ye shall know that I am the Lord.

The Valley of Dry Bones that Ezekiel saw was a concrete picture of a people in exile. There must have been not a few sceptics who were ever ready to hurl their insults at him. Perhaps there were some who established themselves in Babylonia and became prosperous. From later records we learn that not all the Jews returned to Zion when the hour of redemption struck. Such people were prone to see Ezekiel as a dreamer of dreams. While looking into Ezekiel's mind one wonders what faith could do! Babylonia was so powerful, her military might so overwhelming, yet the prophet preached of Israel's rescue.

One of the great lamentations of world literature, "By the rivers of Babylon," came out of this period. It is heart-rending in its grief and overwhelming in its pain. The heart of man, replete with yearning for its native land cries out in all its solemnity and divine dedication to the hope of redemption. Old is the vow, but the Jewish people have never forgotten to remember Jerusalem "above their chief joy."

A tale is told that once Napoleon Bonaparte passed by a synagogue on the 9th of the month of Ab, the national mourning day for the Jewish people, and noticed many Jews sitting and weeping. "Why do these people weep?" asked Napoleon.

Someone answered, "They once had a Temple which was destroyed on that day."

"When did it happen?" asked Napoleon again.

"Thousands of years ago," he was answered.

"Well," Napoleon said, after contemplating upon it for a while, "if a people can mourn the loss of a temple for thousands of years, then it certainly deserves to rebuild that temple and get it back as of yore."

Had Napoleon known Psalm 137, he would not have had to ask.

> By the rivers of Babylon,
> there we sat down, yea, we wept,
> when we remembered Zion.
> We hanged our harps upon the willows
> in the midst thereof.
> For there they that carried us away captives
> required of us words of song;
> and they that wasted us required of us mirth:
> Sing us one of the songs of Zion.
> How shall we sing the Lord's song
> in a strange land?
> If I forget thee, O Jerusalem, let my right hand
> forget her cunning.
> If I do not remember thee,
> let my tongue cleave to the roof of my mouth;
> if I prefer not Jerusalem above my chief joy.
> Remember, O Lord, the children of Edom
> in the day of Jerusalem;
> who said, Rase it, rase it, even to the foundation thereof.
> O daughter of Babylon, who art to be destroyed;

happy shall he be, that rewardeth thee as thou has served us.

Happy shall he be, that taketh and dasheth thy little ones against the rock.

Ezekiel would see that his people did not forget Jerusalem. He would teach them to "sing the Lord's song in a strange land." Ezekiel's visions of redemption and of the restoration of his fatherland are imbued with nobility and idealism. No longer would there be two rival kingdoms, rent asunder by animosity, by self-destructive conflicts, and by shedding of human blood. Before his mind's eye there emerges a unified nation, a kingdom of brotherly love where peace, justice, and truth are the pillars of social life. His faith in man created in the image of God never fails him; for what appears as wholly utopian today may become a reality tomorrow. The prophet is never afraid of being designated a dreamer. Dreams, to him, are not something extraneous to life. How else can the advance of man on the road toward perfection be effected?

Indeed, Ezekiel's dreams kept the exiles together. They saved them from being assimilated or swallowed up by the majority culture. Swayed by the prophetic visions of Ezekiel and encouraged by his disciples, they kept burning in their hearts the hope of national rejuvenation. Purified by their suffering and cleansed of their sins, the exiles abandoned idolatry completely. Preparing themselves for a return to Zion, they turned a new leaf in the history of their people. Here, in Babylonian captivity, far from Jerusalem, the first synagogues must have been founded. In the Houses of Prayer and Learning the exiles found solace and rallied around their leaders and teachers. While praying, they turned lovingly toward Jerusalem, the City of God and the City of Peace, whereby they accentuated their deep-set craving for the restoration of Solomon's Temple in all its glory. In those assembly houses they observed the days of mourning which were established to commemorate the tragic events of the fall of Judah and of the destruction of Jerusalem. Mourning days like the 9th day of Ab and the 3rd of Tishre became national Fast Days. The Scriptures were read and studied publicly. Many of the old traditions—the sanctity of human life, the purity of family life, respect for learning, fear of God, love for Torah—were strengthened and zealously adhered to.

Ezekiel is also known as a great mystic by virtue of the fact that he started out on his prophetic mission with the vision of God's "flaming chariot," drawn by four "beasts," each of them having "four faces": the face of a man, the face of a lion, the face of an ox, and the face of an eagle. It is indeed difficult, if not impossible, to bring his vision of the "chariot" into focus by reason. It towers as a product of poetic imagination, which prevailed in Ezekiel to a high degree. The Vision of the Chariot has been held during the centuries as the mystery of mysteries. It was forbidden to expound it publicly. Mystics have delved into its hidden meanings which were permitted to be handed over only from teacher to teacher under special conditions. It rests on the supposition that God reveals Himself to the selected few through strange and fanciful images (Infra, chapter on "Cabala").

Ezekiel's imagination is remarkable in his capability of planning out the temple-to-be and in reorganizing a government and a country whose restoration was as yet not realized. His precise instructions concerning every detail, the measurements of the edifice he gives, the regulations of the ritual, are of such a nature as to leave the impression that everything is just ready-made and fixed.

His apocalyptic visions, likewise, are breath-taking (38:1-6, 8-9, 18, 21-22):

> And the word of the Lord came unto me, saying: Son of man set thy face toward Gog, of the land of Magog, the chief prince of Mesech and Tubal, and prophesy against him, and say: Thus saith the Lord God: Behold, I am against thee, O Gog, chief prince of Mesech and Tubal; and I will turn thee about, and put hooks into thy jaws, and I will bring thee forth, and all thine army, horses and horsemen, all of them clothed most gorgeously, a great company with buckler and shield, all of them handling swords: Persia, Cush, and Put with them, all of them with shield and helmet; Gomer, and all his bands; the house of Togarmah in the uttermost parts of the north, and all his bands; even many peoples with thee . . . . After many days thou shalt be mustered for service, in the lat-

ter years thou shalt come against the land that is brought back from the sword, that is gathered out of many peoples, against the mountains of Israel, which have been a continued waste; but it is brought forth out of the peoples, and they dwell safely all of them. And thou shalt ascend, to cover the land . . . . And it shall come to pass in that day, when Gog shall come against the land of Israel, saith the Lord God, that my fury shall arise in my nostrils . . . . And I will call for a sword against him . . . . And I will plead against him with pestilence and with blood; and I will cause to rain upon him, and upon his bands, and upon the many peoples that are with him, an overflowing shower, and great hailstones, fire and brimstone.

Bewildered and dazed, we read those awesome visions of the "last days," when the people of God will make the last stand against evil. A heavenly kingdom on earth, a kingdom that has never yet been realized, will emerge. Then God will be recognized by all the nations. Did Ezekiel visualize all this coming soon? To the prophets, time did not mean much. Remote things, hidden in the womb of the future, looked near and so close at hand that one could perceive them. Their great craving and burning desire to bring God down into man's world and to elevate man to the high level of holiness enabled them to envision the future, whether near or remote, as a reality. And in that consists their greatness—a greatness that has never been duplicated either by philosopher or poet.

ISAIAH II

From the midst of the Babylonian Captivity, from the dreams and visions of restoration, and from the nostalgia and craving of people to return to their native land, there came forth a nameless prophet—the Prophet of Redemption.

His great prophecies, as messages of good tidings, are found in chapters 40-55 (and perhaps more) of the Book of Isaiah. As he remained nameless, we call him Deutero-Isaiah, Isaiah the Second.

Fully entitled to a most exalted place among the prophets, he was therefore placed with the great Isaiah. Perhaps his name was Isaiah or perhaps he was a grandson of Isaiah, and owing to this his writings were collated with the writings of Isaiah. Be that what it may, we have before us a prophet of hope and redemption. All his words are attuned to the joy of his great heart, to the enthusiasm and inspiration that comes from a soul filled with loving-kindness and bliss.

> Comfort ye, comfort ye my people, saith your God.
> Speak ye comfortably to Jerusalem,
> and cry unto her,
> that her warfare is accomplished,
> that her iniquity is pardoned:
> for she hath received of the Lord's hand
> double for all her sins.
>
> (Isa. 40:1-2)

He speaks of God as the God of the universe (Isa. 40:12):

> Who has measured the waters in the hollow of his hand
> and marked off the heavens with a span,
> enclosed the dust of the earth in a measure
> and weighed the mountains in scales
> and the hills in a balance?

As he, the prophet himself, is the servant of God, so is Israel. As the prophet is the teacher of men, so is Israel the teacher of nations. Indeed, one of the sacred tasks of Israel is to be "a light to the nations." Israel had recognized the true God first, whereby she became the servant of God and the servant-teacher of humanity, not to rule over others, but rather to be an example to others, instructing others by wisdom and endurance, inner conviction and self-sacrificing.

Why did Israel suffer? Of course she had sinned, but her suffering was not entirely the result of her sins. There is a higher reason underlying her tribulations. Great missions can never be realized without suffering. The greater the ideal, the weightier the responsibilities and the more difficult the realization. Is not the prophet the most despised and rejected by men? Is he not one acquainted with grief and sorrows? So is Israel, the servant of God (43:1-4):

> But now thus saith the Lord that created thee, O Jacob,
> And He that formed thee, O Israel:
> Fear not, for I have redeemed thee,
> I have called thee by thy name, thou art Mine.
> When thou passest through the waters, I will be with thee,
> And through the rivers, they shall not overflow thee;
> When thou walkest through the fire, thou shalt not be
>   burned,
> Neither shall the flame kindle upon thee.
> For I am the Lord thy God,
> The Holy One of Israel, thy saviour;
> I gave Egypt for thy ransom,
> Ethiopia and Seba for thee.
> Since thou wast precious in my sight,
> Thou hast been honorable, and I have loved thee;
> therefore will I give men for thee,
> and peoples for thy life.

This was a great promise by the eternal God.

> That men may know, from the rising of the sun,
> and from the west, that there is none besides me:
> I am the Lord, and there is no other.
> I form light and create darkness,
> I make peace and create evil.
> I am the Lord, who do all these things.
>
> (45:6-7)

"I make peace and create evil"—*evil?* This phrase must be taken in the context of the time. It was the time when the Persians and the Medes, led by the great Cyrus, appeared on the world scene, destined to become the rulers of a greater empire than the Babylonians ever had. In the year 558 Cyrus ascended the throne of Persia. Nine years later he became the master of Media, the ruler of a dual monarchy—Persia and Media. In 547, he defeated Lydia and her allies. King Croesus, famous for his riches, surrendered to him. Cyrus was preparing for greater spoils: to invade Babylonia and capture Babylon. In 538, Cyrus attacked. Babylonia, she that had brought others low, she that destroyed Judah and Jerusalem, was gobbled up by the Persians and the Medes. Belshazzar, the king of Babylon, did not put up even a real fight. The fall of Babylonia was acclaimed (Isa. 14:4-7):

> How the oppressor has ceased,
> the insolent fury ceased!
> The Lord has broken the staff of the wicked,
> the scepter of rulers,
> that smote the peoples in wrath
> with unceasing blows,
> that ruled the nations in anger
> with unrelenting persecution.
> The whole earth is at rest and quiet;
> they break forth into singing.

And the song of the nations follows (14:12-15):

> How you are fallen from heaven,
> O Day Star, son of Dawn!
> How you are cut down to the ground,
> you who laid the nations low!
> You said in your heart,
> I will ascend to heaven;
> above the stars of God
> I will set my throne on high;
> I will sit on the mount of assembly
> in the far north;
> I will ascend above the heights of the clouds,
> I will make myself like the Most High.
> But you are brought down to Sheol,
> to the depths of the Pit.

Indeed, the Prophet of Redemption viewed Cyrus as the appointed of God. However, the faith of the Persians was not the faith of Israel. The Persians believed in two gods: Ormuzd, the spirit of light; and Ahriman, the spirit of darkness or evil. These two beings were constantly at war with one another. Sometimes Ormuzd came out the temporary victor and sometimes Ahriman. This war of the gods was supposed to go on for a long time, but in the end Ormuzd would become the sole ruler of the universe; then happiness would prevail. This could be equated with the "last days" predicted by the great prophets, but the dualism of gods could never be accepted by a Hebrew prophet. Fearing that Israel by her enthusiasm for the Persians might be misled to accept the faith of their redeemers, the Prophet of Redemption came out strongly against dualism: There is no god of darkness and there is no god of light; light and darkness, life and death, good and evil are two sides of the *same* coin.

The Prophet of Redemption lifted suffering and martyrdom for an ideal to the highest. The self-sacrificing ordeal of the ideal man or nation was one of the noblest acts of life. The sanctification of God's name by suffering was a mark of distinction. Probably more than any other prophet did this great teacher wish to bring the truth to the whole of mankind. The God of the universe must be the God of all nations. Israel's selection aimed at bringing the idea of the universal God to all. But before that could really happen, Israel must be true to her mission. She must, like the true prophet, be prepared to suffer for her ideals.

OTHER PROPHETS

More prophets preached and wrote during what we call the Prophetic Age than the seven great figures just discussed. Surely there were some who left no writings at all, and likely the other prophets whose writings we mention now wrote more than the short works that have come down to us. In any case, in the spirit of this brevity, a few sentences about each must suffice.

Zephaniah

Zephaniah was an aristocrat, a descendant of one Hezekiah, probably King Hezekiah of Isaiah's time. He prophesied in the early reign of King Josiah (620-630 B.C.E.) and was presumably present when the Book of the Law was discovered in the Temple. He must have participated in the great reform of those days. His message was one of scathing judgment upon Judah for her religious and social corruption; his images of destruction are dramatically poignant and almost unrelenting. Yet, hope is found in a "remnant of Israel."

Nahum

Only a few years after the prophecy of Zephaniah, Nahum sings in joy at the destruction of Nineveh (612) by the Babylonians. The fall of the Assyrian empire, built upon plunder and annihilation, had to have had a great impact upon people's thinking at that time. Nahum's descriptive powers were keen; his poetic qualities approached the best parts of Isaiah's work.

Habakkuk

Most scholars date Habakkuk at the end of the 7th century. He finds that the Babylonians are proving to be as cruel and aggressive as the Assyrians. *Why* do the unjust prosper? *Why* do the just suffer? Habakkuk agonizes with the assurance that righteousness is rewarded, that justice will triumph.

> O Lord, how long shall I cry,
> and thou wilt not hear?
> I cry out unto thee of violence,
> and thou wilt not save!
>
> (1:2)

At last Habakkuk understood that divine justice is not to be measured by the shortness of man's life; God gives a special patience.

> And the Lord answered me:
> Write the vision, and make it plain upon tablets,

that he may run who reads it.
For still the vision awaits its time;
it hastens to the end—it will not lie.
If it seems slow, wait for it;
it will surely come, it will not delay.
Behold, he whose soul is not upright in him shall fail,
but the righteous shall live by his faith.

(2:2-4)

Obadiah

There was no love lost by the Hebrews on their neighbor Edom.
At the fall of Jerusalem in 586, the Edomites had aided the Babylonians in the looting of the city and the capture of fleeing Judeans.
The Book of Obadiah, the shortest in the scriptures, is a prophecy
of the downfall of Edom.

Haggai and Zechariah

Second Isaiah viewed Cyrus as the appointed of God. Not only
did Cyrus conquer Babylonia, but in 537 B.C.E. he issued a decree
permitting all Hebrew exiles in Babylonia who wanted to do so to
return to their homeland. Some went, but poor land, poor crops,
poverty, and discouragement were their lot. Then, in 520, Haggai
arose to challenge his people in and around Jerusalem: Rebuild
the Temple and God will bless us and prosper us. Two months
later, another prophet, Zechariah, joined Haggai in calling the
people to repentance and a rebuilding of the Temple. Within four
years the Temple was indeed finished. It was not as grand as
Solomon's, but it was rebuilt and it functioned as a central focus
for the life of Israel.

Malachi

Half a century after the rebuilding of the Temple, the purity of
religious practice was sullied, priestly laxness and corruption was
prevalent, doubts ate away the previous hopes and faith of the
people, divorce and intermarriage were rife, social injustice prevailed. It was to this flawed and disillusioned society the prophet
Malachi spoke. He assured them of God's love for them, that God
had not forgotten them. He urged the priests and people to purge

their worship ritual and look to the attitudes behind the sacrifices. For example, he reproved them for offering for sacrifice to God a sick animal they would be ashamed to offer even to the Persian governor. Malachi's emphasis on the Law and on the institutions of religion represents an attempt to embody the prophetic spirit and principles in more tangible forms—a move which came to more creative fruition with Ezra and Nehemiah a few years later.

Joel

Still later, about the end of the 5th century, another half century after Ezra and Nehemiah, the prophet Joel takes the occasion of a terrible locust plague and a drought which are blighting the country to issue a call to Judah for repentance. His dramatic and poetic descriptions are rich and powerful. All the people—young and old, priests and peasants—come together for prayer and fasting, and God promises restoration (2:25, 26):

> I will restore to you the years
> which the swarming locust has eaten . . . .
> You shall eat in plenty and be satisfied.

Jonah and Daniel

There are two prophetic books which differ in two respects from the others we have discussed. In the first place, these two books appeared probably after the canon had been closed on the prophetic books; therefore, they are not, strictly speaking, classified among the Prophets, but among the Writings. In the second place, each book is about a prophet, rather than by a prophet. Nevertheless, because both Jonah and Daniel were prophets and because we have been looking at prophetic books, they are included here.

The Book of Jonah has all the earmarks of a folk story. The rebellious prophet fleeing from God, the raging storm at sea, the casting of lots to determine on whose account God had sent the storm, the monster fish which swallowed the guilty one—these are motifs not only familiar to us today from the ancient story of Jonah, but familiar also to the people who read it when first written, perhaps the 3rd century B.C.E. The message of the book is the universalism of God. He is everywhere: on the land, on the sea, under the sea. No man can flee or hide from God (cf. Amos 9:2-4). Furthermore, God cares for everyone: chosen Israelite, fugitive Jonah, pagan Ninevite. The God of the Hebrews is the God of all men.

The Book of Daniel relates the experiences and visions of Daniel in Babylonia. He interprets the king's dreams and reveals Babylonia's downfall. He envisions Israel's deliverance and destiny. Many scholars date the book as late as 168 B.C.E., suggesting that it was written during the terrible days of Antiochus Epiphanes as a passionate plea for the Jews to hold fast and be loyal to their faith and religious practices, even as had Daniel and Shadrach, Meshach, and Abednego years earlier.

אׇ / 3

POETIC WORKS

HEBREW POETRY

The structure of Hebrew poetry differs from classic poetry as found in Greek and Latin literatures. Rhyme in Hebrew poetry is very rare; assonance and alliteration are frequent; acrostics are sometimes used. Rhythm or balance within a line, in terms of words and stresses (not syllables), is common to almost all Hebrew poetry. All of these characteristics are impossible to reflect adequately, if at all, in any translation. However, the basic form of Hebrew poetry, parallelism, is amenable to translation and can be illustrated in English. Parallelism, referring to the relationship between the lines or to the movement of thought between the lines, can be classified as: synonymous, antithetical, synthetic. In one sense, it can be said that Hebrew poetry rhymes thoughts instead of words. Finally, the normal unit in Hebrew poetry is the couplet, or distich, although the single line occurs occasionally and three-line, four-line, etc. combinations are not uncommon.

Synonymous parallelism refers to lines where the same thought is repeated in different but equivalent terms. Lamech's song, which we noted in an earlier chapter, carries a good example of this (Gen. 4:23):

Adah and Zillah, hear my voice;
you wives of Lamech, hearken to what I say.

Or from Deborah's song (Jud. 5:3):

To the Lord I will sing,
I will make melody to the Lord.

A sequence of couplets opens Moses' song in Deuteronomy (32:
1-3):

Give ear, O heavens, and I will speak;
and let the earth hear the words of my mouth.

May my teaching drop as the rain,
my speech distil as the dew,

as the gentle rain upon the tender grass,
and as the showers upon the herb.

Or from the Psalms (21:2):

Thou hast given him his heart's desire,
and hast not withheld the request of his lips.

This example of the less common triplet is also from the Psalms
(93:3):

The floods have lifted up, O Lord,
the floods have lifted up their voice,
the floods lift up their roaring.

Antithetical parallelism refers to contrasting lines; that is, a
thought is enhanced with opposite statements, again as illustrated
from the Psalms (30:5, 18:27):

For his anger is but for a moment,
and his favor is for a lifetime.

> Weeping may tarry for the night,
> but joy comes in the morning.

> For thou dost deliver a humble people;
> but the haughty eyes thou dost bring down.

Deborah's song again offers another illustration (Jud. 5:2):

> That the leaders took the lead in Israel,
> that the people offered themselves willingly,
> bless the Lord.

A prophetic poem in Zechariah also serves as an example (13:8):

> Two thirds shall be cut off and perish,
> and one third shall be left alive.

The Proverbs are replete with examples; one will suffice (10:1):

> A wise son makes a glad father,
> but a foolish son is a sorrow to his mother.

Synthetic parallelism is where the second line supplements the idea of the first. The opening of Moses' song after the Red Sea crossing illustrates this (Ex. 15:1):

> I will sing to the Lord, for he has triumphed gloriously;
> the horse and his rider he has thrown into the sea.

Again from the Psalms (3:5, 121:2):

> I lie down and sleep;
> I wake again, for the Lord sustains me.

> My help comes from the Lord,
> who made heaven and earth.

One example from Proverbs (21:9):

It is better to live in a corner of the housetop
than in a house shared with a contentious woman.

THE PSALMS

If there is a book saturated in tears, a book that has driven despair from the human heart and given it hope, it is the Psalms, a
collection (by our present arrangement) of 150 lyric poems. The
human heart speaks here directly to God. It tells Him its anguish,
its tribulations, its troubles, its fears, its hopes, its aspirations, its
visions; it pleads with man, with God; it turns unto itself in humility; it meditates upon the world, upon sin, upon kindness; it seeks
to convey the very loftiest in man; it sings while instructing and instructs while beseeching God. One almost dare not speak *about* the
Psalms; they must be read and re-read so that every word be heard
inside the soul. Here the greatest singers of Israel, the God-seekers
of yore, are represented; the teachers and wise men; the followers
of the great prophets; the very best of the human race.

How many persons have gone to their graves accompanied by
the lovely words, "The Lord is my shepherd"? How many persons have contemplated the words of "The Prayer of Moses, the
man of God"? How many among us have meditated upon the
Psalm of David, "The heavens declare the glory of God"? It is
a people's book that has inspired Jew and non-Jew alike. It is the
greatest prayer book.

The whole range of human life, its joy and its woe, its
light and its shadow, and its daily routine, is treated in the
psalter. There are psalms of common worship, pilgrim
songs and processional hymns, calls to worship, hymns of
praise and thanksgiving for individual or national deliverance, for the harvest and the joys of nature. There are national psalms, prayers for deliverance from external or internal foes, for national restoration, prayers of trust in
national peril and of praise for past deliverance, battle
songs, and odes of victory. There are royal psalms, cor-
onation and wedding odes, prayers for the king's just and

ideal rule, for God's help in battle or thanksgiving for victory. There are psalms of individual piety with its longings for communion with God and its joy in the experience of it; with its prayers for help and healing, for forgiveness and purification; with its songs of faith and trust and its hymns of thanksgiving and praise. There are didactic psalms, with the warm, insistent teaching of the fear of God, the divine government in the world, retribution for pious and wicked alike; with their warnings against trust in riches, and concerning the vanity and brevity of life; with their teachings of true worship and true sacrifice, of the blessedness of forgiveness and of charitableness toward others, of the joys of home and of nature and law; and with their lessons from Israel's great history in the past. Out of the heart of life they sprang, and to the heart they speak. Many poets have contributed; some of them were original geniuses of poetic power, others were common versifiers. They are not grouped according to any chronological, topical, or other principle. Varied as life itself, they are also tossed together in the same kaleidoscopic manner as life's experiences themselves. . . .

To grasp the variety of the religious life which finds its expression in the psalms it is necessary to group those that belong together. Since many were not used in the temple we may divide them into psalms for the public worwhip either of the whole community or of the individual, and psalms of private devotion, edification, and instruction.[1]

Psalm 8, a hymn of praise, would be an example of a song for public worship in the Temple:

> O Lord, our Lord,
> how majestic is thy name in all the earth!
>
> Thou whose glory above the heavens is chanted
> by the mouth of babes and infants,
> thou hast founded a bulwark because of thy foes,
> to still the enemy and the avenger.

When I look at thy heavens, the work of thy fingers,
the moon and the stars which thou hast established;
what is man that thou art mindful of him,
and the son of man that thou dost care for him?

Yet thou hast made him little less than God,
and dost crown him with glory and honor.
Thou hast given him dominion over the works of
    thy hands;
thou hast put all things under his feet,
all sheep and oxen,
and also the beasts of the field,
the birds of the air, and the fish of the sea,
whatever passes along the paths of the sea.

O Lord, our Lord,
how majestic is thy name in all the earth!

Praise and joy did not always fill the Temple. Psalm 90 is a lament about God's displeasure toward man's sinfulness and a prayer for the restoration of divine favor:

Lord, thou hast been our refuge
in all generations.
Before the mountains were brought forth,
or ever thou hadst formed the earth and the world,
from everlasting to everlasting thou art God.

Thou turnest man back to the dust,
and sayest, "Turn back, O children of men!"
For a thousand years in thy sight are but as yesterday
    when it is past,
or as a watch in the night.

Thou dost sweep men away; they are like a dream,
like grass which is renewed in the morning:
in the morning it flourishes and is renewed;
in the evening it fades and withers.

For we are consumed by thy anger;
by thy wrath we are overwhelmed.
Thou hast set our iniquities before thee,
our secret sins in the light of thy countenance.

For all our days pass away under thy wrath,
our years come to an end like a sigh.
The years of our life are threescore and ten,
or even by reason of strength fourscore;
yet their span is but toil and trouble;
they are soon gone, and we fly away.

Who considers the power of thy anger,
and thy wrath according to the fear of thee?
So teach us to number our days
that we may get a heart of wisdom.

Return, O Lord! How long?
Have pity on thy servants!
Satisfy us in the morning with thy steadfast love,
that we may rejoice and be glad all our days.
Make us glad as many days as thou hast afflicted us,
and as many years as we have seen evil.
Let thy work be manifest to thy servants,
and thy glorious power to their children.
Let the favor of the Lord our God be upon us,
and establish thou the work of our hands upon us,
yea, the work of our hands establish thou it.

Private worship in the Temple is seen in Psalm 5, a morning
prayer by an individual worshipper in the sanctuary:

Give ear to my words, O Lord;
give heed to my groaning.
Hearken to the sound of my cry,
my King and my God,
for to thee do I pray,
O Lord, in the morning thou dost hear my voice;

in the morning I prepare a sacrifice for thee, and
    watch....

I through the abundance of thy steadfast love
will enter thy house,
I will worship toward thy holy temple
in the fear of thee.
Lead me, O Lord, in thy righteousness
because of my enemies;
make thy way straight before me....

Psalm 42 is clearly the cry of an individual not worshipping in
the Temple, because his anguish is precisely over his inability to
make the pilgrimage to the sanctuary:

As a hart longs for flowing streams,
so longs my soul for thee, O God.
My soul thirsts for God,
for the living God.
When shall I come and behold
the face of God?
My tears have been my food day and night,
while men say to me continually, "Where is your
    God?"...

Why are you cast down, O my soul,
and why are you disquieted within me?
Hope in God; for I shall again praise him,
my help and my God....

Psalm 37 is the reflection of an old man upon that troublesome
question of the suffering of the righteous and the prosperity of the
wicked. He opens with his conclusion, which he elaborates at
length for the remainder of his psalm:

Fret not yourself because of the wicked,
be not envious of wrongdoers!
For they will soon fade like the grass,

and wither like the green herb.

Trust in the Lord, and do good;
so you will dwell in the land, and enjoy security.
Take delight in the Lord,
and he will give you the desires of your heart....

A final example of the Psalms combines a number of themes. Psalm 15 asks, "Who can worship in the sanctuary?" The answer is given in terms of social justice, reflective of the prophets' message:

O Lord, who shall sojourn in thy tent?
Who shall dwell on thy holy hill?

He who walks blamelessly, and does what is right,
and speaks truth from his heart;
who does not slander with his tongue,
and does no evil to his friend,
nor takes up a reproach against his neighbor;
in whose eyes a reprobate is despised,
but who honors those who fear the Lord;
who swears to his own hurt and does not change;
who does not put out his money at interest,
and does not take a bribe against the innocent.

He who does these things shall never be moved.

JOB

The Book of Job is regarded as one of the great masterpieces of world literature. It has been compared by some critics to such works as Aeschylus' "Prometheus Bound" and Shakespeare's "Hamlet." Perhaps it surpasses both.

There are two central themes or questions which run through the Book of Job. One is, again, that of retribution: Why do the righteous suffer and the wicked prosper? The other: Is a truly God-fearing and God-loving man able to endure all kinds of suffering and still remain faithful to his God? Is faith in God strong enough to compensate man for all possible tribulations?

If one assumes that the righteous prospers and the upright lives in good health to a ripe old age, that the wicked is beset with woes and the sinner cut down early in his unrighteous life, then when calamity strikes the good man he can only look into his secret self for unknown or hidden sins. God knows our hearts and God punishes sin. Therefore, if suffering befalls one, it is because of one's sin. Such was the reasoning of many of the Jews. The author of the Book of Job meets this belief head on.

The man Job is a righteous man. God himself is proud of Job and calls him "a blameless and upright man, who fears God and turns away from evil." (1:8) Satan questions Job's faithfulness; Satan suggests that Job is good because it pays—expedient righteousness. God agrees to a test of Job. Thus Job loses his possessions, his children, his friends, his health. "Friends" come to console Job, who argues with them his uprightness (29:12-17):

> Because I delivered the poor that cried,
> and the fatherless, and him that had none to help him.
> The blessing of him that was ready to perish came
>   upon me;
> and I caused the widow's heart to sing for joy.
> I put on righteousness, and it clothed me;
> my judgment was as a robe and a diadem.
> I was eyes to the blind, and feet was I to the lame.
> I was a father to the poor; and the cause which I
>   knew not
> I searched out.
> And I brake the jaws of the wicked, and plucked the
>   spoil
> out of his teeth.

The "friends" reject this. They use the common retribution argument and insist that Job is a sinful man and that his unrighteousness has brought his losses, his woes, his loathsome diseases upon

himself. God is punishing him; Job must repent. Job protests
still his innocence. Job agonizes. But he never denies the existence
of God. He criticizes. He condemns. But he still declares that
even if brought to the portals of death, he would cling to God.
What he demands is an explanation. *Why? Why?* He wants God
to be just.

Finally, God appears to Job, not with an answer of explanation,
but with an overwhelming of rhetorical questions out of the whirl-
wind (38:4-7, 29, 34-35; 39:26-27):

> Where were you when I laid the foundations of the
>   earth?
> Tell me, if you have understanding,
> who determined its measurements—surely you know!
> Or who stretched the line upon it?
> On what were its bases sunk,
> or who laid its cornerstone,
> when the morning stars sang together,
> and all the sons of God shouted for joy?
>
> From whose womb did the ice come forth,
> and who has given birth to the hoarfrost of heaven?
>
> Can you lift up your voice to the clouds,
> that a flood of waters may cover you?
> Can you send forth lightnings, that they may go
> and say to you, "Here we are"?
>
> Is it by your wisdom that the hawk soars,
> and spreads his wings toward the south?
> Is it at your command that the eagle mounts up
> and makes his nest on high?

Job sees man's insignificance. "Behold, I am of small account."
(40:4) Job experiences the insignificance of his own suffering, of
man's suffering. Job never learns *why* he suffered, but his vision
of God suffices. He knows he has God's favor; and he knows that
God's favor can be bestowed on one regardless of the external

appearances of poverty, loss of health, and other calamities. We all question; we all seek answers. The craving to know, to understand, is perhaps the penalty we must pay for being endowed with a mind that is ever searching for a meaning in life. The Book of Job will ever be studied as one of man's attempts to penetrate the mystery of life.

SONG OF SONGS

Song of Songs, or Song of Solomon, is a collection of love poems and wedding songs composed probably at various times. Tradition attributes them to King Solomon. More likely the songs root in Near Eastern marriage customs, whereby a week before a wedding the villagers assembled to work out details. A threshing board was set up as a throne, on which the couple took their seats as "king" and "queen." Songs of praise of the physical charms of the young pair were recited and dances were held. The "king" could have been called Solomon and the "daughters of Jerusalem" the village maidens in attendance on the bride. These practices are still to be found in some Syrian villages, for example.

This is one description the shepherdess gives of her lover (5:10-16):

> My beloved white and ruddy,
> the chiefest among ten thousand.
> His head is as the most fine gold,
> his locks are bushy,
> and black as a raven.
> His eyes are as the eyes of doves
> by the rivulets of water,
> washed with milk, and fitly set.
> His cheeks are as a bed of spices,
> as sweet flowers;
> his lips like lilies, dropping sweet smelling myrrh.
> His hands are as gold rings set with the beryl:
> his belly is as bright ivory overlaid with sapphires.

His legs are as pillars of marble,
set upon sockets of fine gold:
his countenance is as Lebanon,
excellent as the cedars.
His mouth is most sweet:
yea, he is altogether lovely.
This is my beloved and this is my friend,
O daughters of Jerusalem.

This and other descriptions throughout of a flaming love are, of course, physical and figurative, but not overly erotic. It is simple love, natural and innocent. The outpouring of emotion on the part of the lovers is as pure as anything in nature. Two hearts speak to each other. A Tanna like Akiba ben Joseph sensed it long ago. He called the Song of Songs a holy poem. During the many centuries of Israel's dispersion among the nations, pious Jews interpreted the poems as an allegory, picturing the mutual love between Israel and the God of Israel. It does no harm to read the Song of Songs allegorically, as long as we keep in mind that at heart it is a beautiful love poem, as this springtime-of-love passage reminds us (2:8-13):

My beloved spake, and said unto me,
Rise up, my love, my fair one, and come away.
For, lo, the winter is past,
the rain is over and gone.
The flowers appear on the earth;
the time of the singing is come,
and the voice of the turtle is heard in our land;
the fig tree putteth forth her green figs,
and the vines with the tender grape spread their aroma.
Arise, my love, my fair one, and come away.

PROVERBS

Proverbs and Ecclesiastes belong to the Wisdom Literature of the Hebrews. The Wisdom Literature is teaching literature, primarily addressed to individuals, not to the community or the nation. It is good, sober counsel; sage and common sense observations put into pithy sayings; wisdom covering the range of personal and social everyday life.

The scriptural Book of Proverbs is a collection of proverbs, maxims, epigrams, discourses attributed to King Solomon, whom tradition credits as perhaps the wisest of sages and the world champion proverb maker. Actually, even within the book itself certain sections are attributed to others—e.g., Agur, King Lemuel And certainly the list of authors is long and anonymous. Fortunately the charm and instructiveness of the proverbs lie not in their authorship, but in their intrinsic value.

Get wisdom; get insight.
Do not forsake her, and she will keep you;
love her, and she will guard you.

(4:5-6)

Do not enter the path of the wicked,
and do not walk in the way of evil men.
Avoid it; do not go on it;
turn away from it and pass on.
For they cannot sleep unless they have done wrong;
they are robbed of sleep unless they have made someone
stumble.
For they eat the bread of wickedness
and drink the wine of violence.

(4:14-17)

When pride comes, then comes disgrace;
but with the humble is wisdom.

(11:2)

Like vinegar to the teeth, and smoke to the eyes,
so is the sluggard to those who send him.

(10:26)

Like a gold ring in a swine's snout
is a beautiful woman without discretion.

(11:22)

The way of a fool is right in his own eyes,
but a wise man listens to advice.

(12:15)

He who is slow to anger is better than the mighty,
and he who rules his spirit than he who takes a city.

(16:32)

Even a fool who keeps silent is considered wise;
when he closes his lips, he is deemed intelligent.

(17:28)

Bread gained by deceit is sweet to a man,
but afterward his mouth will be full of gravel.

(20:17)

If your enemy is hungry, give him bread to eat;
and if he is thirsty, give him water to drink;
for you will heap coals of fire on his head,
and the Lord will reward you.

(25:21-22)

Do not rejoice when your enemy falls,
and let not your heart be glad when he stumbles;
lest the Lord see it, and be displeased,
and turn away his anger from him.

(24:17-18)

He who closes his ear to the cry of the poor
will himself cry out and not be heard.

(21:13)

If you have found honey, eat only enough for you,
lest you be sated with it and vomit it.

(25:16)

ECCLESIASTES

Ecclesiastes (Hebrew: Kohelet) is traditionally attributed to King Solomon. The word Kohelet, a derivative of the root Kahal, meaning "assembly," is interpreted as one who addresses an assembly or a member of an assembly; literally, as Jerome takes it in his translation, a preacher or reciter. It may simply be a proper name. We do not know the book's author. We do not know its date, though it was probably written about 200 B.C.E.

Ecclesiastes contains in the first few chapters autobiographic details about the author's searching after happiness, wealth and honors, pleasures and comforts, which he attained; nevertheless, nothing seemed to satisfy him. He felt that everything in human life was meaningless (1:2):

Vanity of vanities, says Kohelet,
vanity of vanities! All is vanity.

Kohelet does not find any purpose in life. He declares that all his experiments with various forms of study, pleasure, and enterprise in the hope of finding the meaning of life came to nought. Disgusted and frustrated in his long search and seeing that it was all in vain, he was forced to conclude that there was no purpose to it all

What does man gain by all the toil
at which he toils under the sun?
A generation goes, and a generation comes,
but the earth remains forever.
The sun rises and the sun goes down,
and hastens to the place where it rises.

The wind blows and returns again. The rivers flow to the sea and then flow again.

> All things are full of weariness;
> a man cannot utter it . . . .
>
> What has been is what will be,
> and what has been done is what will be done;
> and there is nothing new under the sun.
>
> (1:3-9)

Kohelet could not give easy acceptance to the doctrine of retribution: God will punish the wicked and reward the righteous. His experience taught him otherwise (3:16; 7:15; 9:11):

> I saw under the sun that in the place of justice, even there was wickedness, and in the place of righteousness, even there was wickedness.
>
> There is a righteous man who perishes in his righteousness, and there is a wicked man who prolongs his life in his evil-doing.
>
> The race is not to the swift, nor the battle to the strong, nor bread to the wise, nor riches to the intelligent, nor favor to the men of skill; but time and chance happen to them all.

Man cannot know God's workings. "However much man may toil in seeking, he will not find it out." We cannot know whether God loves us or not. (8:17-9:1)

What does Kohelet conclude? If life is purposeless and worthless, it would seem that man should cease life. But Kohelet is far from advocating despair or suicide. Though death comes, live life!

> Light is sweet, and it is pleasant for the eyes to behold the sun. (11:7)

In fellowship with others, live and work and enjoy pleasures. But do not act in excess, and do not act immorally.

> There is nothing better for a man than that he should eat and drink, and find enjoyment in his toil. (2:24)

Is this all? It is enough.

Kohelet is a moral man. He is deeply skeptical, even cynical. He believes strongly in God. He is not irreligious. As we read his wisdom, we encounter contrasting motifs. We hear him say:

> Apart from God who can eat or who can have enjoyment? For to the man who pleases him God gives wisdom and knowledge and joy; but to the sinner he gives the work of gathering and heaping, only to give to one who pleases God. (2:25-26)

> I said in my heart, God will judge the righteous and the wicked, for he has appointed a time for every matter, and for every work. (3:17)

> The end of the matter; all has been heard. Fear God and keep his commandments. (12:13)

Are these simply contradictions? Are they somehow an integral part of Kohelet's wisdom? Are they later additions by a more pious editor? We cannot be absolutely certain. Let us then agree that all in all Ecclesiastes is a book which makes an account of life in toto without reaching an absolute conclusion. Perhaps the historian Herbert J. Muller echoes Kohelet when he suggests that in the final analysis there is no final analysis.[2]

ך | 4

HISTORICAL
WORKS

FOLKLORE AND HISTORY

Long before Herodotus, the Greek "father of history" (5th century
B.C.E.), history was being written by the Hebrews—a comprehensive
history which dealt with Israel in the context of world history, a
history which had movement and unfolding and purpose, a history in universal and divine and human terms. This unique
achievement was not, of course, of uniform quality; it did not
spring full-blown from the mind of some Hebrew philosopher of
history. Hundreds of tale tellers and writers participated; there
were great intellects and common minds. Many traditions, different perspectives, and various types of materials went into the
making of the historical works of the Hebrews.

There is a level of analysis which studies these works in terms,
for example, of the distinct points of view in different sources such
as the J, E, D, P documents (abbreviations referring, respectively,
to materials using the name Jehovah for God, using Elohim for
God, emphasizing the Deuteronomic Code, emphasizing the Priestly
Code). These matters, and similar issues, we leave to the critics
and other scholars. Suffice it here for us to glance at a few of
the pieces used in the Hebrews' historical mosaic.

Historical records were kept: accounts of internal affairs and of contacts with other peoples, both in war and peace. Genealogies were registered. We know, for instance, that at the time of David in the 10th century there was in the royal palace an official secretary who kept records of events. The great prophet Isaiah was at one time such a scribe serving as a historian of the Kingdom of Judea. The scribes were more than historians, since they inserted in the records stories that either appealed to their imagination or carried a moral idea with an instructive character. Such historians-moralists looked upon themselves as teachers of the people.

The historical works contain legends, tales, national interpretations of events, parables, genealogies, proverbs, biographical sketches, excerpts of songs from older books—a rich range of folklore and history. As we have noted earlier, some of the material was handed down orally generation after generation, some was written, some was lost, some was preserved.

TWELVE BOOKS

Following the Pentateuch, in our arrangement of the Bible, there are a dozen books whose thrust is historical.

Joshua and Judges

These two books cover a period of about 300 years from the death of Moses to Eli the high priest of Shiloh. They deal with the important events in the life of Israel after the death of Moses: the conquest of Canaan, the division of the land among the tribes, the tribulations from domination of neighboring peoples, the judges, or tribal leaders, who arose at various times, especially to rally the Israelites in war against the oppressors.

1 Samuel and 2 Samuel

These books open with the story of the birth of the prophet Samuel and tell how he eventually became leader of the people. Samuel was the last judge, for in his old age, with his help but against his wishes, the institution of monarchy emerged. Samuel anointed Saul, son of Kish, a peasant, as king. After a short victorious reign, Saul showed himself to be what we might call psychopathic. As a result of a conflict between Samuel and him, he was driven by an "evil spirit." Abandoned and depressed, Saul was eaten by jealousy and fear lest young David, a shepherd from Bethlehem, take his crown away. He hunted David like a criminal. David, however, escaped all threats to his life. Finally, after Saul fell on the battlefield in the war against the Philistines, David was crowned in Hebron—king of Judah and later king of both Judah and Israel, a unified kingdom. He subjugated all the surrounding peoples.

1 Kings and 2 Kings

These books begin with the death of David and the ascension of Solomon to the throne. In contrast to David the warrior-king, Solomon was a king of peace. He undertook great building projects: the Temple of Solomon, a sumptuous palace for himself, fortifications in many parts of the country. Immediately following his death, an insurrection occurred under the leadership of Jeroboam, an Ephraimite rebel, resulting in the secession of ten tribes. The country was thus divided into two kingdoms: Israel and Judah. The history of the two kingdoms is told. There are folk stories. There are long narratives about persons and events. We read about insurrections and usurpations in Israel, the bloody conflicts between rivals for the throne, the activities of such prophets as Elijah and Elisha. The story jumps back and forth between Israel and Judah. After the last days of the Kingdom of Israel, destroyed by the Assyrians, the rest of the book is devoted to Judah, especially the reforms of Hezekiah under the leadership of Isaiah, the invasion of Sennacherib, the reformation of King Josiah, and the final destruction of Judah at the time of Jeremiah.

1 Chronicles and 2 Chronicles

Whereas the books of Samuel and Kings seem to have been written from a prophetic perspective, the Chronicles were written more from the priestly point of view. They start with a lengthy genealogy from Adam to the time of David. The books laid heavier stress upon Judah. Special emphasis was given to Temple worship, Jerusalem, and the Davidic dynasty.

Ezra and Nehemiah

These two books were originally parts of the Chronicles, but were later separated. The Book of Ezra opens with the edict of Cyrus the Great who permitted the Jewish captives in Babylonia to return to their homeland. Then it goes on to give a register of the families who returned to Judah and their struggles with the Samaritans who opposed the rebuilding of the Temple. The Book of Nehemiah continues the story of Ezra. Nehemiah, the cupbearer of King Artaxerxes, tells his own story of how he arrived in Jerusalem and found it desolate, and what he did to restore it and to safeguard the people from being assimilated among the surrounding peoples.

These two books were written partly in Chaldaic, which became the vernacular of the Jewish people during the Babylonian exile; it was at this time that Hebrew as a spoken language almost disappeared.

Ruth

This is a simple story, called by Goethe the finest idyllic masterpiece in world literature. After the death in Moab of her husband and two sons, the Hebrew mother, Naomi, prepared to return to Bethlehem. She admonished her two Moabite daughters-in-law to remain, but Ruth refused. In a voice of love and self-sacrifice which still across the centuries touches our heart, Ruth said to Naomi (1:16-17):

> Entreat me not to leave thee, or to return from following after thee. For whither thou goest, I will go; and where thou lodgest, I will lodge; thy people shall be my people, and thy God my God; where thou diest, will I die, and and there will I be buried; the Lord do so to me, and more also, if aught but death part thee and me.

The two women came to Bethlehem and soon Ruth married Boaz, a wealthy and influential man in the community. We have seen the hard line Ezra and Nehemiah took against mixed marriages. The author of Ruth is in his own way transcending race and nationality, and suggesting that God blesses righteousness wherever it is found.

Esther

The story of Esther belongs to the period when the dual empire of the Persians and Medes dominated southeastern Asia from India to Ethiopia. The high point of the account is the conspiracy of Haman, an ardent Jew-hater, who is out to destroy the Jewish people scattered throughout the empire. He secures a royal decree, signed and sealed, to massacre all the Jews on the 13th day of the month of Adar; he makes all necessary preparations. Underlying this human side of the story is the mysterious hand of God active in history. Esther, a simple Jewish girl, the adopted daughter of Mordecai, is selected as queen of Persia. Mordecai, long before Haman's plot, had saved the king's life by exposing two would-be assassins. The king belatedly proposes to reward Mordecai, and in a twist of events Haman is hanged on the gallows he prepared for Mordecai. The Jews are saved and Mordecai is given Haman's post as vizier. Good triumphs over Evil.

To commemorate this delivery, the Feast of Purim was instituted among the Jews by Mordecai and Esther on the 14th and 15th days of Adar. The story of Esther became a symbol, a warning, to all Jew-hating Hamans that their end was certain to come, because evil could never succeed.

SAMPLE STORIES

The Scroll of Esther is what we today would call historical fiction. The genealogical lists from the Chronicles we would designate as one source from which historians begin to create their treatises. Within this range, as we noted earlier, there is a wealth of diverse materials. Let us look at three examples of the sort of folk stories found in the Bible.

Anti-Monarchy Sentiment

On the death of Gideon, one of the early judges, the children of Israel began again to worship the idols of the surrounding countries. Gideon's son, Abimelech, conspired to kill all of Gideon's other sons and make himself king.

> Speak, I pray you, in the ears of all the men of Shechem:
> What is better for you, that all the sons of Gideon, which
> are three score and ten persons, reign over you, or that
> one reign over you? (Jud. 9:2)

With the help of the Shechemites, the wholesale slaughter was carried out; all the brothers were killed, except Jotham, "for he hid
himself." When the Shechemites were crowning Abimelech king,
Jotham suddenly appeared nearby and addressed the crowd. He
told a parable predicting their downfall (Jud. 9:8-16,19-20):

> The trees went forth on a time to anoint a king over them;
> and they said unto the olive tree, Reign thou over us. But
> the olive tree said unto them, Should I leave my fatness,
> wherewith by me they honor God and man, and go to
> rule over the trees? And the trees said to the fig tree, Come
> thou and reign over us. But the fig tree said unto them,
> Should I forsake my sweetness, and my good fruit, and
> go to rule over you? Then said the trees unto the vine,
> Come thou and reign over us. And the vine said unto
> them, Should I leave my wine, which cheereth God and
> man, and go to rule over you? Then said all the trees un-
> to the bramble, Come thou and rule over us. And the bram-
> ble said unto the trees, If in truth ye anoint me king over
> you, then come and put your trust in my shadow: and if
> not, let fire come out of the bramble, and devour the cedars
> of Lebanon. Now therefore, if ye have done truly and sin-
> cerely, in that ye have made Abimelech king, and if ye
> have dealt well with Jerubbaal and his house, and have
> done unto him according to the deserving of his hands, re-
> joice ye in Abimelech, and let him also rejoice in you. . . .
> But if not, let fire come out from Abimelech, and devour
> the men of Shechem, and the house of Milo; and let fire
> come out from the men of Shechem, and from the house
> of Milo, and devour Abimelech.

This was the first time that an Israelite aspired to become king
in Israel before the establishment of the monarchy by the prophet
Samuel against his will. His condemnation of the monarchy is
probably the oldest such denunciation in history (1 Samuel
8:11-20):

And Samuel said: This will be the manner of the king that
shall reign over you: he will take your sons, and appoint
them for himself, for his chariots, and to be his horsemen; and some shall run before his chariots. And he will
appoint him captains over thousands, and captains over
fifties; and will set them to plow his ground, and to reap
his harvest, and to make his instruments of war, and instruments of his chariots. And he will take your daughters
to be confectionaries, and to be cooks, and to be bakers.
And he will take your fields, and your vineyards, and
your oliveyards, even the best of them, and give them
to his servants. And he will take your menservants, and
your maidservants, and your goodliest young men, and
your asses, and put them to his work. He will take the
tenth of your sheep: and ye shall be his servants. And ye
shall cry out in that day because of your king which ye
shall have chosen you; and the Lord will not hear you
in that day. Nevertheless the people refused to obey the
voice of Samuel; and they said, Nay; but we will have
a king over us; that we also may be like all the nations;
and that our king may judge us, and go out before us,
and fight our battles.

Nathan's Parable

The parable of Nathan the Prophet, recited to King David after
the latter had committed the crime of causing the death of Uriah,
an army officer, and then taking his wife Bath-sheba as one of his
wives, is a classic. We see here a confrontation between a powerful
king and the prophet who fearlessly tells him the truth and condemns him (2 Samuel 12:1-13):

And the Lord sent Nathan unto David. And he came unto
him saying, There were two men in one city; the one rich,
and the other poor. The rich man had exceeding many
flocks and herds. But the poor man had nothing, save one
little ewe lamb, which he had bought and nourished up;
and it grew up together with him, and with his children;
it did eat of his own meat, and drank of his own cup, and
lay in his bosom, and was unto him as a daughter. And

there came a traveller unto the rich man, and he spared to take of his own flock and of his own herd, to dress for the wayfaring man that was come unto him; but took the poor man's lamb, and dressed it for the man that was come to him.

And David's anger was greatly kindled against the man; and he said to Nathan, As the Lord liveth, the man that hath done this thing shall surely die: And he shall restore the lamb fourfold, because he did this thing, and because he had no pity.

And Nathan said to David, Thou art the man! Thus said the Lord God of Israel, I anointed thee king of Israel, and I delivered thee out of the hand of Saul. And I gave thee thy master's house, and thy master's wives unto thy bosom, and gave thee the house of Israel and of Judah; and if that had been too little, I would moreover have given unto thee such and such things. Wherefore hast thou despised the commandment of the Lord, to do evil in his sight? Thou hast killed Uriah the Hittite with the sword, and hast taken his wife to be thy wife, and hast slain him with the sword of the children of Ammon. Now therefore the sword shall never depart from thine house; because thou hast despised me, and hast taken the wife of Uriah to be thy wife.

Thus said the Lord, Behold, I will raise up evil against thee out of thine own house, and I will take thy wives before thine eyes, and give them unto thy neighbor, and he shall lie with thy wives in the sight of the sun. For thou didst it secretly: but I will do this thing before all Israel, and before the sun.

And David said unto Nathan, I have sinned against the Lord. And Nathan said unto David, The Lord also hath put away thy sin; thou shalt not die.

Solomon's Wisdom

King Solomon is described as the wisest man. This is what the chronicler tells us about him (1 Kings 4:29-34):

And God gave Solomon wisdom and understanding ex-

ceeding much, and largeness of heart, even as the sand that
is on the sea-shore. And Solomon's wisdom excelled the
wisdom of Egypt. For he was wiser than all men: than
Ethan the Ezrahite, and Heman, and Chalcol, and Darda,
the sons of Mahol; and his fame was in all nations round
about. And he spake three thousand proverbs; and his
songs were a thousand and five. And he spake of trees,
from the cedar that is in Lebanon even unto the hyssop
that springeth out of the wall; he spake also of beasts, and
of fowl, and of creeping things, and of fishes. And there
came of all people to hear the wisdom of Solomon, from
all kings of the earth, that had heard of his wisdom.

How did Solomon obtain such "exceeding" wisdom? It came directly
from God (I Kings 3:5-7, 9-13):

In Gibeon the Lord appeared to Solomon in a dream by
night; and God said, Ask what I shall give thee.

And Solomon said, Thou hast shewed unto thy servant
David my father great mercy, according as he walked before thee in truth, and in righteousness, and in uprightness, and in uprightness of heart with thee. . . . And now,
O Lord my God, thou hast made thy servant king instead
of David my father; and I am but a little child; I know
not how to go out or come in. . . . Give thy servant an
understanding heart to judge thy people, that I may dis-
cern between good and bad; for who is able to judge this
thy so great a people?

And the speech pleased the Lord, that Solomon had
asked this thing. And God said unto him, Because thou
hast asked this thing, and hast not asked for thyself long
life; neither hast asked riches for thyself, nor hast asked
the life of thy enemies. . . . Behold, I have done according
to thy words; lo, I have given thee a wise and an understanding heart; so that there was none like thee before
neither after thee shall any arise like unto thee. And I have
also given thee that which thou hast not asked, both riches
and honor.

Soon enough Solomon was given a chance to prove his wisdom
(I Kings 3:16-28):

Then came there two women that were harlots, unto the king, and stood before him. And the one woman said, O my lord, I and this woman dwell in one house, and I was delivered of a child with her in the house. And it came to pass the third day after I was delivered, that this woman was delivered also; and we were together; there was no stranger with us in the house, save we two in the house. And this woman's child died in the night, because she overlaid it. And she arose at midnight, and took my son from beside me, while thine handmaid slept, and laid it in her bosom, and laid her dead child in my bosom. And when I rose in the morning to give my child suck, behold, it was dead; but when I had considered it in the morning, behold, it was not my son, whom I did bear. And the other woman said, Nay; but the living is my son, and the dead is thy son. And this said, No; but the dead is thy son, and the living is my son. Thus they spake before the king.

Then said the king, The one saith: This is my son that liveth, and thy son is the dead; and the other saith, Nay; but thy son is the dead, and my son is the living. And the king said, Bring me a sword. And they brought a sword before the king. And the king said, Divide the living child in two, and give half to the one, and half to the other.

Then spake the woman who was the mother of the living child, for her bowels yearned upon her son, and she said, Oh, my lord, give her the living child, and in nowise slay it; she is the mother thereof.

And all Israel heard of the judgment which the king had judged; and they feared the king; for they saw that the wisdom of God was in him, to do judgment.

ה 5

THE SECOND COMMONWEALTH

FROM BIBLE TO TALMUD

From Ezra the Scribe (mid-5th century B.C.E.), who edited most of the Hebrew scriptures, to Judah the Prince (mid-2nd century C.E.), who compiled the Mishnah, there is a period of 700 years, almost the entire lifespan of the Second Commonwealth (from Ezra-Nehemiah to the destruction of the Second Temple in 70 C.E.). During that time, after the fall of the Persian empire, Judaism met Hellenism in the person of Alexander the Great (356-323 B.C.E.), to whose rule it submitted. For more than a century, there was little conflict; they were simply two different worlds. Then the two worlds clashed; then there was the Maccabean revolt. For a time Judah won her independence. But inner conflicts, clashes between various parties and sects, weakened the country. Mighty Rome entered the scene and became overlord. Then it was all over. The Temple was destroyed, the Second Commonwealth was ended, and the Jewish people were dispersed throughout the then known world. Another terrible catastrophe had befallen the Jews.

Had the Jews only been a nation like others, they would, like the powerful Carthaginians, have become extinguished with the end of their state. Had they been a religious community bound to some local sanctuary, and with no universal outlook, . . . they would have been exterminated, or have perished for want of a living spirit. But Judaism represented both a nation with a remarkable past and with a still more soaring vision of the future, as well as a religion which, incontestably the purest and highest of antiquity, embraced within its range the whole of mankind, and even in its practical workings showed itself adaptable to every clime and civilization.[1]

Since Ezra's time, the religious cult which was mainly centered around the Temple in Jerusalem was gradually widening to include a new institution—the synagogue. The synagogue, both as House of Learning and House of Prayer, must have appeared at first in Babylonia. The captives from Judah, finding themselves strangers in a strange land, could hardly identify themselves as Jews without assembling somewhere to pray to the God of their forefathers, or to listen to a teacher who was willing to expound the Torah. We know, for instance, that the elders among the captives came to Ezekiel for instructions. In captivity they turned their faces toward Zion while praying. The synagogue grew out of those communal assemblies; it was a replacement or substitute for the Temple.

When they returned to Zion they brought the new institution with them. In fact it must have grown into larger proportions at home, particularly in the outlying districts. In the synagogue there was no priest and no ritual other than praying or learning; here emerged the popular teacher, one who was later called rabbi, which means master, teacher, instructor (cf. last section of next chapter).

The elders and the wise men, then, began to direct the destiny of the people. The influence of the priesthood changed. The prophet's word became less a focus of leadership. The written word was to become more and more important, though the spoken word was by no means lost. Ezra, for example, was neither a prophet nor a priest; he was a scribe, a redactor of the sacred writings. The Sopherim (scribes) issued decrees and ordinances based on their interpretation of the Torah.

The Men of the Great Assembly, at first convoked by Ezra and then continuing until the time of Simon the Just, composed prayers and instituted them. Portions of the Torah were read in the synagogue on Saturdays. Since Ezra replaced the ancient Hebrew script with the square script called Assyrian, all the Biblical writings had to be rewritten. Consequently, competent people were needed to safeguard the texts from possible errors by either omission or commission. The Sopherim fulfilled that task. No small wonder that the interpreters of the Law multiplied. Appearing before the people during the national holidays and on the sabbaths, their object was to teach. One single passage in the Scriptures sufficed sometimes as a theme for a lengthy dissertation. Thus the later method of teaching, known as Talmudic or Midrashic, had its beginnings in the early days of the Second Commonwealth. It was oral teaching, an unwritten form of expounding the words of the Torah, which was handed down from generation to generation. Thus the Sopherim were the predecessors of the later Pharisees.

During the more than two hundred years of Persian rule, Judah did not fare badly. Their religious autonomy was secure as long as the Jews paid tribute to the Persian rulers. The Jewish people turned into themselves and apparently enjoyed their seclusion and peace. But with the advent of Hellenism into Asia, after Alexander's great conquests (332 B.C.E.), this wall of seclusion was cracked. Though at first Judaism and Hellenism seemed to live in peace, as Judaism and Persian culture had, soon enough the shadows of dark days to come were creeping in. The peaceful years of the rule of the Egyptian Ptolemies over Judah and later of the Syrian-Greek dynasty of the Seleucids were a silence before a storm. The Hellenizing process, which first took root in Egyptian Jewry, reached at last the upper classes of Judean society. Judaism and Hellenism, hitherto relatively indifferent to each other, suddenly found themselves as mortal foes on the world scene. Judaism had had to contend only with Asian cultures. Now East and West clashed, resulting at long last in the Maccabean revolt. It was a struggle for survival which the Jewish people undertook, a struggle not only for the liberation of the national soil, but for the saving of the people's soul.

The Maccabean revolt (168 B.C.E.) started in a little town,

called Modein, where an aged priest, Mattathias the Hasmonean, a father of five heroic sons, stood up against the Syrian officials who had ordered the populace to offer sacrifices upon the altar of the pagan gods erected in the marketplace. The old priest killed both the Syrian official and the Jew who had stepped forward to officiate at the ceremony. Thereupon, Mattathias and his five sons retreated into the hills. Soon masses of pious Jews followed them. They were vehemently opposed to the ways of the Greek-Syrians and ever ready to die for the Torah and the laws, the practice of which had, at the penalty of death, been forbidden by the rulers. Mattathias' followers began a harassing guerrilla warfare upon the foreigners.

When Mattathias died, his son Judas Maccabeus took over the command of the rebels. Desperate battles were then fought. Finally, after several defeats, the Syrian army retreated and Jerusalem was liberated. Thus the first war for religious freedom was won (165 B.C.E.).

The victory over the Greek-Syrians halted for a while the Hellenizing process in Judah. But the Hellenization process that was going on outside Judah was not halted. In Egypt, for instance, there were large Jewish communities, especially in Alexandria, which were undergoing a process of assimilation. The youth were educated in Greek, and the old Hebrew language was unknown to many. The Jews of Egypt tried to counteract assimilation by teaching the Torah in Greek or by using philosophy to strengthen the fundamental tenets of Judaism. Many books were composed in Greek purporting to demonstrate the rational basis of the Torah. Whatever could not be explained rationally was taken allegorically and symbolically. The most characteristic thinker of this type was Philo of Alexandria, an observant Jew but at the same time a great admirer of Greek philosophy, particularly of Plato; Philo tried to harmonize Judaism and Greek philosophy. Philo was one of the leaders of Egyptian Jewry, a defender of the faith of his forefathers. He went to Rome to plead in the name of Egyptian Jews before Emperor Caligula. With all of this he still did not exert much influence on Jewry as a whole. His main ideas, considerably changed, were later used by certain Christian thinkers.

On the other hand, Hillel, a contemporary of Philo, worked more closely within the confines of Judaism; he was the recognized Jewish leader both in Judah (Judea, so called by the Romans) and in the Diaspora. This great leader and moral personality served as a bridge between the post-Biblical world and the Talmudic world that was shaping into concrete form. With him and by him the Talmudic period really started, but it would take time until its contours would be seen by all.

Indeed, Hillel was one of the strongest links in the chain of Jewish continuity. The second greatest creative work of the Jewish people—the Talmud—was to be completed in the next 600 years. It would be a collective monument, the accumulated results of debates, decisions, pronouncements, interpretations of hundreds, perhaps thousands, of scholars in the various academies of Palestine and Babylonia. Jewish literature would become a people's literature in which both sage and common man participated—something that the world had never seen before.

THE CHAIN OF TRADITION

> Moses received Torah from Sinai, and handed it over to Joshua; Joshua to the Elders; the Elders to the Prophets; and the Prophets handed it over to the Men of the Great Assembly. They said three things: Be deliberate in judgment; raise up many disciples; and make a fence around the Torah. (Aboth 1:1)

Who were those Men of the Great Assembly? What did they do? We do not know much about them but we do know a little.

The rebuilding of the Second Temple and the restoration of the Commonwealth, resulting from the proclamation of Cyrus the Great (537 B.C.E.), came to their completion in the year 444, when Ezra and Nehemiah effected a cultural, religious, and social revolution. Ezra the Scribe was the one of whom it was later said that he restored the Torah which had been forgotten; according to the Talmud, he restored "the crown of the Torah to what it had been before the Babylonian captivity." Empowered by a decree of King

Artaxerxes Longimanus of Persia, Ezra returned from exile to Judah with over 1,500 people, called together the leaders of the people to Jerusalem, and re-introduced the Torah of Moses as the basis of Jewish life and thought—a measure that more than any-thing else secured the continuance and vitality of Judaism. He also took energetic steps against assimilation by insisting that all Jews divorce any foreign wives; all future mixed marriages would be forbidden. In this reform he was greatly aided by Nehemiah, a cupbearer to Artaxerxes. Nehemiah came to Jerusalem twice, carrying out the necessary plans for fortifying Jerusalem against the surrounding enemies.

During the Persian rule, in fact up to the year 332 B.C.E., the re-ligious leadership was in the hands of the Men of the Great Assem-bly, a sort of Synod which issued decrees, interpreted the Laws, preserved the Scriptures, and generally directed the autonomous life of the communities. Their actual program is expressed in the three principles cited in the Talmudic passage above.

"Be deliberate in judgment" meant that everything pertaining to the development of Jewish religious tradition and life must be carefully considered both in the light of the political and economic conditions and in the light of the inner meaning of the tradition itself. "Raise up many disciples" meant that the Torah be made the central point of the community as a whole; that schools of learning be established; that the masses of people, not only the learned, be brought close to the Torah. "Make a fence around the Torah" meant the issuing of such decrees and ordinances that would serve as a protection against encroachment by foreign cults. It also meant the preservation of the old sacred texts in their purity, safeguarding them against errors or extraneous ad-ditions. Only those Scriptures considered to be expressive of the true religious and national spirit of the people were to be included among the Sacred Writings. All others were to be excluded (S'forim Hitzonim: "books that remained outside").

The Men of the Great Assembly, all or a great part of them, were known as Sopherim (scribes), because they were followers of Ezra the Scribe. In the Talmud the Sopherim were so called be-cause "they counted every letter of the Torah" (sophar means "counting" in Hebrew). The attention paid by scribes to the letters of the Hebrew Scriptures can perhaps best be illustrated by an example given by Christian David Ginsburg (1831-1914) in his Introduction to the *Massoretic-Critical Edition of the Hebrew Bible* (1897):

> I possess a manuscript of the Pentateuch in which every two pages are followed by a page containing two tables. These tables register, line for line, the number of times each letter of the alphabet occurs in the two corresponding pages, as well as the number of words in each line. At the end of each table, the sum total is given of each separate letter, and of the words in the pages in question.

VARIOUS SECTS

"Sect" may not be entirely accurate to describe all the groups, parties, communities, and sects which are lumped under this one label, but it will serve. The Bible acquaints us with sects among the Israelites. Perhaps the oldest we know of are the Rechabites, founded by Jonadab, son of Rechab. They were ascetics, living a nomadic life in the wilderness and retaining the old pre-settlement, pre-agriculture customs; they lived in tents and sowed no seed, as per Jonadab's commandments (Jer. 35). They were, like Elijah, fiery opponents of the worship of Baal. They refrained from wine. At the time of Jehu (c. 842 B.C.E.), their leader, Jonadab, seems to have participated in or at least approved of the revolt against the Omri dynasty (2 Kings 10:15-17). At the time of Jeremiah, two-and-a-half centuries later, this sect was still in existence.

Other sects, much better known, were very active during the Second Commonwealth, when probably two dozen or more flourished, some more political than others, some entirely religious. A few of the more important ones deserve our attention.

Samaritans

The Samaritans were the descendants of those settlers from foreign lands brought by the Assyrians after the destruction of the Kingdom of Israel (721 B.C.E.), or the descendants of those Israelites who remained in the land but assimilated with the new colonists. We hear about them at the time of Ezra. There was a split then between the Jews and the Samaritans that apparently could not be repaired. The Samaritans later separated completely and built their own temple on Mount Gerizim. They recognized only the Five Books of Moses and the Book of Joshua as their scripture. The prophets were rejected. This sect, still in existence today, counts about 200 members. They adhere to the ancient custom of sacrificing a paschal lamb publicly. In the Talmud they are called Kuthim. There is a special set of laws regulating the relations between Jews and Samaritans, some of them favorable, others antagonistic. The parable of the good Samaritan, as told by Jesus in the New Testament, is well known.

Pharisees

The three most active and influential groups of this Second Commonwealth period were the Pharisees, the Sadducees, and the Essenes. The Pharisees were the popular party, the leaders of which were the most learned and pious Jews. The origin of the name is unclear. Some scholars say it comes from a root word meaning "to separate"—i.e., to pull apart from unclean things and be holy. Other scholars suggest the root word means "to interpret," thus translating "Pharisee" as "expounder of the law." In any case, the Pharisees were pious *and* were learned interpreters.

The Pharisees formed a Haburah (brotherhood or association: they called themselves Haberim, "associates") and admitted only those who, in the presence of three members, pledged themselves to the strict observance of Levitical purity, to the avoidance of close association with Am Ha-Aretz (the ignorant and careless boor), to the scrupulous payment of tithes to the priests and to the poor. Josephus describes the Pharisees as extremely virtuous and sober, and as despising luxuries. Their ethics was based upon the principles: "Be holy as the Lord your God is holy" and "Love thy neighbor as thyself."

The Pharisees maintained that besides the written law (Torah) there was the oral law in the form of interpretations deduced from the written text. This was their explanation and elaboration of the Mosaic law, designed as guides for new circumstances of life not explicitly covered in the written law; it was also their attempt to "make a fence around the Torah." Most of the Pharisees came from the common people. They could not pride themselves upon their noble birth or upon being wealthy. Their only distinction was their zeal and love of Torah. Their progressive outlook on life enabled them to interpret the Law of Moses in such a manner as to safeguard its spirit and at the same time make it possible for the people to adjust and live under foreign domination. Simon the Just and Hillel are good examples of Pharisaic leadership, learning, and sainthood. The Talmud is a direct result of the Pharisaic method. We can count the Pharisees as a major link in the chain of Hebrew tradition, cherishing and keeping alive the best in Judaism.

Why then are the Pharisees in the New Testament vainglorious hypocrites? Why are the Pharisees slandered as divorcing morality from religion, when everywhere they declared virtue, probity, and benevolence to be the essence of the Law? There were, of course, some hypocrites among the Pharisees. The Talmud recognized this; it condemned them as "destroyers of the world" (Sotah 3:4) and as a "Pharisaic plague" (Yer. Sotah 11:19a). There was a kind of justifiable pride the Pharisees could take in their talented and inspired interpretation of the scriptures. This must have gone to the heads of a few individual Pharisees. However, the evidence does not support the image of the New Testament Pharisee.

Sadducees

Most Sadducees were aristocrats; many were priests. Their name (Hebrew: Zaddukim) denoted "adherents of Zadok," or descendants of Zadok, the High Priest at the time of King David. The Sadducees admired the Hellenistic culture, including the theater and the sports of that time. They rejected the more progressive and liberal interpretations of the Law proposed by the Pharisees. They denied the immortality of the soul or the existence of any Hereafter. Instead of learning and prayer, they emphasized Temple worship and the offering of sacrifices. They insisted that the written Torah should remain precisely as is; oral interpretations were neither needed nor permitted. In his *Antiquities of the Jews,* Josephus said that the Pharisees delivered to the people

> a great many observances by succession from their fathers which are not written in the laws of Moses; and for that reason it is that the Sadducees reject them, and say that we are to esteem those observances to be obligatory which are in the written word, but that we are not to observe those which are derived from the tradition of our forefathers [i.e., the oral tradition].

Many Sadducees were very close to the ruling power, and it was simply more advantageous for them to take a less nationalistic stand. Because they were generally wealthy, aristocratic, priestly and in charge of the Temple worship, and catered to the Hellenistic ruling power, the Sadducees for a time wielded power out of proportion to their small numbers. With the destruction of the Second Temple in 70 c.e., however, they disappeared from history.

Essenes

The Essenes formed small communities in the outlying districts throughout Palestine. The groups were a combination of what we know as monastic orders and intentional communities. North American counterparts in the 19th and 20th century might be the Amish, the Hutterites, or the Shakers. The Essenes led a collective mode of life; the members worked, ate, studied, and worshipped together, and property was held in common. They lived an ascetic life dedicated to the service of God and the Torah. Their clothing and food and housing were simple; luxuries and pleasures were rigidly outlawed. Some communities insisted on celibacy. The Essenes' aims in life were purification of soul and body, learning and praying, and honest work. Hired help was forbidden; a community could not keep slaves or servants. Josephus describes the Essenes as follows:

> They reject pleasures as an evil, but esteem continence and the conquest over our passions as a virtue . . . . And as for their piety toward God, it is very extraordinary; for before sunrise they speak not a word about profane matters but

put up certain prayers . . . . After this every one of them is
sent away by the curators to do some work until late in the
afternoon when they undergo a second water purification.

The Essenes were opposed to the priesthood in Jerusalem. Both
Philo and Josephus numbered the Essenes at 4,000, which seems
small in comparison with their influence; their reputation spread
to Rome where Pliny wrote favorably of them. The derivation of
their name is uncertain, but probably meant the "pious ones."

Therapeutai

This was a small sect described at length by Philo. It resem-
bled the Essenes in Palestine, but its communities were scattered
throughout the Mediterranean world, especially in Egypt, where
their center seemed to be near Alexandria. Also, their members
tended to come from the upper classes rather than the poor. They
turned to mysticism and a contemplative way of life because they
could not find gratification in the social and political turmoil of
the times. Weary and discontented, they retired into seclusion
where they hoped to find a cure for their souls. Their very name
means "healers."

Messiah-believers

In the early days of Christianity, the believers in Christ as the
Messiah formed small communities in various parts of the country.
The only feature that distinguished them from their Jewish brethren was their belief that the Messiah had already come. They were
awaiting his return. No one could have envisioned at that time
that this small sect was destined to become a world religion.

THE DEAD SEA SCROLLS

Another sect active during this same period was the Dead Sea
Covenanters. They were very similar to the Essenes and may actually have been identical, coming down to us in the form of two
names for the same sect. They lived in the Qumran region near
the Dead Sea in Palestine. The discovery of the Dead Sea Scrolls

in 1947 in a Qumran cave, along with other finds that followed, was one of the most sensational religious events of the 20th century, and necessitates our giving a separate section to this sect.

Ancient documents of over 2,000 years ago suddenly emerged from behind the heavy fogs of time to tell an astounding story to people of today. A period in history, prior to Christianity, came out of the caves; new light was shed upon Christianity and Hebrew literature was enriched by a series of writings unknown until now to the world. The world was aghast. Scores of books were published on the Dead Sea Scrolls as scholars the world over sat down to decipher every point and letter of the documents.

Here is the story of how the documents were discovered. A bedouin lad called Muhammed Adh-Dhib had lost some goats he had been grazing in the vicinity of the Dead Sea. Having been searching for them among the ravines and rocks on the western shores, he noticed a hole in one of the cliffs. He thought that his strayed goats might have escaped into the hole, and in order to drive them out, he tossed stones into it. The goats did not emerge but the sound of a broken jar reverberated through the empty air of the devastated place. Frightened, Muhammed ran away. The next day Muhammed, accompanied by another boy, came back to the place. They both decided to squeeze through the hole and enter the cave. Inside, they found a number of large clay jars, with lids attached to the tops. Removing the lids, they noticed old scrolls made of leather and inscribed with strange letters arranged in parallel columns. They brought them to their Taamirah tribe. Five scrolls were sold to a Syrian Metropolitan by the name of Athanasius Yeshue Samuel for perhaps £50 British money. This was, of course, the 1947-48 period when political turmoil reigned in the area, with Jews and Arabs at each other's throats. Travel was difficult, passes were necessary, bombings were frequent, gunfire was threatening. Further, secrecy, doubts about the authenticity of the documents, and simple chance occurrences all combined with the turmoil of the times to make the year following the discovery of the scrolls a wildly complicated one. Even today accounts of who saw what and who bought what and for how much are not agreed upon by the participants, some of whom have died or been killed. There are even two or three different versions of

how Muhammed Adh-Dhib found the scrolls than the story related
above. Suffice it to conclude that eventually a number of Biblical
and Qumran community scrolls were discovered, along with thousands of fragments of scrolls, not to mention hundreds of additional items of historical value but not of such sensational interest:
coins, letters, contracts, and general artifacts from a larger area
than the original cave. Most of the material has been gathered together at the Palestine Museum in Jerusalem and is being studied
by scholars. Further, the buildings of the Qumran have been ex-
cavated and much has been learned of this Second Commonwealth
Jewish sect. Truly, events of bygone ages have emerged from the
stone and the dust.

The Dead Sea Scrolls and the fragments discovered with them
really represent a library. It is called the Library of Qumran. It
consists of at least the following writings:

1. The so-called Manual of Discipline, containing a system of
regulations initiated by a then existing brotherhood, a collective
society that went into the desert to live isolated from the rest of the
world.

2. An apocalyptical book which tells of the War of the Sons of
Light and the Sons of Darkness, and the final victory of Good
over Evil.

3. Two copies of the Book of Isaiah, one complete and the other
a considerable portion.

4. Commentaries on parts of Habakkuk, Micah, Nahum, and
Psalm 37.

5. An oration by Moses to the people of Israel.

6. The Thanksgiving Psalms.

7. The Copper Scrolls, presumably containing accounts of treasures of gold and other costly things hidden somewhere in the area.

The Manual of Discipline

The so-called Manual of Discipline is a remarkable document.
It parallels another ancient document known as the Zadokite Doc-
ument discovered by Dr. Solomon Schechter in 1896-7 in the Cairo
Genizah (Genizah means "hiding place": a repository for dam-
aged sacred manuscripts or books, attached to some synagogues).
Dr. Schechter found it in the Ezra synagogue in Fostat, Egypt,

and published it. Both historic documents coincide at some points and bring to light details about a Brotherhood that existed over 2,000 years ago. The Brotherhood was a kind of monastic community similar to the organization of the Essenes characterized above. Those God-fearing men were convinced that the Day of God, the day of punishment for social injustice and evil predicted long ago by the great prophets of Israel, would soon come. Only those who separated themselves from evil and lived in accordance with God's laws, as promulgated by Israel's Torah, might hope to escape the dire consequences.

One would naturally expect the Brotherhood to have been eagerly searching for new members; presumably this was not the case. New members were put through a rigorous two-year period of probation. Only after the first year was a new member permitted to eat from the same table as the regular members. But he was still on probation for another year. Members were sworn to the following principles: to honor God and man, to study the Torah, to act justly in accordance with the Mosaic Law, to shun the path of evil, to join the community under the covenant with God. Living in accordance with God's laws meant acting truthfully and righteously, purifying the soul from evil intentions, stubbornness, false pride, and arrogance.

The members prayed and studied in groups of ten under one who was appointed for that task in recognition of his knowledge. The priests and Levites served as the expounders of the Law to the whole community. The covenanters considered themselves as "servants of God" and also as "the remnant of Israel," whose most sacred duty it was to uphold the Covenant of God in a sinful and wicked world which was gradually approaching its doom.

The Last War

The last war on earth will be the War of the Sons of Light and the Sons of Darkness. Who are the sons of Darkness? They are the army of Belial, the power of evil. They will surround the Sons of Light from all sides in an attempt to destroy them. However, the Sons of Light, consisting of the tribes of Judah, Benjamin, and Levi, returning from "their exile among the nations," will march against them in battle array and defeat them all. The mighty armies of Edom, Moab, Philistia, the Kittians of Egypt, and the Kittians of Assyria will be overcome and destroyed. Wickedness will perish from the face of the earth. A new light will shine forth from one end of the world to the other. The Era of God will come. Peace and happiness will descend upon humanity. Seven times, one after another, will the Sons of Light defeat their enemies, but every time the Sons of Darkness will try their luck again. In the seventh battle the Sons of Light will completely triumph. God Himself will march in front of them. The Sons of Darkness will all be destroyed to the last man. This is an apocalyptical vision of the "last days," before the coming of the Messianic Age, a remarkable representation of the future redemption of humanity interspersed with breath-taking details of the last war and of the ultimate triumph of the Sons of Light.

Isaiah and Habakkuk

The complete text of Isaiah, the later Isaiah text (incomplete but substantial), and the almost complete text of Habakkuk (with its accompanying commentary) give us Biblical works of very ancient date which fruitfully aid scholars in their exegetical and linguistic study. The Isaiah scroll, for example, has given scholars the opportunity to compare the Masoretic or traditional Hebrew text with a Hebrew text of Isaiah at least a thousand years older than any such text known prior to the 1947 discovery.

Thanksgiving Psalms

A most original work is the collection of about twenty hymns. This work has to remind one of the Book of Psalms in the Bible, although the latter is by and large of slightly higher quality. Nevertheless, the Qumran hymns are a true expression of the human heart, of its yearnings toward God, and of its clinging to the hope of man's ultimate redemption. From the standpoint of Hebrew literature, they represent a new spiritual treasure.

The Qumran men appear in the hymns in all their sublimity and idealism. They tell God about the scoffers around them, their enemies who mock at them, and the evil that surrounds them. Their trust in God not only sustains them, but imparts to them courage, hope, consolation, and, above all, a meaningful life which overflows their souls. While reading these wonderful out-pourings of the soul of man, one perceives the meaning of true faith. One cannot help thinking of the ideal in man, the divine sparks in his soul as he stands face to face with God. One trusts those hymn writers simply because they are zealously dedicated to their way of life and to the teachings of their elders. The ancient Hebrew words sparkle with life, telling us a story of long ago about people who, steeled by resolve and faith, would brave the desert rather than remain in a society where injustice reigned. Leading a good life in a community of good people meant to them more than all the comforts that the city life could ever offer.

The freshness and the vigor of the Hebrew words is difficult to capture in a translation, but these excerpts will give some sense of the poetic impact of this book of hymns (translations from the original Hebrew by the author of this present volume):

> I praise thee, O God, for putting my soul among
>   the Living,
> and for protecting me against the snares of perversion.
> Evildoers sought to destroy me because I upheld Thy
>   Covenant.
> But they are a league of deceit and a union of evil-doing.
> They do not know that Thou hast made me stand up.
> Thou in Thy mercy hast come to my help;
> and with Thee I stepped forward.
> Because of what you have done for me they assailed me.

Here we can hear how the writer thanks God for saving his life from the hands of the wicked people who sought to destroy him. Although we do not know who the writer's persecutors were (how we would like to know it!) or why they wanted to destroy him, we nevertheless feel the trembling of his heart as he stands before God:

> I said: Cruel men surrounded me with their weapons,
> they shot their arrows without letup,
> their spears were like flames consuming wood,
> their voice like the roaring of mighty waters,

like a bursting stream of great destruction . . . .
And I, while my heart was melting like water,
was clinging to Thy covenant.
Their foot was caught in the very net
they had spread for me.

In another passage the writer brings forth some autobiographical details of his life:

They had banished me from my country
like a sparrow is banished from its nest;
all my acquaintances and friends
alienated themselves from me,
and regarded me as a broken vessel.
They were advocates of lies
and visionaries of falsehood.
They conspired against me.
They wanted flatteries to replace
Thy teaching which Thou hast inscribed
upon my heart.

And here is another short passage which contrasts man with the greatness of God:

I am dust and ashes — What can I plot if Thou
    dost not wish it?
What do I account for—if Thy will be not there?
How may I stand up—if Thou dost not support me?
What can I say—if Thou hast not opened my mouth?
And how can I answer—if Thou didst not give me
    wisdom?

APOCRYPHA, PSEUDEPIGRAPHA, APOCALYPSE, APOLOGY

The definitions of these terms can get as confusing as the title of this section looks, but it is important to understand them as we look at types of literary activity especially prominent during the last two or three centuries of the Second Commonwealth period.

Apocrypha

By 100 C.E. the Jews had drawn up a list of their authoritative sacred writings; the canon was closed. The rabbinical designation for noncanonical books was "outside works." Many of these "outside works" were treasured religious books, interesting and important to hosts of the Jewish people. The Egyptian Jews had already, during the two centuries prior to the fixing of the canon, incorporated some of these works into their scriptures and given them official recognition in their synagogues. Further, the Alexandrian Jews believed that divine inspiration for writers was still active; whereas the Palestinian Jews believed it had ceased at the beginning of the Second Commonwealth period. This became an issue in the final canonization of Hebrew scriptures, when it was determined that a criterion for inclusion was whether the book had been written prior to the time of Ezra and Nehemiah, prior to the cessation of divine revelation to writers. This is why the authorship by King Solomon of Ecclesiastes, Proverbs, and the Song of Songs became so important; if they could be attributed to Solomon then they could be canonized, but if they were written as late as the 3rd century B.C.E., as some parts seemed to be, then they would be "outside works." The early Christians, of course, used for their scriptures the Jewish scriptures; but they, those outside Palestine at least, used the Greek version (the Septuagint) of the scriptures, and this version contained those works which the Jews came to designate "outside," but which the Christian church continued to use officially in their worship and instruction. It was St. Jerome (c. 340-420 A.D.) who gave the term "apocrypha" to these "outside works," though in his Latin translation of the Bible, and in other Christian versions of the Bible, the works remained for years distributed among the various Old

Testament books. It was Martin Luther (1483-1546), in his German translation of the Bible, who first grouped the Apocrypha as a separate unit; though he granted that the apocryphal books were "profitable and good to read," he insisted that only the Hebrew canon books were the true word of God. This Protestant-Catholic difference continued and became accentuated. Today the Protestants exclude the Apocrypha from their Bible; the Roman Catholic Church includes them. The apocryphal books for Protestants and Jews are:

1 Esdras
2 Esdras
Tobit
Judith
The Rest of Esther
The Wisdom of Solomon
Ecclesiasticus
Baruch with the Epistle of Jeremiah
The Song of the Three Holy Children
The History of Susanna
Bel and the Dragon
The Prayer of Manasses
1 Maccabees
2 Maccabees

Pseudepigrapha

For Catholics, since the above apocryphal books are part of their scripture, the term Apocrypha applies to another group of books, which for them are their non-Biblical works. These include The Psalms of Solomon, Martyrdom of Isaiah, The Assumption of Moses, Enoch, Sibylline Books, and others. Of course, these works are also non-Biblical for Jews and Protestants, but they use the designation Pseudepigrapha for them. The word comes from the Greek, meaning "writings under assumed names"; this refers to later actual authorship ascribed to earlier Biblical figures in order to give the books authority. To complicate matters further, we must admit that the Jewish-Protestant Apocrypha contains books of a pseudepigraphal nature: e.g., Baruch with the Epistle of Jeremiah.

We must not ask for too much precision from these labels. Suffice it for us simply to refer to any ancient religious book not in the Jewish scriptures as an "outside book." A few examples:

1 Maccabees is a historical record of the period 175-135 B.C.E. It tells in detail about the struggle of the Maccabees from the first uprising of Mattathias to the death of Simon the High Priest. The name of the author is unknown. Originally written in Hebrew, it was known also as the Book of the Hasmonean House. It came down to us in its Greek translation. Except for its late origin, its historical value and its piety and patriotism would surely have qualified it for canonization.

2 Maccabees covers a similar but shorter period of the Maccabean rebellion, detailing additional events, especially martyrdoms and a focus on the courage displayed in this struggle for religious freedom—one of the first such struggles in the history of the world. The author claims that his book is a condensation of a larger work of five volumes by one Jason of Cyrene. The editor-author admits that his abridgement was not easy, "just as it is no easy matter for a man to prepare a banquet and strive to benefit others."

3 Maccabees contains a long story about the Jews in Alexandria, Egypt, who were in peril of their lives by one of the Ptolemies. However, the king changed his mind in time and all of the Jews were saved.

4 Maccabees discusses the question of piety versus reason and attempts to adapt Jewish ideas to Greek thought. The author takes much of his illustrative material from 2 Maccabees.

The Scroll of Antiochus, or the Scroll of the Hasmoneans, contains some accounts of the Maccabean wars. Its final version must not have been completed until sometime in the 7th century C.E., since many later Midrashim are quoted in the book. It contains many beautiful legends and fanciful Aggadic stories which contributed to its popularity. The Yemen Jews still consider it as part of their liturgy. In the Middle Ages, this Scroll was read in the synagogues in some countries on Hanukkah, the festival commemorating the Maccabean victory. The Jews in the Middle Ages knew little about the Maccabean rebellion, because the Maccabees Books, being "outside works," were not part of the canon. The

Scroll of Antiochus, therefore, apparently served them as their only ready source of information on this subject, excepting the details found about it in the Talmud.

Hymns of Solomon, written in Hebrew in Palestine about the middle of the 1st century c.e., is a collection of eighteen songs similar to the canonical Psalms.

Judith is the story of a woman who endangered her life to save her people from the besieging Assyrians. Modest and pure—and scrupulous in following all Jewish practices—Judith offered herself to the Assyrian commander, Holofernes, but succeeded in killing him before he had a chance of touching her.

Tobit is the story of an upright man and his son, Tobias, their good deeds, and their reward. It was written as early as the late 3rd century b.c.e. Tobit allegedly lived in Nineveh during the time of King Sennacherib, and being a pious Jew, Tobit made it his business to bury any Judean who had been executed by the state. The tyrant, enraged, sentenced Tobit to death, but he escaped. In the book, Tobit instructs his son Tobias what a good man is supposed to do: to treat his fellow man justly, to extend a helping hand to the needy, to pay the wages of a worker immediately, and "not to do anything to anyone which is hateful to you."

Apocalyptic Literature

Apocalyptic literature is a revelation of hidden things (from the Greek word meaning "to uncover"); it generally represents an attempt to reveal the mysteries of God's workings to an anxious people in a troubled time, an attempt to make sense of persecutions and wickedness in a world God appears to have forgotten. The period of the Maccabean rebellion and the Roman occupation of Palestine was an era ripe for the creation of such literature. We find apocalyptic motifs in Biblical books such as Ezekiel, Zechariah, and Daniel, but apocalyptic works seemed to proliferate during the course of Israel's national distress from approximately 200 b.c.e. to 100 c.e. What characterizes an apocalyptic work? Visions, symbols, expectations, angels, demons, Messiahs, catastrophic world endings, great judgments, terrible punishments for the wicked, a coming Golden Age, a new heaven and a new earth, bodily resurrection for the righteous. By picturing the wonders of

God's power and the mysteries of God's ways, in a lavish and imaginative use of imagery and symbols—for example, nations and persons as animals, events in history as occurrences of nature (earthquakes, storms); and by envisioning even greater divine manifestations in the near future, the apocalyptic writer offered hope and encouragement in the dark days of persecution. God would ultimately triumph and establish his kingdom—and "ultimately" would surely be very soon. Examples of apocalyptic works are as follows:

Enoch contains a history of the world in successive stages, secrets of the unseen world, and revelations about the Messianic kingdom.

Testaments of the Twelve Patriarchs are testaments ascribed to the twelve sons of Jacob. Each contains a historical account of his life, a summary of lessons to be learned and warnings to be heeded from the sins and virtues of this life, and an apocalypse dealing with the immediate future of his own period. The ethical content of the Testaments is admirable; the treatment of the concepts and practice of love and forgiveness, for instance, ranks with the best of Second Commonwealth writings.

The Assumption of Moses protests the mixing of political and religious ideals. The writer eschews a Messiah, but sees the Kingdom soon coming, preceded by a time of woes and supernatural signs and great repentance.

In the Revelation of Rabbi Joshua ben Levi, this Tanna is given the opportunity of seeing before his death the place awaiting him in paradise. He saw seven portions. In the first dwelt the proselytes to Judaism; in the second, repentant sinners; in the third, the Patriarchs and the Israelites who came out from Egypt; in the fourth, the perfectly righteous; in the fifth, Elijah and the Messiah; in the sixth, those that died in piety; and in the seventh, those who died for the sins of Israel. Rabbi Joshua also entered the inferno, where he saw pagans burned by angels in pits of fire.

In the Hebrew Elijah Apocalypse, the angel Michael reveals to the prophet Elijah what is to happen at the "end of the days." The last wicked king who will rule upon earth will instigate three wars and will also "stretch out his arm against Israel." Then the Messiah will appear from heaven, accompanied by angels, to wage war against the enemies of God. After this, Israel will be secure for forty years. Then Gog and Magog will arouse the heathen against Israel, but they will be annihilated. Finally the dead will be awakened to new life and peace will reign forever among men.

The Wars of King Messiah tells how the kingdom of Edom will spread over the whole world and Israel will be persecuted most cruelly during nine months. Then Messiah ben Joseph will appear and restore the worship of the Temple in Jerusalem. But his reign will not last; he will be slain in battle against Armilus, the commander of the heathen. Then Messiah ben David will come. Armilus will be defeated. The Israelites, heretofore dispersed over all the lands, will be gathered into Jerusalem.

2 Esdras (same as most of 4 Ezra) inquires into the relationship between the justice of God and sin and suffering. A 20th century Christian scholar makes an interesting comment:

> It is nothing less than astonishing that the close affinities [of St. Paul's New Testament writings] with the Apocalypse of Ezra do not receive any recognition. In this work there are elaborate discussions of the problem of sin, the Fall of our first parents, Election, the wrath, long-suffering, and mercy of God, the prerogative of Israel, the significance of the Law, the temporal and eternal Jerusalem, of the prospect of dying or surviving to the Parousia, the tribulation of the times of the End and the Judgment.[2]

Apocalyptic literature is, of course, richer and more numerous than these few examples, but they will suffice.

Apologetic Literature

Hebrew apologetic literature are those works composed during the centuries in defense of Judaism and the Jewish people. Its aim was to strengthen the bonds of Judaism internally by enlightening the Jew about his faith and explaining it in appealing terms; externally, apologetics sought to defend Judaism against attacks by its enemies or to present the faith attractively for proselyting purposes. There was a spate of apologetic literature written by the Jews during the Second Commonwealth period; as a matter of fact, during that period the earliest Jewish apologetic works known to us were written: The Wisdom of Solomon, 4 Maccabees, Sibylline Books. Of course, the Jews continued to produce apologetic literature for 2,000 years more, and will continue.

The Wisdom of Solomon, written about 50 B.C.E., probably by an Alexandrian Jew, exalts Judaism and presents the Torah as the true wisdom. He sees no difference between the highest ideals of Greek philosophy and the ideals of Judaism. Condemning the natural religions of the pagan world, he tries to prove the superiority of monotheism and the harmony that exists between true wisdom, that is, the philosophy of reason, and the wisdom of Israel's Torah based as it is upon revelation.

Similar in aim but not in form are the Sibylline Books. They take their inspiration and their form from a practice common in the Hellenistic and Roman world: seeking divine guidance by consulting a sibyl—a prophetess or oracle. These Books contain oracular utterances by Hebrew sibyls predicting the triumph of Judaism over idolatry and contrasting the lofty ethics of the Jewish people with the low morals of paganism. The writer clothed the work in a Greek dress in order to commend Judaism to the Greek world. Some of these oracles are said to have been later interpolated with statements favorable to Christianity.

In 4 Maccabees, the writer seeks to harmonize Greek and Hebrew thought by arguing that Greek philosophy is embodied in the Mosaic Law.

No one made a more thorough effort to combine Greek philosophy and Jewish religious beliefs than Philo, the Jewish philosopher born late in the 1st century B.C.E. He was a Jewish apologist par excellence and we discuss him in more detail later.

ECCLESIASTICUS

The title "Ecclesiasticus" comes from St. Jerome's Vulgate, but the Jews call it Sirach, or Ben Sira, for its author, Joshua ben Sira. This book of wisdom literature is one of the "outside works," from the Apocrypha, but it is being considered here separately in order to give it more space. The Book of Ben Sira is quoted in the Talmud and Midrash, was cited by Saadia Gaon in the 10th century, and has been cherished by the Jews for centuries.

Ben Sira's ideas mark a summary of the Hebrew thinking of his time. As a spokesman for the priesthood, Temple worship and sacrificing are to him the pillars of religion; but simultaneously with this he requires man to be charitable and conscientious. He never speaks of the resurrection of the dead, nor of the immortality of the soul. An upright man should enjoy life here on earth as much as is compatible with morality and a good life, for "there is no joy in Sheol [underground]." He is critical of women, of skeptics, of people who pose as thinkers, of false friends. He opposes fatalism and offers faith in God as the best way to happiness. He speaks of a time when Israel would be delivered from domination by strangers, a kind of Messianic age but without a Messiah. He never mentions that the Messiah would come from the Davidic dynasty. On the contrary, he asserts that the House of David had not lived up to the compact with God, since only three kings of the Davidic dynasty remained faithful to God. Only the solemn compact with Aaron would endure forever; that is, only the priesthood would last into the Messianic Age, because it is worthy of God's favor.

Israel Levi evaluates this work as follows:

> The Wisdom of Ben Sira marks an epoch in the history of Jewish thought, on account both of what it teaches and of what it silently ignores. While the author advocates the offering of the prescribed sacrifices and the veneration of priests, he condemns all hypocrisy and urges the union of the outward practice of religion with a pure conscience and with the doing of charity. . . . The view has been expressed that this work, early in date as it is, bears traces of Hellenic influence. The author, in his travels, may possibly have come in contact with Greek civilization, since he speaks of foreign poets and moralists whose fame was spread abroad. The customs which he describes are taken from Greek rather than from Hebrew society. The fatalistic philosophers whose opinions he contests were doubtless the Stoics. . . . Ben Sira's maxims show a profound knowledge of the human heart, a fraternal sympathy with the poor and the oppressed, and a sincere, enlightened piety.[3]

Joshua ben Sira, a Jerusalemite, wrote his book in Hebrew about the end of the 3rd century B.C.E. In 132 B.C.E., his grandson translated it into Greek. Scholars consider the book an important source for understanding this period of the Second Commonwealth. Akin to the Book of Proverbs, the work contains epigrams, poems, maxims, and practical observations on human conduct. Ben Sira has something to say about parents and children, husbands and wives, rich and poor, masters and slaves. "A trustworthy slave," ben Sira writes, "should be guarded as your own life." Though the rod is sometimes needed for a rebellious slave, avoid it as much as possible, counsels ben Sira. Maintain compassion and good will toward all. Ben Sira is a pure monotheist, as his prayers scattered through the book testify. That ben Sira was gifted as a poet may be seen from the following poem written in honor of Simon the High Priest, the son of Johanan (50:1-24):

> Great among his brethren, and glory of his people,
> Was Simeon the son of Johanan, the priest;
> In whose generation the House was repaired,
> And in whose days the Temple was fortified;
> In whose generation a cistern was digged,
> A pit like the sea in its abundance;
> In whose days a wall was built—
> Turrets for protection in the temple of the King;
> Who took thought for his people against the spoiler
> And fortified the city against the besieger.
> How glorious when he looked forth from the Tent,
> And when he went out from the sanctuary!
> As the morning-star from amid thick clouds,
> And as the full-moon in the days of the solemn feast;
> As the sun dawning upon the temple of the king,
> And as a rainbow seen in the cloud.
> As a bud in the branches in the days of the solemn feast,
> And as the lily by the watercourses;
> As the flower of Lebanon in the days of summer,
> And as the fire of incense upon the meal-offering:
> As a gold vessel . . .
> That is set with precious stones;

As a green olive full of berries,
And as a wild olive-tree with branches full of sap.
When he put on robes of honor,
And clothed himself with robes of glory;
When he ascended the altar of majesty,
And made glorious the court of the sanctuary;
When he received his portions from the hand of his
    brethren,
While standing by the altar-fires:
Round him the garland of his sons,
Like cedar plants in Lebanon.
And they compassed like the willows of the brook—
All the sons of Aaron in their glory;
With the fire-offerings of the Lord in their hands,
Before all the congregation of Israel;
Until he had finished serving the altar,
And arranging the fires of the Most High.
Then sounded the sons of Aaron, the priests,
With trumpets of beaten work;
And they sounded, and made their mighty voice heard,
To bring to remembrance before the Most High.
All flesh hastened together,
And fell down on their faces to the ground;
Worshipping before the Most High,
Before the Holy One of Israel.
And the choir uttered its voice,
And over the multitude they made sweet melody.
And all the people of the land chanted,
In prayer before the Merciful;
Until he had finished serving the altar,
And had brought his customary offerings unto it.[4]

Ben Sira's proverbs and epigrams reflect the ideas of a practical
man who speaks from experience. He teaches man to be practical
and to do righteousness, because it is more advantageous. Ben
Sira accepts the principle that the good are rewarded and the
wicked punished.

Bread and water, a house and a robe to cover your nakedness—this is sufficient for a man's life.

*

The love of gold is a stumbling block to everyone; those who run after it must stumble and fall.

*

Degrading a righteous man who is poor and honoring a wicked man who is rich—both are abominable.

*

What comradeship can there be between a copper pot and an earthen vessel? When they meet, the first strikes and the second is broken.

*

Do not join the wine drinkers; many are those who are wine's victims.

*

Do not expect favors from rulers or to enjoy yourself among them. When a ruler speaks to you pleasantly, do not rely on his words. If needs be, he may break his word and instead of favoring he may imprison you.

*

Love thy servant as thyself; do not rob him of his free time.

*

Do not burden thy family, and do not brutalize thy slave.

*

Give not over thy soul to sorrow.

*

Gladness of heart is the life of man; joyfulness lengthens man's life.

*

Envy and wrath shorten man's days; care bringeth old age before the time.

*

Sorrow hath destroyed many, and there is no profit therein.

THE SEPTUAGINT

In the history of Western culture, the Septuagint—the translation of the Hebrew scriptures into Greek—marked a turning point. It brought East and West together. For the first time Jerusalem spoke the language of Hellas; and Moses, the divine lawgiver of the Hebrews, addressed himself to the forums of Greece and to the higher circles of Greek thought. Nothing like it had happened before. Israel's Torah, the Mosaic Law, was ushered into the West in the 3rd century B.C.E., perhaps even with the greatest honors—by the royal house of the Ptolemies, the Greek rulers of Egypt. It is impossible to determine precisely how this great event came about. Fact and fantasy seem irrevocably mixed in the tales handed down to us from antiquity. Major sources of our information are Philo of Alexandria, Flavius Josephus, certain Talmudic passages, and the pseudepigraphal Letter of Aristeas. All in all, this is how the traditional story goes:

In the first quarter of the 3rd century B.C.E., Alexandria was one of the greatest cultural centers in the world. The royal library there had grown to be not only a treasure house of rare manuscripts and books but also a center for scholars and intellectuals. Once, we are told, King Ptolemy Philadelphus, a patron of art, philosophy, and science, asked the number of volumes the library contained—to which the librarian, Demetrius Valerius, answered that it contained "twenty times ten thousand" but that very shortly it would contain "fifty times ten thousand." Then Valerius added, somewhat sadly, so the story goes, that he had encountered difficulties in obtaining for the library a set of books written a long time ago by the Wise Men of the Hebrew people. Of course, he could get them in Hebrew, but the language barrier would stand in the way of reading them. What he would like to do is to translate them into Greek and thus make them available to the intellectual world. The king agreed and sent a special envoy to Jerusalem requesting scholars and translators for the project. He also sent gifts for the Temple: gold, gems, and money for buying sacrifices in his name. Eliezer, the High Priest, selected six men from each tribe, seventy-two scholars. Another version has seventy scholars chosen—thus the name Septuagint, Latin for

seventy (or as often abbreviated into the numerical symbol: LXX).
In any case, in Alexandria the translators were accorded a royal
reception. Here is how Philo, in the early 1st century c.e., continues the story:

> Reflecting how great an undertaking it was to make a full
> version of the law given by the voice of God, where they
> could not add or take away or transfer anything, but
> must keep the original form and shape, they proceeded to
> look for the most open and unoccupied spot in the neigh-
> borhood outside the city . . . . In front of Alexandria lies
> the island of Pharos, stretching with a narrow strip of
> land toward the city and enclosed by a sea not deep but
> most consisting of shoals, so that the loud din and boom-
> ing of the surging waves grows faint through the long
> distance before it reaches the land. Judging this to be the
> most suitable place in the district where they might find
> peace and tranquility, and the soul could commune with
> the laws with none to disturb its privacy, they fixed their
> abode there; and, taking the sacred books, stretched them
> out toward heaven with the hands that held them, asking
> of God that they might not fail in their purpose . . . . Sit-
> ting here in seclusion, with none present save the elements
> of nature—earth, water, air, heaven—the genesis of which
> was to be the first theme of their sacred revelation, for
> the laws begin with the story of the world's creation, they
> became as it were possessed, and under inspiration wrote,
> not each scribe something different, but the same word
> for word, as though dictated to each by an invisible
> prompter.

Josephus recites another episode connected with the translation,
how Ptolemy, after having acquainted himself with the content of
the Torah, expressed his amazement at the fact that neither the
poets nor the historians of Greece had ever mentioned the existence
of such wonderful legislation. Demetrius explained it in his own
way: Many did not dare touch this subject because they lacked the
required knowledge, and the few that did dare write about it were
struck by sickness or blindness, as was one Theodoctes, a writer
of tragedies. Thereupon one of Ptolemy's intimate friends, Aristeas

by name, reminded the king of his promise to free 100,000 Jewish slaves upon the completion of the translation. Most of those slaves were captured by his father, Ptolemy Logos, during the wars that he waged in Syria, Phoenicia, and Judea. A royal decree was issued and duly put into effect.

The Jewish community of Alexandria, the most prosperous in Egypt, and all other communities throughout the land, decided to celebrate the day when the translation was completed. A celebration was also observed for hundreds of years following on the island of Pharos.

Begun about 250 B.C.E., the translation continued, not only through the Torah, but until all the Hebrew scriptures were translated into Greek, which was during the 1st century B.C.E. Not only did the Septuagint serve the intellectuals, as Ptolemy had proposed, but all Jews in the Hellenistic world who lacked knowledge of Hebrew. They were happy to have their sacred scriptures in the vernacular, and with justice prided themselves that now the non-Jewish world had a chance to acquaint itself with the Mosaic Law and with the wisdom and poetry and great prophets of Israel.

A few other ancient translations of Hebrew scriptures should be briefly noted.

The Samaritan Pentateuch was in the West Aramaic dialect, which was spoken by the Samaritans, who recognized only the Torah and the Book of Joshua. Some scholars think that this version is even older than the Septuagint. They assign it to the 4th century B.C.E. It differs from the Hebrew text in many places.

The Peshitta is the Syriac translation of the Hebrew Scriptures. It was probably made in Mesopotamia during the 1st century.

Aquila's Greek translation was made under the guidance of Rabbi Joshua ben Hananiah and Rabbi Akiba. Only fragments of this translation have come down to us. Aquila was a proselyte.

Symmachus, a Samaritan convert to Judaism, made (about 200 C.E) another translation into Greek. At about the same time, a Christian by the name of Theodotion, perhaps a native of Ephesus, made his own translation.

Targum Onkelos is an Aramaic translation which is still in existence. Onkelos was a proselyte. The Aramaic translation of the prophets is attributed to Jonathan ben Uzziel, one of Hillel's disciples.

It is said that the Bible was translated into over 2,000 languages and dialects.

PHILO JUDAEUS
(c. 20 B.C.E.-50 C.E.)

Philo Judaeus, or Philo of Alexandria, was one of the earliest interpreters of Judaism in the Hellenistic world. A prolific writer, well versed in philosophy as elaborated by Plato, a traditional Jew, and a student of the Bible in its Greek translation (Septuagint), he introduced Judaism to the non-Jewish world and to those Jews who were culturally Hellenized. The Jewish communities in Egypt, as well as in other Hellenistic countries, had to defend their religion against various philosophies and religions of the day. Philo therefore undertook the task of expounding the values of Judaism in the light of Greek philosophy. His aim was to bring Judaism and philosophy into harmony. Where reason balked, he employed the allegorical method. Thus, anthropomorphic representations of the Godhead in the Bible were interpreted as symbolic. Passages that appeared to him as too particularistic or nationalistic were rewritten in a spirit of universalism. He also underscored the ethical nature of the Bible. Philo greatly influenced the Christian world, but rabbinic Judaism in Babylonia and Palestine ignored him almost completely.

A good illustration of Philo's approach is to be found in an essay in which he takes up the question of God's existence and His nature. Man, according to Philo, should search for an answer to the questions of God's existence and of His nature, since both are directly related. God's existence, however, can be demonstrated more easily than His essence, which is "not only difficult to explain but perhaps impossible to solve altogether." We know that anything and everything that exists presupposes one who has made it. One looks at statues or paintings, houses or ships, clothes or furniture not as objects which have made themselves; but rather as things that were made by someone. A well-ordered city does not spring up ready made and from nowhere by itself; such a city tells clearly that it is being directed by wise and good rulers. The world is likened to such a city: its orderliness, the fixed laws that govern the changes of day and night, the seasons, the seas and rivers and lakes teeming with life testify to the existence of a Ruler and Creator. The universe is an artistic creation of the most perfect order. Hence there must be someone whose great knowledge and perfection enables this world not only to come into being but also to be maintained constantly in the course He laid down.

Concerning the essence of God, Philo thinks that despite the fact it is difficult if not impossible to comprehend it, it is still man's duty to seek it. "For nothing is better than to search for the true God." In fact, those who sought God testified that the very seeking, even without finding, was blissful. It is as with the sun. Although we cannot look at the sun when it shines forth in all its brightness, we can feel the emanation of the rays as they reach us. Likewise, though the knowledge of God's essence has been denied us, we may still experience His actions in the world. Philo writes:

> Thus Moses, the sacred guide, most dearly beloved of God, had this in mind when he besought God to reveal Himself to him. But God replied, "Thy zeal I approve as praiseworthy, but thy request cannot be granted . . . . I freely bestow what is in accordance with the recipient; for not all that I can give is within man's power to take, and therefore to him that is worthy of my grace I extend all the boons which he is capable of receiving . . . . But I readily and with right good will admit you to a share of what is attainable. That means that I bid you come and contemplate the universe and its contents, not by the eye of the body, but by the unsleeping eyes of the mind."
> . . . When Moses heard this, he did not cease from his desire, but kept the yearning for the invisible aflame in his heart.

The philosophic problem of how a transcendental God whose essence is incomprehensible might have created a material world as ours was solved by Philo as follows: God did. not create the material world directly. Between God and the world there was an intermediary called Logos (word), a sort of angel, a secondary divine power. This power appears in various forms, spiritual as

well as material. Man, according to Philo, is a part of the material
world, but by virtue of his reason belongs to the Logos. His body
is a sort of prison to his spirit, and the high aim of man is to
liberate himself from his body-prison and return to the original
source whence his spirit came. Morality leads man toward that
goal.

The question then arises: What are the moral virtues? Philo indicates four of them: Courage, Prudence, Temperance, and, above
all, Justice. There are also secondary virtues: good fellowship,
love of peace, mercy, and nobility. Philo regards philanthropy as
one of the major virtues, deviating in this respect from the Greek
philosophers. Perhaps this is due to Philo's Jewish upbringing.
Philo also includes in his list of moral excellence prayer, repentance,
and learning. While he accepts the concept of free will for man, he
declares that nothing can be done without God, that man needs
God's help even while doing good.

Although some of Philo's ideas were basically non-Biblical in
character, as, for instance, his Logos as an intermediary power
between God and the world, he himself thought otherwise. Philosophy and Judaism seemed to him as pursuing one and the same
goal—moral excellence and happiness. Centuries later, in the Middle Ages, Jewish religious philosophers, like Saadia and Maimonides, seeking to find a modus vivendi between two world conceptions,
did almost the same as Philo had. Yet we must admit that Philo's
main influence was exerted upon Christianity and not upon Judaism. Christian theologians studied his works and borrowed from
them extensively, whereas he was almost forgotten by Jewish thinkers in Talmudic and post-Talmudic times. Only in the last few
centuries has interest in Philo arisen.

Ignored by Jewish theologians and historians though he was,
Philo was a loyal member of the Jewish community of Alexandria, ever ready to defend it against its enemies, not only with his
pen but also with his personal presence. This is illustrated in the
story of a Jewish delegation from Alexandria that went to Rome.
The Alexandrian Jews had been victimized by a horrible pogrom
instigated by the Roman prefect Flaccus and eagerly perpetrated
by a populace who wreaked mass violence and death. Philo wrote
a vivid and heart-rending description of those agonizing days; the

reader is referred to his essay, "Flaccus," for his masterful treatment. Suffice it here for us to read a shorter example of Philo's style, his account of the audience his delegation had with Emperor Caligula (Gaius Caesar) at a villa outside Rome, in order to plead for relief for the Jews of Alexandria:

The moment we entered we knew from his look and movements that we had come into the presence not of a judge but of an accuser more hostile than those arrayed against us. For this is what a judge would do: he would sit with assessors selected for their high merit, as the case under examination was of the greatest importance . . . : the opposing parties would stand on either side of him with the advocates who would speak for them, and he would listen in turn to the accusation and the defense for the space of water-time allowed! then he would rise and consult with his assessors as to the verdict which in full accordance with justice they would publicly declare. The actual proceedings showed a ruthless tyrant with a menacing frown on his despotic brow. Instead of doing anything that I have just mentioned he sent for the stewards of the two gardens belonging to Maecenas and Lamia near to each other and the city, in which gardens he had been spending three or four days. For this was the stage where the tragedy which was aimed against our whole nation was to be performed with us who were present as the immediate victims. He ordered them to leave all the villas completely open as he wished to make a careful survey of each of them. When we were brought into his presence the moment we saw him we bowed our heads to the ground with all respect and timidity and saluted him addressing him as Emperor Augustus. The mildness and kindness with which he replied to our greeting was such that we gave up not only our case but our lives for lost! In a sneering, snarling way he said, "Are you the god-haters who do not believe me to be a god, a god acknowledged among all the other nations but not to be named by you?" And stretching out his hands towards heaven he gave utterance to an invocatory address which it was a sin even to listen to, much more to reproduce in the actual words. How vast was the delight which at once filled the envoys on the other side! They thought that Gaius's first utterance had secured the success of their mission. They gesticulated, they danced about and invoked blessings on him under the names of all the gods.

Seeing that he was delighted at being addressed as of more than human nature the virulent sycophant Isidorus said, "My lord, you will hate still more these people here present, and those of whose nation they are, if you understand their malevolence and impiety towards you. For when all men were offering sacrifices of thanksgiving for your preservation they alone could not bear the thought of sacrificing. And when I say 'they' I include also the other Jews."

We cried out with one accord, "Lord Gaius, we are slandered; we did sacrifice and sacrifice hecatombs too, and we did not just pour the blood upon the altar and then take the flesh home to feast and regale ourselves with it as some do, but we gave the victims to the sacred fire to be entirely consumed, and we have done this not once but thrice already, the first time at your accession to the sovereignty, the second when you escaped the severe sickness which all the habitable world suffered with you, the third as a prayer of hope for victory in Germany."

"All right," he replied, "that is true, you have sacrificed, but to another, even if it was for me; what good is it then? For you have not sacrificed to me."

When we heard these words following on his first remark we were seized by a profound terror which spread till it became visible in the countenance. While he was saying this he was going on with his survey of the houses, the different chambers, men's or women's, the ground floors, the upper floors, all of them, and some he censured as defective in structure, and for others he made his own plans and gave orders that they should be more magnificent. Then driven along we followed him up and down mocked and reviled by our adversaries, as they do in the mimes at the theatres. For indeed the business was a sort of mime; the judge had taken on the role of accuser, the accusers the role of a bad judge who had eyes only for his enmity and not for the actual truth . . . .

After giving some of his orders about the buildings he put to us this grave and momentous question, "Why do you refuse to eat pork?" The question was greeted by another outburst of laughter from some of our opponents because they were delighted, while with others it was a studied attempt to flatter him, intended to make the remark seem witty and sprightly. The laughter was so great that some of the servants following him were annoyed at it as showing disrespect for the emperor, with whom even a tempered smile is unsafe except for quite intimate friends.

We answered, "Different people have different customs and the use of some things is forbidden to us as others are to our opponents."

Then someone said, "Yes, just as many don't eat lamb which is so easily obtainable," whereupon Gaius laughed and said, "Quite right too, for it's not nice." Under such befooling and reviling we were helpless.

Then tardily going on a different tack he said, "We want to hear what claims you make about your citizenship."

We started to speak and give him the information but when he had had a taste of our pleading and recognized that it was by no means contemptible, he cut short our earlier points before we could bring in the stronger ones, and dashed at high speed into the large room of the house, and walked round it and ordered the windows all round to be restored with transparent stones, which in the same way as white glass do not obstruct the light but keep off the wind and the scorching sun.

Then he advanced in a leisurely way and said in a more moderate tone, "What is it that you say?" and when we began on the points which came next in the thread of our argument he ran again into another room and ordered original pictures to be put up there.

So with the statement of our case thus mangled and disjointed, one may almost say cut short and crushed to pieces, we gave up, for there was no strength left in us, and since we all the time expected nothing else but death, in our deep distress our souls had passed from within us and went forth to supplicate the true God that he should restrain the wrath of the pretender to that name. And God taking compassion on us turned his spirit to mercy; he relaxed into a softer mood and said just this, "They seem to me to be people unfortunate rather than wicked and to be foolish in refusing to believe that I have got the nature of a god," and saying this he went off bidding us be gone also.

Such was this combination of a theatre and a prison in place of a tribunal, theatre-like in the cackling of their hisses, their mockery and unbounded jeering, prison-like in the strokes inflicted on our flesh, the torture, the racking of the whole soul through the blasphemies against God and menaces launched upon us by this mighty despot, who resented the affront not to another, since then he might easily have changed his mind, but to himself and his desire of the deification to which he supposed the Jews alone did not assent and could not pledge themselves to subscribe. From this prison we had escaped and were just able to breathe again, not because we clung to life and cringed from death, which we would gladly have chosen as being immortality, if thereby we were going to get restoration of our institutions, but because we knew that we should prove to have thrown ourselves away for no useful purpose and to our great discredit. For whatever ambassadors suffer recoils upon those who sent them. For the above reasons we were able to lift our heads above water to some extent but the other circumstances alarmed us in our trepidation and suspense as to what he would decide, what verdict he would declare, on what grounds the judgment would be given. For had a hearing been given to our case by him who heard some points only to misunderstand? Surely it was a cruel situation that the fate of all the Jews everywhere should rest precariously on us five envoys.[5]

FLAVIUS JOSEPHUS
(c. 37-100 c.e.)

Joseph ben Mattathias the Priest was a member of a priestly family in Jerusalem. He was well versed in Torah, a gifted writer, and a student of Greek literature and philosophy. He visited Rome and was deeply influenced by the power and glory of the Roman Empire.

During the revolt against Rome which broke out in Judea in the fateful year 66 c.e., Joseph ben Mattathias was appointed governor of Galilee by the Sanhedrin in Jerusalem, whereupon he went to the north, raised an army of more than 100,000 men to defend the province, and fortified the boundary towns that lay in the path of the Roman legions. However, unlike another priest Mattathias of another Jewish revolt (Maccabean) over 200 years earlier, this Mattathias did not go down in history as a hero for Judaism. From the very beginning of the campaign, Joseph ben Mattathias' heart was not in the war. As a matter of fact, hardly had he taken command of the battle force then he was charged with unfaithful intentions.

After the fall of Jotapata to the Romans, he clandestinely negotiated with the enemy, and surrendered. The Roman commander, Vespasian, and his son Titus, became his patrons. Under the protection of the Emperors, Josephus lived in Rome in great comfort. Both Vespasian and Titus, who ruled the Empire, adopted him as one of the royal family and changed his name to Flavius Josephus. In the security and comfort of the Roman court, Josephus devoted many years to writing. His main works, originally written in Aramaic and translated into Greek, were the following: *The Wars of the Jews,* a complete history of the revolt against Rome; *Antiquities of the Jews,* a history of the Jews since early times; *Against Apion,* an attack on anti-Semitism; and *The Life of Flavius Josephus,* a brief autobiography.

In his autobiography, Josephus justifies his actions as commander of Galilee and places the blame for the fall of the province upon the local Jewish leaders. In *The Wars of the Jews,* he deals with this same revolt, but details the preparations for the war, the courage of certain Jewish leaders in Jerusalem, and the fighting itself. Josephus' conduct during and after the war has always sullied his reputation among the Jews. On the one hand, two of Josephus' contemporaries, Justus of Tiberias and John of Giscala, openly accused him of treachery. On the other hand, Josephus himself insisted that he fought

> as long as it was possible for us to make any opposition.
> I was then seized on by the Romans, and became a cap-
> tive. Vespasian also and Titus had me kept under a guard,
> and forced me to attend them continually. At the first I was
> put into bonds.[6]

A middle position might see Josephus as simply a realist who firmly believed that the Jews could never stand up against the Romans, that some sort of submission was necessary, and that he was the one to negotiate it. We can never know for sure the true nature of Josephus' role in that 1st-century Jewish uprising. We do know, however, that Josephus was largely ignored by Jewish scholars for centuries. He is not even mentioned in the Talmud. Some scholars think that the Talmud tractate Hallah 4:11 refer-ence to Joseph Ha-Kohen is to Josephus, but this seems doubtful. It was not until the 16th century, in the re-evaluation by Azariah dei Rossi (1513-1578), that Jews began to give some credence to Josephus as a historian. It was the Christian church which pre-served the works of Josephus, because of their importance in il-luminating the history of New Testament times and because of cer-tain notes dealing with Jesus and John the Baptist.[7] In modern times, Josephus gets a mixed review from the *Jewish Encyclopedia:*

> It can not be denied that he possessed extraordinary liter-
> ary talents; and his desire to glorify his people ought not
> to be accounted to his dishonor. It is true that he was dis-
> ingenuous in his dealings with his people; but he wrote an
> exemplary apology for them. He was vain and self-seek-
> ing; but he also fought and worked much; and his con-
> demnation by such historians as J. Salvador and Graetz
> is certainly too severe.[8]

Josephus' longest work is his *Antiquities,* containing

> all our antiquities, and the constitution of our government,
> as interpreted out of the Hebrew Scriptures . . . to explain
> who the Jews originally were, what fortunes they had been

subject to, and by what legislator they had been instructed
in piety, and the exercise of other virtues, what wars also
they had made in remote ages . . . . Those Antiquities contain the history of 5,000 years, and are taken out of our
sacred books; but are translated by me into the Greek
tongue.[9]

He began with the creation of the world and ended with his own
time. But the non-Jewish world did not believe Josephus. Surely,
they said, the Jewish people are not *that* old. Why have we not
heard of their ancient history before this man Josephus came
along to tell us this tale? So Josephus wrote another book,
Against Apion.

Since I observe a considerable number of people . . . will
not believe what I have written concerning the antiquity of
our nation, while they take it for a plain sign that our nation is of a late date, . . . I, therefore, have thought myself
under an obligation to write somewhat briefly about these
subjects, in order to convict those that reproach us of spite
and voluntary falsehood, and to correct the ignorance of
others, and withal to instruct all those who are desirous
of knowing the truth of what great antiquity we really
are.[10]

When critics asked why they had not read about the Jews in the
Greek historians, Josephus answered by pointing out *where* in
the Greek writers references to the Jews could be found. As a matter of fact, St. Jerome, reflecting 300 years later upon Josephus'
apology, marveled

how one that was a Hebrew, who had been from his in-
fancy instructed in sacred learning, should be able to produce such a number of testimonies out of profane authors,
as if he read over all the Grecian libraries.

But Josephus had a few questions and comments for his critics.
There is a kind of oblique humor to be seen in his straightforward
approach. Before citing the Greek sources, he asked why "we must
attend to none but Grecians, when we are inquiring about the
most ancient facts." After all, he continued,

almost all which concerns the Greeks happened not long
ago; nay, one may say, is of yesterday only. I speak of

the building of their cities, the invention of their arts, and
the description of their laws; and as for their care about
the writing down of their histories, it is very near the last
thing they set about . . . . It was also late, and with difficulty, that they came to know the letters they now
use . . . .

How can it then be other than an absurd thing for the
Greeks to be so proud, and to vaunt themselves to be the
only people that are acquainted with antiquity, and that
have delivered the true accounts of those early times after
an accurate manner![11]

The following long excerpt touches again on this Greek motif,
capsules Josephus' characterization of Hebrew scripture, and
espouses briefly his ideas about writing history:

We have not an innumerable multitude of books among
us, disagreeing from, and contradicting one another [as
the Greeks have], but only twenty-two books, which contain the records of all the past times; which are justly believed to be divine; and of them five belong to Moses,
which contain his laws and the traditions of the origin of
mankind till his death. This interval of time was little short
of 3000 years; but as to the time from the death of Moses
till the reign of Artaxerxes, king of Persia, who reigned after Xerxes, the prophets, who were after Moses, wrote down
what was done in their times in thirteen books. The remaining four books contain hymns to God, and precepts
for the conduct of human life. It is true, our history hath
been written since Artaxerxes very particularly, but hath
not been esteemed of the like authority with the former by
our forefathers, because there hath not been an exact suc-
cession of prophets since that time; and how firmly we have
given credit to those books of our own nation, is evident
by what we do; for, during so many ages as have already
passed, no one has been so bold as either to add anything
to them, to take anything from them, or to make any
change in them; but it becomes natural to all Jews, immediately and from their very birth, to esteem those books to
contain divine doctrines, and to persist in them, and, if oc-

casion be, willingly to die for them. For it is no new thing
for our captives, many of them in number, and frequently
in time, to be seen to endure racks and deaths of all kinds
upon the theatres, that they may not be obliged to say one
word against our laws and the records that contain them;
whereas there are none at all among the Greeks who would
undergo the least harm on that account, no, nor in case
all the writings that are among them were to be destroyed;
for they take them to be such discourses as are framed
agreeably to the inclinations of those that write them; and
they have justly the same opinion of the ancient writers,
since they see some of the present generation bold enough
to write about such affairs, wherein they were not present,
nor had concern enough to inform themselves about them
from those that knew them; example of which may be had
in this late war of ours, where some persons have written
histories, and published them, without having been in the
places concerned, or having been near them when the actions were done; but these men put a few things together
by hearsay, and insolently abuse the world, and call these
writings by the name of Histories.[12]

The remainder of Book I in *Against Apion* is taken up citing references to Jews in the historical writings of other nations. Though
Josephus' accuracy may not have been 100 per cent, his point
was made.

I have demonstrated our antiquity, and confirmed the
truth of what I have said, from the writings of the Phoenicians, and Chaldeans, and Egyptians. I have, moreover,
produced many of the Grecian writers, as witnesses thereto. I have also made a refutation of Manetho and Cheremon [Egyptian historians] and of certain others of our
enemies.[13]

Book II is a refutation of Apion and Apollonius Molo, Alexandrian anti-Semites. Apion's calumnies brought about death to
Jews. He aroused the mobs in Alexandria to kill and to oust the
Jews from the city. He was the first Jew-hater to charge Jews with
ritual murder. Josephus fought also against the charge that in
ancient days, at the time of Moses, the Hebrews were afflicted with

leprosy and were driven from the country, the Egyptians fearing an epidemic would race through the land.

In *Against Apion,* Josephus also discusses certain Jewish theological notions. Of special importance, of course, is an understanding of the superiority of the Mosaic Law.

Now, since time is reckoned in all cases the surest test of worth, I would call time to witness to the excellence of our lawgiver and of the revelation concerning God which he has transmitted to us. An infinity of time has passed since Moses, if one compares the age in which he lived with those of other legislators; yet it will be found that throughout the whole of that period not merely have our laws stood the test of our own use, but they have to an ever-increasing extent excited the emulation of the world at large.

Our earliest imitators were the Greek philosophers, who, though ostensibly observing the laws of their own countries, yet in their conduct and philosophy were Moses' disciples, holding similar views about God and advocating the simple life and friendly communication between man and man. But that is not all. The masses have long since shown a keen desire to adopt our religious observances; and there is not one city, Greek or barbarian, nor a single nation, to which our custom of abstaining from work on the seventh day has not spread, and where the fasts and the lighting of lamps and many of our prohibitions in the matter of food are not observed. Moreover, they attempt to imitate our unanimity, our liberal charities, our devoted labor in the crafts, our endurance under persecution on behalf of our laws. The greatest miracle of all is that our Law holds out no seductive bait of sensual pleasure, but has exercised this influence through its own inherent merits; and, as God permeates the universe, so the Law has found its way among all mankind. Let each man reflect for himself on his own country and his own household, and he will not disbelieve what I say. It follows, then, that our accusers must either condemn the whole world for deliberate malice in being so eager to

adopt the bad laws of a foreign country in preference to
the good laws of their own or else give up their grudge
against us. In honoring our own legislator and putting
our trust in his prophetical utterances concerning God,
we do not make any arrogant claim justifying such odi-
um. Indeed, were we not ourselves aware of the excellence
of our laws, assuredly we should have been impelled to
pride ourselves upon them by the multitude of their admirers.[14]

Josephus adds a question: "Why should we envy other nations
their laws when we see that even their authors do not observe
them?"

Unity and identity of religious belief, perfect uniformity in
habits and customs produce a very beautiful concord in
human character. Among us alone will be heard no contradictory statements about God, such as are common
among other nations, not only on the lips of ordinary individuals under the impulse of some passing mood, but
even boldly pronounced by philosophers; some putting
forward crushing arguments against the very existence
of God, others depriving him of his providential care for
mankind. Among us alone will be seen no difference in the
conduct of our lives. With us, all act alike, all profess the
same doctrine about God, one which is in harmony with
our Law and affirms that all things are under his eye.[15]

Nothwithstanding this twit against philosophers, Josephus actually
respected the Greek philosophers and saw much common ground
between them and Moses. True, Moses brought his teaching to
the masses, whereas the philosophers addressed themselves to the
few; Moses made religion the all-inclusive governing power in life,
whereas the philosophers looked at religion as one branch of human life. But as he said, basically the philosophers "were Moses'
disciples," whether they knew it or not. Josephus' respect for the
philosophers is seen again in his comments about the Greek gods:

Who, in fact is there among the admired sages of Greece
who has not censured their most famous poets and their
most trusted legislators for sowing in the minds of the
masses the first seeds of such notions [polytheism] about

the gods? They represent them to be as numerous as they choose, born of one another, and engendered in all manner of ways. They assign them different localities and habits, like animal species, some living underground, others in the sea, the oldest of all being chained in Tartarus. Those to whom they have allotted heaven have set over them one who is nominally Father but in reality a tyrant and despot, with the result that his wife and brother and the daughter whom he begot from his own head conspire against him to arrest and imprison him, just as he himself had treated his own father.

Justly do these tales merit the severe censure which they receive from their intellectual leaders. Moreover, they ridicule the belief that some gods are beardless striplings, others old and bearded; that some are appointed to trades, this one being a smith, that goddess a weaver, a third a warrior who fights along with men, others lute players or devoted to archery; and again that they are divided into factions and quarrel about men, insomuch that they not only come to blows with each other but actually lament over and suffer from wounds inflicted by mortals . . . . The noblest and chief of them all, the Father himself, after seducing women and rendering them pregnant, leaves them to be imprisoned or drowned in the sea, and is so completely at the mercy of destiny that he cannot either rescue his own offspring or restrain his tears at their death. Fine doings are these, and others that follow, such as adultery in heaven, with the gods as such shameless onlookers that some of them confessed that they envied the united pair . . . Then there are the gods in bondage to men, hired now as builders, now as shepherds; and others chained, like criminals, in a prison of brass. What man in his senses would not be stirred to reprimand the inventors of such fables and to condemn the consummate folly of those who believed them?

The genuine exponents of Greek philosophy were well aware of all that I have said. That was why they rightly despised them and agreed with us in forming a true and befitting conception of God. From this standpoint Plato declares that no poet ought to be admitted to the republic, and dismisses even Homer in laudatory terms, after crowning and anointing him with unguents, in order to prevent him from obscuring by his fables the correct doctrine about God.[16]

II

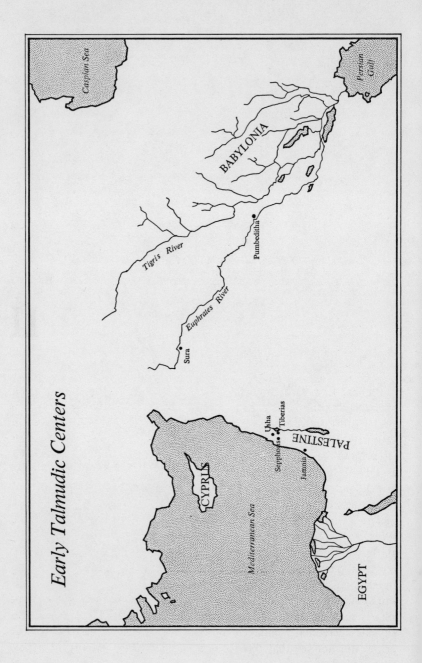

Early Talmudic Centers

٩ | 6

THE
TALMUDIC
PERIOD

TORAH AND TALMUD

Biblical Law as embodied in the Pentateuch has sometimes been slighted, as compared, for instance, to the Prophets, who seemed to overshadow it. Moses, as lawgiver, was often placed below such prophets as Amos and Isaiah. Or, to put it another way, Torah (the Law) has by some been dated very late chronologically in Israel's history, Ezra the Scribe viewed as the real lawgiver of Israel, and the Great Prophets credited with advancing the idea of Monotheism.

The Talmud fared worse. Since early times, through the Middle Ages, to our own time, the Talmud has been described, mostly by those who have had little if any knowledge of it, as a work of dry legalism or of casuistry; even those who have tended to be less harsh often denied it a place in literature qua literature. To the uninitiated, the great Talmudic academies in Jamnia and Usha, Sepphoris and Tiberias, Sura and Pumbeditha seemed mere debating societies perennially engaged in sophistry or mental acrobatics. The critics did not see that the Talmud was a literary activity of a particular kind.

The Torah was Israel's greatest achievement. Just as the Greek mind and spirit have found fulfilment in art and philosophy, so the Hebrew mind and spirit have found fulfilment in the moral law, expressed in Prophetic Judaism and in the searching after justice of the Talmudic sages. As a law based on morality and ethics instead of primarily on the power of the state, Judaic law was essentially different from Roman law. Israel's law stemmed directly from their monotheistic world view and the Biblical conception of life.

Monotheism did not appear upon the world scene as a metaphysical theory. From the beginning, it was a Way of Life. As a law-making process and as a normative force, the Torah was meant to regulate human life by creating, at first, a special people as an example to other peoples. It was not just monotheism which the Jews exhibited to the world, but rather *ethical* monotheism. This was the very core of the Sinaitic revelation and also the central idea that animated both the prophets and the later Talmudic sages. The literary activity of the Jewish people, therefore, rested squarely upon the foundation of the moral law. Neither the prophets nor the Talmudists looked at civil and criminal law as something separate from religious law. The Torah took human life as a *whole*. Laws regulating relations between man and man were not set aside from those regulating relations between man and God. The prophets, for instance, did not fight against ritualism because they were opposed to it per se. Rather, they wanted a meaningful ritualism, one in which the heart of man and his very spirit prevailed. They aspired to attain the high ideal of bringing the whole of man upon the altar of God. The Talmudic sages followed in their footsteps by applying the prophetic aspirations and ideas of justice to every branch of human endeavor, to every case in practical life.

This kind of literature, created as it was under the egis of the moral law and the prophetic ideals, did not intend to amuse or entertain the people. It was studied and read for the sake of normalizing life. The very word Torah, usually rendered as Law, literally means teaching, instruction. Learning Torah, then, means to learn how to act justly, in full accord with the Law. The more legalistic portions of Israel's Torah, including the Talmud, represent instructions and elaborate discussions which point one toward the highest goal of moral life. In this respect the Torah is more than faith, more than what is often meant by the word "religion," and more than what we mean by "literature." Indeed the Torah has been called "A Torah of Life." These are the true aspects of the Torah as a direct product of the monotheistic world view.

Saadia Gaon, the noted philosopher and Talmudic scholar, attributed the existence of Israel among the nations to the fact that it was a people "of two Torahs"—the Written Law, the Pentateuch; and the Oral Law, the explanatory part, handed down from generation to generation until committed to writing in what came to be called the Talmud. This particular oral tradition goes back to ancient times, even before the time of Ezra the Scribe (c. 450 B.C.E.). The Mosaic Laws, viewed as the basic Constitution of Judaism, had always been in need of explanation and elaboration, as any constitution comprised of general principles needs to be interpreted and expounded. The Torah contains 613 Mitzvot (commands)—248 specific "good deeds" and 365 prohibitions. All 613 Mosaic precepts are considered to be contained, in essence, in the Ten Commandments. How can one deduce from ten short sentences the entire compendium of laws found in the Torah? The Talmud says: "Whatever a well-versed student of the Torah might ever expound had been given already to Moses on Mount Sinai" (Berakhoth 2). In the same way, the Torah contains provisions for all times and it is only a matter of interpreting aright the hidden meaning of the Torah.

The process of expounding the Torah, that is, the Written Law, had been going on in various schools founded by Torah scholars for centuries before the destruction of the Second Temple in the year 70 C.E. Naturally, the interpretations of the Law as applied to particular cases varied in accordance with the opinions of the scholars and in consonance with the localities in which their academies were located. Innumerable controversial verdicts were issued by different schools. The Oral Law became so voluminous that it was impossible for students to remember it all by heart or to know how to apply it. As a result, Judah the Prince, in the 2nd century C.E., decided to compile all these oral traditions into one book, which became known as the Mishnah, comprising brief decisions on various cases plus the opinions of individual scholars who did not agree with the decisions of the majority. The word Mishnah means both "repetition" and "learning." All the scholars mentioned in the Mishnah are known as Tannaim (learners).

Now, the Mishnah, written as it was in brief passages (each passage is also called Mishnah), failed to present fully the reasons behind the verdicts of the Tannaim, leaving it to the student to find them out. Consequently, it needed "completion" or a supplement. This was supplied by the Gemara (Gemara means "completion"), which makes a thorough-going analysis of each Mishnah, comparing a particular case to other similar ones and arriving at a definite conclusion. Gemara thus became a lengthy commentary upon the Mishnah and the Written Torah as well. It also included scholarly views upon life in general, comments upon the lives of the Tannaim and other historical figures, elucidations of the Scriptural text, and other materials touching upon every phase of life. Gemara actually forms the bulk of Talmudic materials. Mishnah and Gemara together are known as Talmud (Talmud is a derivative of "Lamad"—learning).

It is not possible to describe adequately the Talmud. It is, as suggested above, interpretations of the general principles of the Torah, elaborated, adjusted, and applied to life through the generations and to the needs of the moment. But it is more. It is wisdom and tradition and reason. And it is more. It is an immense encyclopedia containing laws and discussions, theological and juridical dicta, historical observations and national reminiscences, precepts and maxims touching upon every phase of life, proverbs and uplifting legends, fables and poetic tales, peculiar customs and long discourses upon the minutest point of morality. And more. Only those who have "broken their backs" over the heavy volumes of the Talmud, plus its innumerable commentaries, and who have learned its terminology and its methods, might claim, after many years of effort, to have *sensed* the spirit of the Talmud. As Gustav Karpeles said:

> In the whole range of the world's literature there are few
> books with so checkered a career, so curious a fate, as the
> Talmud has had. The name is simple enough, it glides
> glibly from the tongue, yet how difficult to explain its import

to the uninitiated! Futile to seek an answer by comparing this gigantic monument of the human intellect with any other book; it is *sui generis*. Suffice it to say that it is a great national work, a work of first importance, the archives of ten centuries, in which are preserved the thoughts and opinions, the views and verdicts, the errors, transgressions, hopes, disappointments, customs, ideals, convictions, and sorrows of a people—a work produced by the zeal and patience of thirty generations, laboring with a self-denial unparalleled in the history of literature.[1]

ROME AND THE JEWS

The destruction of the Temple by Titus (70 c.e.) and the downfall of Judea was a catastrophe that struck at the very existence of the Jewish people. Defeated and broken in spirit, they were threatened by eventual extinction, except for a few leaders who, looking beyond the tragic present, would not abandon all hope.

Foremost among those leaders was Johanan ben Zakkai, Hillel's venerable disciple, a man of great vision. Amidst the violence and confusion and the state of starvation in the besieged city of Jerusalem, Johanan decided to save the Torah; that is, save Israel's culture from the conflagration. Saving the soul of the people was, to him, the same as saving the people from extinction. During the third year of the war (68 c.e.), Johanan devised a scheme. Having instructed his disciples to declare him dead, he was carried in a coffin outside the city walls, ostensibly to be buried. This strange funeral party soon, of course, encountered a Roman patrol. Johanan, brought before Vespasian, then the commander-in-chief of the Roman legions, asked one favor: the Romans should spare the little town of Jamnia (Jabnah, Yabneh) and its local school—a wish that Vespasian granted him.

This seemingly insignificant permission actually saved Judaism, for Jamnia became within time a center which radiated new energy and life into the bleeding body of fallen Judea. Replacing Jerusalem, which lay in ruins, Jamnia was a rallying point for teachers and spiritual leaders. Johanan's Academy and Synod was known at that time as the Vineyard of Yabneh. It produced good fruit at a time of greatest national despair. The Torah was studied with zeal and devotion, and instruction and inspiration went forth to all Jewish people to persevere until the raging storm was over.

The Bar Kochba (Simon ben Cozeba) revolt (132-35), which occurred some sixty years after the destruction of Jerusalem, was the last attempt by the Jewish people to win back their independence. The rebellion was ruthlessly, though slowly, crushed; but even this last and greatest catastrophe was not to be the last chapter of Israel's history. The revived spirit at Jamnia stood firm. Despite the cruel policies of persecution by the Romans to uproot the Torah and its adherents, the inspired scholars continued at the peril of life to teach and to learn. Many died a martyr's death but many others replaced them. Furthermore, Rome's attitude toward the Jews was ambivalent; it alternated among persecution, neglect, recognition, honor. For instance, even after the destruction of Jerusalem in 70 c.e., the Jews were accorded a form of religious autonomy. Not only had approval been given to the academy at Jamnia, but Rome recognized a Jewish leader as a kind of ambassador between the government and the Jewish communities. In 85 c.e., Gamaliel II, a descendant of Hillel, was chosen Nasi, president of the Sanhedrin and titular head of Judaism. As then constituted, the authority of the Sanhedrin was confined to religious matters; civil law remained in the hands of the Romans.

TWO TALMUDS

In addition to the Palestinian religious center at Jamnia, and later at Usha, there had developed the important Jewish communities in Babylonia, which would, for hundreds of years to come, outstrip Palestine in significance and in contributions to Jewish life and learning. After the Cyrus Proclamation in 537 b.c.e., many Jews returned to Palestine at the time of Zerubbabel. Three-quarters of a century later, under the leadership of Ezra and Nehemiah, many more Jews returned from Babylonia to Zion. But many

Jews remained. Under Persian rule, and later under the Parthians, Jewish communities in Babylonia were relatively prosperous. The government recognized a religious autonomy for the Jews, in a way similar to that granted by Rome to Palestine. A descendant of the Davidic dynasty was chosen and called Prince of the Captivity (Resh Galutha); his task was to direct the affairs of the Jewish communities in Babylonia.

Academies of learning developed in Babylonia. In 219 c.e., for example, Abba Arika, known as Rav (Master), returned from Palestine where he had spent years in study of the Torah; he established an academy at Sura. Samuel Yarhinai, physician and astronomer, famous for both his Torah and secular knowledge, established another academy at Pumbeditha. Scholars traveled among the many centers of learning in Babylonia, among the academies in Palestine, and between Babylonia and Palestine, thus maintaining a continuity and exchange between the two Jewries.

After the Mishnah was canonized in the 2nd century c.e., it became the standard work on Jewish laws and customs in both the Babylonian and the Palestinian academies. However, interpretation of the Mishnah text varied. The lengthy discussions of the scholars revolving around the differing interpretations came to be called Gemara. And as a result of the many elaborations and discussions in both centers of Judaism, there emerged two Talmuds: one composed in Palestine and called the Jerusalemite Talmud (Yerusalmi) and the other composed in Babylonia and called the Babylonian Talmud (Talmud Babli).

The Jerusalemite Talmud was completed during the 4th century, years before the final closing of the Palestinian academies by Roman decree. The Babylonian Talmud was completed in 499 c.e. The great academies in Babylonia existed for another 500 years after the closing of that Talmud, until 1034-38, when the last Babylonian academy was also closed and the center of Jewish learning shifted to Spain.

The Babylonian Talmud has long overshadowed the Jerusalemite Talmud, because of the length of time which went into its composition, because of its sheer bulk (it is three times longer), and because of the greater intellectual brilliance of the Babylonian Gemara. The Babylonian Talmud thus became the Book of the

Law second only to the Scripture: next to the Bible, the normative book for the Jewish people. Today when one speaks of "the Talmud," it is understood that he means the Babylonian Talmud.

THE TALMUD

The Talmud's influence has pervaded and regulated their lives wherever Jews resided, despite the fact that due to their scatteredness among the nations they have lived under the most adverse conditions: usually a small minority surrounded by a ruling majority. The Talmud is a monumental cultural creation without which Israel could never have survived.

The Talmud is monumental quantitatively as well. It contains about two-and-a-half million words. Its sixty-three tractates, with commentaries, fill from ten to twenty printed volumes. It takes years to study the Talmud. It is being studied all over the world by thousands of Jews today, one page each day. Some Hebrew and Yiddish periodicals announce in advance the page number to be studied, so that all students can be studying the same page on the same day. The usual cycle of study through the entire Talmud is completed in seven years.

There is probably no other collection of books in the world as the Talmud so loved by the people who created it and so misunderstood or despised by many others. Its fate in the world was equal to the fate of Israel among the nations. Those who sought to destroy Israel wanted also to destroy the Talmud, which they regarded as the diabolical force which secured Judaism's existence and future. The Talmud was burned at the stake as Israel, as Jerusalem, as individual Jews were burned. It was calumniated in the Middle Ages as "the book of Satan."

Vicious charges were made against the Talmud, including those of advocating ritual murder and of instructing the Jewish people to deceive their non-Jewish neighbors. Such slander was often launched by Christian churchmen who had never read the Talmud. Henricus Seynensis, a fanatical Dominican of the Middle Ages, insisted that the Talmud must be destroyed. He was such a "specialist" on the Talmud that one speech he made in an inquisitorial court evoked embarrassed laughter in the church. He used the phrase *ut narrat Ribbinus Talmud* (Rabbi Talmud relates), presumably not even knowing that Talmud was a book and not a person.

On the other hand, Johannes Reuchlin, a Hebrew scholar and author of a Hebrew grammar, pleaded with his fellow Christians in the 15th century: "Do not condemn the Talmud before you understand it. Burning it is not an argument. . . .Instead of burning all Jewish literature, it were better to found chairs in the universities for its exposition."

The Talmud's Mishnah consists of six orders covering the following general subjects:

1. Agricultural laws.

   This order is called Zerayim (seeds) and is devoted to the regulative laws of priestly gifts, first-fruit offerings, charity and help to the poor in an agricultural society. The first tractate of this order deals with benedictions and prayers.

2. Festivals and fasts.

   This order is called Moed (holidays) and covers the laws of the observance of the sabbath and the holidays, including the national fast days in commemoration of historical events, of both sorrow and joy.

3. Family laws.

   This section is called Nashim (women) and deals with the laws of marriage and divorce, sexual questions, ritual purification of women, etc.

4. Civil and criminal jurisprudence.

   The name of this section is Nezikin (damages). It covers court procedures, commercial regulations, trade laws, penalities. It includes also regulations about dealings with idol-worshipers and ends with a treatise known as Pirkei Aboth, which contains short Sayings of the Fathers.

5. Sacrifices.

   This order is called Kodashim (holy things). It is devoted mainly to the ritual of the Temple in Jerusalem, to sacrifices, and to rules governing the slaughter of animals, etc.

6. Clean and unclean.

This order is called Toharot (purities) and deals with the regulations related to ceremonial purity and impurity.

The Talmud is written primarily in the Eastern Aramaic dialect which was spoken by the Jewish masses in the early Talmudic period. Hebrew is found mainly in the Mishnah. Occasionally Latin or Greek words occur, probably because there were no Hebrew or Aramaic equivalents or because the foreign words were more popular at the time.

The student of the Talmud encounters certain difficulties at first, which, though not insurmountable, are formidable. Not only is he expected to know both Hebrew and Aramaic, but he must become acquainted with the special framework and terminology of the tomes. The text contains no punctuation marks, for example. Furthermore, inasmuch as many sections are reports of discussions in the academies, one must learn how to distinguish between a question and an answer. Also, reference is often made casually to other texts, mentioning only a few words about them, relying upon the reader to know and pick up the full context. Commentaries were therefore necessary from time to time; such were indeed composed throughout the centures, some printed side by side with the text and others at the end of a volume.

One interesting feature of the Talmud is the way in which it incorporates into itself disputes and differing interpretations of the Law. Take, for example, the case of Hillel and Shammai. In the late 1st century c.e., two opposing houses of learning were established in Jerusalem; each soon counted hundreds of students and each leader was considered a foremost Tanna, master teacher. Shammai and his followers were rather strict and legalistic in their interpretation of the Torah. Hillel and his students stressed more liberal, more flexible principles. The leniency of Hillel was closer to the interest of the people and his teachings prevailed among the masses and among most of the leaders. Yet the Mishnah records Hillelite *and* Shammaite verdicts, declaring that the decisions of *both* houses are "the words of the living God." If the majority of the scholars and the people rejected the Shammaite interpretations, why were they quoted? The Mishnah itself gives the answer:

If and when in the distant future a more worthy court of religious law would find a decision of the House of Hillel unacceptable, it could turn in such a case to the Shammaites' decision. Such a case may occur in the Messianic age or even earlier.

While the aim of the discussions was to arrive at a conclusion, sometimes the question simply remained open, occasionally for several generations, until finally decided one way or the other. Generally, concrete cases from life were taken as examples, though sometimes the discussion focused upon theoretical or imaginative problems. The primary purpose of the Talmudic scholars was to legislate for practical, daily life. The most insignificant appearing detail, as long as it touched upon human life, was important; small items and large issues were dealt with seriously and conscientiously.

The hub of the discussion was the Mishnah, which was analyzed point by point, detail by detail, each of the participants being given full opportunity to question and discuss. The exchanges were directed at bringing forth the meaning of the Mishnah or at straightening out contradictions or at revealing new phases in the interpretation of the Law. During such discussions, the teachers became students and the students teachers. In the Gemara, the recording of these discourses, the students usually remained anonymous whereas the teachers were mentioned by name, whether their elucidation was original with them or they simply quoted their own teachers or former Tannaim; for the Talmud was very careful in according honor to a teacher.

Underlying all this scholarly work was the fundamental attitude toward the Torah. The Talmudic sages, from the earliest Sopherim (scribes) to the Tannaim (teachers) down to the Amoraim (interpreters of the Tannaim), assumed that the Torah did not contain even one superfluous word; every letter carried special meaning. The interpreters were looking for the correct key to the intent of the Torah. In a real sense, there were no "new" judgments or verdicts; all interpretations were essentially "revealed Torah," something that had been there from the time when the Torah was given to Israel on Mount Sinai. The students of the Torah believed that by exposing its secrets, by explaining it, they were making it an inexhaustible spring of living water.

Although the form of the Talmud is a sort of stenographic re-

port of a class discussion in an academy, in which professors and
students participated, and although the interpretation of the law
was indeed the business at hand, yet the content is not just dry,
legalistic logic. Talmudists included in their discussion much illustrative and inspirational material which we would call folk
stories, fanciful moral teachings, life stories of famous persons,
words of wisdom, homilies, parables. This is known as the Midrashic motif, which makes up almost a third of the Talmud. This
material is also called Aggada or Haggadah (Hagged, saying,
narration), as opposed to Halakha (law, conduct), which reflects
a more direct concentration upon the law. In an oversimple characterization, Halakha material in the Talmud can be said to appeal to the head, Haggadah material to both the heart and head.

A Midrashic story admirably illustrates the difference between
Halakha and Haggadah: Two Amoraim, Hiya bar Abba, an authority in the Law, and Abbahu, an Aggadist, happened to have
come into one town. The people flocked to listen to Abbahu who
fascinated them with his stories and parables, whereas his greater
colleague drew only a small number of people. Abbahu comforted
the disappointed scholar with a charming parable. Two merchants
came once to a town. One displayed gems and pearls for sale, the
other displayed cheap things: gaudy ribbons, trinkets, needles, and
pins. To whom would the crowd flock? Certainly to the one who
offered little ornaments, since not every one was a customer for
costly stones. Thus it is with us, said Abbahu. There was a time
when the struggle for existence was not as fierce as it is today. The
people then had more leisure and patience so that they could listen
better to the profound teachings of the Torah. Now times are
changed and people need the little things that the Aggadist might
offer them by way of consolation and hope.

Thus Abbahu humbled himself in order to console Hiya. The
Aggadist was always something of a popular poet. He was closer
to the masses and tried to speak to the heart and imagination of
the common people whose wounds he was ever ready to bandage.
This was probably the reason that even after the closing of the
Talmuds, the Midrashic literature kept growing for hundreds of
years until it became a rich literature by itself. Thus the Hagga-
dahic sections one finds in the Talmud form only a part of the extensive Midrashic literature.

The word Midrash occurs twice in the Hebrew Scriptures (2

הבית והעלייה של שנים שנפלו...

גמ׳ ...

מתני׳ הבית והעלייה...

גמ׳ ...

Sample Babylonian Talmud page from tractate Babba M'ziha, chapter 10, page 116. To the left of the tractate text is Rashi's commentary; to the right is Tosafot. Marginal notations carry emendations and page numbers of other tractates quoted in the text. This format was established in the first complete printed edition of the Babylonian Talmud, which appeared in Venice in the 1520s, from the press of Daniel Bomberg, a Christian printer and publisher; all subsequent editions have followed the Venice edition format and pagination.

Chron. 13:22; 24:27) and in both cases is usually translated into English as "story." Perhaps a more accurate translation would be "commentary," though even this does not capture its essence. Midrash is a figurative or allegorical, rather than literal, interpretation of the Biblical text—what we might call poetical literature. Seven works among many are noted as samples of this rich collection: Mekhilta, commentary on Exodus; Sifra, on Leviticus; Sifre, on Numbers and Deuteronomy; Pesikta, on various sections of the Torah; Tanhuma, on the entire Pentateuch; Midrash Rabba, on the Pentateuch, plus Esther, Ruth, Lamentations, and the Song of Songs; Yalkut, an anthology of Midrashim.

There is no better characterization of the Haggadic literature than the one that Henrich Heine, the great poet, gave in his famous Ramanzero series of poems, as he himself in his childhood and youth had been charmed by it:

> Where the beauteous, ancient sagas,
> Angel legends fraught with meaning,
> Martyr's silent sacrifices,
> Festal songs and wisdom's sayings,
> Trope and allegoric fancies—
> All, howe'ver by faith triumphant
> Glow pervaded—where they gleaming,
> Glis'ning, well in strength exhaustless.
> And the boyish heart responsive
> Drinks the wild, fantastic sweetness,
> Greets the woful, wondrous anguish,
> Yields to grewsome charm of myst'ry,
> Hid in blessed worlds of fable.
> Overawed it hearkens solemn
> To that sacred revelation
> Mortal man hath poetry called.[2]

SAMPLE MISHNAH VERDICT

This sample from the Mishnah (tractate Babba M'tzi'a; Mishnah

1) is characteristically spare and to the point:

Two [people] are holding one Tallith [mantle; prayer-shawl]. This says, "I have found it," and the other says, "I have found it." This says, "It is wholly mine," and the other says, "It is wholly mine." This one is to swear that not less than one half is his, and the other is to swear that not less than one half is his. And then they divide it equally between themselves.

The discussions which swirl around the Mishnah pronouncements are what make up the bulk of the Talmud. The following discussion and explanation of the Mishnah quoted above is drawn from the Gemara and commentaries relating to it; in my translation I have slightly paraphrased and considerably summarized, in order to give the reader simply a flavor of the sort of reasoning involved:

The case is such that neither of the two claimants is able to produce proof, since no witnesses were present at the time. It presents two possibilities: either both found the shawl simultaneously or one really found it and the other saw it only from a distance. Thus both stand under the suspicion of lying altogether, that is, of being charged to have made a false claim, or of making a claim on the fact of "seeing" alone. Hence justice has only one way open to it, namely, that they divide equally between them the shawl or the price accruing therefrom. But since justice, by such a verdict, may be compensating a possible liar, it is entitled to put up an obstruction. This is the purpose of the oath placed upon each, for sometimes a man would not be willing to perjure himself publicly before God and men for a little gain; also, instead of both undergoing the procedure of an oath, they might prefer to reach a compromise between themselves. Such a reconciliation would be a direct contribution to peace in society.

The Talmud, of course, includes actual question-answer exchanges which went on in the academies. Here is an example pertaining to the Mishnah quoted above:

Question: Why does the Mishnah read: "This says, 'I have found it,' and the other says, 'I have found it,'

this says, 'It is mine,' and the other says, 'It is mine'?"
Why not [Does it not read] as one? [Note: the claim
of each litigant is divided into separate parts, unnecessarily.]

Answer: It is one. [This presupposes a regrouping of the
words in the order required.]

Question: Let the Mishnah read, "I have found it," which
would clearly indicate that he claims it. What do we
need the repetition for?

Answer: The Mishnah uses both phrases in order to avoid
a misunderstanding, because 'people usually assume
that by seeing a thing [even without picking it up]
they can claim it as their own. Hence it is necessary
that each claimant should declare distinctly before the
court that it is "wholly" his.

Question: How can you argue this? We know that Ravnayi
[Rabina] declared that whenever the Scriptures use the
phrase "you found it," it means that the object was
actually picked up [not just seen].

Answer: This is true as far as the text of the Scriptures is
concerned. However, in popular parlance it is not taken
that way. The Mishnah simply uses the word in its
common connotation. The same answer is applied to
the other half of the claim. [Hence both are needed.]

Then Rab Pappa, an Amora, is seen to present an entirely different interpretation of the Mishnah passage:

The two-sided claims deal with two separate cases: One,
concerning an object that was found; the other concerning
an object that was bought by two men. However, one case
cannot be deduced from the other, because the motivation
is dissimilar. In the case of a "finding," we may rightfully
say that the oath imposed is absolutely necessary, because
the claimant might think: Look, that fellow did not invest
anything, getting something for nothing, and since I have
noticed it, why can I not claim it and then get a part of it?
It is therefore necessary to impose an oath upon him. But
in the case of a purchased object, such justification cannot
be applied, so no oath be imposed on them. Therefore, the
Mishnah distinctly imposes the oath in the case of a pur-

chase, too. On the other hand, if a purchased article would have been dealt with [expecting us to deduce therefrom the case of a "finding"], another dissimilarity would stand in our way. For concerning a purchase, a man may say to himself: I have bought it and he has bought it; now, since I need the article, I shall get it and let him buy another one. Therefore, an oath is required in this case. But in the case of a "finding," no such motivation exists or can be applied, consequently there is no need for an oath. Thus both cases must be expressly and distinctly indicated.

In the Talmud the discussion about this Mishnah passage continues and elaborates many other points in the attempt to clarify the principles of the law and detail its application to life. However, from the samples above it should be clear that the Talmudic expounders did their utmost to bring to light the various angles of the case in question. The student who diligently studies such cases always finds them to be rationally sound. They sharpen his mind and teach him how to compare cases. True, Rab Pappa's elucidation is a little complicated or strained, but at the same time it is highly rewarding by reaching out into the psychological motivations of people and showing how alibis can be used as justifications. It also explains the necessity of the oath in both cases. (The question of how one purchase by two persons is possible and how we could not find out from the merchant who the real buyer was is discussed further at length in the same tractate.)

SAMPLE TALMUDIC ARGUMENTATION

Mishnah (tractate Makkoth 7a; middle of Mishnah):

A sanhedrin has jurisdiction within the land and outside. A sanhedrin that executes once in seven years is called "destructive." R. Eliezer b. Azariah says once in seventy years. R. Tarphon and R. Akiba says were we members of a sanhedrin no person would ever be put to death.

Amoraic comments:

A sanhedrin has jurisdiction . . .

Question: How was this inferred?

Answer: The sages based it on the following [Scriptural]
passage: "And these things shall be for a statute of
judgment unto you throughout your generations in all
your dwellings." (Num. 35:29) This includes every
place both in the Land of Israel and outside it.

Question: If that be so, what do we learn from the passage: "Judges and officers shalt thou make thee in all
thy gates which thy God giveth thee tribe by tribe"?
(Deut. 16:18) [This seems to contradict the first
passage.]

Answer: In your gates [Land of Israel] you set up
tribunals in every district as well as in every city. In
other countries in every district but not in every city.

A sanhedrin that executes . . .

Question: Is R. Eliezer's comment a censure or a mere ob-
servation?

Answer: It remains undecided.

R. Tarphon and R. Akiba . . .

Question: How could they have done it [while serving as
judges in homicide case]?

Answer: Both R. Johanan and R. Eleazar suggested that
they could do it by examining the witnesses so long
that they had to answer questions pertaining to the
health or fatal affection of the victim [which could hardly
be answered by them as laymen].

Rab Ashi added: If they testified that the victim was healthy, they
might be asked whether they were certain that the sword did not
sever an internal lesion [and he was killed accidentally].

SAMPLE MISHNAH WITH DUAL SOLUTION

Mishnan (tractate Babba M'tzi'a 14):
Two [persons] deposited with a [trustworthy] man money;
one deposited one hundred Zuz [an ancient coin], the other

200 Zuz. When they returned after a long absence, each of them claimed that he had deposited 200 Zuz.

The Mishnah proposes two ways of resolving the problem. The first Tanna (name not given because he represents the majority opinion) decreed that since each deposited at least one hundred Zuz, each should get one hundred Zuz, and the third one hundred Zuz should be retained by the tribunal until the coming of the prophet Elijah, that is, until one of the two could bring evidence that the money belonged to him. However, Rabbi Jose, a second Tanna, objected to this verdict on the ground that since one of the two is certainly a deceiver, it is wrong to give the latter whatever he had deposited and retain the money that belongs rightfully to the honest one. His objection is clear-cut: "What does the deceiver lose?" Hence, R. Jose proposes that the entire sum of 300 Zuz be retained by the court in the hope that the deceiver would surely come and confess, since he would realize after a time that not only did he gain nothing but in addition he lost his own money. This seems to be a psychological solution.

The final decision, not following Rabbi Jose's judgment, was rendered on the assumption that both persons had made their deposits in the presence of one another and did not ask for receipts. The honest man, therefore, forfeited his right and must wait for the recovery of his one hundred Zuz.

TALMUDIC TEACHINGS ON GOD, MAN, AND THE WORLD

God

The conception of God was elevated by the Talmudic sages to the highest. God is one, unique; nothing preceded Him and nothing would ever succeed Him; He is eternal; He is the holy one, the Creator and maintainer of the universe, the Master of the World. He has no associate, no brother, and no son. (Exodus Rabba 29) Everything that exists is His servant: the sun, the stars, and the elements. He is not material or corporeal. "God said to Moses: 'Tell them that I was, I am, and I shall be.'" (Exodus Rabba

3) "God remains in His holiness, whether they sanctify Him or not." (Sifra, K'doshim 1) He is peerless, unique. (Berakhoth 6) The prophetic visions of Isaiah, Ezekiel, and Daniel were human representations. Isaiah envisioned God as a "big city" man, Ezekiel as a villager. The sages themselves represented God as one who studies the Torah, or as a father who bewails the suffering and tribulations of his children—the people of Israel—this being a method of teaching; for "the Torah speaks in the language of men." God knows man's thoughts and feelings; He is a personal God and simultaneously the God of history and the God of the universe.

Truth, Justice, Mercy

God is the highest Truth, His justice is true Justice. All His words are eternally true, because He is Truth Himself. (Pesikta Rabbati 14) God has never issued a verdict without justice. (Berakhoth 8) His justice is always combined with mercy. He is a jealous God, but ever patient even with the wicked. "He is showing mercy unto the thousandth generation of them that love Him." (Exodus 20:6) His truth, His justice, and His mercy are unique as He Himself is.

The World

"God created the world out of nothing and without effort. "Not with work and not with toil the Holy One created the world" (B'reshith Rabba 10). The mystery of Creation is hidden: "Let no man ask what had been before creation of the world" (Haggigah 11). Many worlds were created and afterward destroyed, until God created this world, and said, "This one I like." The world testifies that there is a Creator just as the house testifies that there is a builder, and the cloth that there is a weaver.

Creation Of Man

"God created a single man in order to demonstrate that there is only one God"; (Sanhedrin 36) also, because He wanted to teach man that all are equal in His eyes. Adam represented "mankind." God created man "in his own image," that is, He endowed him with reason and free will. By virtue of man's free will, both the way of life and the way of death are open to him, and he may choose one of the two. "Who is strong? He who controls his passions, the Yetzer HaRa, the evil instincts, which try to overwhelm and destroy man. (Sanhedrin 91) But God had prepared a remedy: Torah. Yetzer HaRa is a false God dwelling in man. Since man was created last, God loves him like a father loves his youngest son. When one studies the Torah and performs good deeds, his evil instincts cannot mislead him. (Abodah Zara 5) Hence, learning the Torah is one of the highest ideals in life.

Israel And Torah

From all the peoples of the world Israel was chosen by God, but not for the sake of dominating others. Israel was chosen to get the Torah and thereby become "a light to the peoples" (Is. 60:3). God said to Moses: "Tell the children of Israel they are my firstborn son" (Shabbath 31). When they do God's will they are His children and He is their father. The highest ideal of Israel is to "sanctify God's name," because the Torah was given Israel for no other purpose but to sanctify God's name in the world. Israel said to God: "Be favorably inclined towards me, because I have been the one to proclaim your name in the world" (Menohot 53). Israel's existence is secured by the Torah; it is as eternal as the heavens. As the world cannot exist without winds, so it cannot exist without Israel (Taanith 3).

Fear And Love Of God

One who knows the Torah but has no fear of God is likened to a treasurer to whom the inner keys were given but the outside keys were not given. How can he enter? (Shabbath 31) Whoever has the fear of God in his heart his words are being listened to (Berakhoth). But much higher than fear of God is love of God, and greater is the one who does good out of love of God than the one that does good out of fear (Sotah 31).

Love Of Man

"Thou shalt love thy fellow man as thyself" is a great principle of the Torah (Sifra Kedoshim 4). Hillel said: What you do not like (that someone should do to you) you should not do to your fellow man; this is the whole Torah and the rest is a commentary (Shabbath 31). Love people and bring them close to the Torah.

With love comes mercy. God is merciful to him who is merciful to his fellowman (Sifre 117). The children of Abraham distinguish themselves by being merciful (Betza 32). Love of man includes love of the stranger; there is no distinction between a Jew and a non-Jew. It is forbidden to deceive or oppress the stranger. Love of man includes also charitableness. He who hides himself from giving charity is like one who worships idols (Ketuboth 68).

Rabbi Akiba used to say: "Beloved is man, for he was created in God's image"—Man and not Jew; love thy neighbor as thyself—Jew and Gentile alike. Thus there is related (Tanna d'bei Elijah 16) the story of a Jew who sold to a non-Jew four measures of olives. Instead of giving him the correct measure, he took the latter into a dark room and cheated him of two measures. Later Elijah met him on the street and said, "My son, it is written, 'Thou shalt not rob thy fellow man.' Your fellow man should be regarded as your brother."

Attitude To Labor

The Talmudic Sages, in conformity to the laws of the Torah, were deeply concerned about protecting the rights of labor. The general rule was laid down that in a conflict of interest between an employer and a worker, the worker has the upper hand. The employer was forbidden to keep the worker longer than the customary time of work in the locality where he worked. The employer was obligated to specify the kind of food he would serve during the working hours. The workers were privileged to get the best food and be paid at nightfall, at the end of the day. Many of the Talmudic Sages were themselves artisans and workers; a man must earn his livelihood by and through honest work. In contrast to the Greeks and Romans who deemed manual work undignified for a free man, Judaism from the earliest times upheld the dignity of labor and extolled industry above idle piety (Berakhoth 8a) Idleness was branded the fruitful mother of many evils, and declared to be the mistress alike of lewdness and insanity (Ketuboth 59b).

Gossiping, Lying, And Flattering

Four categories of men do not dwell in God's Presence: mockers, liars, flatterers, and gossipers.

He who gossips and he who listens to it deserve to be thrown to the dogs (P'sahim 108).

The tongue of man may be in one place and slay someone in Rome (P'sikta 32).

He who does not live up to his word is like one who worships idols (Sanhedrin 92).

A liar even when he tells the truth is not trusted. This is his penalty (Sanhedrin 29).

God hates those whose hearts are not one with their mouths [They do not speak what they mean or do not mean what they speak] (P'sahim 113).

Mercy And Charity

God is merciful to those who are merciful to others (Sifre 117).

A man of charitableness seeks those who are in need (Shabbath 104).

Even a poor man who lives on charity should give charity (Gittin 7).

Greater than Moses is the one who gives charity anonymously (P'sikta 103).

Give charity with a joyful heart (VaYikra Rabba 34).

One who helps his fellow man by granting him a loan is greater than the one who gives him charity (Shabbath 63).

The poor of your city come before the poor of other cities (Babba M'tzi'a 71).

Lovingkindness is greater than charity. Lovingkindness may be expressed in any form; charity may be given only in the form of money or things (Sukkah 49) Lovingkindness is one of the three pillars upon which the world stands (Aboth 1:2).

The world exists on three things: truth, justice, and peace (Aboth 1:18). Do not favor either the poor or the rich when they are wrong. Bribe, whether in the form of money or in the form of words, blindfolds "the eyes of the wise" (Ketuboth 105).

Envy, Jealousy, And Revenge

Jealousy, passion, vanity drive one out of the world (Aboth 4).

Do not say, I love scholars and hate disciples, I love disciples and hate simple people. Love all (Aboth di R. Nathan 16).

If your enemy is hungry give him bread to eat and if thirsty give him water to drink. Even if he came to kill you, give him food if he is hungry or water if he is thirsty (Midrash Mishle 27).

Humility

Man should be very humble, for his hope is vermin (Aboth 4).
Whoever humbles himself, God elevates him; whoever is proud, God brings him down. Whoever runs after honors, honors run away from him. (Erubin 13).

Faith And Trust In God

Many should thank God both for evil and good (Berakhoth 89). When a man suffers let him examine his deeds (Berakhoth 54). Whoever truly believes in God justifies God's ways (even when evil befalls him) (Taanit 8).

Praying And Learning

While praying man must attune his heart to God (Berakhoth 31). Learning Torah is higher than anything else (Peah 1).
Torah is the Supreme Good, the Truth, a Tree of Knowledge. (Aboth 6).

TALMUDIC AND MIDRASHIC PROVERBS AND PARABLES

Rivalry of scholars advances wisdom.
*
Truth is heavy, therefore few care to carry it.
*
The soldiers fight and the kings are the heroes.
*
The place honors not the man; it is the man who honors the place.
*
Teach thy tongue to say: "I do not know."
*
He who is loved by man is loved by God.

Rather flay a carcass then be idly dependent on charity.

*

The best preacher is the heart; the best teacher, time; the best book, the world; the best friend, God.

*

A miser is as wicked as an idolator.

*

He who takes from a thief smells of theft.

*

Alas for the bread which the baker calls bad.

*

Tell no secrets for the wall has ears.

*

Silence is a fence around wisdom.

The Martyrdom of Rabbi Akiba

When the wicked Roman government decreed that the Israelites should not study the Torah, Pappos, son of Judah, met Rabbi Akiba, who publicly called assemblies at which the Torah was studied. Pappos said: Akiba, fearest thou not the government? Rabbi Akiba replied: I shall tell you a parable. A fox once walked about by the riverside and perceived fishes that were fleeing from place to place. He said to them, Why do you flee? They answered: Because men spread nets to catch us. The fox said: Better go up to the land, so that you and I may live together in peace. They said: You talk like a fool. If we are terror-stricken in the place where we live, how much greater our fear in the place where we are sure to die. And Akiba added: This is our case. If we are in such distress now that we study the Torah, concerning which it is written: For it is thy life and the length of thy days, how more deplorable would be our position, if we ceased to study the Torah. Before many days Rabbi Akiba was seized and imprisoned, and one day he was led forth to be put to death. While they tore his flesh with iron combs, he took upon himself the yoke of the kingdom of heaven. His pupils asked, O master, thus far? Is this the verse: Thou shalt love Thy God with all thy heart, all thy soul ... I used to say: When shall I have the opportunity to fulfill it?

And now that I do have the opportunity, shall I not use it? And he prolonged the word Ehod (One God) until his soul departed. (Berakhoth 61b)

Jeremiah Consoles an Unhappy Mother

Jeremiah said: While going up to Jerusalem, I lifted up mine eyes, and saw a woman sitting on the top of a mountain. She was clad in black, her hair dishevelled. I drew nigh unto her and asked her who she was. She answered: I am she who had seven children and a beloved husband. My husband died in a city across the sea and my seven children were killed when our house fell upon them. Now I know not for whom I shall weep more. I said, Thou art not better than my mother Zion, who has become pasture for the beasts of the field. She answered, I am thy mother Zion. Jeremiah said: Thy misfortune is like the misfortune of Job: Job's sons and daughters were taken away from him, and likewise thy sons and daughters were taken away from thee. I [the prophet speaks now in the name of God] took away from Job his silver and gold, and from thee, too, did I take away the silver and gold; I cast Job on the dunghill, and likewise thee did I make into a dunghill. And just as I returned and comforted Job, so shall I return and comfort thee; I doubled Job's sons and daughters, and thy sons and daughters shall I also double; I shook Job from the dunghill, and likewise concerning thee it is written: Shake thyself from the dust; arise, and sit down. O Jerusalem. (Pesikta Rabbati)

Good Traits

It was said of Johanan ben Zakkai: He never spoke facetiously; he never walked four ells [five feet] without Torah or T'fillin (phylacteries); he never slept or took a nap in the House of Study; no one ever came to the House of Study before him, or left after him; he never thought of sacred matters in unclean places; no one ever found him sitting in idle silence, but only sitting and learning. No one else opened the door for his disciples; and he never uttered anything that he did not hear from his teachers. He never said, "It is time to leave the House of Study," except on the Eve of

Passover and the Day of Atonement, when the meal at home is more important than study. His disciple, Rabbi Eliezer, emulated his teacher in all these things. (Tractate Sukkah 27)

A Will With a Riddle

A man died and left a will which no one understood. His three sons asked the help of Rabbi Banaa. He read: "Give my oldest son a barrel of dust, my second son a barrel of bones, and my youngest son a barrel of threads." The Rabbi asked: "Did your father leave land, cattle and cloth?" "Yes," was the answer. "Then," said the Rabbi, "the oldest receives the land; the second, the cattle; and the third, the cloth." (Babba Batra 143)

Evil Within The Law

Rabbi Johanan said: Jerusalem was destroyed because the people acted evilly within the law. A story illustrates it: A former apprentice who had become rich was enamored of his master's wife. She returned his love and often visited him by stealth. Once the master needed money and informed his erstwhile apprentice of this. The latter offered to lend him the money and suggested that the master send his wife for it. They remained together for three days, and just as she left her lover, the husband arrived, inquiring for his wife.

"She left me within the hour of her arrival," said the apprentice. "But I have heard a rumor that she has been unfaithful to you."

"What shall I do?" asked the master.

"Divorce her," said the apprentice.

"But her marriage settlement is large, and since it is only a rumor, I must pay it."

"I shall advance you the money," said the apprentice.

As soon as the divorce was effective, the paramour married the woman. Soon he sued his former master for the money, and the latter, being unable to pay it, was compelled to agree to work off his debt by labor. While he waited at the table, his tears trickled down his cheeks and fell into the cups of wine he was serving.

Then it was that the decree was sealed in Heaven that Jerusalem should be destroyed. No actual crime had been committed; it was entirely legal as to procedure, and well within the law, yet it merited a harsher penalty than an actual crime would have brought on. Justice may not be deliberately blind. (Gittin 58a)

The Unsatisfied Eye

The great king Alexander [of Macedononia] asked for admission at the Gate of Paradise.

"Only the righteous may enter here," was the reply.

He then pleaded for a gift, and a piece of human skull with one eye open was thrown to him. Alexander wished to weigh it on his scales, and placed on the balance gold and silver, but the skull was heavier. More gold was added, but to no avail. Acting upon the advice of the Sages, he placed some earth on the eye, and at once the gold became heavier.

"This teaches," they said, "that a human eye is not satisfied with all the gold that exists until it is covered with the earth of the grave." (Tamid 31)

Man and Beast

Once the great Alexander visited a king in an outlying corner of the world. The king acted as magistrate and invited his guest to sit beside him. Two men came before the court. One said: "I have bought a house from this man, and while repairing it, a treasure was found. I offered to return it to him, but he refuses to accept it."

The other said: "I knew nothing of the treasure, and it does not belong to me. Since I sold him the house and the lot, the treasure is his property."

The king said: "Have you a son?" and to the other: "Have you a daughter?" "Yes," was the answer from each. "Then," continued the king, "let them marry and keep the treasure as their dowry."

Alexander smiled, and remarked: "In our country the law is that the king takes unto himself whatever is found."

His host looked at him in astonishment, and replied: "Does the sun shine in your land? Does the rain ripen grain and fruits?"

"Yes," responded Alexander.

"Are there beasts in your land?" the king inquired.

"Yes," answered Alexander.

"Then surely the sun and rain come to your land for the sake of the innocent beasts, not for the sake of unjust men. In our land, however, the sun shines and the rain descends for the sake of men, and the beasts receive their food for our sake." (Introd. to Tanhuma Buber 152)

The Stolen Beaker

Once when Mar Zutra sojourned at an inn, one of the guests stole the innkeeper's silver beaker. Mar Zutra watched the actions of the guests. He saw a man wash his hands and wipe them on the robe of another who was not present.

Mar Zutra advised the landlord to search through this man's effects, and lo, the beaker was discovered.

He said: "He who does not care for the property of another is not an honest man." (Babba Metźia 23)

The Piercing of a Slave's Ear

According to the Mosaic Law, a Hebrew could become a slave under one of two conditions: (a) he might be sold following conviction for theft, (b) he might sell himself because of poverty. However, after six years of service he was to be freed. In case the slave refused to be freed, the Law required the master to bring him to the doorpost where he would pierce the slave's ear with an awl.

Johanan ben Zakkai asked: Why was the ear singled out from all the other organs? And he answered: This ear heard when I proclaimed on Mount Sinai that unto me the children of Israel are servants; they are My servants and not servants of servants. Yet this man went and got a master for himself; let his ear be pierced. (Kidushin 22)

On Patience and Tolerance

A certain man wagered a large sum on angering Hillel, president of the Sanhedrin in the last century before the Common Era. The man ran before Hillel's house on a Friday, just at the time when Hillel was bathing in preparation for the Sabbath. In a loud voice he shouted:

"Hillel, who is Hillel and where is he?"

Hillel wrapped himself in a cloak and came out saying:

"I am Hillel. What do you want, my son?"

"I want to ask you a question," the man replied.

"Ask, and whatever I know I will tell you."

"I want to know," the man said, "why the Babylonians have round heads."

"It is because the Babylonians do not have skilled midwives; the heads of the newborn children become rounded in their hands."

A moment later the man shouted again:

"Where is Hillel?"

"Again Hillel came out and said: "What do you want, my son?"

"Can you tell me," the man asked, "why the eyes of the people of Tadmor are weak?"

"You have asked well," Hillel said. "It is because Tadmor is located in a sandy region and dust gets into people's eyes."

A moment later the man called Hillel again. Hillel came out again.

"I want to know," the man said, "why the feet of the Africans are so wide?"

"It is a result of their going barefoot in swampy land."

Therefore the man said: "I wish to ask you other questions but I fear that you will be angry."

"You may ask as many questions as you wish and I shall answer them to the best of my ability."

"Are you Hillel?"

"I am."

"Then I wish the Jews that there should be no more like you among them."

"Why do you wish them this?" Hillel asked.

"Because through you I have lost a large sum of money. I wagered that I will make you angry and now I do not know what to do to make you angry."

To this Hillel replied, "Even if you were to lose twice that sum, still you could not anger me." (Shabbath 30)

Two Stories of Beruriah

One Sabbath Rabbi Meir, Beruriah's husband, had been in the academy all day teaching the crowds that eagerly flocked to his lectures. During his absence from home, his two sons, distinguished for beauty and learning, died suddenly of a malignant disease. Beruriah bore the dear bodies into her sleeping chamber, and spread a white cloth over them. When the rabbi returned in the evening, and asked for his boys that he might bless them, his wife said, "They have gone to the house of God."

She brought the wine cup, and he recited the concluding prayer of the Sabbath, drinking from the cup, and, in obedience to a hallowed custom, passed it to his wife. Again he asked, "Why are my sons not here to drink from the blessed cup?" "They cannot be far off," answered the patient sufferer, and suspecting naught, Rabbi Meir was happy and cheerful. When he had finished his meal, Beruriah said: "Rabbi, allow me to ask you a question." With his permission, she continued: "Some time ago a treasure was entrusted to me, and now the owner demands it. Shall I give it up?" "Surely, my wife should not find it necessary to ask this question," said the rabbi. "Can you hesitate about returning property to its rightful owner?" "True," she replied, "but I thought best not to return it until I had advised you thereof." And she led him into the chamber to the bed, and withdrew the cloth from the bodies, "O, my sons, my sons," lamented the father with a loud voice, "light of my eyes, lamp of my soul. I was your father, but you taught me the Law." Her eyes suffused with tears, Beruriah seized her grief-stricken husband's hand and spoke: "Did you not teach me to return without reluctance that which has been entrusted to our safekeeping? See, 'the Lord gave, and the Lord hath taken away; blessed be the name of the Lord.' "

"Blessed be the name of the Lord," repeated Rabbi Meir, accepting her consolation, "and blessed, too, be His name for your sake; for it is written: 'Who can find a virtuous woman? For far above pearls is her value. . . . She openeth her mouth with wisdom, and the law of kindness is upon her tongue.' " (Midrash Yalkut on Proverbs)

Another story about Beruriah is characteristic of her personality and learning. Once we are told Rabbi Meir was so incensed at the evil-doings of certain people that he prayed for their destruction. But Beruriah objected to it: "How can you do that?" Beruriah asked her great husband. "Do not the Scriptures say: 'May sins cease from off the earth, and the wicked will be no more.' When sin ceases, there will be no more sinners." Beruriah asked Rabbi Meir rather to pray that they repent, and amend their ways. (Berakhoth 10a)

SAYINGS OF THE FATHERS
(Pirke Aboth)

Sayings of the Fathers, or Ethics of the Fathers, is a small tractate, which was added to the end of the order Nezikin (damages) in the Mishnah. It contains pithy sayings, epigrams, maxims, observations by distinguished teachers, who flourished during a 500-year period from the time of Simon the Just to the 2nd century c.e., when the Mishnah was compiled. The Sayings are generally concise, concentrated, including the most possible in the least number of words.

"Aboth" (Fathers, Sages), as this tractate is called, is a sort of summary of Talmudic conceptions; some call it "The Small Talmud." It is a book of practical wisdom, a truly human and humane work. Next to the Tanakh, or the Jewish Scriptures, Aboth was the most popular book among the Jews, eventually becoming incorporated in the Siddur, or Prayer Book. From Passover to Rosh Hashanah (Jewish New Year), Jews the world over study every Saturday afternoon a chapter of the Sayings. Since the book contains six chapters (in the Mishnah there are only five; the sixth was added later), it is usually completed in six weeks. It is then studied from the beginning for another six weeks, and a third time, too.

Not only has Aboth been extremely popular and influential in the life of the Jews, but among the non-Jewish community it has also, with the universality of its message, found ready acceptance.

The Talmud itself says of the Sayings: "He who wants to become truly pious and virtuous, let him study and practice the teaching of Aboth" (Babba Kamma 30a).

Selections from the Sayings

Upon three things the world is based: Torah, worship [literally: work], and lovingkindness (1:2).

*

Let thy house be a meeting place for the wise; sit amidst the dust of their feet; and drink their words with thirst (1:4).

*

Let thy house be open wide; let the poor be as the members of your household; and engage not in much conversing with the woman [gossip] (1:5)

*

Make a teacher for yourself, obtain a friend, and judge every man in the scale of merit (1:6).

*

Keep far from an evil neighbor, associate not with the wicked. Expect retribution [even if it is late in coming] (1:7).

*

Love peace and pursue peace. Love mankind and bring people nigh to the Torah (1:12).

*

He who makes great his name [self-aggrandizement] loses it; he who adds not [knowledge] destroys it; he who does not learn deserves to die (1:13).

*

If I am not for myself who will be for me? And when I am only for myself what am I? And if not now, when? (1:14).

*

Specify a time for Torah [learning]. Say little and do much. Receive every man cheerfully (1:15).

All my days I have grown up among the wise, and I have not found anything better than silence. Study is not the chief thing, but action (1:17).

*

Be cautious with the ruling power: it befriends a man for its own benefit (2:3).

*

Separate not thyself from society. Trust not thyself until the day of thy death. Judge not thy fellow man until thou reachest his place. The diffident cannot learn. The angry cannot teach. Not everyone who does much business is wise. In the place where there are no men [good men], try to be a man (2:5)

*

He [Hillel] saw a skull floating on the surface of the water, so he said to it: Because thou hadst drowned others, they have drowned thee, and the end of those who have drowned thee shall be that they themselves will be drowned (2:7).

*

More flesh, more worms.
More wealth, more anxiety.
More maid servants, more promiscuity.
More men servants, more robbery.
More Torah, more life.
More counsel, more understanding (2:8).

*

Let the honor of thy fellow man be as dear to you as thine own. Do not get angry on any light pretense (2:15).

*

An evil eye, evil thinking, and hatred of people drive a man out of this world (2:16).

*

Let the property of thy fellow man be as dear to thee as thine own (2:19).

*

Reflect upon three things, and thou wilt not come to commit transgression: Know whence thou camest; know whither thou art going; and know before whom thou art about to give account and reckoning (3:1).

Pray for the welfare of the government, since but for the fear thereof men would swallow each other alive (3:2).

*

He with whom the spirit of men is pleased, the spirit of God is also pleased (3:13).

*

Merriment and levity accustom a man to lewdness (3:17).

*

Everything is given on pledge, and a net is spread for all living: The shop is open, and the dealer gives credit; and the ledger lies open, and the hand writes; and whosoever wishes to borrow may come and borrow; and exact payment from man whether he wills or not; and they have whereon they can rely in their demands; and the judgment is a judgment of truth; and everything is prepared for the feast (3:20).

*

Who is wise? He who learns from every man.
Who is mighty? He who subdues his passions.
Who is rich? He who rejoices in his portion.
Who is honored? He who honors others (4:1).

*

There are three crowns: the crown of Torah, the crown of priesthood, and the crown of kingdom; but the crown of a good name excells them all (4:17).

*

Pacify not thy fellow in the hour of his anger (4:23)

*

Seven things are in a clod, and seven in a wise man: The wise man does not speak before him who is greater than he in wisdom; does not interrupt the words of his companion; is not hasty to answer; questions according to the subject matter, and answers according to the rule; speaks upon the first thing first, and upon the last last; what he does not understand, he says: "I do not understand"; acknowledges the truth. The opposites of these are in a clod (5:10).

*

There are four characters among men.
He that says: "What is mine is mine, and what is thine is thine."

This is the average character (some say it is the character of Sodom).
He that says: "What is mine is thine, and what is thine is mine." This is a boor.
He that says: "What is mine is thine, and what is thine is thine." This is the pious.
He that says: "What is thine is mine, and what is mine is mine." This is the wicked (5:13).

*

Love which depends upon something else is no more when the thing is no more (5:19)

*

Whosoever has these three attributes is of the disciples of Abraham our father: a good eye, a humble mind, and a lowly spirit.
An evil eye, a haughty mind, and a proud spirit are the signs of the disciples of Balaam the wicked (5:22).

SHORT LIFE STORIES OF SAGES

Brief sketches of a few of the Tannaim associated with the Sayings give a more personal flavor to Aboth. These sketches are based primarily on Talmudic and Midrashic sources.

Hillel (c. 75 B.C.E.-10 C.E.)

Hillel, one of the greatest figures in Jewish history, was a descendant of the house of King David. He was born in Babylonia but little is known of his life until he came to Palestine to enroll in the school of Shemaiah and Abtalion. There, we are told, he hoped to clarify certain doubtful points of the Law.

As he was young and without relatives or friends, he barely managed to eke out a livelihood by hard work. The little he did earn he divided in two: one part for bread, and the other for payment of the entrance fee to the doorman at the academy. Once, on a cold and wintry night, Hillel, unable to pay the fee, lay on the roof of the academy in order to hear the discussion of the teachers. When he was taken down from his perch, he was nearly frozen to death.

Later, when he had become the foremost student of the academy, his fame spread quickly both as a scholar and as a moral personality. His accession to the high office of Nasi (president of the Sanhedrin) was hailed by the people as a step in the direction of restoring the "Kingdom of David," at least so far as the Torah was concerned. It meant that a great scholar was occupying the throne of David.

The situation in which the people found themselves at that time was one of abuse and tyranny. The ruler of the country, Herod the Edomite, a despot and an oppressor, was a tool in the hands of Rome. The bloody campaigns he undertook against the neighboring countries were looked upon with ill favor by the people who were themselves groaning under a foreign yoke. If it had not been for their innermost yearning for salvation and their great hope that God would save them, their suffering would have been unbearable. This yearning and this hope found in the person of Hillel, scion of the Davidic dynasty, the man of the hour.

The great influence which Hillel exerted, his profound scholarship, his personality as a moral teacher and leader of men, were regarded by the people as a sign that not everything was lost. As a lover of peace and as a lover of mankind, Hillel swayed the hearts of the people by his unassumed simplicity, his democratic way of living, his humaneness, and above all, by his inexhaustible and proverbial patience.

Hillel's famous maxim, "Do not do unto your neighbor [fellow man] what you would not have him do unto you," a paraphrase of the commandment of the Torah, "Love thy neighbor as thyself" (Lev. 19:18), continued to place the principle of brotherly love as the very basis of Judaism.

Hillel, on his part, exemplified this principle in and through his own life.

Johanan ben Zakkai (1st century c.e.)

A disciple of Hillel, Johanan was one of the foremost religious leaders before the destruction of the Temple (70 c.e.). In the

Talmud the following epithets were accorded to him: "Father of Wisdom," "Father of the Coming Generations," "Light of Israel," "Pillar of the Sanctuary."

After the collapse of the revolt against Rome, Johanan was recognized as the only leader. The circumstances in which the Jews found themselves then was indeed desperate: Jerusalem lay in ruins and beseiged; the country was devastated; and the people, beaten and vanquished, awaited their bitter fate at the hands of a cruel foe.

Days on end Johanan had brooded over the problem what to do and how to save from final destruction whatever might be saved under the circumstances. Land, people, Torah—which of them comes first? He was aware that the enemy viewed the people as material for exploitation and the land as conquered territory. But Torah, learning? Here was the solution: A properly preserved Torah would tend to keep the light of Israel burning and when times would change for the better the people and the land would be saved, too.

Thus came about that unusual escape we noted earlier, in which Johanan's disciples carried his body outside the beleaguered city in a coffin, as if he had died. Following the escape, he appeared before the Roman commander, Vespasian (who later became Emperor), and petitioned that the small town of Jamnia be designated as a place of refuge for the learned.

There followed, last but not least, Johanan's work to reconstruct the spiritual life of the people, consoling them and giving them guidance in their despair. This man is indeed an example of great leadership, genuine wisdom and foresight, and a model of inspired idealism which only the great possess and are able to apply at the most critical moments in the life of peoples and nations.

Johanan did not occupy officially the high office of Nasi; he was, nevertheless, regarded as the uncrowned head of Israel both in Palestine and in all other countries where Jews lived. Leaders everywhere turned to the school at Jamnia as previously they had turned to Jerusalem, and Johanan's word was revered as the word of God.

He was exemplary in his love for the people and the Torah. Teaching was to him a labor of love, and to it he dedicated his life. "If thou hast learned much," Johanan said, "do not keep it to thyself; for thereunto wast thou created." A "good heart" was to him the supreme thing—"the good way to which a man should cleave." That Israel has survived to this day is due in part to Johanan whose unselfish love inspired him to build a Realm of the Spirit for a people without a homeland and without a national life.

Hanania ben Teradyon (died c. 135 C.E.)

One of the "Ten Martyrs," Hanania ben Teradyon was burned at the stake after having been arrested by the Romans on the charge of learning the Torah in violation of the governmental decree.

Because the book of the Torah was found hidden next to Hanania's chest, the executioner was ordered to wrap his body in parchment and place moist wool over his breast in order to prolong his agony. The execution was carried out publicly. His daughter and his disciples were forced to witness it. They all wept at seeing his suffering, but Hanania did not complain nor call for help. He assured them that God would avenge in due time his death.

When one of his disciples asked him: "Rabbi, what do you see?" he replied from amidst the flames, "I see the parchment burning but the letters on it are flying upward."

Akiba ben Joseph (c. 60-135 C.E.)

Akiba was one of the greatest, if not the greatest, expounders of the Torah. He was of lowly station, or, as some have it, of proselytic descent. As he himself relates (Pesathim 49), he was in his youth not only ignorant, but also hostile to learning and the learned.

Very late in life (tradition has it that he was forty years of age) he entered one of the academies and started his course of studies, beginning with the alphabet. Due to his diligence and intelligence, he became the foremost student of the academies established by Nahum Gamzu and Rabbi Eliezer ben Hyrcanus, and later was destined to be one of the foremost scholars of his time.

In addition to his scholarship and intellect, Akiba was also a man of character and individuality, one who towered above his contemporaries in martyrdom and sainthood. Such incomparable praises were showered upon him, that it is doubtful whether even Hillel the Elder or Johanan ben Zakkai ever succeeded in setting fire to the people's imagination as did this humble man. "Secrets that were not disclosed to Moses have been disclosed to him" (Bamidbar Rabba), and "Moses himself said to God that Rabbi Akiba is greater than he"—these and many similar comments were made about him by the learned.

His method of learning the Torah was unique, for he held that every word, even every letter and marking, contains more than the superficial meaning, and that the inner meaning of the Torah could become accessible to everyone by following certain rules. Thus Akiba succeeded in creating a basis in the Torah for many customs and traditions prevalent among the people, an accomplishment which was tantamount to proclaiming new laws for the safeguarding of Judaism. In this field he was superior to all, so that after his death it was said: "After Akiba died the arms of the Torah fell down and the fountains of wisdom were blocked" (Sotah 49).

As a patriot and revolutionary, Akiba joined Bar Kochba and participated in the campaign against the Romans, encouraging and urging the masses to stand by their military leaders. He also journeyed to distant lands—tradition has it that he reached even into Gual—to bestir other people to rise against their oppressors.

His faith in God was a flaming one, and like a flame it spread far and wide, inspiring people to emulate the Master. His was a belief that bore no doubts, no hesitations, no vacillations. It was as clearcut and as certain as life itself. To Akiba, God was not only a fountain of goodness and supreme justice in man's time of rejoicing, but also in man's hour of suffering. For, "beloved is man who was created in the image of God." And, "whatever God doeth is for the best, . . . the world is judged by grace."

Akiba ben Joseph died a martyr's death in 135 c.e.

Judah the Prince (135-219 c.e.)

Judah ha-Nasi (the Prince) was the son of Rabbi Simeon ben Gamaliel II. As a man of rare talent, Judah seems to have prepared himself from early youth for his exalted position as a leader in Israel. Having studied under the guidance of his father, he had absorbed not only the knowledge of the Torah as transmitted from generation to generation, but also acquainted himself with the various methods advanced by other scholars. In addition, he was provided with tutors who instructed him in secular subjects, so that the door to the alien world might also be open to him. At a later period in his life, Judah visited different schools. In some of them he tarried for a time, enrolling as a student and participating in the discussions. Thus Judah came in close contact with the keenest minds of his generation.

When he had assumed the office of Nasi, Judah bent all his efforts to enhancing the prestige which this position had formerly commanded. He apparently increased by his own initiative the immense wealth inherited from his father. This he used generously for building up a great center of learning and for the support of scholars and students who flocked to his academy.

His prestige grew through the years, both as a defender of the people's interests against the encroachments of the rulers and as the greatest teacher since Hillel. So great was the admiration he commanded that he was the only one in the long line of Tannaim to be called by the title "Rabbi" alone—without mentioning his first name; or sometimes he was referred to as Rabbenu HaKadosh, our holy teacher.

In his relations with the authorities, Rabbi Judah displayed his masterly qualifications, both as a man of the world and as a man of practical wisdom. Thus many of the Roman officials became his closest friends, notably Antoninus who was then Governor. Rabbi Judah used this friendship for the benefit of his people.

He was a charitable man and gave generously to the poor. During periods of exceptional need, as during the years of famine, it was upon Judah's orders that wheat and corn were distributed to the hungry.

Although his contributions were many and vast, his greatest achievement and his life work was the compilation of the Mishnah, the code in which he collected the opinions and decisions of both his predecessors and contemporaries. Previously the Oral Law, transmitted from generation to generation, was studied in the academies and decided in accordance with the opinion of the majority. And long before the period of Judah the Prince, some of the learned had realized the difficulties involved in memorizing the various interpretations. Both Rabbi Akiba and Rabbi Meir had started the codification of the laws. But it was Rabbi Judah who carried this process on to completion. In this gigantic work he was aided by all the scholars of his academy, where the material was sifted and systematized and then written down in a clear and concise Hebrew. This work was immediately accepted as the standard book of the law, second only to the Pentateuch. Completed about 200 c.e., this codification was to become the basis for both the Babylonian and the Jerusalemite Talmuds.

PERSONAL PRAYERS BY TALMUDIC SAGES

In the Babylonian Talmud (Berakhoth 16-17), there are a number of prayers composed by various sages as expressions of their individual feelings. Through them we can look into the inner world of Israel's religious leaders.

Rabbi Eliezer used to say:

> May it be Thy will, O Lord our God, to cause to dwell in our lot love and brotherhood and peace and friendship, and mayest Thou make our borders ricn in disciples and prosper our latter end with good prospect and hope, and set our portion in Paradise, and confirm us with a good companion and a good impulse in Thy world; and may we rise early and obtain the yearning of our heart to fear Thy name, and mayest Thou be pleased to grant the satisfaction of our hearts.

R. Johanan:

> May it be Thy will, O Lord our God, to look upon shame and behold our evil plight, and clothe Thyself in Thy mercies and cover Thyself in Thy strength.

R. Zera:

> May it be Thy will, O Lord our God, that we sin not nor bring upon ourselves shame or disgrace before our fathers.

Rab Abba Arika:

> May it be Thy will, O Lord our God, to grant us long

life, a life of peace, a life of good, a life of blessing, a life
of sustenance, a life of bodily vigor, a life of fear of sin,
a life free from shame and confusion, a life of riches and
honor, a life that we may be filled with the love of Torah
and the fear of heaven, a life in which Thou shalt fulfill
all the desires of our heart for good.

R. Judah the Prince:

May it be Thy will, O Lord our God and God of our
fathers, to deliver us from the impudent and from impu-
dence, from an evil man, from evil happenings, from the
evil impulse, from an evil companion, from an evil neighbor, and from the destructive Accuser, from a hard lawsuit and from a hard opponent, whether he is a son of the
convenant or not a son of the covenant!

Mar Huna, the Son of Rabina:

O my God! guard my tongue from evil and my lips from
speaking guile; and to such as curse me let my soul be
dumb, yea, let my soul be unto all as the dust. Open my
heart to the Law, and let my soul pursue thy commandments. If any design evil against me, speedily make their
counsel of none effect, and frustrate their designs.

At Jamnia this prayer was recited:

I am God's creature, and my fellow is God's creature.
My work is in the town, and his work is in the country.
I rise early for my work, and he rises early for his work.
Just as he does not presume to do my work, so I do not
presume to do his work. Will you say, "I do much and
he does little?" We have learned: One may do much or
one may do little; it is all one, provided he directs his
heart to heaven.

THE TITLE "RABBI"

Since the Talmudic period, the title "Rabbi" has undergone
changes, making our modern concept of "Rabbi" basically different from the ancient usage. Originally, this title was accorded only

to the Tannaim, those scholars whose opinions and verdicts were incorporated in the Mishnah. As soon as the Mishnah was compiled and completed, the title was not used any more. The successors to the Tannaim, the Amoraim, carried the title of "Rab" (master), but not "Rabbi."

He who was accorded the title of "Rabbi" during the Tannaitic period (from c. 10 B.C.E. to 220 C.E.) had a chance of being elected to one of three positions: (a) mastership in rendering verdicts in civil and ritual cases; (b) leadership in the judiciary, that is, to become Ab Bet Din, president of a court; (c) Nasi, president of the Sanhedrin.

A Rabbi was not just a leader in a congregation. He was a leader in Israel, one whose position was recognized by all. He was revered for integrity and piety, wisdom and knowledge in various fields, but primarily for his profound knowledge of Torah. Deep learning and good deeds were the primary distinctive signs of a leader, not to mention sainthood and great dedication to the needs of his people.

Many Rabbis in Talmudic times earned their livelihood by hard work as simple workers or artisans: R. Hanina and R. Oshaya were shoemakers (Pesahim 113b); Abba b. Zemina, a tailor (Yer. Baba Kamma 10:10); R. Yose, a tanner (Shabbath 49b); R. Joshua, a blacksmith; Johanan Hasandlor, a sandalmaker. Some Rabbis were merchants and peasants.

In the Tosifta to tractate Edyot (end) the following definition is given of the title Rabbi: "He who has disciples and whose disciples have their own disciples is called Rabbi; when his disciples are forgotten [when he is too old and has more than a third generation of disciples] he is called Rabban."

The true meaning of Rabbi is "my master"; the personal pronoun "my" is attached to the word "Rab."

Most of the Tannaim who carried that title were founders of their own academies, in which they served as professors without remuneration. Those who did not organize academies joined others. Since Torah was not regarded as an aristocratic distinction, and most of the learned came from the broad masses, Rabbis were distinguished by their saintly and simple conduct, by their deep insight into human life, by their understanding of the strivings of the human heart, and by their all-around wisdom which reached into various areas: psychology, social duties, economic life, human relations. They had no need of oratory because they swayed people by their personality and character. Their teaching was in short and concise sentences, with no embellishments. They influenced others by serving God and humanity and by their flaming love of Torah to the point of dying for it.

During the Middle Ages, especially after the Babylonian academies were closed and the Geonic period came to an end, the title of "Rabbi" was re-established. The Rabbi then became the spiritual leader of a congregation, and the title Gaon was given only to such that excelled as great scholars. No remuneration was designated for the Rabbi's services. Even later when a Rabbi obtained some reward, it was rather regarded as a reward for loss of time sustained by him since he was unable to do something else.

Zacharias Frankel (1801-1875), one of the founders of the school of historical Judaism, defines the role of the Rabbi thus: "In Judaism there is no power endowed with the right to bind and to loose; there are no clergymen who by higher inspiration stand above the laymen; but only teachers, who expound the Law and give information".[3] The Rabbi is no priest, no apostle, but rather a moral leader whose supeior learning, true dedication to Judaism, and purity of conduct and character give him the right to lead other people upon the pathway towards a righteous and God-fearing way of life.

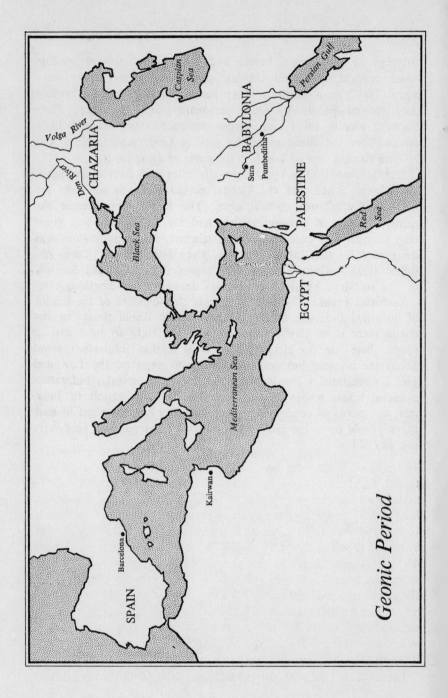

Geonic Period

ק | 7

THE
GEONIC
PERIOD

BABYLONIA AND THE JEWS

The Babylonian Talmud was closed in the year 499 c.e., when Rabina, the last Amora (interpreter) and editor, died. There followed a short period of approximately seventy-five years, during which the final touches on the completion of the work were made. Those scholars who did the work of checking the texts and adding their own short annotations were called Saboraim (from the Aramaic word Sabora, explanation). From about 576 c.e. started the long period of the Geonim (Gaon, singular, excellence, eminence). It lasted in Babylonia until 1038, when the two great academies of Sura and Pumbeditha were closed. During that long time, about 450 years, many things happened which effected Hebrew letters considerably, though not everything is as yet well understood because the records of old are scanty. What little we do know about this period can be summarized as follows: (a) The Talmud became the standard law book; (b) the so-called Responsa literature was developed to a high degree; (c) Hebrew liturgical poetry came into its own; (d) Jewish mysticism became extremely popular.

Let us look briefly at the political situation in the eastern Medi-

terranean lands where the Babylonia center was located. The short
period of the Saboraim, mentioned above, fell at the end of the
Persian rule. The government, having been weakened internally,
began persecuting the Jews. As a result, the great Talmudic academies in Babylonia were in a critical situation. Torn from the rest
of Jewry, their existence was precarious. Fortunately a new force
emerged from the Arabian desert—Islam, which changed the situation completely. Hardly a decade after Mohammed's death (632),
the sons of the desert, under the leadership of the second calif,
Omar, holding the sword in one hand and the Koran in the other,
swept over Western Asia. A little later Omar undertook a campaign against Persia, which tottered under his heavy blows. The
Jews and the Chaldean Christians, and possibly other persecuted
groups, were hostile to the Persian rulers. Perhaps they were in
contact with the enemy and helped him from within. Naturally,
when Persia fell under Arab rule, Omar conferred special privileges upon the Jewish communities in all the conquered lands.
The former restrictions against Judaism were abolished. A scion
of the Davidic family, Bostanai by name, was reappointed as the
Prince of the Captivity, that is, as the official representative of Jewry,
and the two academies at Sura and Pumbeditha were reopened
and restored to their former dignity and influence.

From then on new titles of honor came into use: the Prince of
the Captivity or Resh Galutha gave way to Exilarch, and the
leaders of the academies were called Geonim. The Gaon of Sura
was regarded as the supreme religious leader, the Gaon of Pumbeditha ranking next to him. The Sura academy received two-
thirds of the contributions sent by the communities and the liturgic
order of prayers was formulated by the Gaon of Sura. On the
death of an Exilarch, the Gaon of Sura officiated until a new Exilarch was chosen. Generally a Gaon was elected by the scholars,
but occasionally he was appointed by the Exilarch and then approved by the academy faculty. The function of the Geonim consisted primarily in directing the academies and in interpreting the
Talmudic law. Just as the Amoriam interpreted the Mishnah in
which the verdicts of the Tannaim were incorporated, and just as
the Saboraim completed the work of the Amoraim, so the Geonim
re-interpreted the laws and customs as they applied to the cases

involved. In some instances they even changed or abrogated a regulation or custom if conditions demanded it, though this was rarely done. The Geonim were consulted on questions of religion not only by their immediate constituents, but by Jews from France to India, and their decisions were honored throughout the Diaspora.

While religious leadership of the Jews was vested in the two Geonim, political leadership lay with the Exilarch, who represented the Jewish communities to the government authorities. Living in a royal palace as an eastern potentate, the Exilarch enjoyed great privileges at court.

Nathan HaBabli, who visited Babylonia sometime in the 10th century, gave an eyewitness report about the installation ceremony of an Exilarch:

> The members of the two academies, Sura and Pumbeditha, led by the two heads [the Geonim] as well as by the leaders of the community, assemble in the house of an especially prominent man before the Sabbath on which the installation of the Exilarch is to take place. The first homage is paid on Thursday in the synagogue, the event being announced by trumpets, and every one sends presents to the Exilarch according to his means. The leaders of the community and the wealthy send handsome garments, jewelry, and gold and silver vessels. On Thursday and Friday the Exilarch gives great banquets. On the morning of the Sabbath, the nobles of the community call for him and accompany him to the synagogue. Here a wooden platform covered entirely with costly cloth has been erected, under which a picked choir of sweet-voiced youths well versed in the liturgy has been placed. This choir responds to the leader in prayer, who begins the service with Baruk she-amar [a prayer]. After the morning prayer the Exilarch, who until now has been standing in a covered place, appears; the whole congregation rises and remains standing until he has taken his place on the platform, and the two Geonim, the one from Sura preceding, have taken seats to his right and left, each making an obeisance. A costly canopy has been erected over the seat of the Ex-

ilarch. Then the leader in prayer steps in front of the platform, and, in a low voice audible only to those close by, and accompanied by the "Amen" of the choir, addresses the Exilarch with a benediction prepared long beforehand. Then the Exilarch delivers a sermon on the text of the week, or commissions the Gaon of Sura to do so. After the discourse the leader in prayer recites the Kaddish, and when he reaches the words, "during your life and your days," he adds the words "and during the life of our prince, the Exilarch." After the Kaddish he blesses the Exilarch, the two heads of the schools, and the several provinces that contribute to the support of the academies, as well as the individuals who have been of special service in this direction. Then the Torah is read. When the Kohen and Levi[1] have finished reading, the leader in prayer carries the Torah roll to the Exilarch, the whole congregation rising; the Exilarch takes the roll in his hands and reads it while standing. The two heads of the schools also rise, and the Gaon of Sura recites the Targum [translation] to the passage read by the Exilarch. When the reading of the Torah is completed, a blessing is pronounced upon the Exilarch.

After the Musaf prayer, the Exilarch leaves the synagogue, and all, singing, accompany him to his house. After that the Exilarch rarely goes beyond the gates of his house, where services for the community are held on the Sabbaths and feast days. When it becomes necessary for him to leave his house, he does so only in a carriage of state, accompanied by a large retinue. If the Exilarch desires to pay his respects to the king, he first asks permission to do so. As he enters the palace the king's servants hasten to meet him, among whom he liberally distributes gold coins, for which provision has been made beforehand. When led before the king his seat is assigned to him. The king then asks what he desires. He begins with carefully prepared words of praise and blessing, reminds the king of the customs of his fathers, gains the favor of the king with appropriate words, and receives written consent to his demands; thereupon, rejoiced, he takes leave of the king.[2]

RESPONSA LITERATURE

During the long existence of the Geonate, the literature known as Responsa, i.e., answers to questions posed to the Geonim, grew to immense proportions. More than 900 collections of such legal treatises came down to us, reflecting not only various phases of Jewish life but containing also interesting details of the life of the peoples among whom the Jews lived. Hence the Responsa are of great historic value for the study of conditions of the past.

Questions and answers are, of course, a major motif of the Talmud, but not until the Gaonic period did there emerge an independent branch of Jewish literature, Responsa, which was patterned entirely around this format. Responsa flowed from the academies in Babylonia and Palestine and later in Europe; although many Responsa have been lost throughout the years, those extant number probably half a million.

The Responsa literature, written in Hebrew, Aramaic, and Arabic, was extensive and highly informative, since it was by no means restricted to problems of legalism or ritualism as one might think. It touched upon all branches of human life: theology and philosophy, history and social problems, economy and politics. The questions posed to the Geonim by communities and individuals required sometimes an elucidation touching upon the relations between Jews and non-Jews, and many other such things that had nothing to do with religion per se.

In the Geonic period the text of the Talmud was already fixed and accessible to scholars who lived in distant lands. When a question arose as to a certain case, or there was a controversy between two factions or scholars, people turned to the Babylonian academies for a final decision. The question was referred to the Gaon of Sura, who called it to the attention of his colleagues. A discussion about it ensued, but instead of giving a ruling of "yes" or "no," the Gaon authorized his secretary or secretaries to compose a Responsum, an answer that dealt with the question at length. Passages of the Talmud were cited, comparisons between various cases were made, until the verdict was clearly brought to light. In order to avoid any serious misunderstandings regarding other cases, the Gaon had to clarify all possible consequences.

At first, questions were received from Babylonia itself or from the nearby countries, but as time passed communities in distant lands turned to the Geonim for answers. In order to see how seriously the Geonim took their task, an introductory remark to one of the Responsa serves well as an illustration:

Amram ben Sheshna, head of the academy of the city of Mehasya [Sura], to all scholars and their disciples and to those of our brethren of the house of Israel who dwell in Barcelona [Spain], and who are dear beloved, and revered unto us, may their prosperity increase and wax great! Receive ye greeting from us and from R. Zemah, the president of the court, from the heads of the Kallah, from the authorized teacher, and from all other scholars and disciples of the academy, all of whom ever pray for your health, that God in His great mercy may have compassion on you. The questions which ye have laid before us we have caused to be read unto us, while the president of the court and the Allufim [honored Torah students] and the other sages and disciples sat before us. We have studied them, and weighed all that is written in them, and with divine help have given to them the following answers.[3]

The answer was frequently concluded with the formula "thus is the final decision" or "thus is the correct practice."

In some Geonic responses, they said that the decision rendered was approved after consultation with the scholars who were members of the "small sanhedrin" of thirty and also with those who belonged to the "great sanhedrin" of seventy. This indicated that the Geonim shared their leadership with other scholars.

The Geonate revived the ancient custom of the Kallah months, during which thousands of students and common people assembled in the academies to study the Torah. These were the month of Adar before the Passover holiday, and the month of Elul before New Year (Rosh Hashnah). It was customary to read before the public some of the questions referred to the Geonate and then the answers were discussed at length.

SAMPLE RESPONSA

Some Responsa are in the form of long and elaborate discussions, reflecting the thinking of generations past as well as the social and economic conditions of the Jewish communities throughout the Diaspora. Three examples of short Geonic Responsa will illustrate their form and content.

Mar Rab Sar Shalom, Gaon of Sura during the decade c. 949-59, was asked about stealing from a Gentile or deceiving him in any other way. He responded:

> As to what you have asked: "How is it with regard to to the theft of non-Jewish property in cases where it has not been forbidden as a desecration of the divine name?" thus is our ruling: The prohibition of theft has naught to do with the desecration of the divine name, but is a clearly established law which forbids any theft whatever from a non-Jew. Desecration of the divine name is mentioned only in association with objects which have been lost. According to Rabbi Phinehas ben Yayir, "Whensoever it leads to a desecration of the divine name, one is forbidden to appropriate anything which a non-Jew has lost." The vine said to have been taken from the garden of a Gentile by Rab Ashi was evidently taken in return for compensation.[4]

Sar Shalom Gaon also responded in a characteristic way regarding certain customs observed in some communities in northern Africa and in other parts of the world:

> As to what you have asked: "After the burial of a corpse many wipe their hands on the ground." No such custom prevails among us. And as to what you have heard: "While returning from the cemetery many are wont to wash their hands before reaching the house and to sit down on the way; what is the reason for this?" thus is our opinion: The washing of the hands is not obligatory, but where it is the custom one should wash them. The bid-

ding of the sages that one must sit down seven times while returning from a corpse is intended to apply solely to the case in which one goes to the place of burial and returns from it, and solely for the kinsmen, and solely for the first day, and, above all, solely for those places where the usage is customary. The sevenfold repetition of sitting down is on account of the evil spirits which follow the returning mourners, that a demon may disappear each time the bereaved sit down.

The great Talmudic scholar, Isaac Hirsh Weiss, has this to say about this Responsum: "Whoever looks deeper into Sar Shalom's words can see that he was averse to such customs, and, moreover, he personally did not believe in spirits who follow the returning mourners. Had he believed, he would have accepted it as obligatory upon all and not just as a local custom."[5]

A Responsum of historic significance is the 11th century one by Rabbi Hananeel of Kairwan, Africa, famous Talmudic commentator and a disciple of Hai Gaon. It deals with the question of conscious and unconscious sins.

As to what you have asked, about the Talmudic saying that it is better to let the children of Israel transgress laws unconsciously which they would transgress consciously were they fully instructed, whether this is not contradictory to many passages of Scripture, such as Leviticus 19:17, commanding us "to rebuke our neighbor" and such-like admonitions as in Ezekiel 33:9 and Proverbs 24:5. This is the answer: It is true that the children of Israel are commanded to rebuke one another and thus it is written in the prophets and the "writings" (hagiographa), whether one man or an entire community be guilty of a transgression. If the violation of the words of the Torah is conscious, the transgressor must be warned, and, if necessary, he may be punished, while, on the other hand, all efforts must be made to win him back to righteousness. If, however, all this is without avail, then "thou hast delivered thy soul" [Ez. 33:9; i.e., "thou hast saved thy soul" by doing everything possible, which means "you are not responsible any longer."] In case the transgression is unconscious and there is reason to suppose that the children of Israel would obey if they were instructed, they must be warned and enlightened concerning the teachings of the Law and the way of righteousness. It is otherwise, however, when what is forbidden is regarded as permitted, and when a prohibition is regularly taken with little seriousness on account of the assumption of the presence of due precaution against violation of the Law. Thus, on the eve of the Day of Atonement folk sit to eat in broad daylight, but their meal lasts until evening draws near. Those who eat intend to finish the meal in due time and wish to fix the proper moment arbitrarily. They say: "It is still time," while darkness is approaching; and though we should warn them they would not listen. In such cases it is better for us to remain silent, and not to cause them to become guilty of conscious sin. This case is to be differentiated from one in which we see another transgress a law consciously, for then we are duty bound to lift up our voices against him on the chance that he may harken to us.[6]

Remarkably enough, Rabbi Hananeel evades the issues of banning altogether, although there were two degrees of excommunication according to Talmudic law, known as Niddui (interdict) and Herem (complete excommunication). The former was usually imposed upon a transgressor for thirty days, but if he did not submit he was excommunicated.

GEONIM

Many Geonim achieved fame for their literary contributions. Some of them were not only legal authorities but also poets and scholars in other fields. For instance, Zemah Gaon (Gaon of Sura, 872-895) compiled an Aramaic dictionary. Saadia Gaon (b. 892) was a noted Aristotelian rationalist and theological reformer. Sherira Gaon (b. 900) was a historian. His famous Iggereth Sherira Gaon, or Epistle of Sherira, written as a Responsum, de-

tails the period of the Tannaim, Amoraim, Saboraim, and the
Geonim; without his Letter much of the era would be lost to us.
Sherira was the third to last Gaon in Babylonia before the closing
of the academies in 1038. His son, Hai Gaon (b. 940), was the
next to last.

Hai was a scholar interested in astronomy and other secular
subjects, a worldly man with a practical bent of character. His
book on the regulations of buying and selling is still regarded as
the best summary of Talmudic law in this field. His Responsa are
clear-cut and broad-minded, reflecting a superb deductive method.
In synthetical thinking and methodical application of general rules,
Hai was one of the great minds in the Geonic period.

Hai was also a liturgical poet of note, though his poems are
more didactic than imaginative, for he was primarily a moralist.
As an admirer of science, Hai tried to show that Judaism is not
averse to secular knowledge. In one of his proverbs, he sums up
his approach to knowledge: "Do not acquire gold and silver. Acquire knowledge. Study science even when it does not come easy
to you."

A man in North Africa addressed a letter to Hai Gaon in Babylonia regarding belief in magic and mysticism in general. The
questions referred to the following: (a) the Ineffable Name of God
and similar names of Angels through means of which people believe they can make themselves invisible, save themselves from
robbers, or perform other miracles such as calming the sea, bringing a dead body back to life, and shortening the way by traveling
immense distances in no time; (b) mysterious books which can
cause calamity and premature death if not used aright; (c) incantations and amulets which can influence the destiny of man for
good or evil.

Hai replied calmly and logically to every point of the inquiry.
He warned Jews not to put too much credence in such things.
What people say is one thing, and what may be witnessed with
one's own eyes is something else. He went on to say that in his
own college there are such books, and that one of his predecessors
was known to have been addicted to such things; but one should
be careful in accepting anything upon the basis of hearsay. "Only
a fool," he wrote, "believes everything." As for the books with
formulas:

We have a number of them, such as the book called Sefer
Hayashar and the book called The Sword of Moses which
commences with the words, "Four angels are appointed to
the Sword," and there are in it exalted and miraculous
things; there is, further, the book called The Great Mystery,
besides minor treatises which are innumerable. And many
have labored in vain to find out the truth of these things.

This goes far to prove that mystical books were written and
published long before the 11th century. Such literature apparently
was very popular among Jews in the Byzantine empire and
throughout the Middle East.

Solomon ibn Gabirol, who was still young at the time of Hai's
death, eulogized him as follows:

> Who would take over his leadership,
> And who is suited to occupy his judge's chair,
> And who would defend the oppressed,
> And who would by his wisdom still my spiritual thirst,
> And who would replace Hai?

EARLY LITURGICAL POETRY

During the Geonic period, the first liturgical poets appeared. Because the records of that period are fragmentary, we do not know
much about these poets, but it is generally recognized that their
influence upon the synagogue was of great significance in the development of Hebrew letters. We have almost no details at all on
any liturgical poets in Babylonia, through our evidence suggests
that is where the encouragement came from. We do, however,
have some records of Palestinian poets.

It appears that the series of prayers that had come down from
Talmudic times was insufficient for the time that people were wont to
spend in the synagogues during the Geonic period, since the synagogue became more a House of Prayer than a House of Learning. Hence the liturgical services had to be expanded, particularly
on the High Holidays, by adding new material to be recited. The

Geonim, having recognized the need for expansion, apparently encouraged the poets to compose new prayers.

One of the earliest poets to serve the synagogue with his pen was Jose ben Jose Ha-Yathom (orphan). Very little is known of his life, either about his birthplace or his residence. It is assumed that he flourished in Palestine.

Jose did not use either rhyme or metre. His model was the poetry of the Bible. His poems carried an alphabetic acrostic. Sometimes the acrostic was running in the regular alphabetical order and sometimes in reverse—from the last letter to the first. This style was not an innovation, since the acrostic was used already in Biblical times (though never in reverse).

This liturgical poetry is called in Hebrew, Piyyut, the word perhaps having been derived from the Greek. The poet was called Payyetan. Such Piyyutim were composed in the hundreds and most of them were included in the prayer book for the holidays known as Mahzor. They are still being recited by the Orthodox today.

Eleazar HaKalir (late 7th century) was a prolific poet, a disciple of another poet named Yannai. HaKalir's style is somewhat heavy and complicated, because he allowed himself to coin new words, sometimes against the accepted grammatical rules or possibly in conformity to rules that had been in vogue at that period and were abandoned later. Abraham ibn Ezra severely criticized HaKalir for such extravangances. Ibn Ezra declared: "HaKalir had made the Hebrew language a wall full of breaches." Modern critics, however, agree that HaKalir's poetry possesses emotional power, notwithstanding his verbosity.

His cherished form is a dialogue between Israel and God. HaKalir bewails the plight of his people in exile, their degradation and humiliation. While he uses freely legends from the Talmud and the Midrashim, he bestows his own personality upon them.

In one of his poems, which is recited on the 9th of Ab, the mourning day for the destruction of Jerusalem and the Temple, HaKalir makes the prophet Jeremiah say to the Patriarchs: "Beloved ones, how can you lie at rest, while your children are banished, pierced through with the sword?" The Patriarchs, emerging from their graves, cry with bitter lamentations. They turn to God and plead with him to have compassion. But God answers them: "They changed my glory for vanity; they had no fear of me; when I hid my face from them, they longed not for me." Then the faithful shepherd Moses, appears on the scene. He complains to the Most High who had left his people without a shepherd. Only when the mothers, Leah and Rachel, lift up their hands to heaven to plead for their children, God assures them that Zion's children will be redeemed and returned to their home.

HaKalir's Piyyut, "Open the Gates," given below, is recited during the last service of the Day of Atonement, called Ne'ila or Ne'ilat She'arim (Closing of the Gates). In the Talmud there is a double interpretation of this "closing." Rabbi Johanan says it means the closing of the gates of the Temple in Jerusalem, but Abba Arika (Rav) interprets it as the closing of the gates of heaven. Rav's interpretation was traditionally accepted by the people, and special prayers composed by various Payyetanim (liturgical poets) are recited late in the afternoon on the Day of Atonement.

The mystical "gates of heaven" must have appealed to Ha-Kalir, who is known as a mystic. Modern scholars have discovered traces of the mysticism of the old Sefer Yetzirah (Book of Formation) in HaKalir's poems. The esoteric ideas of that book must have fascinated the poet. The phrase "Open the gates—of the armies celestial" clearly indicates what he means. The "Temple" he mentions in the first line is certainly the "heavenly temple."

Open the Gates[7]

Open the gates—the gates of the Temple,
Swift to Thy sons, who Thy truths have displayed.

Open the gates—the gates that are hidden,
Swift to Thy sons, who Thy Law have obeyed.

Open the gates—of the coveted Temple,
Swift to Thy sons who confess and seek grace.

Open the gates—of the armies celestial,
Swift to Thy sons, Judah's tearful-eyed race.

Open the gates—the radiant portals,
Swift to Thy sons who are lovely and pure.

Open the gates—of the crown of fidelity,
Swift to Thy sons who in God rest secure.

Another liturgical poet of that period was Yannai. One of Yannai's extant poems is "And It Came To Pass at Midnight," which is recited on the Eve of Passover at the Seder ceremony. The poet draws his theme from Jewish history, starting with the Patriarch Abraham, "to whom God revealed the true faith," and coming down to his own time when the people of Israel were exiled and scattered among the nations. Yannai pleads with God to redeem his oppressed people. This poem in Hebrew is chanted in accordance with a special melody.

Yannai is said to have been Eleazar HaKalir's teacher. Most of his poems are lost; some are still extant but it is difficult to ascertain whether they are really his or they belong to another early poet who remained unknown by name. The poem given here is ascribed to Yannai, though proof is lacking. There is also an old legend to the effect that Yannai was jealous of his disciple Eleazar HaKalir, who surpassed his master. Yannai, unable to contain himself, allegedly slew his disciple.

Both Yannai and HaKalir probably lived in Palestine at a time when that center was practically extinguished. The Palestine Patriarchate was abolished in the year 425, almost 300 years before these two poets. How their Piyyutim reached the Babylonian academies is not known. It is quite possible that the scholars who immigrated into Babylonia, in order to save themselves from the religious persecutions in Palestine, brought them.

This English translation of Yannai's poem is, of course, not an exact rendition, but it brings forth the spirit in which it was written.

And it came to pass at midnight[8]

Unto God let praise be brought
For the wonders He hath wrought
Response: at the solemn hour of midnight.

All the earth was sunk in night
When God said: "Let there be light!"
Resp.: Thus the day was formed from midnight.

So was primal man redeemed
When the light of reason gleamed
Resp.: Through the darkness of the midnight.

To the Patriarch, God revealed
The true faith, so long concealed
Resp.: By the darkness of the midnight.

But this truth was long obscured
By the slavery endured
Resp.: In the black Egyptian midnight.

Till the messenger of light
Sent by God dispelled the night
Resp.: And it came to pass at midnight.

Then the people God had freed
Pledged themselves His law to heed
Resp.: And it came to pass at midnight.

When they wandered from the path
Of the Lord, His righteous wrath
Resp.: Hurled them into darkest midnight.

But the Prophets' burning word
By repentant sinners heard
Resp.: Called them back from darkest midnight.

God a second time decreed
That His people should be freed
Resp.: From the blackness of the midnight.

Songs of praise to God ascend,
Festive light their glory lend
Resp.: To illuminate the midnight.

Soon the night of exile falls
And confined within the walls
Resp.: Israel groans in dreary midnight.

Anxiously with God they plead
Who still trust His help in need
Resp.: In the darkest hour of midnight.

And He hears their piteous cry:
"Wait! be strong, my help is nigh"
Resp.: Soon 't will pass—the long-drawn midnight.

Tenderly I cherished you
For a service great and true
Resp.: When 'tis past, the long-drawn midnight.

O, Thou Guardian of the Right
Lead us onward to the light
Resp.: From the darkness of the midnight.

Father, let the day appear
When all men Thy name revere,
Resp.: And Thy light dispels the midnight.

When no longer shall the foe
From th' oppressed wring cries of woe
Resp.: In the darkness of the midnight.

But Thy love all hearts shall sway,
And Thy light drive gloom away
Resp.: And to midday change the midnight.

KARAITES

In the midst of the Geonic period, about the year 762, a new
Exilarch had to be elected from the nearest kin of the Bosta-

nai family. There were two pretenders: Anan ben David and his younger brother Josiah (or Hanihah). The two Geonim and the leaders of the communities elected Josiah, because Anan had been known as an anti-Talmudist, as an advocate of a return to a simpler Judaism based upon the Pentateuch, and as a man of a disposition antagonistic to the established leaders. Immediately two factions formed: Ananites on one hand and anti-Ananites on the other. Anan's adherents then refused to submit to the dictates of the academies and declared Anan Exilarch against the will of the leaders. Anan was then arrested and imprisoned. Later he escaped and formed a new sect which became known as the Karaites. This sect represented an open revolt against traditional Judaism and particularly against the Talmud.

In intent and form, this movement might be compared, for purposes of understanding, to later protests within Christendom. For example, in the 12th century in France and Italy, there arose reformers, Albigenses and Waldenses, who urged a return to the one true scripture of their faith: the New Testament; and who deplored the trappings of the Roman Catholic Church which had developed since the days of Jesus. Or in the present-day United States, the Amish sect within Protestantism can, by analogy, perhaps illumine our insight into this ancient Jewish reformation. There have for centuries been Christian reform movements demanding a return to the simple gospel of Jesus and to a simpler life style less compromised by intercourse with the political and economic urban forces of the day.

In the 8th century, discarding the traditions of the Rabbis and their schools, Anan asserted that the Talmudic sages misinterpreted the Mosaic laws. He called his adherents to return to the original sources of the Bible, according to his own interpretations, which he claimed were the right ones. He thus set himself up as the supreme tribunal and sole reformer of Judaism. He produced a code of laws which rested upon his own understanding of Judaism and which lacked the experience and insight of generations. In many respects his new regulations, represented as truly Biblical, were much harsher than the Talmudic regulations which he so strenuously opposed.

As a matter of fact, Anan's regulations were not even accepted by most of the dissenters. Instead of Ananists they started to call themselves Karaim, or Karaites (From "karah," to read), because they held on to the Written Torah called Mikrah (Scriptures) as against the Talmud which was known as the Oral Law.

A littler later, about the end of the 8th century, there appeared another leader of the Karaites—Benjamin b. Moses Nahawendi, from Nahawend, Persia, who overshadowed Anan. Benjamin wrote in both Arabic and Hebrew, and was more lenient toward the Talmud. In his books Sefer Denim (Book of Laws) and Sefer Mitzwot (Book of Precepts), he re-adopted many Talmudic ordinances which Anan had rejected, though he left them to the free choice of the individual Karaites, thus holding on to the original tenets of Karaism that the Talmud was not authoritative. He even decreed that a son may differ from his father, a disciple from his master, provided they can prove their views. That meant that he opened the door for free inquiry in religious matters. Small wonder that Karaism soon underwent a process of fragmentation into small sects which were fighting each other.

Aggressive opposition against the Karaites by the established leaders of Judaism waxed and waned during the Geonic period, but in the 10th century there emerged a group of Karaitic scholars who assulted the Talmudic fortress again with such force that a counterattack was a must. Armed with a thorough knowledge of the Bible and Hebrew grammar, these Karaites emphasized the "inconsistencies" of the Talmud in interpreting the Torah. Their threat to the Rabbinites, as the Karaites called the Talmudic Jews, was a real one. Traditional Judaism needed a man for the times, a man of wide knowledge and forceful intellect. Such a man appeared: Saadia Gaon; he struck at the Karaites with conviction and effectiveness.

Although a few thousand Karaites still exist today, the movement long ago lost any influence it had within Judaism. Its contributions were significant, however. It did prompt correction of some abuses of religious practice among the Jews. Also, it aroused Talmudic Jewry to pay more attention to the Bible and to make the Bible more available to the masses; Saadia, for example, translated the Bible into Arabic for the people. Furthermore, Karaism inspired established Judaism to devote more time to the study and development of Hebrew philology and grammar.

SAADIA BEN JOSEPH
(892-942)

Saadia ben Joseph, born in the year 892 in Dilaz, a village in Fayyum, Egypt, was the first Talmudic scholar to formulate and systematize a complete religious philosophy of Judaism. Prior to him, only partial attempts were made at a philosophical approach, as shown, for example, by the work of Isaac ben Suleiman Israeli (845-940), a physician and Hebrew philologist. It is not known where and how Saadia acquired his general and Talmudic education. Egypt at that time was not a great center of learning. We do know, however, that in 915 he visited Palestine and remained there for some time. Later he visited also Syria and Babylonia.

In the year 928, at the age of thirty-six, he was invited by David ben Zaakai, the Exilarch, to occupy the chair of Gaon of Sura. Thus he became the acknowledged religious leader of all the Jewish communities in the Diaspora. However, his leadership created a major rift between Gaon and Exilarch. In 930, in a probate case, Saadia refused to sign the verdict of Exilarch David ben Zakkai, as was the custom. The Gaon of Pumbeditha signed, but Saadia considered the verdict unjust, and his conscience dictated against ratification. The Exilarch, enraged, deposed Saadia and appointed another Gaon. Saadia countered by conferring the office of Exilarch on David ben Zakkai's brother, Hasan. Hostile factions formed, a pamphlet war broke out with each side exchanging severe attacks, and Saadia finally left Sura and devoted himself to writing his scholarly and polemical works. Seven years after the break, the two enemies were reconciled and Saadia was reinstated as Gaon of Sura.

Even before he first settled in Sura, Saadia had gained a reputation as a scholar and an ardent advocate of Judaism. Saadia's first work, while he was still a young man, was *Agron*, a small

Hebrew dictionary, the first of its kind. He intended it primarily for use by poets. Saadia himself was a poet, though he cannot be reckoned among the great. Some of his prayer-poems were included in his Siddur, known as Saadia's Prayer Book, which contained the entire ritual for weekdays, Sabbath, and the festivals, with explanations in Arabic. The most important poems are his "Azhoroth" (warnings and instructions) about the 613 precepts of the Torah.

His position as one of the first Hebrew grammarians is acknowledged by many. Though his grammatical work has been lost, it is known that it exerted a deep influence upon the development of Hebrew lexicography, exegesis, and grammar. Saadia was also one of the founders of comparative Hebrew philology, as he explained many Hebrew words by the Arabic.

Of all Saadia's works, his polemics against Karaism exerted the greatest influence. Perhaps the majority of Saadia's religious, grammatical, theological, and philosophical writings have been lost to us; nonetheless, we know that he wrote at least 100 titles in Hebrew and 200 in Arabic. Saadia's greatest work was his *Beliefs and Doctrines*, written originally in Arabic and later rendered into Hebrew. In his introduction to his book, he wrote:

> Deep was my grief at seeing how people are drowned in the sea of doubts; the misleading waves of atheism overwhelmed them, and there was no experienced diver who would save them, no kindly swimmer appeared to extend to them a helping hand. But God endowed me with something which may be of help to those people....I know well how limited is my understanding. I am not superior nor wiser than my generation. I therefore wish only to do as much as I can, with the little that I possess. I hope that God would not abandon me; He would grant me his mercy and support. Not because I deserve it as a reward for my good deeds, but because He knows well my innermost wish and desire.

It was a time of crisis in the life of traditional Judaism, which struggled on many fronts for its survival. The spread of Islam was a threat. Furthermore, Judaism met anew the challenge of Greek philosophy, but this time in Arab garb. There was also the battle between Talmudists and Karaites. Swayed by the philosophical beliefs in vogue at the time, many Jews questioned the tenets of Judaism as they had come down to them from Talmudic times. Other Jews, swayed by the "fundamentalist," non-philosophic approach of the Karaites, questioned Talmudic Judaism. New conditions demanded new answers, and Judaism had to be re-thought.

For Saadia, reason and faith are not in conflict. The differences between true philosophy and Judaism are only apparent. What is Judaism's highest aim? He answers his question: Its aim is to lead man toward the highest ideals of life. Philosophy in turn aims at the same goal. If their goal is the same, then their differences which express themselves mainly in method can be resolved. Thus, according to Saadia, there are two roads leading to the Good Life: The road of Torah and the road of philosophy or reason. The question then arises: If one could attain the same end by human reason, what would one need revelation for? Saadia answers as follows: Not everyone is by nature inclined to philosophize and not everyone is capable of doing it for himself. Also, human reason strays easily from the right path. What the Torah teaches is accessible to all and can easily be pursued by anyone.

An Arab poet, contemporary with Saadia, wrote: "There are two kinds of people in the world, those who have intelligence but no faith and those who have faith but lack intelligence." Saadia tried to build a bridge between reason and faith, to make the intelligent faithful and the faithful intelligent.

Let us see how Saadia approaches the question of the existence of God and of the world. How can one explain the existence of the world? asks Saadia. There are three answers: First, the world created itself; second, the world existed eternally; third, the world was created by a supreme power. The first answer is unthinkable. How could the world create itself before it had existed, and from what had it created itself? Hence we remain with two answers. Saadia selected the third. The universe must have had a beginning, and if there were a beginning, the next conclusion must be someone who had made that beginning. The one who made that beginning he calls God. Saadia admits that this answer is not easy to explain. The alternative, however, the world's eternal existence, is far more difficult to accept. The changeability of the world simply denies its eternity. And here Saadia presents some speculative reasons, Greek philosophical deductions, in support of his idea that the world must have had a beginning:

(a) Everything on this earth that was created out of smaller elements is new. First it didn't exist and then it came into existence.

(b) No one thing can create itself when it already exists.

(c) Every beginning has an ending, and where there is an ending there once was a beginning. If something had a beginning it was created by something else which existed earlier.

(d) Every whole from which a part can be removed, whose separate parts had a beginning and an ending, also had a beginning and ending and is not eternal. Only that which is eternal and from which no part can be removed has no beginning and no ending. As soon as we try to split a small and separate portion from eternity, then the smaller part has a beginning and it is no longer eternal. Eternity is complete and never divisible.

These four rules Saadia assumes are absolute, consistent, and confirmed by the rational world. Following these rules, we conclude that our world is not eternal. There must be something else which is eternal and which created it, and that eternity existed before creation. Based upon these reasons, Saadia arrives at the conclusion that the world had been created by a Supreme Being who is himself eternal. However, as soon as reason reaches out to that point it means that it agrees with the Torah, that is, with Revelation. Once God is recognized as Creator, He must necessarily be taken as one; for two or more gods could not have made a world that was the product of one creative Will.

While discussing the unity of God, Saadia takes a strong hand against the Christian doctrine of the Trinity. He also, in the course of argument about the existence of God and of the world, explicitly refutes twelve specific theories about the origin of the world put forth by Arab philosophers.

When man recognizes God as the Creator of the world, then his heart fills with a sense of sublimity and gratefulness that gives direction to his life. One sees himself as part of a whole which had been created with and for a purpose; not at random, but in accordance with a plan conceived and elaborated in advance; not a particle tossed around aimlessly by the storms of fate. This Creator then is the Great King and Master of the world to whom man is fully responsible for his actions. This is the meaning of the phrase "walking with God," a phrase that truly characterizes the saintly in Israel during all the centuries. Thereby man is able to attain true happiness, the pinnacle of ethical perfection. The same aim should inspire the true philosopher, that is, the one who seeks to show man the way to an ideal life.

In Saadia's judgment, people are gravely mistaken in thinking that belief and reason are facing each other as opposites. Both are different expressions of truth. How do we reach truth? There are four main sources, according to Saadia: (a) sense perceptions; (b) judgments; (c) logical inference; (d) tradition transmitted from past generations. Of course, such traditions, in order to be deserving of our trust, must have been preserved with the utmost care. As a matter of fact, the experiences of others are as vital to us as are our own. Were we to reject all the experiences of past generations and rely only on our own experience, our knowledge would be poor indeed. Faith is not only related to religious experience but to all phenomena of life. We must rely on others in many things, for without such reliance life would be impossible. Israel's Torah and the theophany on Sinai were facts of life, events that occurred before the eyes of an entire people. Judaism therefore stands squarely upon the experience of Israel. The Law as given by Moses and the testimony of Israel's prophets guarantee its truth.

Saadia, while accepting every word of the Bible as divine, insisted that the truth of the Torah rests upon reason and, like Maimonides later, claimed that wherever the Bible seems to contradict reason it must be interpreted metaphorically (Emunoth we-DEot 2:44, Beliefs and Doctrines). In interpreting miracles he generally follows the Talmudic sages: "When God created the world he made an agreement [that at a particular time] the sea would divide, the fire not hurt, lions not harm, the fish not swallow persons singled out by God; and thus the whole order of things changes whenever He finds it necessary." (Genesis Rabba 5,4) The underlying idea is that miracles were foreordained by God's creative wisdom, and appear only to man as something extraordinary. The sages also decreed that miracles not be invoked as testimony in a legal controversy about the interpretation of the Torah (Babba Me'ziah 59b). The daily wonders of life were extolled by some above miracles. "The wonder of the support of a family in the midst of great distress is as great as the parting of the sea for Israel." (Pesahim 118a).

Saadia's fight against Hiwi Al-Balkhi is an interesting chapter in the story of his life. Hiwi, a Jew from the town of Balkh, Persia, wrote a book against the Bible, the first known work in Hebrew composed by a skeptic and heretic. In this book it is said Hiwi presented two hundred objections to and questions about the divine origin of the Bible. Only a few of his questions were preserved in quotations by other writers. Three examples: Why did God prefer to live among unclean mankind instead of living among the clean angels? Why did manna from heaven no longer descend in the desert of Sinai? Why did God require sacrifices and shewbread if He did not eat them? Hiwi also pointed to discrepancies and contradictions in the Bible, and inferred from all the divergence and questions a non-divine authorship of the Scriptures. The passing of the Israelites through the Red Sea Hiwi explained by the natural phenomenon of the ebb tide; Exodus 34:29, where we are told that Moses' face shone, he explained as referring to "the dryness of his skin" due to long fasting (ibn Ezra's commentary on that passage).

Saadia unleashed his full intellectual powers against this critic and skeptic. He analyzed Hiwi's every objection and tried to demonstrate Hiwi's ignorance of the true spirit of the Bible. Hiwi became anathema both to Rabbinical Jews and to Karaites. Abraham ibn Ezra even changed Hiwi Al-Balkhi's name whenever he used it; by transposing the letters, he called him Al-Kalbi—the dog-like.

As the Gaon of Sura, Saadia must have written many Responsa, but unhappily they were not preserved, excepting one which came down to us in its entirety. This Responsum is sufficient, however, as an illustration of his extensive Talmudic knowledge. Saadia shows himself to have been methodical in his treatment. His style is lucid, to the point, and highly concentrated. Referring first to the Biblical sources, he then cites the Talmud, and finally applies his own reason to bring forth his verdict.

Of Saadia's writings on Halakha (legal decisions), one commentator said: "As in his other writings, Saadia is fond of stating the number of possibilities which may arise in connection with a given subject. . . . His conclusions proceed from sound judgments and a sober spirit."[9]

Saadia's commentary on the Sefer Yetzirah was an attempt to explain a mystical book in the light of rational terms, especially by the system of Hebrew phonology in which he was a master. Although he regarded this mystical book as worthy of his study, he was far from a mystic himself. Perhaps this sort of distant sympathy to mysticism explains why, when he discussed the problem of creation in his *Beliefs and Doctrines,* he never mentioned any of the mystical theories of creation put forth in Sefer Yetzirah.

Saadia's contribution to religious philosophy was of inestimable value for Jews and non-Jews alike. His influence reached far and wide both into the Islamic and the Christian worlds. He wanted to clarify certain aspects of Judaism in the light of reason and place some philosophical ideas side by side with revelation. By employing this method he hoped to bring back the cultured doubters into the fold of Judaism. The very fact that a religious leader of his stature, an observant and God-fearing Talmudic scholar, endeavored to present the Scriptures from a philosophical point of view was significant. It opened new vistas and served as a starting point for a rationalistic interpretation of the Bible which was further developed by other thinkers.

Saadia died at the age of fifty of "black gall," which undermined his otherwise delicate health.

ESOTERIC, MYSTICAL, AND FANTASTIC WORKS

It is a remarkable fact that just as during the post-Biblical period there was a rich crop of apocalyptic books which remained outside the Hebrew Scriptures, so during the post-Talmudic period, at the time of the Geonim, there appeared many works of an esoteric

and mystical and fantastic character which were also placed outside the mainstream of Hebrew literature. Some of these books
were altogether lost to posterity and only their titles are known;
others came down to us in fragments. But there are several which
were published in the Middle Ages and later in their entirety. They
have been studied by both Jewish and non-Jewish scholars as
amazing productions of man's imagination and as works with an
influence upon the development of later and modern mystical
literature.

SEFER YETZIRAH
(Book of Formation)

Adolph Franck in *The Kabbalah* says the Sefer Yetzirah is
probably the oldest document in Hebrew mysticism. No one knows
exactly when this mysterious book was composed nor who the author was, though it has been ascribed to Abraham the Patriarch
and to Rabbi Akiba. Scholars now generally conclude that it was
written during the Geonic Period by someone who maintained ano-
nymity even in his own time.

Sefer Yetzirah came down to us in two versions: one, a thauma-
turgical work mentioned in the Talmud (tractate Sanhedrin 65b,
67b); the other devoted to speculations concerning God and the
angels. The Aristotelian Saadia, the Neoplatonist Solomon ibn
Gabirol, the Cabalists of France, and the mystics of Germany derived some of their doctrines from this remarkable book. It is variously regarded as pre-Christian, Essene, Mishnaic, Talmudic, and
Geonic. Scholars attribute some ideas of the book to Gnosticism
and to Egyptian and Greek sources. It is also the oldest known
Hebrew grammar, since the linguistic theories of the unknown author are an integral component of his cosmogony. It was first
printed in Mantua in 1562, and it contained two recensions in which
there were textual variations. It is noteworthy that in neither version of Sefer Yetzirah is the word "Israel" mentioned; also, God
is not mentioned as the God of Israel, but rather as the Creator
of the universe. The book was studied by Christian scholars since

the time of Johannes Reuchlin. Twenty commentaries were written on the work from the beginning of the 10th to the end of the 19th centuries.

Sefer Yetzirah is the earliest attempt by a Jewish mystic to explain the emergence of the world. It presents thirty-two "marvelous paths of wisdom" with and through which God brought the universe into being. These "paths" were the twenty-two letters of the Hebrew alphabet and the first ten numbers, "1" representing God, the first Sefirah or the very source of everything that exists. The other nine Sefirot are derivatives from 1, reflections in which the power of God is mirrored. The second Sefirah, the closest to God, is called "breath;" it contains the twenty-two letters of the alphabet, which by various combinations make up the "word" by which God ordered the world to become what it is. The third Sefirah is "water" and the fourth is "fire." The remaining six Sefirot represent the six sides of the world: east, west, north, south, height, depth.

The letters of the Hebrew alphabet are divided into three groups: three "mothers" (Matras Lectionis), seven "doubles" (letters having two pronunciations: a hard and a soft), and twelve "simples." This classification of the letters is perhaps the oldest, from before the time when Hebrew grammar became a subject for study. Sefer Yetzirah, however, uses this classification for another purpose, namely, for explaining certain phenomena. The numbers 3, 7, and 12 are given mystical connotations. A 3 represents the three-fold appearance of morality: a) the scale of merit, b) the scale of culpability, c) the law which decides between the two. The Seven Doubles represent "contraries:" good and evil, happiness and unhappiness, life and death, and others. The Twelve Simples represent the signs of the Zodiac, the twelve months of the year, and the principal parts of the human body. Thus numbers and letters actually govern the world. The Sefer Yetzirah purports to show man the road to God by revealing the secrets of the universe.

> God's substance is at the bottom of everything, and therefore all things bear His imprint and are symbols of His supreme intelligence and Wisdom.... There are ten Sefirot. Ten and not nine, ten and not eleven. Try to understand them in thy wisdom and thy intelligence. Constantly train on them thy researches, thy speculations, thy knowledge,

thy thought, and thy imagination. Rest all things on principle, and restore the Creator on His foundation.

The Ten Sefirot of the Cabala are mentioned in the book, though with an entirely different connotation; yet the Sefer Yetzirah must have had a great influence upon the development later of Cabala.

The knowledge of the twenty-two letters, according to the Sefer Yetzirah mystic, is very important in life. Man can perform great miracles by the knowledge of these letters, for "God drew them, hewed them, combined them, weighed them, interchanged them, and through them produced the whole creation and everything that is destined to come into being."

Instead of explaining the world as a creation "ex nihilo," out of nothing, the Sefer Yetzirah outlines a series of emanations. God is regarded as the first cause, but not as the immediate efficient cause, for between Him and the world stand the Sefirot.

The Jewish Encyclopedia gives a good summary evaluation of the importance of the Sefer Yetzirah:

> The history of the study of Sefer Yetzirah is one of the most interesting in the records of Jewish literature. With the exception of the Bible, scarcely any other book has been the subject of so much annotation. Aristotelians, Neoplatonists, Talmudists and Cabalists have used the book as a source, or at least thought they did. Two points must be taken in consideration in judging the importance of the work: the influence which it exerted on the development of Jewish philosophy, especially on its mystic side, and the reputation which it enjoyed for more than a thousand years in most Jewish circles.

HEKALOT RABBATI

This is a mystic book often attributed to Ishmael ben Elisha, the famous Tanna of the 1st and 2nd centuries, a colleague of Akiba. Modern scholars, however, have assigned it to the Geonic period. Hai Gaon stated in a Responsum that the author was one of the mystics known as "Yorede Merkabah" (Riders in the Heavenly Chariot), who claimed that by virtue of praying and fasting divine secrets of the other world were disclosed to them. "Hekalot" in Hebrew means "halls" and "Rabbati" means "large." This book is known to have existed in two versions, the second a smaller, abridged version of the original. The smaller version has been lost and the original has come down to us not in its entirety but in thirty fragments.

The Hekalot Rabbati tells about the chosen. Those who are chosen to enter the divine world, or worlds, concealed from ordinary people, see things that could never be seen with the eyes of flesh. A "Rider in the Heavenly Chariot" is endowed with such gifts as seeing through the souls of men, differentiating between good and evil. He is also armed with a miraculous power to protect himself against those who would hurt him, for anyone who would do something against him is certain to be severely punished. A "Rider" would not, or could not, associate with ordinary people.

When one is looking at the "Chariot," one trembles from fear and ecstasy. It is an awful sight. Not only humans are terrified by it, but even angels who see it more frequently go through a terrible time. This kind of fear, however, is much different than ordinary fear. In order to secure the beholder against such seizures, the book offers a number of incantations and formulas that could help the "Rider" along. By virtue of those incantations, the "Rider" could visit the "Divine Halls," numbering seven in all. In fact, a detailed description of each "Hall" is given. Not less than eight fiery angels are guarding each "Hall." The seventh "Hall" is, however, the most formidable, because it is guarded by angels with drawn swords, angels whose eyes emit fire.

To be privileged to enter those "Halls," one must prepare himself by a long process of gaining knowledge, of purifying the soul from all the dross of material existence, and by contemplation and prayer of raising himself above everything that man calls "life." Such a man, endowed with will power and helped by God, attains the highest wisdom and true happiness.

This esoteric book is said to have greatly influenced the early liturgical poets. Eleazar HaKalir, for instance, is believed to have been swayed by its mysteries, and traces of them are to be found in some of his poems

The first printed edition of the book appeard in Venice in the year 1601; it was reprinted in Cracow in 1648. The Venice edition is titled "Pirke Hekalot." There are also two later editions: one by Yellinek and the other by Werteimer, which contain some variations as compared to the earlier editions.

SHI'UR KOMAH

The Shi'ur Komah purports to give the "exact" measurements of Adam Kadmon (Primal Man) who, like the Logos of Philo, mediates between the mundane world and God. How were the detailed measurements of the Primal Man revealed? Metatron, the closest angel to God, revealed them to those worthy of that knowledge.

The idea of Primal Man in Shi'ur Komah has some analogous roots in the prophet Ezekiel's vision:

> Out of the midst came the likeness of four living creatures; they had the likeness of a man. And every one had four faces, and every one had four wings. And their feet were straight feet; and the sole of their feet was like the sole of a calf's foot; and they sparkled like the color of burnished brass. (Ez. 1:5-7)

The Shi'ur Komah author's imagination is clear in this brief excerpt from his description of Primal Man:

> The soles of his feet fill the entire world and their height is three myriad times 1,000 parasangs; the right foot is called parsimya atar ratatat and the left foot agtamon. The distance between the sole and the ankle is 1,000 myriads and 500 parasangs [ca. 1,500 miles].

The words "parsimya atar ratatat" and "agtamon" are not Hebrew, and their meaning is unknown.

The words Shi'ur Komah mean "the measurement of stature," and the entire book consists of measurements, such as those just quoted, applied to the hands, trunk, head of Primal Man. It is a true anthropomorphic representation of a demigod.

This esoteric book was written at least prior to the early 9th century, since it is mentioned by Bishop Agobard of Lyons (c.

920) and by the Karaite Solomon ben Yeruham (b. 886). Leopold Zunz and Heinrich Graetz assign the book definitely to the
Geonic period, but others (e.g., Gaster) think that it might have
been composed even as early as the 1st century. It shows traces
of Gnosticism. It is known that Sherira Gaon and Maimonides
studied it, the latter declaring it a forgery. It is printed as a part of
the mystic book Raziel.

OTHER MYSTICAL BOOKS

Other mystical books of the Geonic period are known to have
existed:

1. Alphabeth de Rabbi Akiba, a book that explains the mysteries of the Hebrew consonants, with which God was supposed to have created the world.
2. Gan Eden (Paradise), printed in different versions.
3. Gehinnom (Inferno).
4. Harba de-Moshe (The Sword of Moses), consisting of mystical names by means of which man may protect himself
   against enemies and sickness, and may even subjugate nature. It is a theurgic book, replete with incantations and
   talismans.
5. Raza Rabbah (Great Mystery).
6. Raziel, assigned to the 13th century, but containing much
   older parts. Raziel was supposed to be an angel who revealed the mysteries of heaven to man.

THE BOOK OF YOSIPPON

The Book of Yosippon is a popular history of the Jewish people
from the time of the destruction of Babylon (539 B.C.E.) to the
destruction of the second commonwealth of Judea (70 C.E.);
a few chapters are devoted to early Biblical history. It was widely
read during the Middle Ages and regarded as a valuable histori-

cal account. It fascinated its readers by its popular style and with
the hundreds of fantastic tales which the author related with zeal.
It is written in a pure Hebrew style, easily read and understood,
abounding in many highly poetic passages. Occasionally the author indulges in philosophical speculations, but in an easygoing
manner.

Modern scholars point out many errors and inconsistencies in
the Yosippon. Because the book went through numerous editions
it is likely that errors were multiplied as copyists attempted to
make it more intriguing with elaborations upon the fantastic tales.
It was also rendered into Arabic, Latin, French, Yiddish, and
other languages. Portions were also translated into English and
German. During the Middle Ages, Yosippon was read avidly by
the Jewish masses. In the somber ghettos of Europe and Asia and
Africa the glorious stories of ancient times, glistening like gems in
the dark, served to inspire a weary and persecuted people.

Who wrote the book, and when? No one knows. The book
claimed, in its text, to have been written by the famous 1st century Jewish historian Josephus Flavius and included sections
from Josephus' known works. For centuries this attribution was
accepted, and the book was often called The Smaller Josephus.
But no one today holds to a Josephus authorship, and Yosippon
is more likely to be referred to as The Pseudo-Josephus.

The Muslim writer, Ibn Hazin (d. 1063), owned a copy of the
Yosippon in Arabic, translated by a Yemenite Jew, so we can at
least conclude that the book was written no later than the end of
the Geonite period. In the Yosippon there is a brief history of
Hannibal and an account of the crowning of a Roman emperor.
The French historian, Basnage, in his *Histoire des Juifs* (1710),
maintained that this account referred to Otto the Great's corona-
tion in 962, thus dating Yosippon no earlier than the last part
of the 10th century. Leopold Zunz maintains that the author lived
not earlier than the middle of the 9th century. Tieber says it was
written in the 4th century. And, regardless of its authorship, medieval Jews placed its composition in the 1st century. No one knows.
We only know that it was a popular and influential book, loved
by the masses for centuries.

The first printed edition in Hebrew appeared in Mantua near the end of the 15th century. The first Yiddish translation was printed in Zurich in 1546.

ELDAD HA-DANI

One of the most fantastic figures to have visited Babylonia during the Geonic period, sometime during the 9th century, was Eldad ben Mahli Ha-Dani, a merchant and traveler, whose life and story became legendary. He called himself Ha-Dani because he claimed to have come from the tribe of Dan, which he said then inhabited an independent Jewish sovereign state in eastern Africa. Eldad's appearance in Babylonia, in Spain, in Kairwan revived the legend of the Ten Lost Tribes, for he brought with him reports and documents purporting to prove that these hidden Jews were living isolated from northern and eastern Mediterranean Judaism, but living in accordance with the Mosaic laws. These laws were introduced by Joshua ben Nun, Moses' successor (by Orthniel ben Kenaz, according to another version), but they did not correspond to the Talmudic ordinances; it was a "pure" Biblical Judaism still existing in the form of tribes living in Africa, Arabia, Armenia.

Eldad's story went as follows: The tribe of Dan emigrated to the land of gold, Havilah (Kush), shortly after the separation of Judah and Israel. The tribes of Naphtali, Gad, and Asher joined the Danites later. They have a king called Adiel ben Malkiel, a prince by the name of Elizaphan, of the house of Eliab, and a judge named Abdan ben Mishael, who has the power to inflict the four capital punishments prescribed in the law. The four tribes lead a nomadic life, and are continually at war with the five neighboring Ethiopian kings. Each tribe is in the field three months, and every warrior remains in the saddle without dismounting from one Sabbath to the next. They possess the entire Scriptures, but they do not read the Scroll of Esther (not having been included in the miraculous salvation mentioned in it) nor (tribe of Levi). The river Sambation encircles their land. It rolls sand and stones during the six working days and rests on the Lamentations (to avoid its disheartening influence). They have a

Talmud in pure Hebrew, but none of the Talmudic teachers is mentioned. Their ritual is introduced in the name of Joshua, who had received it from Moses, who in his turn had heard its contents from the Almighty. They speak only Hebrew.

On "the other side of the river of Kush" dwell the Bene Mosheh (tribe of Levi). The river Sambation encircles their land. It rolls sand and stones during the six working days and rests on the Sabbath. From the first moment of Sabbath to the list, fire surrounds the river, and during that time no human being can communicate with the Bene Mosheh from the borders of the river. The Bene Mosheh dwell in beautiful houses, and no unclean animal is found in their land. Their cattle and sheep as well as their fields bear twice a year. No child dies during the lifetime of its parents, who live to see a third and fourth generation. They do not close their houses at night, for there is no theft or wickedness among them. They speak Hebrew, and never swear by the name of God.

Eldad then told how he came to visit other Jewish tribes in the course of the journey which eventually brought him to Babylonia. When he last left the land on "the other side of the river of Kush," he traveled with a man of the tribe of Asher. A great storm wrecked the boat, but God prepared a plank for him and his companion, on which they floated until thrown ashore among a cannibal Ethiopian tribe called Romrom. The Asherite, who was fat, was immediately eaten, while Eldad was put into a pit to fatten. Soon afterwards, another tribe attacked the cannibals, and Eldad was taken prisoner. He remained in captivity four years. Then his captors brought him to the province of Azanian, where he was ransomed by a Jewish merchant for thirty-two pieces of gold. Eldad continued his journey, and fell in with the tribe of Issachar, dwelling among high mountains near Media and Persia, their land extending ten days' journey on every side. They are at peace with all, Eldad said, and their energy is devoted to the study of the law; their only weapon is the knife for slaughtering animals. Their judge and prince is called Nahshon, and they use the four methods of capital punishment.

The tribe of Zebulon occupies the land extending from the province of Armenia to the river Euphrates. Behind the mountains of Paran, the tribe of Reuben faces them. Peace reigns between these two tribes; they war as allies and divide the spoils. They possess the Bible, the Mishnah, the Talmud, and the Haggadah. The tribe of Ephraim and half of Manasseh dwell in the southern mountains of Arabia, and are very warlike. The tribe of Simeon and the other half of Manasseh are in the land of the Chazars. They take tribute from twenty-eight kingdoms, and many Muslims are subject to them.[10]

Eldad's account spread like wildfire and was told and retold from community to community. Even the Christians listened with interest—and with consternation; for they believed that no Jews would ever be restored as a free people until they recognized Jesus as the Messiah. A book incorporating Eldad's tale was published and has come down to us in at least eight versions.

Hasdai ibn Shaprut, the leader of Spanish Jewry, and Talmudic authorities such as Rashi and others accepted Eldad's story as true. When the Gaon of Sura, Zemah ben Hayyim, was asked about Eldad, he replied favorably about Eldad's character and personality. Record has come down to us of only two Jewish leaders in the Middle Ages who doubted Eldad's account: Meir of Rothenburg and Ibn Ezra. Some modern scholars mark off Eldad as simply a charlatan; others suggest that he was a Karaite missionary intending to discredit the Talmud.

THE RIVER SAMBATION

The river Sambation, which Eldad mentioned, is found in the old Midrashic literature, but in connection with the Assyrians, who exiled the inhabitants of the Kingdom of Israel in the 7th century B.C.E. Josephus was the first one to place it somewhere in Syria. His account reads as follows:

> When Titus marched from Berytus [Beirut] to the other Syrian cities, he saw a river of such a nature as deserves to be recorded in history, it runs in the middle between Arcea, belonging to Agrippa's kingdom, and Raphanea. It has something very peculiar in it: for when it runs, its current is strong and has plenty of water; after which its

springs fail for six days together and leave its channel
dry,...after which days it runs on the seventh day as it did
before;...it hath also been observed to keep its order per-
petually and exactly; whence it is that they call it the Sab-
batic river (Sabbation or Sambation)—that name being
taken from the sacred seventh day among the Jews.[11]

Pliny, in his Historia Naturalis (31:2), mentions a river that runs
six days and stops on the seventh day.

According to another legend, Alexander of Macedon discovered
a similar river in Egypt. It flowed with water for three days and
with sand for three days. Also, Arab writers reported a river in
Egypt which rests on Saturday.

As late as the 17th century, the legend still prevailed. Gershon
b. Eliezer ha-Levi wrote about a river in India that casts stones
six days and rests on the seventh day.

LAND OF THE CHAZARS

During the Geonic period, from 740 to 969 c.e., there flourished
in southern Russia, between the Volga and Don, up to the shores
of the Black and Caspian Seas, the Kingdom of the Chazars,
which was ruled by a long line of kings who accepted Judaism.

The first king, Bulan by name, who ruled that country in the middle of the 8th century (A. Harkavy dates it at 620 c.e.), decided
to find a new faith for his people. After he consulted a Christian
scholar, a Muslim scholar, a Jewish scholar, and a philosopher, he
selected Judaism. He and his whole family accepted the Jewish faith.
His people, however, were not converted. Nevertheless, King Bulan
and his successors provided an enlightened regime at a time when
enlightenment did not reign in western Europe. In Chazaria, the Supreme Court was composed of two Jews, two Christians, two Muslims,
and one neutral who represented the Russians and Bulgars of the
country. The royal family founded synagogues and schools where
the Bible and the Talmud were studied by those who converted to
Judiaism. Enjoying a flourishing trade and religious and intellectual
freedom. Chazaria served as a refuge for people fleeing persecutions.

Whether the Jews in Babylonia knew of Chazaria is not known. The country is not mentioned in any of the Responsa which have survived, nor in any other work of the Geonic period we have today. We do know that the last king of Chazaria, Joseph, and the great Jewish statesman of Spain, Ibn Shaprut, exchanged correspondence in the early 960s. Furthermore, at one time Chazaria was so powerful that both Persia and Byzantium entered into close commercial and political relations with the Chazars.

In 969, Sviatoslav, the duke of Kiev, conquered Chazaria and razed their capital. Later the rise and fall of the land of the Chazars inspired the great Jewish poet, Judah Halevi, to compose his work, "Ha-Kuzari," through which the Chazars left their imprint in Hebrew literature.

VOCALIZATION AND ACCENTUATION

Two important innovations that exerted a great influence upon the development of both Hebrew grammar and Biblical exegesis are ascribed to the Geonic period. One was the introduction of vowel points and the other the placing of accents on each word in the Hebrew Scriptures. These arrangements, invented and introduced around the 8th century, are being used today.

Until about the 7th century, Hebrew, like most of the Semitic languages, was a consonantal language. It was lacking graphical vowel signs, excepting several consonants which were occasionally employed as vowels. Many Hebrew words might be read differently, and one could hardly distinguish a word unless he paid close attention to the context. Thus, to be able to read correctly, one had constantly to guard against pitfalls. The introduction of vowel points into Biblical Hebrew was, therefore, of crucial importance.

The second innovation was known as accentuation. It had three purposes: a) Punctuation: Since there were no marks of interpunction in the Scriptures, the accents served as such marks; they divided or combined words. b) Interpretation or Meaning: The division or combination or words served also as a logical interpretation of the text. c) Memory: Since every word in the Bible received a special tone, passages could be chanted in accordance with a simple melody; the music helped the reader to remember entire parts.

This combination of vowel points and accentuation, in general use today, is known as the Tiberian Systems of Vocalization and Accentuation, so known because the arrangements were invented and introduced into the text in Tiberias, Palestine, which was at the time one of the great centers of learning. The people who dedicated themselves to this work were called Baale Ha-Masorah, Masters of the Masorah (tradition), and Baale Hanikud, or Nakdonim (punctuators). Today we use the general name Masoretes. The Masoretes of the 7th and 8th centuries were the guardians of the Masorah, that is, of the old traditions as to the integrity of the Scriptural texts. Their marginal notes as to the spelling of words, missing or superfluous letters, and other peculiarities of the texts have come down to us in a gigantic critical work completed during many centuries: the Masorah Magna (large), and an abbreviated version, Masorah Parva (small).

Aaron ben Moshe ben Asher, from Tiberias, was a scion of a family of Masoretes—six generations back to Asher the Elder who lived in the middle of the 8th century. Aaron devoted his life to bring forth a corrected copy of the Bible. In the year 916, he finished his codex of the Hebrew Scriptures, completely vowel pointed and accented. His codex was generally accepted by all scribes (This codex copy is now in Jerusalem). Aaron is regarded as one of the last punctuators and accentuators. During the Middle Ages, many more punctuators worked in this same field, but primarily as grammarians and scribes, and some made slight changes.

Until the year 1839, the Tiberian Systems were the only ones known. In that year, however, old manuscripts were discovered in the Cremea representing another system. This is the so-called Babylonian System of both vowel points and accents, which was used in Babylonia. In 1894, a third system, probably the oldest of the three, was discovered in Syria and Egypt; it is called now the Palestinian System. Both of these systems were superlinear; that is, the vowel points and the accents were generally placed above the words, instead of under the words as was usually the case in the Tiberian Systems.

Until the beginning of the 16th century, people believed that the vowel points and accents were very old indeed. But Elijah Levita (1468-1549) was the first, in a major work, to point out their post-Talmudic origin. His book, Masoret Ha-Masoret, published in Venice in 1538, was translated into Latin by his student, S. Munster. Levita's theory, although not altogether new, provoked a great controversy among both the Jews and the Christians. Many felt that some vowel point and accentuation system was at least as old as the 5th century B.C.E. and was used or introduced during the period of Ezra. The Masoretes insisted that they were maintaining, without change, a system from pre-Talmudic times. Many followed Levita's lead and believed the vowel point and accentuation arrangements to be of more recent origin. The debate continues today and we are still not certain of any of the systems' beginnings.

III

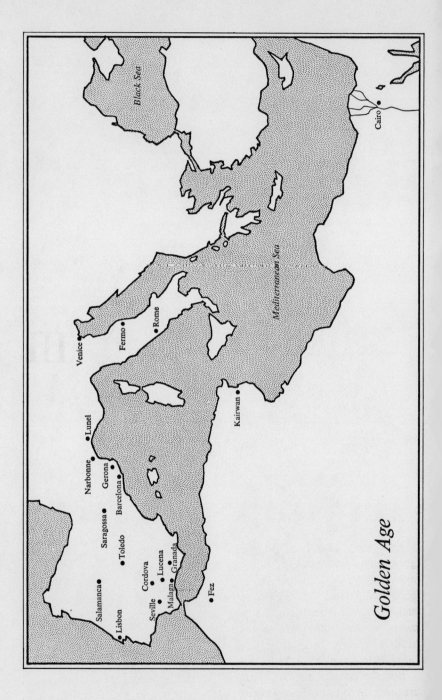

Golden Age

ח | 8

THE GOLDEN AGE

The servant of God does not withdraw himself from
secular contact lest he be a burden to the world and the
world to him; he does not hate life . . . . On the contrary,
he loves this world and a long life.

Judah Halevi (12th century)

FROM BABYLONIA TO SPAIN

Less than one hundred years after the death of Saadia, the
great Babylonian center, which had been leading world Jewry for
over 700 years, reached its end (1038 C.E.). An observer with a
penetrating and historically oriented eye might have early de-
tected signs of decay in the Babylonian academies. Jealousies between leaders, the Karaitic rift, rivalry between the two principal
academies were being intensified. Indeed, the sun was fast setting
on the great center of the East.

But fortunately for Judaism, while the shadows of night were
creeping in on the East, a new light emerged in the far West—in

231

southern Spain, which was then, like the East, under Arab domination. Small and insignificant at first, the Jewish communities in Spain were slowly but surely growing into independent centers of learning. What they needed in order to be able to take over the cultural hegemony from Babylonia were a few leading spirits, men of insight and influence. Such men Providence had apparently prepared for Spanish Jewry: For example, the leader with whom the Golden Age of Hebrew Literature actually began, Hasdai ibn Shaprut, diplomat and financial adviser to Calif Abd al-Rahman, ruler of Andalusia.

The Hebrew Golden Age, or as some designate it, the Hispano-Jewish epoch, lasted, roughly speaking, from about the middle of the 10th century to the end of the 15th, a period of approximately 550 years, during which Spanish Jewry succeeded in creating a rich and meaningful literature, which left its imprint far and wide in both Jewish and general history.

Spanish Jewry's creativeness assumed three different forms, in each of which it attained a high level of spiritual development: poetry, philosophy, Biblical exegesis and Hebrew philology.

The neo-Hebraic poetry born under the sunny skies of southern Spain was altogether different in comparison with the heretofore popular liturgical or synagogal poetry created in Palestine and Babylonia. It was no more the Piyyut (prayer-poem) of previous generations: it was now free, welling with life, ever singing—whether in grief or in joy—instead of lamenting, attuned to the heart of the individual poet instead of the penitent masses.

Religious Jewish philosophy, the second child of the Golden Age, although resembling in some respects the philosophy of Saadia Gaon, was more daring, more profound, and all-inclusive. This process of re-thinking the tenets of Judaism in the light of a more advanced age reached its zenith in the work of Maimonides. Problems that had never been touched by God-fearing Jews were brought forth. New vistas were opened and new answers were given. Gabirol, Halevi, Maimonides—thinkers of great power—stood in the forefont of life and what they had to say reverberated through the centuries.

Simultaneously with the brilliant development of Hebrew poetry, Hebrew philology and Biblical exegesis were advanced by such great researchers as Judah ibn Daud Hayyuj and Jonah ibn

Janah. The ancient Hebrew language, neglected during many centuries, came into its own. Poets and grammarians worked hand in hand to perfect the instrument of man's creativeness—language. No small wonder that the work of those early grammarians even today dominates the study of Hebrew, and the rules laid down by them have never been invalidated.

This spiritual renaissance was a result of two main factors: the re-awakening of interest in classical Greek philosophy and the meeting of two cultures: Judaism and Islam. The new social, cultural, and political conditions in the Arab world were such that both Arabs and Jews were impelled to re-think their past in the light of the new changes. Faith and reason seemed to clash, and either a reconciliation between religion and philosophy was necessary or faith would be submerged in a sea of doubt and skepticism. It was Islam versus Aristotelianism, the Koran versus reason, Judaism versus the Greeks, Moses versus Aristotle. In both Islam and Judaism, reconciliation turned out to rule. Thus intellectuals among the Jews and the Muslims met upon the same spiritual plane.

Precisely when Christian Europe was enveloped in darkness, and the light of reason was flickering, science, philosophy and literature in the Arab world blossomed forth as never before. Working hand in hand with learned Syrians and Arabs, the Jews became transmitters of culture, the apostles of knowledge; they served also as a connecting link between the Biblical world outlook and the philosophical thought systems of classical Greece, as re-interpreted by the Arab thinkers.

For years and years, prior to the Muslim conquest of Spain in the 8th century, Jewish communities on the Iberian peninsula had suffered persecutions ranging from restrictions to confiscation of property to forced baptism. When the Moors invaded and conquered southern Spain, the oppressed Jews joined the side of the invaders. Under the reign of Abd al-Rahman (912-961) and his son al-Hakim, southern Spain became an asylum for oppressed Jews from the north. Jewish communities grew rapidly in such cities as Cordova, Malaga, Seville, Toledo, Saragossa, and Lucena. Jews prospered by their far-flung commercial connections in remote regions of the then known world. Jewish scholars and poets, diplomats and financiers, merchants and physicians of great repute appeared all over the Arab world. Excepting short periods during which a fanatical wave was sweeping over some Arab lands, Arab rulers were more tolerant than the Christians toward the Jews. This, apart from all other factors, contributed greatly toward the spread of culture generally and toward the development of the religious Jewish philosophy of the Middle Ages in particular.

Out of the crucible of peoples in the Arab world, out of the clash of ideas and views, emerged that brilliant religious philosophy which reached its zenith in Maimonides and that brilliant scientific development—all of which contributed so significantly to the growth of Western thought.

Abraham ibn Daud Halevi, in his Sefer HaKabalah (Book of Tradition), tells the following story about the beginning of Spanish Jewry. Sometime about the middle of the 10th century, four scholars from Babylonia embarked on a ship sailing west, their object being to collect money for the Babylonian academies, which were then in dire straits. Captured by Moorish sea pirates, they were held for ransom. One of the four was Moses ben Enoch, an eminent Talmudic scholar, who was ransomed by the Jews of Cordova, although they at first did not know who he was. Out of humility, he did not disclose his identity. Later, there arose a legal question in the local school which could not be satisfactorily answered by the regular teacher or rabbi. In such a case the community usually turned to the Babylonian authorities for a decision. This time, however, there was no need to do so, for Rabbi Moses disentangled the problem and resolved it on the spot. The people who listened to him immediately recognized the humble rabbi as an authority in the Law. Hasdai ibn Shaprut, the leader of the Jewish communities in Andalusia, invited him to become the religious leader of Cordova. He also assisted him financially to establish a Talmudic academy in the city. Thus, according to this story, the first Torah center in Spain came into being.

The other three scholars, we are told, were also ransomed. One of them, Shemariah ben Elhanan, settled in Cairo. Another, Hushiel by name, was brought to Kairwan, North Africa, and the last one reached Narbonne. Each of them established an academy of his own.

It is interesting to note that not one of the four Talmudic scholars, when freed, returned to Babylonia. Taken symbolically, the story briefly and pointedly pictures the Golden Age of Hebrew Literature: the decline of the Babylonian center, the vigorous growth of religion and knowledge in Spain, and the spread of Talmudic centers around the Mediterranean.

RENAISSANCE BEGINNINGS

Hasdai ibn Shaprut (c. 915 to 970)

Under the intellectual leadership of Hasdai ibn Shaprut, Jewish scholarship flourished in Cordova, Spain. Under his inspiration and financial support, neo-Hebraic poetry was born. His role at the beginning of the Golden Age of Hebrew Literature was major. He is considered the first leader of Spanish Jewry.

The son of a wealthy Jew of Jaen, Hasdai was well trained in the sciences of his day. For example, he translated Dioscorides' *Plant Lore*, a book that served as a chief botanical textbook for medieval Europe. By profession Hasdai was a physician; his reputation as a doctor led to his appointment as personal physician to Calif Abd al-Rahman.

Hasdai showed himself to be not only a physician but also a clever diplomat, a practical statesman, and a good and wise friend. Within time he was second only to the calif, practically the vizier. Hasdai was also the confidant of Abd al-Rahman's son, Al-Hakin. He conducted the foreign affairs, controlled the customs and ship dues, and concluded trade treaties with many countries. Hasdai received the delegations that came to Cordova. As a master of Hebrew, Arabic, and Latin he was in a position to personally negotiate with both Christian and Islamic dignitaries. Among the Arab diplomats it was rare to find one who knew Latin, the diplomatic language at that time. Johannes of Gortiz, the envoy of the German emperor Otto I, met Hasdai on a visit to Cordova and characterized him as follows: "I have never seen a man of such subtle intellect as the Jew Hasdai." The queen of Navarre described Hasdai as the calif's faithful counselor; she accepted his advice to submit to the calif a proposal of a treaty of peace. A Jewish poet of Hasdai's time described him as a man who won his high position "by the charm of his words, the strength of his wisdom, the force of his cunning, and his thousand tricks."

Hasdai was a proud Jewish prince who dreamed of the Messianic redemption of his people, as his letter to King Joseph of the Chazars testifies [supra, "Land of the Chazars," p. 224]. The vision of a Jewish kingdom between the Volga and the Don touched the most sensitive fibers of his heart. Hasdai's first attempt to contact the land of the Chazars was thwarted by the political conditions prevailing at the time in Christian Europe and in the Asiatic countries; travel from country to country was complicated, and Hasdai's personal envoy, Isaac ben Nathan, whom he sent with gifts to King Joseph, had to return to Cordova without ever reaching Chazaria.[1] Hasdai persisted; another letter was sent, and after a long delay a reply was received. Both letters are regarded as significant historial documents.

Ibn Shaprut stands out in Jewish history as an exalted prince, a patron of Torah and literature and science, a personality who opened a new epoch in the history of a people. A great age breeds great men but the reverse is also true. Perhaps it is mutual, a product of both time and leadership. We know that at the time of Hasdai, the Jewish community of Cordova came to the forefront. Although not a large community, the Jewish population was already conspicuous. One of the gates of the beautiful city was known as "The Jew's Gate." Cordova attracted many scholars who came from as far as Egypt. Soon Cordova became a world center for Jewish learning. To be sure, Hasdai was not the only patron of literature in Muslim Spain, but he was certainly one of the chief supporters. No small wonder that his name became a symbol for many generations.

Hasdai, as patron, was midwife to the birth of neo-Hebraic poetry. This name distinguishes it from the old liturgical poetry which served mainly as a medium of expression for penitents. The prayer-like idiom was replaced by a lighter tone and the range of subjects widened enormously. Born in Andalusia, it reflected the sunny landscape of southern Spain, and written in Arabic metre, it assumed a dancing pace and a singing rhythm.

But the adopted metric forms which the Hebrew poets transplanted from Arabic into Hebrew did not represent the only changes. The Hebrew language itself was enriched and greatly improved by the searching studies of the poets, who were also grammarians and rhetoricians of the first order. In this field two outstanding personalities distinguished themselves: Menahem ben Saruk and Dunash ben Labrat.

Menahem ben Saruk (10th century)

A native of Tortosa, Spain, Menahem ben Saruk moved to Cordova at an early age. Hasdai's father, Isaac, extended a helping hand to a poor young man. When Isaac died, Menahem wrote a touching eulogy which was widely acclaimed. He returned to Tortosa, but Isaac's son soon persuaded him to come back to Cordova as his private secretary. It was in this role that Menahem later wrote the historic letter which Hasdai sent to the king of Chazaria. Hasdai was also concerned to encourage and support Menahem in work on his magnum opus. This Menahem completed in 955: the Mahberet, a dictionary of the Hebrew language and a collection of grammatical rules, the first lexical treatment of the Biblical vocabulary. Menahem's work was long considered definitive. The great 11th century commentator, Rashi, regarded Menahem as the master grammarian.

However, Menahem did not fare as well with his contemporaries. Hasdai at this time supported a second protége, Dunash ben Labrat, and in response to Mahberet, Dunash composed a special treatise in verse attacking Menahem and his work.

Dunash ben Labrat (10th century)

Dunash's family came originally from Bagdad, but Dunash was born in Fez, North Africa. As a young man he came to Sura in Babylonia where he enrolled as a student of Saadia Gaon. There he started to write Hebrew poetry, employing for the first time Arabic metric forms. When he showed Saadia his verses, the latter is said to have exclaimed: "Such a thing has hitherto been unknown in Israel." From that time on, Arabic metre was adopted in Hebrew poetry. All the great poets of the Golden Age followed in his footsteps. His pupil Jehudi ben Sheshet characterized Dunash in the following words: "He created a new foundation for our poetry, such as did not exist in the days of our fathers." After Saadia's death (942), Dunash returned to Fez and then went to Cordova.

In Spain he met some scholars for whom he did not have much admiration. The poverty-stricken Menahem was one of them. Menahem in turn paid Dunash in the same coin; he dared criticize Saadia, who was adored by Dunash, for he prided himself not only on his knowledge of Hebrew grammar and his poetic talent, but also on his Babylonian study under Saadia. There were undoubtedly simply intellectual differences between Menahem and Dunash. There may also have been professional jealousies. Furthermore, the complications of Saadia's tutelage and of Menahem's and Dunash's having the same patron may have contributed to the problem. We cannot know the details. In any case, the Menahem-Dunash differences grew into a public controversy and a personal feud, with enmity on both sides. Hasdai took sides and withdrew his support from Menahem. In one sense, this might be seen as no catastrophe for Menahem, inasmuch as Hasdai had in the past often been sparing in his support; but Menahem did rely upon the support he got from Hasdai. He soon found himself destitute, and sent a heart-rending letter of appeal to his former patron. Hasdai replied laconically: "If you are guilty, the suffering I caused you has led you to repentance; if you are innocent, the undeserved suffering I brought upon you has assured you eternal bliss in the life to come."

In historical perspective, the Menahem-Dunash controversy did have at least one beneficial outcome. The controversy drew into itself many scholars from Cordova and other cities, as a result of which a deeper interest in Hebrew was awakened and a livelier exchange between scholars established: a renaissance flowered.

Work in Hebrew grammar and Biblical exegesis was zealously continued, for example, by Judah ibn Daud Hayyuj (born c. 950), a disciple of Menahem and one of the founders of Hebrew philology. Hayyuj applied the methods of the Arabic grammarians to Hebrew and succeeded in opening new understandings of the language's origin and development. He broke new ground with his works on punctuation, on verbs containing weak letters, and on verbs containing double letters.

Greater than Hayyuj was his disciple, Jonah ibn Janah (born c. 985), a prominent physician by profession. His chief work was Kitab al-Tankih (Book of Minute Research), a complete exposition of Hebrew grammar and vocabulary, and a treasure for Biblical exegesis, rhetoric, syntax, and hermeneutics.

A long line of grammarians and exegetes followed these two masters. For example, Isaac ibn Gikatilla, Moses ibn Gikatilla, Judah ibn Bal'am, Isaac ibn Yashush, David ben Hagar, Abraham ibn Ezra, the Kimhi family—Joseph, Moses, and David. The latter was known as Redak, abbreviated from Rabbi David Kimhi; he authored a Bible dictionary, a Hebrew grammar, and a very popular Bible commentary.

Spanish Jewry did not neglect the Talmudic studies. To the participants in this new era, the heritage of the old was as dear as the new. Thus, in Cordova, Granada, Lucena, Saragossa, great academies grew and students from Spain and other countries flocked to hear the Torah teachers.

SAMUEL IBN NAGDELA
(992-1055)

Samuel ibn Nagdela, also known as Samuel Ha-Naggid (prince), was a Talmudist, poet, linguist, statesman, one of the greatest leaders produced by Spanish Jewry, second after Hasdai ibn Shaprut. Born in Cordova, the Andalusian center of learning, his father gave him the best education possible at that time. His teachers were the best: Judah Hayyuj for Bible and grammar, Rabbi Enoch for Talmud, non-Jewish masters for Arabic, Latin, and Berber. His career and his future was assured.

But civil war came to Cordova and persecution of the Jews followed; thousands of Jews fled the city. Samuel went to Malaga;

he was twenty years old. Having lost most of his possessions, he opened a small store from which he derived a scanty livelihood; he devoted his free time to the study of the Talmud. A quirk of fate brought Samuel into the world of diplomacy and government.

Apart from his mastery of the Arabic language, spoken and written, Samuel was also a very talented calligrapher. A servant girl of the vizier, Abu al-Kasim ibn al-Arif, patronized Samuel's store; through her he obtained report-writing jobs which he did during off hours. These reports came to the attention of al-Kasim, who was impressed with their style and calligraphy. Samuel was summoned to the vizier and became his private secretary. From that time on, Samuel also became al-Kasim's counselor, because he did nothing without Samuel's advice. In 1027, the vizier fell ill, and before he died he confessed to King Habus that all his good fortune had been, for many years, due to Samuel. Thereupon the king appointed Samuel katib, minister of state for Granada.

Habus did not regret this appointment, for Samuel excelled in all his duties. Patient, cool-headed, courteous, and honest, he was admired and respected by all, including his initial detractors who had resented having a Jewish superior. An interesting story is told of Samuel. A fanatical Arab, a merchant, once insulted him in the presence of the calif. Samuel had taken it in good stead but Habus, incensed at the merchant's arrogance, ordered his friend to punish the offender by cutting out his tongue. Samuel tacitly accepted the harsh order, saying nothing. Later, the calif noticed that the arrogant Arab still spoke, and he asked for the reason. Samuel answered, "I indeed have torn out his *angry* tongue, and given him a *kind* one instead." The wise diplomat turned an enemy into a friend.

Samuel ibn Nagdela, despite his great political responsibilities, served as chief rabbi of Granada and as the acknowledged leader of the Jewish communities in that country. He was a supporter of scholars and students, spending large sums for books which he presented to both, especially to the poor among them who could not afford such things. He was also in close contact with the leaders of Israel in other lands, corresponding with them upon issues important to Judaism.

"In Samuel's time," wrote Moses ibn Ezra (1070-1139), the great poet, "the kingdom of science was raised from its lowliness, and the star of knowledge once more shone forth. God gave unto him a great mind which reached to the spheres and touched the heavens, so that he might love knowledge and those that pursued it, and he might glorify religion and her followers."

A contemporary Arabic poet sang Samuel's praises in verse:

> If man could tell the true and false
> and could the difference understand,
> instead of kissing Mecca's stone,
> they would, O Samuel, kiss thy hand.

Samuel's own poetic compositions are numerous; though distinguished by their exaltation, they did not reach the high level of creativity found, for instance, in Ibn Gabirol's poetry. Of Samuel's many Responsa, only two are extant. We do have his Mebo ha-Talmud, An Introduction to the Talmud. It contains two parts: a list of scholars from the Great Assembly down to the time of Enoch, Samuel's teacher, and methodological rules for the study of the Talmud. This work was translated into Latin and published at Leyden in 1633. Samuel also wrote Ben Mishle (Son of Proverbs or New Proverbs), Ben T'hilim (New Psalms), and Ben Kohelet (New Ecclesiastes), all somewhat in imitation of the three Biblical books. Ben Kohelet, which was lost, contained Samuel's philosophical meditations. The former, from which the following are taken, contained his aphorisms and proverbs.

> He who has toiled and bought for himself books
> But his heart is empty of what they contain—
> Is like a lame man, who engraved on a wall
> The figure of a foot, and tried in vain to stand!
>
> *
>
> Turn from one who enjoins the doing
> of right, but himself is a man of wrong!
> How shall he heal the malady
> Who himself suffers from its pain?
>
> *

The wise of heart forsakes the ease of pleasure,
In reading books he finds tranquillity;
All men have faults, thine eyes can see them,
The wise heart's failing is—forgetfulness?

*

When men commend thee with their lips,
Unto their words apply thine heart;
And if they laud for parts not thine,
Strive hard to justify their praise!

*

The wise is beloved of all
And loveth all whom he meeteth;
The fool is hated of all,
And hated by all who may see him;
Therefore keep watch and ward,
To be a brother of wisdom,
And keep far thy name from the name
Of all the brothers of folly.

*

Woe to the man who stands awake,
Yet seeth not his path;
Happier he who lies asleep,
And has eyes within his heart!

*

When thou art poor, ride on the back of a lion,
To seek thy sustenance, and beg of none!
Nor covet other's wealth, for in such envy
Thine own heart thou painest more than another's.[2]

ISAAC ALFASI
(1013-1103)

The first Talmudic codifier was Isaac Alfasi, who was recognized by later generations as one of the three greatest legal authorities, the other two being Maimonides and Asher ben Yehiel (known as

"Rosh"). Alfasi was born in a village near Fez, North Africa, in the year 1013. He was a disciple of Rabbi Hananel and Rabbi Nissim.

He won his position as an authority in the Law by his work known as Halakot, the first Talmudic code. Alfasi separated what he considered the essential from the nonessential Talmudic material. He eliminated the lengthy argumentations which led up to the legal decisions in the Talmud, then he restated these legal decisions clearly and concisely. He also left out the Aggadic portions: proverbs, stories, and such. It was the legal decisions which comprised his Talmudic text. However, he did not cover all the Talmudic laws, but only those relating to life outside the Holy Land; laws pertaining to Palestine were omitted. Alfasi's codification nevertheless deeply impressed the scholars of his day with its finality and exactness and was of vital importance to all of Judaism.

Ever since the closing of the Talmud, attempts had been made to give clarity and finality to the Talmudic legal decisions. For example, Simon Kahira, Yehudai Gaon, Ahai of Shabha tried their hands at this task, but none succeeded in bringing it to completion. Maimonides, in the introduction to his commentary on the Mishnah, evaluates Alfasi and his work:

> The Halakot of our great teacher, Rabbenu Isaac of blessed memory, have superseded all their predecessors, because there is included therein everything useful for the understanding of the decisions and laws at present in force; that is, in the time of the exile. The author clearly demonstrates the errors of those before him when his opinion deviates from theirs, and with the exception of a few Halakot whose number at the very utmost does not amount to ten, his decisions are unassailable.

Alfasi's code was studied with the same zeal and seriousness as the Talmud, and commentaries were written on it.

In addition to his major work, we have extant a number of Alfasi's Responsa; the collection touches upon 320 civil questions.

At the age of seventy-five, Alfasi was forced under fear of death to flee from Africa, someone having slandered him as being in-

volved in a political affair, a serious charge at that time under
Muslim rule. Without means, and barefooted, he sought refuge in
Cordova.

Alfasi was received by the Jews of Cordova with open arms.
They honored him as a great scholar and saintly man. But he
could not long remain in Cordova. Two other scholars, Isaac
Albalia and Isaac ibn Ghayyut, envying his position, criticized his
code severely. They attacked him for his independence in the
treatment of the Talmud and for taking upon himself to render
final verdicts in legal questions. As a result, Alfasi left Cordova
and settled in Lucena, where he established a great Talmudic
academy.

The historian Heinrich Graetz tells this story:

> Upon his death bed, Isaac Albalia charged his seventeen-
> year-old son, Baruch, who was weeping bitterly at the
> destitution that awaited him after his father's demise, to re-
> pair to Alfasi in Lucena, and to tell his enemy that, at the
> brink of the grave, he forgave him all that he had ever said
> or written against him, in the expectation that he would be
> forgiven in return, and in the hope that Alfasi would deal
> kindly with his enemy's son. Baruch carried out his father's
> wish. Alfasi embraced his enemy's son with tears in his eyes,
> promised to be a father to him, and kept his promise.

Graetz adds: "One does not know whom to admire most, the one
who reposed the greatest confidence in his enemy's generosity or
the one who did not disappoint that confidence. Baruch ibn Albalia
became one of Alfasi's most distinguished disciples."[3]

Another of Alfasi's disciples, Joseph ibn Migash, was the teacher
of Maimonides. He succeeded Alfasi as head of the academy at
Lucena.

On a tombstone found at Lucena, the following inscription was
engraved:

> It was for thee the mountains shook
> on the day of Sinai;
> for the angels of God approached thee
> and wrote the Torah on the tablets of your heart;
> they set the finest of its crowns upon thy head.

SOLOMON IBN GABIROL
(1021-1058)

Solomon ibn Gabirol was born in Cordova, but shortly afterwards, due to Berber disturbances, the family fled to Malaga. There Solomon's parents soon died, leaving him a sickly orphan. The plight of the child was called to the attention of the Jewish nobleman, Jekuthiel ibn Hasan, Saragossa statesman and scientist. Jekuthiel took him under his protection and Solomon grew up under his guidance, until 1039, when Jekuthiel was involved in a palace revolt and was slain.

Solomon lamented his erstwhile benefactor in a long poem of 200 verses, in which he portrayed Jekuthiel as a man

> Whose mouth was a fountain of salvation,
> whose heart was overflowing with generosity,
> and whose lips uttered always the truth. . . .
> If Jekuthiel could pass away,
> the skies themselves are transitory.

Even a few years earlier, Solomon was well known as a poet, and in a poem he wrote in 1037 we can already hear the urgent cries of a poet's heart which will echo throughout Solomon's poetry:

> My song is warped with care, and mixed with sighs my joy;
> And see I laugh, my heart for very anguish cries.
> O friend! Shall I but mourn, a sixteen-year-old lad,
> Who should with childhood play, as a lily with the dew.

After Jekuthiel's death, Solomon wandered aimlessly, embittered at the unfriendliness he found in Saragossa when Jekuthiel was no longer alive. He finally returned to Malaga, where Samuel ibn Nagdela became his patron.

Here, at the age of twenty, he composed a complete Hebrew grammar in verses arranged alphabetically (only ninety-five lines of this work are extant). To make a long poem out of such a dry subject required genius!

Dissatisfactions plagued Solomon—dissatisfactions with himself which made him querulous, dissatisfactions with others who failed to give him the recognition he felt he deserved. He seemed to seek solace in solitude and to make philosophy and poetry his only friends and companions.

> My body trudges upon the earth,
> My spirit soars among the clouds.
> But my heart—it feels
> The weight of eighty years.

Nevertheless, or because of this, under Solomon's magic wand, the ancient Hebrew language suddenly came to life again in a rainbow brilliance that had not been seen for many centuries. Former poets, such as Yannai and Kalir, had known only the way to the synagogue; they had always bewailed the destiny of their people in exile. Theirs were mostly poetic prayers. Gabirol, having rejuvenated the old tongue, made it sing of the individual's suffering. He could speak for the people, but his own anguish and loneliness was too deep and poignant to be contained within his soul without conveying it in verse.

Here is a poem in which Solomon seems to be speaking at one and the same time of both the destiny of his people and the heart-cry of an individual:

The Cry of Israel[4]

> Thou knowest my tongue, O God,
> Fain would it bring
> A precious gift—the songs
> Thou makes me sing!
>
> Thou guidest my steps from old;
> If boon too high
> I ask—Thou gavest me speech,
> Spurn not my cry!
>
> My thought hast Thou made pure
> As whitest fleece:

Thou wilt not that mine heart
Shall ne'er have peace.

O, be my refuge now,
Even as of yore.
My God, my Saviour, Thou—
Tarry no more!

The original Hebrew conveys so much better the strength of ibn Gabirol's poems, but even in translation one feels here the soul-vibrations of the awe-inspired poet:

At the Dawn I Seek Thee[5]

At the dawn I seek Thee,
Refuge, Rock sublime,
Set my prayer before Thee
in the morning,
and my prayer at eventide.
I before Thy greatness
Stand and am afraid:
All my secret thoughts
thine eye beholdeth
Deep within my
bosom laid.
And withal what is it
heart and tongue can do?
What is this my strength,
and what is even
this my spirit in me too?
But indeed man's singing
may seem good to Thee;
So I praise Thee, singing,
While there dwelleth
Yet the breath of God in me.

We are caught up short when we come across a frivolously written piece by Gabirol. A poet of humor as well as of suffering? Yes.

Water Song[6]

When monarch wine lies prone,
By water overthrown,
How can a merry song be sung?
For naught there is to wet our tongue
  But water.
Of wine, alas! there's not a drop,
Our host has filled our goblets to the top
  With water.

No sweetmeats can delight
My dainty appetite,
For I, alas! must learn to drink,
However I may writhe and shrink,
  Pure water.
Of wine, alas! *etc.*

Give Moses praise, for he
Made waterless a sea—
Mine host to quench my thirst—the churl!—
Makes streams of clearest water purl,
  Of water.
Of wine, alas! *etc.*

To toads I feel allied,
To frogs by kinship tied;
For water drinking is no joke,
Ere long you all will hear me croak
  Quack water!
Of wine, alas! *etc.*

May God our host requite;
May he turn Nazirite,
Ne'er know intoxication's thrill,
Nor e'er succeed his thirst to still
  With water!
Of wine, alas! *etc.*

The summit of Gabirol's creative ability is to be found in his divine song Kether Malkhuth (The Crown of the Kingdom), in which he brings forth his conception of the Unity and All-inclusiveness of God.

> Yours, O God, is the greatness, might, magnificence,
>   eternity, and glory.
> Yours, O God, is the Kingdom, exaltation over everything,
>   wealth and honor,
> Everything in heaven and on earth bears testimony that
>   you live forever, but everything else is perishable.
> Yours is the might whose secrets our weak mind is
>   unable to fathom, because you overwhelm all our powers.
> Yours is the mystery of power, the secret of matter and
>   form.

Thus Gabirol describes stanza after stanza and with ever greater power the God of the Universe. His awe and veneration, his humility and flaming love, as he looks at God's handiwork, are overwhelming.

> Thou [God] art the Foundation of all Existence;
> Everything that exists is but a reflection of Thy light. . . .
> Thou art the One, the beginning of all numbers
>   and the Foundation of all phenomena. . . .
> The secret of Thy Unity is a riddle for the greatest
>   and the wisest. . . .
> The whole world, everything that exists, praises God
>   the creator, even the pagans and the animals.
> Thy glory is not diminished by those who serve other gods,
> For in their ignorance they still crave after Thee
>   like blind people who think they follow the right path,
>   though they stray into crooked byways. . . .

> Behold, all the endless distances are too small to
>   serve as Thy abode. . . .

> Yet in my mind Thou dwellest, O God.

It is a poem in which the poet and the thinker embrace, a poem full of sublimity and humility. No small wonder that it became a prayer to be recited on the Day of Atonement, the holiest day of the year for the Jew.

All his doubts, all his questions, all his fears, all his tribulations recede and vanish when he looks at the greatness of God. At such a moment he feels that the individual is not a lonely splinter carried by the waves of a vast sea, but a vital part of a Whole, which reflects the wisdom of the Creator. Gabirol's universal God is the God of Israel.

> Three do I see constantly before my eyes that remind
>   me of Thy holy name, O God:
> Contemplate I the remote skies above, I hear their
>   testimony as to Thy infinite greatness;
> The earth under my feet reminds me of Thee, the
>   eternal builder and creator;
> And my heart that feels and thinks remembers Thee,
>   shouting, "At all times bless your God, my soul!"

Gabirol cried, "I am Master and the song is my slave." Indeed, the Hebrew language in his hands was like clay in the hands of the potter. The poetic Muse did his bidding. The poet Moses ibn Ezra (1070-1139) said:

> Solomon ibn Gabirol was the youngest among the poets of
> his generation but excelled them all. He was the knight of
> poetry, the master of the song. His greatness is to be seen
> in his scope. Aiming at the loftiest, he reached indeed the
> very heights of the human mind.

Poetry was Gabirol's first earthly friend and companion. Philosophy was his second. Early in his life, he wrote, in Arabic, *On the Improvement of the Soul*, a system of morals cast on a rational basis, independent of religious dogmas. Ibn Gabirol's next and more important philosophical work was the *Fountain of Life.* This work, in Latin *(Fonce Vitae)*, was very influential among European Christians. Albertus Magnus and Thomas Aquinas took pains to refute parts of *Fonce Vitae*. Duns Scotus and Giordano

Bruno frequently referred to it. In the struggle between the Scotists and the Thomists, it occupied a prominent place as late as the 14th century.

Until 1846, *Fonce Vitae* was thought to be written by the Arab, Avicebron, but the scholar, S. Monk, showed that Gabirol was actually the author.

Fountain of Life is written in the form of a Platonic dialogue between master and disciple, discussing such questions as: What is the nature of the soul? What is the main aim of human life? How did God who is absolutely perfect create a world which appears to be somewhat defective? The book is strictly a philosophical work, based on reason, with no reference to the Bible. This might help explain its unpopularity among the Jewish community. Furthermore, Gabirol espoused basically a neo-Platonism, the mystical philosophy rooted in Plotinus (204-270 c.e.).

Gabirol also compiled Mibhar Hap'ninim (Choice of Pearls), a collection of aphorisms:

> The sage [Aristotle] was asked, "How is it thou hast more wisdom than thy fellow?" He replied: "Because I spent on [midnight] oil more than they spent on wine."

*

> I search not, said the sage, for wisdom with the hope of ever coming to the end of it or attaining it completely; rather do I search for it as not to be a fool, and the intelligent man should have no other motive than this.

*

> Man is only wise during the time that he searches for wisdom; when he imagines he has completely attained it, he is a fool.

*

> He who cannot control his temper is defective in intellect.

*

> I find humility a greater help to me than all my fellow men.

*

> To drink a deadly poison is better than worry.

*

He who seeks more than he needs hinders himself from
enjoying what he has.

*

Contentment is better even than intellect.

*

It is meet for an intelligent man to perceive [the spirit of]
his age, guard his tongue, and attend to his business.

*

It is easier to tolerate a whole fool than half a fool, i.e.,
a fool who wishes to appear clever.

*

The eye of a needle is not narrow for two friends, but the
world is not wide enough for two enemies.

*

Treasure thy tongue as thou treasurest thy wealth

*

None is so poor as the man who is fearful of becoming
poor.

*

I have tasted the bitterness of things, but I have found
nothing so bitter as the taste of begging.[7]

A legendary story of the tragic death of Solomon ibn Gabirol
tells much about the place which he held in the hearts of the Jews.
A jealous Muslim poet, who became his mortal enemy, slew him
and buried his body under a fig tree. It so happened that the fig
tree bore such wonderful fruit that the people of Valencia started
to wonder. Some of them took the trouble of digging beneath the
fig tree and found the poet's body. The murderer then paid with
his own life for the crime he had committed.[8]

BAHAYA BEN JOSEPH IBN PAKUDA
(first half of 11th century)

Bahaya ibn Pakuda, one of the foremost moral teachers of the
Golden Age, the author of the popular book, Hobot Ha-Lebabot

(Duties of the Heart), flourished in Saragossa, Spain. Almost nothing is known of his life, neither his day of birth nor his day of death, excepting the fact that he served as Dayyan (judge) in the local rabbinical court.

His book, however, by virtue of which he became famous, was one of the most beloved Jewish books during the centuries. It went through numerous editions, having been regarded as a standard for the highest moral conduct. Ibn Pakuda is not concerned with philosophy as such. What concerns him most is guiding man on the path of ethical life. In his introduction, Bahaya indicates his avowed purpose in writing his book:

As the science of religion deals with two parts, external and inward religion, I studied the books of the ancient writers who flourished after the Talmud and who composed many works dealing with the precepts, in the expectation of learning from them the science of inward religion. . . .I found however that this department of knowledge, the science of the Duties of the Heart, had been entirely neglected.

Outward observance of religion, without being inwardly involved, will not do. It does not produce that type of religious man who is ever willing and ready to perform life's duties. "I am certain that even the practical duties cannot be efficiently performed without willingness of the heart and desire of the soul to do them. . . .It is clear that we are under the obligation of inward as well as external duties, so that our service shall be perfect and complete, and shall engage mind as well as body." Bahaya told the parable of a man who found a buried treasure, a mass of silver blackened with tarnish. He scoured it and polished it to its original luster. "I wish to do the same with the hidden treasures of the heart: namely, to bring them to light and exhibit their shining excellence so that any one who desires to draw near to God and cling to him may do likewise."[9] Bahaya appealed to the reader to study his book not for the purpose of "winning a reputation or gaining glory" but rather for the purpose of instruction and guidance. "Bring it close to your mind and heart, my brother. If you see any error, correct it; any omission, supply it."

The whole world testifies to the Divine Wisdom: (a) the order of the cosmos itself and the manner in which it is regulated; (b) the human species, which constitutes a world on a small scale, a little universe; (c) the human body with its wonderful physical structure, and above all the light of reason which distinguishes man from the brute; (d) all other living animals, from the least to the greatest; (e) plant life and minerals, which constitute a variety of objects used largely for the benefit of life; (f) the sciences, arts, and crafts, products of the mind, which the Creator bestowed upon us; (g) Israel's Torah, in which one God is proclaimed.

The world is not a product of mere chance, for wherever there is purpose and plan there must have been Wisdom at work. Ink spilled accidentally upon paper cannot produce a poem or a philosophic composition. All causes and principles of things point to one principal cause; the wonderful harmony in nature, the interdependence of all things and creatures indicate a supreme designer —one Creator. Two or more creators would not do, because they could never produce that unity which the universe presents. They could not be infinite either, because one would limit the other. God's unity is not like any other unity that we may think of. He is *real* unity, whereas all other unities are composites. The question then is: How can man come in contact with God? Not by the help of reason alone, but rather by the longing soul which craves to unite with and cling to its Creator. Reflection on the greatness and goodness of God, as manifested throughout Creation, enables man to come nearer to Him. If, as it often happens, men fail to do so, it is either because they are ensnared in the web of material pleasures or dissatisfied with their lot.

Trust in God, says Bahaya, is one of the greatest treasures—if not the greatest—that man can ever possess. "It is greater than the magical power of the alchemist who creates treasures of gold by his art; for he alone who confides in God is independent and satisfied with what he has, and enjoys rest and peace without envying anyone."

Bahaya's *Duties of the Heart* contains many brilliant sayings and words of wisdom compiled from various books, both Jewish and Arabic. Its deeply religious spirit endeared it to generations of Jews. It was translated into Portuguese, Italian, German, and other languages. Two original Arabic manuscripts of the book exist: one in the Bodleian Library, Oxford, and the other in Paris.

The first printed copy of Ibn Tibbon's translation in Hebrew appeared in Naples in 1489. Six commentaries on *Duties of the Heart* have been written during the centuries.

MOSES IBN EZRA
(c. 1070-1139)

Moses ibn Ezra, one of the three greatest poets of the Golden Age—the other two being Ibn Gabirol and Judah Halevi—was born into a wealthy family in Granada. Apart from his Talmudic education, he was versed in Arab philosophy, mastered Arabic, Greek, Latin, and of course Hebrew. His teacher was Judah ibn Ghiat, poet and scholar.

Moses was the first Hebrew poet to celebrate so enthusiastically the enjoyment, the joy, of life, though in later years, as a result of a personal love tragedy, he became a penitent, so much so that the epithet Ha-Salah (poet of penitent prayers) was attached to his name. But in the early years of his life, Moses seems to have known no sorrow.

"How can I be in sorrow," asks Ibn Ezra in one of his poems, "when I hear the chirping of the birds and I rest, enwrapt in sweet slumber, under the shadow of a blossoming tree on a bed of aromatic flowers? Let us be joyful, brethen. Let us go into the orchards. No worries and no grief."

Moses does not shun even erotic love. "The full-grown breasts of my beloved pierced my heart like with spears. . . . But the days that separate me from my beloved are black like her black tresses."

Then the spring of his life came to an end. He fell in love with the daughter of his older brother, a love that was as "strong as death." His three older brothers declared that they would never permit him to marry her. The entire family and all his friends stood against him. Another version was that the girl was his niece who had rejected his love and married one of his brothers, but right after her marriage died. Be that as it may, Moses left his native city and wandered about the country. Later he ventured into business, and lost everything he possessed. It so happened that those who had deceived him became his enemies. His erstwhile friends abandoned him. Thus grief and melancholy became his constant companions.

With the passing of the years, the lonely poet found some consolation in philosophy and poetry. In his poem, "I Awoke From The Slumber of My Thoughts," he described how his poetic visions had faded away before the emergence of his philosophical thoughts; how his reasoning faculties had overcome his passions; and how in the dark recesses of his inner self, God revealed himself to him, and the divine rays of eternal truth fell upon him.

Ibn Ezra's main poetic work is known as Tarshish (chrysolite). Written in the Arab form of Ttadjins, that is, in stanzas ending with rhymes that are the same words but carrying different meanings, it bristles with melancholy and repentence. It is called Tarshish because this word, when taken numerically, that is, in accordance with the numbers represented by the letters, gives one the number 1,210—the number of lines the book contains. It is divided into ten chapters, each containing the twenty-two letters of the Hebrew alphabet according to their traditional order.

Ibn Ezra discusses the following subjects in this book: (a) Love and poetry; (b) the beauty of nature; (c) the frustrations of love; (d) the betrayal of false friends; (e) old age and death; (f) trust in God. Ibn Ezra's sad moods seem often to hold sway over him even in those parts where he appears as a light-hearted singer.

Ibn Ezra and Omar Khayyam were contemporaries. As one begins the poem, "Joy of Life," from Tarshish, he cannot but be reminded of the well known lines from the Rubaiyat: "A book of verses underneath the bough,/ A jug of wine, a loaf of bread—and thou."

> A beautiful woman, a cup of wine, and a garden;
> The song of bird and the sound of murmuring waters;
> These are balm to a lover, and joy to the sad one,
> And welcome to the stranger,
> And wealth to the poor, and healing to the sick.[10]

Ibn Ezra admires nature and describes it colorfully, but soon enough grief comes along to eradicate the little joy. While bewailing his youth that passed away, his sole consolation is that in old age he will be completely free from passions. Four poems from Tarshish:

The Beauty of the Stars[11]

I gaze upon the beauty of the stars
That cover the face of the sky,
And think of them as a garden of blossoms—
Until the white dawn rises like a dove,
From beneath the wings of a raven that flees away.

The Young Dove[12]

The young dove that nests in the tree top
In the garden of spices—
Whereof should he lament?
The brooks deny him not their waters,
The palm bough is a shade unto his head;
His nestlings disport before him,
and he teaches them his song.

Mourn, little dove, mourn for the wanderer
And for his children, that are far away,
With none to bring them food.
He sees no one that has seen their faces,
None can he ask of their welfare,
Save wizzards and mutterers.
Oh, lend him thy wings,
That he may fly unto his loved ones,
And rejoice in the dust of their land!

Thou Who Art Clothed[13]

Thou who art clothed in silk, who drawest on
Proudly thy raiment of fine linen spun,
Bethink thee of the day when thou alone
Shalt dwell at last beneath the marble stone.

How can'st thou ever of the world complain,
And murmuring, burden it with all thy pain?
Silence! thou art a traveller at an inn,
A guest, who may but overnight remain.

Man is a weaver on the earth, 'tis said,
Who weaves and weaves—his own days are the thread,
And when the length allotted he hath spun,
All life is over, and all hope is dead.

Elegy[14]

My thoughts impelled me to the resting-place
Where sleep my parents, many a friend and brother.
I asked them (no one heard and none replied):
"Do you forsake me, too, Oh father, mother?"
Then from the grave, without a tongue, these cried,
And showed my own place waiting by their side.

Ibn Ezra's other poems, mostly penitential, are to be found in the Sephardic Mahzor (Prayer Book for the High Holidays). In them the poet calls man to mend his ways, describing the frustrations and sorrows resulting from the seeking of pleasure, and the account that the sinner will have to give in the Day of Judgment. There are many Piyyutim in which Ibn Ezra attains great heights of emotion.

In addition, in the Bodleian Library of Oxford, there is a manuscript, written by Moses ibn Ezra, containing 300 secular poems (It is marked Hebrew Mss No. 1792—the Diwan of Moses ibn Ezra.)

Ibn Ezra also wrote a treatise on rhetoric and poetry, which includes a review of the history of Spanish Jews since early times. Moses also wrote a treatise on philosophy, *Garden Bed of Perfume* (Arugat Ha-Bosem), which was translated from Arabic; only seven chapters are extant.

Judah al-Harizi, one of the most distinguished poets of the Golden Age, characterized Ibn Ezra as follows: "Moses ibn Ezra draws pearls from the well of thought." (Tahkemoni 3)

JUDAH BEN SAMUEL HALEVI
(born c. 1086)

Heinrich Heine, greatest German-Jewish lyric poet, described Judah Halevi in the following ecstatic lines:

> All pure and true, without a stain,
> Such was his song, such was his soul.
> When by the hands of God was shaped,
> He, self-complacent, stamped
> Upon this beautiful soul a kiss,
> And every song the poet sang
> Thrills with the echo of that kiss,
> Made sacred by that gift divine.

Indeed, Halevi was one of the greatest singers of the Hebrew Golden Age, if not the greatest. A melodious and divinely gifted poet, his heart was throbbing with love for God, Israel, and the Holy Land. Unlike Ibn Gabirol, Judah Halevi did not view the world as a dismal place to live in. All of life's treasures were open to him, love prevailed in everything he wrote. He could sing as well of rosy lips and raven hair, of blue waters and golden fields, of bright skies and blood-red wine, of joy and the desire of youth, of the charm of woman and flaming lust.

Aside from his poetic power and his mastery of the Hebrew language, Judah was a man endowed with an insatiable thirst for knowledge. A physician by profession, he was an avid student of philosophy and the natural sciences, and above all a Talmudic scholar. His knowledge of Hebrew grammar and of the Scriptures was second to none.

The great Jewish historian Heinrich Graetz evaluates Judah Halevi in the following words:

> Judah Halevi had a more correct conception of poetry than his Arabic and Jewish contemporaries. Poetry, to him, was something sacred and of divine origin; the poetic impulse must be something original, innate, and not an art that may be learned. . . . In each word and turn the great master is recognized who has the power to draw a

finished picture with a few bold strokes. His descriptions
of nature can be favorably compared with the best products of poetry in any language. One can see in his lines
the flowers bud and glisten; one inhales their fragrance;
one sees the branches bending beneath the weight of golden
fruits, and hears the songsters of the air warble their love
songs. With the hand of a master he paints the sunshine
and the gentle breeze. When he describes the fury of a
storm-tossed sea, he imparts to his readers all the sublimity and the terror which he himself felt.[15]

The height of ecstasy and inspiration was reached by Halevi
in his cycle of the Songs of Zion. Here he wears the laurel crown
of a national poet. His grief and deep sorrow at seeing Zion's
children scattered all over the earth and degraded to the very dust
are so deep and irresistable that the reader must weep with him.
The poet's heart is wide open, and his wounds are bleeding before our very eyes. Past glories and present lowliness are con-
trasted, and one hears Jeremiah's lamentations coming to life
again.

O Zion, wilt thou not inquire[16]

O Zion, wilt thou not inquire about the peace of thy
    captives,
They that seek thy peace and are the remnant of thy flocks?
From west and east, from north and south, greetings
    from them that are far and near take thou on all sides.
Greetings also from a slave of yearning, who sheds his
    tears like Hermon's dew, and longs that they fall on thy
    mounts.

I am like a jackal to bewail thy woes; but when I dream
    of thy restoration, I am a harp for thy songs.
My heart moans for Beth-el, and Peniel, and Mahanaim,
    and all the meeting-places of thy pure ones.
There God's Presence dwells near thee, and thy Creator
    opened thy gates toward the gates of heaven.
The glory of the Lord alone was thy light; the sun,

the moon, and stars illumined thee not.

I yearn that my soul be poured forth in the place
    where God's spirit was poured out on thy chosen ones.
Thou art a royal house, thou art the thrones of God,
    how then can bondmen sit upon the thrones of thy
    princes?

Would that I were roaming about in the places
    where God appeared unto thy seers and messengers!
Who would make me wings, that I may fly away?
I would cause my broken heart to move amidst thy
    mounts of Bether!
On thy ground fain would I lie prostrate; I would take
    pleasure
    in thy stones, and would love thy dust!
Then standing by the sepulchres of my fathers, I would
    gaze with rapture on thy choicest graves in Hebron.
I would pass through thy forest and Carmel, and stand
    in Gilead,
And gaze with rapture on Mount Abarim;—Mount Abarim
    and Mount Hor, where are buried thy two great
    luminaries,
    thy teachers who gave thee light.

I will pluck and cast away the beauty of my locks, and
    curse fate
    which defiles thy Nazirites in an unclean land.
How can it be pleasant unto me to eat and drink,
    when I see that the curs drag thy young lions?
Or how can the light of the day be sweet to my sight,
    when I see the flesh of thine eagles in the mouths of ravens?
O cup of sorrow, gently! desist for a while!
For my reins and soul are already filled with thy bitterness.

But just as Halevi could bewail Zion's ruins and Israel's exile,
so he might draw upon his poetic treasures to portray a spring
day in Castile, Spain.

Spring[17]

But yesterday the hot earth drank like a child
with eager thirst the autumn rain.
Or like a wistful bride who waits the hour
of love's mysterious bliss and pain.
And now the spring is here with yearning eyes
midst shimmering golden flower beds,
on meadows a tapestry of bloom o'er all,
and myriad-eyed young plants upspring,
white, green or red like lips that to the mouth
of the beloved one sweetly cling.
Come, go we to the garden with our wine,
which scatters sparks of hot desire,
within our hand it's cold, but in our veins
it flashes clear, it glows like fire.

The above poem is one of those he wrote in his youth. As a boy of fifteen years he already was known as a poet. Many of his songs testify conclusively that his youth was joyful and gay. Such expressions as: "wide and full as the sea is my heart" and "the days dance before me, revolving like a wheel of joy" tell their tale. The young poet drank the wine of life from a brimful goblet. He wrote then songs of wedding feasts, wine-poems, witty epigrams. Here are two stanzas from Judah's wedding songs:

Rejoice, O young man, in thy youth,
And gather the fruit thy joy shall bear,
Thou and the wife of thy youth,
Turning now to thy dwelling to enter there.

Thy glory shall rise, nor make delay;
And thee shall He call and choose; and thy light,
In the gloom, in the darkness of night,
then shall break forth like the dawn of day;
And out from the shining light of the morn
Shall the dew of thy youth be born.[18]

The immersion of Halevi's soul in God, his striving to reach the fountain of life and light, may be seen from a little poem, the stanzas of which are replete with yearning to become one with the eternal.

> Lord! where art Thou to be found?
> Hidden and high is thy home.
> And where shall we find Thee not?
> Thy glory fills the world.
> Thou art found in my heart,
> And in the uttermost ends of the earth.
> A refuge for the near,
> And for the far, a trust.
> The universe cannot contain Thee,
> How then a temple's shrine?
> Though Thou art raised above men
> On Thy high and lofty throne,
> Yet art Thou near unto them,
> In their spirit and in their flesh.
> Who can say he has not seen Thee!
> When, lo! the heavens and their host
> Make, silently, Thy presence manifest.[19]

Details of Halevi's life that have come down to us are indeed few. Even the date of his birth is not known for certain. Some think that he was born in the year 1080 and died about 1142. What we do know is the fact that he was born in the Christian part of Castile, Spain, in the city of Toledo. His father sent him to Lucena, where he enrolled as a disciple of the great Talmudic scholar, Isaac Alfasi. He studied medicine and later became a prominent doctor. Having learned Arabic, he acquainted himself with Greek philosophy as expounded by the Arab thinkers of that time. Moses ibn Ezra, who was then already famous both as a poet and critic, proclaimed Halevi as "the star from Castile which will illuminate the world." When Halevi returned to Toledo, he practiced medicine, but his greatest love was Hebrew poetry. The ancient Hebrew words opened for him new vistas: They expressed the most profound sentiments of his soul as a man and a Jew; they submitted to his will when he became an advocate for his sorely tried people; and they helped him to become the National Poet of the Hebrew Golden Age—"the Harp of Zion." Never, since the Prophets and the Psalmists, had Hebrew poetry attained such heights.

Halevi's contribution to religious philosophy was his famous work, Ha-Kuzari, written originally in Arabic but later translated into Hebrew, in which he tried to show the truth of Judaism as against the philosophical theories current at the time. The inspiration for the writing of Ha-Kuzari was the 10th-century exchange of letters between Hasdai ibn Shaprut and King Joseph of Chazaria (supra, "Land of the Chazars," p. 224; "Hasdai ibn Shaprut," p. 236). Halevi began with the actual event in Jewish history: the conversion to Judaism of King Bulan in the 8th century, after hearing a symposium of scholars—a Christian, a Muslim, a Jew, and a philosopher. The lengthy discussions themselves are, of course, Halevi's creation.

In Ha-Kuzari, the philosopher was the first to propose his theories, but the king found them too abstract and unadaptable to the life of the common people. When he turned to the Christian and Muslim for enlightenment on the subject, he was amazed to hear that both of them based their faith on the Hebrew Scriptures, on the Patriarchs and the Prophets. If this is the case, mumbled the king, then there is no other choice but to listen to what the Jew has to say in the matter. From this point on, a lengthy discussion in the form of a dialogue, consisting of questions and answers, is carried on, in which every phase of Judaism is dealt with in a masterly way.

Halevi, in the figure of the Jewish scholar, argues that philosophy, especially Aristotelianism, so widespread in the Arabic world, cannot express the whole essence of man's life. Of course, reason is important, but it is not the only source of knowledge, nor for that matter the most important one. To the philosopher, the question of the existence of God is like any other speculative question; it is theory not practice. Judaism, on the other hand, is not theory. Concerned with man's ethical conduct, his way of life, it takes man as a whole, intellectually as well as emotionally.

The philosopher's god, Aristotle's First Cause, the Immovable

Mover, is not the God of Abraham who is personal, close to the human heart. True religion is not interested in making a man of good intentions, but rather in creating a man of good deeds, teaching him how to act justly. This aim cannot be attained by philosophy, which is constantly wavering as one may see from the fact that each philosopher proposes a different view of life. The disagreement among the philosophers testifies to the flimsiness of their views. As a matter of fact, "the study of the philosophy of religion is detrimental to true faith." The wisdom of the Greeks "bears only flowers but not fruit."

The religious training that Judaism proposes is based upon a set of traditions the truth of which has been demonstrated by the experience and the history of the Jewish people. Philosophy lacks the certainty of prophetic Judaism. Had Aristotle had a trustworthy tradition in support of some of his views, he would not have accepted the eternity of matter vis-a-vis his First Cause. He would have accepted, instead, one Creator, as the Torah proposes. To Judah Halevi, the Torah is the Truth which does not need any other truth in corroboration of its tenets. The survival of the people of Israel in Egypt, their delivery from bondage, their wandering in the desert, the giving of the Law on Mount Sinai, their later history among the nations, their preservation under the most adverse conditions—all this is proof enough of the divine essence of the Torah, the only true faith given by God. The question as to why the Torah was given to Israel and not to all of mankind is put by Halevi on the same plane as the question as to why animals were not created men.

The suffering and dire tribulations of the Jewish people are taken by Halevi as proof of the truth of Judaism. That the Jewish people are downtrodden and in exile should not be regarded as a refutation of the truth of the Torah, for whoever clings to an ideal must suffer for it. Arrogance and pride, might and success are not criteria of truth. Israel among the nations, states Halevi, is like the heart in the human organism: it bears the brunt of all afflictions that strike the body.

Another long exchange from Ha-Kuzari illustrates how Halevi elaborates his views.[20] The king asks the Jewish scholar: Who is a pious man? How does he behave? The scholar answers that the pious man treats his country carefully, provides all the inhabitants whatever they need, acts justly, never deceives anyone, never gives one more than what he is entitled to get. The king interrupts: I did not ask you about a ruler; I asked you about a pious man. The Jew replies:

The pious man is comparable to a prince. He is obeyed by his senses, and by his mental as well as by his physical faculties, which he governs corporeally, as it is written: "He that ruleth his spirit [is better than he] that taketh a city" (Prov. 16:32). He is fit to rule, because were he the prince of a country he would be as just to his people as he is to his body and soul. He subdues his passions, keeping them in bonds, but giving them their due in order to satisfy them as regards food, drink, cleanliness, etc. He allows them all the freedom necessary for coping with material wants, and for solving scientific problems; but not so much as to be betrayed into doing evil. He allows the senses their due, according as he requires them for the use of hands, feet, and tongue, as necessity and desire arise. The same is the case with hearing, seeing, and the kindred sensations which succeed them: imagination, conception, thought, memory, and will power. He commands all these and makes them subservient to the will of the intellect. He does not allow any one of these faculties to go beyond its special task, or to encroach upon another. Having satisfied each of them, he calls upon his whole being as a respected prince calls upon his disciplined army, to assist him in reaching the higher or divine degree which is to be found above the degree of the intellect. He arranges his being in the same manner as Moses arranged his people round Mount Sinai. He orders his will power to accept every command issued by him, and to carry it out forthwith. He makes his faculties and limbs do his bidding without contradiction, forbids them evil inclinations of mind and fancy, forbids them to listen to them, or believe in them, until he has taken counsel with the intellect. If he permits, they can obey him; but not otherwise. In this way his will power receives its orders from him, carrying them out accordingly. He directs the organs of thought and imagination, relieving them of all worldly ideas mentioned above, charges his imagination to produce, with the assistance of memory, the most splendid pictures possible, in order to resemble the divine things sought after. Such pictures are the scenes of Sinai, Abraham and Isaac on Moriah, the Tabernacle of Moses, the Temple service, the presence of God in the Temple. He then orders his memory to retain all these, and not forget them; he warns his fancy and his sinful promptings not to confuse the truth or to trouble it by doubts; he warns his irascibility and greed not to influence to lead astray, not to take hold of his will, nor subdue to wrath and lust. As soon as harmony is established, his will power stimulates all his organs to obey it with alertness, pleasure, and joy. They stand without fatigue when occasion demands, they bow down when he bids them to do so, and sit at the proper moment. The eyes look as a servant looks at his master, the hands drop their play and do not meet, the feet stand straight, and all limbs are frightened and anxious to obey their master, paying no heed to pain or injury. The tongue agrees with the thought, and does not overstep its bounds, does not speak in prayer in a mere mechanical way as the starling and the parrot, but every word is uttered thoughtfully and attentively. This moment of prayer forms the heart and fruit of his time, while the other hours represent the way which leads to it. He looks forward to its approach, because while it lasts he resembles the spiritual beings, and is removed from merely animal existence.

Ha-Kuzari was translated into Latin (by Buxtorf, 1660), Spanish, German, and English. Six commentaries have been written on it. It has served as one of the most forceful of Jewish bulwarks against threats from without (e.g., Aristotelians) and from within (e.g., Karaites).

In his old age, Halevi decided to leave his family and friends in Spain and visit Palestine. About the year 1141, he sailed from his native land and reached Egypt, where he was received by the Jewish communities with great honors. From there he went to the Holy Land, which was then under the rule of the Crusaders. But no one knows what happened to him. Legend has it that while he prostrated himself at the Wailing Wall he was trampled by Arab cavalry, dying as a martyr.

In the village of Kabul, a tombstone was found carrying the following inscription:

A man inquired where mercy doth abide, where gentleness
and where humility; the graces three assembled and replied:
Here where Judah is—there are we.

ABRAHAM BEN MEIR IBN EZRA
(1088-1167)

Abraham ben Meir ibn Ezra's fame rests mainly upon his Biblical commentaries and his grammatical works. The latter, e.g., Safha Brura, Sepher Zahut, all written in Hebrew, are still regarded as basic compositions.

The commentaries, especially on the Pentateuch, were Abraham's crowning achievement of his life. His greatness consisted in presenting a simple, sober, and textually consistent interpretation based chiefly on Hebrew grammar, on the meaning of the words, to the exclusion of Midrashic exposition, which had been in vogue prior to his time. In this respect his approach was that of a keen critic who, utterly unconcerned about anything extraneous to the Scriptures, dared to express doubts as to the integrity of the text and the Mosaic authorship of the Pentateuch; but fearful of being pronounced a heretic, he employed his great mastery of Hebrew to hide his remarks in riddle-like phrases, which challenged the mind of the scholar. At times he used such prases as: "And the wise will understand" or "And the wise will keep silent." He was also the one who indicated that the Book of Isaiah contained chapters—from chapter 40 to the end—that do not belong to Isaiah and were written later in Babylonia; likewise some Psalms attributed traditionally to King David were declared by him as of a much later date.

Ibn Ezra, however, was not a systematic thinker, despite his great knowledge and experience as a man of the world. On the contrary, he was a man of contradictions and glaring contrasts. While he appeared to be a free-thinking expositor, endowed with a deep insight and a sharp analytical mind, he was nonetheless a fanatical believer in astrology. The rational and the mystical appeared to live within his soul in perfect harmony and peace. Also, while he himself was such a critically disposed commentator, he was far from tolerant to others similarly inclined.

Ibn Ezra was also a poet. Al-Harizi (1190-1240) assigns an honorable place to Abraham among the poets of the Golden Age. "The poems of Ibn Ezra," he writes, "provide help in time of need, and cause refreshing rain in time of drought. All of his poetry is lofty and admirable in its content." (Tahkemoni 4) Leopold Zunz, on the other hand, is more reserved. "Through him," Zunz declares, "the gap between Piyyut [synagogal or liturgical poetry] and classic style came clearly to be recognized. Yet poetry was not his special line of activity. Number and measure lurk in his verses, and flashes of thought spring from his words—but not pictures of the imagination." History's judgment favors Zunz's. Ibn Ezra's poems are not of the highest order; they are overly didactic and frequently lack emotional impact. Some of his liturgical hymns can be found in the prayer books for the holidays.

One curiosity in Hebrew literature is Abraham's chess poem, in which he followed the Arabic designation of pieces: foot soldier is pawn, elephant is bishop, wind is rook.

The Song of Chess

I will sing a song of battle
Planned in days long passed and over.
Men of skill and science set it
On a plain of eight divisions,
And designed in square all checkered.
Two camps face each one the other,
And the kings stand by the battle,
And 'twixt these two is the fighting.
Bent on war the face of each is,
Ever moving or encamping,
Yet no swords are drawn in warfare,
For a war of thoughts their war is.
They are known by signs and tokens
Sealed and written on their bodies;
And a man who sees them, thinketh,
Edomites and Ethiopians
Are these two that fight together.
And the Ethiopian forces
Overspread the field of battle,
And the Edomites pursue them.

First in battle the foot soldier

comes to fight upon the highway,
Ever marching straight before him,
But to capture moving sideways,
Straying not from off his pathway
Neither do his steps go backwards;
He may leap at the beginning
Anywhere within three checkers.
Should he take his steps in battle
Far away unto the eight row,
Then a Queen to all appearance
He becomes and fights as she does.
And the Queen directs her moving
As she will to any quarter.
Backs the elephant or advances,
Stands aside as 'twere an ambush;
As the Queen's way, so is his way,
But o'er him she hath advantage,
He stands only in the third rank.
Swift the horse is in the battle,
Moving on a crooked pathway;
Ways of his are ever crooked;
Mid the squares, three form his limit.

Straight the wind moves o'er the war path
In the field across or lengthwise;
Ways of crookedness he seeks not,
But straight paths without perverseness.
Turning every way, the King goes,
Giving aid unto his subjects;
In his actions he is cautious,
Whether fighting or encamping.
If his foe come to dismay him,
From his place he flees in terror,
Or the wind can give him refuge.
Sometimes he must flee before him;
Multitudes at times support him;
And all slaughter each the other.
Mighty men of both the sovereigns

Slaughtered fall, with yet no bloodshed.
Ethiopia sometimes triumphs,
Edom flees away before her;
Now victorious is Edom;
Ethiopia and her sovereign
Are defeated in the battle.

Should a King in the destruction
Fall within the foeman's power,
He is never granted mercy,
Neither refuge nor deliv'rance,
Nor a flight to refuge city.
Judged by foes, and lacking rescue,
Though not slain he is checkmated.
Hosts about him all are slaughtered,
Giving life for his deliverance.
Quenched and vanished is their glory,
For they see their lord is smitten;
Yet they fight again his battle,
For in death is resurrection.

Ibn Ezra's epigrams, riddles, and sarcasms are masterly and striking:

I strove to acquire wealth,
but the stars are hostile to me.
Were I to deal in shrouds,
not a man would die;
were I to deal in candles,
the sun would not set
until my dying day.

*

I call on my lord in the morning,
but am told that on horseback he's sped;
I call once again in the evening,
and hear that his lordship's abed.
But, whether his business is riding,
or whether my lord is asleep,

I am perfectly sure disappointment
is the one single fruit I shall reap.

My Cloak[21]

Like to a sieve is that old cloak of mine,
A sieve that wheat and barley might refine.
I spread it tent-like in the mid of night,
and view through it the stars in endless line;
The moon, Orion, and the Pleiades
And countless constellations through it shine.
I weary counting all its numerous holes,
Jagged and cleft like a saw in their design.
The threads with which my cloak is patched exceed
The warp and weft by more than nine times nine;
And should a fly fall in its mazy web,
He'd speedily despair and to death resign. . .
O God, exchange it for a cloak of praise,
But make its seams much stronger, Power Divine!

Ibn Ezra was a scholar with scanty means, yet—driven partly
by persecution of Jews in Spain and partly by his own restlessness
—he succeeded in traveling over most of the then known world. His
wanderlust drove him on from southern Spain into Egypt, Palestine,
Babylonia, and back again through Europe to Rome into southern
France and from there to London. During his long travels, he composed one work after another. It is said that he was the author of
108 works, but most were lost.

The Jewish Encyclopedia calls Ibn Ezra's travels a "historic
mission." Basically he took to many European Jews, who were
unacquainted with Arabic, their first genuine understanding of science and scientific methodology. Furthermore, his Biblical learning
and teachings enriched the minds of scores of scholars, Jewish
and non-Jewish alike.

The name "Rabbi ben Ezra" is also marked off in a well known
poem of that name by the English poet, Robert Browning. Browning knew Ibn Ezra's work. For example, in 1854 he translated
Ibn Ezra's "Song of Death" and used it as the final nine stanzas

of his own poem, "Holy-Cross Days." Perhaps Browning was fascinated by the fact that Ibn Ezra, during his long wanderings, reached London and lived there for a while. In any case, many of Browning's poems employ Jewish and Arabic themes and personages, and we know in this case that Abraham ben Meir ibn Ezra was in part the inspiration for "Rabbi ben Ezra."

JOSEPH BEN JACOB IBN ZADDIK
(d. 1149)

Joseph ben Jacob ibn Zaddik—rabbi, poet, and philosopher—is known to have served as a member of the rabbinical court at Cordova jointly with Rabbi Maimon, father of Maimonides. The date of Joseph ben Jacob's birth cannot be ascertained. He died at Cordova in 1149.

Al Harizi describes him as a highly gifted poet. Some of his poems were incorporated in the Sephardic prayer book for the High Holidays. To the literature of the Golden Age he contributed a small treatise in Arabic which was translated into Hebrew under the title Olam Katan (Small World).

In the first part of his book, Joseph discusses various philosophical problems: matter and form, substance and accidents, man and his position in the world. Man, according to Ibn Zaddik, is a small world unto himself, a microcosmos, whereas the outer world is the macrocosmos. From this follows his idea that in order to understand the world one must study the physical and psychological structure of man. Socrates' principle, "Know thyself," is thus taken by Ibn Zaddik as basic knowledge.

The comparison between the Large World and the Small World is made as follows: man's organism is constituted from the four principal elements, air, water, fire and earth, in the same manner as the outer world; man has the characteristics of the minerals, plants, and animals. He nourishes and reproduces himself like the plant and he has feeling and life like the animal. Like the tree, he stands erect. His hair grows like grass. His veins and arteries remind one of rivers.

Due to his composition constitution, man possesses three souls: a vegetative, an animal, and a rational soul. The third soul is, of course, the highest. Its modes are justice, benevolence, truth. Due to the knowledge of his spiritual self, man can reach his Creator.

Thus Joseph ibn Zaddick develops his entire theory of life from the body of man. Following in the footsteps of earlier thinkers, he arrives at the conclusion that man must know three things: that there is a Creator, that everything is known to God, that God can only be served by good deeds.

Ibn Zaddik is not regarded as an original thinker, because most of his ideas were derived from Arabic philosophy, but he did stamp them significantly with his own personality.

ABRAHAM BAR HIYYA HANASI
(12th century)

Abraham bar Hiyya Hanasi, known among Christians as Abraham Judaeus, was one of the most distinguished Spanish scientists and philosophers of the 12th century, though very little of his life is known, except that he wrote copiously on scientific and philosophical subjects. Bar Hiyya, like Solomon ibn Gabirol, was a neo-Platonist.

The following list of some of his works gives the range of his intellectural interests: (a) The Foundations of Understanding and the Tower of Faith, which covered mathematics, geometry, optics, astronomy, music; only fragments of this encyclopedic work have come down to us. (b) Form of the Earth, on geography. (c) Calculations of the Courses of the Stars. (d) Scroll of the Revealer, predicting the coming of the Messiah in the year 5118 (1358). (e) A book on the calendar. (f) Work on scientific methodology, perhaps his greatest contribution. (g) Meditation of the Soul. Written in the form of sermons exhorting the reader to lead a life of devotion to God and to follow the highest moral principles, he quoted freely from the works of ancient "pagan" sages, urging that though they lacked Torah they discovered many truths and attained a high degree of godliness.

All of Bar Hiyya's works were written in Hebrew, but he was also an active translator from Arabic.

Interesting is Bar Hiyya's viewpoint on Judaism. He divides the laws of the Torah into three classes: the Decalogue, containing the fundamental laws; laws intended for creating a "Holy Congregation"; legislation intended for an agricultural society to be formed into a "Kingdom of Justice." In the Messianic age, however, when brotherhood and love will reign supreme, no other laws than the ones given in the Decalogue will be needed. "Men, imbued solely with love for their fellows, free from sin, will rise to the standard of the God-devoted man, and, like him, share in the eternal bliss of God."

Abraham bar Hiyya occupies an important place in the history of science. He contributed greatly to the education of the Jews of Spain, Provence, and Italy, who at that time were placed in the position of intermediaries between the Christian and the Islamic worlds.

ABRAHAM IBN DAUD HALEVI
(1110-1180)

Abraham ibn Daud (David) Halevi, one of the first Jewish Aristotelians, was an astronomer, a philosopher, and a historian. He was born in Toledo about the year 1110 and died as a martyr for his faith about the year 1180. His main works are: Emunah Rama (Sublime Faith) and Sefer Ha-Kabbalah (Book of Tradition). In the latter work he established the chain of tradition from Moses to his own time. The historic facts he gathered about the Geonic period and the Spanish Jews are of inestimable value to the historian.

In the field of religious philosophy, Ibn Daud was a forerunner of Maimonides. Although he touched upon many phases of Aristotle's philosophy as related to Judaism, he nevertheless failed to reach either the depth or the scope of Maimonides whose *Guide for the Perplexed* actually overshadowed Ibn Daud's book.

Ibn Daud mentions two philosophical works which were at his disposal at the time he composed his *Sublime Faith*: Saadia's *Beliefs and Doctrines* and Ibn Gabirol's *Fountain of Life*. He followed, of course, in the footsteps of Saadia, having viewed him as a pathfinder in Judaism, though he takes exceptions to certain of his views. Gabirol was a neo-Platonist, whereas Ibn Daud was an Aristotelian in the fullest sense of the word. To him, Aristotelianism, as propounded by the Arab philosophers Alfarabi and Ibn Sina, was the last word in philosophy, the very truth that the human mind can no more attain. A rationalist to the very core, he saw in Gabirol's explanation of reality no more than illusions. Like Maimonides, he sought to reconcile Judaism and philosophy, faith and reason. Like Maimonides, Ibn Daud encountered the question of Biblical creation versus the eternity of matter; but whereas Maimonides rejected the idea of eternity of matter, Ibn Daud seems to have left this difficulty unresolved.

The study of Ibn Daud's *Sublime Faith* is particularly interesting from the standpoint of Maimonides' religious-philosophical theories, which can better be understood by following these two contemporary thinkers. That is, by comparing the two, one can see Maimonides' contributions to medieval thought in a much clearer light.

MOSES BEN MAIMON (MAIMONIDES)
(1135-1204)

Moses ben Maimon (called by the Christians Maimonides; often called by the Jews Rambam, abbreviation for Rabbi Moishe ben Maimon) was unquestionably the greatest Jewish religious philosopher of the Middle Ages. He was also one of the great codifiers and systematizers of Talmudic law. His personality, his life's work, his position as a leader in Israel bordered upon the legendary even during his life; the legend grew with the passing of time. Later generations knew him as the "Great Eagle" or "Our Teacher," whose epoch-making contribution has been compared to the work of Ezra, Hillel, Judah the Prince. The well known epigram, "From Moses [ben Amram] to Moses [ben Maimon] there was no one like Moses," truly expressed what people have thought of Maimonides. No higher distinction could have been given to a historic figure. He still stands out above Israel's leaders of the last 800 years as one of the most brilliant stars, whose luster has not faded.

Born in 1135 in Cordova, Spain, Moses was recognized as a prodigy from his childhood. Among his first teachers was his father, Rabbi Maimon, who excelled in mathematics and astronomy. Later he was instructed by Joseph ibn Migash, scholar and poet. Scion of a family of pious and learned Jews in a long chain of eight generations back to the founder, Obadiah, and the son of a prominent rabbi, Moses followed in their footsteps. Blessed with a wakeful and absorbent mind, and endowed with reasoning powers second to none, he matured mentally very early in life.

At thirteen years of age Moses already felt what it meant to be a Jew. In the year 1148, Cordova was conquered by the Almohades, a fanatical Muslim sect, who not only persecuted the Jewish population but demanded of them, under the threat of the sword, to accept Islam. The family had no other choice but to flee Cordova. They wandered from place to place for more than ten years and finally reached Fez in North Africa. But even here life was far from secure. Maimon and his family then decided to emigrate to Egypt. On their way they tarried for a short time in Palestine and finally settled in Fostat, near Cairo, Egypt. There old Maimon died. David, the younger son, established a jewelry business from which the two families derived a livelihood. Moses devoted all his time to studying. Later, David sailed to India and perished in a shipwreck. Destitute, with two families on his hands, Moses fell sick and was bed-ridden for a year. Nevertheless, he succeeded in completing one of his first great works, a commentary on the Mishnah, in Arabic, a work started during his wandering years. It is known in Arabic as the Siraj (Illumination). It represents a methodical treatment of the Mishnaic law, something that had never been done by anyone before. Every point of the law, which touched upon anatomy, physics, or any other branch of science known at the time, was thoroughly examined and expounded. Commenting upon the Mishnah, Maimonides tried to bring to light the general principles upon which the law rested. Heretofore Judaism had been viewed as a conglomerate of precepts, "Thou shalt do's" and "Thou shalt not's." Maimonides constantly searched for the rational basis of the Mishnaic law. In his commentary, he elaborated the thirteen principles, which were later generally accepted as the philosophy of Judaism: Belief in (1) God's existence; (2) God's unity— one God; (3) God's incorporeality; (4) God's immutability; (5) God's eternity; (6) worship; (7) prophecy; (8) prophetic supremacy of Moses; (9) the Torah's divinity; (10) the Torah's immutability;

(11) reward and punishment; (12) the coming of the Messiah; (13) resurrection.

Maimonides' greatest work, completed about 1180, is his Talmudic code, known as Mishneh Torah (Repetition of Torah) or Yad Hahazakah (Strong Hand), arranged in fourteen books, a literary structure of the first order. Written in the Mishnaic dialect, it represents the first complete presentation of the entire Talmudic Law, divided and classified according to proper headings, and given with amazing finality, orderliness, and perfection. It overshadowed all other attempts that had been made before. Only Isaac Alfasi's code of the 11th century had even come close to approaching the ambition and thoroughness embodied in this 12th-century codification. Only those who have delved into the intricacies of the Talmud might appreciate the achievement of the author.

The value of the Code both as a teaching instrument and a sum total of Talmudic Law cannot be overestimated. A contemporary of Maimonides put the case well:

> Before this work reached Spain, the study of the Talmud was so difficult for the Jews that they had to depend upon the decision of the rabbis, since the laymen could not ascertain the definite legal results in the complexity of the discussions. But as soon as they obtained the work of Maimonides, which was easily accessible to them on account of the lucidity of its language and its orderly arrangement, their eyes were opened and they realized its value. They absorbed themselves in it, and young and old gathered to study it and to acquire its contents. Now there are many who are familiar with the law, and in the case of a legal dispute, are in a position to know what the law is. They are also able to watch over the decisions of others.

Later in his life, about the year 1190, Maimonides completed an equally famous and contentious work. This was Moreh Nebuhim (Guide for the Perplexed), written originally in Arabic and translated into Hebrew just before Maimonides died. Its Latin translation greatly influenced Christian thinkers: Thomas Acquinas, Albertus Magnus, Duns Scotus, and others. The work has also been rendered into many modern languages.

All was not praise, however, for Mishneh Torah and Moreh

Nebuhim. Both provoked controversy and opposition. Maimonist and anti-Maimonist groups formed in many Jewish communities throughout the world. Meir ben Todros Abulafia, one of the famous Talmudists of Spain, strongly objected to Maimonides' views. Many scholars joined Abulafia, but convinced that the opposition was not aggressive enough, he turned to the rabbis of France for support against these threatening and heretical ideas. There Abraham ben David of Posquieres was a harsh critic of Maimonides' Talmudic codification. Solomon ben Abraham of Montpellier vigorously attacked the *Guide*. But events got out of hand in France. Solomon and two of his disciples, David ben Saul and Jonah of Gerona, banned the *Guide* and warned that they would excommunicate any Jew in southern France who read the book. Jews rose in protest against the ban. The rabbis of Lunel, Beziers, and Narbonne demanded that Solomon and his followers retract their threat. When they did not, the anti-Maimonists were excommunicated. Fights and brawls broke out in the streets and in synagogues. The conflict spread back into Spain; communities were divided.

Solomon sensed that he was losing and he took an extraordinary step. In desperation he turned to the Inquisition and denounced Maimonides' works as a threat to the Church and religion. The Inquisitors were only too happy to encourage dissension among the Jews and impede their growth. And so it happened that in the 1230s Maimonides' books and the Talmud were burned in the streets of Paris and Montpellier. Neither Solomon nor Maimonides lived to see this tragic denouement, nor could they see the wave of repentence which swept over many Jewish communities as a result. Jonah Gerondi, a follower of Solomon, repented of his share in the anti-Maimonist campaign, and vowed to make a pilgrimage to Tiberias, Palestine, to ask forgiveness at the grave of Maimonides. A satiric Maimonistic poet penned an epigram which reflects the mood of the times:

> What say ye arrogant knaves and fools purblind,
> The precious books were to the flames consigned?
> An all-consuming fire, and words that burn,
> How can they be by flames consumed in turn?
> Elijah-like their way they skyward wended,

And angel-like amidst the flames ascended?

What was the controversy all about? Let us return to *Guide for the Perplexed* and examined the position Maimonides worked out. The aim of writing the *Guide* is explained by Maimonides:

I have composed this work neither for the common people, nor for beginners, nor for those who occupy themselves only with the law as it was handed down, without concerning themselves with its principles. The design of this work is rather to promote the true understanding of the real spirit of the law, to guide those religious persons who, adhering to the Torah, have studied philosophy and are embarrassed by the contradictions between the teachings of philosophy and the literal sense of the Torah.

Generally speaking, Maimonides' task is described in various ways. He tried to harmonize philosophy and Jewish tradition, and for him philosophy meant Aristotle. He re-thought the basic tenets of Judaism in the light of Aristotelian philosophy. He "judaized Aristotle and aristotelized Judaism." There is truth in these descriptions, but the truth is perhaps deeper. Maimonides actually believed that Torah and philosophy were not two separate domains. Torah was originally based upon philosophical ideas, but during the long periods of suffering and sojourn of the Jewish people, these dropped out of consciousness. Nevertheless, these ideas and principles were still in the Torah, hidden, implicit, only to be dug out, to be made explicit again. When this is done, it will be seen that a universal Reason underlies the Torah, that the Torah roots in Aristotelian philosophy. Reason, as extended and elaborated by Aristotle, discovered many of the truths expressed in the Torah.

The highest point that Greek philosophy had reached, according to Maimonides, was the idea of a First Cause, the ultimate cause of all causes—God. At this point Aristotle met Moses. Whatever differences remained between the two could be easily straightened out as long as this point did not stand in the way. Since Aristotle arrived at the conclusion that there is only one cause, it meant that he recognized Monotheism, though a little differently than the Torah did. *One cause* meant the same as *one God.*

The compatibility of Moses and Aristotle was not a notion new with Maimonides. It was a strong belief in the Middle Ages that Aristotle had derived many of his ideas from Judaism. Earlier, Josephus referred to a passage from Clearchus, a student of Aristotle, about a meeting with a Jewish sage:

> In his first book on Sleep he relates of Aristotle, his master, that he had a discourse with a Jew; and his own account was that what this Jew said merited admiration and showed philosophical erudition. To speak of the race first, the man was a Jew by birth and came from Coelesyria [Palestine]. These Jews are derived from the philosophers of India [!]. In India, the philosophers call themselves Kalani; and in Syria, Jews, taking their name from the country they inhabit, which is Judea; the name of their capital is rather difficult to pronounce: they call it Jerusalem. Now, this man, who had been the guest of many people, had come down from the highland to the seashore. He was a Greek not only in language, but in soul; so much so that, when we happened to be in Asia in about the same places whither he came, he conversed with us and with other persons of learning in order to test our wisdom. And as he had had intercourse with a large number of sages, he imparted to us more knowledge of his own. (*Contra Apionem* 2, 17)

Joseph b. Shem-Tob quotes an old book to the effect that "Aristotle at the end of his life had become a proselyte." Another legend had it that Aristotle obtained some of his philosophical ideas from writings by King Solomon, writings which Alexander of Macedon brought from Jerusalem.

It was true for Maimonides that perhaps Aristotle, all his reasoning notwithstanding, could not furnish as full a conception of the Deity as the Jews had through revelation. That was not crucial; Maimonides would go with Aristotle as far as he could, and then, if necessary, leave him behind.

In the *Guide*, Maimonides elaborated his discussion of the nature of God begun with his thirteen principles in Siraj, especially the first five principles. For example: God's incorporeality. The Biblical God is not corporeal, material, man-like; this principle he placed as the very basis of the Biblical conception of God. In this respect, it is extremely important to see Biblical anthropomorphisms as symbols or metaphors. True, as the Talmud says, "The Torah speaks in the language of man," but we must never forget that the "hand of God" or the "eyes of God" or even more subtle expressions are symbolic, allegorical. For example, Maimonides quotes Isaiah 13:10:

> For the stars of heaven and the constellations thereof shall not give their light; the sun shall be darkened in his going forth, and the moon shall not cause her light to shine.

Then he comments:

> I cannot imagine that anyone would be so foolish and blind as to take those allegorical and figurative phrases as real, that is to say, to the effect that the prophet meant to say that Babylonia's doom would cause such radical changes in nature.

Having emphasized the incorporeality of God, Maimonides then discusses at length the question of divine attributes. May we ascribe any attributes to God? No. Any attributes, any quality that we may ascribe to God, would be no more than a man-like attribute. Let us take "omnipotence" as an example. Do we have a concept of such power? No; our concept of power is taken directly from our experience. Likewise, "omniscience," which we usually ascribe to God: How can we present Him as such when we do not know, due to our own limitations, what it is? Even His Oneness and uniqueness are grasped differently by us from what they really are. "One," to us, represents a beginning followed by two, three. . .etc., whereas God is ONE that stands alone, without antecedent and with nothing succeeding him. One must remember that God is not one of a class or one of a species like any other object. When we ascribe an attribute or quality to any object we do it on the basis of comparison of one thing with another. A cat is recognized as a cat and not as a dog because it possesses the qualities attributed to the cat class. It is otherwise with God, who does not belong to a class, because He is conveived as only one, and consequently cannot be likened or compared to anything else; for if we do compare Him we violate His essence and ascribe to him something that is altogether alien.

If this be the case, then the question arises: Can we have any conception of God? Maimonides' decision is Yes, but we must remember that what we cannot do we cannot do. No positive attribute can be given to God; nevertheless, we can ascribe to him negative attributes, which, in His case, may serve to give us a limited conception of Him, a sort of partial description of His reflected essence. What is a negative attribute? The attribute of omnipotence cannot be ascribed to God, not because He is not necessarily omnipotent. He might be that for all we know, but we are in truth unable to do it because we are not all-powerful ourselves. However, we have a right to say that God is not as non-powerful as we are, that He is not as impotent. Eternity is not known to us, because we ourselves are temporary or non-eternal, but we can say that God is not as non-eternal as we are. We cannot say that God is omniscient, because omniscience is not within our experience, but we can say that He is not as non-knowing as we ourselves. Thus, by employing negative terms we can ascribe certain qualities to God without violating His essence, while simultaneously guarding ourselves from attributing something to Him the knowledge of which is not given to us as human beings.

Maimonides then raises the question of God's existence. Enumerating all twenty-six principles upon which Aristotle based his theory of the First Cause, he agrees with twenty-five of them, excepting the last one: that matter is co-existent with God. Instead, he accepts the principle of "creatio ex nihilo," that God created the world out of nothing. Here Maimonides admits that his rejection of Aristotle's principle of the eternity of matter is not a result of Biblical knowledge. It is rather because better arguments can be advanced for the principle of "creatio ex nihilo" than for the eternity of matter. Furthermore, he claims, Aristotle himself left this question open.

Maimonides quotes Aristotle as follows: "There are things which escape our judgment, or are too high for us. To explain why things have such and such properties is as difficult as to determine whether the world existed eternally or not"; Maimonides then adds this comment:

> We have mentioned this because we know that the majority
> of those who consider themselves wise, although they know
> very little about science, accept the theory that the world

is eternal, relying upon the authority of learned men. They refuse to accept the words of the prophets, because they say that the latter did not use scientific methods, and relied entirely upon divine inspiration. However, since Aristotle himself had left the question open, it would mean that the Biblical answer is by no means averse to reason.

What does Maimonides say about reason and morality? "Moral conduct," he asserts, "is a preparation for intellectual progress, and only a man whose character is pure, calm, and steadfast can attain to intellectual perfection—that is, acquire correct conceptions." (Guide 1, 34)

> Let there not enter your mind the belief of the fools among other peoples and also of the many uninformed men among the Israelites, that the Holy One, blessed be He, decrees concerning the human being, from his birth, whether he is to be righteous or wicked. The matter is not so. Every man has the possibility of becoming as righteous as Moses our teacher, or as wicked as Jeroboam—wise or stupid, kind or cruel, miserly or generous, and similarly with all the other qualities . . .In the same way that the Creator willed that all created things should have the tendency which He desired, so did He desire that a man should be possessed of free will, that all his actions should be under his control, and that there should not be anything to compel or to withhold him, but that of his own accord and by the mind which God had endowed him with, he should do all that man is able to do (Mishneh Torah, T'shubah 5:1-4).

As to the goal that man may reach by moral excellence and knowledge, Maimonides has this to say: If and when man actually reaches by his own effort and acts the level of the highest moral life, dedicating all his thoughts and deeds to God and purifying his soul by the control of his passions, he would actually be ready to accept the gift of prophecy. The prophetic spirit is a combination of both reason and imagination elevated above the sensual and freed entirely from the dross of material life. The prophets see things in the mirror of God, although the seeing appears in gradations; some see clearer visions; others see things like in a dream. The greatest prophet was Moses who saw God "face to face." He removed all the veils that corporeal existence puts on the soul, whereby he attained the highest degree of prophecy. The truth that descended upon him, Moses transmitted to his people. This is what we call Revelation—Israel's Torah, which contains not only the divine teaching, laws, and regulations that lead to the Good Life but also the underlying general principles of God, world, and man. In the fulfilment of its precepts, man can find health for the body and gratification for the soul—true happiness. In it and through it one can converse with God and see Him as the prophets saw Him.

The highest aim of man's life on earth, Maimonides holds, is to learn Torah for her own sake and to love God for His own sake, without expectation of honors, riches, or anything else. A perfect man is not supposed to say: I fulfil the commandments of the Torah because I shall get my reward in this life or in the after life; nor should he say: I do this or do not do this because of fear of punishment.

The idea of reward and punishment may be better understood, writes Maimonides, by a simple parable. When a little boy starts learning he has no interest in learning per se; in fact it is burdensome to him because he wants rather to play than to learn. But the teacher who knows the value of learning induces him to do so by giving him sweetmeats or honey. To the boy the sweetmeats are the important thing, whereas to the teacher they are only a means to an end. Only when the boy grows to maturity may he start to appreciate what learning really means. Likewise the imperfect man takes reward and punishment as the aim worthy of pursuing; to the contrary, the perfect man knows that the real reward, if any, lies in the learning itself, just as the punishment for not doing it lies in the fact of being ignorant. The first one is like the little boy that is brought to school; the latter one is in the position of the mature man who appreciates perfection. Certainly the greatest perfection that man can attain is in loving knowledge for knowledge's sake and in loving God for the sake of loving God. True faith in God and true love of God mean that nothing in the world, either wealth or power or honors, means anything to man; that the entire world fades into nothingness in comparison with the Creator of all. This is Perfection. (see Mishneh Torah, Snhedrin)

An interesting insight into Maimonides' views on moral conduct can be gained by noting his eight degrees of charity (listed in order of decreasing quality): (1) when one aids a man in want by offering him a gift or a loan, by entering into partnership with him, or by providing work for him, so that he may become self-sufficient; (2) when he who gives and he who receives are not aware of each other; (3) when the giver knows the recipient, but the recipient does not know the giver; (4) when the recipient knows the giver, but the giver does not know the recipient; (5) when the giver puts the alms into the hands of the poor without being asked; (6) when he puts the money into the hands of the poor after being asked; (7) when he gives less than he should, but does so cheerfully; (8) when he gives grudgingly.[22]

Maimonides' writings in other fields were voluminous. A mere listing of his works would show him as the encyclopedic mind, the renaissance man, he was. Just a sampling: At the age of sixteen he wrote a book on logic (Millot Hahigoyon). Ibn Tibbon translated it into Hebrew; Sebastian Munster translated it into Latin. Moses Mendelssohn wrote a commentary on the book. He did a work on the calendar, based on principles of astronomy. In medicine, he authored works on sexuality, on poisons and their antidotes, on hemorrhoids, on asthma, on hygiene; he believed that most diseases originate in the stomach and can be effectively cured by a healthy diet. Maimonides composed aphorisms, in imitation of Hippocrates, as instructions to doctors. He carried on an extensive correspondence and wrote many Responsa; a collection of the latter appeared in 1520 in Constantinople.

Maimonides was not only a scholar, a writer, the leader of the Jewish community in Egypt. He was also a practicing doctor, and physician to the sultan of Egypt. In a letter to his translator, Samuel ibn Tibbon, Maimonides opens a window for us onto his busy life, which touched and influenced and healed so many other lives.

My duties to the Sultan are very heavy. I am obliged to visit him every day, early in the morning; and when he or any of his children or the inmates of his harem are indisposed, I dare not quit Cairo, but must stay during the greater part of the day in the palace. It also frequently happens that one or two of the royal officers fall sick, and I must attend to their healing. I do not return home until the afternoon. Then I am almost dying with hunger; and I find the waiting-room filled with people, both Jews and non-Jews, nobles and common people, judges and bailifs, friends and foes—a mixed multitude—all waiting for my return. I dismount from my animal, wash my hands, go to my patients and entreat them to bear with me while I partake of some slight refreshment, the only meal I have in twenty-four hours. Then I attend to my patients and write prescriptions and directions for their various ailments. I prescribe for them while lying down out of sheer fatigue, and, when night falls, I am so exhausted that I can scarcely speak. As a result, no Jew can have a private interview with me except on the Sabbath. On that day the whole congregation, or at least the majority of the members, come to me after the morning service, when I instruct them as to their proceedings during the whole week. We study together a little until noon, then they leave. Some of them return, and read with me after the afternoon service until evening prayers.

Maimonides died December 13, 1204, in Cairo. His body was brought to the Holy Land and buried in Tiberias.

JUDAH AL-HARIZI
(1190-1240)

The last great poet of the period was Judah al-Harizi, a humorist and satirist par excellence.

Born in Spain and reared in the tradition of Spanish Jewry, in which Judaism and secular knowledge went hand in hand, Harizi was a master of both Hebrew and Arabic. A restless genius, he wandered from land to land, reaching as far as the Holy Land and Babylonia. He frequently complains of the complacency shown him in the Eastern lands. "For the fathers of poetry [the great Hebrew poets who preceded him], the sun in the West-land was always shining. They were rewarded for their poems with gold. But I came late. The sun had long set. Those poets dwelt on the banks of blessed rivers, but I have to starve in the scorching desert."

His greatest work is his book, Tahkemoni, meaning "an assembly of the wise or a place where the wise congregate." It is written in the Makama form, a literary form invented by the Arabic poet Hariri. The Hebrew word Tahkemoni is the equivalent of the Arab word Makama, a place where public matters are discussed. It is midway between an epic and a drama, a dialogue form in which the chief narrator tells about some curious episodes and another one asks questions, comments, and urges the first one to tell more. This form opens for Harizi a wide field for his talent; he showers the reader with witty epigrams, wise sayings, frivolous observations, and humorous scenes.

Harizi's aim in composing this book, as he indicated in the introduction, was two-fold: to prove that Hebrew can bring forth all possible poetic forms, including the difficult Makama-form; to amuse and bring joy into the life of the people. His characters, Heber the Kenite and Heman the Ezrahite, visit all sorts of places: marts, alleys, hidden corners in the orchards. The scenes change kaleidoscopically. Everything and anything is material for the poet. Now he makes his hero speak seriously, and soon enough he reappears as though from nowhere full of frivolity and jest.

Having been the first Makama writer among Jews, he furnished a model for all that followed him; as the first genuine Jewish humorist, he brought joy into sorrowful and aggrieved hearts. His humor, as any good humor, carries within it a vein of melancholy.

Here is a sample of Harizi's verses in which he reveals his inner self:

> Within my heart I held concealed
> My love so tender and so true;
> But overflowing tears revealed
> What I would fain have hid from view.
> My heart could never more repress
> The woe that tell-tale tears confess.

And here is a frivolous drinking song, which shows Harizi as a pleasant friend and companion:

> Here under leafy bowers,
> Where coolest shades descend,

Crowned with a wreath of flowers,
Here will we drink, my friend.
Who drinks of wine, he learns
That noble spirits' strength
But steady increase earns,
As years stretch out in length
A thousand earthly years
Are hours in God's sight,
A year in heav'n appears
A minute in its flight.
I would this lot were mine,
To live by heav'nly count
And drink and drink old wine
At youth's eternal fount.[23]

The following short poem illustrates the power of Harizi's diction:

The Song of the Pen[24]

My Muse, though airy, glides softly along.
Singing full oft a voiceless song;
My pen, though frail and slim of figure,
has a serpent's tooth and a lion's vigor.

The following example is from the Tahkemoni (Makama 10), though it loses much in the translation, of course:

From Siddim's vale
to Chaldea's pale
I went
and when arrived
the thought revived
to try
all to see
that there might be
rising, growing,
coming, going
of the worst and the best

east and west.
As I strode
on the road
one day I espied on a stone
all alone
at the highway side
a stranger sitting
resting. As befitting
I addressed him
aiming at interesting him
as travelers do
when a few
or two
chance to meet
in a country street.
And I said, What cheer
neighbor dear?
Whence hast thou strayed
and what thy trade?
He said, From daring feat
to daring feat
as it chances
my roving pleasure ever glances.
A fox I chase
or run a race
with the mountain sheep
no hill too steep
for me to pace.
Said I, Tell me, since thou so much hast wandered
some wondrous thing thou hast pondered.

Another example of Harizi's versatility (again from the Tahkemoni, but this time impossible to translate) is one poem written in Arabic, Aramaic, and Hebrew, each of the three languages taking a third of the space. The Arabic rhymes with the Hebrew, and the Aramaic portion uses only two-syllabled words, each of which is rhymed to the next throughout.

Harizi was a full-blooded poet of the earth and of life. He was in love with nature, in love with beauty, in love with life itself. He sings of luxurious gardens and orchards, where the young meet to enjoy life. Time and again he indicates that the charming daughters of mother Eve are not strangers to him. His best weapon is his humor: he laughs, mocks, ridicules, and taunts. The targets are the hypocrites, the misers, the rascals, and the mediocre do-nothings.

Harizi is famous not only as a poet but also as a keen critic. In several Makamas he presents an appraisal of the poets of previous generations. He also wrote Mahbereth Uthiel, another book in the Makama style; some short essays on the art of writing; and a translation of Maimonides' *Guide for the Perplexed,* which was not as popular as Ibn Tibbon's translation.

PARABLES, FABLES, HUMOR

A contemporary of Judah al-Harizi was Joseph ibn Zabara, author of the mock-heroic poems known as Sefer Sha'ashuyim (Book of Diversions). This book was also written in the Makama style. Zabara freely used parables and fables gathered from Jewish, Greek, Arabic, and Hindu sources. Many of these stories originating in the Orient were unknown in Europe until Zabara introduced them into European literature.

Earlier, in the 11th century, Peter Alfonsi, a converted Jew, presented thirty-three such stories in his Latin book, Disciplina Clericalis. Georg Depping regards this Alfonsi story presentation as the beginning of the European novel.[25]

Another contemporary of Judah al-Harizi was Judah ibn Sabbatai, a physician in Cordova. He wrote *The Misogynist,* a story about a man named Serah who had promised his dying father never to marry, "because women are the cause of all evil in the world." Serah gathers three other men of like minds and they go forth together to propagate their point of view. The campaign is successful; multitudes of women are furious. The women empower Korbi, an old hag, to find a young temptress to woo Serah away from his promise. She succeeds. Serah marries, only to discover after the wedding that an old lady has been substituted for his beautiful seducer. He requests a divorce, but the women insist that he is stuck with his old wife. Sabbatai himself was no woman-hater; he was just interested in a fun story.

About 1240, Berechiah of Natroni compiled a book of Arabic parables. About 1244, Isaac Abu Sahula of northern Spain compiled a collection of beautiful fables. Abraham ben Hasdai of Barcelona wrote *The Prince and the Nazarite,* a compilation of parables from the Talmud and from Hindu sources. "The Prince and the Dervish" is one such parable, told by the dervish to his prince to illustrate the nature of human life in this world and the need for preparing good deeds for the world to come. The story went like this:

In the Far East there was a little island, the inhabitants of which had some strange customs, notably in regard to their selection of a king to reign over them. Being averse to a hereditary monarchy, they used to go once every year to the seashore and choose as their king the first poor shipwrecked passenger whom they happened to meet there. As such, he was driven in a state coach to a magnificent palace, and there he was permitted to enjoy for a year all the rights and privileges of an Eastern Potentate. But as soon as the year of his reign was over, the king was stripped of his royal garments, brought back to the very spot where he had been found, and there left to himself.

Once, however, it so happened that the stranger, whom they had selected as their king, was a prudent man and experienced in worldly affairs. Astonished at his sudden elevation, he made enquiries of one of the islanders whose confidence he had gained, and learned from him the real reason. He accordingly devised a plan, from which he hoped that he and his friend would derive some lasting advantage. They were simply to go on a dark night to the state treasury, and to take away a quantity of jewels, which by right were the king's property for the time being, and hide them in a cave near the sea; they would thus have some means of subsistence when the year of the king's reign was ended. The plan was speedily effected. After his year's reign was over he was taken back to the place whence he had come, stripped of his royal robes, told he was no longer king, and left to fend for himself. He and his friend took possession of their hidden treasure, and with it they went on board a passing ship, which brought them to a foreign country, where the sale of their valuables enabled them to live a life of comfort and happiness.

Kalonymos ben Kalonymos (1286-1328) wrote Eben Bohan (Touchstone), a satire imbued with a lofty conception of life. In one of his most graceful chapters, he tries to demonstrate how better off woman is in comparison with man. It starts with a satiric elegy about the sorrowful state in which man finds himself. "His life is like a field laid waste"; he is exposed to "scorn and contumely," but—

> Were I, for instance, a woman,
> How smooth and pleasant were my course.
> A circle of intimate friends
> Would call me gentle, graceful, modest.
> Comfortably I'd sit with them and sew,
> With one or two mayhap at the spinning wheel.
> On moonlight nights
> Gathered for cozy confidences,
> About the hearthfire, or in the dark,
> We'd tell each other what the people say,
> The gossip of the town, the scandals,
> Discuss the fashions and the last election.

Kalonymos enumerates many more advantages of womanhood, such as falling in love with a "youth of handsome mien, brave and true, with heart filled with love for me." Then, since "the sages tell us everywhere" that we must be satisfied with our lot:

> So I will force my lips, however they may resist,
> to say the old blessing:
> "My Lord and God accept my thanks
> that thou hast made of me a man."

THE TIBBON AND KIMHI FAMILIES
(1120-1304)

Many families were influential in the growth of Spanish Jewry. Two outstanding families, the Tibbons and the Kimhis, are worthy of special note, as illustrative of the continuity of contribution made generation after generation by uncounted families.

Among Jews, Judah ben Saul ibn Tibbon (1120-1190) is called "The Father of Translators." He was a master of both Hebrew and Arabic. As translator he is best known for rendering into Hebrew the works of Saadia ben Joseph, Jonah ibn Janah, Solomon ibn Gabirol, and Bahaya ibn Pakuda, thus enabling the Jews of Christian Europe to study the works of these religious and intellectual giants. As a student of philosophy and a lover of books, Judah collected a rich library. He also wrote an original work on rhetoric and grammar, but it was lost. Preserved for us is one of the finest human documents known: his ethical will written for his son.

Judah was born and educated in Granada, but persecution of the Jews by the Almohades forced him to flee Spain. He settled in Lunel, in southern France, where his son, Samuel, was born in 1150. Samuel translated into Hebrew the works of the Arab Averroes and Ali ibn Ridwan. His greatest contribution was the translation of Maimonides' *Guide for the Perplexed*. He also wrote a commentary on the entire Bible, but only portions of it remain.

Moses, Samuel's son, continued the translation tradition, rendering into Hebrew many works on philosophy, mathematics, astronomy, and medicine. He also wrote Biblical commentaries.

Moses' son, Jacob ibn Tibbon (1236-1304), was well known by his Latin name, Don Profiat Tibbon or Profatias Judaeus. He was a prominent physician and well versed in astronomy and other sciences. Some of his own works were translated into Latin and quoted by Copernicus, Reinhold, and Clavius. Jacob translated the geometry of Euclid into Hebrew and prepared a compendium of Ptolemy's work, Almagest. He also wrote a treatise on the quadrant and its use and prepared important astronomical tables, which were used by scientists of his day and for generations.

Joseph Kimhi (1105-1170), as did Judah ibn Tibbon, fled Spain under persecution. He settled in Narbonne, Provence, where his fame grew as a grammarian, exegete, poet, and translator. Much of his work is lost to us, but extant is Sefer Habrit (Book of the Convenant), an apologetic work attempting to prove the truth of Judaism as against Christianity. Joseph's sons became more famous than their father.

David Kimhi (1160-1235), known also as Redak, wrote an extensive commentary on the Bible, which was a model of exegetical simplicity. He also composed the two-part Miklol, a complete Hebrew grammar and Biblical dictionary.

MOSES BEN NAHMAN
(1195-1270)

Moses ben Nahman, known also as Nahmanides and Bonastruc da Porta, was born in Gerona in the year 1195. He was famous as a Talmudist, Bible exegete, and physician. He was also well versed in philosophy, though he tended to be critical of its use by Jews; he remained a traditionalist in his views.

In the year 1263, he was called upon by the king of Aragon to enter into a public disputation on the truth of Judaism. His opponent was Pablo Christiani, a Jewish convert to Christianity, who out of hatred of his former co-religionists tried every means at his disposal to calumniate Judaism. The church, of course, was interested to expose the folly of Talmudic Judaism, whereby it hoped that the Jews would be persuaded to accept Christianity. The open disputation between Nahmanides and Christiani was held in Barcelona in the presence of King Jayme and his court. Many dignitaries of the church took part in the debate that lasted four days. Nahmanides was the only defender of Judaism. He stood up for his faith with such fearlessness, and defended every tenet of it with such dignity and acumen, that the king presented him with a money reward. The Dominican judges, however, spread rumors that the Jew had been defeated on all points, whereupon Nahmanides published a refutation in the form of a complete report on the

disputation, Viku'ah (Disputation). He gave all the questions
posed and the detailed answers to all of them. Nahmanides' report
indicated that the debates covered such topics as whether there is
evidence in the Talmud that the Messiah already came, the godliness of the Messiah, whether the Messiah died for humanity, whether
the Torah was to be abrogated after the Messiah's coming. The
exchanges took such form as follows:

At first Pablo referred to Genesis 49:10, which reads: "The
sceptre shall not depart from Judah, nor the ruler's staff from between his feet until Shiloh comes." Since the Talmud interprets
Shiloh as the Messiah, Pablo argued, it is clear that the kingdom
shall not depart from Judah till the coming of the Messiah; but
with his coming, Judah would no more hold the sceptre. This
happened at the time of Jesus: Judah lost her independence.
Nahmanides refuted it upon the basis of history. Judah, he declared, lost her independence at the time of Nebuchadnezzar
(586 B.C.E.) and never regained it except for the short period at
the time of the Hasmoneans. Judah did not wield a sceptre almost
600 years before Jesus.

Pablo then cited a story from Midrash Eikha Rabba, 1:16, about
an Arab who told a Jewish peasant that when the Temple was destroyed the Messiah was born at Bethlehem. The Jewish peasant,
having heard such a good report, went to Bethlehem and found
the mother and the baby-savior. He presented her with some gifts,
but when he visited her a second time, the child had disappeared.
Pablo insisted that the child was Jesus. Nahmanides answered that
he did not believe in such legends, but even if he were to believe, it
had nothing to do with Jesus who had been born before the destruction of the Temple, according to the New Testament.

Nahmanides' book so incensed the Dominicans that they brought
charges against him that he had insulted Christianity and the
church. The king advised Nahmanides to leave Spain, which he
did. He and his family settled in Palestine at Acre, where he spent
the rest of his life studying, teaching, and writing. He gathered
disciples, who considered him one of the great lights of Jewry.

Early in life, Moses had composed a book titled Milhamot
Adonai (Wars of God), in which he defended Isaac Alfasi's code
against the criticisms of Zerahiah Halevi of Gerona. In Acre he

wrote his chief work, a commentary on the Pentateuch. With varying intensity, he attacked the approach or interpretations of Rashi,
of Abraham ibn Ezra, of Aristotle, of Maimonides. Some of Maimonides' ideas he considered "sinful" even to hear. Nahmanides
was an admirer of Cabala and he interspersed his commentary,
though cautiously, with Cabalistic ideas. The commentary went
through many editions and was considered first-rate.

Nahmanides also wrote works on Talmudic law, in addition to
his earlier *Wars of God*. He died in 1270 and was buried at
Haifa.

SOLOMON BEN ABRAHAM ADRET
(1235-1310)

Solomon Adret, a disciple of Nahmanides and of Jonah of Gerona, was the most eminent rabbi of Spain, recognized as the
greatest Talmudic authority. Legal questions were referred to him
from Portugal, Italy, France, Germany, and even from Asia Minor.
His Responsa show him to have been a man of wide experience,
systematic thought, and deep insight. Although an opponent of
philosophy and somewhat inclined towards Cabala, he did not
manifest any hostility towards those who studied philosophy, nor
did he show too much zeal for Cabala. Primarily Adret was a
Talmudist.

Yet Solomon Adret was pushed into a position where he had
to take measures against philosophy even when his heart was not
in the act. The man who forced it upon him was Abba Mari b.
Moses ha-Yarhi, a sworn enemy of philosophy. Abba conducted a
campaign against heresy. He corresponded with the rabbis of
France about the danger to Judaism due to young people's at-
traction to philosophical ideas. Abba Mari collected his correspondence and published it in a book, Minhat Kanaot (The Offering of Jealousy). Adret tried at first to keep an impartial position, but finally he was forced to take a stand. In the year 1305,
Solomon Adret, in conjunction with his colleagues of the Barcelona
rabbinate, issued a ban against studying philosophy before the

age of thirty. We assume that with their aversion to philosophy, neither Abba Mari nor Adret drew upon Aristotle's advice in the Nicomachean Ethics (I, 3), which suggests that philosophy is not for the young. In any case, a second ban was pronounced against interpreting the Bible allegorically. The bans were by no means popular in Spain; nor were they rigorously enforced.

Solomon Adret, known by his abbreviated name, Rashba, left numerous Responsa which were later published. He also wrote a refutation of the charges of Raymund Martini, a Dominican monk of Barcelona, who composed a book entitled *Pugio Fidei*, in which he attacked the Talmud. Adret also refuted a work by a Muslim who charged that the priests had falsified certain parts of the Bible. In everything he wrote he demonstrated his keen intelligence and profound knowledge of the subjects discussed.

ISAAC ALBALAG
(second half of 13th century)

Isaac Albalag lived during the second half of the 13th century in Spain. Nothing of his life and activities is known. Some of his philosophical views, especially his liberal interpretation of the Creation story in Genesis, stamped him as a heretic in the eyes of his contemporaries.

According to Albalag, the six days of Creation have the purpose only to show the relative order of things as they proceeded one after the other, but not as an exact account of Creation. He accepts Aristotle's eternity of matter, in opposition to Maimonides' "creatio ex nihilo." The Genesis creation account, therefore, becomes with him nothing more than a kind of "coming out" or evolvement from matter that had already existed. How does one treat the conflict between Scripture and philosophy? How could matter co-exist eternally with God? Albalag answers: Indeed both philosophy and the Bible give different answers, yet they are both true—the one from the point of view of philosophy and the other from the standpoint of theology. Since the Creation account was written by prophets, it is to be understood only by prophets, because the common people, not being philosophers, might understand it only in a concrete form as presented by the Torah. "Therefore," Albalag insists, "one errs doubly who rejects a philosophical truth on account of its apparent contradiction of Scripture; second, because thereby he declares the real argument of philosophy inconclusive." Philosophy demonstrates, whereas religion teaches; in teaching, various methods may be used.

Albalag shows leanings toward the Cabala, though he opposes excessive mysticism. He translated Al-Gazzali's *Logic and Metaphysics* from Arabic into Hebrew.

IMMANUEL BEN SOLOMON
(1270-1330)

Immanuel ben Solomon or Immanuel of Rome, satirical poet and scholar, was born in 1270 at Rome and died about 1330 at Fermo, Italy. He was endowed with an easy, humorous, and witty talent. Writing both in Hebrew and Italian, he was held in high regard in Italian literary circles. Some Italian critics placed him beside Dante. Hebrew criticism, however, does not accord him such an exalted position.

He introduced into Hebrew poetry the form of the sonnet, which was popular in Italy. In his old age he collected all his poems and published them in a diwan entitled Mehabberot. They all deal with Jewish life of his time. His satire is sharp and biting, funny and replete with fine allusions. At times Immanuel is frivolous.

> Virtue dwells rarely in the bright-eyed and fair,
> But in the wrinkled old crones with silver-white hair.

> Of what good can Paradise be,
> When the company there is so boring,
> Homely old hags always snoring?[26]

Immanuel also wrote a long poem entitled Ha-Tofet weha-Eden (Hell and Paradise), which is patterned on Dante's Divine Comedy.

This book, however, is not of the same literary quality as Dante's, although it occupies a respectable place in Hebrew literature, thanks to Immanuel's fine style and mastery of language.

As a member of a wealthy family, Immanuel received a good Talmudic and general education. He was well versed in mathematics, astronomy, medicine, philosophy. He wrote Italian, Arabic, Latin, Hebrew, and perhaps Greek. He was stimulated to write poetry by his cousin, Judah Romano, who distinguished himself in philosophy and translating.

Following his predecessors, Immanuel wrote commentaries on the Bible, the greater part of which was lost. Only small portions came down to us in manuscript form.

Gustav Karpeles makes the following interesting remark about Immanuel:

> With amazement we see the Hebrew Muse, so serious aforetimes, participate in truly bacchanalian dances under Immanuel's guidance. It is curious that while, on the one hand, he shrinks from no frivolous utterance or indecent allusion, on the other, he is dominated by deep earnestness and genuine warmth of feeling, when he undertakes to defend or expound the fundamentals of faith.[27]

LEVI BEN GERSHON
(1288-1344)

Levi ben Gerson, known as Gersonides or Leon Hebraeus, was a philosopher, astronomer, mathematician, and Biblical exegete, whose works made a deep imprint on medieval throught among Jews and Christians alike. Levi wrote extensively on various branches of science: on algebra, a special treatise titled Sefer Hamispar (Book of Number); a treatise on astronomy; a work on syllogism and logical thinking, Sefer Hahekkesh Hayashar (Book of Right Analogy). In his work on astronomy, consisting of 136 chapters, extant only in manuscript form, he criticized the systems of Ptolemy and Al-Bitruji, and described an instrument which he had invented and used to make precise astronomical observations. Pico de Mirandola highly praised the book, and Pope Clement VI ordered that it be translated into Latin. Kepler was so interested in the astronomical tables printed in the book that he obtained a copy in order to make a special study of the tables.

As a philosopher, Gersonides' fame rests on his work titled Milhamot Adonai (Wars of God). Among all the Jewish religious philosophers in the Middle Ages, Gersonides dared to take a stand against the Biblical theology if it was not in agreement with reason. He laid down the principle: "The law cannot prevent us from considering to be true that which our reason urges us to accept." (Introduction to Milhamot Adonai)

Such a statement was daring enough in the 14th century, when one could have been proclaimed a heretic. In his Biblical commentaries, he did away with miracles altogether. The passage in Joshua 10:12, "Sun, stand thou still upon Gibeon," he explained as merely a wish that "the sun should not set before the defeat of the enemy." Likewise, the 10° retrogression of the sun in 2 Kings 20:8-11 he expounded as meaning not the sun but the shadow. Gersonides took miracles as natural events which were distinguished from regular occurrences, if at all, by the fact that the former occurred rarely and for the sake of special purposes.

Gersonides criticized many tenets of Maimonides' philosophy, especially the notion that God can only be known by negative attributes. Gersonides argues that negative attributes and positive attributes are different only in degree, not in kind. Were they different in kind, we would have no way of knowing anything about God. Knowledge and being, both of them positive attributes, can certainly be ascribed to God, argues Gersonides.

As to the question of "creatio ex nihilo" versus the eternity of matter, Gersonides takes a middle course. "There existed," he declares, "before the beginning of creation a kind of inert, undeterminate substance which had been no more than potentiality." At a given moment God bestowed upon this potentiality form, motion, and life and thus everything that exists proceeded therefrom, excepting some heavenly "intelligences" that had been directly emanated from God.

Some of Gersonides' ideas were incorporated by Benedict Spinoza in his Theologic-Political Tractate. Some orthodox scholars regarded them as heresies. Gersonides' book was called at times not Wars of God but rather Wars against God. Even his Biblical commentaries were condemned by some of the learned, despite their admiration for his Biblical and Talmudic knowledge.

HASDAI CRESCAS
(1340-1410)

Hasdai Crescas, Talmudist and philosopher, has the distinction of having been one of the greatest opponents of Aristotelianism in the Middle Ages at a time when Aristotle seemed to reign supreme over the minds of men. Crescas undertook to demolish this philosophic stronghold, thereby freeing Judaism from the bondage of Greek philosophy. His main target was, of course, Maimonides, who had brought Greek philosophy into the vineyard of Israel. Hasdai deplored the fact that Maimonides, whose scholarship he respected and honored, should have accepted Aristotle, whereas it could be easily shown that most of his arguments fall apart under critical analysis. This is what Hasdai attempted in his book, Or Adonai (Light of God)—to demonstrate the weakness of Aristotle's philosophy, the vulnerability of his principles and his arguments.

Aristotle's propositions, numbering twenty-six, were accepted by Maimonides, excepting the last one: the eternity of matter. To Maimonides, the twenty-five propositions were all axiomatic, self-evident truths. But under Hasdai's sharp critique, they were not self-evident at all. He argued against Aristotle's assertion that an endless chain of causes is unthinkable and therefore we must assume a First Cause. Whence comes the certainty that an endless chain of causes is unthinkable? How do we arrive at the conclusion that there must be an ultimate cause that has no antecedent? Philosophy is unable to prove anything like that, said Crescas; it is not within the competence of metaphysics to arrive at such conclusions. And even if an ultimate cause is posited, it does not mean that one has proved unity; for there might be several ultimate causes. Even if God is omnipotent, it does not mean that other gods with other functions might not still be in existence.

Crescas disagreed with Maimonides on another point. It is not reason or knowledge that brings man to God and secures his happiness, but rather love—God's love which seeks to meet man half-way and man's love of God when kindled by a desire to do good in correspondence to God's will. Crescas also denied Maimonides' contention against ascribing positive attributes to God. Why not? he asked. It is true perhaps that by employing such attributes we might obtain an imperfect or even erroneous concept, but this would be only subjective; that is, *we* would fail, but it would not mean that the implied imperfection resides in God. We might say that the attributes we ascribe to God simply fall short of His perfection. But what of it? God does not lose anything by our having imperfect conceptions of Him. Hence positive attributes can and may be given to the Godhead.

Maimonides made prophecy contingent upon the cultivation of the intellect and the imagination. Hasdai disagreed again. The requirement of knowledge is not a necessary condition for being endowed with the prophetic gift. Communion with God stems from love and reverence. Philosophical speculation is not needed as a help to the prophet.

Maimonides stated that it is useless to search for the ultimate purpose of life, since man's mind is limited and can never hope to discover the secrets of creation. Hasdai disagreed again. In his judgment, there is such a purpose, and one does not have to look for it, because it is within man. The purpose is *the happiness of the soul*. The soul of man is constantly striving after union with the divine. The Torah, when fulfilled with love and devotion, helps to realize that striving, so that man is happy. Not knowledge, but love, creates the soul. Filled with love, the soul yearns after the source whence it came. Man's highest aim in life is to do God's will as revealed in the Torah; God's will is to make man happy in this world and make him worthy of a higher world—in the Hereafter.

Hasdai's *Light of God* was a trumpet call to return to traditionalism, but apparently the time was not ripe for such a return. Hasdai's book was not hailed enthusiastically by those he wanted to reach; it went through only a very few editions. Hasdai felt he had failed to dislodge the intellectual rule of Aristotle.

JOSEPH ALBO
(c. 1380-1444)

Joseph Albo was a disciple of Hasdai Crescas. Nothing of his life is known except the fact that he participated in the religious debate held at Tortosa in the years 1413-14. He was a preacher and theologian.

We know best Albo's work on the fundamentals of Judaism, Sefer Ikkarim (Book of First Principles). The principal question that Albo poses is: What principles are indispensable to a religion that is both divine and true? His answer is that there are three fundamental principles which form the basis of a true and divine religion: belief in the existence of God, revelation, reward and punishment. All other articles of faith such as incorporeality and unity of God, which Maimonides included in his thirteen principles of faith, are inferences that follow from Albo's three basic principles. According to Albo, the first fundamental principle, belief in God's existence, comprises the following secondary inferences: unity, incorporeality, eternity, and perfection. The second basic principle, revelation, contains the following inferences: prophecy, Moses as the greatest prophet, and the binding force of the Mosaic Law. The third principle, reward and punishment or retribution, comprises one corollary: resurrection.

Opinion has varied about Albo's book. S. Back and Munk praise it as building a valid philosophical foundation for Judaism. H. Graetz is critical, charging Albo with "shallowness," "verbosity," and "fondness for platitudes." The latter charge likely stemmed, in part, from the fact that the style of Albo's work is homiletic. Notwithstanding such charges, Albo's book did exert considerable influence on the development of Jewish thought in the Middle Ages, especially in polemics with Christianity and Islam.

DON ISAAC ABRAVANEL
(1437-1508)

With the expulsion of the Jews from Spain, the cultural achievement of Spanish Jewry, which enriched civilization for over 500 years, came to its end. Yet there remained some scholars who left their imprint in Hebrew literature.

Don Isaac Abravanel was one of them. A statesman and a great Biblical scholar, he was the son of Dom Judah, the royal treasurer of Portugal. When his father died, he occupied the same position. In 1483, he was involved in a political affair, and was forced to flee into Spain. The king of Castile, aware of his ability, appointed him his state treasurer. Abravanel served in that capacity until 1492, when Ferdinand and Isabella issued the decree of expulsion of the Jews. Abravanel is said to have offered the royal pair a large sum of money to revoke the decree, but to no avail. He personally was permitted to stay in Spain, but chose to lead his brethren into exile.

He settled in Venice, Italy, and devoted his time to studying and writing. Abravanel was a copious writer. His works deal with Biblical exegesis, religious philosophy, and apologetics. Many Christian scholars, such as Buddeus, Carpzov, the Buxtorfs, quoted Abravanel. In his Biblical commentaries especially he manifested his great knowledge of political and social life. His observations on monarchy are particularly interesting:

> In an elected government in which there is nothing crooked or perverse, no man lifts his hand or foot to commit any manner of trespass.
>
> *
>
> The existence of a monarch is not necessary; nay, it is harmful and a great danger.
>
> *
>
> Behold the lands where the administration is in the hands of kings, and you will observe their abomination and corruption. Each king does what is right in his own eyes, and the earth is filled with their wickedness. On the other hand, we see many lands where the administration is in the hands of judges. Temporary rulers are elected there, and over them there is a chief against whom there is no rising up.
>
> *
>
> When the turn of other judges or officers comes, these will be able to investigate whether the first ones have not failed in their trust.

It is more likely that one man should trespass, through
his folly or strong temptations or anger, than that many
men taking counsel should trespass. For if one of them
turns aside from the right path, the others will protest
against him. Moreover, since their administration is
temporary, and they must render account after a short
while, the fear of men will be upon them.

*

I think that kings were at first set up not by the consent of
the people but by force. They made themselves masters, as
if God gave them the earth, and they leave it to their children as an inheritance, as if it is a plot of land which one
acquires for money.[28]

Judah Abravanel, son of Don Isaac, was a prominent physician,
poet, and philosopher. He was also known as Leo Hebreus. His
most important work, Dialogi di Amore (Dialogues of Love),
written in a polished Italian style, was published at Rome in the
year 1535, the year of Judah's death in Venice. It was very popular and went through five editions in twenty years. It was translated into Spanish, French, Latin, and Hebrew.

ABRAHAM BEN SAMUEL ZACUTO
(c. 1450-1510)

Abraham Zacuto—astronomer, mathematician, historian—was a
professor at the University of Salamanca, his native city, and later
at the University of Saragossa. After the expulsion of the Jews
from Spain in 1492, Zacuto settled in Lisbon, Portugal.

When Vasco da Gama projected his expedition to circumnavigate
Africa, the king of Portugal consulted Zacuto on the feasibility of
the project. Zacuto, as the court astronomer, encouraged the king
to subsidize da Gama. The ships fitted out for the expedition were
equipped with Zacuto's perfected astrolabe, an instrument used for
obtaining the altitudes of planets and stars. It is also known that
Columbus used astronomical charts prepared by Zacuto. He also
wrote books on astronomy.

When persecutions of Jews were started in Portugal, Zacuto fled first to Tunis and then to Turkey. There he wrote a chronological history of the Jews from the Creation to the year 1500. This book is known as Sefer Ha-Yuhasin. It is of great value to the student of Jewish literary history.

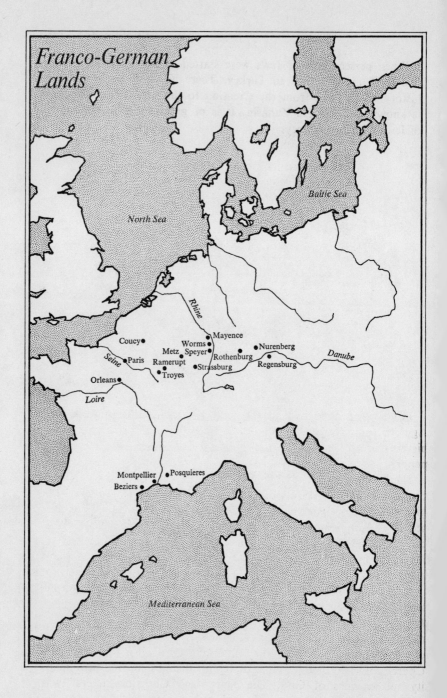

Franco-German Lands

Baltic Sea

North Sea

Rhine

Coucy
Mayence
Worms
Metz Speyer
Nurenberg
Seine Paris Ramerupt Rothenburg Danube
Strassburg Regensburg
Orleans Troyes

Loire

Montpellier Posquieres
Beziers

Mediterranean Sea

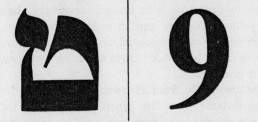

THE FRANCO-GERMAN LANDS

AGE OF DARKNESS

The division of history into specific periods—Dark Ages, Middle Ages, Renaissance, Reformation—generally applied to European history, is neither helpful nor valid for the history of the Jewish people.

The entire range of Jewish history in Europe since the 4th century, except for brief periods of time and some geographical regions, can be designated one long Age of Darkness—an age of persecutions, confiscations, banishments, tortures. It continued practically into the 18th century and in some countries even much later, involving most of the peoples of Europe, excepting little Holland after it had freed itself from the Spanish yoke in the 16th century.

As early as Biblical times, Israel was likened to a flock of scattered lambs. This metaphor was a reality in the Middle Ages. The Jewish communities in Europe, like scattered flocks, were surrounded by ferocious wolves: the mobs, the feudal lords, and some of the Church dignitaries. They all combined against the Jews. The Church, officially, lodged charges against them as enemies of humanity and enemies of God. The charge of "Christ-murderers" was

309

hurled at rich and poor, young and old, man and woman. Pope Innocent III insisted at the Fourth Lateran Council convoked in 1215 that all the regulations enacted against the Jews formerly must be put in operation with utmost stringency. Every Jew was to wear a yellow badge or cap in order to mark him or her off as a creature condemned to degradation and as a convenient target for those ever eager to wreak vengeance upon the Jews by robbing them of their possessions.

Driven systematically from economic life, confined within dank ghettos, and isolated from the general population, the Jews were pushed into moneylending, although only a small number could indulge in such an occupation. The greater majority were, of course, poor, and lived from hand to mouth. Yet the charge of usury was hurled against all the members of the "despicable" race. It was charged that the Talmud, one of the most ethically oriented works, second only to the Bible, taught the Jews to deceive and rob the Christians in business and even to murder innocent children for ritual purposes. Many believed that before the Passover holiday, pious Jews actually kidnapped Christian children, killed them, and drained their blood to be kneaded into dough for matzos. Too often, when a Christian child got lost, the Jewish community was accused, and before anything rational could be done, the mob was already at work: robbing, murdering, or driving the Jews like wild animals and mutilating them.

In France, volumes of the Talmud as well as other sacred books were burned publicly.

When the Black Plague struck Europe in 1348, the Jews were the first to be blamed. The filthy conditions in the cities and towns of Europe were little taken account of. It was the Jews who had poisoned the wells in order to wreak vengeance upon the Christian population.

In most cases Jews were helpless. The state authorities collaborated with the Church in cleaning out the infidels, the perfidious Jews, the mortal enemies of society.

Since 1096, when the First Crusade began, massacres of Jews were frequent in France and Germany. Another Crusade started in 1147, and a third in 1189. The literature of these Crusades is replete with tales of chivalrous acts of heroic knights who went forth to liberate Jesus' grave from the Muslims; it was a story of religious dedication in a war for the sake of Christianity. But the annals of the Jewish people present a different picture of this enterprise. Rivers of Jewish blood were spilled all over Europe by those Knights of the Faith. "Death to the Jews" was their motto. Entire Jewish communities were destroyed by fire and sword.

The last stage in the persecution of Jews was banishment. In England, Edward I decided in 1290 to get rid of the Jews. First they were robbed of their possessions, and when they were already homeless and beggared, he ordered them to leave the country altogether. In France the Jews had lived from time immemorial, but in the year 1300 an edict was issued for their banishment. Later they were returned but they had to leave again. In Germany the situation of the Jews was similar to France, though here due to the division of the country into separate provinces under different lords, the Jews who survived the massacres could wander from one province to another. The expulsion of the Jews from Spain in 1492 was only a climax of a long line of persecutions and unimaginable inquisitorial tortures perpetrated and executed against the Jews for hundreds of years.

While one studies the Hebrew literature of the Middle Ages one wonders: How could those scholars and thinkers, poets and visionaries, teachers and students, moralists and preachers, commentators and interpreters dedicate themselves to thinking and writing while such terrible events were going on before their eyes? Whence did they derive that stamina, courage, inspiration, and patience to compose such works? In the face of such adverse conditions, they could still summon strength and unimaginable endurance to create a world of the ideal in the midst of an inferno, where pillage and murder were raging unhindered. Precisely when in Mayence alone about 6,000 Jews were slaughtered in the light of day, and when in Strassburg the whole Jewish population was burned as a public spectacle, Jewish scholars were still writing books delving into the mysteries of God and his creation, and translating into Hebrew many works written in Arabic.

Jewish mysticism, or Cabala, flourished during this Age of Darkness as it never had before. The Cabala as a whole, with its mysteries and secret incantations, with its flight into imaginary worlds, its spells and magic rites, its parables and interpretations of the sacred writings, its enchanting calls for redemption, and its dreams of the Messianic age that would soon come, stands out as something wonderful. There was the rigid Talmudist, there was the liturgic poet calling people to repent their sins and pray for forgiveness, there was the learned Jew who desired to harmonize his faith with philosophy and reason—and there was the Cabalist with his theories of the En-Sof (the endless), the Sefirot (emanations), and the entire "hidden science" of numerology and other secret mystic lore which underlay the Scriptures and gave true meaning to God's word.

Perhaps Cabala embodied the will to live which emerged despite the troubles of the time. Perhaps the medieval Jews, while their sorrows piled up around them, found refuge in a world not of this world, a world of imagination rather than the world of reality that seemed all grief and tragedy. There is some parallel for understanding, and some irony, in relating Cabala to the New Testament book of Revelation. With its Messianic visions, its mystic numbers, its triumphal conquest of evil, the book of Revelation gave hope and courage to beleagured Christians persecuted by a Roman world. Centuries later, the Jews, persecuted by a Christian world, found light, warmth, hope, vigor in Cabala.

Thus, we see that the Jews continued during the Middle Ages in Europe to produce works ranging over the entire spectrum of Hebrew literature: poetry, Biblical exegesis, grammar, philosophy, ethics, mysticism. One historian has said: "The Franco-German scholars did not attain to the polish and versatility, as well as the philosophical breadth of view, which distinguished their Spanish brethren; but, if the Northerns lacked the love of philosophizing, they at least possessed in an abundant measure moral earnestness and deep piety."

The very beginning of the Franco-German schools is credited to the arrival in Narbonne of Nathan ben Isaac, one of the four Babylonian scholars who were captured by the Moors in the 10th century. Nathan was ransomed by the Jews of Narbonne, where he established a great Talmudic academy. His disciple, Judah ben Meir, took up his master's mantle and continued his work. But it remained for Rabbenu Gershom to lay strong foundations for Torah-learning all over Germany and France.

The Spanish and Portuguese Jews and their descendants all over southern Europe and the East belong by their origin, distinctive religious ritual, and pronunciation of Hebrew to that section of the Jewish people known as Sephardim (from Sephard: Obadiah 20, which was erroneously interpreted as meaning Spain). The Jews of northern and eastern Europe are called Ashkenazim (from Ashkenaz: Genesis 10:3, which is understood as the name for Germany).

During the 10th-15th centuries, the Ashkenazic center of Judaism was overshadowed by the Sephardic culture of Spain; but with the expulsion of the Jews from Spain in 1492, the Franco-German schools dominated Hebrew learning and literature.

GERSHOM BEN JUDAH
(b. 960)

The first great personality of the Franco-German schools was Gershom ben Judah, known as Rabbenu (our master) Gershom, or Ma'or Hagolah (Light of the Exile). He stood at the head of all the Jewish settlements on the Rhine and all the communities scattered in northern and southern France.

Rabbenu Gershom was born in Metz in 960. His teacher was Judah ben Meir HaKohen, a renowned Talmudist. Gershom himself became a learned Talmudist and Jewish leader, and in addition a poet, a grammarian, and a Masorete. When Gershom settled in Mayence, he established his own academy; students from all over Europe flocked to him, and Jewish communities from Europe and Africa turned to him with their legal problems; his decisions were revered throughout the Jewish world. Among his disciples were such personalities as Jacob ben Yakar, Rashi's teacher, and Eleazar ben Isaac ha-Gadol (the Great).

In addition to his far-flung Responsa, Gershom maintained a constant correspondence with the leading rabbis in France and Germany. With special concern for the regulation of Jewish life in the Franco-German lands, Gershom, with the concurrence of many other rabbis, issued four edicts around the year 1000: (a) No divorce shall be granted by a rabbinical court without

the consent of both husband and wife. (b) Apostates under com-
pulsion shall be treated with friendliness and compassion. (c) Letters addressed to one person shall not be opened by another.
(d) Polygamy shall be prohibited.[1]

The apostate edict was soon to prove tragically personal. In
1012, when the Jews were driven from Mayence, Gershom's son
forsook Judaism. It is characteristic of the man that when his
apostate son died, Gershom bewailed him, observing all the traditional customs prescribed for the period of mourning. His compassion for those who submitted to baptism under duress was
proverbial. For example, in his synagogue he permitted former
apostates to pronounce the benedictions and perform other
services.

The Franco-German schools distinguished themselves mainly
in Talmud learning. In Biblical exegesis they followed the simple
meaning of the text interspersed with Midrashic interpretations.
The French Jewish religious leaders were not interested in philosophy or in literature as such. Their "philosophy" and "literature"
were the Talmud and the Midrashim. Their poetry was purely
liturgical, reflecting the suffering of Israel in exile, the hope for redemption, and the prayers for forgiveness. This was the course
which Ashkenazic Jewry would pursue for centuries to come. Piety
first and foremost, all else secondary.

SOLOMON BEN ISAAC (RASHI)
(1040-1105)

Solomon ben Isaac, or Solomon Izhaki, known by his abbreviated name, Rashi (the first letters of Rabbi Shloime Izhaki), is the
greatest commentator of both the Talmud and the Bible. He became
the recognized teacher of generations of men, Jews and Christians
alike.

Rashi became a legendary figure during his lifetime, and fascinating tales were told about his parents and birth. According to
tradition, Rashi's father obtained a gem that had served as an eye
for an idol. Pious Christians offered him a large sum of money for

it, but he refused, because he did not want to benefit by something that came from an impure source. He therefore cast the precious gem into the sea, whereupon he heard a heavenly voice announcing that a son was to be born to him who would be a "Light in Israel."

Another legend was told about Rashi's mother during her pregnancy. While she passed through a narrow alley in Worms, she was pushed to the wall by a rushing chariot of a feudal lord. She could have been killed if not for a miracle that occurred: The wall momentarily bent, forming a niche, and thus both the pregnant woman and the unborn child were saved.

A third legend purported to demonstrate Rashi's wisdom, though the same story was told about others, too. A local lord who was about to lead his troops into war in the East came to Rashi and ordered him to predict through which gate he would enter the city upon his return home. The city walls had two entrances: a large gate and a smaller one. Rashi promised to submit his prediction as soon as he was notified of the ruler's return. When the returning lord stood in sight of the city, he started to figure what to do. Logically he would have to use the large gate but he reckoned that to do this would give Rashi a chance to guess correctly. He therefore decided to use the smaller one. On second thought, however, he was fearful that the Jew might also think the same way; therefore it would be better to enter through the larger gate. But what would happen if the Jew had also reasoned similarly? Hesitating what to do, he decided to make a new entrance. On his arrival at the castle, he obtained Rashi's note which contained the following words: "A ruler breaks a fence and passes through." The learned Jew, following the same train of thought, reached the same conclusion.

Later generations attributed to Rashi divine inspiration and prophetic insight into the Torah; otherwise he could not have composed such a commentary as he did, for the consummation of that gigantic task required not only genius but the fullest measure of divinity which Rashi allegedly possessed in abundance.

Another legend illustrates Rashi's love for the land of Israel. A Christian pilgrim returned from Jerusalem and presented him with a leaf torn from a tree in the Holy Land. When Rashi looked at that leaf, tears welled from his eyes at remembering the tragic life of the Jewish people suffering in Exile. The tears dropped on the leaf, which started to grow again as though it were on the twig of the tree. Rashi, while weeping, prayed for the restoration of the land of Israel and the return to Zion.

In his early youth, Rashi left his home town of Troyes, in Champagne, to study in the great academies of Mayence and Worms. Rabbenu Gershom was not his teacher, although Rashi studied in the academy which he had established. His first teacher was Jacob ben Yakar, a man of great learning and piety. He mentioned his teacher in various places in his commentaries, speaking of him with great admiration.

Rashi was not an official rabbi, although he might have served as such. He derived his livelihood from his vineyards and from manufacturing wine. His business was apparently attended to by others, and he was able to devote his time to learning. At the age of twenty-five, he returned to Troyes and established there his own academy, which was destined to eclipse all others in northern France and the Rhenish provinces. It did not take him long to attract the best students, men to whom learning was indeed the highest ideal in life.

Rashi's style is simple and to the point. Scholars have demonstrated that if a word stands out as seemingly unnecessary or superfluous in his comment, it is upon deeper analysis found to be an answer to a possible question. Many a time one is amazed at the logical penetration into the text which Rashi manifests casually as it were. He not only observes the minutest discrepancies of the text he currently discusses but also the connection between one passage and another found somewhere else in the Scriptures. His versatility is phenomenal.

The Aggadic citations from various Talmudic and Midrashic sources are gems of thought. Rashi was endowed with a sense for the poetic, legendary, and fantastic; and when he came across something which fascinated him, he readily included it in his commentaries. Some scholars fond of Peshat (simple interpretation) do not appreciate an intermingling of legend and fact, but Rashi valued it. This trait of his probably contributed greatly to the popularity of his commentaries. Rashi knew how to speak to the imagination of common folks and how to warm their hearts. He knew also how to enter into the hearts of children who would study his commentaries. For them a dry text with no more than interpretations of words would not suffice. An Aggadic interpretation, coupled with an occasional moral principle, would make the learning more intriguing. Thus Rashi's comments became an integral part of the text. They were inseparably interwoven and closely linked. The great teacher loved both the Torah and the people; therefore he tried to make the Torah the possession of the many instead of the possession of a few. His grandson, Samuel ben Meir (Rashbam), reported that Rashi said had he been younger he would have written a simpler commentary. Perhaps he would have done so, but still his commentary was a spiritual treasure house *for the people,* and loved by them.

Rashi's Aggadic method may be illustrated by a few examples. From Genesis 1:1, Rashi wants to establish the right of the Jewish people to ownership of the Holy Land. He therefore asks in the name of Rabbi Isaac the following: Why did the Bible start with the story of Creation, whereas it would have been more proper to start with the first Law given to Moses in Egypt as to the preparing of the Paschal Lamb? And Rashi answers as follows: He started with Genesis because it is written: "He hath declared to his people the power of his works, in giving them the heritage of the nations." (Ps. 111:6)

> If the people of the world will say to Israel: You are robbers because you have conquered the land [Canaan] of seven peoples, so Israel will answer and say, "The whole earth belongs to God; He created it and gave it to whomever He pleases; when He willed it He gave it to you; and when He willed it he took it away from you and gave it to us.

Another illustration is to be found in Genesis 47:28-31, where Jacob asks Joseph to bury him in Canaan and not Egypt. A little later (48:7), after Joseph brought his two children to receive blessings from the patriarch, Jacob mentions the death of his beloved Rachel who was buried on the road to Bethlehem. Jacob is made by Rashi to say the following:

> Although I trouble you [Joseph] with my burial, I did not act in the same manner when your mother died. I buried

her on the road and did not bring her body to Bethlehem, and I know that you feel a sort of resentment toward me for that. But remember, my son, that I just did what I had been bidden by God to do. When Nebozarhadden, the Babylonian commander, will chase my posterity from their homeland and they will pass by mother Rachel's grave, Rachel will emerge to pray for her children, as it is written:

Thus said the Lord:
A voice is heard in Ramah,
Lamentation, and bitter weeping,
Rachel weeping for her children
refused to be comforted for her children,
because they were not.
Thus saith the Lord:
Refrain thy voice from weeping,
and thine eyes from tears.
For thy work shall be rewarded, saith the Lord:
and they shall come again from the land of the enemy.
(Jer. 31:15-16)

Thus Rashi explains Jacob's action while at the same time extending a word of hope and consolation to his sorely tried people. This excerpt quoted above was chanted by Rashi's students in accordance with a special melody.

Characteristic of Rashi's methodology is his way of deducing ethical principles from the Biblical text. He cited freely from the Midrashic literature. For example: In Genesis 1:16, we are told that on the fourth day, "God made two great lights," to all appearances the sun and the moon, though they were not mentioned by name. Then, in the same verse, we read that the "greater" (big) light was designated to rule the day and the "lesser" (small) light to rule the night. The question here is about the expression "two great lights," followed immediately by a description of one as big and the other as small. Abraham ibn Ezra, for instance, resolved the seeming contradiction in a simple manner. "They are at first," he writes, "called big in comparison to the stars which seem to us small." Rashi, however, selected rather an Aggadic explanation.

At first, he says, the two heavenly bodies, sun and moon, had been both equally "big." But the moon, being jealous, came before the Throne of God with a complaint. "Almighty God," the moon said, "it is not right that two kings should wear the same crown."

The moon, of course, having begrudged the sun his greatness, expected that the Creator would make the sun smaller. God, however, replied, "If this be true, then go and make yourself smaller."

The ethical meaning of this story was more important to Rashi than the verbal interpretation of the text. Begrudging someone what he has carries with it a penalty; instead of winning more, one ends up with less.

Thus Rashi's selections of Aggadic citations inserted amid his other interpretations sparkle like diamonds. Here and there he brings a word of consolation to his oppressed brethren, a ray of hope from the ancient sources. Concerned as he is with the plain meaning of the text, he still finds occasion to enlighten the student as to what former sages had thought regarding this or another passage. The vast Midrashic literature being open to him, he used it freely.

Rashi's Talmudic and Midrashic knowledge was most extensive and profound. Familiar with all the works that had been written before his time, he explained with facility every obscure part of the Talmud, bringing forth the most significant points in a manner commensurate with the understanding of a student who was in need of a good teacher. Rashi's commentaries on the Talmud are more concise than his commentaries on the Bible. Wherever there arose a question of law, he was careful to place every important point in the proper perspective. While expounding the meaning of the text, Rashi also revised it if he felt that it needed revision, either because it contradicted another passage or it contained some errors of a careless copyist. His corrections were generally accepted.

The terrible times that came upon Franco-German Jewry during the Crusades, the frequent expulsions and the burning of the Talmud in 1240 in Paris, brought about the destruction of many institutions of learning. No small wonder that under such dire circumstances the Jews cherished Rashi's commentaries, which enabled them to study without a teacher. They carried them to their refuge places, studied them with zeal and veneration. Rashi accompanied the student in the course of studying the Talmud, and he also accompanied the common people who were eager to understand better the Torah and the prophets. He became a people's teacher, his works a wandering university, which everyone could enter freely. The great popularity of Rashi is attested by the fact that, to the people, he became an integral part of both the Bible and the Talmud. Studying them without Rashi was almost unthinkable.

Rashi's commentaries enjoyed this phenomenal popularity not only in the Franco-German lands, but also to some extent in Spain, Africa, and the East as well, although a few scholars gave cautious reception to Rashi's works. For example, Abraham ibn Ezra was somewhat critical of Rashi's interpretations, especially where the Aggadic portions were concerned. But all critics acknowledged Rashi's great erudition, and it was Abraham ibn Ezra himself who wrote of Rashi:

> A star shone forth in France —
> A mighty commentary he wrote on Torah.
> Therefore he is called Parshandata [Interpreter
> of the Law].

Rashi's commentaries were popular not only among Jews. In the Middle Ages, Christian scholars studied Rashi, and some of his interpretations were cited in their work as the Rabbinical point of view. Nicolas de-Lyra (1279-1340), in his work on the Bible, refers to Rashi in many instances; and Martin Luther, while translating the Bible into German used de-Lyra's comments. Thus, Rashi's influence was embodied in the Protestant Bible. At that time a witty saying in Latin was popular: *Si Lyra non lyrasset, Luther non saltaset.* Had Lyra not played, Luther would not have danced.

JACOB BEN MEIR TAM
(1100-1171)

Jacob ben Meir Tam, or Rabbenu Tam, grandson of Rashi, poet, grammarian, and one of the greatest Talmudists of the 12th century, was a worthy heir to his grandfather. Born in Ramerupt, on the Seine in the year 1100, he was at first taught by his father, Meir ben Samuel.

Jacob's principal work is the Sefer Hayashar (Book of the Pious), but most of his interpretations were incorporated in the Tosafot to the Talmud in which he demonstrated his keen mind in solving legal problems and in smoothing out seeming contradictions in the Talmud. Jacob revised certain passages in the Talmud, in accordance with the Talmudic text of R. Hananeel, the text then accepted as the most correct copy. Wherever contradictions appeared in the text itself or in comparison with other sources, Jacob tried to reconcile them. In this respect he claimed simple logic as the means to his end. He opposed those who invented difficulties in order to show their power and ability in learning. Yet some scholars think that Jacob Tam was not always careful, since at times he himself gave involved answers.

After his father's death, Jacob took over the leadership in the academy of Ramerupt. His name was already widely acclaimed. Rabbenu Tam also proved to be an important link between Jews and Christians. At his time, French and German Jews kept up closer relations with their non-Jewish neighbors. There was, therefore, a need for certain new regulations. As a practical man, Jacob knew well the ways of the world, and with his erudition and keen logic he rendered verdicts which were readily accepted. When Jacob took up a problem, he proposed all possible answers and then demonstrated the untenability of all but one.

On May 8, 1147, on the second day of the Feast of Weeks (Shovuot), a band of crusaders entered Rabbenu Tam's home. They took everything they could lay their hands on, and dragged him into the fields outside the city. They tortured him and inflicted five wounds upon his head. Finally they prepared to kill him. They told him that they had nothing against him personally, but they wanted to wreak vengeance upon the Jews who had crucified their Savior, and the blood of the most prominent leader in Israel would surely atone for the spilled blood of Jesus. Jacob readied himself to die, but, miraculously, a prince passed by just at that moment, and Jacob begged him for mercy. After promising to buy a horse for the prince, Jacob was released to him, and the prince assured the crusaders that he would, within a few days, either persuade Jacob to be baptized or return the Jew to them to do with him what they wanted.

After this incident, Jacob Tam moved to Troyes. In the year 1160, an assembly of rabbis was convoked at which Jacob took a prominent part. A second assembly took place later, and at a third assembly Jacob presided together with Moses of Pontoise. Many regulations were passed at those assemblies, the most important of which was that disputes between Jews be settled in a Jewish and not in a Christian court. The ban against polygamy pronounced by Rabbenu Gershom was re-enacted, and a regulation against divorcing a wife without a sufficient reason was approved.

Tam was also a poet. He was greatly influenced by the poets of the Golden Age. Following in their footsteps, his style was graceful and gentle. When Abraham ibn Ezra reached France, he met Rabbenu Tam, who greeted him with a special poem written in his honor. Ibn Ezra read it with great astonishment, saying, "Who has admitted the French into the temple of poetry?"

Rabbenu Tam was also deeply interested in Hebrew grammar. Taking up the old controversy between Menahem ben Saruk and Dunash ben Labrat from the mid-10th century, Jacob defended Menahem. This called forth some opposition; for example, Joseph Kimhi devoted an entire book to refuting Jacob's position.

Nevertheless, like his grandfather Rashi, Jacob's knowledge was honored by all. Students came to him from as far away as Bohemia and Russia. Talmudic authority Asher ben Jehiel (Rosh) declared that Jacob Tam superseded even Maimonides in knowledge of Torah.

ABRAHAM BEN DAVID
(c. 1125-1196)

Abraham ben David of Posquieres was one of the greatest Talmudic scholars of France, ranking with Alfasi, Rashi, and Maimonides. Because he was the first severe critic of Maimonides' Code, he is known as Baal Hasagot (master of critical notations). His critical notations, written on the margins of Maimonides' text, were brief and sharp, at times derogatory, but never malicious. Abraham spoke with an authoritative voice. He knew his subject to perfection and could stand his own against his famous contemporary, Maimonides

A fervent opponent of philosophy in general and of Maimonides' ideas in particular, Abraham ben David believed that faith does not rest on abstract and speculative conceptions. An extreme anti-rationalist, he did not even reject the anthropomorphic representation of God. Maimonides declared that whoever represented God anthropomorphically was to be regarded as an apostate. Abraham's caustic response to this was: "Why does he call such persons apostates? Men better and much worthier than he have held this view, for which they believed they have found authority in the Scriptures."

In brief, Maimonides and Abraham ben David did not share the same outlook. Maimonides was a Sephardi, a Spanish Jew, who saw Judaism from the standpoint of a rationalist. His aim in composing the Code was primarily to save time and effort for the intellectual Jew, in order that he could devote part of his time to philosophy and science. Abraham ben David was an Ashkenazi, a mystically inclined Jew whose rationalism was circumscribed by the Talmud. In his view, the Jew could find fulfilment only in the Talmud. The fact that Maimonides composed a Code without showing the sources upon which he had based his decisions was a break with tradition. Abraham had no quarrel with Alfasi's Code, because it was not given such finality and also because Alfasi held onto the form of the Talmud. Maimonides' Code, however, claimed finality, and the author attempted to gather in everything pertaining to the Law; therefore, it appeared to some as if he intended his work to replace the Talmud entirely, a hint he tacitly gave in his introduction to Mishneh Torah. This frightened Abraham ben David.

TOSAFISTS
(c.1100-1300)

After Rashi, and possibly while the great commentator was still alive, there emerged the first school of the Tosafists, in which the work of their teacher in the field of interpretation was energetically continued. The word "Tosafot" means additions or addenda. These were composed in the form of argumentation about various points of the law. This argumentation was supposed to take care of seeming contradictions between one text and another, similar cases in which the verdicts differed in their result, and interpretations that could not stand under a rigorous analysis.

Most of the Tosafists were followers of Rashi, admirers of the great commentator and his work, but that did not mean that they followed everything he had written. With them it was not the authority of Rashi that prevailed, but rather the logic of things, the penetration into the meaning of the law, and the bringing forth into light final decisions. This independence of thought which was characteristic of the Tosafists was truly remarkable. Agreement or disagreement with the teacher did not matter as much as to judge aright.

When one looks at a page of the Talmud one sees the Talmudic text in the center of the page printed in square Hebrew letters. To the right side of the page stands Rashi's commentary, and to the left there is the column of Tosafot. While studying a page of the Talmud, one is expected to learn a few lines of the Talmudic text, then look up what Rashi has to say. When everything is understood in that particular passage, one would turn to study what the Tosafist added. If one wants to know the final decision one can look up at the end of the tractate the brief and concise decisions as they were made at the time when the Tosafists were active.

The object of the Tosafists was two-fold: Learning per se and translating learning into deeds. Learning in itself was regarded as a worthwhile aim. The Talmud and its commentaries formed a veritable Republic of Thought, a gigantic palace of literature into which the Jews might escape when needed. Outside, the Jew found himself surrounded by mortal enemies; derision, mockery, enmity were raging on all sides. Inside, on the pages of the Talmud, pure thought prevailed. Here great minds contended among themselves in the name of justice and truth. Little things, cases of slight importance in themselves, grew into grave problems because they touched upon the meaning and intent of God's laws. While studying the Talmud, the Jew actually conversed with generations of learned men, listening to their opinions, analysing their reasons, and eventually taking sides with one Gaon or the other. All of them were alive, actually sitting right there before the very eyes of the Jew, who was eagerly listening to their expounding of the Torah. What else could be compared with such a blissfull moment?

The Tosafists enhanced the happiness of such moments by their love of learning as well as by their logical exposition. As it happens, such argumentations might have gone sometimes to an extreme, assuming a form of hair-splitting discussions known later as Pilpul, which became popular in some schools of learning in Poland; but this was not the object of the Tosafists.

The period of the Tosafists lasted close to 200 years. A whole literature grew up in this field of endeavor. Only a part of the vast Tosafistic literature was included in the Tosafot printed as marginal commentaries with the Talmudic text. All the various schools, and there were many, were rooted in the great work performed by Rashi.

The chief home of Tosafot literature was France and Germany, this work having been started by the disciples of Rashi. The first famous Tosafists were Rashi's two sons-in-law, Meir ben Samuel of Ramerupt and Judah ben Nathan. The greatest of all was Rashi's grandson, Jacob ben Meir Tam, whose style was adopted by his successors. His most prominent successor was Isaac ben Samuel Hazaken (The Elder). In Germany, the greatest Tosafists were Baruch ben Isaac of Regensburg, Meir ben Baruch of Rothenberg. In Italy, Isaiah de Trani was the most famous

Other principal Tosafists were the following: Samson of Sens, Moses of Evreu, Eliezer of Touques (who edited the regular Tosafot and also special ones), Joseph ben Isaac of Orleans, Moses b. Jacob of Coucy, Moses b. Meir of Ferrara, Samuel b. Meir (Rashbam), Samuel b. Natronai, Jehiel b. Joseph of Paris (d. 1286), Jacob ot Chinon, Abigdor b. Elijah Ha-Kohen, Elhanan b. Isaac, Eliezer b. Joel Halevi, Samuel b. Solomon of Falaise, Perez b. Elijah of Corbeil, Issac b. Asher Halevi, Simhah b. Samuel of Speyer, Joseph Porat, Samuel of Evreu.

JOSEPH BEN ISAAC BEKOR SHOR
(12th century)

Joseph ben Isaac Bekor Shor of Orleans—French Tosafist, exegete, poet—was a pupil of Jacob Tam and Samuel ben Meir (Rashbam). He composed a Biblical commentary in which he demonstrated his keen critical faculties and his rational approach towards many questions. For example, Joseph admits that there are duplicate narratives in the Bible; when one remembers that this was in the 12th century and that the admission was made by a leading Talmudist, it seems almost incredible. In interpreting the "Tree of Life" in Genesis, Joseph says that it was not a "Tree of Eternal Life" but rather a "tree of healing" (Hai in Hebrew connotes also "health"). Another rational explanation concerns the story about Lot's wife: Lot's wife did not believe that Sodom and Gomorrah would actually be destroyed; hence she tarried on the road. She looked backward to the cities of the plain, curious to see what would happen, and overtaken by the rain of brimstone and fire, which was mixed with salt, she subsequently perished. The Biblical story says, of course, simply that Lot's wife was turned into a pillar of salt.

Joseph was also conversant with Christian Biblical exegesis. He also composed a number of liturgical poems. But his chief work, however, is as a Tosafist. In this field he showed himself to be one of the keenest minds of that epoch.

JUDAH BEN SAMUEL HA-HASID
(last half of 12th century)

Judah ben Samuel ha-Hasid of Regensburg, ethical writer and mystic, descended from a family of Cabalists. His father, who was also called ha-Hasid (pious), died when Judah was very young. In 1195 Judah settled in Regensburg (Ratisbon), where he founded an academy. One of his most prominent disciples was Eleazar of Worms.

The principal work attributed to him is the Sefer Hasidim (Book of the Pious). It contains ethical and mystical instructions. In it Judah endeavors to deepen the feeling of devotion of the Jew which he considers as more important than studying. In this respect he is a forerunner of later-day Hasidism which gave prayer preference over studying. Judah lacked philosophic training, and consequently he was unable to systematize his ideas, but his *Book of the Pious* was very popular in Germany. Here are a few excerpts:

> If a man sees his children, relatives, or pupils doing wrong things and does not do anything within his power to correct them, because he would be considered a peaceful and meek man, this is sinful meekness.
>
> *
>
> He who does a good deed in order to be honored, or for the purpose of praising himself thereby, is displaying sinful kindness.
>
> *
>
> There are people who give charity for sinful purposes. Such as when one supports adulterers, supplies weapons of destruction to murderers, provides food or other things to robbers. The one that does such things is an accomplice to crimes.
>
> *
>
> A man should give no charity at all rather than give it publicly.
>
> *
>
> If a man gives charity while he cannot pay his debts, his charitableness is no more than robbery.

Leopold Zunz characterizes Judah in the following words:
> To vindicate whatever is noble in human endeavors, and the highest aspirations of the Israelite, and to discover the inmost truths alluded to in the Sacred Books, seemed to be the ultimate purpose of a mind in which poetic, moral, and divine qualities were fused.

ELEAZER BEN JUDAH BEN KALONYMUS
(1176-1238)

Eleazar ben Judah ben Kalonymus of Worms—Talmudist, Cabalist, moralist, scientist, poet—was a disciple of Judah ha-Hasid, under whose influence and instruction he became a Cabalist.

Eleazar's wife, Dulcina, supported the family with a business in parchment scrolls, thus freeing her husband from financial pursuits and enabling him to devote his time to studying and writing. In the fall of the year 1196, when Eleazar was writing his commentary on Genesis, one night two Crusaders broke into his house and killed his wife, his two daughters, and his son. Despite this great tragedy, he never lost his cheerfulness, patience, and love of humanity.

Eleazar, apart from his Talmudic and Cabalistic knowledge, was interested in science. He was an astronomer, a poet endowed with a lucid style, and a moral personality who swayed people by his piety and honesty. As a Cabalist he claimed to be privy to the secrets of nature and God; he was engrossed in the theoretical Cabala of Isaac the Blind. He brought into the Cabala his system of performing miracles by the numerical values of the Hebrew letters and by expounding the names of God. Eleazar wrote a number of mystical books, whereby Cabala, not previously very popular in Germany, spread widely throughout the country. Eleazar also wrote commentaries on the Bible, treatises on the Talmud (Tosafot), a history of part of the Third Crusade, and many liturgical poems. However, his contribution lies mainly in the field of morals. His most famous work, Ha-Rokeah, is replete with ethical instructions. Here is a sample from Ha-Rokeah:

No crown carries such royalty with it as doth humility.
*
No monument gives such glory as an unsullied name.
*
No worldly gain can equal that which comes from observing God's laws.
*
The highest sacrifice is a broken and contrite heart.

The highest wisdom is that which is found in the Law;
The noblest of all ornaments is modesty.

*

The most beautiful of all things man can do is to forgive
wrong.

*

Cherish a good heart when thou findest it in any one.

*

Hate the haughtiness of the overbearing man, and keep the
boaster at a distance.

*

There is no skill or cleverness to be compared to that
which avoids temptation.

*

There is no force, no strength that can equal piety.

*

All honor to him who thinks continually with an anxious
heart of his Maker, who prays, reads, learns, and all these
with a passionate yearning for his Maker's grace.

During the Middle Ages, another form of ethical literature which
began to reappear among the Jews was the ethical will, presumably rooting in Biblical times (cf. Gen. 49:1; Kings 2:1-10; Jer.
35:6-8). Some scholars regard Jewish ethical wills as unique in
world literature. Eleazar ben Judah wrote such a testament, from
which these excerpts are taken:

Never turn away a poor man empty-handed. Give him
what you have, be it much or little.

*

As to games of chance, I entreat my children never to engage in such things.

*

I earnestly beg my children to be tolerant and humble to
all.

*

Seek peace and pursue it with all the vigor at your command. Even if you suffer loss thereby, forbear and forgive.

By avoiding scandal, falsehood, money-grabbing, you will surely find tranquillity and affection.

*

Against all evils, silence is the best safeguard.

*

My children, eat and drink only what is necessary, refraining from heavy meals, and holding the glutton in destestation.

*

Do not listen to gossip and scandal; for if there were no receivers there would be no bearers of slanderous tales.

*

I ask, I command, that the daughters of my house be never without work, for idleness leads first to boredom, then to sin. Let them spin or cook or sew or do anything useful.

*

Be cautious as to promises. The breach of one's undertakings leads to many lapses.[2]

MOSES BEN JACOB
(13th century)

Moses ben Jacob of Coucy, codifier and Tosafist, was one of the foremost Talmudic scholars of the 13th century. His fame rests on his work known as Sefer Mizvot Hagadol (Large Book of Precepts), which won for him a position among the codifiers.

In 1235, Moses, who was an eloquent preacher and master of the French, Spanish, and Arabic languages, traveled over France and Spain. Visiting the principal communities, he delivered lectures which drew large crowds. In his lectures he emphasized the principle that mere observance of the law is not sufficient; justice and brotherly love, irrespective of creed and race, must accompany the observance of the precepts. At that time, mixed marriages between Jews and Muslims and Jews and Christians were widespread in Spain. Moses criticized this practice. In his travels, he also witnessed the rift in many Jewish communities caused by the Maimonists versus anti-Maimonists dispute, and Moses tried, with some significant success, to heal these wounds and bring peace and harmony once again to these communities.

In 1250, Moses was one of the four rabbis who defended the Talmud at the Paris disputation. Another member was the well known Tosafist, Jehiel of Paris. The Jewish delegates ably defended the Talmud, but the Churchmen condemned it just the same. The Talmud was publicly burned at Paris that year.

An excerpt from the ethical will left by Moses of Coucy:

> It is because man is half angel, half brute, that his inner life witnesses such bitter war between such unlike natures. The brute in him clamors for sensual joy and things in which there is only vanity; but the angel resists and strives to make him know that meat, drink, sleep are but means whereby the body may be made efficient for the study of the truths, and the doing of the will of God. Not until the very hour of death can it be certain or known to what measure the victory has been won. He who is but a novice in the love of God will do well to say audibly each day, as he rises: "This day I will be a faithful servant of the Almighty. I will be on my guard against wrath, falsehood, hatred, and quarrelsomeness, and will forgive those who wound me." For whoso forgives is forgiven in his turn; hardheartedness and a temper that will not make up quarrels are a heavy burden of sin, and unworthy of an Israelite.

MEIR BEN BARUCH
(1215-1293)

Meir ben Baruch, known as Ma'aram of Rothenburg, was one of the great Talmudists of the 13th century, a Tosafist and a liturgical poet, ranking among the foremost leaders of Ashkenazic Jewry.

Born in Worms about the year 1215 in a family noted for piety and scholarly attainments, Meir was at first instructed by his father, who was a scholar in his own right. Later he studied for

some time in Warzburg and thence he went to Paris where he
studied under the guidance of the famous Tosafist, Jehiel of Paris.
When he returned to his home town, Meir organized his own
academy, which soon attracted students from all over Germany
and other countries. His saintly life and his devotion to Torah
were widely recognized, and although there is no evidence that
he served as the chief rabbi of Germany, some scholars are inclined to accord him that title. He served as rabbi in the principal cities: Rothenburg, Nuremberg, Mayence, and others.

Meir's name stands at the very top among the great leaders of
Ashkenazic Jewry. The appellation Ma'or Hagolah (Light of the
Exile) was attached to the names of only two others—Rabbenu
Gershom and Rashi. He was also one of the few leaders whose
influence reached far into other lands. Even Solomon ben Abraham
Adret, the greatest Talmudist of Spain, turned to him for deci-
sions. Meir's great disciple, Asher ben Jehiel, who settled in Spain,
honored his teacher by quoting him widely.

From two decisions rendered by Meir of Rothenburg, we can
learn the extent of his influence. In the year 1282, Emperor Ru-
dolph allocated some parts of his kingdom to his son Albrech.
The Jewish communities of Austria, Styria, and Carinthia refused
to pay their portion of taxes to the Emperor's treasury, contending that they became citizens of another state and therefore were
not liable for the unpaid taxes. This was a delicate question
fraught with perils for the German Jews as well as for the Jews
directly involved. It was therefore decided by the leaders of the
communities to turn to Meir for a dicision on the matter. The
great rabbi deliberated long and decided against the communities.
His verdict was accepted and fully honored.

Another decision involved those Jews who had been ransomed
from the hands of pirates or local captors. It so happened that
some of them, after having been freed, refused to repay the communities the ransom that had been paid. Meir issued the verdict
that the communities must be reimbursed. Moreover, the communities were fully justified in confiscating the properties or other possessions of the ransomed Jews. In a question that involved the
community versus the individual, the community's interest prevailed. Since cases of captured Jews for ransom were frequent

and the only way of saving them was through the community funds, it was absolutely necessary to reimburse the communities and thus make possible for other Jews to be ransomed. This decision also was fully obeyed.

Meir was a productive writer. Having the entire Talmudic literature practically at his finger tips, he wrote copiously on almost every subject of the law. He was also well versed in the Masorah. Manuscripts containing important Masoretic notes by Meir of Rothenburg are kept in Oxford and in the Vatican Library. Some Cabalistic works are attributed to him but modern scholars have shown that he was not their author. He definitely was not a mystic.

Meir of Rothenburg was also a liturgical poet. Nineteen of his poems were included in the German Mahzor. His model was Judah Halevi's poetry, though he did not attain the height of the bard of Spain.

There follow excerpts from a poem by Meir. This is part of the Kinnah recited on the 9th of Ab, mourning the burning of the Talmud in Paris in the 13th century.

The Burning of the Law

Ask, is it well, O thou consumed of fire,
 With those that mourn for thee,
That yearn to tread thy courts, that sore desire
 Thy sanctuary;
That, panting for thy land's sweet dust, are grieved,
 And sorrow in their souls,
And by the flames of wasting fire bereaved,
 Mourn for thy scrolls;
That grope in shadow of unbroken night,
 Waiting the day to see
Which o'er them yet shall cast a radiance bright
 And over thee?
Ask of the welfare of the man of woe,
 With breaking heart, in vain
Lamenting ever for thine overthrow,
 And for thy pain;

Of him that crieth as the jackels cry,
    As owls their moaning make,
Proclaiming bitter wailing far and nigh,
    Yea, for thy sake.

ASHER BEN JEHIEL
(c. 1250-1328)

Asher ben Jehiel, the religious leader of Ashkenazic Jewry, was
know as Rosh (abbreviation of Rabbenu Asher). Harassment of the
German Jews by the emperor—for example, the imprisonment
and death of Meir of Rothenburg—prompted Asher to leave Germany in 1305 and settle in Toledo, Spain, where he was received
with honors and admiration. He became the rabbi of Toledo upon
the recommendation of Solomon Adret, then the most eminent
rabbi of Spain.

Asher was a disciple of Meir of Rothenburg. As an Ashkenazic
leader, he was averse to philosophy, rigid and outspoken against
its use. Philosophy, according to Asher, is based on critical research, whereas religion is founded upon tradition. Consequently,
there is no way of reconciling the two; they are opposites.

In Talmudic learning, to which he devoted all his time, Asher
was second to none. In this field he demonstrated his independence
of thought. His basic principle was: "We must not be guided in
our decisions by admiration of great men; and in the event of a
law not being clearly stated in the Talmud, we are not bound to
accept it, even if it be based on the works of the Geonim." His
greatest work is an abstract of the Talmud, known as "Rosh,"
in which all the Aggadic portions are omitted and only the practical Halakot left intact. In this work he brought forth final verdicts, after having quoted the opinions of Alfasi, Maimonides, and
the Tosafists. This work was accepted with approbation by the
learned, and it was printed at the end of the Talmudic tractates.
Later Talmudists wrote special commentaries on the "Rosh."

Asher had two sons, Jacob and Judah, who distinguished themselves as leaders in Israel, particularly the first who is regarded

as one of the great Talmudic codifiers. Jacob (d. 1340), known as the Baal Haturim (Master of the Rows), composed a complete Code in four parts, dealing with all ritual laws, family regulations, and civil laws. This Code was regarded as the standard for both Sephardic and Ashkenazic Jews until it was superseded later by Joseph Caro's Code, Shulhan Aruk (The Prepared Table).

Jacob composed two commentaries on the Pentateuch. One of them consists of short comments based on Gematria, that is, on the numerical values of the words of the text, or Nortaricon, that is, on the enlargement of each letter into a word. These two methods were employed by the Cabalists. However, Jacob was not a Cabalist, but just interested in drawing out certain moral ideas from each word of the Torah's text. The method as a whole was predicated upon the belief that the Scriptural text contained some hidden ideas which would be revealed through the numerical values of the letters. Learners were fond of this kind of interpretation and frequently indulged in it as a pastime.

Judah ben Asher (1292-1349), the second son of Rabbenu Asher, is known as a great moral teacher. After his father's death, he was chosen as the religious leader of Toledo. Aside from his many Responsa, published under the title Sikron Yehudah by David Cassel, in 1846, he left an ethical will for his children. He was a pious and humble man who influenced people by his saintly life. Neither he nor his brother, Jacob, were philosophers. Like their great father, they remained Ashkenazic scholars concerned only with the Talmud in spite of the fact that they were leaders of Spanish Jewry. Their works were composed in the tradition of the Franco-German schools.

Later generations honored Rabbenu Asher and his two sons as the greatest Talmudic minds after Alfasi and Maimonides.

Excerpts from the ethical will of Asher ben Jehiel:

My son, make not gold the foremost longing of thy life; for that is the first step to idolatry.

*

Do not struggle vaingloriously for the small triumph of showing thyself in the right and a wise man in the wrong. Thou art not one whit the wiser therefor.

*

Be the first to extend courteous greeting to everyone, whatever be his faith; provoke not to wrath one of another belief than thine.

Excerpts from the ethical will of Judah ben Asher:

A wise man was once asked why he honored every man,
to which he replied, "I have not met a man who has not
excelled me. If he be old, I say to myself, 'This man must
have performed good deeds more than I.' If he be young,
I say to myself, 'I must have committed more sins than
he.' If he be rich, I say, 'This man must have given more
charity than I.' If he be poor, I say. 'This man must have
suffered more than I.' If he be wiser, I honor him for his
wisdom. If he be not wiser, I say, 'This man will surely
not be punished as severely as I will.' "

*

Once there was a wicked man who committed all kinds of
sins. One day he asked a wise man to teach him the way
of repentance. "Refrain from telling lies," replied the wise
man. The sinner accepted it gladly because he thought this
was easy. Later, however, he found out that it was not
easy. When he wanted to steal, he asked himself: "What am
I going to say if someone asks me whither I go? Admitting
the truth would be a confession of my criminal intentions;
but if I lie, I would violate my promise to the wise man."
Thus, by refraining from lying, he refrained from stealing
too.

BEHYA BEN ASHER
(d. 1340)

Behya ben Asher was the first Cabalistic commentator of the
Pentateuch. The novelty of his commentary consists in the fact
that he employs all the four methods of interpretation simultaneously: Peshat, the simple exposition; Midrash, Aggadic exposi-

tion; Reason, philosophic interpretations; and the mystical exposition. In order to be able to do that, Behya must have examined all the commentaries that had been written prior to his time. His Cabalistic commentary rests on the belief that the Biblical text comprises mysteries apart from the simple meaning of the words. In order to prepare the learner for what Behya regarded as essential in the understanding of the Torah, he wrote short prefaces to each weekly portion. Then he analyzed each passage by posing questions with the view of involving the learner in what was being told. Finally he proposed his answers. His Cabalistic interpretations are interesting for a variety of reasons, the most important of which are the drawing of new meanings from the Biblical texts and the relationship between one method and another. No small wonder that Behya's commentary made a special niche for itself in the Biblical exegetical literature.

A second work by Behya is his book, Kab Hakemah (Flour Jar), which was very popular during the centuries. Written not for the intellectual but rather for the common man, it is lucid and easily understood by all. A wide range of topics are touched upon, among which are: fear of God, love of mankind, righteousness and honesty towards non-Jews and Jews, sacredness of the oath, justice and truth. In this popular book, one senses the piety of the author, his loving-kindness and charitableness, and the nobility of a great teacher. It was first printed in Constantinople in 1515 and since then has been reprinted in numerous additions.

JEDAIAH BEN ABRAHAM BEDERSI
(1270-1340)

Jedaiah ben Abraham Bedersi—poet, philosopher, physician— was born in Beziers, France. He was scarcely fifteen years old when he published his first work, Bakkashat ha-Memim (Mem Prayer), a hymn of one thousand words, each of which begins with the Hebrew letter "mem." It was something that had never been done by anyone. It is often obscure, but as a whole it is an astounding feat, particularly when one considers the age of the author. At seventeen Jedaiah composed a treatise on ethics known as Sefer Hapardes (Book of the Orchard). At eighteen he completed two more books, Zilzal Kenafayim (Rustling of Wings) and Oheb Nashim (Lover of Women). The latter book he wrote against the early 13th century poet, Judah ibn Sabbatai, author of Soneh Hanashim (Misogynist). In 1305, when Solomon Adret, the prominent Spanish rabbi, pronounced a ban on studying philosophy before the age of thirty, Jedaiah wrote his famous Iggeret Hitnazelut (Letter of Apology), in which he appealed to Adret to revoke his ban. Jedaiah was primarily a philosopher-moralist, a follower of Maimonides.

Jedaiah's fame rests on his poetic book, Behinat Olam (Examination of the World), in which he presented his outlook upon human life. This book was so popular that it went through sixty-seven editions and was translated into French, German, Italian, and English.

Three excerpts from *Examination of the World*, the third being from his famous treatise, "The Nothingness of Man and His Pursuits":

Do not, child of man, accuse the Author of nature for the evils that overwhelm thy short and frail existence. The evils thou complainest of are of thy own making.

*

There is nothing in human life worthier than the soul which the Creator gave man. Celestial by origin, the human soul, so long as it is attached to the body, groans under a shameful slavery. The occupation worthy of its noble extraction is therefore to direct all its faculties toward the worship of the Creator, the happiness of one's fellow-creatures, and the triumph of truth. This result can be attained only by keeping the commandments of God.

*

The world is a tempestuous sea of immense depth and breath, and time is a frail bridge constructed over it, the beginning of which is fastened with the cords of chaos that preceded existence, while the end thereof is to behold eternal bliss, and to be enlightened with the light of the King's countenance. The width of the bridge is a cubit of a man, and it lacks borders. And thou, son of man, against thy will art thou living, and art continually travelling over it, since the day thou hast become a man. When thou considerest that the path is narrow and that there is no way to turn either to the right or to the left, shalt thou glory in position and fame? When thou seest that destruction and death are unto thee a wall on thy right and on thy left, shall thy heart endure, or shall thy hands be strong? Even if thou pridest thyself on the desirable acquisitions and the abundance of possessions which thou hast amassed and discovered with thy arm, hast sought with thy bow, and hast gone down to possess with thy net, what wilt thou do against the tempest of the sea and the roaring thereof, when it rages, overflows, passes through, so that even thy dwelling-place is about to be broken? Glory thou over this immense sea in whose midst thou art; rule over the horsemen and chariots thereof; go out now, I pray thee, to fight against it. For even while thou reelest to and fro and staggerest with the wine of thy rebellious arrogance which deceived thee, and with the juice of the pomegranates of thy haughtiness which misled thee, thou wilt soon incline slightly toward one side or another, and wilt perish in the terrible depths, and none will seek thy blood from them; thou wilt go from abyss to abyss, perplexed in the depths of the sea, and none shall say: "Restore."[4]

׳ 10

CABALA

WHAT IS CABALA?

We are about to enter an orchard full of exotic plants, trees laden with strange fruit, and paths meandering between the thick shrubs and leading in various directions while losing themselves in dark corners.

One asks himself: Is this a real world or is it no more than a creation of man's imagination? Is it poetic philosophy that has nothing to do with reason? Is it philosophical poetry? How could so many great minds, persons endowed with exceptional reasoning faculties, be so deeply engrossed in it? Those who have studied the subject have tried to find an answer to those questions, but they have not succeeded. We stand before a sphinx.

One thing is clear: Cabala (tradition) is predicated upon one all-inclusive premise which, as any premise, must first be accepted before one can contemplate anything that Cabala teaches. This premise is the following: There is a divine world beyond the material one, a world which man can communicate with, can influence, and be influenced by, a world in which all secrets stand revealed to the select. By means of constant spiritual communion with God it is possible for man to secure clear mental vision, the gift of prophecy, and even perform miracles. Hasidism, which came later, sometime in the first half of the 19th century, used those principles to advantage and built up the worship of the Zaddik (righteous man), who thus became the mediator between the Hasid and God.

In the literature of the Cabala we find the queerest collection of various ideas, expressions of the soul, wonderful teachings, prayers of great inspiration, visions of Paradise and of worlds beyond, descriptions of angels and Seraphim, Messianic predictions, magic numbers, and combinations of the numerical values of words and divine names.[1] Cabala wanted to lift man to heaven, bring him ever closer to the ideal world beyond, where God's glory prevailed. Since life in the material world was almost unbearable, the question of the why and the wherefore was pressing hard the soul of man. Surely there must be a higher purpose in the suffering of Israel, and only by an approach to the fountain of light and life could one find consolation and hope. Cabala undertook to bring that hope and that consolation to the sorely tried people who needed it so badly. It explained the origin of the world, the unity of nature and God, the mission of Israel, and the meaning of suffering for an ideal.

The Cabalistic literature of the Middle Ages had two phases: theoretical Cabala and practical Cabala. Theoretical Cabala is a metaphysical system of thought and imagination which attempts to give man a conception of the universe and its secret: how it came into being and how man can penetrate into its mysteries. It purports to show the learner how he can get in communion with God. Practical Cabala undertakes to instruct the initiate how he can influence the forces of nature. It reveals mystical names by means of which man can guard himself against sickness and enemies. When man knows how to apply the Cabalistic formulas and incantations, he is able to control the natural forces and bring about changes in the course of regular events. This borders upon magic, but Cabala claims that it is not the same as "black magic," which stems from the "other side," for the theurgic Cabala comes from the source of "Kedusha," that is, "sanctity," which is directly connected with God. On the other hand, magic comes from an impure source and its purpose is to bring forth profanity and mischief. The exponents of Cabala spoke in the name of the highest ideals of justice and truth. Its ultimate aim was to redeem the world of wickedness and evil and thus open the way for the coming of the Messianic age.

But aside from its intrinsic value as a metaphysical conception of the universe, and its aspirations for a better world, Cabala did present some obnoxious aspects. The Jewish Encyclopedia summarizes its evaluation of Cabala as follows:

> The beneficial influences of the Cabala are, however, counterbalanced by several most pernicious ones. From the metaphysical axiom that there is nothing in the world without spiritual life, the Cabalists developed a Jewish magic. They taught that the elements are the abode of beings which are the dregs or remnants of the lowest spiritual life. Demonology, therefore, occupies an important position in the works of many Cabalists; for the imps are related to those beings that are generally designated as demons, being endowed with various supernatural powers and with insight into the lower realms of nature, and even occasionally into the future and the higher spiritual world. Magic may be practiced with the help of these beings, the Cabalists meaning white magic in contrast to the black art.

Cabalistic ideas also exerted a deep influence on the Christian world. Luther and Melanchthon adopted some of the ideas of the Cabalists as part of the Protestant dogmas. German mystics like Valentin Weigel (1533-88), Knorr Baron von Rosenroth, and Athanasius Kircher (1602-82) translated some Cabalistic works and distributed them widely among Christians. Johannes Reuchlin was interested in Cabala as a divine revelation. Pope Sixtus IV asked for a Latin translation of the Cabalistic book, Sefer Zohar, seeing in it support for the Catholic faith.

Maaseh Bereshit and Maaseh Merkabah (Work of Creation and Work of the Chariot) are two Talmudic terms signifying the esoteric teachings about the creation of the world and about the divine chariot in Ezekiel 1. Maimonides interprets them as meaning physics and metaphysics, respectively, but apparently there was

something more to those subjects than this, as the following story
given in Tosefta, Hag. 2, 1 indicates: Rabbi Eleazar ben Arak was
riding on a mule behind Rabbi Johanan ben Zakkai, when he
asked for the privilege of being initiated into the secrets of the Merkabah. The great master demanded proof of his initiation into the
gnosis, and when Eleazar began to tell what he had learned thereof, Rabbi Johanan immediately descended from the mule and sat
upon the rock. "Why, O master, does thou descend from the mule?"
asked the disciple. "Can I remain mounted upon the mule when
the telling of the secrets of the Merkabah causes the Shekinah [God's
presence] to dwell with us and the angels to accompany us?" was
the answer. Eleazar continued, and behold, fire descended from
heaven and lit up the trees of the field, causing them to sing an-
thems, and an angel cried out, "Truly these are the secrets of the
Merkabah." Whereupon R. Johanan kissed Eleazar upon the fore-
head, saying, "Blessed be thou, O father Abraham, that hast a
descendant like Eleazar b. Arak." Subsequently two other disciples
of R. Johanan walking together said to each other: "Let us also
talk together about the Maaseh Merkabah," and no sooner did R.
Joshua begin speaking than a rainbow-like appearance was seen
upon the thick clouds which covered the sky, and angels came to
listen. On hearing the things related by R. Joshua, R. Johanan
blessed the disciples and said: "Blessed the eyes that beheld these
things! Indeed I saw myself in a dream together with you, seated
like the select ones upon Mount Sinai; and I heard a heavenly
voice saying: 'Enter the banquet hall and take your seats with
your disciples and disciples' disciples, among the elect, the highest
[third] class'."

The mystic Jewish teaching known as Cabala is generally traced
back to the 13th century. That does not mean that there were no
mystic books in existence prior to that time. We know that during
the Geonic period esoteric books were popular. Even in Talmudic
times there were sages who trafficked with such subjects as the
"Act of Creation" and the "Divine Chariot", which were forbidden to
be studied publicly. In the 13th century there occurred a revival
of interest in mysticism. A beginning or rather a renewal was made
by a man about whom not much is known: Isaac the Blind (c.
1190-1210), the son of Abraham b. David of Posquieres. Isaac

was regarded at that time as a saint. He had two disciples: Azriel and Ezra (some think they are one man), both from Gerona. Azriel is known to have set out on a journey to a number of cities in both Spain and France, with the view of spreading his master's teaching. He claimed to have received from his master certain secrets relating to God, the creation of the world, the soul, etc. In his book, Ezrat Adonai, he admitted, however, that his trip was not successful. "The philosophers", he declared, "believed in nothing that cannot be demonstrated logically." Disappointed, he returned to his hometown, Gerona, and established a school. Azriel also organized a small circle of adherents who eagerly studied the secrets of Cabala. Among those who came to listen to his lectures was Nahmanides, a young man at the time.

The following is a conversation between Azriel and one of his disciples. It is imaginery, but is based on Azriel's own commentary, in which he expounds the meaning of the Ten Sefirot. It is given in question-answer form, as Azriel's book and some other Cabala books were.

Question: What is meant by the term En Sof by which the Cabalist designated God?

Azriel: En Sof means simply "no-end," infinite, which is the only true name we as humans may give God. He is everything, everywhere, and there is nothing outside Him. He is the whole of existence; matter, time, space may be included in Him but He is more than all of them together. What else may we call the Whole? The closest phrase is: "there is no place devoid of Him," or "His glory fills the universe." En Sof is, however, better than all other appellations that we may employ.

Question: How do we know that En Sof exists?

Azriel: Everything that exists is a mid-process, with no beginning and no end. At what point can we place the beginning of time? At what point can we place the end of time? How did it all start? How will it end? Where is the beginning of space, and where does it end? What is there where it ends? What was there before it had begun? All this indicates that En Sof is the only existence that we know of. It is the only reality that can ever be. All else is just part of it, and not a very important part either.

Question: Can we ascribe some positive attributes to the En Sof?

Azriel: Never. Every positive attribute we may give the En Sof would reflect sensualism. God would become man-like, Adamic. Even negative attributes should not be employed, though if one would remember that they are only arbitrary and man-made they may serve a temporary purpose. When we talk about the En Sof we must condition it thus: The En Sof cannot be taken as having desire, thought, word or doing any action. It can only be viewed as a Negation of All Negations, as Endless, all-inclusive.

Question: If this be so, How can we ever conceive Him (God), not to say come in contact with Him?

Azriel: We can see Him through His works, through the universe that has come from Him.

Question: Through His creation?

Azriel: We do not accept the idea that the world was created.

Question: That does not correspond to the Torah, which declares that God created the world out of nothing.

Azriel: This will be explained a little later. Meanwhile I shall say this: We agree with those philosophers who say that "from nothing comes nothing." We therefore reject completely "creatio ex nihilo."

Question: You accept then the idea that the world is eternal?

Answer: No. We only say that the universe is part of God; it existed within the En Sof.

Question: How then did the world come into being?

Azriel: It came into being, for instance, as the rays that flow from the sun. The sun is prior to the rays. This we call emanation. Just as the sparks and colors are latent in the coal, so the universe was latent in the En Sof. Creation did not consist in producing an absolutely new thing; it was merely a transformation of potentiality into actuality.

Question: How did an imperfect world emerge from God, the most perfect being?

Azriel: The material world, being limited and imperfect, certainly could not have come out from the perfect directly. There must have been intermediaries between it and the En Sof. These intermediaries are the Ten Sefirot. The first Sefirah, Kether, being close to the original source, was of the same purity. The second Sefirah was a little less pure because it was farther away, and so on from the second Sefirah to the last one.

Question: Do the Sefirot depend upon each other, or has each an independent existence?

Azriel: They are all contingent upon the En Sof.

Question: Was the En Sof diminished in any way by those emanations?

Azriel: Not at all. Take, for instance, a flaming candle. Is it not capable to ignite an infinite number of candles without diminishing its own light?

Question: Why *Ten* Sefirot?

Azriel: The Ten Sefirot were needed just as the ten first numbers are needed in mathematics. Just look: "One" (1) is contained in every possible number, so much so that it can be said that every number ad infinitum is only a re-occurrence of one, whether only once or an nth time. If "one" would be missing, no other number could possibly exist; "one" is the foundation for all foundations. It generates itself till it reaches "ten," which is the same "one" (1-0). All other numbers are no more than "repeats" of "one" and "ten."

SEFER HA-BAHIR

The Sefer Ha-Bahir (Book of Brightness) is traditionally attributed to a Tanna by the name of Nehunyah b. Hakanah, a contemporary of Johanan b. Zakkai (first century). Modern scholars, however, have assigned it to the 13th century. Nahmanides is the first authority to have mentioned this book. In the literature prior to the 13th century it had not been mentioned by anyone. Some scholars ascribe this mystic book to Isaac the Blind, since it starts with a sentence from Job 37:21, which reads: "And now men see not the light which is bright in the skies." It is a kind of motto, but unrelated to the text immediately following. It is therefore taken as an allusion to Isaac the Blind who lacked the sight of his eyes, but nevertheless had seen the light "which is bright in the skies."

It speaks of the "Or Ha-Ganuz", the hidden light, which had once emanated from the En Sof. It discusses the Ten Sefirot, or emanations, which proceeded also from the En Sof. There is no doubt that this book was composed under the influence of the old Sefer

Yetzirah. Scholars consider both as important works for the history of mysticism.

Sefer Ha-Bahir is written in the form of questions and answers. The unknown master who answers the questions accepts, for example, the theory of Ghilgul, the transmigration of souls, whereby he explains why the just suffer in this world and the sinful prosper. "The just," says the author, "may have been wicked in their former life and the wicked righteous." Thus one is getting rewarded and the other punished. The author uses the letters of the Hebrew alphabet and their numerical values to prove some of his points.

The HaBahir is a forerunner to Sefer Zohar (Book of Splendor).

ABRAHAM BEN SOLOMON ABULAFIA
(b. 1240)

Abraham Abulafia was one of the most eccentric Cabalists—dreamer, visionary, adventurer. Born in 1240 in Saragossa, Aragon, he received a good Talmudic and general education. At twenty years of age, a few years after the death of his father, he left Spain. First he reached Palestine whence he planned to go on a journey to find the legendary river Sambation and the lost Ten Tribes. In Palestine, however, the desolation caused by the Crusaders made it impossible for him to proceed. He then decided to go to Italy. There he tarried for quite a number of years, during which he studied the religious Jewish philosophy of the Middle Ages, particularly Maimonides. He was also engrossed in the Sefer Yetzirah and the commentaries written on it since the time of Saadia. He was greatly influenced by the mystic Eleazar of Worms. Thus Abulafia, a visionary of great power, became an ardent Cabalist himself. He believed that he was endowed with a prophetic vision and could perform miracles by the secret formulas of Cabala.

Abulafia left Capua, Italy, wandered around and reached Patras, Greece. Here he completed his first prophetic book titled Sefer Hayashar (Book of the Righteous). In 1280 he appeared in Italy again, with the avowed object of converting Pope Nicholas III to Judaism. The Pope was then in Suriano, and when he was told

about it, he issued orders "to arrest the Jew and burn him at the
stake." Abulafia ignored the danger and went straight to the place
where the Pope stayed. A stake was actually prepared for him,
but Abulafia avoided death, for the Pope had an apoplectic stroke
the night before. Abulafia was arrested and cast into prison for
four weeks. Soon enough he appeared in Sicily where he proclaimed himself as the Messiah. A letter arrived from Rabbi Solomon
ben Adret, the most prominent religious leader of Spanish Jewry,
in which the Jews of Palermo were warned not to listen to this
impostor. Abulafia was compelled to leave Sicily. Imre Shefer
(Words of Beauty), his last work—one of twenty-one books he
composed—was written about 1291. After this we hear nothing more
of this adventurer.

Abulafia distinguishes his own Cabalistic teaching from his predecessors. He calls his system not plain Cabala, but Prophetic
Cabala, because he claims that he has had direct communion with
God. This "communion" he attained thanks to his knowledge of the
right use of Hebrew letters as numerals and particularly because
he knew the secret of how to use the Tetragrammaton—YHWH,
the mysterious name of God.

A. Yellinek gives the following evaluation of Abulafia:

In the Spaniard Abraham Abulafia of the 13th century,
Essenism of old found its resurrection. Preaching asceticism and the highest potentiality of the spirit through communion with God, effected by a perfect knowledge and use
of His names, he was thoroughly convinced of his prophetic mission, and considered himself to be the God-sent
Messiah and Son of God. He differs, however, from the
Messiahs who have risen at different times in his many-
sided philosophical training as well as in his perfect un-
selfishness and sincerity. He addresses himself not to the
masses, but to the educated and enlightened, and does not
confine his mission to his coreligionists, but is filled with
the desire to extend it to the adherents of the Christian
church also. It seems that, for the sake of influencing
these, he tried to construct a Trinitarian system, though it
was a Trinity in form only, and did not touch the essence
of God's personality. Before his vision stood the ideal of

a unity of faith, the realization of which he longed to bring about. Imbued with this spirit, his disciples worked in Spain and Italy, emphasizing still more the Trinitarian idea while treating of the Ten Sefirot, in order to win the adherents of the Church. Hence we have the terms Father, Mother, Son, and Holy Ghost, borrowed from the Christian creed, in the Cabalistic literature of the 13th century. In order to understand Abulafia psychologically and judge him correctly and without bias in the light of history, it must be borne in mind that his cradle was in Spain, the home of religious ecstasy, and that the age in which he lived was that of the Crusades, so favorable to mystic speculation, an age in which many longed to see the barriers separating Judaism, Christianity, and Islam broken down, and in which the Messianic hopes of the Jews found new nourishment in many hearts.[2]

MOSES DE LEON
(1250-1305)

Moses b. Shem Tov de Leon, born at Leon, Spain in 1250, is regarded as either the author or the editor of the Cabalistic book, Sefer Zohar. He was well versed in the philosophy of ibn Gabirol and Maimonides and in the literature of the mystics. He was a prolific writer, mostly on Cabala themes in which he excelled. Several works, some of which exist in manuscript only, were composed by him. They are: Sefer ha-Rimmon, ha-Nefesh ha-Hakamah (The Wise Soul) or ha-Mishkal, and Shekel ha-Kodesh. In his book Sefer ha-Sodoth (Book of Secrets), completed in 1293, he discussed the question of heaven and hell. De Leon also wrote a commentary on Ezekiel's Heavenly Chariot.

Toward the end of the 13th century, Moses published the Zohar, which he claimed to have discovered. He attributed it to the Tanna Simon ben Yohai, who lived in the 2nd century. From the outset the book aroused suspicions, because it was never mentioned by any of Moses' predecessors. It is the opinion of some scholars that Moses de Leon was the editor of the book, which is probably a collection of various, partly ancient, writings. One of the noted Cabalists of the 13th century, Isaac of Acro by name, having heard about it or having read parts thereof, went specially to Spain to meet Moses and find out from him how he had discovered the manuscript. They met at Valladolid. Moses promised to bring the original manuscript from Avila, where he then resided. But on the way home he took sick and soon after died. Another story is told about a rich man who offered a large sum to de Leon's widow for the original. She admitted that her husband was not the author.

The Zohar was idolized by both Jews and non-Jews as a book of divine revelations.

SEFER ZOHAR
(Book of Splendor)

The Tanna, Simon b. Yohai, who according to the Talmud hid himself in a cave for thirteen years at the time of the Hachian persecutions in the 2nd century, is represented as addressing his disciples, who formed a closed circle around him. He disclosed to them the hidden secrets of the Torah. The form of the Torah as it is is nothing more than her outer garb or "robe." Underneath that garb lies the inner meaning of it. This inner meaning is the Truth, the Divine Wisdom. The Zohar distinguishes two domains. The Domain of Holiness (Kedushah), the domain of God, the world of light emanates from the source of life. The second domain is to be found on the other side, being the "shell" (Klipah) that surrounds the "light." Evil thrives only in the shell, in the dark side, or Sitra Ahra (the other side). All evildoers are servants of the dark side; the pious and the saintly belong to the side of Holiness and Light. The attachment of man's soul to either of those two sides is represented as a form of conjugal union, resting upon the division of "male" and "female." One can "unite" with the "holy" as well as with the "unholy" or "unclean."

The principal ideas of the Zohar seem to have been derived partly from the old Sefer Yetzirah, which was known already in the Geonic period, and partly from the Sefer Ha-Bahir. Those ideas, however, were amply elaborated and enlarged with new features.

The Zohar assumes four kinds of interpretation of the Torah, abbreviated in the word Pardes (orchard), spelled without vowels as Prds, each of its four letters standing for one complete word, namely: "P" for Peshat, simple meaning; "R" for Remez, allusion; "D" for D'rash, homiletics; "S" for Sod, mystic. In reference to Sod, Simon b. Yohai says:

> Woe unto the man who asserts that the Torah intends to relate only commonplace things and secular narratives; for if this were so, then in the present times likewise a Torah might be written with more attractive narratives. In truth, however, the matter is thus: The upper world and the lower are established upon one and the same principle; in the lower world is Israel, in the upper world are the angels. When the angels wish to descend to the lower world, they have to don earthly garments. If this be true of the angels, how much more so of the Torah, for whose sake, indeed, the world and the angels were alike created and exist. The world could simply not have endured to look upon it. Now the narratives of the Torah are its garments. He who thinks that these garments are the Torah itself deserves to perish and has no share in the world to come. Woe unto the fools who look no further when they see the elegant robe! More valuable than the garment is the body which carries it, and more valuable even than that is the soul that animates the body. Fools see only the garment of the Torah, the more intelligent see the soul, its proper being, and in the Messianic time the "upper soul" of the Torah will stand revealed (Zohar 3:152).

Thus, the Zohar teaches that besides the "outer" meaning of the Torah there is an "inner" meaning. This principle is to be applied not only to the Torah but also to the visible world, which must be seen from the "inside" in order to be understood aright. Since the universe represents a series of emanations—Ten Spheres, one below the other—it can be grasped by a series of ascensions. At first man can only see it through the mirror of "indirect light." Later in the process of purification a higher stage may be reached which enables the initiate to see the world through the mirror of "direct light." The third stage is attained by the help of intuition, and the fourth one through love of God. From this point on there comes the highest state of ecstasy. This is represented by seven stages, one higher than the other, through which one may enter the heavenly halls (Hekalot), one more beautiful than the other. Rabbi Simon describes such a state:

> Once I was plunged in a contemplative ecstasy, and I beheld a sublime ray of a brilliant light which illumined 325 circles, and amid which something dark was bathing. Then the dark point, becoming bright, began to float toward the deep and sublime sea, where all the splendors were gathering. I then asked the meaning of the vision, and I was answered that it represented the forgiveness of sins.

The Cabala rests on the all-inclusive principle which asserts that "all that exists originates in God, the source of light eternal," or that "there is no place devoid of God." God Himself is the mystery of mysteries, and His essence can never be known. He can only be recognized through the things in which He manifests Himself. From the divine source which is hidden, there emanated four different worlds: a) The world of Aziluth (nobility), which is governed by the first Sefirah - Kether (crown), representing the first emanation; b) The world of Bri'ah (creation), which is governed by three Sefirot; c) The world of Yetzirah (formation), which is governed by the next three Sefirot; d) The world of Asiya (making), which represents the material world. The Ten Sefirot are: Kether (crown), Hokhma (wisdom), Beenah (understanding), Hesed (grace), Gheburah (strength), Tif'eret (beauty; splendor), Nezah (eternity), Hod (majesty), Yesod (foundation), Malkhut (kingdom). Man is able to share in the bliss of these worlds because God endowed him with three separate "souls" or "essences": a) Nefesh, a soul for the world of Asiya, which soul he shares with all animals; b) a higher soul called Ruah, which, if cultivated, is adaptable to the higher world—Yetzirah; c) Neshamah, an entirely spiritual essence that can penetrate into the world of Bri'ah; this third soul is the immortal part of man.

Cabala proposes a method by which man can become one with the world-all—God. Man must first shake off the dust of the material world and liberate himself from all the desires of the flesh, by living a life of purification and sainthood. Fasting, prayers, learning, and concentration are the means to that end. When one attains the higher levels of spiritual sight, one sees all of existence in the mirror of eternity and obtains true happiness and bliss.

The Zohar is a book rich in lofty ideas and conceptions, but simultaneously with them occur many fantastic assertions and long descriptions of mysterious places, heavenly chambers and halls, angels and diabolical creatures. Suddenly, also, one encounters what we would call rather scientific statements, such as this one:

> In the book of Hamnuna the Elder we learn through some extended explanations that the earth turns upon itself in the form of a circle; that some are on top, the other below; that all creatures change in aspect, following the manner of each place, but keeping the same position. But there are some countries on the earth which are lighted while others are in darkness; and there are countries in which there is constantly day or in which at least the night continues only some instants. . . .These secrets were made known to the men of the secret science, but not to the geographers (3:9b).

The Zohar appeared in the 13th century, but for two centuries only small groups studied it. It was not until the great tragedy of the expulsion of the Jews from Spain and Portugal occurred and multitudes of people had been uprooted that the Cabala emerged from relative obscurity. The first Cabalists who settled in Safed, Palestine, near the grave of Simon b. Yohai at Miron, tried to solve the problem of suffering by giving it a higher purpose and relating it to the mysteries of the universe and of God. Jacob B. Agus gives the following answer to the question of why the Zohar exercised such peculiar fascination over the minds of the Jewish people for many centuries:

> Doubtless, it was the whole-souled reaffirmation of the supreme worth of Judaism, at a time when the Jewish faith was challenged at every step. The Zohar was taken to be a new revelation, confirming every belief in Judaism,

strengthening every hope in the breast of the Jew and in-
flating the importance of every aspect of Jewish life into
cosmic proportions. In a motherly spirit, wiping away the
tears of her beaten child, the Zohar conjured up an aura
of cosmic glory to balance the deepening tragedy of Spanish Jewry. As the unhappy lot of medieval Jewry reached
successive depths of misery in the 14th and 15th centuries,
the Zohar grew in popularity, displacing the works of the
rationalists whose philosophy seemed pale and ineffectual
in a trying age, offering but cold comfort to bruised souls.
Following the supreme tragedy of 1492, the brutal expulsion from Spain, the Zohar was exalted to the highest pinnacle of esteem, the unhappy exiles finding in its pages the
assurance of speedy redemption and the knowledge that
their daily sacrifices for the faith were fully justified. In the
"revealed" world of physical existence, the Jew was a
wretched pariah, homeless, helpless and adrift, but in the
"hidden" world, as it was depicted with powerful pathos
and rich imagery in the Zohar, the Jew held in his hands
the trembling scales, in which the fate of the universe was
weighed; he was the high priest of humanity, the destiny
of creation. [3]

The mystic theories of the Cabala appealed even to the Talmudic
rationalists. Thus it is known that such personalities as Nahmanides, Solomon ibn Adret, Joseph Caro, author of the last Talmudic
code, Moses Isserles, Don Isaac Abravanel, Elijah of Wilna, and
innumerable others were also adherents of Cabala. The Zohar's
conception of the En Sof was viewed by many scholars as no more
than an extension of the old God-conception. "Come and see", wrote
the Zohar, "thought is the beginning of everything that is; but as
such it is contained within itself and is unknown. The real [divine]
thought is connected with the En Sof and never separates from it.
This is the meaning of the words [Zech. 16:9] 'God is one, and His
name is one'." (Zohar Wayehi 1:246b)

This mystic book won adherents not only among Jews, but
many Christian scholars studied it zealously. Among the Christians who delved into its mysteries were Johannes Reuchlin, Pico
de Mirandola, Egidius of Viterbo, and scores of others. Many com-

mentaries were written on it. Parts of it were translated into Latin and other languages, from its original Aramaic.

Here are a few excerpts from Sefer Zohar:

One loved a woman who resided in the street of tanners. Had he not loved her, he would never have entered such an evil-smelling place; but, since his beloved lives there, the place smells to him like a place full of perfumes. (3:116b)

*

One should honor his father and mother as one honored God. All three have been partners in his creation. (3:93a)

*

Hunger dominates the world when justice is not tempered with mercy. (1:81b)

*

An ideal man is strong as the male and compassionate as the woman. (4:145b)

*

A wealthy man who is sick is poor; likewise, one who has lost his reason. (5:273b)

*

A river with abundant water is slower in freezing than the river with little water. Likewise, the one who has little knowledge is more critical of faith than the learned. (1:152a)

*

One should not ask God to destroy the wicked. If Terah would have been destroyed, Abraham might not have been born. There would have been no Israel, no Torah, no prophets, and no Messiah. (Zohar Hadash 105)

*

He who praises himself shows that he is ignorant. (4:193)

*

Love without jealousy is not true love. (3:245)

*

Even in the Messianic age we can expect only the weakening of the Evil Impulse but not its total removal. The Good Impulse yearns for the joy of Torah; the Evil impulse seeks women, wine, arrogance.

*

Evil in relation to man is manifold in that it takes semblance for substance, and tries to get away from the divine primal source instead of striving to unite with it.

*

Happy are the righteous in the world to come, for upon them all who are above and below are dependent. Thus it was said, "The righteous [man] is the foundation of the world." (1:245b)

CABALA CENTER AT SAFED

The Cabala reached its highest development in Safed, Palestine, under the leadership of Isaac Luria and his disciple Hayyim Vital Calabrese. The latter collected the teachings of Luria and published them in a six-volume work known as Ez Hayyim (Tree of Life). The Cabala circle at Safed included scholars such as Joseph Caro, Solomon Alkabiz, Moses Cordovero, Israel Saruk, Elijah de Vidas, Joseph Hagiz, Elisha Galadoa, Moses Bassala, Moses Alshech, Israel Najara, and many others.

The mystics of Safed led a life of hermits isolated from the material world and dedicated entirely to God. They spent most of their time in prayer and meditation, fasting days on end and denying themselves any comfort beyond the bare necessities. Only on the Eve of Sabbath they put on white robes, and, walking in a group to the fields around Safed, they sang Psalms, thus inviting the Sabbath Bride to enter the Holy City of Safed, where close by was the grave of the Tanna, Simon ben Yohai, the alleged author of the Zohar. The mystics firmly believed that the time of the coming of the Messiah was near at hand, and that with the help of prayer and dedication they might sway heaven and their hope become a reality.

But Safed was not the only place where Jews hoped for the coming of the Messiah. Practically all over the Diaspora there were people waiting for something miraculous to happen. The frequent expulsions of the Jews, beginning in the 14th century in France and ending with the expulsion from Spain in 1492, the cruel laws enacted against them in various countries, the massacres perpetrated and executed in many cities, turned the minds of the survivors away from the dark present into a visionary world in which life is blissful. In addition, the evil times were seen as the culmination point of the long-drawn-out exile and as the sign of the redemption promised by the Prophets and Sages of long ago. The Cabala actually brought hope into wounded and bleeding hearts. The ghetto was stirring. It was a yearning for security and life.

The hope of the coming of the Messiah was an old one. At times, when the Jew was left alone, it just flickered. However, when life was imperiled and there was no hope save relying upon God, it came back in all its strength. But how could one be sure that the day of redemption is near? The all-knowing, mysterious Cabala said the wonderful word; it also gave the proper signals in advance of time.

DAVID RE'UBENI and SOLOMON MOLKO
(early 16th century)

David Re'ubeni (died 1541) and Solomon Molko (1500-1532) appeared in Europe, both contributing to firing the imagination among the mystically inclined Jews and non-Jews. For in some instances Christians were involved, too. David Re'ubeni came to Europe as a representative of some Jewish tribes in Arabia who were waging war against the Muslims. His aim was to obtain financial aid for his brethren from Christian countries. Having negotiated directly with the Pope and with the king of Portugal, he is said to have been promised some help. When David was in Portugal, he came across Solomon Molko, a marano who was influential in the royal court. Solomon, a mystic and visionary, believed that the Messianic Age was near. He decided to return to Judaism. Both Molko and Re'ubeni visited many Jewish communities, predicting that the Messiah would soon appear. Molko even designated the year of his coming: 1540. The romantic stories about Jews in distant lands fighting against their enemies fascinated the Jewish masses in the ghettos of Europe. Both Re'ubeni and Molko paid with their lives for such tidings. Molko was burned at the stake by the Inquisition in Mantua, Italy, in 1532, and Re'ubeni was imprisoned in Spain and died in 1541.

However, the hope for redemption did not die with them.

JOSEPH CARO
(1488-1575)

Joseph Caro, the greatest codifier since Maimonides, was born either in Spain or Portugal. His father, Ephraim, became one of the exiles from the Iberian peninsula. After several years of wandering, the family settled in Nicopolis, Bulgaria, which was then part of Turkey. When Joseph was yet a young man he established an academy in Adrianopol. There he started to write his famous commentary on the Turim (Four Rows) of Jacob ben Asher, which took him twenty years to complete. This commentary he called Beth Joseph (House of Joseph). He was recognized as the greatest Talmudic authority.

In Adrianopol he met Solomon Molko, the mystic from Spain, who impressed Caro. Caro decided to settle in Safed and join the circle of Cabalists. When the information reached him that Solomon Molko was burned at the stake in Mantua (1532), Caro wanted to die in the same manner—"for the sanctification of God's name". He prayed for it, but his wish was never fulfilled. In Safed he composed his commentary on Maimonides' Mishneh Torah. His main object in writing it was to show the sources of Maimonides' decisions. Caro's versatility in this field was phenomenal; he showed himself to be conversant with every detail of the Law.

His next great work was the Shulhan Aruk (Ready-Made Table), his own Code in which he surpassed all his predecessors. After a time it became the standard law book for Jewry. Moses Isserles (1520-1572), Talmudist and religious philosopher, contributed greatly to Caro's fame. As one of the eminent leaders of Ashkenazic Jewry, he added his notations to the Shulhan Aruk; he included all the customs and traditions of the Ashkenazic Jews, whereas Caro covered only the traditions of the Sephardic Jews.

Enlarged thusly by Moses Isserles, the work was the last great Code, which culminated the efforts of the few major codifiers of the past 500 years: Jacob ben Asher, Maimonides, Isaac Alfasi. Caro's Code ruled Jewish traditional life for centuries.

The most amazing story in the life of this great codifier is the one about the Maggid (popular preacher) who it is said appeared to him in visions. The Maggid, the personification of the Mishnah, was reported to be a spirit who disclosed to him secrets of the Torah. A book entitled Maggid Mesharim (He Who Tells Righteous Things) was later published in which the discussions between Caro and the Maggid were recorded. Some of Joseph Caro's contemporaries testified that they had personally heard the instructions of the Maggid. Caro claimed that the Maggid promised him that his works would have a widespread circulation. Not only did he instruct Caro in writing his books, promising him that his name would become world famous, but he also advised him how to conduct himself in practical life. Caro's position in the cultural history of the Jewish people was not due, however, to his visions. His position was won by hard work which reflected his overall knowledge of the Law.

Excerpts from Shulhan Aruk:

Everyone is obliged to contribute to charity. Even a poor man who is himself maintained by charity should give a portion of what he receives.

*

He who wishes to be deserving of divine reward shall conquer his evil inclinations and open wide his hand, and everything done or given in the name of heaven shall be of the best and the finest.

*

Charity should be given with a friendly contenance, with joy, and with a good heart; the giver should sympathize with the poor man, and should speak words of comfort to him.

*

If a man and his father and his teacher are captives, he himself comes before his teacher; his teacher before his father; but his mother comes before all. A woman is to be redeemed before a man. If a man and his wife are captured, the wife is to be ransomed first, and the court may seize his property to ransom her.

*

There is no act of charity more meritorious than ransoming captives; therefore, money collected for any worthy purpose whatsoever may be used as ransom, even if originally collected for the erection of a synagogue.

MOSES ALSHECH
(16th century)

Moses Alshech, a disciple of Jospeh Caro, belonged to the circle of the Cabalists in Safed, but his works are not Cabalistic. In the introduction to his commentary on the Pentateuch he writes:

I never aimed at things too high or beyond me. From my earliest days the study of the Talmud was my chief occupation. The nights I devoted to research and the day to Halakah. In the morning I read the Talmud and in the afternoon the Posekim [post-Talmudic authorities]. Only on Fridays did I find time for the reading of the Sciptures and Midrash in preparation for the lectures on the Sidra [portion of the week] and similar topics, which I delivered every Sabbath before large audiences, eager to listen to my instructions.

Alshech's lectures were written down and later published. In his comments Alshech employs a special method. Discussing a passage, he first poses a number of questions as to its meaning. Then one answer removes all the questions. His main purpose is to bring to light the moral significance of the passage. He constantly pleads with the learner for repentence and the performing of good deeds, which would help in the realization of the Messianic age on earth.

Alshech was a prolific writer, having composed eighteen books. His Responsa were collected in a separate work.

SOLOMON ALKABIZ
(16th century)

Poet and Cabalist, Solomon Alkabiz stands out as a leading

light in the Safed Cabala center. As the teacher of Moses Cordovero, one of the great Cabalists at that time, Alkabiz's ideas
must have formed part of Moses' world conception.

However, Alkabiz's fame rests mainly upon his liturgic poems,
particularly the Sabbath poem known as Lekah Dodi (Come,
My Friend), which is recited throughout the world on Friday
evening in all synagogues. This ecstatic poem proclaims the coming of the Messianic Age, calling upon Israel to reawaken and
make preparations for the coming of the Redeemer. The Sabbath
is represented as the Bride waiting for her Bridegroom. Alkabiz
does not lament the Exile, nor does he ask forgiveness for sins.
He sings of the restoration of Jerusalem and the in-gathering of
the exiles. The joy of redemption is reverberating from every
word. This poem appeared at the right time, when the hope for
restoration inspired the broad masses of the Jewish people, and
was a balsam for their wounds. It soon became the Song of a
People, sort of a national anthem. Alkabiz composed other poems,
but only Lekah Dodi attained such popularity. Famous cantors
have composed special musical compositions for this Sabbath
song.

Come, My Friend

Come, my friend, to meet the bride,
Let us welcome the presence of the Sabbath.

"Observe" and "Remember" the Sabbath day,
The only God caused us to hear in a single utterance:
The Lord is One, and his name is One,
To His renown and His glory and His praise
                              Come, my friend . . .

Come, let us go to meet the Sabbath,
For it is a wellspring of blessing;
From the beginning, from of old it was ordained—
Last in action, first in thought.
                              Come, my friend . . .

O Sanctuary of our King, O regal city,

Arise, go forth from thy overthrow;
Long enough hast thou dwelt in the valley of weeping;
Verily He will have compassion upon thee.

Come, my friend . . .

Shake thyself from the dust, arise,
Put on the garments of thy glory, O my people!
Through the son of Jesse, the Bethlemite,
Draw Thou nigh unto my soul, redeem it.

Come, my friend . . .

Arouse thyself, arouse thyself, for the light is come;
Arise, shine!
Awake, awake! Give forth a song!
The glory of the Lord is revealed upon thee.

Come, my friend . . .

Be not ashamed, neither be confounded.
Why art thou cast down? And why art thou disquieted?
The poor of my people trust in thee,
And the city shall be built on her mound.

Come, my friend . . .

And they that spoil thee shall be a spoil,
And all that would swallow thee shall be far away:
Thy God shall rejoice over thee,
As a bridegroom rejoiceth over his bride.

Come, my friend . . .

Thou shalt spread to the right and the left,
And thou shalt reverence the Lord.
Through the offspring of Perez [David]
We also shall rejoice and be happy.

Come, my friend . . .

Come in peace, thou crown of thy husband,
With rejoicing and with cheerfulness,
In the midst of the faithful of the Chosen People:

Come, O bride; come O bride.

Come, my friend . . .

MOSES CORDOVERO
(1520-1570)

Moses b. Jacob Cordovero (known by his abbreviated name Remak) was a disciple of Joseph Caro in Talmudic studies and of Solomon Alkabiz in Cabala. His basic work, Pardes Rimmonim (Orchard of Pomegranates), represents a complete exposition of his own views on Cabala as well as of the Zohar theories. Cordovero deals only with theoretical Cabala, keeping himself aloof from touching practical Cabala with its magic formulas and incantations.

Since everything that exists is in God, Cordovero arrived at the following conclusion:

The perfection of creatures consists in the support they get from their being united with the primary source of existence, and they sink down and fall from that perfect and lofty position in proportion to their separation from it.

The question as to God's knowledge and man's knowledge Cordovero answered as follows:

God's knowledge is different from that of His creatures, since in the case of the latter, knowledge and the thing known are distinct, thus leading to subjects that are again separate from Him. This is described by the three expressions—the cogitation, the cogitator, and the subject of cogitation. Now, the Creator is Himself Knowledge, the Knower, and the object known. His knowledge does not consist in the fact that He directs His thoughts to things outside him, since in comprehending and knowing Himself He comprehends and knows everything that exists. There is nothing which is not united to Him, and which He does not find in His own substance. He is the archetype of all existing things, and all things are in Him in their purest and most perfect form.

Cordovero's God-conception as set forth in another work extant in manuscript is identical with Spinoza's. In a letter to his friend Oldenberg, Spinoza wrote that he owes his theory to an old Jewish philosopher. Some scholars think that this "philosopher" was Cordovero. The paragraph in which Cordovero propounds his conception reads as follows:

And the Holy one—blessed be He!—shines in the ten sefirot of the world of emanation, in the ten sefirot of the world of creation, and in the ten heavenly spheres. In investigating this subject the reader will find: that we all proceed from Him, and are comprised in Him; that our life is interwoven with His; that He is the existence of all beings; that the inferior beings, such as vegetables and animals, which serve us as nourishment, are not outside of Him; in short, he will discover that all is one revolving wheel, which ascends and descends—all is one, and nothing is separated from Him.

ISAAC LURIA ASHKENAZI
(1534-1572)

He is called Ari (an abbreviation of Ashkenazi Rabbi Isaac), or the saintly Ari, because all his life was entirely dedicated to Torah and Cabala, to piety and good deeds. Ari (pronounced A-ree) means lion, connoting that he was like a lion among the circle of adherents and disciples around him. He was a Cabalist theoretician, and although he did not write anything himself, his disciples, particularly the greatest among them, Hayyim Vital, left books filled with their teacher's interpretations. Vital's principal work is Ez Hayyim (Tree of Life), a very popular book which went through many editions.

Luria accepted the Zohar's basic idea that the world is an emanation of God, but here a question arose: How could have the world come into being, when God filled the "space" even before the beginning of creation? How did God make room for the universe? To this question Luria gave his own answer: It had been done by Tzimtzim, meaning simply "contracton"; that is, God "contracted" Himself in order to make room for the universe. Naturally, in the "void" that remained there was place enough for the "emanation" that went forth from the source of light. The farther the "rays" penetrated the grosser they became. Our lower world, being so far from the original source, is consequently grossly material; on the other hand, the closer to the source the spheres are, the more refined and divine they are. However, God's radiance as it was flowing forth from the "source of light" was so powerful that the Creator provided special "shells" or vessels in which to contain it. Indeed, the vessels received the powerful rays and held them for a long time. Then they "broke" and the radiance spilled outside. The sparks were dispersed and intermingled with darkness and thus "evil" (contamination) entered the world. This "evil" became "the other side," the shell, the impure force.

The Creator then, having brought forth man into the lower world, gave him a sacred task, namely, to gather the "sparks" (Nitzotzot) and bring them back to their source. Man could do this only by good deeds. When all the sparks would be gathered, the Messianic Age would immediately become a reality. Jews who fulfil the commandments of the Torah and cling tenaciously to God by prayer are the ones that can bring the Messianic Age closer. The salvation of Israel, and by the same token the salvation of humanity, lies in the hands of the good people. God actually is waiting for man to do the right thing. All the problems, all the tribulations and suffering of man, might be resolved in no time, if man only wanted it. As Israel is in exile, so the Shekinah (God's presence) is in exile. For God has gone into exile together with his people.

Isaac Luria's teaching, despite its mysticism, is the most profound expression of the craving for redemption. Outwardly, it looks like a theory which is extraneous to life, but inwardly it is a practical way of conduct upon which the salvation of humanity depends. Luria placed the pious and God-fearing Jew in the forefront of the struggle for the complete redemption from evil and sin.

HAYYIM VITAL CALABRESE
(1543-1620)

Hayyim Vital was Luria's most prominent disciple. Some tall
tales were told about him, as a man destined from his childhood
to perform great things. When he had reached twelve years, a chiro-
mancer predicted that Hayyim would reach a crossroads at exactly
twenty-four years of age; he would then have to select the right
road. Another story about him was to the effect that Joseph Caro
the famous Talmudist, foretold him a great future. A third one
was about the prophet Elijah who was said to have appeared to
him in a dream and subsequently transported him to a beautiful
garden, which was filled with birds. In the midst of the garden
there was a throne upon which God sat in all His majesty. The
birds were not just birds: they were the souls of the saints that
gathered to listen to God teaching the Torah. Apparently Vital
was fond of such stories about himself.

In 1572 Isaac Luria appointed Vital as his spiritual heir. Since
Luria did not leave any writings, Hayyim wrote down everything
his teacher had said. He posed as a miracle man who was able
to call out the spirits of the dead from the other world by the power
of Cabalistic formulas.

One incident, however, in Vital's life indicated that he was not
as sure of himself as he pretended to be. On a visit to Egypt he
was called to the governor's office. The governor, Abu Sufia by name,
challenged him to rediscover the aqueduct King Hezekiah had built
in Jerusalem in Biblical times. Vital was supposed to indicate the
exact place in Jerusalem, and Abu Sufia was determined to find out
whether it was correct. The all-knowing Cabalist did not lose time:
he fled from Egypt at night and subsequently reappeared in Damascus.

In Damascus he soon found some adherents. There he completed
a work on the patriarch Abraham, a book filled with Cabalistic
incantations. Later he returned to Safed and submitted his manuscript to a wealthy Jew named Joshua b. Nun, who bought it from
him for a considerable sum and published it.

According to Vital the old Cabala had outlived its time. The real

Cabala was the one taught by Isaac Luria to whom great secrets were revealed anew. He also claimed that Moses Cordovero appeared to him in dreams and disclosed many hidden things.

At one time Vital proclaimed himself as Messiah ben Joseph, who was supposed to appear before the real Messiah, a scion of the Davidic dynasty. In Damascus, where he had organized a circle of adherents, he lectured freely about it. Two prominent rabbis of that time, Menahem di Lonzano and Jacob Abulafia, warned against him. Di Lonzano, in his book Imre Emet (True Words), condemned him as an impostor. Vital retracted for a while.

ISRAEL BEN MOSES NAJARA
(16th century)

Among the Cabalists of Safed at the time of Isaac Luria was Israel ben Moses Najara, one of the most prominent poets of the 16th century, whose hymns were included in the prayer books of various countries, particularly Italy and Palestine. Najara also wrote Z'mirot (Sabbath Songs) to be chanted at the Sabbath meals.

The saintly Isaac Luria is said to have declared that "Najara's hymns were listened to with delight in heaven". A number of Najara's poems appeared in a book titled Z'mirot Israel (Songs of Israel).

Najara himself picked up some Turkish and Arabic melodies and subsequently composed poems to correspond to the music. He also wrote poems of love using Turkish, Spanish, and Greek metric forms.

Loved of my soul[4]

Loved of my soul! Father of Grace!
Lead on Thy servant to Thy favoring sight;
He, fleetly as the hart, shall speed his pace
To bow him low before Thy glorious might.
Sweet is Thy love to him beyond compare,
Sweeter than honey, fairer than things fair.

Splendor of Worlds! Honored, adored!
My soul is sick with pining love of Thee;
My God! I pray Thee, heal her: be implored;
And o'er her let Thy holy sweetness be
A soothing strength to stay her yearning sore;
And joy shall be for her for evermore.

Source of all good! Pity Thou me!
And be Thou moved for Thy beloved son.
Ah! Would that I could rise aloft and see
The beauty of Thy strength, Thou mighty one!
These things my soul desireth: Lord, I pray,
Grant me Thy mercy; turn Thee not away.

Be Thou revealed, dearest of mine!
And spread o'er me Thy canopy of peace;
Lo! with Thy glory all the earth shall shine,
And we shall know a joy that shall not cease.
Hasten, beloved, for the time is nigh,
And have compassion as in days gone by.

אי|11

LITURGICAL
POETRY

There is an old story, conceived by the sages and handed
down age to age, that when God had finished the world,
He asked one of the angels if aught were wanting on
land or on sea, in air or in heaven. The angel replied
that all was perfect; one thing only was lacking—speech,
to praise God's works. And the Heavenly Father approved
the angel's words, and soon thereafter He created man,
gifted with the muses. This is the ancient story, and in
consonance with its spirit, I say: "It is God's peculiar
to benefit man, and man's work to give Him thanks."

Philo Judaeus (1st century)

Numerous poets, known and unknown by name, contributed
during the centuries to the rich liturgical division of Hebrew literature, their poems becoming prayers recited on various occa-
sions. The prayers cover the whole year: weekdays, Sabbaths,
holidays, fast and mourning days commemorating national ca-
tastrophes. Collected into separate books, they formed special
anthologies:

1. Siddur: Prayers, Psalms, and excerpts from Bible and Tal-

mud for weekdays and Sabbaths. The word Siddur is a derivative of Seder, meaning "order," and Sadder, "to arrange."

2. Mahzor: Prayers and poems (Piyyutim) for the holidays.
Mahzor is a derivative of Hazor—"to come back," repeat, meaning a cycle, an annual repetition.

3. Selihot (S'lihot): Prayers of forgiveness and repentance,
usually recited before Rosh Hashanah (New Year) and Yom Kippur (Day of Atonement), many nights prior to Rosh Hashanah
and during the ten penitential days between Rosh Hashanah and
Yom Kippur. Selihot, from word meaning penitence.

4. Zemirot (Z'mirot): Sabbath songs chanted at the table during the meals. They were included in many of the traditional
prayer books. Zemirot, songs.

5. Haggadah: Passover songs and prayers recited the first
two nights of the festival of freedom.

The oldest complete prayer book was arranged in the Babylonian academies. It is known as Siddur of Amram Gaon (846-864),
and served as the basis of other later prayer books. The Siddur
of Amram Gaon, apart from being the oldest compilation, contains important notes on customs which prevailed at that early
time, and also homiletic interpretations not found in the regular
Siddur. Another prayer book, discovered in Al-Fayyum, Egypt,
is attributed to Saadia Gaon (10th century). It contains poems
and moral exhortations by Saadia. The most important early
compilation of prayers is to be found in the famous Mahzor
Vitry, composed by Simhah ben Samuel of Vitry (d. 1105), a
disciple of Rashi. It is ten times as voluminous as the Siddur of
Amram Gaon. It contains also some historic notes. The first
printed copy of the regular prayer book appeared in 1486. It
was used in the Franco-German communities, that is, by the
Ashkenazic Jews. The first printed Sephardic prayer book used
by the Spanish Jews appeared in 1524.

The Siddur appeared in various editions, differently arranged.
Prayer books contained varying combinations of the five collections noted above. There is the prayer book arranged by Isaac
Luria (Ari), which is called Siddur Ari; it is Cabalistic in spirit
and content. The Gaon of Wilna, Elijah Gaon, arranged a Siddur,
as did Shneour Zalman of Liadi. In modern times special prayer

books have been published by Reform Jews and other sections of Jewry.

The penitential prayers were originally composed for the Day of Atonement, but later Rosh Hashanah was included. Other Selihot were composed for the nights before Rosh Hashanah. Jews assembled after midnight in the synagogues and recited them. Still later poets composed Selihot for the fast days, too. Prayers of penitence fall into the following categories: historical or Aggadic, exhortations, descriptions of persecutions, commemoration of martyrs, supplications, dirges and lamentations.

The principal authors of Selihot were: Gershom b. Judah (Ma'or Hagolah), Ephraim b. Jacob of Bonn, David b. Meshulam, Joel Halevi, Simon b. Isaac, Solomon b. Judah, Eliezer b. Nathan, Solomon b. Judah Hababli, Shephatiah b. Amittai, Simon b. Isaac Abun, Meir b. Samuel, Meir b. Isaac of Orleans, Zebadiah.

The Haggadah of Passover is an old compilation. One part— the four questions—is even mentioned in the Mishnah. It contains also poems composed in the Middle Ages. The Haggadah was printed in hundreds of editions. In 1890 Adolf Oster collected 230 copies of various printed editions, but S. Wiener succeeded in collecting 895 editions. One copy was printed by Soncino as early as 1486 in Italy. The next printed copy is of the 1505 edition. Many commentaries were written on the Haggadah. The Wilna edition of 1892 carried 115 commentaries. There is a large number of illustrated Haggadahs, artistically decorated. Prayers are recited in accordance with a special chant known as Nusah. Various great cantors have composed musical compositions for the principal prayers.

Hear, O Israel
(Shema Israel)

Hear O Israel: the Lord our God, the Lord is One.
And thou shalt love the Lord thy God with all thine heart, and with all thy soul, and with all thy might. And these words, which I command thee this day, shall be upon thine heart: and thou shalt teach them diligently unto thy children, and shalt talk of them when thou sittest in

thine house, and when thou walkest by the way, and when
thou liest down, and when thou risest up. And thou shalt
bind them for a sign upon thine hand, and they shall be
for frontlets between thine eyes. And thou shalt write them
upon the door posts of thy house, and upon thy gates.

(Deut. 6:4-9)

This is the oldest Biblical prayer. The Tanna Simeon b. Yohai
said (Sotah 42a) that "Shema Israel" was a battle cry of the
priest in calling Israel to arms against an enemy. Akibah b.
Joseph, the martyr Tanna, died reciting it while his flesh was being
torn with iron combs (Ber. 61b). During the centuries while Jews
were tortured they died with Shema on their lips. It was also used
as a password whereby one Jew recognized another. Eldad
Hadani (10th century) reported that it was incribed on the flag of
his tribe in Arabia.

Rabbi Joseph Hertz interprets the Shema prayer:

"Hear, O Israel: the Lord our God, the Lord is One".
These words enshrine Judaism's greatest contribution to
the religious thought of mankind. They constitute the primal confession of faith in the religion of the synagogue.
They rightly occupy the central place in Jewish religious
thought, for every other Jewish thought turns upon it; all
goes back to it; all flows from it. The "Shema" became
the first prayer of innocent childhood, and the last utterance of the dying. It was the rallying-cry by which a hundred generations in Israel were welded together unto one
Brotherhood to do the Will of their Father in Heaven; it
was the watchword of the myriads of martyrs who were
agonized and died for the idea of cosmic unity.[1]

Hin'neni
(I am ready)

The following supplication, composed by an unknown Hazzan
(cantor) in the Middle Ages, reveals the fervor and humility of the
writer as he stood up to pray for his congregation.

Behold, in deep humility,
I stand and plead before Thee, God on high,

Great Lord who art enthroned above all praise,
O hearken and give heed unto my prayer.
Though unworthy of my sacred task,
Though imperfect, too, and filled with awe,
I bow before Thy Holy Presence here,
To crave compassion for my erring folk.
O God of Israel's Patriarchs,
Their children's children send me as their voice
To supplicate Thy pardon and Thy grace,
To ask Thy mercy, Thy continued love.
Though unworthy of the mission, Lord,
Though I stand not flawless in Thy sight,
Condemn Thou not my people for my faults,
Consider but their virtues, Righteous Judge,
Forgive us our iniquities,
And turn Thou our afflictions unto joy.
Thou great, exalted God who hearest prayer,
Hear ours, and bless us all with life and peace.[2]

Prayer for Universal Freedom

And therefore, O Lord our God, let Thine awe be manifest in all Thy works, and a reverence for Thee fill all that Thou hast created, so that all Thy creatures may know Thee, and all mankind bow down to acknowledge Thee. May all Thy children unite in one fellowship to do Thy will with a perfect heart; for we know, O Lord our God, that dominion is Thine, that Thy might and power are supreme, and that Thy Name is to be revered over all Thou hast created.

And therefore, O Lord, grant glory to Thy people who serve Thee, praise to those who revere Thee, hope to those who seek Thee, and confidence to those who yearn for Thee. Bring joy to Thy land, gladness to Thy city, renewed strength to the seed of David, and a constant light to Thy servants in Zion. O may this come to pass speedily in our days.

And therefore, the righteous shall see and be glad, the just exult, and the pious rejoice in song, while iniquity shall close its mouth and all wickedness shall vanish like smoke, when Thou removest the dominion of tyranny from the earth.

According to Rabbi Morris Silverman, these three paragraphs, each beginning with U-v'hane, reaffirm loyalty to a universal outlook and world brotherhood, the well-being of Israel, and the triumph of the moral law. The three forces of internationalism, nationalism, and religion, each retaining its own sphere of influence, but reacting upon one another will hasten the advent of the Kingdom of God and bring salvation to mankind.[3]

And thus great is the work of our God!

In this hymn the author, Meshullum ben Kalonymos, presents the greatness of the Creator as compared to the smallness and insignificance of man. He admonishes man not to rely upon temporary things.

> In the height and the depth of His burning,
> Where mighty He sits on the throne,
> His light He unveils and His yearning
> To all who revere Him alone.
> His promises never are broken,
> His greatness all measure exceeds;
> Then exalt Him who gives you for token
> His marvellous deeds.
>
> He marshals the planets unbounded,
> He numbers the infinite years;
> The seat of his empire is founded
> More deep than the nethermost spheres;
> He looks on the lands from His splendor:
> They tremble and quiver like reeds;
> Then exalt ye in lowly surrender
> His marvellous deeds.

The worlds He upholds in their flying,
His feet on the footstool of earth;
His word hath established undying
Whatever His word brought to birth.
The ruler of hosts is His title;
Then exalt Him in worshipful creeds,
Declaring in solemn recital
His marvellous deeds.

He is master of all He created,
Sublime in His circle of light;
His strength with His glory is mated,
His greatness at one with His might.
So that Seraphim over Him winging,
Obeying an angel that leads,
Unite in the rapture of singing
His marvellous deeds.

But of man—ah! the tale is another,
His counsels are evil and vain:
He dwells with deceit as a brother,
And the worm is the close of his reign.
Into earth he is carted and shovelled,
And who shall recount or who heeds,
When above earth he strutted or grovelled,
His marvellous deeds?

Not so God!—earth on nothing He founded,
And on emptiness stretched out the sky;
With land the great waters He bounded,
And bade all their breeds multiply.
In light He is clad as a raiment:
His greatness no eulogy needs;
Yet exalt, 'tis your only repayment,
His marvellous deeds.[4]

Hymn Of Weeping

Amittai ben Shefatia lived about the end of the 11th century. He recited his own compositions in the synagogue as cantor. This hymn is part of the Ne'ilah service of the Day of Atonement.

> Lord, I remember, and am sore amazed
> To see the cities stand in haughty state,
> And God's own city to the low grave razed:—
> Yet in all time we look to Thee and wait.
>
> Spirit of mercy! Rise in might! Awake!
> Plead to thy Master in our mournful plaint,
> And crave compassion for thy people's sake;
> Each head is weary, and each heart is faint.
>
> I rest upon my pillars—love and grace,
> Upon the flood of ever-flowing tears;
> I pour out prayer before His searching face,
> And through the fathers' merit lull my fears.
>
> O Thou Who hearest weeping, healest woe!
> Our tears within Thy vase of crystal store;
> Save us; and all Thy dread decrees forego,
> For unto Thee our days turn evermore.[5]

Universal Recognition Of God

This poem, written more than 1200 years ago by an unknown author, is remarkable for its universalistic outlook. This is particularly noteworthy since the Middle Ages were marked by intolerance, prejudice, and violence. The poem is from the services of the Day of Atonement.

> All the world shall come to serve Thee
> And bless Thy glorious Name,
> And Thy righteousness triumphant
> The islands shall acclaim.

And the peoples shall go seeking
Who knew Thee not before,
And the ends of earth shall praise Thee,
And tell Thy greatness o'er.

They shall build for Thee their altars,
Their idols overthrown,
And their graven gods shall shame them,
As they turn to Thee alone.
They shall worship Thee at sunrise,
And feel Thy Kingdom's might,
And impart their understanding
To those astray in night.

They shall testify Thy greatness,
And of Thy power speak,
And extol Thee, shrined, uplifted
Beyond man's highest peak.
And with reverential homage,
Of love and wonder born,
With the ruler's crown of beauty
Thy head they shall adorn.

With the coming of Thy Kingdom
The hills shall break into song,
And the islands laugh exultant
That they to God belong.
And all their congregations
So loud Thy praise shall sing,
That the uttermost peoples, hearing,
Shall hail Thee crowned King.[6]

Highest Divinity
(From the Rosh Hashanah prayers)

Highest divinity,
Throned in the firmament,
Potentate paramount,

Hand superdominant,
Lord of infinity.

Highest divinity,
Great in performing all,
Sure in decreeing all,
Stern in unbaring all,
Lord of infinity!

Highest divinity,
Speaking in holiness,
Vestured in righteousness,
Heedful of suppliants,
Lord of infinity!

Highest divinity,
Time is His dwelling place,
Goodness e'erlastingly
Spanning the firmament,
Lord of infinity!

Highest divinity,
King of the universe,
Piercer of mysteries,
Causing the dumb to speak,
Lord of infinity!

Highest divinity,
Propping, sustaining all,
Slaying, surviving all,
Seeing, unseen of all,
Lord of infinity!

Highest divinity,
Crowned with omnipotence,
Right hand victorious,
Savior and Shelterer,
Lord of infinity!

Highest divinity,
Sleeping nor slumbering,
Center of restfulness,
Awed angels chanting His praise,
Lord of infinity!

Lowly humanity,
Doomed to go down to death,
Grave-ward and lower still,
Vain is man's heritage,
Sovran of Vanity!

Lowly humanity,
Sleep is his daily end,
Deep sleep his final goal.
Darkness flows over him,
Sovran of Vanity!

Highest divinity,
Dynast of endlessness,
Timeless resplendency,
Worshipped eternally,
Lord of Infinity![7]

For We Are Thy People
(Prayer of the Day of Atonement, from unknown medieval poet)

For we are thy people, and thou art our God;
We are thy children and thou art our father.
We are thy servants, and thou art our master;
We are thy congregation and thou our portion.
We are thine inheritance, thou our lot;
We are thy flock, thou our shepherd.
We are thy vineyard, and thou art our keeper;
We are thy work, and thou our creator.
We are thy faithful ones: thou art our beloved;
We are thy chosen: thou art the Lord our God.
We are thy subjects, thou our king;

We are thine acknowledged people.
Thou our acknowledged Lord.

Sabbath of Rest
(Zemira, or table hymn for the Sabbath, by Isaac Luria)

This day is for Israel light and rejoicing,
A Sabbath of rest.

Thou badest us, standing assembled at Sinai,
That all the years through we should keep Thy behest—
To set out a table full laden, to honor
The Sabbath of rest.
Refrain: This day. . . .

Treasure of heart for the broken people,
Gift of new soul for the souls distrest,
Soother of signs for the prisoned spirit—
The Sabbath of rest.
This day. . . .

When the work of the worlds in their wonder was finished,
Thou madest this day to be holy and blest,
And those heavy-laden found safety and stillness,
A Sabbath of rest.
This day. . . .

If I keep Thy command I inherit a kingdom,
If a treasure the Sabbath I bring Thee the best—
The noblest of offerings, the sweetest of incense—
A Sabbath of rest.
This day. . . .

Restore us our shrine—O remember our ruin
And save now and comfort the sorely opprest;
Now sitting at Sabbath, all singing and praising
The Sabbath of rest.
This day. . . .[8]

Hymns of Refuge

The first stanza of a S'lihah, prayer of forgiveness, by Isaac ben Samuel, who probably lived between the 10th and 12th centuries:

> The shade of His hand shall cover us
> (under the wings of His presence);
> He surely will pity, trying thus
> The wrongful heart, to show the righteous way.
> Arise, Lord, I beseech Thee:
> My help! help now, I pray;
> Lord, now let our crying reach Thee.[9]

The first stanza of a S'lihah by Solomon ben Samuel, 13th century:

> "Forgiven", He will let us hear
> (He in his secret dwelling);
> His hand shall bring salvation near
> The people, poor and lowly and astray.
> While we to Thee be crying,
> Help wondrously we pray;
> Lord, now be Thou replying.[10]

Dirge for the Ninth of Ab

O thou afflicted, drunken not with wine!
Cast to the earth thy timbrel; strip thee bare;
Yea, make thee bald; let not thy beauty shine;
Despoil of comeliness thy presence fair;
Lift up a wailing on the mountain height;
Turn thee to all the borders; seek thy flight.
> And cry before the Lord
> For thresholds waste,
> For thresholds waste;
> Cry for thy little ones
> Slain of the sword;

Lift up thine hands to Him,
To Him implored.

How hath to Zion come the foeman dread,
Into the royal city entrance found!
How do the reckless feet of strangers tread
With step irreverent on the hallowed ground!
Lo! when the spoilers stormed the sanctuary,
They fell on priests, the guards of sacred rite,
Watchmen who kept their charge, and fearlessly
Stood by, unflinching 'mid the deadly fight:
Until their blood was shed, profuse as when
Of yore the Nile was turned to bloody flow;
Within the curtain burst unholy men,
Yea, even where the High Priest feared to go.
They stript of gold thy walls' majestic heights,
And the fair windows of Thy narrowed lights.
            Refrain: And cry . . . .

The voice of Zion's daughter sore doth moan,
She waileth from afar in anguish deep,
Uttereth the cry of Heshbon* overthrown,
And with the weeping of Mephaath* doth weep:
Woe! I have drunk the cup, have drained it! Woe!
Lions with savage fangs have me undone,
Daughter of Babylon, that liest low!
Daughter of Edom, O thou guilty one! —
Wherefore, O Zion, art bewailing thee
Over this thy doom? For lo! Thy sin is known:
By the abundance of iniquity
Beholdest thou the exile of thine own;
For that thy watchman true thou didst forsake,
To hearken unto words false omens spake.
            And cry . . . .

Rejoice not, O mine enemy, o'er my pain,

* Amorite cities (see Joshua 13:17-18)

O'er the destruction that hath come to me,
For though I fall I shall arise again;
The Lord yet helped me; yea, even He
Who scattered, in His burning wrath, His flock,
Shall gather me once more within His fold;
He shall deliver me from thee; my Rock
Shall free His servant to thy bondage sold.
Then unto thee shall pass the brimming bowl,
The cup whose bitterness hath filled my soul.
    And cry . . . .[11]

O Soul of Mine!

O soul of mine!
Resolve to school yourself
With such self-discipline,
That fear and loss of faith
Can never threaten you again.
Let no exuberance
Of loud prosperity cajole you
Into fantastic structures of belief.
Remember that I am a child of God
And wealth and power cannot add to that,
Nor loss of them detract from it.
Within my inmost self
My worth is centered
Impregnable, unconquerable and supreme.
Then keep it so and do not sully it
By lack of self-control.[12]

                                 Israel Baal Shem

Rabbi Amnon's Prayer and Death

During the reign of one of the bishops in Metz, so the story goes, there lived a Jew in that city, who was called Rabbi Amnon. He was of illustrious family, of great personal merit, rich and respected by the Bishop and the people. The Bishop frequently pressed him to abjure Judaism and embrace Christianity, but without the slightest avail. It happened, however, upon a certain day, being more closely pressed than usual, and somewhat anxious to get rid of the Bishop's importunities, he said hastily, "I will consider the subject, and give thee an answer in three days." As soon as he had left the Bishop's presence, however, his heart smote him, and an unquiet conscience blamed him for admitting, even in this manner, a doubt of the true faith. He reached home overwhelmed with grief; meat was set before him, but he refused to eat; and when his friends visited him and ascertained the cause of his low spirits, he refused their proffered consolation, saying, "I shall go down mourning to the grave for these words." On the third day, while he was still lamenting his imprudent concession, the Bishop sent for him, but he refused to answer the call. Having refused several of the Bishop's messengers, they were finally ordered to seize him, and bring him by force before the prelate.

"Amnon," said the Bishop, "why didst thou not come to me, according to thy promise, to inform me of thy decision in regard to my request?"

"Let me," answered Amnon, "pronounce my own doom for this neglect. Let my tongue, which uttered those hasty words be cut out; a lie I uttered, for I never intended to consider the proposition."

"Nay," said the Bishop, "I will not cut out thy tongue, but thy feet, which refused to come to me, shall be cut off, and the other parts of thy obstinate body shall be also punished and tormented."

The toes and thumbs of Rabbi Amnon were then cut off, and after having been severely tortured, he was sent home in a carriage, his mangled membes beside him. His life after this was of course to be measured by days. The Feast of the New Year came round, while he was living, and he desired to be carried to the synagogue. He was conveyed there, and during the service he requested to be allowed to utter a prayer. The words proved to be his last:

> I will declare the mighty holiness of this day, for it is
> awful and frightful. Thy kingdom is exalted thereon; thy
> throne is established in mercy, and upon it thou dost rest

in truth. Thou art the Judge, who chastiseth, and from Thee nought may be concealed. Thou bearest witness, writest, sealest, recordest, and rememberest all things, aye, those which we imagine long buried in the past. Thou unfoldest the records, and the deeds therein inscribed tell their own story, for the seal of every man's hand is set thereto. The great shofar is sounded, and a still small voice is heard. The angels in heaven are dismayed and are seized with fear and trembling, as they proclaim, "Behold the Day of Judgment!" For the hosts of heaven are to be arraigned in judgment for in Thine eyes even they are not free from guilt. All who enter the world dost Thou cause to pass before Thee, one by one, as a flock of sheep. As a shepherd mustereth his sheep and causeth them to pass beneath his staff, so dost Thou pass and record, count and visit, every living soul, appointing the measure of every creature's life and decreeing its destiny. On the New Year is is written, on the Day of Atonement it is sealed. All Thy decrees are recorded. Who is to live and who is to die. The names of those to meet death by fire, by water, or by the sword; through hunger, through thirst, and in the pestilence. Those who are to have tranquility, those who are to be disturbed. Those who are to be troubled, and those who are to be blessed with repose. Those who are to be prosperous, and those for whom affliction is in store. Those who are to become rich or poor; who exalted, who cast down; but penitence, prayer, and charity, O Lord, may avert all evil.[13]

A Modern Hebrew Poet on the Old Prayer Book

The old tear-stamped prayerbook will I take in my hand
And call upon the God of my fathers in my distress.
To the God of my fathers who was their Rock
And Refuge in ages past,
I will pour out my woe
In ancient words, seared with the pain of generations.
May these words that know the heavenly paths

Bring my plaint to the God above,
And tell Him that which is hidden in my heart,
What my tongue is incapable of expressing.
These words, faithful and true, will speak for me before God.
They will ask his pity.
And God in heaven who has heard the prayers of my fathers,
Perchance He will hear my prayer, too, and my distress,
And will be a shield unto me as He was unto them.
For, like them, I am left a spoil unto others,
Degraded and despised,
A wanderer over the face of the earth.
And there is none who can help and sustain me
Except God in heaven.[14]

Jacob Cohen

IV

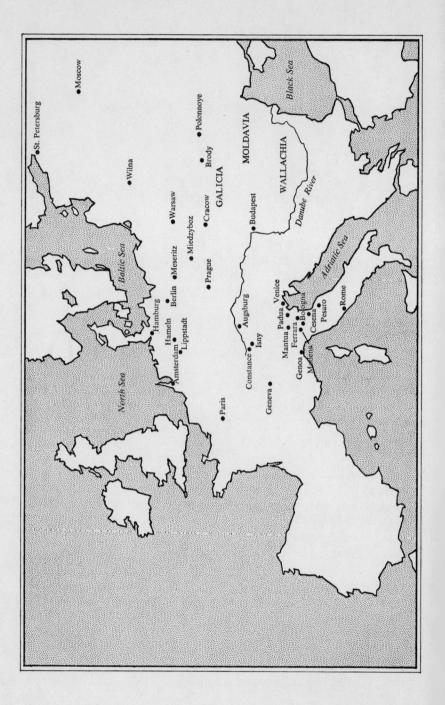

Moscow

St. Petersburg

Wilna

Polonnoye

Brody

Cracow

GALICIA

Warsaw

Miedzyboz

MOLDAVIA

Black Sea

Baltic Sea

Berlin

Meseritz

Prague

Budapest

WALLACHIA

Danube River

Hamburg

Hameln

Lippstadt

Augsburg

Venice

Padua

Adriatic Sea

Amsterdam

Constance

Isny

Mantua

Ferrara

Bologna

Cesena

Pesaro

Rome

North Sea

Paris

Geneva

Genoa

Modena

יב|12

PERIOD
OF
TRANSITION

QUESTIONS AND REEVALUATIONS

Europe of the 16th, 17th, and 18th centuries was experiencing what we look back and refer to as an Intellectual Revolution. Nurtured on Renaissance humanism, inspired by new discoveries and new forces—the discovery of America and other new lands, the impact of the Protestant Reformation, the use of the printing press—and captivated by an avalanche of new scientific methodologies and formulations, men and women revised old ways of seeing and doing and thinking. The Jews participated in this experience. Liberal ideas penetrated the ghettos; there was a yearning for something new, a groping for change. This quest, this questioning, took two forms: one more activist, another more intellectual. A number of movements arose, expressions of dissatisfaction with and rebellion against the life the Jew had too long known. Scholarly and philosophical questions about the Jewish intellectual and religious tradition were raised.

In Holland, a haven now for Jews, a New Jerusalem, where a Jew could live as a free man, some thinkers went beyond the bounds thought proper by the Jewish authorities. Uriel da Costa and Baruch

389

Spinoza, for example, were banished from the Jewish community. In Italy, Leon de Modena and Joseph Solomon Delmedigo raised penetrating questions about traditional Judaism. It was indeed a time of intellectual reevaluation.

Four movements within Judaism symbolize the controversy and the innovations which characterized this period of transition for the Jews. In 1538, there erupted a quarrel between the rabbis of Jerusalem and the rabbis of Safed, under the leadership of Jacob Berab. The split threatened the integrity of Judaism; the problem involved the restoration of the ancient custom of rabbinical ordination. What Jacob Berab did was simple. He assembled a rabbinical court of twenty-five Talmudic scholars in Safed and decreed that rabbinical ordination was to be reintroduced into Jewish life, an act seemingly not in any way dangerous to anyone. But the rabbis in Jerusalem, under the leadership of Levi ben Jacob ibn Habib, protested vehemently, condemning the action as detrimental to Judaism. What was behind Berab's actions? The expulsion of the Jews from Spain in 1492 had shaken Judaism to its core. The 16th century witnessed the establishment of hundreds of new Jewish communities in Europe and the Mediterranean world as the result of this new Diaspora. New conditions and new problems confronted many, many Jews; old ways of doing things were proving questionable. Stability and unity among Jews were crumbling; there was no single authority to whom one might appeal. Each rabbi took it upon himself to decide the gravest matters of religious life. Jacob Berab conceived the idea of a central spiritual authority in Safed, then the largest Jewish community in Palestine. He thought to begin unobtrusively with rabbinical ordination, intending later to enlarge his ordaining body into a Sanhedrin to whom all rabbis would be subject. Such a central authoritative religious body within Judaism had not existed for over a thousand years. Jerusalem, jealous of its position, objected to Berab's plan; contentious factions developed. Berab died several years later and his dreams died with him.

A little over a hundred years later there arose a figure with even grander ambitions. He tried to redeem Israel from exile. He proclaimed himself Messiah. His name was Sabbetai Zevi (1626-1676). He had from his youth been attracted to Cabala. Believing that by asceticism and the mortification of the body one could communicate with God, he followed all the mystic instructions to the letter. His tall majestic figure, the charming features of his face, his princely behavior, won for him many adherents who regarded him as a holy man. The belief that the redemption of Israel was near and the Messiah would soon appear was widespread not only among Jews but also among Christians. The Book of Splendor (Zohar) was widely cited to the effect that the year 1648 was to be the year of redemption and restoration of the Jewish people in their old homeland. The suffering of the Jews, the massacres of Jews in the Ukraine, the annihilation of hundreds of Jewish communities in Poland, were taken as the signals before the coming of the Messiah. In Italy, Holland, Germany, Palestine, and elsewhere Sabbetai's good tidings enthused multitudes and centers were opened for his adherents. The most fantastic stories were accepted as true. Thousands of Jews sold their businesses and possessions in order to be ready for the return to the Holy Land. But in 1665 the great vision suddenly faded. Sabbetai was imprisoned by Turkish authorities and, threatened with death, abandoned Judaism for the Muslim religion. Many of his followers accepted this apparent betrayal as a temporary step which the Messiah in his wisdom had to take, but the majority were frustrated and disillusioned. The movement withered away after Sabbetai's death.

In the mid-18th century, another false Messiah appeared to claim Sabbetai's legacy—Jacob Frank, a simple charlatan, who organized a sect which integrated sexual immoralities into its practices. In a few years Jacob and his followers were involved in a wholesale conversion to Christianity. Thus the Frankists completely disappeared from the Jewish scene.

Also in the 18th century, there emerged the great popular movement known as Hasidism, which exerted such a deep influence on modern Jewry and on Hebrew literature. It will be discussed in more detail later in this chapter, as will the intellectual and literary developments of this transition period. These discussions, focusing around the personalities involved, are grouped into four geographical areas: southern Europe (Italy), western Europe (Holland), central Europe, and eastern Europe.

OBADIAH BERTINORO
(d. 1500)

Italian Jewry brought forth two great commentators: Obadiah Bertinoro, commentator of the Mishnah; and Obadiah Sforno, commentator of the Pentateuch.

Bertinoro left his native Italy in 1488. On his way to Palestine he stopped for a considerable time in Egypt and Greece, where he wrote letters to friends and relatives in Italy. These letters, translated into German, French, and English, proved of historic significance because of the acute descriptions of social and economic life among the Jews and non-Jews of Egypt and Greece. Having settled in Jerusalem, Bertinoro established an academy, which became famous. His prestige was so great that the Jews of Egypt, Italy, and Turkey supported him liberally. Since the 4th century, when the Palestinian academies closed, Jerusalem had not been a center of learning; but Betinoro restored the Holy City's position in this respect.

Bertinoro's name reached far and wide. His saintly way of life and his conscientious work as teacher and leader in Israel were acknowledged both in the West and the East; Jews in Arab lands, as well as in Italy and other European countries, referred their legal problems to him. He was a leading rabbi in the best tradition of the word, viewing his function as a religious duty to be fulfilled without monetary compensation. In his commentary, he reproved other rabbis for receiving payments, going so far as to call them "robbers."

Bertinoro's commentary on the Mishnah became popular as soon as it appeared. He usually followed Rashi in his interpretations, but he was more explicit and thoroughgoing in his explanations. Among students of that day, studying the Mishnah without Bertinoro's elucidations was unthinkable. Bertinoro became known as Rab (master).

Bertinoro also composed a number of poems. Some of his liturgical poems exist in manuscript at the Bodleian Library, Oxford.

OBADIAH SFORNO
(c. 1475-1550)

Obadiah Sforno was a Talmudist, a Biblical scholar, a philosopher, and a prominent physician in Italy. When Johannes Reuchlin visited Rome in search of a scholar who would instruct him in Hebrew, Cardinal Domenico Grimani recommended Sforno as the ablest scholar in Italy; Reuchlin subsequently became Sforno's diciple. In 1525, Sforno moved from Cesena, his native city, to Bologna, where he established his own academy.

In his commentary on the Pentateuch, Sforno was a rationalist, frequently applying philosophical ideas to explain the text, as long as his religious beliefs were not compromised. The commentary is distinguished by its simplicity; Sforno's comments were short and concise, sober and clear. The commentary was highly honored by learners.

Sforno authored another book, Or Amim (Light of Peoples); this was his attempt to refute some of Aristotle's ideas. He translated it into Latin and sent it to King Henry II of France. It remained in manuscript.

ELIJA LEVITA
(1468-1549)

One of the famous Hebrew grammarians, Elija Levita, occupies a high position in the history of Hebrew literature not only as an author of important works but also as a teacher of Christians. His most prominent disciples were Cardinal Egidius of Viterbo, Paul Fagius, and Sebastian Münster, as well as others who wanted to perfect themselves in the knowledge of the ancient language. Levita was by no means the only Jewish scholar known in the Christian world. His contemporaries were such well-known personalities as Judah Abravanel (Leo Hebreus); Jacob Mantion, personal physician to Pope Paul III; Benet di Lattes, astronomer. However, in the field of Hebrew grammar, Levita was regarded as one of the greatest scholars.

At first he lived in Padua, but after the city was conquered by the army of the League of Combray, Levita lost all his possessions and was destitute. He then escaped to Rome where he turned to Cardinal Egidius for help, because he heard that the Cardinal was interested in learning Hebrew. He accepted Levita as his teacher and agreed to maintain him and his family in his palace. Levita remained there thirteen years.

During that period he composed valuable works. One of them was his Sefer Ha-Bahur, a Hebrew grammar published in 1518 and dedicated to his disciples. In his introduction he explained the word "bahur," his family surname, as denoting "youth" and "selected." The same year another book was published, Sefer Ha-Harkabah, in which he compiled all the irregular verbs found in the Bible. In order to enable the student of Hebrew to have a systematic comprehension of the structure of Hebrew grammar, Levita completed another work, Pirkei Elija, comprising lectures on the peculiarities of the language. Levita's works were soon translated into Latin and were received with approbation in the scholarly world. Many Christians wanted to learn Hebrew in order to better acquaint themselves with the literature of the Old Testament.

In 1527, Rome was sacked by the Imperialists, and Levita was one of the victims; he was robbed again of his possessions. He escaped with his family to Venice where he met Daniel Bomberg, a Christian who established a Hebrew printing press, where the famous Rabbinical Bible and the Talmud were printed. Bomberg employed Levita as a proofreader. Levita continued his Hebrew teaching. Among his distinguished students in Venice was George de Selve, then serving as ambassador of France but later appointed Bishop of Lavaur. De Selve made it possible for his teacher to complete his work on the Masorah, Sefer Ha-Zikronot (Book of Memories). Levita worked on this book twenty years and sent the manuscript to Paris to be published at his own expense. For some unknown reason it was never published, but the manuscript is still kept in the Bibliotheque Nationale in Paris.

Levita's name as a scholar was so popular that Francis I offered him the chair of Hebrew studies at the University of Paris. He politely declined on the ground that he would not make his home in a city where his coreligionists were forbidden to reside. Other invitations by Cardinals and Princes were also rejected.

Levita's subsequent work was his Masoret Ha-Masoret (1538), in two parts, in which he explained various phases of Biblical spelling of words in accordance with the marginal notes of the Masoretes. In this work Levita demonstrated the theory that the Hebrew vowels

were invented and introduced in post-Talmudic times, in contradistinction to the general belief that they came down from Biblical times.
Two years later he published a book on the Hebrew accents, Tob
Taam, propounding a similar theory of post-Talmudic origin. Levita's
theories soon aroused a heated debate among both Jews and Christians. Jewish Orthodox elements regarded the theories as heresy.
Besides, they were antagonistic toward Levita on another ground:
Notwithstanding that his Christian students publicly announced
they were studying Hebrew primarily to find arguments in the
Scriptures against Judaism, Levita continued teaching them. Among
Christian scholars, Levita's theory about the Hebrew vowels started
a controversy that continued for almost three centuries, in which
such Hebraists as the Buxtorfs and others participated. Levita's
book went through a number of editions. It was translated into
Latin by Nagel (1758), into German by Christian Gottlob Meyer
(1772), and later into English by Christian D. Ginsburg (1867),
a Jewish convert who specialized on the Masorah.

In 1540, Levita's former student, Paul Fagius, established a Hebrew printing press at Isny and later at Constance. Levita was in
charge of the press. There he published the following works: Tishbi,
a Talmudic dictionary of 712 difficult words with explanations in
German; Meturgaman, an Aramaic dictionary; Yiddish versions of
the Pentateuch and of the Haftorot (Biblical passages read on Sabbath in the synagogues).

Levita was also the author of the so-called Bovo-Bukh (Baba-
Bukh) in Yiddish, a book of romances based upon the Italian model
known as Buovo D'Antona, which was an adaptation of the Anglo-
Roman romance of Sir Bevis of Hempton. Yiddish scholars consider
Levita as one of the early progenitors of Yiddish literature.

The following epitaph was engraved on Levita's tombstone in the
Venice Jewish cemetery:

> The stone cries from the wall,
> and mourns for all passersby
> over this grave—
> over our Rabbi who has departed,
> and ascended to heaven.
> Elijah is gone to the Lord in a whirlwind!

He who has shed light
on the darkness of grammar,
and turned it into light.
He went up at the end of Shebat
in the year 5309 [1549]
and his soul is bound up in the bundle
of life.[1]

AZARIAH BEN MOSES DEI ROSSI
(1531-1578)

Italian scholar and physician, author of the Me'or Enayim (Light of Eyes), a book that attracted the attention of both the Jewish and the non-Jewish scholarly world, Azariah dei Rossi occupies a special place in Hebrew literature. A man possessed of an insatiable desire for learning and remarkable intellectual faculties, Azariah was well versed in Hebrew, Latin, and Italian literatures. He studied medicine, archeology, history, Greek and Roman antiquities, philosophy. His book Me'or Enayim reflects his wide knowledge and education and his independent thinking in the field of religion. In the third part, under the title "Imre Binah" (Words of Reason), he makes a survey of the history of the Jewish people at the time of the Second Commonwealth, records the origin of the Jewish settlements in Egypt and Cyrene, and describes the Bar Kochba revolt aginst the Romans. He also criticizes some Talmudic interpretations, particularly Aggadic passages which he considers as only symbolic in nature. In his approach to many phases of Jewish life, dei Rossi follows scientific methods instead of tradition. Naturally, such a book could not have been ignored by the traditionalists. It immediately aroused opposition. Prominent among his critics were Moses Provencal of Mantua, Isaac Finzi of Pesaro, and others. Joseph Caro condemned the book and was ready to draw up a decree banning it. He died, however, before signing the decree and the rabbis of Mantua only prohibited its reading before the age of twenty-five.

The Me'or Enayim contains also an interesting description of the earthquake of 1571 which occurred in Ferrara, in which 200 persons perished. Dei Rossi lived then in that city and his house was partly destroyed. The account of the earthquake, written shortly after, is a historical document. It forms the second part of the book and is titled Kol Elohim (Voice of God).

The greater part of the book was translated into Latin by Bartolocci and others. Dei Rossi was also a poet; some of his poems are liturgical in character.

LEON DE MODENA
(1571-1648)

Leon (Judah Aryeh) de Modena could have attained the loftiest position among Jews and non-Jews alike on account of his great intellect. He was a rabbi of distinction at Venice, an orator whose eloquence enchanted multitudes, a scholar in both Talmudic and secular subjects, a man who had an entry into the highest circles of Italian society, a teacher, a poet, and a man of the world with a cultural background second to none. But, unhappily, this great man suffered from a weakness that constantly dragged him down. Leon was a gambler; he could not curb this passion.

At twelve, Leon already demonstrated his poetic capability by translating into Hebrew the first canto of Ariosto's *Orlando Furioso,* and at thirteen he composed an essay in the form of a dialogue against gambling. It was a literary curiosity which became so popular that it went through ten editions. It was also translated into French, Latin, German, and Yiddish. The author, however, remained a gambler the rest of his life.

De Modena was a victim of fate in other respects. Of his five children, one son was killed; another died of sickness; a third led an irresponsible life and fled to Brazil, never to be heard of again; only one daughter remained with him. To climax it all, Leon's wife lost her reason. All those misfortunes notwithstanding, Leon de Modena kept on writing and producing one work after another.

Two works of his represent something that is, mildly speaking, phenomenal. They are his books Kol Sacal (Voice of a Fool) and Sha'agat Aryeh (Roar of a Lion)—the first an attack on traditional

Judaism, the other a defense of Judaism. In the Kol Sacal, published under the pseudonym Amittai ibn Raz Alkala, de Moden attacked the Talmud in no uncertain terms. Taking the stand that the Talmudic sages misinterpreted the Torah, he tried to prove that many laws were not valid at all. He therefore demanded reforms in the synagogal services, the abolition of the dietary laws, changes in the manner of performing circumcision, and the abrogation of many rites. Some of his arguments against the Talmud he had taken from the Karaite literature with which he was apparently conversant, but some of them were his own. As a Talmudic scholar he knew where to strike most effectively. In his Sha'agat Aryeh, he took the opposite view and appeared as the advocate of Judaism, advancing one refutation after another.

For centuries people believed that the Kol Sacal was really written by an opponent of the Talmud, or by a Karaite, because no one could imagine that a rabbi of the stature of De Modena had written such a work. It was left to modern scholars to delve into the contents of the two books, in order to discover that the author was none other than the same man.

De Modena composed many other works, some of which are extant in manuscript. He was the author of a commentary on the Sayings of the Fathers and a history of ancient Israel in Italian, which was translated into French, English, Dutch, and Hebrew. He also left a collection of responsa, 400 sermons, Hebrew poems, and a number of Selihot (penitent prayers).

JOSEPH SOLOMON DELMEDIGO
(1591-1655)

Rabbi, philosopher, and physician, Delmedigo was a man who stood between two worlds—the world of traditional Judaism, in which he was raised and educated, and the world of free thinking and science. Born in Candia in 1591, he received a good Talmudic and secular education. At the age of fifteen he arrived in Padua, Italy, where he enrolled as a student in the university. He studied various sciences, especially astronomy. In the latter he attended the classes of Galileo. From time to time, Delmedigo visited Venice where he came in close contact with Leon de Modena. This free thinking rabbi must have exercised a strong influence upon the young student. Delmedigo subsequently returned to Candia, but he could not stay there long. From then on he was wandering from country to country. Having visited Wallachia and Moldavia, he reached as far as Wilna. From there he went to Hamburg and later to Amsterdam. For some years he officiated as rabbi in those cities. Finally he settled in Prague, where he practiced medicine.

Delmedigo composed numerous works on scientific subjects: arithmetic, geometry, astronomy, logic, metaphysics, optics. In his book Mazref Lahokmah (Crucible of Wisdom) he tried to harmonize faith with philosophy, but his ideas were not always clearly expressed on account of his constant fear of being declared a heretic. He looked for the middle way which he did not readily find. Like de Modena he remained on the borderline of two worlds.

He died in Prague in the year 1655. In Hebrew he is known as Yashar of Candia.

DEBORAH ASCARELLI
(17th century)

In the 17th century, when Humanism reached a high point, there lived in Italy two Jewish poetesses who actively participated in the general cultural life of Venice. Although details about them are scanty, what we do know of their lives is highly intriguing.

One was Deborah Ascarelli of Venice, wife of Juiseppe Ascarelli, a rabbi. She was well versed in Hebrew and a master in Italian. Deborah translated the second part of Moses Rieti's Hebrew book, Mikdash Me'at (Little Temple). Rieti flourished at the time of Dante (1265-1321), and composed his book in imitation of the *Comedia Divina*. In that section which Deborah translated, the author described a symbolic journey through the realm of heaven, where the spirits of the saints dwelt. Passing through the celestial synagogue, he arrived at the City of God where he introduced the teachers of the Talmud, the Geonim, and the later-day luminaries of Judaism. While

Rieti was far from being a Dante, and his poetry in the judgment of critics falls short from the creations of the Golden Age, his work still occupies a significant place in Hebrew literature. In her translation, Deborah contributed much of her own talent and fiery temperament.

Deborah was also famous for the hymns of praise to God which she composed for the Italian synagogues. A contemporary Italian poet, enchanted by her talent, wrote the following lines about Deborah:

> Let other poets of victory's trophies tell,
> Thy song will e'er thy people's praises swell.

SARAH COPIA SULLAM
(d. 1641)

The second poetess, not less famous, was Sarah Copia Sullam. She was also a Venetian and enjoyed a high standing in the world of art and science. An admirer portrayed her as follows: "She revelled in the realm of beauty, and crystallized her enthusiams in graceful, sweet, maidenly verses. Young, lovely, of generous impulses and keen intellectual powers, her ambition set upon lofty attainments, a favorite of the muses, Sarah Copia charmed youth and age".

Sarah suffered from an unfortunate and strange love for an old Italian priest-poet by the name of Ansaldo Ceba, whose greatest passion in life was to convert her to Christianity. The connection between Ansaldo and the proud, sensitive Jewish poetess was sensational in itsclf. Ansaldo lived in Genoa where he published an epic in which Esther of the Bible was the heroine. Sarah read that poem and was enchanted by Ansaldo's verses. In her enthusiasm, she wrote a letter of gratitude to the old priest, a total stranger to her. Replying to her letter, he requested her picture. From this point on a correspondence between the two developed. Two souls exchanged their verses: Sarah holding on firmly to the faith of her forefathers, saying: No! and the old priest, steadfast in his faith, trying to take her over to his side whereby he believed he would save the soul of

his beloved. Ansaldo tried his utmost to awaken sympathy for his
old age in the heart of the gentle Jewish girl:

> Life's fair, bright morn bathes thee in light,
> Thy cheeks are softly flushed with youthful zest.
> For me the night sets in; my limbs
> Are cold, but ardent love glows in my heart.

What did the Jewish poetess answer? We do not know. Only
Ansaldo's verses were published. The Church probably had seen
to it that Sarah's replies be destroyed. In another poem we hear
Ansaldo singing:

> How long, O Sarah, will thou liken me
> To those great singers of olden days?
> My God and faith I sought to give to thee,
> In vain I proved the errors of thy ways.
> Their song and charms more potent than my own,
> Or art thou harder than a beast or stone?[2]

Sarah had her own troubles. She suddenly took sick and then
her father died. A fanatic named Balthasar Bonifacio, envious of
her standing in Venetian society, published a brochure in which he
accused her of rejecting the immortality of the soul. She was in danger of falling into the hands of the Inquisition. Sarah wrote a brilliant essay defending herself against her calumniator. She wrote
also a number of sonnets in which she brought forth her great
faith in God.

> O Lord, Thou know'st my inmost hope and thought,
>   Thou know'st whene'er before Thy judgment throne
>   I shed salt tears, and uttered many a moan,
> 'Twas not for vanities that I besought.
> O turn on me Thy look with mercy fraught,
>   And see how envious malice makes me groan!
>   The pall upon my heart by error thrown
> Remove; illume me with Thy radiant thought.
>   At truth let not the wicked scorner mock,

O Thou, that breath'dst in me a spark divine.
The lying tongue's deceit with silence blight,
Protect me from its venom, Thou, my Rock,
And show the spiteful sland'rer by this sign
That Thou dost shield me with Thy endless might.

Sarah proved she could stand on her own; exonerating herself, she
exposed the evil intentions of her malicious enemies. Ansaldo was
informed of all she was living through, but he rejected her letters,
insisting upon her conversion. He died soon after his last rejection.

Sarah died in 1641. The entire Jewish community of Venice
mourned her death. Leon de Modena, who had known her closely,
wrote the epitaph engraved on her tombstone.

URIEL DA COSTA
(1590-1647)

Uriel da Costa was a tragic figure—restive, rebellious, dissatisfied,
contradictory. His end was as tragic as his life, perhaps more. A
descendant of maranos, he fled, like many others who were sought
by the Inquisition, to Amsterdam. There he and his family would
be free to practice Judaism openly and with no molestation by the
Church. Like many others he should have been happy. But this was
not the case with Uriel: The Jews of the Netherlands were not as he
had envisioned them in Portugal; they did not live up to the standard of the Torah as Uriel interpreted it. It all stemmed from his
former marano life. Uriel was well versed in the Bible and filled with
a burning zeal for the Law, but far from adequately knowledgeable
and learned in Talmudic and post-Talmudic literature. In his judgment, the Jewish people were unnecessarily burdened with regulations and ordinances extraneous to the original Torah. Outspoken
and honest, Uriel, the erstwhile marano who had lived for years
under the shadow of death for his Judaism, protested vehemently.
A fiery critic by nature, he condemned the rabbis and the Jewish
community. A man with a skillful pen, he was prepared to compose
a book in which he would prove that he was the real Jew.

No small wonder that the Amsterdam Jews were greatly irritated.

Such a rebellious Jew in their midst could not be tolerated. Uriel was undermining the very foundation of their community, leading others astray Besides, they did not recognize him as a competent judge. How did he dare propose basic reform in Judaism which was so sacred to them? Uriel was warned by the rabbis and the leaders of the community that he would be excommunicated if he were to continue his subversive activities. Their warnings were ignored. The rebel was obstinate. Finally Uriel was excluded from the synagogue. All social connections with him were cut off. Isolated, he suffered for a time, and unable to bear it longer, appeared before the community leadership and repented. He was reinstated to his former status. But Uriel was not the man to keep silence. He started to speak again. A second ban was pronounced upon the rebel, and when he repented a second time, they did not trust him. The people decided therefore to put the heretic to shame, degrading and wearing him down. They flogged him publicly and spit on him. In his Latin autobiography, *Exemplar Humanea Vitae,* written shortly after he had been publicly disgraced, Uriel described what he lived through:

> Many of them spit upon me as they passed me in the streets and encouraged their children to do likewise. The only reason why they did not stone me was because they wanted power. This persecution lasted for a period of seven years, and should I relate all that I suffered it would seem incredible. For two parties violently persecuted me—the whole Jewish community and my family who sought their revenge in my disgrace. . . . When I was sick nobody would attend me. If I suffered any other misfortune, it became a triumph and joy to them; if I proposed any one of them to act as judge between us the proposal was rejected.

One wonders at the tragic irony: People who were either themselves victims of the Inquisition or the offspring of those victims employing such inquisitorial methods against one of their own. Perhaps this is how human nature operates: The persecuted learn the ways of the persecutor. Yet one should perhaps try to remember that the coin had another side. To both Jews and Christians, their faith was dearer than life itself, and tolerance often seemed tantamount to communal suicide; thus, banning a dissenter was felt to be their only means of defense.

Da Costa at first opposed the Talmud as against the Bible, but later he seems to have rejected the Mosaic laws altogether. In his autobiography, he declares:

> Sometimes after this I asked myself whether the Law of Moses be considered the law of God inasmuch as there were many arguments which seemed to persuade or rather determine the contrary. At length I came to the conclusion that it was nothing but a human invention, like many other religious and legal systems in the world, and that Moses was not really its author. I noted that it contained many things contrary to the laws of nature, and God who was the author of those laws could not contradict himself which he must have done, had he given to mankind rules and regulations contrary to the laws of nature.

Such opinions must have sounded very strange in the ears of people who had suffered so grievously and long for their faith. That would go far to explain their indignation at the rebellious Uriel.

Da Costa could hardly endure his isolation from the community. One day he said to himself: Enough! and shot himself.

MANASSEH BEN ISRAEL
(1604-1657)

A colorful personality was Manasseh ben Israel of Amsterdam: a man of affairs and a teacher; a dreamer and Messianist; a defender of Jews and a diplomat; a writer, printer, and publisher; a linguist; a Talmudist. His knowledge and personality won for him many friends among non-Jewish scholars.

Above all, credit is due to Manasseh for opening a country—Britain —to Jews, a feat unique in the history of the Jewish people. There were old Jewish communities in England. In 1066, William the Conqueror brought with him a number of Jews. Some of them became prosperous merchants. But under the reign of King Edward I, severe laws were enacted against them. They were forbidden to hold public office and ordered to wear the Jewish badge. In 1209, the king ordered them to leave the country. Their houses and lands were confiscated. Sixteen thousand souls, men, women, and children, were put on boats and forced to seek refuge somewhere else. They settled in Flanders and France. England freed herself of her Jewish population, and for 300 years no Jew could step on British soil. When the Puritans came to power under Oliver Cromwell (1599-1658), after Charles I had been beheaded, Manasseh ben Israel felt that the time was at hand to open England for Jewish immigration. His belief rested upon the fact that the Puritans on the whole might be more tolerant to other faiths, particularly to the Jews as the people of the Bible.

Thus Manasseh went to England to plead for his brethren. He met Cromwell and made a profound impression on him. Cromwell was sympathetic, but there were others whose prejudices against the Jews blinded them. The opposition was so powerful that nothing was accomplished, and Manesseh returned to Amsterdam a frustrated man. Ten years later, however, England opened her doors to Jewish immigrants, but Manesseh did not live to see it.

Like many others of his time, Manasseh was a strong believer in the approach of the Messianic era, contingent upon two main conditions: suffering of the Jewish people and their being scattered all over the globe. It seemed to him that the Spanish Inquisition and the resulting suffering of the Jews fulfilled the first condition. On the other hand, the fact that England, the most northern country of Europe, was closed to Jews was contrary to the second condition; for the "ingathering of the exiles" must proceed, in accordance with the prophetic promises, from *all* the corners of the earth: north and south, east and west. If, Manasseh hoped, Britain were to be opened to Jewish immigration, it would serve as a signal for the coming of the Messiah and the redemption of Israel, as well as the redemption of the world as a whole.

Another important achievement of Manasseh was his setting up the first Hebrew printing press in Holland. Although he obtained his livelihood from teaching, Manasseh learned the printing trade in his spare time. Many books composed by him and other writers issued from his press. Manasseh was a prolific writer in Hebrew and Latin as well as in Spanish, Portuguese, and English. He completed his chief work, *El Conciliador*, in Spanish. In this book he discussed all the passages in the Hebrew Scriptures that seemed to conflict with one another and it was one of the first books written in a modern language by a Jew to win a large Christian audience. He corresponded with the most prominent scholars of the day: Hugo Grotius, Caspar Barleus, Cunaeus Bochart, and others. Rembrandt etched a portrait of Manasseh. Salom Italia made an engraving of him in 1642. Other writers were active in Holland at that time: David Neto, David Abenator Melo, who translated the Psalms into Spanish, and Daniel de Barrios, poet and critic. Manassah collaborated with them and helped them in their work. He was also recognized as one of the best orators in Amsterdam.

From Manasseh's press appeared such works as a Hebrew prayer book, an index to the Midrash Rabbah, a Hebrew grammar by Isaac Uzziel, Manasseh's teacher, and an elegant edition of the Mishnah. One sensational book was Manasseh's own *Esperanza de Israel* (Hope of Israel), in which he identified the North American Indians with the Ten Lost Tribes of Israel. He translated the work into Hebrew and Latin. The book created a furor in England and several replies were written against Manasseh's claim.

BARUCH SPINOZA
(1623-1677)

Baruch (Benedictus) Spinoza is one of the world's great philosophers. He, like Uriel da Costa, was a descendant of Spanish Jews, but his character, his disposition, and his scope were of a different mettle. He received a good Jewish education under the tutorship of Manasseh ben Israel and Rabbi Isaac Abuob. He was well versed in the Bible and knew Hebrew grammar to perfection; he composed a Hebrew grammar in Latin. He studied zealously the commentaries of Abraham ibn Ezra. Having delved into the mysterious passages of ibn Ezra, he noticed the critical phases of the great commentator. Thus Spinoza himself became a critic of the Scriptures and started to doubt the integrity of the Biblical texts. Thirsty for knowledge, he studied various philosophical systems, particularly the philosophy of Descartes (1596-1650).

Soon enough Spinoza's opinions were known to the Amsterdam Jews, and as in the case of da Costa, they were aroused against him. The leaders made several attempts to bring the young rebel back to the fold, including offering special privileges, but Baruch was not a man to compromise on convictions. At long last he was excommunicated, in 1656. Spinoza left the Jewish community for good. Living among his Christian friends, he found work which would not take too much time from his studies; he ground lenses. He lived scantily, withdrawn from the noise of the world, dedicating himself to perfecting his philosophical system. A sick man—he suffered from tuberculosis—he knew that he was living on borrowed time. He was humble, tolerant, and forgiving. When he was offered a chair at the University of Heidelberg, he declined, preferring to remain where he was. We are told that when a Christian woman asked him once what religion he would recommend to her, he replied calmly: "All religions are good that lead one to a good life."

Some phases of Spinoza's system can be shown to have had their origin in his study of Jewish religious philosophers of the Middle Ages: Maimonides, Gersonides, Crescas, and others. He was perhaps also influenced by the Cabalists, with their central emphasis upon Unity. However, the elaboration of his philosophy expressed his originality.

Spinoza's system is a form of pantheism, a form of monism, which identifies mind and matter, the finite and the infinite, making them manifestations of one universal or absolute being, which he conceived as Substance or God or the Whole. In this Whole, cause and effect ruled supreme. Nothing could ever remain outside. Nothing was, or is, free. The iron law of necessity was preeminent everywhere. If man wanted to live in this universe he must accept it in full. Free will was no more than a chimera. The basic principle of life was self-love. The highest ideal of man is Love of God, a sort of abstract Love of the Whole.

Spinoza's philosophy is extremely anti-Judaism. Instead of the personal God of Judaism, indispensable to faith, Spinoza gave man the abstract concept of Substance and the Whole, an impersonal God unconcerned with the welfare of individuals. Instead of a transcendent Creator of nature, Spinoza urged a God immanent within nature.

For about one hundred years after his premature death, Spinoza's name was anathema both in the Jewish and Christian worlds. Later, however, interest in him was awakened and many scholars went out of their way to bring his works to the attention of the world. His basic works—*Ethics* and *Tractatus Theologico-Politicus*—have been studied zealously. A whole library of critical and interpretive works accumulated around Spinoza. The lonely philosopher of Amsterdam became a world thinker in the fullest sense of the word, for even those who disagreed with him recognized his greatness and his genuine dedication to what he regarded as the Truth.

DAVID BEN SOLOMON GANS
(1541-1613)

David Gans was born in Lippstadt, Westphalia in 1541 and died at Prague in 1613. On his gravestone he was designated Ha-Hasid (pious). Gans was well versed in Rabbinical literature. He studied with Judah Löw ben Bezalel of Prague and the Talmudic genius Moses Isserles (1520-1572) of Cracow. Gans' fame, however, rests not on his Talmudic knowledge, but on his contribution to history. His principal work, Zemah David (Plant of David), published at Prague in 1592, is considered the first attempt at writing a history of the Jewish people in the Hebrew language, coupled with a review of general history, which was based upon the writings of Spangenberg, George Cassino, and others.

Other works by Gans were Zurat Ha-Eretz or Gebulat Ha-Eretz, a work on cosmography, and Maggen David, an astronomical treatise. He was deeply interested in secular sciences, especially mathematics and astronomy. Before settling in Prague, Gans lived for some years at Nordheim, where he studied geometry and trigonometry. He later came in contact with the famous astronomers Johannes Kepler (1571-1630) and Tycho Brahe (1546-1601). Gans translated the Alphonsine Tables from Hebrew into German for Brahe.

It was Moses Isserles who encouraged Gans to write his scientific and historical books. Isserles himself, known as Rema, possessed an extensive knowledge of astronomy and was fond of history. Isserles, for example, in his notations to Joseph Caro's Shulhan Aruk, took exception to Caro's urging that one must devote all his time to the study of Torah. According to Isserles, one may not only study secular sciences diligently, provided he guards himself against heretical ideas, but he may also read nonreligious works even on the Sabbath, if they are written in Hebrew. Gans followed his master.

JUDAH LÖW BEN BEZALEL
(d. 1609)

Judah Löw ben Bezalel, known as the Maaral of Prague, was born about the middle of the 16th century and died in 1609. He was one of the great leaders of his time. Regarded by his contemporaries as a Gaon and "a light in Israel," he composed a number of books on Halakah. He was also interested in philosophy and science, particularly in mathematics. Although well versed in Cabala, Maaral wrote mainly on Talmudic subjects. His philosophical and scientific ideas, however, were conspicuous in his writings.

Maaral is also famous as the creator of a Golem. What is a Golem? It is a body, artificially made by man, a moving figure of clay in the shape of a man lacking both emotion and understanding, but given a "soul" by the saint who makes it. Cabalists claimed to possess the knowledge and capability of creating a Golem. It is also mentioned in the Talmud that certain sages had created Golems. Legend has it that Maaral of Prague performed such a feat for the sake of the Prague Jews who were in need of help against their adversaries. According to the legend, Judah Löw restricted the Golem's activities to the weekdays only. Friday afternoon, on the coming of the Sabbath, God's name, placed in the Golem's body, was removed, so that he could not do any mischief on the holy day of rest. During the weekdays, however, the Golem was active: he did whatever he was bidden to do. Maaral controlled him rigidly, keeping him only for emergencies. Such an emergency came once when the Prague Jews were assaulted by a band of hooligans; the Golem appeared on the scene and drove them away. Then a change occurred in the Golem; having tasted blood, he became bloodthirsty. One Friday, before the Maaral had had time to remove his "soul," the Golem grabbed an axe and went out into the street and started to split heads. Frightened, the Jews of Prague came running to their rabbi. The appealed to him to stop the Golem. Maaral did their bidding, and soon enough the Golem was changed into a lump of clay. Because it was not entitled to be buried as a human body, Maaral placed the clay corpse in the attic of the Prague synagogue.

This fantastic story was popular among Jews for centuries. Various legends have been created around it. In modern times, the Yiddish poet H. Leivick took up the legendary threads of this story, developed it in his own way, and composed a poem-drama, *The Golem*, which has been performed on the stage both in Yiddish and in Hebrew. Leivick wove into the story many other ideas, legendary figures, and characters, and widened its scope to include the idea of the Messianic Age. It is a symbolic drama of great power and suggestiveness.

No one can explain why the Maaral was chosen by the popular imagination to be the hero of the Golem story. In his own works, the great rabbi shows himself to have been rather a rationalist, a keen logician, and a man far removed from such fantastic attempts. Perhaps the Golem legend as a whole was no more than a result of the deep craving for redemption that was animating the Jewish masses at the time. Helpless and defenseless against their adversaries, they needed a sustaining hope which was found in legend and fantasy instead of in real life.

MOSES GERMANUS
(d. 1702)

Johann Peter Spaeth was born at Venice in the first half of the 17th century and died at Amsterdam in 1702. His father, a shoemaker, was a devout Catholic, who fled from Italy on account of an impending war. He settled at Augsburg. Unable to take care of his son, Johann Peter, he handed him over to the Jesuits to be raised and educated. In the year 1680, however, Peter abandoned Catholicism and accepted Lutheranism. A little later he returned to the fold, but he soon regretted it and abandoned Catholicism again. At that time Peter decided to take up the study of Hebrew in order to be able to read the Scriptures in the original. He studied also the Talmud and the Cabala for a number of years and finally decided to renounce Christianity altogether and become a Jew. On being converted, Peter renamed himself Moses Germanus. In his critical works he vehemently attacked Christianity. Even the Sermon on the Mount did not find favor in his eyes, since "it proposed ideals that were impossible of realization by human beings as they are constituted by nature." Moses composed five works in German and in Latin in defense of Judaism. In one of these he explained how he arrived at the decision of becoming a Jew:

> I once dropped a crucifix, which was picked up by a Jew who said: "This is Israel, the man of sorrow." I now understood the 53rd chapter of Isaiah: The Jews bore the sins of the heathen, while they were daily persecuted by them. From time immemorial they had been treated in a shameful manner. As the whole history of the passion tended to render the Jews odious, so the same sort of thing happens nowadays. For instance, the Jews are said to have murdered a child, and to have distributed the blood in quills for the use of their women in childbirth. I have discovered this outrageous fraud in time; and, therefore, I abandon Christianity, which permits such things.

GLUECKEL OF HAMELN
(1646-1724)

She was a mother of twelve children, became a widow, and lived to a ripe old age—seventy-eight. She wrote seven books of memoirs in the language she knew—Yiddish. She left her literary heritage to her people and thus became Glueckel of Hameln, a mother-writer of great power.

Glueckel is straightforward and openhearted as to why she sat down to write. Her husband died. He was a good husband and a good father. The burdens of the entire family were laid upon her shoulders. "This way I have managed, my children, to live through many sleepless nights."

Glueckel was God-fearing and pious and a highly intelligent woman. Versed in Torah and in ancient lore and possessed of practical wisdom, she wrote on many subjects.

When God sends evil days upon us, we shall do well to remember the remedy suggested by the physician in the following story: A great king once imprisoned his physician and had him bound hand and foot with chains, and fed him only a small portion of barley bread and water. After months of this treatment, the king sent some relatives of the physicians to visit him in prison and find out what the unhappy man had to say. To their astonishment, he looked as hale and hearty as when he had entered the cell. He told his relatives that he owed his strength and well-being to a beverage of seven herbs which he had prepared before he went to prison, and of which he drank a few drops every day.

"What magic herbs are these?" they asked, and he answered: "The first is trust in God; the second is hope; the third patience; the fourth repentance of sins; the fifth contentment because my suffering is not worse; the sixth the expectation of something better in afterlife; the seventh the realization that God can set me free at any time."

Here is how Glueckel looked at another aspect of life:

Above all, my children, be honest in money matters with Jews and non-Jews alike. If you have money or possessions belonging to other people, take better care of them than you would if they were your own. A man may work ever so hard to amass money dishonestly; he may, during his lifetime, provide his children with rich dowries and leave them a generous inheritance at his death; and yet, I say, woe shall it be to that wicked man who, because he tried to enrich his children with dishonest money, he forfeited his share in the world to come![3]

ISRAEL BAAL SHEM TOV
(1700-1760)

The life of Israel ben Eliezer, or Israel Baal Shem Tov (Master of the Good Name), founder of the Hasidic movement, like the life of other founders of religions and sects, is enveloped in a legendary and mysterious web, in which fact and fiction are inextricably interwoven. We shall select only those details that seem to be more realistic.

Israel Baal Shem, known as Besht, was born in the town of Okop, not far from the border between the Ukraine and Bessarabia. His father, and possibly his mother, died when Israel was a child, and the community had to take care of him. We are told by the early Hasidic writers that the boy showed peculiar traits. For instance, he often disappeared from Heder (traditional school) and would be found sitting alone engrossed in thought in some secluded place, or straying in the forests around the town. At twelve, he hired himself out as a helper to a Melamed (teacher), carrying upon his back the younger children of the town to and from school. Later he became an assistant sexton in a synagogue. Most of the nights he spent in praying and learning. At fifteen, he married a poor girl, but she died soon after. Israel then left his birthplace and settled in Brody, Galicia, where he married the sister of a cantor—Gerson from Kutov. He then left Brody. During many years he led a secluded life in the Carpathian mountains. For a short time he was an innkeeper in a village.

At long last, at the age of thirty-six, there came the time for Israel to reveal himself. The Hasidim describe it as a "divine call." Israel was soon recognized as a Baal Shem who performed miracles, cured the sick, and drove out devils. He indeed radiated love and compassion. Humble and kindhearted, full of joy and ever ready to help the needy and downtrodden, his name went before him. Wandering from town to town and coming in contact with the masses— the unlearned, the poor, the sick, the destitute—Israel became a popular hero, a teacher, and a leader. Later, when his adherents num-

bered already in the thousands, he settled in Miedzyboz, which became a center of Hasidism. People from all walks of life flocked to
him. Thus Israel found himself as the uncrowned head of a popular
pietist movement which spread far and wide.

The Hasidic movement spread with lightning rapidity all over
Poland, Hungary, Rumania. It brought a quickening influence, an
overflowing consolation, to the weary masses of Jews who, confined
to the ghetto, needed an elixir of life. From the very first, Hasidism
was bitterly opposed by the leading rabbis. It looked like a revolt
against the old order of things. The admiration and devotion displayed by the Hasidim toward their teachers frightened many; the
movement might turn into a false Messianism, as at the time of Sabbetai Zevi (1665), or into a sect, such as the Frankists, which
ended in wholesale conversion. The miraculous deeds attributed to
the Hasidic leaders indeed looked suspicious. The opponents of
Hasidism, called Mitnaggedim, turned therefore to the famous
Elijah of Wilna, the most learned and saintly leader at that time.
The result was that the Hasidim were excommunicated. Hundreds
of communities were split. A terrible struggle between those two opposing factions went on for a long time. The progress of Hasidism,
however, could not be stopped.

After the death of Israel Baal Shem, two of his most prominent
disciples—Baer of Meseritz and Jacob Joseph Cohen of Polonnoye—
contributed to the spread of Hasidism. Baer of Meseritz became the
recognized leader of the movement. Jacob Joseph, author of the
book Toldot, is regarded as the expounder of Hasidism. He laid
the foundations of Hasidic literature, which grew extensively and
was read avidly by the Jewish masses in Eastern Europe. Four
prominent disciples of Baer of Meseritz can be noted: Elimelech of
Lizianka (Lisansk), Levi Isaac of Berdychev, Nahum of Chernobyl, and Shneor Zalman of Liady. Elimelech is known as the
author of the Hasidic book, Noam Elimelech, in which he develops
the idea that the Zaddik (saint) is the mediator between God and
the common people. Levi Isaac is famous for his homiletic book,
K'dushat Levi, and for his folk songs which are an expression of
his fervent love for the common people. Shneor Zalman founded a
principal branch of Hasidism—Habad Hasidism.

After the death of Baer of Meseritz, Hasidism had no central leadership. It branched out into separate divisions headed by the disciples of the original leaders. Later the cult of Zaddikism was developed, according to which leadership was inherited from father to son. This contributed greatly to the eventual decline of Hasidism.

Israel Baal Shem Tov did not leave any books. He was not a writer. His wise proverbs and parables, his interpretations of the Torah, and his teaching were spoken orally. His disciples, however, wrote down some of his teachings.

Israel was not concerned with the philosophical side of religion. To him, God was more than a metaphysical concept; his relation to God was rather a matter of the heart than of the mind. Where is God? God is everywhere. Is not the world great enough for one to see the imprint of God in every part of it, in the little pebble as well as in the stars that shine above our heads? Who is so blind as not to see God's hand in everything around us? Just look with open eyes at the world and God reveals Himself to you. Israel's teaching was based upon the Cabalistic principles accepted by him as axioms of life: "The world is but an emanation from God and nature; the world as it appears to us is but the garb of God under which His Presence and Glory are hidden." "There is no place devoid of God." These were taken in their fullest sense, as in Isaiah 6:3, "The whole earth is full of His glory." God's "holy sparks," then, were scattered all over the material world and it was man's task to seek them out and bring them up to their source.

> When a man sees anything, and is afraid of it, he should say to himself: Why should I be afraid? My enemy is a man like myself, a garb which manifests God's potency. Hence if I am afraid of him, how much more do I have to fear God? If he sees a beautiful woman, let him meditate thus: Whence does her beauty comes? Were she to die, she would not have that beauty any more, and since this is the case then her beauty comes from the divine source. Why then should one covet the beauty of an insignificant part? It is better to unite oneself with the source of all the worlds.

Worship of God is the Hasid's greatest task; it is in fact the aim of human life. Sorrow and grief, however, are stumbling blocks. God must be worshipped joyfully, with a heart full of enthusiasm and ecstasy. Even when man is sinful he should not let himself

fall into the pit of sadness. The union of man's soul with the Creator and the ecstasy attained by banishing all profane thoughts and
communing with God represent the greatest happiness that man
can achieve. It gives him courage and power to withstand all the
sorrows and dangers of the world. In fact, as soon as man learns
to attain this higher plane, all the sorrows vanish. A great joy pervades his whole being. True faith envelopes his soul. While he
looks at the world, he knows that he looks at God and that God
looks at him, for there is nothing in the world that does not carry
within itself His exuberance and power. He knows then that there is
nothing but God to be afraid of and nothing but God to rely upon,
because everything else is perishable, transitory, and temporary.

The Baal Shem thus rejected the old Cabalistic teaching of physical deprivations and mortification of the body as a way of approaching God. He emphasized prayer as against learning of Torah,
since through prayer one could come closer to God. Thus he taught
that one did not have to be well versed in Torah in order to attain
a high level in the worship of God; for prayer, recited from the
depth of the heart, might do the same or even more. Hence, the
simplest of the simple, the common people, could find a place in
God's world. Weeping while praying, he said, was bad, because
man was to serve God out of joy. Only tears of joy were good.

When the Baal Shem was still seeking the proper way
to serve the Lord, he found that the observance of the Sabbath according to the injunctions of the later rabbis practically prohibited any movement and filled a man with anxiety lest he should transgress some strict regulation. He believed that this contradicted the command of Isaiah to
"call the Sabbath a delight." He pondered on this for a
a long time, and in the night he had a dream:

An angel took him up to Heaven and showed him two
vacant chairs in the highest place in Paradise, brilliantly
illumined, as if with varicolored gems. "For whom are
these intended?" he asked. "For thee," was the answer,
"if thou makest use of thy intelligence; and also for a man
whose name and residence I am writing down for thee."
He was next taken to Gehenna at its deepest spot and
shown two vacant seats, burning with a hellish flame. "For

whom are these intended?" he asked. "For thee," was the answer, "if thou makest no use of thy intelligence; and also for a man whose name and residence I am writing down for thee."

In his dream the Baal Shem visited the man who was to be his companion in Paradise. He found him living among non-Jews, ignorant of Judaism, except that on the Sabbath he gave a banquet for his non-Jewish friends, wherein he greatly rejoiced.

"Why do you hold this banquet?" asked the Baal Shem. "I know not," replied the man, "but I recall that in my youth my parents prepared admirable meals on Saturday, and sang many songs; hence I do the same." The Baal Shem wished to instruct him in Judaism, inasmuch as he had been born a Jew. But the power of speech left him for the moment, since he realized that the man's joy in the Sabbath would be marred if he knew all his shortcomings in the performance of religious duties.

The Baal Shem then departed, in his dream, to the place where his companion in Gehenna dwelt. He found the man to be a strict observer of Judaism, always in anxiety lest his conduct was not correct, and passing the entire Sabbath day as if he were sitting on hot coals. The Baal Shem wished to rebuke him, but once more the power of speech was taken away from him, since he realized that the man would never understand that he was doing wrong.

Thereupon the Baal Shem meditated on the whole matter and evolved his new system of observance, whereby God is served in joy which comes from the heart.[4]

The Baal Shem once told the following parable:

There was once a king who was told that humility lengthens man's life. Deciding to live humbly, the king dressed himself in rags, lived in a small hut, and forbade his courtiers to bow before him. A wise man, having noticed that the king was proud of his accomplishments, remarked: "This is not the right way, O King. Dress like a king; behave like a king; let people serve you like a king. Yet be humble in your heart. That is what humility means.

Another parable:

The highest knowledge is to know that we don't know. There are, however, two attitudes toward this kind of "knowledge": There is one who seeks it and then arrives at a conclusion; but there is one who arrives at the conclusion without seeking it. To what may they be likened? They may be likened to two men who wanted to see the king, but were told they could not, though they might visit the inner chambers of his palace. The first man said: "I'll visit the palace and see the king's riches and perhaps be fortunate enough to see the king too." The second man said· "If I cannot see the king, what do I need the palace for?" The first man observed so many wonderful things in the palace that he visualized the greatness of the king. The second one, however, did not see either the palace or the king, whereby he had lost everything.

The Baal Shem talked about the nature of faith:

There are two kinds of believers in God. One believes in God because his father and grandfather believed. Such a man has an advantage: His faith in God stems from a source close at hand. Hence it might possess great power. But he is exposed also to a disadvantage: His faith does not rest upon conviction; he just follows others.

There is another kind of believer, one who himself searched after God and reached his own conclusion as to the existence of God. This is a great advantage, but at the same time he is exposed to a disadvantage: Since his faith rests on his own reason, there may come another who is endowed with a better reasoning faculty and convince him otherwise.

What is the remedy? The right way is to let faith in God rest on both, that is, on tradition and reason together. He who possess such a faith would enjoy the advantages and evade the disadvantages.

Finally, a short saying by the master:

Sinning against a fellow man is worse than sinning against God. God is everywhere, so forgiveness can be sought everywhere and at any time. Man is mortal, so sometimes a wrong committed cannot be righted.

ELIJAH BEN SOLOMON
(1720-1797)

Elijah of Wilna, known also as Vilna Gaon—Talmudist, Cabalist, grammarian, exegete, mathematician—was the personification of both sainthood and learning, an "eternal student" whose whole life was dedicated to Torah and God. It is said that Elijah never slept more than two hours each day; the remaining twenty-two he devoted to learning. There was almost no book he had not perused, and there was not a saying that the Gaon might not locate, indicating instantly the folio number and the exact subject it was related to. Wilna was famous at that time as a city of highly learned men, being called for that reason the Jerusalem of Lithuania and the City of Torah; but when there arose a question of law that no one in Wilna could answer properly, it was referred to Elijah and an answer was obtained on the spot.

While yet a child, Elijah demonstrated his extraordinary memory. At seven he knew already several Talmudic treatises by heart. At ten he did not need a teacher any more. He studied for himself with such marvelous dedication that the Jews of Wilna viewed him as a saint. As a man of Torah, he was sparing in words, and when he spoke it was only in reference to learning. This great saint studied everything that came his way; mathematics, astronomy, history interested him. He believed that in order to understand the Talmud aright one needs general knowledge. True, he devoted to secular knowledge only a small part of his time, but endowed as he was with a fertile and penetrating mind he succeeded in learning any subject quickly. He wrote a book on algebra, geometry, and trigonometry entitled Ayil M'shulash. He also compiled a complete geographical outline of the Holy Land, a rare thing at the time, and a reconstruction plan of Solomon's Temple.

In conformity with a custom among pious Jews—to suffer and taste "the bitterness of exile and poverty"—Elijah wandered about Poland and Germany for five years. On his long trips he kept on studying.

In 1748, he returned to Wilna and was received with great honors. He was then only twenty-eight and was not an ordained rabbi —he was never ordained—but Wilna acknowledged him as the religious leader, the Vilna Gaon.

A man of utmost humility, Elijah did not mingle with people, nor did he participate in communal affairs. From time to time he lectured to a select group of people. Nonetheless his fame spread far and wide, and many people came to Wilna just to see the Gaon sitting in his secluded corner studying the Torah. Because he was always studying in a certain synagogue, sitting there day and night, it was called the Gaon's House of Learning. Food was brought to him from home and left there on the sill of a window. Many a time it was found the next day untouched. Wilna Jews felt it their sacred duty to see to it that the Gaon not be disturbed by anyone. If little boys started to play around the place, making a noise that could have disturbed the holy man, there was always a Jew who asked them to leave the place and go somewhere else.

Elijah did become involved in one controversy; this was the major issue of the nature of Hasidism. Convinced that Hasidism endangered Judaism, Elijah encouraged the bans of 1771 and 1781 against it. As the representative leader of Talmudic Judaism, the Gaon was fully convinced that he was fulfilling his most sacred duty to God and Israel by checking the spread of Hasidism, and no one could move him from this stand, notwithstanding the ruinous conflict among families and communities which resulted from the Hasidim-Mitnaggedim (opponents) factions. Historically, Elijah was in error in his judgment, because Hasidism was simply another pietist movement and not the radically undermining force he envisioned, but he believed otherwise and acted accordingly.

Illustrative of Elijah's influence in the Hasidism controversy are these two stories. It is said that when Baer of Meseritz, who had become the leader of the Hasidim after Israel Baal Shem, was on his deathbed and heard of the ban against Hasidism, he burst into tears; however, he begged the Hasidic leaders not to criticize Elijah and "not to say even one bad word about him," so high was the prestige of the Gaon even in the eyes of his opponents.

Shneor Zalman of Liady came to Wilna to explain Hasidism to Elijah, but the Gaon refused to even see him, though the great rabbi of Liady wept at his door as a child and appealed to him time and again. Finally, Elijah left the city and refused to return until Shneor Zalman was gone. The Jews of Wilna, wanting of course their venerable teacher back, urged the Hasidic rabbi to go home to Liady.

Elijah's knowledge of Judaism was so extensive that he was among the few who emended the Talmud and the Midrashim. His textual corrections were short and to the point. In many instances one word resolved a contradiction and avoided superfluous controversies and discussions. Elijah made his notations on the margins of his books; later his disciples gathered his emendations and published them together with the texts. As a Biblical exegete, Elijah also wrote commentaries on parts of the Bible. He also composed a Hebrew grammar and a commentary on Sefer Yetzirah. In addition he arranged a special Siddur, known as the prayer book of the Gaon of Wilna, and prepared his own Code of Laws.

The Gaon's personality had a significant impact upon Jewry. In Wilna he was viewed as "an angel of God in the shape of a man." He was indeed one of the great spiritual giants.

SHNEOR ZALMAN OF LIADY
(1747-1813)

Shneor Zalman of Liady, a disciple of Baer of Meseritz, who succeeded the Baal Shem as the leader of the Hasidic movement, was the founder of the Habad Hasidism. This branch is still well organized and powerful today despite the fact that Hasidism as a whole has lost its influence, lingering on in small and widely scattered circles. Habad is strong both in America and in Israel.

The founder of Habad was unquestionably not only a great leader of men but also a thinker in his own right. He was a Cabalist of the first order, a Talmudic genius, and an original interpreter of Judaism. His piety and saintliness were recognized by all during his lifetime and by the generations that followed. The Shneorson family brought forth great Hasidic rabbis who led, and still lead today, tens of thousands of people. Shneor Zalman's basic work, Tanya, is a source book for Habadism. The book is an expression of man's complete submergence in God, the most distant point to which Cabala could raise man's soul and imagination. Shneor Zalman maintained that this is the only way that leads to "knowing" and true bliss.

What is Habad? The word is an abbreviation of three Hebrew words: Hokhmah (wisdom), Binah (understanding), and Da'ath (knowledge), each of which had a special connotation given it by the founder. For instance, Hokhmah was understood as an intuitive flash which strikes the mind of man at certain moments, emerging as a sporadic "seeing." Binah is that sort of "understanding" which becomes an actuality by reflection and profound meditation. Da'ath is that "knowledge" which becomes part and parcel of the thinking person. This three-fold knowing can be illustrated from the area of aesthetics:

> Hokhmah is the bare notion of beauty which enables a man to see that a splendid building, for example, is truly beautiful. When he pauses to reflect on why he finds it beautiful, when he considers that his pleasure is caused by his appreciation of such things as the harmonious proportions and the skilful blending of colors, he attains to Binah. He now knows why he finds it beautiful. Da'ath is both the interest in beautiful things which moves him in the first place and the powerful attraction invoked by his reflections.[5]

Shneor Zalman applied these terms to contemplation about the world and God. Real knowledge does not consist in looking at the world as a complex of separate things, but rather as Unity; however, that high level can never be attained without Da'ath. Man has to go through the three stages of knowledge in order to stand on a point from where he can contemplate everything as a whole.

In conjunction with the older Cabala, Shneor Zalman defines God as the En Sof, the endless, eternal, and infinite. About God nothing positive can be said. He is above space and time, above all the categories of understanding; He is Ayin (nothingness), as far as we are concerned. We know that He *is*, but we do not know, nor can we ever know, *what* He is. The question: How did the En Sof create the universe? is answered by Cabala that the world is nothing more than an emanation of God. The old theory of Sefirot is applied here. But at this point Shneor Zalman brings in his own idea. From our point of view, God is an Ayin and we are a Yesh (something); but from the absolute and ultimate standpoint of God, He is the true Da'ath, because this and only this gives us some knowledge of the Unity which is God. This is what is meant by the verse: "The whole earth is full of His glory." (Isa. 6:3)

According to Shneor Zalman, man has not one soul but rather two: an animal soul and a divine soul. When he follows the animal soul, then good and evil are intermingled. All his actions, thoughts, and emotions are then directed by what is grossly material. But, fortunately, man has also a divine soul, which is truly a spark from the En Sof. This spark ever strives to be united with the source whence it originally came.

The Hasid is expected to meditate long and thoroughly on the idea that all is in God. As a result of profound meditation on this theme, man's love can awaken to the extent that he has no will but for God. It is said that Shneor Zalman was once overheard saying: "I do not desire Thy Paradise. I want Thee alone." For Habad, the virtue of humility does not mean that man thinks little of himself, but that he does not think of himself at all. This is the mystical Hasidic ideal of Bittul Hayesh, "self-annihilation," "nullification of the something."[6]

In support of Shneor Zalman's wish, Habad Hasidim cite an old Midrashic tale, "The Four Gates of God's Glory":

"Show me, I pray Thee, Thy glory," Moses asked God. Thereupon a Gate of Light, beautifully decorated, appeared before his eyes.

"Who are the privileged ones to enter this Gate?" Moses asked.

"The students of the Torah," God answered.

Soon enough another pair of Gates appeared.

"And these?" asked Moses.

"These are for those who pray to me with their whole heart."

A third pair appeared.

"For whom are these?"

"For those who help the needy," answered God.

A fourth pair appeared, even more charming than the previous ones.

"For whom are these?"

"These are for those who dedicate everything to Me. They are wholly Mine because they sanctify my name."

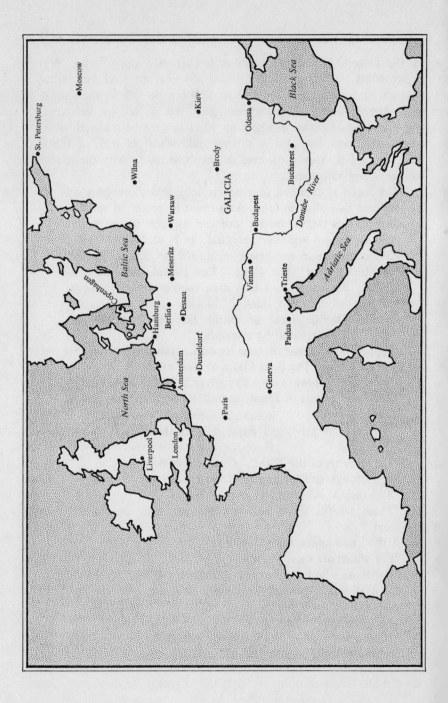

יג | 13

ENLIGHTENMENT AND EMANCIPATION

I will train a lasting nation, which, far from being annihilated by other nations, shall rather exercise its beneficial
influence on their existence. Like the precious Ark of the
Covenant which I have constructed in the midst of this nation wherein I deposited my sacred principles, I will also
construct a kind of ark and launch it as a vessel into the
midst of the people. I will avail myself of the hardest wood
and strongly fasten together its joints. Winds and tempests
will shake and toss it, and reduce it to a most wretched
condition, yet be unable to engulf it. It will survive all, in
order to carry to their destination those riches which I con-
fided to it. Joseph Salvador (1796-1873)

FROM DARKNESS INTO LIGHT

During the Middle Ages and into the 18th century, Jews were deprived of freedom as we understand it. Confined to the ghettos, they
lived under rigid restrictions, economically and politically. A Jew

was forbidden to establish his residence outside the ghetto or to engage in an occupation in competition with the guilds or the artisans' associations. Regarded as aliens, they were steadily exposed to the whims of the rulers.

The Renaissance and the Reformation brought some religious freedom to Europe. Secular literature, science, democratic ideas circulated somewhat among the people. Basic changes were slowly effected. But the situation of the Jews in Europe remained practically unchanged. Few glimmers of freedom illumined the ghettos. The Age of Darkness continued in the ghettos until the 18th century.

In Germany, Gotthold Ephraim Lessing (1729-1781), poet, critic, and dramatist, was among the first non-Jewish writers to criticize dislike of the Jews as a "stupid prejudice." In his drama, *Nathan der Weise* (Nathan the Wise), he presented Nathan the Jew, modeled largely on his friend Moses Mendelssohn, as a sympathetic figure. Lessing looked upon Judaism as a free thinking man should have. But the Lessings were few and far between.

Most liberal minded Christians who tended to say a good word about the Jews spoke at most only in the name of "tolerance." Jews were simply to be tolerated, not as a matter of right, but rather as a favor accorded by the majority. The first practical step toward liberating the Jews from the chains of medieval restrictions, made by Emperor Joseph II of Austria in 1782, reflected this motif. He issued his Edict of Tolerance, in which some of the restrictions on education and trade were removed. The door was opening, but not too wide. It was just a beginning.

The French Revolution moved in the direction of genuine freedom and rights for the Jews. Influenced by humanism and following the example of the American Revolution as embodied in the Declaration of Independence, the French Assembly in 1789 passed the Declaration of the Rights of Man and Citizen. At first only the Sephardic Jews were granted equal rights, but two years later all French Jews were given citizenship rights. When Napoleon became ruler of France and subsequently master of most of Europe, the Jews of other countries outside France were also partially liberated; some restrictions still remained intact. Then Napoleon fell, and the victors —Russia, Prussia, and Austria—reimposed the reactionary measures of the Middle Ages upon the peoples of Europe. The Jews found themselves again in the position of pariahs.

In 1848 there came the so-called Spring of the Nations, when freedom swept most of Europe. The new liberalism that emerged brought more freedom to the Jews, too. France, Sweden, Denmark, Greece revoked many restrictions, and England, Germany, Italy gradually followed suit. Russia and Rumania remained the only countries in Europe which still barred their Jewish population from participating freely in political and economic life.

HASKALA

How did the Jews react to 18th-century change? Two very significant movements appeared, one in eastern Europe, in the Ukraine, and the other in Germany. The first was Hasidism, which was discussed earlier; the second was Haskala, or Enlightenment. Haskala was basically an assimilation movement. It was a Jewish cultural thrust which aspired to adapt to the outside world. Jewish exclusiveness must be abandoned, secular knowledge must be disseminated, "objectionable" customs and traditions must be abolished, the Bible and its language must be stressed to supplant any preeminence of the Talmud or rabbinical literature.

Thus there emerged three branches of Judaism:

1. The Orthodox or Rabbinical Jews. They were those who held onto the old way of living. Their model was Elijah of Wilna, in whom learning and sainthood were combined. The Rabbinical Jews who opposed Hasidism were called Mitnaggedim (opponents). The battleground between Mitnaggedim and Hasidim extended over all of eastern Europe, especially in Lithuania.

2. Hasidim. Hasidism was a pietist movement, an offshoot of the Cabala. It aimed to generate joy and hope in Jewish life, not from the outside but from the inner sources of man's soul. It sought to help the Jew forget his plight and to regenerate his spirit by an emphasis on prayer. Israel Baal Shem was the Hasidim's prototype.

3. Maskilim. These were the Haskala Jews, the liberals who urged assimilation in order for the Jews to realize full emancipation. Maskilim were freethinking people whose center was Berlin. They often opposed the Hasidim even more than the Mitnaggedim did.

Maskilim looked to Moses Mendelssohn as their progenitor. Mendelssohn, though regarded as the Father of the Enlightenment Movement, was actually a traditional Jew in his practical life. But his circle of adherents were the outspoken ones, advocating reforms and publishing their views. For example, they founded the first Hebrew journal, Ha-Measef (The Gatherer), which contained articles on natural science, the Bible, and Jewish history. The principal contributors to the journal were: Isaac Satanow, author of Mishle Asaf (Parables of Asaf); S. Dubno, a Bible scholar; Judah ben Zeev, a noted grammarian; I. Eichel, a critic; Solomon Pappenheim, a philologist; Naphtali Hirz Wessely, a well known poet.

A second Haskala center was formed in Brody, Galicia, around Nahman Krochmal, scholar and philosopher, who was regarded as the Mendelssohn of Galicia. The target of the Galician Maskilim was Hasidism. Two powerful satirists, Joseph Perl and Isaac Erter, ridiculed the Hasidim and their "Rebbes" (Rabbis or Zaddikim), and otherwise agitated for modernized schools.

A third stronghold of Haskala, still later, was formed in Wilna, Lithuania. Two influential writers stood at the center of the Maskilim there: M. A. Ginzburg and Abraham Lebensohn. Ginzburg wrote an autobiography entitled Abi'ezer, which was very popular at the time; he criticized the old Jewish educational system. Lebensohn was both a poet and critic who exerted a strong influence upon the Maskilim of Russia. Other writers, such as Kalman Schulman and Samuel Joseph Fuenn, were active in Wilna.

MODERN HEBREW LITERATURE

The questioning of the old and the quest for new ways of seeing and doing and thinking, which we spoke of in the previous chapter, found full fruition in the 18th and 19th centuries. Modern Hebrew literature was a direct product of the Haskala. It was inspired by a love for the Bible and the Hebrew language, though there was often a tension between this love and the Haskala drive for assimilation. The Hebrew Maskilim, however, turned out to be the early progenitors of national regeneration, and from their ranks came the first pioneers in Palestine and the founders of the agricultural colonies.

Joseph Klausner, Hebrew historian and critic, distinguishes three main periods since the time of Moses Hayyim Luzzatto (1707-1747). The delineations are, of course, not to be taken as absolute; there are overlaps and rough edges. Yet the divisions are helpful in viewing the 18th and 19th centuries. Klausner's three periods are: Romanticism, Realism, National Regeneration.

Although Luzzatto, the first modern Jewish writer to be influenced by the humanist trends outside the ghetto, is regarded as the father of modern Hebrew literature, the period of Romanticism actually started with Mendelssohn. Luzzatto was not a Maskil, but rather belonged intellectually and emotionally to the pre-Enlightenment epoch. With Mendelssohn the real movement toward the outside world began. The writers in each of the principal centers of Haskala —Berlin, Brody, Wilna—looked with condescension and criticism at Jewish life as it was then. The outside world was attractive, good, fascinating; life as it had been lived by the Jews was to be completely reshaped. Enlightenment was "the daughter of heaven"; the Bible as against the Talmud was a poetry vis-à-vis casuistry; the old traditions were shabby, wornout, meaningless ceremonials. Romanticism pervaded Hebrew literature from the time of the Measfim to Sholem Jacob Abramovich, a span of roughly one hundred years.

The period of Realism started with Isaac Mayer Dick (1808-1893) and Isaac Joel Linetzki (b. 1839), predecessors of Abramovich. The works of Dick and Linetzki reflected the realist motto: Describe life as it is seen and make all other aims secondary to that. But the descriptive power, the clarity of purpose, the overall knowledge of these two early realists could not match those of Abramovich. Hence it was he who laid the lasting foundations for Realism in both Hebrew and Yiddish. His followers pursued the realist aim perhaps even more rigorously, and in them Hebrew literature reached maturity. It became European, modern in the fullest sense of the word.

The period of National Regeneration was ushered in by Zionism. The Palestinian center, though small at the beginning, grew with the passing of the years. Many of the great writers in various lands settled in Israel. They became the teachers and educators in the settlements throughout the country. At first they had drawn upon their

experiences in other lands, but soon enough dedicated their pens to
life in Israel. Some of the younger writers were born in Israel and
therefore did not have to deal with this problem of shift in focus. To
them, land and people were indissolubly combined.

MOSES HAYYIM LUZZATTO
(1707-1747)

Moses Hayyim Luzzatto of Padua, Italy, is regarded by historians
as the father of modern Hebrew literature. A poet of true dramatic
gifts, he succeeded in producing several poetic dramas that have
not lost their value even today; though unadaptable to the stage,
they were great literary creations in themselves.

Luzzatto was not only a master of the Hebrew language and a
writer of genuine power, but also a Talmudic scholar, a logician, a
great poet, a moralist, and a mystic-Cabalist. In his personality all
these merged into one, although at times one or the other came
most strikingly to the surface. More than anything else, Cabala en-
thralled him. He was even accused of posing as a Messiah, a charge
levelled at him in the heated atmosphere of frustrations resulting
from the false Messianism of Sabbetai Zevi. He was in peril of being
excommunicated. Finally he and his family emigrated to the Holy
Land, where he fell sick and died.

His first drama was *Samson and the Philistines,* written when he was
yet seventeen years of age. Only fragments are extant. Its meter was
superb; the style powerful and ripe. His next production was Migdal
Oz (Tower of Victory), a romantic drama in which nature, simple
pastoral life, innocence, integrity, and moral purity was idealized.

His greatest artistic achievement, however, was the dramatic long
poem, Layyesharim Tehilla (Praise unto the Righteous), in which
he exhibited his power as a Hebrew stylist of the first order. The
first act is dedicated to a description of man's evil ways. In a world
in which deceit frequently replaces truth and injustice disguises as
justice, there is no place for a virtuous and honest man. Hence the
pious sage retires from the world and finds refuge in solitude. In
the second act, however, the poet describes the innermost hope of the
righteous man, since evil by its nature can never come out victorious.

The third act is replete with praise for truth and justice. The characters of the drama were symbols, personifications of ideas. While Luzzatto employed the devices in vogue in the Italian drama at the time, a new epoch in classical Hebrew literature was inaugurated by the way he presented his ideas. Thus, for example, "lust" or "desire" was introduced as a lad with wings, who carried bow and arrow—in imitation of Pallas-Athena, goddess of love. "Bribe" appeared in the form of a blind man holding a scale in his hands, one of the shells of which was hanging lower. "Deception" was a young and beautiful woman, holding in one hand honey and in the other a snake.

Some critics think that in his love of nature, with its harmony and tranquillity, Luzzatto was under the influence of Guarini (1538-1612), whose Il Pastor Fido (The Faithful Shepherd) extolled nature and made the shepherd a hero. In any case, Luzzatto's works were, in Jewish life, the first time that a call to go out from the ghetto into God's great world was heard. In this alone one can see Luzzatto as an innovator, a messenger of a new era.

The scholar, Franz Delitzsch, evaluated Luzzatto in these words:

All the fragrant flowers of Biblical poetry are massed in a single bed. Yet the language is more than a mosaic of Biblical phrases; it contains the rarest of elegant expressions in the Bible. The peculiarities of the historical writings are carefully avoided, while all modifications of style peculiar to poetry are gathered together to constitute what may fairly be called a vocabulary of poetic diction.[1]

Apart from his poetic works, Luzzatto was destined to become one of the most beloved moral teachers of the Jewish people. His prose work, Mesilath Yesharim (The Path of the Righteous), a treatise on morals, was so popular in eastern Europe that multitudes of people knew it by heart. It went through many editions, and even today it is popular among the pious.

The influence of Luzzatto upon the development of Hebrew literature went far and wide. Almost all writers during the period of Enlightenment regarded him as their progenitor. Among the writers who followed in his footsteps was David Franco Mendes (1713-1792) from Holland, who composed a Biblical drama. Mendes spent some time with Luzzatto when the latter visited Amsterdam. Another writer, Shalom Cohen (1772-1845), asserts in his introduction to one of his dramas that he followed Luzzatto and, moreover, that he selected some of his characters from Layyesharim Tehilla. The same may be said about S. L. Romanelli (1757-1814).

Luzzatto was a combination of a mystic and a thinker. The Lurian Cabala, which was popular at that time, enchanted him; but simultaneously he was a clear-thinking scholar. The same hand that wrote his Cabalistic interpretations wrote also a book designed to show the way of studying the Talmud systematically, and another one dealing with rhetoric and logic. As a mystic one may characterize him as "a man drunk with the glory of God"—an expression applied to Spinoza. Nature simply revealed to him the glory of God. All phenomena appeared to him as the embodiment of holiness; the spirit of God was hovering over everything. Thus poet, mystic, and thinker became one.

MOSES MENDELSSOHN
(1729-1786)

Moses Mendelssohn, the father of the Jewish Enlightenment movement, was born in Dessau, capital of the small German principality of Anhalt. His father was a Torah scribe and a Hebrew teacher. Moses, a sickly child and a hunchback, raised in poverty and deprivation, was possessed by a will to learn. As a lad of only fourteen, he decided to leave his hometown and go to Berlin. After a tedious journey, he reached the Rosenthal Gate, but was stopped by a guard because Jews were not permitted then to reside in Berlin without a special royal permit. Interrogated about his intentions, the boy's answer was short and concise: "To study!" Mendelssohn did not have any relatives in Berlin. His only friend there was Rabbi David Frankel, who had been his teacher in Dessau. But only twenty years later this erstwhile lonely and sickly boy with a life-long stutter was famous all over Germany. The Berlin Academy of Sciences awarded him first prize for a philosophical treatise which he had submitted in a contest with none other than Immanuel Kant, the great German philosopher. Mendelssohn was called the Socrates of Germany.

How did this stuttering hunchback Jew of Dessau succeed in gaining such fame in the Germany of Fredcrick the Great while the walls of the ghetto were still intact? The answer lies in Mendelssohn's breaching these walls and in his thirst for knowledge which led in this direction. Studying was the breath of his life, one of his loftiest ideals brought to Berlin from the ghetto. Whoever possessed knowledge would become his teacher; whatever he learned he would bring back to the ghetto. Israel Zamosz, a Polish Jew with liberal ideas who tarried in Berlin, knew mathematics, so young Mendelssohn became his pupil. He wanted to learn Latin, so he found a young physician from Prague, Abraham Kirsch, who taught him. Mendelssohn studied it on his own at night by the dim light of the lamp. Locke's philosophical treatise *An Essay Concerning Human Understanding* fell into his hands in a Latin translation; so, with indescribable toil, he read it with the help of a Latin dictionary. He wanted to learn French and English, so he found himself a teacher in the person of Aaron Solomon Gumperz. During those years this indefatigable student lived in the most abject poverty, deprived of the essential things that make life livable. Yet, this physically weak man, almost alone but supported by an indomitable will, attained great proficiency in mathematics, literature, philosophy, languages.

Gotthold Ephraim Lessing, Mendelssohn's closest friend, was among the first Germans to recognize genius in Mendelssohn. He anticipated in him a second Spinoza, in terms of superb intellect. Lessing introduced Mendelssohn to the bookseller Friedrich Nicolai, who in 1756 started to publish his Library of Fine Arts. Mendelssohn was invited to be a member of the staff, but soon enough he stood at the head of the project. We have already noted that Lessing used Mendelssohn as a model for his hero in *Nathan Wise,* an extremely popular play which altered the general image the Germans held of the Jews. Also in this drama Lessing proclaimed that all religions were praiseworthy as long as the ideals they set forth were realized by the adherents. This was actually one of Mendelssohn's beliefs, too, reflected most vividly in his controversy with Johann Kaspar Lavater, a Swiss theologian. Lavater publicly challenged Mendelssohn either to accept Christianity or to disprove that Christianity was based on reason. Reluctantly he took up the fight. His point of view was as tolerant and broad-minded as a man of good will can promulgate. All faiths are good as long as they lead man to live in accordance with morality. Hence let everyone stick to his own faith: the Jew to Judaism, the holy heritage handed down to him from his ancestors, and the Christian to Christianity. To find salvation through conversion is below the dignity of man. Nor should something like that be expected of the Jew. Jews could be good citizens and at the same time hold on to the tradition of their faith. The state has no right to interfere in such questions as freedom of thought and speech.

According to Mendelssohn, Judaism is not a religion of dogmas but rather of laws. Christianity, he argues, stands or falls upon the acceptance or rejection of its basic dogmas: the Trinity, Original Sin, the Atoning Death of Christ. Judaism rests on the precepts of the Torah. The Jew will never abandon Judaism, not even for the sake of equal rights, declares Mendelssohn. If any people or state would ask the Jews to be untrue to their heritage in order to obtain emancipation, Jews would rather remain Jews and reject equality of rights.

Interestingly enough, this confrontation with Lavater seemed to inspire an even more intense and strengthened commitment to Judaism on Mendelssohn's part. Notwithstanding his German education, his fame as a philosopher and secular literary critic, and charges of heresy brought against him by some traditionalist Jews, Mendelssohn actually lived in full accord with Jewish orthodoxy His home, where Sabbath candles were lit every Friday night, became a gathering place for intellectuals and poets who sought his company and respected his wisdom.

In his book *Jerusalem* and in a series of essays, Mendelssohn pleaded for his brethren in the name of progress, culture, and justice. Humble in tone, reserved in his attitude towards other faiths, his words were heard in the highest circles of the country. As one of the most cultured Jews in Germany, he was fighting for Jewish emancipation. He wanted his brethren integrated into German culture, but precisely through the Bible. For the sake of his own children he started to translate the book of Genesis into German. Later it was published with a special commentary (Bi'ur) in Hebrew written by Solomon Dubno. Mendelssohn published it on his own expense. Although this new translation was greeted with enthusiasm, not only in Germany but also in other lands, it attracted its detractors, who denounced the translation and the commentary as heretical. A translation of the whole Pentateuch appeared in 1783 with the collaboration of other scholars such as the poet Naphtali Hirz Wessely, Aaron Jaroslav, and Herz Homberg, all prominent Maskilim at the time. It created a stir among the orthodox elements who placed it under a ban. But Mendelssohn did not lose his temper; he viewed it as a natural reaction against any innovation.

Innovative though Mendelssohn was, his followers went much farther than he and the results were often much different than he would have anticipated. For example, many Jews in Germany, in order to realize emancipation, rejected Judaism. Nevertheless, Mendelssohn's ideas fundamentally influenced modern Jewish literature and life. Mendelssohn foreshadowed changes, changes more radical in character yet to come. His work, his life, his fame became symbols of enlightenment, symbols of the crumbling walls of the ghetto.

In his philosophical essays, Mendelssohn declared himself an adherent of the Leibnitz-Wolffian philosophy, but elaborated his own philosophy of art which was recognized as the basis of all philosophic-esthetic criticism in Germany. Among his intimate friends was Thomas Abbt, a young professor, with whom he corresponded on such questions as life after death, the destiny of man, the indestructibility of the soul. As a result of this correspondence, Mendelssohn composed his chief work, *Phädon,* published in 1767, in which he attempted to prove the immortality of the soul. Written in the form of a dialogue, it was the most widely read book at the time. The elegant style, the lucid ideas of the author, his fine attitude towards the opinions of others, enchanted the thoughtful reader. It was reprinted fifteen times and translated into all modern languages.

No small wonder that the Berlin Academy of Sciences proposed his name as a member—an unheard of distinction for a Jew from the ghetto. Frederick the Great, however, to whom the list of candidates was submitted, struck his name out. It is not unlikely that the king's decision was influenced by Mendelssohn's demonstrated fearlessness in expressing his strong convictions. He had earlier dared to criticize the poems of Frederick the Great and the works of a court preacher. Summoned to appear before the attorney general, Von Uhden, Mendelssohn engaged in the following exchange, so the story goes:

> Attorney General: "Look here! How can you venture to write against Christians?"
>
> Mendelssohn: "When I bowl with Christians, I throw down all the pins wherever I can."
>
> Attorney General: "Do you dare mock at me? Do you know to whom you are speaking?"
>
> Mendelssohn: "Oh yes. I am in the presence of privy councilor and attorney general Von Uhden, a just man."
>
> Attorney General: "I ask again: What right have you to write against a Christian, a court preacher at that?"
>
> Mendelssohn: "And I must repeat, truly without mockery, that when I play at ninepins with a Christian, even though he be a court preacher, I throw down all the pins, if I can. Bowling is a recreation for my body, writing for my mind. Writers do as well as they can."

Another example of Mendelssohn's sharp wit comes from his membership in Berlin's first literary salon, which had opened in 1755. Philosophers, physicians, mathematicians, booksellers frequented the meetings. One evening someone proposed that each member present describe his own defects in verse. Mendelssohn wrote the following lines:

> Great you call Demosthenes,
> Stutt'ring orator of Greece;
> Hunchbacked Aesop you deem wise;
> In your circle, I surmise,
> I am doubly wise and great.
> What in each was separate
> You in me united find,
> Hump and heavy tongue combined.

NAPHTALI HIRZ WESSELY
(1725-1805)

Next to Moses Hayyim Luzzatto, Naphtali Hirz Wessely stands out as the first *modern* Hebrew poet. As a follower of the Mendelssohn school of enlightenment, he was one of the foremost German Maskilim. Wessely studied under the famous Rabbi Jonathan Eybeschutz. When Mendelssohn needed a commentator for the book of Leviticus—a difficult task because the book deals mainly with ritual and sacrificial laws—he invited Wessely.

When Joseph II, the Austrian emperor, issued his Edict of Tolerance, the first official proclamation that granted some rights to Jews, Wessely became an ardent advocate of secular education. He published a pamphlet, Dibre Shalom We-Emet (Word of Peace and Truth), which called upon the Jews of Austria to cooperate with the government; it was a clarion call for enlightenment. Rendered into German, French, and Italian, it reached many other communities outside Austria. This pamphlet aroused opposition among the ultra-Orthodox element. The rabbis of Germany and Poland, determined to check the movement, wanted to excommunicate the writer, but the Italian rabbis refused. Thereupon Wessely published another pamphlet in which he tried to prove that he was an observant Jew and that general education was not in opposition to Judaism.

His lasting fame rested, however, upon his poetic work, Shire Tif'eret (Songs of Glory), in which he presented a series of poems on the Exodus from Egypt. His epic style and his perfect Hebrew diction won for him the position of the leading poet of his time, though in artistic imagination he fell far short of Luzzatto. Wessely was also the author of other works: Sefer Ha-Middot, a treatise on the ethics of Judaism; a commentary on the Sayings of the Fathers; a philological study of Hebrew root words and synonyms.

Born in Hamburg in 1725, Wessely later lived in Copenhagen where his father was purveyor to the king. The poet died at the ripe age of eighty.

SOLOMON MAIMON
(1754-1800)

Solomon Maimon was a man of genius whose mind reached the heights of speculative philosophy, heights attained only by the greatest European thinkers. But, unfortunately, nature forgot to endow him with a will capable of controlling his passions and arranging his life in an orderly way. The result was tragic and heart-rending.

Born in the town of Nieszwiez, Lithuania, he was raised in the traditional Jewish way. He married at the age of twelve, and two years later he was already a father. In order to make a living, he went to a neighboring village to serve as a teacher of the children of an innkeeper. There Maimon spent his nights in studying the Jewish religious philosophy of the Middle Ages, particularly Maimonides, and also the Cabala. From philosophy he reached out to various branches of science which he studied from old German books which came his way. All this was regarded at that time as heresy. Maimon then decided to leave Lithuania and reach Berlin. Without money Maimon set out to enter an alien world. For months he wandered as a beggar.

At long last he appeared in Berlin and presented himself to Moses Mendelssohn, who recognized him as a philosopher despite the fact that he lacked an academic education. Maimon showed Mendelssohn his commentary on Maimonides' *Guide* and also a critical treatise on Christian Wolff's *Metaphysics* composed during his wanderings. The latter work was written in a masterly German and contained original thoughts. Naturally, people wanted to extend a helping hand to this Jewish genius. They wanted him to enter the university as a student of medicine. But Maimon was not the man to accept a planned life. Precisely at this time he became a cynic, frequenting bad society and living a life of irresponsibility. Since he could not stay in Berlin, he went to Holland and from there he reached Hamburg. At one time he was about to embrace Christianity, but the clergyman who was supposed to baptize him refused to do so on listening to his wayward ideas about religion. Later he returned to Berlin. He was again befriended by Mendelssohn but no one could help him when he himself lacked an anchor in life.

All this notwithstanding, Maimon's name was well known among the great. In the years between 1793 and 1797, Maimon published three basic philosophical works: one on the development of philosophy, another expounding a New Logic, and a critical investigation of the human spirit. Prior to those works he had completed a book on Kant's transcendental philosophy. Although Maimon rejected many aspects of that system of philosophy, Kant in a letter to Marcus Hertz indicated that among all his critics and opponents Maimon was the one who understood him best. Others had also acknowledged his great contributions; men like Goethe, Schiller, and Kerner paid him tribute.

One of Maimon's finest works is his autobiography, in which he tells his experiences in life. Openheartedly he uncovers the contradictions of his own character, his moral downfall at certain periods, his troubles and suffering. Maimon criticizes the rabbis who "have burdened the Jewish masses with many prescriptions and prohibitions," but he simultaneously defends the Talmud. Maimon is also known for his account of a visit he made to Meseritz, the center of Hasidism after Israel Baal Shem died; his vivid description of the Hasidim is a historic document.

Maimon was unquestionably a genius who tried to liberate himself from the ghetto. He indeed succeeded in entering the free world, but in the process his life was broken up. His contributions to philosophy demonstrate what he could have done if his life would have been directed in a more orderly course.

MANASSEH BEN JOSEPH OF ILYE
(1767-1831)

One of the early Lithuanian Maskilim, Manasseh of Ilye, was a fervent fighter for reforms in traditional Judaism. He was scholar, critic, and educator. Born in Smorgony, province of Wilna, he displayed extraordinary ability in studying the Talmud, but when he showed his interest in Hebrew grammar and the Bible, his father forbade such subjects lest he neglect his Talmudic studies. Manasseh, however, did not budge from his decision. He organized a small circle of adherents with whom he openly discussed problems in opposition to tradition. He criticized Rashi and Caro's Shulhan Aruk as well as the Talmud itself.

Manasseh is said to have been at one time in close contact with Elijah of Wilna—a rare distinction in those days. But later the saintly Elijah rejected him for his reported sympathies towards Hasidism. The young Maskil was not discouraged. Thirsty for more knowledge, he started to study philosophy, mathematics, and astronomy. His keen mind absorbed everything he studied. He also determined to go to Berlin in order to join the circle of Maskilim around Moses Mendelssohn. In Königsberg he was stopped by the authorities on his way to Berlin. He turned to the village of Ilye where he studied languages, natural philosophy, and mechanics.

Manasseh developed a program of reform for the Russian Jews. In his book Pesher Dabar he wrote as follows: "The Jews are divorced from real life and its practical needs and demands. The Jewish leaders are short-sighted because instead of enlightening their followers, they darken their intellect with casuistic restrictions, in which each rabbi endeavors to outdo his predecessors and contemporaries."

In Shekel Hakodesh, published in 1823, Manasseh speaks of himself thus: "My opponents can scarcely grasp that one could risk his peace by opposing influential rabbis and leaders out of mere love of one's people. In fact, I have never sought wealth, fame, or pleasure. I have lived on bread and water, but the thirst for self-perfection and the search for truth would not permit me to rest until I fulfilled my mission."

Alfe Manasseh has an interesting story behind it: The author had made arrangements with a printer to set it up in type and duly delivered the manuscript into his hands. But when the printer started to work on it he was so enraged at its "heretical" ideas that he threw it into the fire and burned it to the last page. The unhappy author, however, rewrote it from memory in a short time and published it elsewhere.

NAHMAN KROCHMAL
(1785-1840)

Nahman Krochmal, noted Jewish religious philosopher and scholar, was born in Brody, Galicia. Krochmal's fame rests on his great though unfinished work, Moreh Hebuche Hazeman (A Guide for the Perplexed of the Time), which was published posthumously by his friend, Leopold Zunz. It is regarded as a Hebrew classic.

The scholar Julius Guttman characterizes Krochmal's work as follows;

> He interpreted the history of the Jewish people as the outcome of the inner relation between Israel and the "absolute spirit" [God]. Due to this relationship, he maintained that the existence of Israel was not bounded by time, as it is true of other nations. After periods of decay and degeneration, the Jewish people revived anew with the strength of youth.

This interpretation has shed new light upon the historic development of the Jewish people and has generated new hope for a spiritual revival. But how did Krochmal prove his theory and how did he arrive at the conclusion that Israel presents, historically, something different than any other people? How did Israel become an exception to the rule of "decay and degeneration" and was able to be "revived anew with the strength of youth"?

Krochmal started out with the individual and ended with peoples and nations and, finally, with Israel's role in the history of the world. Just as any individual has an "I," a something that we call "soul," "personality," or "self," representing his individuality as a whole, so every nation or people has its own individuality or, if you wish, "culture" or "national spirit," which differentiates it from others. In the past this variation of cultures expressed itself in the forms which idolatry assumed in various civilizations. The "gods" in which a people believed embodied the "spirit" of that particular people. But just as an individual has to go through three periods in his life, namely: youth, maturity, and old age—the last period bringing about one's dissolution and death—so cultures and "national spirits" have to go through the same development. Thus, cultures or civilizations which reached the last stage in their evolution usually perished or were extinguished and another people, younger and more vigorous, would sometimes take over what was worthy of saving, and thus continue anew upon the road of its own development.

This law of life is of course universal; yet Israel's history indicates that the law had been invalidated. The Kingdom of Judah was destroyed in the 6th century B.C.E. Later it was restored, starting life anew. When the Second Commonwealth was destroyed, it appeared that everything was lost again. But a new regeneration occurred in Babylonia, which reached its end during the post-Talmudic or Geonic period. Then came a third cycle, a new revival during the Golden Age of Spain. How did Israel succeed to live from one cycle to another? Krochmal answered it thus: Israel was capable of doing what any other people might not do, because her faith was in the "Absolute Spirit" of the universe, the only true and living God. Israel's national spirit was therefore tied not to a *part* of the whole, as one could observe in the history of other nations of antiquity, but to the *Whole*, to something that is not temporary or subject to time and space. When Israel was driven out of her land and scattered all over the earth, she still clung to the "Absolute Spirit," to the eternal substratum of reality. Hence precisely at the moment when she had reached the lowest point, she did not look up to a fallen or defeated god as other peoples did at the moment of their defeat, but rather to the God of the universe who could have never been defeated by other gods, because He was, and is, the only One. Standing face to face with the loving God, Israel declared herself sinful. That God might be unjust was inconceivable of a God of Justice. The only solution at such a dire moment was repentance, and by mending her ways, return to God. This brought about a revival. Israel became young again and a new cycle of life was started, a cycle of youth, maturity, and old age.

Such historic cycles had taken place in Israel's history three times already, and a fourth one was bound to come soon. Krochmal did not succeed in working out the exact periods of those cycles. A sickly man, he probably could not have done it even if he had lived. In any case, he died before he had time to complete his work. What he did achieve was to give a general outline of his theory. But even in its incomplete form it exerted a strong influence upon his generation and generations to come, even unto our own.

ISAAC BAER LEVINSOHN
(1788-1860)

Scholar, critic, thinker, and leading Maskil, Isaac Baer Levinsohn was regarded as the Russian Mendelssohn, the father of Russian Haskala.

Born in Kremenetz, Russia, he received a traditional education. At ten he was well versed in the Talmud and Bible, and had mastered the Russian language, a rare accomplishment among Jews in those days. Having married at eighteen, he settled in Radzivilov where he served as a teacher and translator. While there he perfected himself in the study of history, philology, and philosophy.

Levinsohn suffered from various neurological ailments, and he visited Brody, Galicia, to consult the doctors. There he came in contact with the Galician Maskilim: Nahman Krochmal, Isaac Erter, Joseph Perl, and Solomon Rapoport. Upon his return to Kremenetz, Levinsohn began his book, Te'udda B'Israel (Testimony in Israel), in which he proposed a complete program of social and cultural reform for the Jews of Russia: widening the sphere of Jewish education to include secular subjects, productivization of the Jewish masses by agricultural colonization and industrial occupations, integration into Russian society by learning the Russian language. Levinsohn's program of reform infuriated the Hasidic elements. They suspected him of being an agent of the Russian government and of working to undermine traditional Judaism. It so happened that his program of reform found favor in the eyes of some Russian Czarist leaders. The pious Jews were afraid that this may lead to either assimilation or conversion into Christianity. No wonder that they regarded him as their enemy. As a result of the enmity he aroused, Levinsohn was compelled to leave his home town for a number of years.

In his introduction to his book, Levinsohn explains how he came to write it: "It was not the yearning for fame that impelled me to write this book. . . . Friends seeking truth and light asked me to point out to them the right way of life; they wished to know what learning, aside from the Talmud and its commentaries, it is necessary for a Jew to acquire for the perfection and refinement of his nature as a man and Jew."

In his second basic work, Bet Yehudah (House of Judah), he undertook to bring to light the spiritual life of the Jewish people: to enlighten the Jews themselves about their cultural heritage and to show the Christian world what Judaism really stood for. Levinsohn therefore presented a clear-cut exposition of Jewish religious philosophy. According to him, Judaism was based upon two general principles: faith in God to the exclusion of all forms of idol worship and love of fellow man regardless of race or creed. He also discussed the great contributions of the Jewish people to learning and civilization.

Prompted by a ritual murder charge lodged against the Jewish community of Zaslavl, Levinsohn, on his sickbed in 1838, wrote Efes Damim (Negation of Blood), which attempted to deal once and for all with this problem which had plagued the Jews since ancient times. Written in the form of a dialogue between a patriarch of the Greek Orthodox Church in Jerusalem and the Chief Rabbi, it attempted to prove conclusively how baseless and false the charge was. The book went through three editions and was published in English during the Damascus Affair in 1840, another ritual murder case. It was also rendered into Russian and German. In Efes Damim, Levinsohn demonstrated his remarkable critical talent, his broad knowledge of history, and his ability as a writer and scholar.

ABRAHAM LEBENSOHN
(1789-1878)

Abraham Lebensohn, known by his surname Adam Ha-Cohen, was born in Wilna. A poet of distinction, a Hebrew grammarian, and a rabbinic scholar, he was one of the most prominent leaders of the Lithuanian Haskala.

His Shire S'fat Kodesh (Songs of the Holy Tongue), published in 1842, marked the beginning of a new epoch in Hebrew creativeness. It was the first work written in a style reflecting the rejuvenation of the ancient language. It established Lebensohn's name as a poet. In 1856 a second volume of his poems appeared and in 1869 a third one. The latter contained a series of poems written by Lebensohn's young son, Micah Joseph. Lebensohn also composed an allegorical drama, Emet We-Emunah (Truth and Faith), the central idea of which was the harmonization of religion and science.

In 1846, when Sir Moses Montefiore, the great Jewish philanthropist from England, visited Wilna in the interests of Russian Jewry, Lebensohn prepared a report on the conditions of the Jewish communities, outlining a detailed program for the improvement of their cultural and social life. Lebensohn blamed the Jews themselves for their backwardness. Like all other Maskilim he proposed reforms through government intervention, ignoring the fact that the Jews of Russia suspected the Czarist government of being mainly interested in the conversion of the Jews to Christianity. The main problems stressed in Lebensohn's report were lack of secular education, the rabbis' adherence to old traditions, early marriages, and non-productive occupations. Lebensohn's analyses, proposals, and intentions, all similar to those of Isaac Baer Levinsohn, were equally mistrusted by the ultra-orthodox leaders in Lithuania.

ISAAC ERTER
(1792-1851)

The Galician Haskala brought forth two powerful satirists: Isaac Erter and Joseph Perl; both won their high place in modern Hebrew literature with their sharp pens.

Erter, a physician by profession, belonged to the circle of Nahman Krochmal in Brody. His fame rests on a collection of satiric tales under the name Ha-Zophe le-Bet Israel (Observer of the House of Israel). He was interested in establishing agricultural colonies for the Galician Jews, but his main target was Hasidism, which was widespread in his Austrian province. Erter also wrote poetry, but satire was his forte.

Of the two great Galician satirists, Erter is the more impressive and powerful. In his Tashlih, he ridicules an old Jewish custom of going the first days of Rosh Hashanah to a river and shaking the pockets as a symbol of shaking off sins. On such an occasion, the satirist tells us, he met Satan and his host. And what did they do? They were gathering the sins of Israel that were just cast into the water. Satan was kind enough to tell the writer about the corruption and wickedness practiced by the penitent sinners. This gave him a chance to enumerate them in detail to his readers.

In his Gilgul Ha-Nefesh (Transmigration of the Soul), Erter satirizes the medical profession with a story of the adventures of a soul during a long earthly career, having passed from one body to another. Finally it left the body of an ass for that of a physician. The soul then gives the physician (the author of the story) the following six rules, by observing which he might succeed in his profession:

1. Powder your hair white, and keep on the table of your study a human skull and some animal skeletons. Those coming to you for medical advice will then think your hair has turned white through constant study and overwork in your profession.

2. Fill your library with large books, richly bound in red and gold. Though you never even open them people will be impressed with your wisdom.

3. Sell or pawn everything, if that is necessary, to have a carriage of your own.

4. When called to a patient, pay less attention to him than to those about him. On leaving the sickroom, assume a grave face, and pronounce the case a most critical one. Should the patient die, you will be understood to have hinted at his death; if, on the other hand, he recovers, his relations and friends will naturally attribute his recovery to your skill.

5. Have as little as possible to do with the poor; as they will only send for you in hopeless and desperate cases, you will gain neither honor nor reward by attending them. Let them wait outside your house, that passersby may be amazed at the crowd waiting patiently to obtain your services.

6. Consider every medical practitioner as your natural enemy, and speak of him always with the utmost disparagement. If he be young, you must say he has not had sufficient experience; if he be old, you must declare that his eyesight is bad, or that he is more or less crazy, and not to be trusted in important cases. When you take part in a consultation with other physicians, you would act wisely by protesting loudly against the previous treatment of the case by your colleagues.

Whatever the issue may be, you will be on the safe side.

Some critics compared Erter to the Greek rhetorician and satirist Lucian (125?-210?) and others found in him something of the withering satire of Heinrich Heine.

JOSEPH PERL
(1774-1839)

Joseph Perl's satire is not as powerful as Isaac Erter's, but at times it is imbued with intense pathos. He is more of a parodist than a stairist. His Megallah T'mirin (Discoverer of Secrets) is a clever parody written in the language of the Zohar. It went through many editions, having been published the first time in Vienna, in 1819. He wrote also two other works, Dibre Zaddikim (Words of the Saints) and Bohen Zaddik (Examiner of a Saint), in the same vein.

Perl was also a sworn enemy of Hasidism, which he regarded as simple charlatanism. The Hasidic Zaddikim (saints), in his judgment, used the ignorance of the people to their advantage. Perl's Megallah T'mirin also ridiculed Hasidism. At first even many of the Hasidim bought it because they thought that it had been written by a Hasid; but soon enough the deeply hidden satire was exposed.

Erter and Perl paved the way for a revival of Hebrew literature in Galicia. The satiric tone and the light manner of dealing with life's problems found favor with the reading public. Both of them were fighting writers to whom the pen was a weapon.

SOLOMON LUDWIG STEINHEIM
(1789-1866)

A philosopher, scientist, and prominent physician, Solomon Steinheim was one of the most profound interpreters of Judaism in Germany. As a scientist, he was famous for his treatise on the pathology of tumors, his work on ecstasis, and his study on the structure of the grasshopper.

His most outstanding work was his four-volume philosophical interpretation of Judaism, *Offenbarung nach dem Lehrbegriff der Synagoge* (Revelation According to the Teaching of the Synagogue), in which he endeavored to prove that Revelation was more than a religious belief. According to Steinheim, all philosophical systems lead to duality, in other words to a fragmentation of reality. Judaism in turn is the only system of thought that stands squarely upon the all-inclusive principle of Unity, because everything which exists stems from God, Who is One. In a fragmented reality, neither religion nor morality can have a real basis, since religion would inevitably fall apart into many religions; and morality, likewise, would assume many forms. This was essentially, according to Steinheim, the struggle of Judaism against idolatry in all its forms. In this struggle, the Biblical theory of Creation, that is, that the world is the product of One God, is basic to Judaism. The fact that no philosophical system has ever reached the principle of cosmic unity, as Judaism did, is adequate proof that by the aid of reason alone it could not have been realized. It was a revealed truth that stood apart from all philosophical speculations, and it remained so even today. Unlike the Jewish philosophers of the Middle Ages, Steinheim did not seek to prove Revelation by external evidence. To him it was an internal experience of the genius of the Hebrew people.

RAHEL LUZZATTO MORPURGO
(1790-1871)

One of the finest poetesses in Italy, Rahel Luzzatto Morpurgo mastered Hebrew to perfection. She was born in Trieste. At the age of twelve she was able to read Ibn Pakuda's Hobot Halebabot (Duties of the Heart) in Hebrew. At fourteen she already studied the Talmud. At eighteen she wrote Hebrew poetry replete with cravings for the Infinite but not overly imbued with religious sentiments. Her poems were worldly, directed at nature and filled with a sense of awe for the vastness of the universe. In her own worldly life, Rahel Morpurgo was poor and earned her living as a seamstress. She was a mystic.

She was a lonely soul even after her marriage and after three sons and one daughter; she constantly sought for something hidden and "outworldly." Her uncle, Samuel David Luzzatto, tells the story: She asked him to get for her the Sefer Zohar, which he did. She then asked him what he wanted for his trouble and Luzzatto replied, "I do not ask anything for it except the following: Do not believe everything written in this book." Rahel answered, "You have asked too much." She was an adherent to the Cabala, believing that the Messianic Age would soon come and that the Temple would be restored in Jerusalem.

One hundred years after her birth, the world reminded itself of her existence. Vittorio Castiglione collected and published her poems under the title Ugab Rahel (Rahel's Flute). Some poems were translated into Italian and English.

Song[2]

Ah, vale of woe, of gloom and darkness molded,
How long wilt hold me bound in double chain?
Better to die—to rest in shadows folded,
Than thus to grope amid the depths in vain!
I watch the eternal hills, the far, far lying,
With glorious flowers ever over-run;
I take me eagles' wings, with vision flying
And brow upraised to look upon the sun.
Ye skies, how fair the paths about your spaces!
There freedom shines forever like a star;
The winds blow through your lofty spaces,
And who, ah, who can say how sweet they are?

SOLOMON RAPOPORT
(1790-1867)

One of the foremost Galician Maskilim, Solomon Rapoport, belonged to the closed circle around Nahman Krochmal in Galicia, despite the fact that he was somewhat conservative in his views on Judaism. Rapoport was a rabbi, a researcher, and a critic simultaneously. Indeed, his fame rests upon his original work in the field of medieval Hebrew literature. Rapoport's critical mind enabled him to investigate the past in the light of the scanty facts that have come down to us. He attained a high degree of perfection in bringing to light such personalities as Saadia, Hai Gaon, Eleazar Kalir, whose roles in history were not too clear. His work on the Geonic period was a masterful contribution. Both Leopold Zunz and Samuel David Luzzatto recognized Rapoport as one of the original research men of the century. Among the builders of the "Science of Judaism" he occupied a special place.

His works in Hebrew include the following: Erek Millin, an encyclopedic dictionary of Judaism; critical notes on the English translation of the travels of Benjamin of Tudela (12th century);, essays on the Ten Lost Tribes, on the Karaites, on the Land of the Chazars.

LEOPOLD ZUNZ
(1794-1886)

Leopold Zunz, Father of the Science of Judaism, dedicated many years of his life to the study of Jewish history, Jewish customs, and synagogal poetry. His original research works were recognized as of inestimable value by Christians and Jews alike. Two factors prompted Zunz to devote almost a lifetime to Jewish research: His inherent love of history and his belief that a scientific approach to Judaism would tend to make the Jews more conscious of their past, whereby assimilation would be checked.

In 1819 Edward Ganz, Moses Moser, and Leopold Zunz came together for the purpose of doing something by way of checking assimilation and conversions among the German Jews. The Haskala in Germany started by Mendelssohn had borne strange fruit. Too many Jews were abandoning Judaism. Among the casualties were such young Jews as Heinrich Heine and Karl Ludwig Börne (1786-1837), the great German political and literary writer, who converted to Christianity. The three young men mentioned above conceived the idea of organizing a society for the promotion of Jewish knowledge and culture among the German Jews by establishing schools where a modernized Judaism would be fostered. As a beginning of their activities, they published a journal for the Science of Judaism. Their hope was never realized, for the movement they started did not take root. Only three numbers of the journal appeared; it was given up for lack of funds.

Zunz was disappointed and subsequently arrived at the conclusion that the only thing he could do under the circumstances was to dedicate his own life to rescue "from the deluge of assimilation the Science of Judaism." Thus, as a result of his personal frustrations, he decided to hold onto this one anchor—research in the history of the Jewish past—whereby he hoped that such work "would radiate an influence in limited circles," so that the awakened interest in the past would reflect itself in the present. Perhaps Jewish Science as he conceived it would do what he had intended to do by way of establishing a Society for Culture and Science of Judaism. As to the real outcome of his activities in this field, Zunz was by no means too sure of himself; he rather left it "to God."

Zunz sat down to learn what the Jewish people accomplished during the centuries.

> When the shadows of barbarism were gradually lifting from the mist-shrouded earth, and the first rays of light universally diffused struck also the Jews scattered everywhere, a remnant of old Hebrew learning attached itself to new, foreign elements of culture. In the course of centuries enlightened minds elaborated the heterogeneous ingredients and fused them into the literature which was called Rabbinical.

This contribution of the Jewish people to world culture was almost unknown at that time. Zunz went all out to present a complete picture of the Middle Ages and the role Jews played during those dark centuries. He delved deeply into Rabbinical literature, especially from the standpoint of history; and into liturgical poetry, particularly as the expression of a people's soul. He brought to light facts that were entirely unknown.

His works were all written in German, in which he was a master. The following books are his best: *Die Synagogale Poesie des Mittelalters* (Synagogue Poetry of the Middle Ages), *Ritus des Synagogalen*

Gottesdienstes (The Ritual of the Synagogue), *Literatur-geschichte der Synagogalen Poesie* (History of Synagogue Poetry), *Zur Geschichte der Synagogalen Poesie* (History of Synagogue Poetry), *Zur Geschichte und Literatur* (Contributions to History and Literature), *Studie zur Bibel-Kritik* (Essay on Biblical Criticism), *Die gottesdienstlichen Vorträge der Juden* (The Jewish Sermon).

What Leopold Zunz's work meant for the growth and development of the Science of Judaism may be gauged by the accomplishments of others who contributed in various related fields. Franz Delitzsch and S. I. Baer published a new edition of the Bible in accordance with the Masoretic text. Zacharias Frankel composed his Darke Ha-Mishnah (Introduction to the Mishnah), in which he presented a scientific history of the Mishnah's development. David Hoffman and Israel Levy investigated the origin and the evolvement of the Talmudic Laws. Jacob Levy compiled lexicographical works to the Talmud and Midrashim. Michael Sachs made a special study of the foreign words found in the Talmud. Special editions of the Midrashim were published: Theodor's edition of Midrash Rabbah to Genesis and Zuckermandel's edition of the Tosefta. Julius Fürst compiled a Hebrew dictionary and a concordance of the entire Bible. The original Arabic texts of the Jewish religious philosophers of the Middle Ages were published. Moritz Steinschneider published catalogs of the most famous collections of Hebrew manuscripts and books; this work opened the spiritual treasures of Israel to the scholarly world and displayed the wealth of Hebrew literary creativity during the centuries.

Jewish history became a subject of intensive investigation and study. New scholars appeared: I. M. Jost, David Cassel, L. Landshuth, L. Herzfeld, A. Berliner, Heinrich Graetz. For the first time in the life of the Jewish people they had a complete history in twelve volumes, covering more than 3,000 years.

This was what Zunz had in mind when he used the term Science of Judaism. He opened the door for a scientific investigation of the Jewish past.

> If there are ranks in suffering, Israel takes precedence over all nations. If the duration of sorrows and the patience with which they are borne ennoble, the Jews are among the aristocracy of every land. If a literature is called

rich in the possession of a few classic tragedies, what shall we say about a National Tragedy lasting for over fifteen hundred years in which the poets and the actors were also the heroes?[3]

HEINRICH HEINE
(1797-1856)

Heinrich Heine, the greatest German lyric poet, at a critical moment of his life let himself be baptized—a wayward act committed in despair, which he regretted the rest of his life. In a letter to a friend he declared: "I was merely baptized, not converted, but I still hold it as a disgrace and a stain upon my honor that in order to obtain an office in Prussia—in beloved Prussia—I should have allowed myself to be baptized."

On his sickbed, or as he called it, "mattress grave," in which he lay over eight years, he rethought his youth and uttered his most profound comments on Judaism and the Jewish people. Agonized by excruciating pains and indescribable loneliness, the great poet wrote:

The Jews may console themselves for having lost Jerusalem, and the Temple, and the Ark of the Covenant, and the golden vessels, and the precious things of Solomon. Such a loss is merely insignificant in comparison with the Bible, the imperishable treasure which they have rescued. If I do not err, it was Mahomet who named the Jews "the People of the Book," a name which has remained theirs to the present day on earth, and which is deeply characteristic. A book is their very fatherland, their treasure, their governor, their bliss, and their bane. They live within the peaceful boundaries of this book. Here they exercise their inalienable rights. Here they can neither be driven along nor despised. Here are they strong and worthy of admiration. Absorbed in the city of this book, they observed little of the changes which went on about them in the real world; nations arose and perished; states bloomed and disappeared; revolution stormed forth out of the soil; but they lay bowed down over their book and observed nothing of the wild tumult of the times which passed over their heads.

Formerly Heine had been an admirer of Hellas and its contribution to world culture, but now, in the agony of death, he changed his mind.

Moses was a remarkable artist: he created a masterpiece called Israel. . .and as it was with the artificer, so it was with his handiwork, the Jews. I have never spoken of them with sufficient reverence, and that, of a truth, on account of my Hellenic temperament, which was opposed to Jewish asceticism. My preference for Hellas has since then decreased. I see now that the Greeks were merely handsome striplings. The Jews, however, have always been men, strenuous and full of power, not only at that time, but even at the present day, in spite of eighteen hundred years of persecution and misery. I have since then learned to value them better, and, if every kind of pride of birth were not a foolish contradiction in a champion of revolution and democratic principles, the writer of these pages might be proud that his ancestors belonged to the noble House of Israel, that he is a descendant of those martyrs who have given to the world one God and a moral law, and have fought and suffered in all the battlefields of thought.

Despite the fact that this great lyric poet has been so popular throughout Germany, and his "Lorelei" was chanted by the young— so much so that even the barbarian Nazi regime did not dare outlaw it—all attempts to erect a monument to his memory in Dusseldorf, his native city, have come to naught. Even presently, more than one hundred years after his death, there is a committee in London working to attain that aim. But the German authorities still refuse to accord him the honor he so richly deserves. Here is "Lorelei," translated by the great Jewish-American poetess, Emma Lazarus:

Lorelei

I know not what spell is o'er me,
That I am so sad today;

An old myth floats before me -
I cannot chase it away.

The cool air darkens, and listen
How softly flows the Rhine!
The mountain peaks still glisten
Where the evening sunbeams shine.

The fairest maid sits dreaming
in radiant beauty there.
Her gold and her jewels are gleaming.
She combeth her golden hair.

With a golden comb she is combing;
A wondrous song sings she.
The music quaint in the gloaming,
Hath a powerful melody.

It thrills with a passionate yearning
The boatman below in the night.
He heeds not the rocky reef's warning,
He gazes alone on the height.

I think that the waters swallowed
The boat and the boatman anon.
And this, with her singing unhallowed,
The Lorelei hath done.

SAMUEL DAVID LUZZATTO
(1800-1865)

Biblical scholar, grammarian, and poet, Samuel David Luzzatto, known as "Shadal," stands apart from all the Jewish scholars of the 19th century as one with an extremely positive attitude towards traditional Judaism, despite the fact that he was in close contact with the Maskilim of Galicia.

Born in Trieste, he was a prodigy. At eleven he already contem-

plated writing a commentary on the book of Job and started to
compose a Hebrew grammar in Italian. At thirteen he studied for
himself, without the help of a teacher. At fifteen he wrote thirty-seven
poems which were later included in his book titled Kinnor Na'yim
(Pleasant Harp).

Luzzatto resurrected Elija Levita's 16th-century thesis about
post-Talmudic origins of Hebrew vowel points and accents. Jewish
scholars had for 300 years often ignored Levita's work, largely
because traditionalists disliked his theory and disapproved of his
close association with the Christian community—he was a principal teacher to Christians of the Hebrew language. Luzzatto, then,
re-urged that since the vowel points were mentioned in the Sefer
Zohar (Book of Splendor), it showed that this Cabalistic book could
not have been written earlier than the Middle Ages. He therefore
rejected the claim that the author of the Zohar was the Talmudic
sage Rabbi Simon ben Yohai. His theory on the vowels formed part
of his work on Hebrew vocalization, Ma'amar Hanikkud.

At twenty, Luzzatto wrote Torah Nidreshet, dealing with philosophical and theological problems. In 1879 it was translated into
Italian and published in book form. As early as 1829 he was appointed a member of the faculty of the Rabbinical college of Padua.
Luzzatto was one of the most prolific scholars. He wrote over
thirty books both in Hebrew and Italian, all of them basic scholarly works. He contributed also many essays to scholarly journals.

Luzzatto was deeply interested in the Aramaic translations of the
Bible. He was the first Jewish scholar to have studied Syriac. He was
also first among the Jewish scholars who emended the text of the
Hebrew Scriptures. Correcting in many places the accentuation in
which he was a specialist, he did something that no other Jewish
scholar had done. He made a special study of Ecclesiastes and arrived at the conclusion that the author was not King Solomon, but
a man whose name was Kohelet, who ascribed it to Solomon. Luzzatto suggested that this author's contemporaries erased the name
Solomon and inserted the right name.

As a traditional Jew, Luzzatto was a staunch opponent of Maimonides, Abraham ibn Ezra, and Spinoza, believing as he did that
real faith and philosophy do not go together. In his opinion, Maimonides was guilty of bringing into Judaism foreign ideas incompat-
ible with the tenets of the Law of Moses. Luzzatto declared that he

studied various systems of philosophy and came to the conclusion that one negates the other and that "the more he read them the more he found them deviating from the truth." While noticing these frequent deviations, he asked himself the question: How could it be that "while one approves one thing the other disproves it"? Finally, he arrived at the conclusion that the philosophers themselves did not know the truth, and they simply misled their students by proposing ever new theories unrelated to life and experience.

The civilization of the world today is a product of two dissimilar elements: Atticism and Judaism. To Athens we owe philosophy, the arts, the sciences, the development of the intellect, order, love of beauty and grandeur, intellectual and *studied* morality. To Judaism we owe religion, the morality that springs from the heart and from selflessness, love of the *good*. Atticism is progressive, for the intellect is capable of continuous development and of new discoveries. Judaism is stationary, its teachings are immutable. The heart is capable of corruption, but not of further perfection. Goodness is inborn, wickedness acquired. . . .There is in human nature an inextinguishable thirst for the good. Beauty and grandeur cannot take the place of the *good* Society needs emotion; but intellect and Atticism, far from inspiring emotion, weaken it and snuff it out. This is why human nature reacts—and always will react—in favor of the heart, of the good, of Judaism. If ever Atticism should suffer defeat, human nature would likewise rally to its defense, for intellectual development is included among its needs. Then Atticism may conquer anew; but never shall it enjoy a lasting preponderance unclouded by opposition and reaction.

MEIR HALEVI LETTERIS
(1800-1871)

At the time when the Galician Haskala was at its height, Meir Letteris was regarded as one of the foremost poets. His first book of poems, Tofes Kinnor We-Ugov (Player of Harp and Flute), was received with enthusiasm. Five years later he published his version of Faust. Both works established his reputation as a Hebrew poet. Letteris also rendered Racine's *Athalie* and *Esther* into Hebrew. Letteris published two more works: Dibre Shir (Words of Song) and Ayelet Ha-Shahar (Morning Star). His long poem Yonah Homiyya (The Muttering Dove) became a folk song chanted in many lands. Therein Letteris bemoaned the homelessness of Jewish people. It touched a delicate fiber in the heart of the Jew.

Letteris made a place for himself in German literature by his book *Sagen aus dem Orient* (Sagas of the Orient), in which he rendered in poetic form some of the Talmudic and other legends. Published in Karlsruhe, in 1847, it secured for him the high position of librarian in the Oriental department of the Vienna Imperial Library, though he did not hold it long. In Vienna, Letteris also edited two scholarly journals.

Waves of the Sea[4]

They wander, they wander,
the waves of the sea.

In haste they are flowing;
their faces are glowing
and sparkling with glee.

And while they're rejoicing
and making us gay,
they are mixing and mingling
and gone are for aye.

Yea, scattered and tossed;
forever are lost!

And others, yea, others,
in haste take their place.

They're flowing, they're streaming
and while with joy beaming
and kiss and embrace,

They're rising and falling
and wander away;
No more are seen rolling,
they gone are for aye.

Yea, scattered and tossed;
forever are lost.

They wander, they wander,
life's pleasure and joys.

Like waves of the ocean,
they cease not their motion;

And while with their toys
they mankind ensnare,
they mingle and blend
with grief and with care;

And onward they wend,
and gone are for aye.

Life's pleasure don't stay;
like waves of the sea,
they wander from thee.

SIMHAH PINSKER
(1801-1864)

Simhah Pinsker was a Hebrew scholar and archeologist whose contribution was outstanding and highly impressive due to his connection with Abraham Firkovich, a Karaite scholar. Firkovich (1786-1874) created a sensation in the 19th century by his discoveries in the Crimea of a collection of old manuscripts, facsimilies, molds from tombstones. Later it was shown beyond a doubt that some of the manuscripts were forgeries. However, those that were geniune were sold for a large sum to the Imperial Library of St. Petersburg, upon the recommendation of Professor Chwolson in 1859. Simhah Pinsker, who lived in Odessa, saw the collection before it was sold. Among the manuscripts there was one of the Later Prophets, which carried a special punctuation altogether different than the regular vowel points and accents used in Hebrew. Pinsker sat down to study the new system and decipher it. From this he published his great work, Mabo el Ha-Nikkud Ha-Ashuri We-Ha-Babli (An Introduction to the Assyrian and Babylonian Punctation). It was one of the dramatic scholarly events of the century.

Another work of Pinsker was his Likkute Kadmoniyyot (Compilations of Ancient Times), a book of original research about the Karaite sect, which he published in 1860.

His son, Dr. Leo Pinsker, a prominent Odessa physician, was the author of the famous 1881 pamphlet, *Auto-Emanzipation* (Self-Emancipation), which advocated the acquisition of land by the Jews for an independent Jewish homeland. A congress of delegates from various countries gathered to discuss the project. Pinsker stood at the head of the Odessa Committee for the establishment of agricultural colonies in Palestine.

ABRAHAM MAPU
(1808-1867)

Abraham Mapu was the first modern Hebrew novelist and one of the leading Russian Maskilim of the 19th century. Born in Kovno, Lithuania, he was brought up in a strictly traditional home. His father, Jekuthiel, was a Talmudist and Cabalist, who believed he could make himself invisible by employing mystic incantations. At the age of twelve, young Abraham studied already the Talmud in private, without the help of a teacher, and was regarded as an Illui (an exceptional, diligent student). Influenced by his father, he started to study Cabala on his own. Later he studied Cabala under the guidance of Elijah Kalisher, rabbi at Slobodka. All this time Mapu was deeply religious.

Remarkably enough, his interest in secular subjects was awakened by a Latin translation of the Psalms. On a visit at Kalisher's home, he found a book which contained the Hebrew original and a Latin translation. It intrigued him so much that he started to learn Latin from that book. After a short time he met a Catholic priest who taught Latin in a country school. The priest, on conversing with Mapu, who served then as a Melamed (teacher) of small children in the village, was astonished to hear that he knew Latin. The priest became his Latin teacher, and Mapu gained such proficiency in that language that he composed a book. From that time on Mapu became deeply engrossed in secular subjects; being a born student, he studied everything that came his way.

However, his fervent love was for the Hebrew language, because the Biblical diction and the grand style of the prophets appealed to his poetic nature. The remote past, as reflected in the poetry of the Psalms, but perhaps even more so in the historical books of the Bible, came to life again before his very eyes. Thus the idea of writing a Biblical novel was born in Mapu's mind. Hebrew literature at that time consisted mainly of poetry and essays. When a book of fiction appeared, it was generally a translation from either French or German. Hebrew writers had shunned the novel. But in 1853, Mapu published the first original modern Hebrew novel, Ahabat Zion (Love of Zion). It was an immediate success. Ahabat Zion is a romantic story of the time of Hezekiah and Isaiah, about the 7th century B.C.E. Through Mapu's vision the reader found himself in Judea. Mapu brought him to the hills and the valleys, the fields and the vineyards there. The language, the romantic story by itself, and the deep love of Zion which pervaded this book won for it the heart of the reader. Having been influenced by such writers as Victor Hugo and Eugene Sue, Mapu knew how to build up a story that would appeal to a larger audience. His characters were natural people who acted in accordance with their instincts. Ahabat Zion was translated into German, under the title *Tamar*, by S. Mandelkern; into English as *Amnon, Prince and Peasant* (1887); and into Yiddish as *In The Days of Isaiah*.

Mapu's second work, Ashmat Shomron (The Guilt of Samaria), was also a Biblical novel, though not as powerful as the first. The story is about the time of King Ahaz: An army of Aram and Israel surround Jerusalem in order to force Judea to join them in their attempt to throw off the yoke of Assyria.

Mapu was famous not only as a writer but as a Maskil, a fighter in the first ranks of the war for enlightenment. Mapu was a sick man, suffering from palsy in his right hand and other assorted pains and aches. But his dedication to writing sustained him. His book Ayit Zabua (Painted Vulture), in which he described the struggle between the Maskilim and the "Hypocrites," as he called the ultra-orthodox, obviously antagonized the traditionalists enormously. Mapu composed a novel, in ten parts, about the time of Sabbetai Zevi, but pious opponents broke into his home and destroyed it. They simply regarded him as their most dangerous enemy, for he appealed to both the minds and the emotions of the Jewish youth. Mapu's popularity could not be dampened; even the students of the Talmudic academies were reading his works in hidden places.

ABRAHAM GEIGER
(1810-1874)

Abraham Geiger was a scholar of the first order, who contributed basic research works to the history of Judaism. Unfortunately his work was overshadowed by his extreme Reformism in the field of religion, a Reformism which carried within it at times seeds of sensationalism. He deserved, however, to be taken for what he was: a critic and scholar.

Geiger's basic contribution was his work, *Urschrift und Uebersetzungen der Bibel*, dealing with ancient scripts and translations of the Bible. His research in the field of Jewish history, particularly of the post-Biblical epoch up to the 1st century of the Common Era, was invaluable. He was also among the first scholars to present a better evaluation of the Sadducees and Pharisees in contradistinction to their New Testament presentation as "legalists" and "hypocrites." Geiger succeeded in gathering facts from various sources which tended to prove that the Pharisees constituted a party of the democratic and progressive elements at that time, a party that was supported by the majority of the people. The Sadducees, on the other hand, were the aristocrats and the priestly caste, who were mostly on the side of the Roman rulers.

In the field of the Aramaic translations of the Bible, Geiger's achievements were impressive and highly rewarding. Geiger distinguished himself in writing monographs on Maimonides, Judah Halevi, the Kimhis, and a number of Italian poets. He composed also a history of Jewish apologetic literature.

His position regarding Jewish nationalism was that of an extremist. "Zion" and "Jerusalem" to him were no more than "old ruined cities" whose names should be venerated as "memorials" of ancient history but not as cities to be restored. The Jewish people were a "religious sect"—Germans or Frenchmen or Englishmen who adhered to the "Mosaic teaching." In his Breslau congregation he fought tirelessly to publish a new prayer book in German in which all prayers for the restoration of Palestine were eliminated; in 1854 he succeeded. It corresponded fully to his idea of emancipation in Germany—that the Jews, in order to be recognized as citizens of the German Reich, must abandon all national aspirations. This of course aroused the orthodox against him. His greatest opponent in this controversy was Rabbi Samson Rephael Hirsch, his former friend.

SAMSON REPHAEL HIRSCH
(1808-1888)

Rabbi Samson Rephael Hirsch was the founder of neo-orthodoxy in Germany. Hirsch was a highly cultured man, a Talmudist of distinction and a scholar well versed in philosophy and science. In 1836 he published his famous *Nineteen Letters About Judaism*, under the pseudonym Ben Uziel, which made a furor in Germany. Written in a refined style by an orthodox rabbi, this work constituted an enlightened defense of traditional Judaism. Hirsch paid tribute to some requirements of the new times, but his stand as to the basic tenets of Judaism was firm and consistent. His main attacks were directed against the extreme wing of Reformism, particularly against Abraham Geiger and his followers. In order to safeguard Judaism at the source, Hirsch made a new translation of the Pentateuch, coupled with a commentary based upon the traditional commentators and the Talmud. This work was published in five volumes. Hirsch's commentary contributed greatly to the regeneration of Jewish orthodoxy in Germany.

HAYYIM SELIG SLONIMSKI
(1810-1904)

Hayyim Selig Slonimski occupies a special place in modern Hebrew literature as the first Hebrew writer to popularize science among the Jews of eastern Europe. An observer of traditional Judaism, long-bearded and wearing a skullcap, Slonimski looked like an old-time rabbi or preacher in the synagogue. In reality he was a Maskil, a scientist, an inventor, and a disseminator of knowledge. He chose the role of a popular teacher. Having established in Warsaw Ha-Zefirah, the first Hebrew daily, he wrote articles on popular science. Such articles were entirely new in Hebrew literature. They awakened a deep interest in science among those who were eager to know more about the world.

Slonimski was well known as an inventor. He perfected a calculating machine which was recognized by the St. Petersburg Academy of Sciences. In 1842 he exhibited this machine and won the Demidoff prize of 2,500 rubles. In 1853 he invented a chemical process for plating iron vessels with lead. He also invented a way to send quadruple telegrams, a device later used by Lord Kelvin in multiple telegraphy.

Slonimski published works in Hebrew dealing with higher algebra and astronomy. Toldot Ha-Shamayim (Origin of the Heavens) was devoted to optics and astronomy. His book Sefer Kukba di-Shebit dealt with the Halley comet and related subjects. All his books went through several editions and were well read. He also wrote and published in Russian and German.

ABRAHAM BAER GOTTLOBER
(1811-1899)

Abraham Baer Gottlober, born in Starokonstantinov, Volhynia (Ukraine), was a fiery Maskil, an agitator for enlightenment. He was an active editor and publisher, a poet, a translator, a research man. Like many other Haskala writers, Gottlober wrote in Yiddish for the masses who did not know Hebrew, though his main preoccupation was with Hebrew literature. At fifteen, he married into a wealthy Hasidic family in Chernigov, but when he joined the Haskala movement and became a freethinker, his father-in-law forced the young couple to be divorced. Thereupon, Gottlober became the enemy of Hasidism. Later he settled in Kremenetz where he became a friend of Isaac Baer Levinsohn. Gottlober was a restless person. From about 1836 to 1851 he traveled from city to city and wherever he tarried for a time he planted the seed of enlightenment. In 1865 he became a teacher in the Jitomir Rabbinical School. He stayed there until the Russian government closed it in 1875. Thence he moved to Dubno and subsequently to Kovno. Finally he settled in Byalistok.

As a writer, Gottlober distinguished himself both in poetry and in original historic research. At his time, he was considered one of the foremost poets. His first collection of poems, Pirhei Ha-Abib (The Flowers of Spring), appeared in 1836; another collection, Ha-Nizanim (The Blossoms), and a third, Anaf Ez Aboth (A Twig of the Tree), followed. A fourth important work was his Bikkoret le-Toldot Ha-Karaim (1865), a critical survey of the history of the Karaites. Later he translated from German into Heþrew Mendelssohn's *Jerusalem* and completed an allegorical drama. He also wrote a critical book on the Cabala, several short Hebrew novels, and translated Lessing's *Nathan der Weise* into Hebrew. Gottlober founded the Hebrew monthly Haboker Or (Morning Light), which existed uninterruptedly seven years, appearing first in Lemberg and then in Warsaw. The foremost writers of that time contributed to his periodical. In his magazine he published his autobiography, in which he included some material about the cultural life of the Russian Jews.

In his old age, Gottlober lost his eyesight. Neglected by his friends and almost forgotten, he ended his days in great poverty. The people for whose welfare and enlightenment he worked during many years did not remember him.

KALMAN SCHULMAN
(1819-1899)

Kalman Schulman, one of the foremost Maskilim of Wilna, was a widely read writer of the 19th century, although most of his works were either elaborations or translations. Writing in an easy Biblical style, he selected themes from history that were likely to arouse in the hearts of his readers love for their people's past as well as admiration for literature and science.

In 1849 Schulman published his work Harisut Better [Destruction of Better), in which he presented the history of the Bar Kokhba revolt against Rome; the fortified city of Better was one of the most important points held by the Jews, and its conquest by the Romans marked the collapse of the revolt. In 1859 Schulman published Milhamot Ha-Yehudim (Wars of the Jews), an elaboration of Josephus' history of the war against Rome during the first century. Both books had the effect of awakening the national consciousness of the Jewish people in eastern Europe.

Schulman's other works were: Halikot Kedem, an ethnographical description of Palestine and the surrounding countries; and a translation of Eugene Sue's novel, *Les Mysteres de Paris*. Sue's novel in Hebrew was widely distributed among the Jews of Russia and gave them a good view of life outside the ghetto. Schulman was also a skillful biographer. His monographs of Jewish scholars won wide audience among the Maskilim.

Although Schulman was an accomplished Talmudist who could have occupied a pulpit, he devoted most of his time to writing, being mainly interested in raising the standard of education of the Jewish people. As one of the leaders of enlightenment in Russia, he exerted a strong influence by producing useful works. His style was light and pleasant, though he could not liberate himself entirely from M'litzah, a flowery Biblical idiom. His works were both informative and highly instructive.

MICAH JOSEPH LEBENSOHN
(1828-1852)

Abraham Lebensohn's son, Micah Joseph Lebensohn, was one of the greatest poets of the Haskala period. His Shire Bat Zion (Songs of the Daughter of Zion) is still considered a first-rate contribution. It was translated into German by Joshua Steinberg, under the title *Gesange Zion's* (1859). The young poet suffered from tuberculosis and lived only twenty-four years. Haunted by fear of oncoming death, he expressed in his poems his deep longing for life. Micah Joseph's poetry is distinguished by the perfection of his rhythm, its deep pathos, and love of nature. He was singing of the past glories of Israel. Micah Joseph's Hebrew style was new and fresh. It was Biblical in tone and content, but far from imitative. The young poet imprinted his own personality upon every verse and succeeded in expressing his profound love for the Land of Israel, his craving for the glorious times of David and Solomon. Micah Joseph Lebensohn died with love on his lips—love for Israel and love for life and nature. The tragedy of his premature death was eulogized by Leon Gordon, the great poet of the Enlightenment period and Micah Joseph's closest friend.

Wine[5]

Like an arrow shot
To Death from Birth:
Such is your lot,
Your day upon earth.
Each moment is
A graveyard board
For moments that
Come afterward.
Now Death and Life
Like brethren act:
Beneath the sky
They made their pact.
So Void and Vita
Destroy, create;

Now swallow up,
Regurgitate.
The past is past;
The future lies
Still overcast;
The present flies.
Who shall rejoice
Us, scatter woe,
Make sweet our life
And bring Death low!
My hearties, wine!
Wine scatters woe,
Makes glad the life,
And brings Death low!

Micah Joseph Lebensohn

LEON GORDON
(1831-1892)

Leon Gordon, or Judah Löb ben Asher Gordon, was essentially a satirist, a poet with a piercing style, biting and stinging. However, he employed his satire not only against the fanatics and opponents of Haskala, but also against the enemies of the Jewish people. Gordon was great also as a re-creator of the ancient past. His Biblical poems are an epopee of romantic love portrayed in grand style, tender and highly colorful. He was also fond of the fable. His collection of a hundred fables in verse—some his own and most from others—was published in 1860 and became one of his enduring works.

Because of the heightened consciousness of enlightenment and emancipation issues during the 19th century, the struggle between fathers and sons, the conflict between generations, was sharpened during Gordon's life. The poet tended to side with the younger generation, and in orthodox circles he was therefore viewed as an apostate and heretic of the worst kind. He paid them in the same coin, reproving them as "rebels against light," dedicated to darkness and ignorance.

In 1872 he was invited to St. Petersburg as secretary of the Society for the Promotion of Culture Among Russian Jews. He served also as secretary of the local Jewish community. But his life there was certainly not to be serene. When conflict between the Hasidim and Mitnaggedim broke out in St. Petersburg over the appointment of a rabbi, Gordon was accused by the Hasidim of having been the cause. In 1879, after an attempt was made against the life of Alexander II, Gordon was thrown into prison. He and his family were exiled to the province of Olonetz. His innocence was soon proved. He returned to St. Petersburg and took over the editorship of the Hebrew periodical Ha-Meliz. The Czarist government conferred upon him the title of "Honorary Citizen," in recognition of his contributions towards the advancement of education among Jews.

Gordon reigned supreme in Hebrew literature until the advent of the great poets like Hayyim Nahman Bialik and Saul Tchernihowsky, who gave Hebrew poetry a new direction, precisely when Gordon was disappointed and wrote his poem, "For Whom Do I Toil?", in which he declared himself as possibly the last poet in the Hebrew language. Indeed, it was a critical time for the movement of enlightenment in Russia and frustration was the order of the day. The great poet-fighter of this period was tired and despair gripped his soul. He could hardly visualize that younger forces would soon emerge who were ready and willing to continue his work.

Gordon's poems were published in four volumes under the title Kol Shire Yehudah (1883). A fifth volume consisting of his stories appeared in Odessa in 1889.

Two illustrations of Gordon's poetry follow. The first is a simple satire. The second, "Simhat Torah" (The Joy of Torah), is replete with pride and exaltation; this is a Jew holding onto his spiritual treasures amid the persecution and misery in Czarist Russia of the 19th century. One hundred years later we can see thousands of Jews gathering at the only synagogue in Moscow during the holiday of Simbat Torah, singing and dancing around the Torah, expressing their anguish at being forced to abandon their own traditions and culture under another oppressive Russian government, unable to wish their brethren Lehayyim (to your health and life) no more than once a year—on Simhat Torah.

Thankful Ought I To Be For That[6]

The doctor famed for surgery,
Like to a lamb for butchery,
Upon the altar bound me,
In ether nearly drowned me,
And made me fall asleep,
A prey to slumber deep.
Upon me then he operated,
With zeal and ardor unabated,
And took a rib away.
I awoke and loudly shrieked with horror:
"I am ruined now for aye!"
"Hush! whence this sudden fright and terror?"
I heard the doctor say,
"Although I did your body rip
And take therefrom a precious rib,
Into an Eve I did not make it
And bring to thee; so calmly take it.
Dispel the horror that hath seized thee".
These words of comfort quick appeased me.
Complacently, I mused thereat:
Thankful ought I to be for that!

The Joy of Torah[7]

Lehayyim, my brethren, Lehayyim, I say
Health, peace, and good fortune I wish you today.
Today we have ended the Torah once more;
Today we begin it anew, as of yore.
Be thankful and glad and the Lord extol.
Who gave us the Law on its parchment scroll.

The Torah has been our consolation,
Our help in exile and sore privation.
Lost have we all we were wont to prize:

Our holy temple a ruin lies;
Laid waste is the land where our songs we sung;
Forgotten our language, our mother-tongue;
Of kingdom and priesthood are we bereft;
Our faith is our only treasure left.

God in our hearts, the Law in our hands,
We have wandered sadly through many lands.
We have suffered much; yet, behold, we live
Through the comfort the Law alone can give.

Two thousand years, a little thing when spoken;
Two thousand years tormented, crushed, and broken!
Seven and seventy dark generations
Filled up with anguish and lamentations!
Their tale of sorrow did I unfold,
No Simhat Torah today we'd hold.

And why should I tell it you all again?
In our bones 'tis branded with fire and pain.
We have sacrificed all. We have given our wealth,
Our homes, our honors, our land, our health,
Our lives—like Hannah her children seven—
For the sake of the Torah that came from heaven.

And now, what next? Will they let us be?
Have the nations then come at last to see
That we Jews are men like the rest, and no more
Need we wander homeless as heretofore,
Abused and slandered wherever we go?
Ah! I cannot tell you. But this I know,
That the same God still lives in heaven above,
And on earth the same Law, the same Faith, that we love.

Then fear not, and weep not, but hope in the lord,
And the sacred Torah, his Holy Word.

Lehayyim, my brethren, Lehayyim, I say!
Health, peace, and good fortune I wish you today.

Today we have ended the Torah once more;
Today we begin it again, as of yore.
Be thankful and glad and the Lord extol,
Who gave us the Law on its parchment scroll.

CHRISTIAN DAVID GINSBURG
(1831-1914)

Christian David Ginsburg, from an orthodox Jewish family in
Warsaw, famous as a Masoretic scholar, was converted to Christi-
anity in the year 1846 and joined the London Missionary Society.
For some years he engaged in missionary work in Liverpool, but
in 1863 he decided to devote his time to scholarly work, particularly to the Masorah. His works include the following: commentaries
on the Song of Songs and Ecclesiastes; essays on the Karaites, the
Essenes, and the Cabala; translation of Elijah Levita's Masoret Ha-
Masoret and of Jacob ben Hayyim's introduction to the Rabbinic
Bible, rendered from Hebrew into English. Most of his time, however, he devoted to the collation and examination of all extant remains of the Masorah. Ginsburg edited *The Masoretic Critical Text
of the Hebrew Bible,* published by the Trinitarian Bible Society. He
also published the text of the Moabite Stone (1871) with explanatory
notes.

Ginsburg was partly instrumental in exposing the forgery of M. W.
Shapira (1830-1884), who offered to sell to the British Museum an
ancient manuscript which he claimed was procured from a Bedouin.
It represented a second text of Deuteronomy with many variations
from the extant one. Shapiro, who is said to have been a missionary, asked a million British pounds for it. Ginsburg examined the
manuscript and wrote an account in the London *Times*. Another
scholar, Clermont-Ganneau, came specially to London to examine
it. The manuscript was declared a forgery. Shapira left for Holland
where he committed suicide in 1884.

The remaining years of his life Ginsburg dedicated to the Hebrew
Scriptures and the Masorah. His scholarly works were of inestimable value in the study of the Bible. As a painstaking research man,

he compared various versions of the Masoretic text one to another, and offered his own conclusions in some cases. His introduction to *The Masoretic Critical Text of the Hebrew Bible,* published together with a volume of facsimiles of the manuscripts, was an important contribution in itself.

CONSTANTIN SHAPIRO
(1841-1900)

Constantin Shapiro was one of the great Hebrew poets, a Maskil with a rich Talmudic erudition. His poems, distinguished by a strong diction and a refined style, were published in many Hebrew periodicals. Shapiro's first collection of poems, Me-Hezyonot Bat Ammi (From the ·Visions of My People), immediately called the attention of the Hebrew literary world to him. Shapiro wrote many other poems which placed him in the forefront of Hebrew poetry. He also translated Schiller's *Resignation* into Hebrew.

A change in Shapiro's life occurred when he moved from Grodno, his native city to St. Petersburg. His object in settling in the Russian capital was to enter the Academy of Art. But being unable to continue his studies, probably as a result of Czarist restrictions against Jews, he became a photographer. As an able photographer, he served the nobility and became wealthy. Then he decided to convert to Christianity. He joined the Russian Orthodox Church and married a Christian woman.

Shapiro regretted this action until he died. It is said that every day he closed himself in a special room where he prayed for forgiveness. His anguish during the years was expressed in a series of heart-rending poems, which are regarded as fine lyric compositions in Hebrew.

PERETZ SMOLENSKIN
(1842-1885)

Peretz Smolenskin was a writer of exceptional talents, who was eaten up by his missionary zeal in behalf of the ideals that he deemed to be the goal of his life. The agitator in him exhausted most of his energy.

Born in a small town, not far from Moghilef, he grew up in poverty. At eleven he entered a yeshiva in Shklov. He was considered one of the best students, but clandestinely he read Haskala literature and was fascinated by the new ideas for reforming Jewish life. He became an ardent critic of traditional Judaism, particularly of Hasidism, which was viewed by the Russian Maskilim as obscurantism. When the yeshiva management found out about Smolenskin, they were glad to get rid of him, fearful lest he spoil others. He left Sklov and for years he wandered from city to city until he reached Odessa.

Smolenskin started to write Hebrew at the age of twenty-five, advancing three main ideas which constituted his credo: dissemination of the Hebrew language, the enlightenment of the Jewish masses through secular education, and the reawakening of the national Jewish spirit. In order to bring his ideas into realization, he planned a periodical. In Russia, under the Czarist regime, it was very difficult to carry out such a plan, especially when one lacked financial means. Smolenskin again became a wanderer, and at long last reached Vienna, where he started to publish his journal, Ha-Shahar (The Dawn). At first he was publisher, editor, manager, and everything else that the publication needed. At times he had to write it himself from the first to the last word. Meanwhile he had to make a living, so he worked for bread at daytime and at night was busy with his journal. Many of his long novels were published in his journal, together with literary contributions by other writers. Smolenskin succeeded in winning a wide audience in Austria as well as in Russia.

Smolenskin's Am Olam (Eternal People) expounded his idea that the Jews were not only a religious sect as Mendelssohn had seen them, but also a national unity. In fact, Smolenskin advocated political emancipation and the return to Zion as early as 1873, long

before political Zionism as advanced by Theodor Herzl (1860-1904)
appeared on the Jewish scene. Am Olam influenced Zionists for over
a quarter of a century.

Other works by Smolenskin include: Ha-Ghemul (The Reward),
published in 1867, a novel about the Polish revolt against Russia;
Ha-To'he beDarke Ha-Hayyim (The Straggler Upon the Roads of
Life), a long novel in four parts, in which he described the life of
Joseph the Orphan and his tribulations and sad experiences. Ha-
To'he was partly autobiographical. It was eagerly read by the
Jewish youth during the last half of the 19th century. As a Maskil
who was out to combat obscurantism, Smolenskin saw only the dark
side of Hasidism. Both the Hasidim and their rabbis came out as
hypocrites and charlatans. But at his time he probably could not
do better. Certainly he believed in what he wrote.

Smolenskin's style is Biblical but without being overburdened
with eloquent expressions (M'litza) which earlier Haskalah writers
had been fond of. He held to simplicity and fluency of diction.

Hebrew to Smolenskin was not just a sacred language but one of
the pillars upon which the existence of the Jewish people rested. "Those
who perpetrate to alienate us from Hebrew perpetrate evil upon
Israel and its honor," he wrote. This was the reason why he sacrificed so much for maintaining the journal against all odds. "Like a
merciful mother who would not spare any effort or work for her
baby, I raised this journal. I did not sleep nor did I enjoy any rest
for years in order to maintain it. I have been writer, editor, publisher, proofreader, bookkeeper, and mailer. There was no one
to help."

Smolenskin was one of the most ardent fighters for the revival
of Hebrew. He awakened the consciousness of the Jewish people
by every means at his disposal: novels, essays, and articles, as
well as by publishing the works of others, who were the forerunners
of Hebrew regeneration. The first article about the revival of Hebrew
as a spoken language, written by Eliezer ben Yehudah, was published in Ha-Shahar. Ben Yehudah became indeed the father of Hebrew revival.

MOSES LOB LILIENBLUM
(1843-1910)

Moses Lob Lilienblum, one of the late-comers in the Russian Haskala period, was born in Keidany, near Kovno, Lithuania. Educated
and raised in a traditional home, he married at fifteen and settled
in Wilkomir. There he continued his studies in Talmud and Rabbinical literature, until he came across the new literature of the Russian Enlightenment, particularly the works of Abraham Mapu and
M. A. Ginzburg, which impressed him deeply. As a good observer
of life, Lilienblum started to criticize severely the life of the town
people, their ignorance and superstitions. They proclaimed him a
heretic and at times even persecuted him. The family into which
he married was against him. His wife and father-in-law viewed him
as a dangerous character. Indeed, here was a man, a long-bearded
Talmudist, a scholar, who had strayed from the right path to propagate subversive ideas against the traditional teaching.

Lilienblum was not satisfied with just talking; he aspired to
become a writer and what he wrote was in opposition to the life the
pious inhabitants of the town held sacred. In 1868, at the age of
twenty-five, Lilienblum completed a long essay entitled "Orhot Ha-
Talmud" (The Ways of the Talmud), in which he tried to demonstrate
that traditional Judaism must be reformed. Taking the stand that
life had changed, he argued that religion must not remain static:
it must change in conformity with the requirements of the time.
As a Talmudic scholar, he attempted to prove by the Talmud itself
that such changes had always been made; if not, Judaism would have
been petrified and might not have developed as it had developed in
the past. This essay was published in Ha-Meliz, a periodical of
the Maskilim. When the printed essay reached Wilkomir, it stirred
the community against the heretic. He was publicly denounced. No
pious Jew wanted to have any relationship with him. Even children
in the streets ran after him, casting stones at him. He was degraded
and insulted. Lilienblum could not stay longer in such an atmosphere
and decided to leave the town and go to Odessa, at that time a great
commercial center. There he planned to perfect himself in secular studies and if possible enter the university as a student.

He studied the Russian language by himself; in a short time he became proficient in Russian literature and the sciences. His name went before him. The Maskilim in Odessa respected him as a man of intellect. But Lilienblum was disappointed, for he soon convinced himself that his struggle for reforms was almost in vain. The Jewish youth who grew up in the big cities had not waited for reforms from a Rabbinical Assembly, as he had demanded, but rather permitted themselves to violate all the traditional laws. Lilienblum concluded that his demands were way behind the times.

Then came the year 1880, when bloody pogroms broke out all over Russia and the Jews were helpless. This struck Lilienblum hard. As a Maskil, he believed that the Jews were deprived of civil rights as a result of their backwardness and their isolation from the general population; as soon as they would be educated and "enlightened" they would be emancipated. However, life showed him that secular education was no panacea against anti-Semitism. Hence it dawned upon Lilienblum that the only real remedy was to be found in a homeland for the Jewish people, where they could develop as a national entity. Having read Dr. Leo Pinsker's booklet, *Self-Emancipation,* Lilienblum became a follower of the idea of Jewish nationalism. Thus Lilienblum was among the first to organize a circle of Hobbei Zion (Lovers of Zion), with the object of building Jewish colonies in Palestine. Many such circles formed at that time. Pinsker became the president of the Odessa Committee and Lilienblum its secretary.

Lilienblum continued his journalistic activities, agitating, in both Hebrew and Russian, for Palestinian colonization. He published his book Hattot Ne'urim (Sin of Youth), in which he confessed his mistakes as a Maskil, bringing to light many facets of his inner life. His style was always sober, clear-cut, and highly impressive. Lilienblum left his imprint on Hebrew literature as a man of deep convictions and as one who had the courage to change his opinions if he found them untenable.

MORDECAI DAVID BRANDSTADTER
(1844-1928)

Mordecai Brandstadter, a Galician short-story writer, was born in Brzeko, where he received a strictly traditional education. After his early marriage, he settled in Tarnow and became a successful businessman. In 1869, he met Smolenskin, who, after having been shown a story written by Brandstadter, encouraged him to write.

Since then, Brandstadter wrote humorous little stories in which he exposed the worst sides of Hasidism. He also exposed the emptiness in the lives of those who called themselves progressives and fighters for freedom and enlightenment. Brandstadter often succeeded in presenting realistic characters taken from life. His style is simple and entirely free from that verbosity which was popular in the early stages of modern Hebrew literature. Brandstadter reigned as one of the masters of the realistic short story for almost fifty years. In his old age, he stopped writing altogether. When he was asked for the reason he is said to have answered:

> There is no secret about it, my friend. As during my entire life which was open to all, I have acted openly and freely. My instinct whispered into my ear at the right moment: Stop! And I have not been misled by it. I have read the creative works of the younger generation, and it was clear to me that the time has come to remove myself from the literary world. As it is, if one would review the literature of a generation ago, he may not ignore a writer like myself, because at a certain time I had fulfilled a task. But had I continued writing, I would have brought upon myself denunciation instead of approbation.

NAHUM MEIR SCHAIKEWITZ
(1848-1905)

N. M. Schaikewitz, better known under his pseudonym Shomer, was the most popular writer in the second half of the 19th century. Writing in both Hebrew and Yiddish, he produced over 200 novels and about thirty plays. He was the Paul de Coque of Yiddish literature. He found his readership among the simple folks, particularly women.

In 1888, Sholem Aleichem, then a newcomer into literature, published his pamphlet Shomer's Mishpat (Shomer's Lawsuit), in which he exposed Shomer's deficiencies and castigated him as a scribbler and mediocre sensationalist, who profaned literature by producing works that were below criticism. This attack left a deep impression on the more intelligent circles of eastern European Jewry. Shomer defended himself in a special booklet entitled Yehi Or (Let There Be Light). But his star was setting fast. Only in the last few decades have some critics admitted that Shomer, all his faults notwithstanding, is to be credited for having maintained a mass readership. As he himself described his work, he had aimed "at satisfying evey plane of intelligence from the householder to the servant girl who could not understand the works of the more refined writers." In Hebrew, Shomer composed the following works: Mumar Le-Ha'kis (Spiteful Apostate), 1879; Ta'ut Goy (Mistake of a Gentile), 1880; Ha-Nidahat, two volumes, 1886.

Shomer was born in Nesvizh, province of Minsk. In 1888 he immigrated to America and settled in New York. He died there in 1905.

REUBEN ASHER BRAUDES
(1851-1902)

Reuben Asher Braudes, a native of Wilna, was one of the fore most writers of the later enlightenment period, close to the advent of Zionism. A novelist of merit, his chief aim was to portray the struggle for changes and reform. What distinguished him, however, from other Maskilim at that time was the fact that he tried to see the other side, too.

In his long novel *Two Extremes,* Braudes presented a two-sided picture of life as seen through two principal heroes: one who craves after the world outside the ghetto and another who succeeds in leaving the small town. After a while the latter returned from the big, free world and found in his native town a haven of refuge for his tired soul. The descriptions reflected the reality of Jewish religious life and simultaneously the yearnings and struggles of those who wanted to rebuild their lives.

In another widely read novel, *Religion and Life*, he described the struggle for enlightenment, but without the personal fervor of the previous Maskilim. He was more a realist instead of an agitator, more an artist interested in the inner life of his characters. This was the reason why Braudes' writing possessed the freshness of life and natural beauty. His style was sober and without too much embelishment.

In 1882, Braudes was among those disappointed in both emancipation and enlightenment as remedies for solving the problems of the Jewish people; revival of piety often resulted in a back-to-the-ghetto movement. Therefore, political Zionism became a rallying ground for writers such as Braudes, which meant that emancipation and piety could be emphasized without such automatic dangers of assimilation and onerous ghetto associations. Political Zionism infused new hope into many writers.

‫ייד‬14

MODERN
HEBREW
LITERATURE

HEBREW LANGUAGE REVIVAL

During this period two great historic events occurred: Hebrew became again a living language and the Land of Israel became an independent and sovereign state. The beginning of this story of revival
and regeneration goes back to the year 1881, when Alexander II,
the so-called Czar-liberator of Russia, was assassinated. A terrible
reaction ensued; pogroms and repressions of the Jewish population
followed. The old hopes of the Maskilim that by internal reforms
and education of the Jewish masses there would eventually come a
radical change in the life of the Jews were dashed to pieces. The
Czarist government did not remove any of the civil and political
restrictions; but instead issued new restrictions, more oppressive
than ever. It did everything to put the blame for the pogroms upon
the Jews themselves. As a result, tens of thousands of Jews decided
that Russia did not offer any future for them and their children. Frustrated and humiliated, they left Russia forever and took the wandering staff in their hands. Most of them immigrated to the Americas,
particularly the United States, bringing almost nothing with them
from their old homes except their desire and ability to work and
their dream for a better life.

Another wave of immigration, much smaller in proportion than the immigration to the Americas, was the one directed to Palestine. Small groups of dreamers and idealists, students and professionals, came from the ranks of the erstwhile Maskilim. The movement known as Hibbat Zion (Love of Zion) thus grew out of the misery and frustration in which Russian Jewry found itself.

Hibbat Zion went hand in hand with the hope of Hebrew revival. Writers, poets, teachers, and scholars were among the pioneers in Palestine. They were the builders who laid the foundation of the neo-Hebraic literature in Israel; when the old centers in the Diaspora were destroyed by the Nazis, the new center in Israel was ready to replace them.

The ground for the pioneering spirit in Israel was fertilized first by Jewish thinkers like Dr. Leo Pinsker (1821-1891), author of the famous treatise, *Auto-Emanzipation* (1881), in which he proposed a plan for a Jewish homeland, be it in Palestine or somewhere else, a territory inhabited by Jews and governed by them as the only solution of the Jewish problem. In Odessa a central committee for the colonization of Palestine was then established, and Dr. Pinsker was elected chairman. Small circles of Lovers of Zion were organized in various cities and towns. The atmosphere was pervaded with the idea of national regeneration in the form of self-help.

Such writers as Sholem Jacob Abramovich and Sholem Aleichem, who stood formally apart from the movement (Sholem Aleichem at one time joined the Lovers of Zion), indirectly served the cause of nationalism with their writings. Abramovich, while portraying the drabness of Jewish life in the ghettos of Russia and the abject poverty of the Jewish masses, helped considerably in the process of awakening the consciousness of the Jews. Likewise, Sholem Aleichem, who caused the Jew to laugh at himself, simultaneously made him think of the anomalies of his situation. Both Hebrew and Yiddish literatures opened new worlds of thought for the Jew.

The revival of the Hebrew language started with Eliezer ben Yehudah (Eliezer Perlman), a fanatic of this idea. He was among the first to propose it publicly, and he was among the first to implement the idea—by using Hebrew as a spoken language in his own home and family. He arrived in Palestine in 1882; there were soon three or four families in Jerusalem that used Hebrew in daily life. Remarkably enough, the insistence upon Hebrew as a living language aroused opposition among the orthodox Jews in Jerusalem. They objected to the use of the sacred language in the marketplace. Ben Yehudah and his small circle were seen as heretics and were at times persecuted, but the fight went on. Ben Yehudah, a sufferer from tuberculosis, sat down to work on his projected dictionary of Hebrew in ten volumes, blending in Biblical Hebrew, Mishnaic-Talmudic Hebrew, the Midrashim, and the Rabbinical literature. Since death was speedily approaching, ben Yehudah could not afford to lose time; he worked indefatigably day and night to complete his work.

In order to appreciate the achievement which this project was, one has to remember that the Hebrew language being resurrected for everyday use had not been used as such for 2,000 years. Everyday, urban-oriented life, as the 19th century passed into the 20th, was hardly the society reflected in the Biblical Hebrew language. To be a modern man and at the same time to think and to speak in Biblical Hebrew required more than a facility with language and a tenacious will. The language itself simply could not handle 2,000 years of change. The Biblical Hebrew vocabulary was, understandably, too limited. Numerous modern concepts lacked Hebrew equivalents, and writers were forced to struggle until they found ways of expressing them. There were no words for scientific terms, for example. Names of animals, birds, flowers, trees as used in the Bible were many, but they could hardly be distinguished one from another; their meanings were forgotten during the long exile of the Jewish people. To make of Hebrew a living language again it was necessary to coin new words for tens of thousands of items and concepts.

Ben Yehudah died in 1922, his vast dictionary project well begun, but unfinished. By the time of ben Yehudah's death, official opinion in Jerusalem had altered favorably in his direction, and a special commission was appointed to complete his work. These scholars reflected ben Yehudah's endurance, great love, and fanatical adherence to an ideal. As work on the dictionary progressed, Hebrew literature continued to grow. Many writers, along with their creative work, were also re-creators of the language. Their double task was doubly meaningful. Teachers vowed to "Hebrewize" the school children, the new generation. All—scholars, writers, teachers—contributed to the rebirth of the language and the literature.

When the State of Israel was proclaimed in 1948, therefore, there was already a well-versed and conscientious generation ready to take the burden upon its shoulders of developing the country and protecting it against those who wanted to destroy it. Never had a literature and a language played such an important role in the re-habilitation of a people's life as Hebrew played in Israel. The word and the book showed themselves to be the most effective tools of re-construction and revival.

SHOLEM JACOB ABRAMOVICH
(1837-1917)

At the beginning of this period stands one great writer: Sholem Jacob Abramovich (Abramowitsch or Abramowitz), known as "the grandfather of modern Hebrew literature," from the title—Der Zeide (the grandfather)—given him by Sholem Aleichem.

Abramovich, the progenitor of both neo-Hebraic and Yiddish lit-eratures, was born in Kopyl, Lithuania, into a middle class and pious Jewish family. His father died when he was fourteen. His sickly mother, unable to support her family, sent the young boy to the Slutsk yeshiva. He stayed there two years, and on returning home found his mother married to a Jewish villager, the owner of a flour mill. Since he did not want to become a miller for his step-father, he returned to Slutsk and for a time sat in the local syna-gogue as a "learner."

When he was seventeen, Sholem Jacob met a wandering mendi-cant named Avreml, who persuaded him to make a trip over the provinces with him in his horse and buggy. Fascinated by the prospect of seeing the world, the lad willingly joined Avreml. He soon discovered what a foul deal he had made with the sly and cruel mendicant. Averml forced him to beg from door to door and to do for him all kinds of chores. In those days, many towns maintained a Hekdesh, a place where beggars could stop overnight; where there was no Hekdesh, the local bathhouse was used for that purpose. Cripples of all sorts—blind, lame, and half paralyzed—stopped for a while on their wanderings. There were also disguised cripples who were out just to collect alms. Abramovich, living among them for a considerable time, learned their ways and observed at close range their actions and reactions. While wandering with them from town to town, he noticed the tragic conditions under which the Jewish masses in general were living at that time, their cultural backwardness, their low civil status in Czarist Russia.

At long last Abramovich liberated himself from the paupers and settled in Kamenetz-Podolsk, in the Ukraine. There he met Abraham Gottlober, the then wandering poet-Maskil, who showed the young man the way to Enlightenment. Influenced by the new ideas, he settled down to study Russian and German, history and literature, and secular sciences. In 1857 Abramovich made his literary debut with a Hebrew-language essay on education. He soon moved to Berdichev and continued his career, writing in Hebrew. Abramovich formulated the true task of a writer as follows: "Cultivation of the people's taste for better literature, portrayal of life, and enlightenment of the masses." This became the credo of his life.

In 1864 Abramowitsch resolved upon the bold step of adopting Yiddish as the main language of his literary expression. At that time the Jewish intellectuals held Yiddish in contempt as a corrupt jargon. Its literature for the most part consisted of simple folk tales, prayer-books (Tehinnoth) for the use of women, and books of pious admonitions. Abramowitsch, however, saw clearly that Yiddish would continue to be the language of the Jewish masses, and that in order to reach them he would have to write in that tongue.

For his purpose he created the figure of a bookseller, choosing this literary device because the bookseller of the time not only traveled widely and came into contact with the masses, but also received a certain deference as possessing a wider perspective and a deeper understanding than the average person. [Thus was born Mendele Mocher Seforim (Mendele the Bookseller.)]

The series of works which followed revolutionized Yiddish literature. They gave a realistic and sympathetic portrayal of the contemporary ghetto world, with its problems and its personalities, its customs and mannerisms, its humorous and its tragic phases. Abramowitsch fought the

battle of the masses against their oppressors with every
weapon in the arsenal of literature—pathos, wit, satire, allegory and invective.[1]

Some twenty years after his shift to Yiddish, Abramovich returned
to writing in Hebrew. He also translated most of his Yiddish works
into Hebrew. Thus Abramovich laid the groundwork for modern
Hebrew literary style and served a key role in the creation of modern Yiddish literature. Furthermore, literary value aside even, one
who wants to acquaint himself with Jewish life as it was lived in
eastern Europe in the last of the 19th century can find no better
teacher than Abramovich.

Among Abramovich's many works (about seven volumes in Hebrew and twenty in Yiddish when collected together), the following
deserve mention: *Dos Kleine Menshele* (The Little Man): This was
such a powerful satire on a government crony, whom the public
recognized in Abramovich's story, that the man lost his reputation.
Social and political critique was also evident in *Die Takse oder die
Bande Shtudt Baale Toboth* (The Meat Tax, or The Gang of City
Benefactors), which attacked a tax imposed upon the poor Jewish
masses by the leaders of the Jewish communities. *Die Klyatshe* (The
Old Mare) is an allegorical story representing the Jewish people as
an old and haggard mare driven to exhaustion. Emek Habaka
(Vale of Tears) is a novel about poverty in the ghettos of Russia.
Toledot Hateba (Natural History) was a translation from H. O.
Lenz's German *Naturgeschichte;* the first volume appeared in 1863.
It was one of the first works in Hebrew on popular science.

Mas'ot Binyamin Ha-Shelishi (The Travels of Benjamin III) is perhaps Abramovich's best known work today. The first Benjamin was,
of course, the famous 12th-century Spanish traveler and author, Benjamin of Tudela. The second was Israel ben Joseph Benjamin, who
wrote as Benjamin II; his travels, in the mid-19th century, took him
to Asia, Africa, and America. Abramovich's Benjamin III was a
visionary and unrealistic small-town husband who left his wife and
friends when he launched forth on a fantastic journey to look for
the legendary River Sambation and the Ten Lost Tribes of Israel.
This work was translated into Polish, Russian, and Ukrainian under
the title *The Jewish Don Quixote*, reflecting Abramovich's sobriquet,
"The Jewish Cervantes." Here is almost all of the first chapter of
Mas'ot Binyamin Ha-Shelishi:

"All my days (so says Benjamin the Third himself)—until my great journey, that is—I have lived in Tuneyadevka [Droneville]. There I was born, there I was raised, and there I had the great good fortune to marry my spouse, the virtuous Zelda, may her days be long in the land!"

Tuneyadevka is a little town, far, far out in the hinterland, so far removed from the great world that whenever, once in a blue moon, some traveler does chance to come, all the windows and doors are flung wide and the people swarm to gawk at the newcomer. Leaning out of their windows the neighbors ask one another: "Who can this stranger be? Where does he hail from? Why has he picked out our town of all places? What's behind all this? Nobody's going to come here without a good reason! Something must be up; we've got to find out what's what!"

Whereupon each one becomes anxious to show his cleverness; conjectures of all sorts fly thick and fast. Old folks recall other strangers who had visited their town in the past, in such and such a year; the town wits are reminded of stories not quite decorous, at which the men stroke their beards and smile, and the older women rebuke the wags, not too seriously, while the young matrons turn their faces away, only to look back furtively and giggle. The surmises concerning the stranger make the rounds, picking up momentum and bulk like a rolling snowball, until they fetch up at the House of Prayer, just as every conceivable topic does, whether it has to do with family squabbles, the political problems of Stambul, Turkey and Austria, finance, Rothchild's fortune as compared to the fortunes of the leading local gentry and other Midases, rumors about government decrees, the legends of the Red Jews [Ten Lost Tribes of Israel] and so on. A committee of local notables is always in session at the House of Study, throughout the day and far into the night, praiseworthily sacrificing not only their own interests but those of their families to the public weal, wholeheartedly devoting their attention to these public affairs, yet receiving no other award for their efforts save such as may accrue to them in the Hereafter. These matters are frequently transferred for further debate to the communal baths, where the elders, duly assembled, dispose of them, once and for all and irrevocably—for even if all the Kings of the East and the West were to view the verdict with disfavor, it wouldn't do them the least bit of good. The Turks once came mighty close to losing their realm at such a palaver—who knows what would have become of them if a few worthy citizens hadn't defended their interests? Rothschild, too, almost lost something like ten to fifteen million rubles here. Several weeks later, however, the good Lord took pity on him and the bathhouse statesmen granted him, during a lively conference in the steam room, a clear gain of something like a hundred million rubles!

The denizens of Tuneyadevka are, God save us all, dreadfully poor. To tell the truth, however, they're a merry lot of poverty-stricken, devil-may-care optimists. Just ask a Tuneyadevka Jew (do it suddenly, however): "How do you get along?" He'll seem flustered, not knowing what answer to make at first, but on regaining his composure he'll answer you in all seriousness: "How do I get along, you ask? Ours is a kind Lord, I'm telling you, Who never forsakes His creatures! He supplies their needs and, I'm telling you, He'll go on supplying them!"

"Yes, but just what do you do for a living? Have you a trade of any kind, maybe, or a little business?"

"Praised be the blessed Name! I have—praised be the Lord—I have, sure as you see me, a gift from the Almighty —a musical voice. So, I'm the cantor during the High Holiday services in the settlements hereabout. Now and then I perform circumcisions, and when it comes to perforating matzahs with the indented wheel, there's nobody like me. I also have a bit of luck once in a while as a marriage broker. I have a seat, as sure as you see me, in the synagogue. Then, too—just between you and me—I run a still that gives a little panther milk; I've also got a nanny goat —may she be spared the Evil Eye!—that's a good milker, and a well-to-do relative, not far from here, who likewise can be milked a little, whenever I'm really hard up. Aside

from all these things, God is our father, I'm telling you,
while the Israelites themselves are merciful and the sons of
the merciful!"

Another thing to the credit of Tuneyadevka's citizens
is that they're invariably satisfied with whatever God may
send them and aren't too choosy when it comes to clothes
or food. . . . When it comes to food—bread and soup (if
you're lucky enough to get them) make a meal that's not
at all bad. And if, of a Friday, you have a loaf of white
bread and a dish of something stewed (if you can but afford them), they are verily a royal feast, the like of which
is not to be found anywhere else in the world. Should any
man tell them of delicacies other than stewed fish or meat,
with carrots and parsnips by way of dessert, they would
think him queer and would be likely to snicker and poke
fun at him, as if he were cracked and were trying to take
them in with a cock-and-bull story.

On the fifteenth day of the month of Shevat they nibble
at a sliver of the traditional carob pod—there's a fruit for
you! The sight of it reminds you of Jerusalem. More than
once will the partaker thereof lift his eyes up to heaven
with a sigh and murmur: "Merciful Father, lead us with
our heads held high into our own Land, where even the
goats feed on carob pods!"

Once, by pure chance, someone brought a date into
Tuneyadevka. How the townfolk flocked to gape at it! On
opening the Pentateuch someone discovered that dates were
referred to in the Holy Writ! Think of it! Dates grew in the
Land of Israel, actually! As they contemplated the date, a
vision of the Holy Land spread out before them; here one
crossed the Jordan; there was the Cave of Machpelah,
wherein the patriarchs and the matriarchs are entombed,
and the grave of our Mother Rachel; over there was the
Wailing Wall; some bathed in the hot springs of Tiberias;
others scaled the heights of the Mount of Olives; others
still ate their fill of carob pods and dates, and stuffed
their pockets with the sacred soil, ultimately to be placed
in pillows under their heads in their graves.

The visionaries sighed and tears welled up in their eyes. . . .

In a word, life in his home town seemed to Benjamin to be good and glorious, even though he lived in poverty and his wife and children went around in rags. However, had Adam and Eve been disconcerted by the fact of their being naked and barefooted while they were still in the Garden of Eden?

Nevertheless, the wonder-tales of the Ten Lost Tribes penetrated to his very heart. . . .

From that time on Benjamin began most fervently to meditate upon Rabbah Bar Bar Hana's journeys over land and sea; later on a volume of Eldad Ha-Dani's fell into his hands, as well as *The Travels of Benjamin* (the First), depicting that noted explorer's wanderings to the very ends of the world, some seven hundred years ago, and such books as *In Praise of Jerusalem* and *The Image of the World*, wherein the Seven Wisdoms and all the world's marvels, and all its strange and unique creatures and creations, are described in seven small pages. These works opened new horizons before him that affected him profoundly.

"Those wonder-tales fascinated me exceedingly. And how often did I cry out in my rapture: 'Would that the Almighty might but help me to see even a hundredth part of all this with my own eyes!' My fantastic visions bore me far, far away."

Thenceforth Tuneyadevka became too small to hold him. He made up his mind to throw off its trammels, break loose from its moorings, to escape, even as a chick escapes its shell, to catch his first glimpse of the fair world without.[2]

ISAAC LOEB PERETZ
(1851-1915)

I. L. Peretz, one of the greatest Hebrew and Yiddish writers, was born in Samoścz, province of Lublin. Raised in a traditional home, he was a diligent Talmudic student. Later he studied secular subjects and graduated as an attorney-at-law.

At first Peretz wrote Hebrew poems. In 1886 he published some of them in the periodical Ha-Asif under the title Manginot Hazman (Melodies of the Time). But his real literary career started when he settled in Warsaw. From then on he devoted all his free time to literature, both in Hebrew and Yiddish. He was a master of the short story. In a few pages he could give a complete picture of life, a little world in itself, with all its light and shadows, a story with an idea deeply imbedded in it.

One of the most remarkable features of Peretz's creative ability was his deep penetration into the human soul. A writer of contrasts, he could portray the shoemaker and the coachman, the tailor and the water carrier with the same sympathy as he portrayed the world of the learned Jew. His Hasidic and folkish tales were superb. As a poet he appreciated the warmth of feeling, the emotional upsurge, and the joyful philosophy of life fostered by Hasidism.

In one of his masterpieces, "Between Two Mountains," Peretz introduced two extremes: the old rabbi of Brisk, a Talmudic scholar, a cold logician; and the young Bialer Rebbe, and erstwhile disciple of the Brisk rabbi. The disciple becomes a Hasid. In the story, told dramatically, one can see the difference between a Man of the Mind and a Man of the Heart, between rigid logic and warmhearted emotion.

Joseph Lichtenbaum, noted Hebrew critic in Israel, says of Peretz:

> In portraying the Jewish street he is seemingly a *realist;* yet there is almost nothing in his writing that is pure realism. Constantly there is something fantastic intervening, something of the dreamland lurking beyond reality. For Peretz has a propensity which tends to go deeper than the surface of reality, a propensity that is the offspring of intellectualism intermingled with imagination. While Peretz gives us a wealth of selected details, simple day-to-day affairs, they are being brought together under a veil of spiritualism which is truly romantic. This shows that reality per se was too narrow to accommodate Peretz's talent. His true gratification lay in the conjunction of the real and the unreal.

A. A. Roback characterizes Peretz as follows: "Peretz was at first a romanticist but this was only one stage in his cultural wanderings. He became in turn an impressionist, a symbolist, and even an expressionist."[3] Roback points to Peretz's versatility as expressed in his dramas, poetry, travel pictures, criticism, essays, epigrams, memoirs, folk tales, and Hasidic stories.

Peretz was always dissatisfied with himself, ever searching for new literary forms. He was a creator of forms, original both in style and in content. His soul seemed constantly to cry for something new; otherwise he could not create. Peretz's world was dynamic; restlessness ruled. As one reads one story after another, one cannot help feeling the inherent unrest of the writer. Peretz himself was born into a restless generation, among searchers after something that was as yet hidden in the womb of time. This was apparently the reason for Peretz's multitude of literary forms. Every theme of his seemed to have required a different form, a new style which he had to furnish anew, because the old forms were not congenial to his purposes.

Peretz was an extraordinary literary leader. Due to him, Warsaw became a literary Mecca. Young writers flocked to Peretz as their teacher and guide. A word from Peretz's mouth was tantamount to a literary franchise. Peretz's following was so strong, both among his disciples and among his vast readership, that over 100,00 men and women appeared for his funeral.

SHOLEM RABINOVITZ (SHOLEM ALEICHEM)
(1859-1916)

Sholem Aleichem (pen name), famous humorist, was born in Pereyaslev, province of Poltava, Russia. At first Sholem Aleichem did not have any aspirations as a writer. At twenty-one he was appointed a crown rabbi, a sort of intermediary between the Czarist government and the Jewish community. A little later he settled in Kiev and tried his hand as a merchant, a commission salesman, and a speculator on the exchange. He came into something of a fortune as administrator of his father-in-law's estate, upon the latter's death in 1885, only two years after Sholem Aleichem's marriage. However, he soon lost the inheritance in bad business and financial ventures.

It was just before his marriage that Sholem Aleichem began to write: short stories and essays on Jewish education and other topics. He wrote both in Hebrew and in Russian, and soon in Yiddish for the masses. By the turn of the century he was devoting his full time to writing. The ghetto reeled with joy and laughter because of his remarkable way of presenting figures and situations. Sholem Aleichem was a people's writer, widely read by young and old, rich and poor. His stories, published in small booklets and sold for a few Russian kopecks, were accessible to all. His motto became known everywhere: "Laugh, Jews, laugh; doctors say laughter is healthy."

Sholem Aleichem was endowed with a great talent. Writing in an easy style, witty and humorous, replete with sympathy and love for the common man, he brought joy into the poor and dark hovels of the small-town Jews. His characters were simple Jews, such as Tevye the dairyman, whose naivite, kindliness, trust in God became proverbial; or Menahem Mendel, a sort of schlemiel, who was constantly scheming to become rich, but was miserably failing in his "enterprises." Sholem Aleichem did not aspire to be a reformer, as almost all Haskala writers had tried to be. He came not to criticize, but to describe life as he saw it.

The monologue is Sholem Aleichem's best medium of expression. Letting his characters speak for themselves seems to be his pleasure. Just think of it. Life was so hard in the Russian Pale of Settlement, consisting of several provinces in which millions of people were confined as in a dungeon. Jews were hampered on all sides by restrictions both political and economic. Poverty, degradation, persecutions of all kinds; excesses, assaults, and pogroms were not infrequent under the cruel Czarist regime. Yet Sholem Aleichem's characters seem not to know what despair is. They do not fall. With Sholem Aleichem, life seems to laugh at what is tragic and painful. Nay, more, tragedy *itself* laughs. Humor, it is said, contains something tragic underlying it; if this be so, Sholem Aleichem's writing is indeed "laughter through tears." That is how the common people, who were the first ones to recognize him, took it—even before the critics noticed Sholem Aleichem. The people felt that here was a writer who wholly belonged to them—a folk writer. Take, for example, Tevye the dairyman: Who would not recognize him as a Jew of Jews, suffering yet still optimistic, beset with grief and sorrows yet trusting in God?

The Bible tells us that God created man in his own image. Perhaps something like it may be said of every real creator: he creates "in his own image." And if it is true with others, it is even truer with Sholem Aleichem. He has given parts of himself in his characters: Tevye the dairyman, Menahem Mendel, and Motel Paysee. Sholom Aleichem could not do it otherwise. Their idiom, their gesticulations, their actions and reactions, their smiles and their innermost pains were *his*.

Part of the tragedy underlying Sholem Aheichem's humor was personal. Note the epitaph which he himself wrote for his tombstone:

> Here lies an ordinary Jew
> who wrote in Yiddish it is true;
> and for wives, and plain folk rather,
> he was a humorist, an author
> poking fun at all and sundry;
> at the world he thumbed his nose.
> The world went on swimmingly,
> while he, alas, took all the blows.
> And at the time his public rose
> laughing, clapping, and making merry,
> he would suffer, only God knows,
> secretly—so none was wary.[4]

Perhaps Sholem Aleichem's most praiseworthy feature is his profound sympathy, his love for those creatures he deemed worthy of portrayal. They are his people, so close and dear to his heart that he actually feels as one of them. There is no distance between them and the writer. Moreover, it is a love that is not confined to human beings alone. It reaches also the dumb animals in the ghetto: the dog Rabtchik, the horse Methuselah, the goat and the cat. He seems to have been born and to have lived without the least bit of malice.

His humor is simple and crystal clear, and it wells from the deepest soul springs. It is open hearted and extremely contagious. Never did the Jew laugh at himself as he laughed with Sholem Aleichem, and never did he feel so good as after seeing himself and his fellow men through the spectrum of this great humorist. No wonder that Sholem Aleichem is as popular today as he has been in the past. Perhaps it is because true humor has something of the eternal which never fades or falters. But certainly the credit is due primarily to Sholem Aleichem himself. Indeed he has won a place for himself in French, Spanish, English, and even in Chinese and Japanese. In Soviet Russia it is reported three million copies of his works were sold between 1917 and 1942. When one remembers that most of his characters are so distinctly Jewish, and much of his humor depends upon the Yiddish idiom, the wonder of his popularity in various lands is still greater.

Curt Leviant, translator of Sholem Aleichem into English, says:
Sholem Aleichem's characters, unlike Peretz', are more types than individuals. . . .

Mendele [Abramovich] wrote from a pedestal. He was, to use a current term, alienated from the reader. There was more antipathy than identification in his works; honey hardly touched his acerbic pen. But Sholem Aleichem loved the people, even while he satirized them; among them he felt at home. He laughs along with his characters; he neither approves nor condemns; he observes. An abundant faith in man shines forth from his writings. Although the Jews of his time had reason enough to be pessimistic—pogroms, social upheaval, the breakup of traditional life were rampant—it does not become a theme in Sholem Aleichem. Optimism reigns.[5]

All of Sholem Aleichem's works were translated into Hebrew by Isaac Dov Berkowitz, Sholem Aleichem's son-in-law and a well-known Hebrew writer himself. Berkowitz actually re-created Sholem Aleichem with his masterly translations, as Hebrew was coming to be more of a living language.

The chief importance of Sholem Aleichem's works lie, of course, in the so-called Sholem Aleichem world which he created, a world peopled with literally many hundreds of distinct, individual types, old and young, men and women, rich and poor, ignorant and learned, good and bad, old-

fashioned and modern—all in full view, with their physical
appearances, mannerisms, ways of expression, inner inconsistencies, struggles for existence and social relationships. Indeed, it has been said that if all other records of
the time were lost, one could reconstruct a true picture of
Jewish life in Russia at the turn of the century on the basis
of Sholom Aleichem's works alone.

Some of his characters have become proverbial.[6]

In 1914 Sholem Aleichem moved to America, where he was known
as "the American Mark Twain." He died in New York City in
1916.

Excerpts from three of his stories will illustrate his approach:

On America[7]

"America is all bluff. All Americans are bluffers. . . ."
That's what strangers say. Being greenhorns, they don't
know what they're talking about. The fact is that America
can't even shine Kasrilevke's shoes when it comes to bluff-
ing. And our own Berel-Ayzik could put *all* the American
bluffers into his side pocket.

You'll realize who Berel-Ayzik is when I tell you that if a
Kasrilevkite starts jabbering a mile a minute, or as they
say in America, talks himself blue in the face, he's shut up
with these words: "Regards from Berel-Ayzik." He gets
the hint and buttons his lip.

There's a story they tell in Kasrilevke about a fresh lout
which tells a lot about Berel-Ayzik. On Easter, the Christians have a custom of greeting one another with the news
that Christ is risen. The other answers by saying: True, he
is risen. Well, once a Christian met up with this fresh lout
of a Jew and said: "Christ is risen." The Jew felt his
stomach churning. What should he do now? Saying "he is
risen," would be against his belief. Saying no, he's not
alive, might get him into a pickle. So he thought about it
and said to the Christian: "Yes, that's what our Berel-
Ayzik told us today." Just imagine, it was this very Berel-
Ayzik who spent a few years in America before he returned

to Kasrilevke. Picture the wonderful stories he told about
that country.

"First of all—the land itself. A land flowing with milk and
honey. People make money left and right. Beggars use two
hands. They rake it in. And there's so much business there,
it makes you dizzy. You do whatever you please. Want a
factory—it's a factory. Want to open a store—fine. Want to
push a pushcart, that's permitted, too. Or you can become
a pedlar, even work in a shop! It's a free country. You
can swell from hunger, die in the street, and no one'll
bother you, no one'll say a word.

"As for its size. The width of its streets! The heights of
its buildings! They have a structure called the Woolworth
building. Its tip scratches the clouds and then some. They
say it has several hundred floors. How do you get to the
top? With a ladder called an elevator. To get to the top
floor, you board the elevator early in the morning and
you reach your floor by sunset.

"Once I wanted to find out, just for the fun of it, what it
looked like up there, and I'm not sorry I went. What I
saw, I'll never see again. What I felt up there cannot even
be described. Just imagine, I stood at the top and looked
down. Suddenly I felt a queer kind of smooth and icy cold
on my left cheek. Not so much like ice as jello, slippery
and nappy-like. Slowly I turned to my left and looked—it
was the moon.

"And their way of life. It's all rush and panic, hustle
and bustle. Hurry-up is what they call it. They do everything quickly. They even rush when they eat. They dash
into a restaurant and order a glass of whiskey. I myself
saw a man being served a plate which had something
fresh and quivering on it. As the man lifted his knife, half
of it flew off to one side, half to the other, and that put an
end to that man's lunch.

"But you ought to see how healthy they are. Men as
strong as steel. They have a habit of fighting in the middle
of the street. Not that they want to kill you, knock your
eye out, or push a few teeth down your throat like they do

here. God forbid! They fight just for fun. They roll up their
sleeves and slug away to see who beats who. Boxing is
what they call it. One day, while carrying some merchan-
dise, I took a walk in the Bronx. Suddenly two young
boys started up with me. They wanted to box. "No, sir,"
I said. "I don't box." Well, we argued back and forth,
but they wouldn't let me leave. I thought it over: if that's
the way you feel about it, I'll show you a thing or two.
I put my package down, took off my coat, and they beat
the daylights out of me. I made it away, my life hanging
by a hair. Since th n, all the money in the world won't get
me to box.

"Not to mention the respect we Jews have there. No people are as honored and exalted there as the Jew. A Jew's
a big shot there. It's a mark of distinction to be a Jew. On
Sukkoth you can meet Jews carrying citrons and palm-
branches even on Fifth Avenue. And they're not even
afraid of being arrested. If I tell you that they love Jews it
has nothing to do with the fact that they hate a Jewish
beard and earlocks. Whiskers are what they call them. If
they see a Jew with whiskers, they leave the Jew alone, but
tug away at his whiskers until he has to snip them off.
That's why most of the Jews don't wear beards or earlocks. Their faces are as smooth as glass. It's hard to tell
who's a Jew and who isn't. You can't tell by the beard
and by the language, but at least you can recognize him
by his hurried walk and by his hands when he talks. But
aside from that, they're Jews down to the last drop. They
observe all the Jewish customs, love all Jewish foods,
celebrate all the Jewish holidays. Passover is Passover!
Matzohs are baked all year round. And there's even a
separate factory for the bitter herbs we use during that
holiday. Thousands upon thousands of workers sit in that
factory and make bitter herbs. And they even make a living from it. America's nothing to sneeze at!"

"Yes, Berel-Ayzik, what you say is all very well and
good. But just tell us one more thing. Do they die in America like they do here? Or do they live forever?"

"Of course they die! Why shouldn't they die? When they drop dead in America, they drop dead by the thousands each day. Ten and twenty thousands. Even thirty thousand. They drop dead by the streetful. Entire cities get swallowed up like Korah in the Bible. They just sink right into the ground and disappear. America's nothing to sneeze at."

"Then what's the big deal with Americans? In other words, they die like us."

"As for dying, sure they die. But it's *how* you die—that's the thing. Dying is the same all over. It's death that kills them. The main thing is the burial. That's it!. . . .

There's No Dead[8]

A month before Rosh Hashana, I returned to Kasrilevke to visit my parents' graves.

The ancient Kasrilevke cemetery was much nicer and livelier than the town itself. Here you found little tombstones finer than the nicest of Kasrilevke houses. What good came of the fact that the ground here was as dry as pepper in contrast to the town's muddy, swampy soil? Here, at least, you saw some green grass and two or three pear trees. You heard the twittering birds hopping from branch to branch, talking to one another in their own language. Here you saw the round, blue, skullcap-shaped dome of the sky and the bright warm sun. Not to mention the air! But what difference did it make? One was just as dead here as in town. There was a difference, though. Here, at the cemetery, the dead all lay in one spot. In town, they still walked around. Here, they were at rest and knew of no troubles. In town, they still had troubles and who could tell how many more there were yet in store for them in this world.

I saw a few women stretched out on the graves, crying, screaming, and pleading. One wanted her mother to rise and see what had become of her one and only daughter. . . .

Another woman came to her father, complaining about
the husband the matchmaker sent her. They thought he
would be a bargain. They said he would be a prize. All
the girls had envied her. But he turned out to be a charlatan, a squanderer who would shell out enormous sums for
honors in the synagogue. He also spent a lot for books.
He'd sell his own mother and father for his books, but he
didn't give a damn about her being skin and bones and
sick, as well.

The third woman came to bring glad tidings to her dead
husband. She was marrying off her eldest daughter and
had no money for the dowry, not even the first half, which
he had promised to pay. She had neither shirts nor shoes,
not to mention money for the wedding expenses—musicians,
waiters, this and that. Where would she get money for that?
She'd go out of her mind if the match were broken. God
forbid. What would she do then?

All the other women cried and bemoaned their troubles,
emptying their bitter hearts by weeping, relieving themselves by talking to their true loved ones. Perhaps this
would make them feel better. When you cried your heart
out, you did feel better.

As I roamed around among the half-sunken graves and
read the old, rubbed-out inscriptions on the slanting tombstones, I was seen by Arye, the red-eyed, flaxen-bearded
gravedigger.

"Who do you want to see?" he asked.

Reb Arye was so old that no one knew his real age, not
even Arye.

Nevertheless, he kept himself clean and neat and pam-
pered himself like a spoiled Mama's boy. His shoes were
shined; each hair of his beard was combed. He ate only
soft foods and drank the essence of boiled herbs and rock-
candy every morning.

"He has it easy," is what Kasrilevke folk said of Reb
Arye, truly envying him

"Hello, Reb Arye. How are you?" I said, approaching
the old man. It was evening. The sun, about to set, lit up

the edges of the tombstones. Reb Arye, shielding his red eyes from the sun, contemplated me and stroked his beard.

"Who are you, my son?" he said. "What do you want here?"

I told him who I was and whom I wanted to see. Then he recognized me and greeted me, smacking his lips and talking with a whistle.

"Oh. Is it really you? I knew your father, even your grandfather, Reb Vevik. What a fine man he was! Your Uncle Pini, too, was a wonderful person. Your Uncle Berke is also buried here. So is your Aunt Khane. I knew them all. They're all dead. All the nicest people have died out. Not a one has remained. Mine have died, too," he sighed, and motioned with his hand. "First I buried my children, all of them. Then my wife died, a saintly woman she was, may I live and be well. Left all alone in my old age. No good."

"What's no good?" I asked him.

"It's no good," he said. "There's no dead."

"No dead?" I asked.

"Have they stopped dying in Kasrilevke?" I asked.

"What has dying got to do with it?" he said. "Sure they still die. But who? It's either children, babies, or poor men. You can't make a thing on them, unfortunately. You've got to pass the hat around for shrouds and then after the orphans say the first mourner's prayer, you've got to give them a piece of bread, too. But what can you do? I have no choice." He pointed his dried-out hand toward the crying women. "Those women are stretched out on the graves like princesses. What do I have from them? They swell up like drums, crying! What do they care? Does it cost them anything? And it's me who has to go and show them where their dead are buried, where their mothers and fathers and uncles and aunts are. I've become their father's footman. Sometimes a woman cries so long that she faints. So I have to bring her to, give her some water. Sometimes even a piece of bread. But where from?

How? From the big income I have? There's no dead and
you have to keep living and marry off your orphaned
granddaughter who's of marrying age. She almost had a
groom, the match was about to be made. He wasn't a
bad young fellow, a porter, a widower with a few children, but he earned his living, a fine living, in fact. That
is—if he had work, he earned money. They even got to
meet each other. But before they got engaged, he said:
'Well, what about a dowry?' 'What dowry?' I said. 'I was
told you were giving fifty rubles for a dowry,' he said.
'May all my wild nightmares seep into my enemies' skulls!
Fifty? Where do I come to having fifty? Do you want me
to steal it, or dig up others' shrouds from my graves and
sell them?' To make a long story short, nothing came of
the match. And if you talk to the Kasrilevke folk they'll
insist that they're right. 'Reb Arye, you've got no ground
for complaints—God bless you,' they say. 'You have yourself an excellent job.' An excellent job! If by some slight
chance there happens to be a fine rich man around, he's
been dead a long time. New ones don't come by. There's
no dead. None at all!"

A Passover Eve Scene

The story is related by a Jewish boy, starting with a scene in the
synagogue where the sexton tries to find a home for a guest from
Jerusalem, a stranger to the town. The boy describes the Jew as
"a strange looking individual, in a fur cap, and a Turkish robe
striped blue, red, and yellow." The boy's father, Reb Jonah, wel-
comed the visitor and brought him home. Everything was prepared
for the Seder ceremony. Someone had to say Kiddush, pronouncing
the benediction on wine. Here the following conversation took
place:

"My father: 'Nu?' (That means, "Won't you please say
    Kidush?")

"The guest: 'Nu-Nu' (meaning, "Say it rather yourself!")

"My father: 'Nu-O' ("Why not you?")

"The guest: 'O-Nu?' ("Why should I?")

"My Father: 'I-O' ("You first!")

"The guest: 'O-Ai' ("You first!")

"My father: 'E-O-I' ("I beg of you to say it!")

"The guest: 'Ai-O-E' ("I beg of you.")

"My father: 'Ai-O-E-Nu?' ("Why should you refuse?")

"The guest: 'Oi-O-E-Nu-Nu' ("If you insist, I must.")"

This entire chat-in-signs-and-sounds, characteristic of Sholem Aleichem's writing, is used because the two Jews do not want to use
colloquial words at the sacred Passover table.

MINOR POETS

Among the poets of the 19th century, there were some who enjoyed exceptional popularity, but later, with the appearance of the
great Hebrew poets, their fame faded somewhat. A few sentences
about half a dozen of these popular poets whom history judged
minor must suffice.

Eliakum Zunser (1836-1913) was both a folk poet and a folk
singer, a "badhan" (a kind of jester), as he was called. He wrote
poetry in Yiddish and Hebrew. The number of his songs in Yiddish
is more than 600. His Hebrew poems were published in 1861 under
the title Shirim Hadashim (New Songs). Among his most popular
songs are: "Di Sokhe" (The Hook Plow) and "Dos Goldene
Land" (The Golden Land). He appeared as an entertainer at wed-
dings. In 1889 he settled in America.

Judah Lob Levin (1845-1925), known by his pen name Yehalel,
wrote poetry in Hebrew, which was socialistic in tendency. He was
very popular in Russia. In 1883 he translated Disraeli's *Tancred*
into Hebrew under the title Nes La-Goyim (The New Crusade).

Naphtali Herz Imber (1856-1909) is famous as the author of
Ha-Tikwah (The Hope), which became the national Jewish hymn.
His poems were published in two volumes under the title Barkai, in
1877 and in 1899.

M. M. Dolitzki (1858-1931) wrote poetry and prose. A collection
of his poems was published in 1895 and another one in 1899, under the title Kol Shire Menahem (Poetical Works of Menahem). He
settled in the U.S. in 1892.

Mordecai Zevi Manne (1859-1886), a Hebrew poet who died at

the age of twenty-seven, excelled in his description of nature. A collection of his poems and essays on art, under the title Mebasser Ha-Abib (Herald of Spring), was published in Warsaw. Manne was also an able painter.

Simeon Samuel Frug (1860-1916) wrote in three languages: Russian, Yiddish, and Hebrew. For a time he was regarded as the national Jewish poet in Russia. Fond of folk themes, Frug expressed his people's suffering in light verses.

DAVID FRISHMAN
(1861-1922)

Modern Hebrew literature brought forth many essayists and critics, who, each in his own way, contributed to the enrichment of the language and the literature. Space does not permit discussing them all. We mention only one as a sample.

David Frishman—essayist, critic, short story writer, and at times poet—dominated Hebrew literature for almost half a century. His satiric and playful pen was a mighty force in both Hebrew and Yiddish literature. A European in the fullest sense of the word, and seemingly conversant with every trend in the modern world, Frishman demanded true creative ability from all.

Frishman began very early to write both poetry and prose in Hebrew periodicals, and his style and originality of views soon attracted attention. His *Notes On The History of Literature*, a series of essays on contemporary Hebrew literature, made a furor at the time. His feuilletons, published in various periodicals, were always read with interest.

HAYYIM NAHMAN BIALIK
(1873-1934)

Hayyim Nahman Bialik is regarded as the greatest national Jewish poet since Judah Halevi. Born in the village of Radi, in Volhy-

nia (Ukraine), he received a strictly traditional education. Unable
to make a living in the village, the family moved to Zhitomire
(Ukraine), where Bialik's father maintained a tavern, but soon fell
sick and died. The young boy was raised by his grandfather for
several years. At sixteen he was sent to the famous Talmudic academy of Volozhin, where he studied for two years. He was caught
up by the Haskala movement, which was then spreading rapidly
in Russia. Many of the students in Volozhin were clandestinely
reading the Haskala literature in Hebrew. Bialik was fascinated by
the new ideas. He became a Maskil. He wrote poetry which was acclaimed by the students as worthy of being published. His first
printed poem was El Ha-Tzippor (To The Bird), which was an expression of deep craving for Palestine.

In 1900 Bialik settled in Odessa, where he was received by the
local literary circle with enthusiasm and admiration. His name was
already known, because he had succeeded in publishing a number
of his poems during the 1890s. His style, diction, and rhythm were
refreshingly new, impressively original in the coinage of new phrases
and in the richness of his powerful language. He was proclaimed an
ever rising star in the firmament of Hebrew letters, overshadowing
all the Haskala poets of the 19th century.

Precisely at a time when the last great Haskala poet, Leon Gordon, asked the question: "For whom do I toil?" (the title of a
famous poem of his), implying thereby that Hebrew was doomed to
extinction as a result of the people's disinterestedness, Bialik appeared—a powerful poet who brought new life into Hebrew. Bialik
was capable of singing in a still voice and in a melancholy vein as
in his little poem "Alone," or ecstatically portraying nature in all
its beauty; but he was at his best when he addressed his people.
When he looked at the tragic state of Israel he was more than a
poet. He turned into a prophet of old, mighty in his condemnation,
lamenting as Jeremiah and wrathful as Isaiah. In the "City of
Slaughter," written after he had visited Kishenev and had seen the
results of a pogrom, his poetic vehemence came to the fore. Bialik
makes God to say: Why do they submit? Why are they praying for
help? Let them stand up and demand compensation for their degradation. Let them split heaven with their cries. Let them break my
throne with their fists. Never before had a Jewish poet spoken either

to his people or to God Almighty in such terms as Bialik did. It was the outcry of a broken heart. Denouncing the Jews for letting themselves be slaughtered like sheep, he called for heroism in the face of death. There and then, in 1904 Bialik was acclaimed as the poet of liberation, of survival. The poet can hardly understand why the people are taking it lying down, with slavish resistance and submissiveness. Where, he asks, is that sign and poignant outcry of a living creature when its life is at stake?

> And great is the pain, and great is the shame.
> And what is greater? — You say it, son of man!

Bialik is a national poet because he loves Judaism, both Biblical and Talmudic. His pain stems from that love spring. In his poem "Shouldst Thou Wish To Know" he speaks of the "House of Study" as the source from which Israel has obtained courage and power.

"The name of Hayyim Nahman Bialik," writes Menahem Ribalow, a contemporary critic, "became a legend in his lifetime. His span of life was only sixty years, but he exercised a tremendous influence upon his generation. Most of the modern Hebrew poets and writers were guided by the light he shed, studied his poetic style, absorbed his linguistic inventions and accepted him as their mentor."

Bialik was also great as a prose writer, though he was not prolific in this area; but whatever he did write was masterly.

As an admirer of Hebrew poetry of the Golden Age of Spain, Bialik published works of that epoch in new editions. Together with his colleague I. H. Ravnizki, he also edited and published an anthology of the Aggadic parts of the Talmud and Midrash, which became very popular with the general public.

Upon The Slaughter[9]

> Heavenly spheres, beg mercy for me!
> If truly God dwells in your orbit and round,
> And in your space is His pathway that I have not found,
> Then you pray for me!
> For my own heart is dead; no prayer on my tongue;
> And strength had failed, and hope had passed:
> O until when? For How much more, How long?

Oh, headsman, bared the neck—come, cleave it through!
Nape me this cur's nape! Yours is the axe unbaffled!
The whole wide world—my scaffold!
And rest you easy: we are weak and few.
My blood is outlaw. Strike, then; the skull dissever!
Let blood of babe and greybeard stain your garb—
Stain to endure forever!

If right there be, —why let it shine forth now!
For if when I have perished from the earth
The right shine forth,
Then let its throne be shattered, and laid low!
Then let the heavens, wrong-racked, be no more!
—While you, O murderers, on your murder thrive,
Live on your blood, regurgitate this gore!

Who cries revenge! Revenge! —accursed he be!
Fit vengeance for the spilt blood of a child
The devil has not yet compiled.
No, let that blood pierce world's profundity,
Through the great deep pursue its mortifications,
There eat its way in darkness, there undo,
Undo the rotted earth's foundations!

Shouldst Thou Wish To Know[10]

And shouldst thou wish to know the Source
From which thy tortured brethren drew
In evil days their strength of soul
To meet their doom, stretch out their necks
To each uplifted knife and axe,
In flames, on stakes to die with joy,
And with a whisper, 'God is One,'
To close their lips?

And shouldst thou wish to find the Spring
From which thy banished brethren drew,
'Midst fear of death and fear of life,
Their comfort, courage, patience, trust,
An iron will to bear their yoke,

To live bespattered and despised,
And suffer without end?

And shouldst thou wish to see the Lap
Whereon thy people's galling tears
In ceaseless torrents fell and fell,
And hear the cries that moved the hills,
And thrilled Satan with awe and grief,
But not the stony heart of man,
Than Satan's and than rock's more hard?

And shouldst thou wish to see the Fort
Wherein thy fathers refuge sought,
And all their sacred treasures hid,
The Refuge that has still preserved
Thy nation's soul intact and pure,
And when despised, and scorned, and scoffed,
Their faith they did not shame?

And shouldst thou wish to see and know
Their Mother, faithful, loving, kind,
Who gathered all the burning tears
Of her bespattered, hapless sons,
And when to her warm bos'm they came,
She tenderly wiped off their tears,
And sheltered them and shielded them,
And lulled them on her lap to sleep?

If thou, my brother, knowest not
This mother, spring, and lap, and fort,
Then enter thou the House of God,
The House of Study, old and gray,
Throughout the sultry summer days,
Throughout the gloomy winter nights,
At morning, midday, or at eve;
Perchance there is a remnant yet,
Perchance thy eye may still behold
In some dark corner, hid from view,

A cast-off shadow of the past,
The profile of some pallid face,
Upon an ancient folio bent,
Who seeks to drown unspoken woes
In the Talmudic boundless waves;
And then thy heart shall guess the truth
That thou hast touched the sacred ground
Of thy great nation's House of Life,
And that thy eyes do gaze upon
The treasure of thy nation's soul.

And know that this is but a spark
That by a miracle escaped
Of that bright light, that sacred flame,
Thy forebears kindled long ago
On altars high and pure.

SAUL TCHERNIHOWSKY
(1875-1943)

Next to Hayyim Nahman Bialik, Saul Tchernihowsky is regarded as the greatest modern Hebrew poet. Some critics are even inclined to allocate first place to Tchernihowsky. He was born in the Crimea, Russia. He studied medicine at Heidelberg. Very early in his life, Hebrew became the language of his soul, and to it he dedicated most of his efforts. He was recognized as an eminent poet as soon as his first poems appeared.

What Tchernihowsky brought to Hebrew literature was his emphasis on nature, beauty, hedonism, protest. Nature and love go hand in hand in Tchernihowsky's poetry. In his love poems he is different from all other poets in Hebrew literature: his verses are fresh, full of joy, flaming. There is no self-pity in them.

Tchernihowsky is in love with ancient Greece, "the wonderland where beautiful and gentle goddesses" roam. Some critics have crowned him "The Greek" because of his strong tendencies to extol classical Greek literature and Greek "paganism."

The poet shouts: "My people has aged, and with it God Himself became old." Tchernihowsky calls for Israel to come back to mother nature; come, weary and exhausted, ready to embrace life, to celebrate heroism and beauty as at the time of the judges or when Solomon's Song was written. In his poem "From the Visions of the False Prophets" he denounces the great prophets of Israel and champions the so-called false prophets, "to whom the land and the State were more important than all the abstract moral ideals." Indeed, the "true prophets" triumphed, but with their triumph the kingdoms of Judah and Israel perished. Now the Jews must return to the original sources, to nature, where power and not morals rules supreme. This same theme is seen in Tchernihowsky's poem "Before the Statue of Apollo," which shocked many readers. How could a Hebrew poet, the heir of the pious singers of the Golden Age, write such lines:

> I kneel to life, to beauty and to strength,
> I kneel to all the passionate desires,
> Which they, the dead-in-life, the bloodless ones,
> The sick, have stifled in the living God,
> The God of gods, who took Canaan with storm
> Before they bound Him in phylacteries.

In Tchernihowsky's poem "What Blood is Seething Within Me?" we hear the outcry of protest and rebellion. The poet asks whether "the seething blood in his veins" is the blood of those who perished in the Chmelnitzki massacres (1648) in the Ukraine, and he answers: No! Is it the blood of those who died at the stakes in Spain? No! "Because I am not a lamb to be led to the slaughter." It is not even the blood of the Maccabees who fought for religious freedom. What blood is it then? It is the blood of those who grew up in the wilderness of Sinai and marched out to conquer Canaan. Had the children of the desert at the time of Moses been inspired by moral ideals they could have never conquered the Land of Canaan. It was the bare struggle for life that is inherent in any living creature which gave them courage and strength. Hence the Jewish people must return to the pristine sources, if they want to become a people again.

In this respect Tchernihowsky went much further than Bialik. The latter demanded that the Jew stand up against the assailant even when life was at stake. Tchernihowsky envisioned an overall return to pagan times after Israel shook off all the prophetic ideals. Bialik has great admiration for historical Judaism, whereas Tchernihowsky is almost wholly negative. The Judaism of the Diaspora is definitely not to his liking; he blames it for all the misfortunes that occurred to the Jewish people.

Tchernihowsky was also a prolific translator. He translated Homer, Moliere, and Goethe into Hebrew, as well as Longfellow's *Hiawatha* and the difficult Finnish epic *Kalevala*.

Tchernihowsky's own credo poem is open to various interpretations. Some read in it the vigorous humanism he continually espoused. Others say they see that he was, after all, far from "The Greek" poet in whose robes he tried to appear.

I Believe[11]

Laugh on, laugh on at all the dreams
I tell thee as I see,
Laugh on, I still believe in man,
For I still believe in thee.
My soul still longs for liberty,
Unbartered and unsold,
I still have faith in the fate of man,
In his spirit fierce and bold.
His spirit breaks the weight of chains,
Lifts him high overhead;
Work fears not hunger, freedom gives
The soul its daily bread.
I still believe that friendship lives,
That I shall find a heart,
That shares my hopes, to which I can
My joy or grief impart.
I still believe a time will come
Although it be delayed,
When nations shall meet and greet in peace,
Share blessings unafraid.

Then will my people blossom forth
And give birth to a race,
Which freed from shackles, shall behold,
Deliverance face to face.
That lives and loves and toils and strives,
By whom true life is found,
And earthly paradise of light,
That knows not bond or bound.
And bards to come shall wake to songs
Of large and noble sound;
And decked with flowers from my tomb,
Shall rise up newly-crowned.

JACOB COHEN
(1881-1960)

One of the foremost Hebrew poets in Israel, Jacob Cohen [Kahan] was born in Slutsk, Russia. He received a good general and Jewish education. Unable to complete his education in Czarist Russia, he went to Switzerland where he enrolled as a student of philosophy.

A fervent Zionist and Hebraist, Cohen organized in Bern a circle of Lovers of Hebrew under the name "Ivria." Very early in life he was known as a poet; his first collection of poems appeared in 1903. It was received with approbation. Ten years later, in 1913, a second book of poems appeared, and in 1928 a third under the title Ne'urim Undudim (Youth and Wanderings). These works placed him in line with Bialik and Tchernihowsky and Schnaiur.

As an admirer of classical literature, Cohen translated some works of world literature into Hebrew. His superb translations won for him a special place among Hebrew writers.

Endowed with a melodious tone, perfection of style, and a deep love for harmony, Cohen is never as rebellious as Tchernihowsky. Rather he is the poet of the balanced phrase and of the measured word. Some of Cohen's poems are pervaded with a deep craving for the Infinite, a craving bordering on the most profound religious feeling, turning at times into the form of a prayer-like poem. Cohen is also fond of the folk legend and the ballad. His love for the Land of Israel, his affinity with everything sacred to the Jewish heart and mind, and his strivings for redemption of the Jewish soul are his ever-recurring themes. In 1934 Cohen immigrated to Palestine, established his home there, and devoted all his time to the advancement of Hebrew culture.

"The Eternal Jew" is characteristic of Cohen's manner of expressing an idea.

The Eternal Jew[12]

A wandering Jew once met a man
With blood-spattered clothes and an axe in his hand.
The Jew whispered "God!" as he started aback.
The man, too, was startled, his visage grew black.
"Why are you wandering here, Jew?" he cried.
The Jew said his word: "God will always abide."
The man cried in fury: "What whisper you there?"
The Jew made reply: "God is judge, I declare."
He swung up his axe, smote the Jew on his head.
The falling Jew cried: "God avenges the dead!"
Now when that same man to the seashore did go,
The Jew he beheld as he walked to and fro.
Astonished, he cried: "What, are you still alive?"
The Jew made his answer: "In the Lord I do thrive."
He seized on the Jew, flung him into the sea.
The Jew sank, and never a word uttered he.
Now when that same man went forth on the chase,
He found the Jew meeting him, face unto face,
He raged and he shouted: "Alive yet are you!"
"With the aid of the Lord!" responded the Jew.
He took him, a bullet right through him he shot.
The Jew fell; and falling, he called on his God.
That night the man dreamt. And what did he dream?
Before him the Jew stood. Alive he did seem.
He stared at him piercingly, and murmured once more:
"God sees what befalls, He is judge as of yore."
He leapt up to clutch him, he brandished his fist.

The Jew rose in air, and he vanished in mist.
In the morning he heard him knock at his door.
In the evening he saw him still striding before.
He returned in his dreams. He returns to this day.
He troubles him dreaming and waking, they say.
What power is hid in him? What secret at call?
He has "God" on his lips in his rise and his fall.

ZALMAN SCHNAIUR
(1887-1959)

A master of the novel as well as of the poem, Zalman Schnaiur occupies a seat in the front rank of modern Hebrew literature together with Bialik, Tchernihowsky, and Cohen. Bialik characterized him as a "young Samson" whose hair grew in one night. He started to write very young and seemed to have matured at once. Vigorous, passionate, at times even erotic, he brought into Hebrew poetry something new, an individualistic tone. Arrogance instead of humility, strength instead of weakness, sensual joy instead of repression of the emotional life—these are the motifs of Schnaiur's poetry. Emphasis upon the spiritual side of life was not for him. What he liked was a full life, expressive of man's five senses; that was what constituted the overall theme of his poetry.

As a poet Schnaiur was the singer of the "big city," but as a novelist he was the writer of the "small town," reflecting his birth and upbringing in Shklov, Russia. He was fond of describing the simpletons, the uncultivated, the boors, the ill-bred. In his first stories his characters were weak-kneed people, melancholy and somewhat sickly. But he soon turned away from them to the butcher, the builder, the coachman, and all other such strong-bodied Jews, to whom abstractions were meaningless.

In his "People of Shklov" he presented a gallery of characters who took life as it was, men who could love as well as hate. Some charged him as a glorifier of power and ignorance, but Schnaiur also wrote poems replete with the finest ideals of humanism. What he did glorify was normal, down-to-earth life, in contradistinction to super-spiritualization of life. In this sense he was the poet of regeneration. That Schnaiur possesses a delicate feeling, apart from what seems gross and robust, can be seen in such gentle poems as "Elijah the Prophet," "Hanukkah Candles," "To a Star," or "Welcome Queen Sabbath."

Welcome Queen Sabbath[13]

Oh, come let us welcome sweet Sabbath the Queen!
The cobbler abandoned his awl and his thread,
The tailor's brisk needle now sleeps in its bed.
Father has bathed, washed his hair, and he says:
Sweet Sabbath is near,
Sweet Sabbath is here,
Oh, come let us welcome sweet Sabbath the Queen!

The storekeeper locked and bolted his store,
The teamster unbridled his horse at the door,
The sexton runs hither and thither and says:
The sun sets in the sky,
Sweet Sabbath is nigh,
Oh, come let us welcome sweet Sabbath the Queen!

The white-bearded cantor has hastened along
To welcome the Sabbath with blessing and song,
Dear mother is lighting the candles and prays:
Day of holiness, rest,
Forever be blest,
Oh, come let us welcome sweet Sabbath the Queen!

Joseph Klausner characterizes the three foremost Hebrew poets: Bialik admires and extolls the past, Tchernihowsky craves for the future, and Shnaiur is fond of the present. Like Bialik and Tchernihowsky, Shnaiur is at war with God; but while the former two declared war on the God of Israel alone, Shnaiur defies also the God of the Universe.

In his powerful poem, "Under The Tunes of the Mandoline," Shnaiur poses the question: How and why did man lose his sense for the beautiful? And answers it thus: Religion is to blame for it. In another poem, "And It Shall Come to Pass in the Last Days," he negates even the Messianic ideal, the hope for world peace and the hope for absolute equality of man. Yet Shnaiur denounces humanity for robbing Israel of all spiritual riches, and while taking on an air of nobility itself, it placed Israel in a position of a pariah. He therefore calls upon his people to return to "the sun" and to the land that lies devasted. In his lyric poem, "In the Mountains," he bewails the son of the ghetto who has been alienated from the "free mountain air." But even in this poem, Shnaiur uses many universal ideas. Due to his general motives, Shnaiur stands squarely in line with the great European poets.[14]

OTHER WRITERS

Solomon Bloomgarden (Yehoash) (1870-1927) was a noted scholar, poet, and Bible translator. He made a significant contribution to Jewish culture in general and to the cultural history of American Jewry in particular. Yehoash settled in the United States in 1890 and for the first ten years in this country he was engaged in business. In 1900 he entered a sanitarium for the treatment of tuberculosis. From that time on he devoted all his free time to writing and publishing. He wrote verse, short stories, essays, and fables in Yiddish and some articles in English. His poems were translated into Russian, Dutch, Polish, Finnish, German, and Spanish, as well as into English and Hebrew. After having visited with his family in Israel in 1914, Yehoash wrote a three-volume work in which he described his trip and his impressions of Palestine. It was later translated into English under the title *The Feet of the Messenger*. A Hebrew version appeared subsequently. Yehoash also enriched Jewish literature with his translations of Jewish and non-Jewish masterpieces, including portions of the Koran, classical Arabic writings, and Sayings of the Fathers (Pirke Aboth). His major work, however, to which he dedicated most of his time was the translation of the Bible into Yiddish. To this task he brought great scholarship and literary skill. His research in producing the most authoritative as well as the most literal translation was enormous. A special volume of his notes was later published. He considered his Bible translation as his life's contribution to Jewish culture. In his introduction he declared that he been given a chance of living three times as long, he would have devoted all his time to this work. He was also co-author with Dr. O. D. Spivak of a dictionary of the Hebrew and Chaldaic elements of the Yiddish language, illustrated with proverbs and idiomatic expressions.

S. Ben Zion (S. Gutmann) (1870-1932) specialized in writing about the Jewish youth, particularly children. His writings were replete with love for historic Judaism and its spiritual values. He described masterfully the suffering of the finer type of Jew under the cruel regime of the Czars.

I. Bershadski (1871-1908) was an outstanding novelist, a realist. His two novels, B'ein Mattarah (Without an Aim) and Negged Hazerem (Against the Current), won for him immediate recognition. In the first he described a godless man, one without principles, whose sole interest was to gratify his lust. In the second novel the principal hero was a Maskil who tried to raise his children in a nationalist-religious spirit, and failed. Bershadski's descriptive powers were superb.

Mordecai Ze'eb Feierberg (1874-1899) died prematurely at twenty-four years of age, but succeeded in making a name for himself by virtue of his individualistic stories, such as "Whither?" and "In The Evening," in which he described the innermost problems of the modernized Jew. Feierberg was a true disciple of Ahad Ha-Am, that is, a cultural Zionist.

Uri Nissan Gnessin (1879-1913) was a powerful writer whose life was cut off prematurely; yet he succeeded in making his mark in literature. Having lived for years under the shadow of death as a very sick man, Gnessin's works are pervaded with melancholy—his characters being almost all children of the twilight, on the borderline between life and death. The titles of some of his stories impress us with their abruptness: "Between," "Before," "To the Side."

A. A. Kabak (1880-1945) was a great writer, well read and beloved by Hebrew readers both in Israel and in other lands. Among his many novels there is one titled Bamishal Hazar (The Narrow Path), in which he portrays life in the first century in Palestine at the time of Jesus.

Sholem Asch (1880-1966)—novelist, dramatist, essayist—was one of the leading Jewish writers of the 20th century. Born in Kutno, Poland, he received a general Jewish education. As a young man he came to Warsaw to see I. L. Peretz, who recognized in Asch a promising talent. Asch wrote both Hebrew and Yiddish and soon showed himself to be a master in both. Later, like many others of his generation, he dedicated himself to Yiddish alone. His novels: *Motke Ganov* (Motke the Thief), *Dos Shtetl* (The Small Town), *Di Mutter* (The Mother), and others, won for him a large readership. His dramas: *Kiddush Hashem* (Sanctification of God's Name), *Got fun Nekomo* (God of Vengeance), and others were very popular. His works were translated into almost all modern languages. His dramas were performed on the stages of the world. Some of his books were "best sellers" in America. Asch became the most widely read Jewish writer of the 20th century. A break in his life came when he published *The Nazarene*, a novel about Jesus, which aroused Jewish public opinion against him, because the portrayal, the critics said, did not give a true picture of the time and the role of the Nazarene. Asch continued to write other Christ-centered works: *The Apostle, Mary, East River*. He emigrated to Israel in his old age and settled in Bath Yam. He died suddenly during a visit to London.

Gershon Schoffman (1880-1971) was a master in portraying loneliness, especially that of the young who found themselves uprooted by the exigencies of war and related calamities. With deep psychological insight, Schoffman, in his novels and short sketches, delved into the souls of his characters. In his stories there was much sorrow and hopelessness. His characters seemed to have drifted away from their native shore, without reaching another shore.

J. H. Brenner (1881-1921) was an essayist-critic and novelist. He portrayed the aimlessness of Jewish life in the Diaspora. An uncompromising critic of the old order of things, he demanded basic changes. In his novels, stories, and essays one sensed the agony of the true idealist. He described the anomalies of Jewish life, the poverty and darkness and ignorance of the Jewish masses, and the decadence of the Jewish intelligentsia. Brenner portrayed the ghetto of London, where he lived for years, in the saddest colors. He settled in Israel as a pioneer, but even there he did not find what he was looking for. At long last this suffering writer and idealist found a kind of peace in the soil of Israel which he loved so dearly: he was murdered by an Arab terrorist. His impact upon the youth of Israel was great; he became a symbol of true idealism.

Isaac Dov Berkowitz (1885-1967) was a master of both Hebrew and Yiddish. With deep sympathy and warmth he described the struggle between parents and sons at a period when traditional Jewish life was crumbling. Berkowitz's stories are particulary distinguished by their classic perfection and sparing style in which every word seems to have just its proper place.

HEBREW LITERATURE IN ISRAEL

Since the last quarter of the 19th century, when the agricultural resettlement in Palestine (Israel) started, a new center of literary activity was established there, apart from the old European centers like Wilna, Warsaw, Odessa, and others. The Israel center grew with the new emigrants who settled there. Historians see this emigration to Palestine, prior to the establishment of the State of Israel, as occurring in stages or waves. The Hebrew name for emigrating to Israel is Aliyah (ascend). Dates vary slightly among historians, but generally five Aliyot are recognized. For example: 1882-1904, 1905-1914, 1919-1923, 1924-1928, 1929-1936.

The first Aliyah consisted mostly of dreamers and pioneers, who, disappointed in the Haskala, left Europe in order to rebuild Jewish life in Palestine. They established the first important foothold for the Jewish people in their ancient homeland.

The second Aliyah consisted in the main of people who wanted to establish not only a Jewish settlement in Palestine, but a Jewish settlement founded upon Jewish labor and social justice.

The third Aliyah, which came in the wake of the holocaust in

Europe, consisted of homeless and destitute people who needed a haven of refuge.

With each wave of emigration there came writers, educators, and leaders, who contributed to the growth and development of Hebrew literature. The revival of Hebrew as a living language became during that long period a fact of life. A basic Hebrew educational system was established. A lively and energetic press appeared. Hebrew literature in Israel came of age and displayed its great potentialities. The most talented forces of Jewry, unable to exist in the Diaspora, escaped into Israel and joined hands with those who carried on the struggle for spiritual survival.

Presently the greatest Hebrew cultural center is to be found in Israel, particularly so since the old centers in eastern Europe were destroyed by the ruthless Nazi regime of Germany.

Space does not permit to discuss in detail every significant writer in Israel of today. The best that one can do is to give the reader a quick view of present-day literary activity in this newly established and still growing center.

SAMUEL JOSEPH AGNON
(1888-1970)

One of the foremost Hebrew novelists in Israel, Samuel Joseph Agnon occupies a special place among contemporary writers. He is the first Hebrew writer to have received the Nobel Prize for literature (1966). In 1937 he received the Bialik Prize.

Agnon was born in Buczacz, Galicia, into a pious Jewish family, and true to his upbringing remained a traditional Jew in the fullest sense of the word: observant to the letter and spirit of the Law, humble and reserved, a lover of the Land of Israel, a man of peace with the world and himself.

His family name, Czarkes, was changed to Agnon long ago, probably as early as 1907, when he emigrated to Palestine. In 1913 he left Palestine and tarried in Europe until 1924. That year he returned to Jerusalem where he established his permanent home.

Agnon is a masterful portrayer of Jewish life in eastern Europe, especially in Galicia, succeeding in bringing to light a whole gallery of types. His best features are folkishness, deep sympathy, and a charming naivité. He is a narrator of great power and ability in his unique way, coupled with a style which is wholly his own, reminding one often of the tales found in the Midrash. His style and structure differ in many respects from the usual literary forms. His tales are so simple and close to the manner people tell a story that it seems as though one listens to a friend relaying what he has just seen or experienced.

One of his best novels is Hahnasath Kallah, published in English under the name *Bridal Canopy*, in which he describes a Jew named Reb Yudel, a father of three daughters who, traveling over Galicia to look for a bridegroom, comes in contact with many people and situations. Reb Yudel emerges from Agnon's pen as a character of inner strength, a man of integrity, imbued with trust in God and confidence in the goodness of man. Agnon illumines his story with his wise humor, little sparks of insight, and characteristic lightness. In fact, he succeeds in resurrecting an entire world which passed long ago, a world with all its shadows and light.

Agnon's glaring stylistic feature is his folkishness. Admiring simple, honest-to-goodness faith, he portrays characters that go through life unscathed by virtue of their deep trust in God. "Reb Yudel," writes Agnon, "completely ignored all his sufferings. Having filled his soul with Torah, he converted his life into a chariot for God's Presence, and having decorated his soul with good deeds, he rejected the troubles of the world." Reb Yudel's innermost wisdom consisted in accepting the world as it was. His was a world ruled and directed by a mighty Master. In a planless world fear would lurk in every corner, but not in God's world. Here one might turn to the Master and ask for help.

In another novel, *And the Crooked Shall Become Straight*, Agnon describes a man who, having fallen into the mire of sin, struggles with his fate. But even in this character there glisten sparks of gentleness. Apparently Agnon cannot see the world otherwise.

Agnon is the author of other novels: Agunot (Forsaken Wives) Gibe'at Ha-Hol (Sandy Hill), and others. He also wrote numerous short stories. From time to time Agnon inserts moral precepts into his story, but he does it so casually that it is integrated into the story; it comes naturally, seemingly with little effort.

Agnon grew up in an atmosphere in which thère was much hostility between Hasidim and Mitnaggedim. Yet to him both sides represented human life striving to attain fulfillment. It is reported that when Agnon lived in Europe he met Martin Buber, who, engrossed at that time in studying the Hasidic way of life, exerted a strong influence upon him by bringing him closer to Hasidism. It might have been true to a degree. Yet Agnon portrayed the anti-Hasidic Jew in the same colorful manner as he portrayed the Hasid. The following might perhaps serve as an illustration of Agnon's approach:

> The house of Reb Abigdor was illuminated. The candles were shedding their light. The table was covered with a white and clean cloth. In order to commemorate the destruction of Jerusalem, a part of the table had been left uncovered. The servant brought a pitcher of water and bowl. They all washed their hands, wiping them off with the towel the servant carried on his shoulder. The Rabbi then pronounced the blessing on the bread and all of them repeated after him. This was a demonstration of man's clinging to God in humility and a rejection of the last bit of false pride and arrogance. The Rabbi expounded a difficult passage in Maimonides' Code and all listened to him in silence. The cantor chanted a prayer, and every one pronounced Amen after him. After having completed the meal, they again recalled Jerusalem and the destruction of the Temple. They all chanted the psalm, "At The Rivers of Babylonia." The Rabbi put on an upper white mantle, took the glass of wine in his right hand, and thanked the Creator loudly, carefully, and word for word, for no man should display his pride of being satiated while standing before God.[15]

OTHER PROSE WRITERS

Shloime Zemah (1886-   ), in short stories and novels, portrayed the characters and scenes of Jewish life in Israel at the turn of the century. His novel *Elijah Margolit* presents us with a good picture of various types of Jewish intelligentsia.

Aaron Re'ubeni (1886-1971) was a poet, a critic, and a novelist. We remember him most as a novelist, especially in terms of his powerful trilogy, a presentation of life in Israel during World War I. Re'ubeni was a realist and a keen observer of life.

Judah Burla (1886-1969) is noted for bringing eastern folklore into Hebrew literature. His novels focused around Sephardic Jews and eastern Jewish life.

Isaac Shami (1888-1948) also portrayed the life of the Sephardic Jews. This literary task contributed to better understanding among the Jews who had come together in Israel from so many different lands.

Asher Barash (1889-1952) was one of the outstanding novelists in Israel, where he was rooted in the land for over forty years. He combined a notion of art with the ethical ideals of the prophets which resulted in a vigorous and optimistic outlook on life.

The characters in the work of Dov Kimhi (1889-1961) are opposites to the life of Asher Barash himself. They come from various countries, but they fail to put down roots in Israel. Kimhi himself deeply admired the true pioneers of Israel, especially the youth, but he chose to write about those who had no anchor in life.

Eliezer Steinman (1892-1970), in an attempt to illumine the dark recesses of his characters' souls, based his novels largely on a study of psychoanalysis, an area rarely touched by Hebrew writers before him. Steinman was also an anthologist of Hasidic stories and teachings.

Hayyim Hazaz (1897-   ), master novelist, reveals with deep understanding a different type of Jew: the Yemenite, the Jew from the Arab world. Originally from Russia, Hazaz, in his earlier work, graphically describes the Russian Revolution, an upheaval he himself lived through. Through all his novels, Hazaz displays a special humor, light and heart-warming.

Aaron Feldman (1899-   ), writing under the name Ever Ha-Dani, concentrates upon the pioneers and the collectives (K'vutzot, Kibbutzim), dealing with the problems of men and women who are in the process of adapting to a new and a communal life.

Johanan Twersky (1900-1967), novelist and biographer, is

noted for his treatment of a number of historic Jewish figures. Twersky settled in Israel in 1947.

Jacob Horowitz (1901-   ) is a first-rate novelist and short story writer. Though he handles 20th century life admirably in his work, he is especially fond of portraying historic events from Jewish history. His characters are strong-willed, often extremists.

S. Yizhar is the pen name for Izhar Smilansky (1918-   ), popular novelist, whose works have found acclaim especially among the youth of Israel.

Novelist Moishe Shamir (1921-   ) is also widely read by the people. Typical of his writings is Melekh Bassar We-Dam (A King, Man of Flesh and Blood), which has as its principal hero King Alexander Janneus of Judea (100 B.C.A.), in whom Shamir finds an ambitious ruler, an empire builder.

POETS

Jacob Fichman (1881-1958) was a critic, essayist, and poet, who settled in Israel after World War I. A native of Bessarabia, the fertile province in Southern Russia, he sings of golden fields, of vineyards and orchards, of plants trembling in the breeze of still afternoons. He is the poet of tranquility, gentleness, and rapturous prayer. As a poet of quietness, he is at his best when he sings of Biblical figures. Ruth, David, Joab, Samson fascinate him, because he is fond of being transported into the world of nature and the primitive approach to life. Fichman leaves the noise of the city, the stone dwellings of man, to be embraced by the vast expanses of nature which opens its heart to him. He is an individualist who seems happiest when alone; solitude enables him to be carried away upon the wings of fantasy. When the European holocaust occurred and the desperate cries of his brethren for help reached his ears, even Fichman lost some of his quietude and burst out in a Jeremiad, lamenting the fate of his people. Yet he will likely be remembered more as the poet of peace of mind, of the "still small voice." As Reuben Wallenrod writes, "Unlike the majestic visions of

Tchernihowsky, Kahan [Cohen] and Schnaiur, his visions are of a quiet afternoon on an autumn day, the rustle of breezes, the longing of the human heart."[16]

David Shimonowitz or Shimoni (1886-1956) came to Israel as a man of twenty-one. Energetic and courageous, he enrolled as a member of Hashomer, the organization of Jewish voluntary guards, whose avowed task was to patrol the vineyards and the fields of the Jewish settlers against Arab marauders, who often came at night to destroy the crops and the vines by fire. Shimoni went through all the hazardous experiences of the early pioneers, who had come to redeem the soil with the sweat of their brow, ever ready to sacrifice their life upon the altar of their ideal. During those sleepless nights, the young poet learned to cherish everything which the land offered. He became an integral part of the landscape, a son of nature, the idyllic poet of Israel. His peaceful tone and melodious rhythm were of a wayfarer, who, having been driven out from his native land, wandered about homeless for many years—then suddenly fortune smiled upon this sorely tried wanderer and he found himself at home. To Shimoni, Israel was that long abandoned but newly found home. Every brook, every hill, every valley became his own, something very close to his heart which pulsated with exaltation and good will.

Jacob Steinberg (1887-1948), in contrast to Fichman and Shimoni, reminds one of Ecclesiastes with his "vanity of vanities; all is vanity." He is a skeptic. Everything he sees carries the hues of decay and dissolution. Time-hallowed Jewish optimism and the old faith in God are gone altogether. Even the Land of Israel has no fascination for Steinberg, although he arrived there in his youth.

There is perhaps no better representative of the Jewish pioneering spirit than the tender lyric poetess known as Rachel (1890-1931), who came to Israel to carry on her shoulder "basket, spade, and rake" — to dedicate herself to the ideal of restoring a land for her people. She did labor in the fields, but sick with tuberculosis she died prematurely with love in her heart for the land and the people come alive. In her poetry, Rachel expressed the most profound feelings of a Daughter of Zion. The youth of Israel picked up her words and soon special melodies were composed for some of them;

they are being sung all over Israel today. These two short poems, even in English translation, capture the cravings of Rachel's gentle heart:

Kinnereth[17]

It may be these things never did occur.
Perhaps, somehow,
I never did arise at break of day
To do my labor in the garden
With the sweat of my brow;

Did never, in the long and fiery days
Of harvest time,
High on the wagon, laden with its sheaves,
Lift up my voice in rhyme;

Did never bathe within the blue
And quiet of thy stream,
O my Kinnereth, O Kinnereth mine!
Were you, indeed? Or did I dream a dream?

Dawn[18]

A jug of water in the hand, and on
My shoulder— Basket, spade, and rake.
To distant fields—to toil—my path I make.
Upon my right, the great hills fling
Protecting arms; before me—the wide fields!
And in my heart, my twenty Aprils sing. . .
Be this my lot, until I be undone:
Dust of thy road, my land, and thy
Grain waving golden in the sun!

In contrast to Rachel is Uri Zevi Greenberg (1894-   ), a fiery poet of protest and denunciation. He is always seeing before his eyes the gallows, the knife, the axe. His powerful and agonized out-cries protest against what the civilized world has done to the Jew during the centuries, including modern times. He is merciless in his prophetic tirades; he condemns, accuses, blames humanity.

Isaac Lamdan (1899-1954) is Israel's poet of work and rehabilitation. When one reads his poetry, he feels as though Lamdan were so engrossed in the process of building Israel that he had no time for love, nature, or personal desires: Time was short and the work was heavy and pressing, so the poet must dedicate himself to the needs of the hour and not indulge in little things which seem important when life is streaming in its normal channels.

Abraham Shlonski (1900-   ) came to Israel after World War I as a Hahalutz and joined the hundreds of young men who dedicated their lives to the resurrection of the then malaria-infested Valley of Jezreel, draining swamps and building roads. Shlonski's poetry is colorful, dynamic, stormy. It reflects both the inferno of pogroms and revolution during the years of civil war in Russia and the struggle and disappointments inherent in rebuilding a devastated land. Shlonski seems to write under a great pressure, feverishly as it were. One senses the same pace as in Lamdan. There is no time left; the work must be done quickly. Shlonski had left his parents, his relatives, his friends in the Diaspora; his people must be saved from the Valley of Tears and Blood. And the Land of Israel is the only haven of refuge left in the world.

רשי | 15

MODERN SAGES

The essence of the Jewish concept of life seems to me to be the affirmation of life for all creatures. For the life of the individual has meaning only in the service of enchanting and ennobling the life of every living thing. Life is holy; i.e., it is the highest worth on which all other values depend. The sanctification of the life which transcends the individual brings with it reverence for the spiritual, a peculiarly characteristic trait of Jewish tradition.

There remains, however, something more in the Jewish tradition, so gloriously revealed in certain of the psalms; namely, a kind of drunken joy and surprise at the beauty and incomprehensible sublimity of this world, of which man can attain but a faint intimation. It is the feeling from which genuine research draws its intellectual strength, but which also seems to manifest itself in the song of birds. This appears to me the loftiest content of the God-idea.

Albert Einstein (1879-1955)

528

MOSES HESS
(1812-1875)

Moses Hess was one of those early Jewish visionaries who fore-
saw and foretold the rehabilitation of Palestine as a Jewish homeland before political Zionism appeared upon the world scene. As
early as 1862, in his work *Rome and Jerusalem*, Hess laid the
foundation of Jewish nationalism by proposing colonization in
Palestine. According to him, Judaism is a combination of nationalism and religion; furthermore, Biblical religion has had from the
very beginning a world outlook and was destined to be embraced
by humanity as a whole.

> The Bible begins with the Creation of the world and the de-
> claration of the natural Sabbath, but the prophets went fur-
> ther and completed the process, embracing as they did the
> entire history of human development and foreseeing the
> final historical Sabbath.

This "historical Sabbath" is, according to Hess, the Messianic Age.

As he views the history of humanity during the last three thousand years, Hess sees three thought currents or viewpoints: the
Greek, the Jewish, the Christian. The Greeks sanctified and worshiped nature in their religious cult "in its finished and harmoni-
ous form." Their culture was therefore primarily static. This was
the reason they excelled in the plastic arts. In philosophy they
searched for the systematic interpretation of the world. The Jews,
on the other hand, deified *becoming*; they worshiped "the God
whose very name expressed past, present and future." They were
striving after organic and cosmic unity.[1] The Christian standpoint,
though an offshoot of Judaism, based its world outlook upon the
idea of the salvation of the individual, whereby it committed both
an act of justice and an act of injustice. Aspiring to extend individual salvation to man, it placed him spiritually outside nature, history, country, and nation. This was a contradiction in
terms. For how could man stand alone in his relationship to God?
This cleavage was unfortunate for both humanity and Christianity.
Only total and absolute Unity would in the end bridge the gap.

Only Judaism has succeeded in upholding the highest unity of
man, world, and God—the unity that pervades both the organic

and cosmic universe and is destined to become the faith of the future.

The realization of this higher unity can be possible only by viewing the Jewish historical religion in a scientific manner. The religion which will be raised to a science is none other than the Bible religion, which preaches the genesis and the unity of cosmic, organic, and social life, and to the development and dissemination of which the genius of the Jews after their regeneration as an independent nation will be devoted.

Thus Hess arrives at the conclusion that the Jewish people, in order to be able to play their part in world history, must return to their original national homeland.

The Jewish nation still preserves the fruitful seed of life, which, like the grains of corn found in the graves of Egyptian mummies, though buried for thousands of years, have never lost their power of productivity; the moment the rigid form in which it is enclosed is shattered, the seed, placed in the fertile soil of the present environment and given air and light, will strike root and blossom forth. . . .It is only with the national rebirth that the religious genius of the Jews, like the giant of legend touching mother earth, will be endowed with new strength and again be reinspired with the prophetic spirit.

Rome and Jerusalem comprised twelve letters addressed to a lady. Hess' leading ideas were that the Jews are a people entitled to obtain the status of nationhood and their return to their original homeland in Palestine would be of mutual benefit to both the Jewish people and humanity. Hess was one of the most gifted opponents of Reform Judaism, which had proclaimed its credo that the Jews were no more than a religious minority with no national aspirations ever to rebuild Palestine. Life and history have indeed partly corroborated Moses Hess' analysis of Jewish history, as we can readily see today in the existence and growth of the State of Israel with its almost three million Jews and its cultural and political development as a national entity.

ISAAC HIRSCH WEISS
(1815-1905)

Isaac Weiss was born in Moravia and settled in Vienna in 1858. He is known as a Talmudic scholar and literary historian. He was influenced by the writings of Nahman Krochmal and Leopold Zunz and had strong Haskala sympathies. Weiss subjected many classic Judaic works to his rigorous critical and linguistic treatment, yet he was a traditionalist in many ways. He ever insisted that modern concepts not be read back into the words of ancient rabbis. He strongly defended the unity of the Pentateuch and its Mosaic authorship. He also provided his people with some very talented biographical sketches of key figures in Jewish history: Abba Arika, Saadia Gaon, Maimonides, Rashi. Weiss' major work was his history of the Talmud, Dor Dor We-Dorshow (Every Generation and Its Interpreters), a history of the Oral Law from Biblical times through the Middle Ages. This study quickly became a standard work and exerted a lasting influence over generations of scholars.

MORITZ STEINSCHNEIDER
(1816-1907)

Moritz Steinschneider was born in Prossnitz, Moravia. Well versed in the Talmud, he could have aspired to be a rabbi. Steinschneider, however, was more interested in research work. He studied languages and became proficient in Arabic, Syriac, French, and Italian. Very early in life he translated the Koran into Hebrew and collaborated with Franz Delitzsch, the famous German Bible scholar, in editing Aaron ben Elijah's work Ez Hayyim (Tree of Life). At the same time he contributed scientific articles to Pierer's *Universal Encyclopedia* and to Gruber's *German Encyclopedia of Science and Arts*. In his research work in the field of Judaism, Steinschneider was particularly interested in the contribution of Jews to medicine, philology, mathematics, natural history.

Steinschneider's fame, however, is as a bibliographer. He was the greatest bibliographer in Jewish history of Hebrew literature and the first to present a systematic survey of Jewish literature through the end of the 18th century. His monumental catalog of Hebrew books and manuscripts in the Bodleian Library at Oxford, a work of thirteen years, initially established his name in a field which he easily dominated. He also cataloged Hebrew books and manuscripts in the large public libraries of Berlin, Hamburg, Leyden, and Munich. He founded, and edited for over twenty years, the periodical *Hebräische Bibliographie* (Hebrew Bibliography). In addition, he compiled a complete bibliography of Hebrew translations of the Middle Ages. All of these works—books, journals, articles—represent an almost inexhaustible source of information on any branch of Jewish literature or history.

HEINRICH GRAETZ
(1817-1891)

The reawakening of the Jewish national consciousness, the searching after solutions to the Jewish problem in many lands, the period of enlightenment and rethinking of traditions—all these 19th-century trends contributed to a renewed interest in the history of the Jews. The 19th century saw many eminent scholars, Jewish and non-Jewish, delving into the rich past of Jewish life. Isaac Marcus Jost (1793-1860), Leopold Zunz, and numerous others did much research and writing.

It remained for Heinrich Graetz, in a heroic one-man effort, to pull together a complete history of the Jewish people from the earliest times to the 19th century. His eleven-volume *Geschichte der Juden* (History of the Jews) was acclaimed and criticized, but it was in any event tremendously influential. Indeed, Graetz's history did suffer from shortcomings. He was not at all consistently objective. For example, his own lack of sympathy for Cabala and Hasidism showed distinctly. There were other biases. And there were numerous inaccuracies. Furthermore, Graetz sometimes seemed to be too sentimental and emotionally involved. He also minimized economic and social factors in history, and practically ignored—except negatively—Judaism in eastern Europe. Nevertheless, Graetz's *Geschichte* was a major and significant event of the 19th century, and was appropriately translated into English, French, Hebrew, and Yiddish.

HERMANN COHEN
(1842-1918)

Hermann Cohen, founder of the so called "Marburg School" of neo-Kantianism and one of the foremost philosophers in Germany, was in the early days of his career somewhat critical of religion, although as the son of a cantor he grew up in a strictly traditional atmosphere. His father wanted him to become a rabbi and in 1859 Hermann enrolled as a student in the Jewish Theological Seminary at Breslau. After two years of study, he decided to devote his time to philosophy. He rejected traditional Judaism as no more than an ancient set of ceremonies, devoid of intrinsic value in modern life.

In the field of philosophy, Cohen showed himself to be a thinker in his own right. His interpretations of Plato and Kant attracted the attention of the philosophical world. In the year 1873, he was invited to join the faculty at the University of Marburg, where he served close to forty years. There Cohen was very productive as a writer, teacher, and philosopher. As an interpreter of Kantian philosophy, he was second to none. He also worked on his own system of philosophy. All those years he was indifferent to Judaism. But in the year 1881, a radical change occurred in his life as a result of the venomous anti-Semitism that appeared then in the academic circles of Germany. From then on Cohen painstakingly and wholeheartedly returned to Judaism. The religious Jewish philosophy of the Middle Ages, particularly Maimonides, interested him greatly. With new vigor he returned to the Bible which he had studied in Hebrew in his boyhood. Aided by his profound knowledge of philosophy, he found in the Bible more than he had ever expected.

In his new study of Judaism, Cohen arrived at the conclusion that there exist two realms which a thinking human being must take account of: the realm of nature, which he called the "realm of being"; and the realm of values, where religion and ethics set the standard. These two realms have only one connecting link: the concept of God. This was essentially what Judaism had given the world long ago: God as the Creator of nature and God as the standard of ethical life.

Questions as to the existence and the essence of God, which are purely metaphysical in form and content, have never preoccupied the Jewish mind, except at times when Judaism was forced to defend itself against outside cultures—as at the time of Philo in a confrontation with Hellenism, or in the Middle Ages when it came face to face with Arab-Greek philosophy. Neither in Biblical nor in Talmudic times had Jews been engaged in elaborating philosophical systems per se. What really concerned the Jewish mind was to maintain a link between man and God. That link was the Law, the Torah. Fulfilling the precepts of the Torah was tantamount to imitating the higher virtues ascribed to God. The Law was the Way leading toward God, the path to ever closer perfection. The aim of a higher moral life was to enhance the Good and the Holy in the world, whereby the Messianic Age and the Kingdom of God would become a reality. By proclaiming God's Uniqueness and Oneness, and by santification of His name in the form of sacrificing limb and life for His law, Jews hoped to bring about the redemption of Israel and the redemption of the world.

Cohen's conception of Judaism stands, therefore, upon three pillars: Creation, Revelation, and Messianism, but his interpretation of those concepts differ from the traditional one. Whereas creation was generally conceived as an event that had occurred once, and the Sinaitic revelation was taken as an experience of the far distant past, Cohen re-interpretated them as ever-recurring and constantly evolving events. The Sinaitic revelation was a "beginning," just as the "beginning" that stands at the origin of the world. The process, however, goes on. Wherever and whenever a new truth is proclaimed it is really a recurrence of revelation. Likewise, God reveals Himself in an infinite process of creation. This is what is clearly expressed in the Jewish prayer which is recited every morning: "He renews daily His work of Creation." This is the *becomingness* of Moses Hess.

Cohen's conception of Judaism greatly influenced the thoughts of Franz Rosenzweig and Martin Buber, who regarded themselves as his disciples, though they found their own paths in their approach to Judaism. Due to his emphasis on Messianism, Cohen was opposed to political Zionism. To him, Israel's mission could only be fulfilled in dispersion among the nations instead of in a political state of their own.

ASHER GINZBERG (AHAD HA-AM)
(1856-1927)

Born in the small town of Skvira, Ukraine, Asher Ginzberg was raised in an ultra-Orthodox home. From his early childhood he displayed exceptional ability both in Talmudic and secular subjects. Like many of the young men of his generation he was caught up with the Haskala movement. His father, a fervent Hasid, opposed it, but nothing availed him. Later in his life Ginzberg settled in Odessa, the great commercial harbor on the Black Sea, which was at that time a center for Maskilim. He joined the Odessa Committee of Hobbei Zion (Lovers of Zion), organized for the purpose of helping to establish Jewish colonies in Palestine. He soon became one of the guiding members of the Committee.

Writing under the name Ahad Ha-Am, Ginzberg became one of the foremost Jewish thinkers of the 19th century and is credited with being the father of the modern Hebrew essay. Never before had the Hebrew reader been given the chance of reading such well-balanced, soberly written, concentrated essays as Ahad Ha-Am produced.

Initially, in the late 1880s, Ginzberg wrote a number of essays, but did not dare send them to any periodical in or outside Russia. Finally, persuaded by a friend, he submitted a manuscript to Ha-Melitz, the oldest Hebrew periodical in Czarist Russia. Prompted by a combination of modesty—he was a clerk in the Wissotzky Tea Company in Odessa—and apprehension about the reaction his essay might evoke, Ginzberg did not sign his own name, but called himself Ahad Ha-Am (one of the people). In 1889, Ahad Ha-Am's first published essay appeared in Ha-Melitz. The article, "Lo Ze Haderek" (This Is Not the Way), caused a furor in the nationalist Jewish circles in Russia. Ahad Ha-Am's central idea was that the national rehabilitation of the Jewish people in their ancient homeland must be preceded by, or at least must go hand in hand with, a cultural and spiritual renaissance. In order to generate such a revival it would be necessary to form small groups of zealous adherents of the idea, groups which would reawaken the consciousness of the people. Such an organization began that very year under the name B'ne Moishe, and continued for eight years.

The return of the Jewish people to Palestine was, according to Ahad Ha-Am, a historic necessity. This movement is not a result of anti-Semitism, he said; it is rather a product of Israel's internal life. The ingathering of all Jews was, Ahad Ha-Am argued, impossible at that time. Consequently, one had to talk not of a State, but of a Cultural Center. In order to bring about a true national regeneration it was necessary to prepare the Jewish people for such a change. The tools to be employed in this work were education and literature. Hebrew literature therefore had a task to perform, namely, to awaken the Jewish consciousness and remove certain defects in the national soul of Israel, defects that had accumulated as a result of the long exile among the nations and as a result of the ghetto conditions. Such changes, however, were impossible without a national spiritual center in Israel, a center that would eventually lead all the Jewish communities in the world. Ahad Ha-Am was more concerned with the survival of Judaism than with the survival of the Jews. Of course, a "Cultural Center" established in Palestine might be the beginning of an organized political state, but this was a matter for the future.

From 1889 to 1902, Ahad Ha-Am published many essays on various topics of Jewish history and philosophy. His interpretations of history were thought provoking and novel. Soon recognized as the foremost essayist in Hebrew, he became a genuine force in modern Hebrew literature. Most of his essays appeared in Kaweret

(Beehive), a publication devoted to Zionism; Ha-Shiloah, a monthly Hebrew magazine which Ahad Ha-Am edited; and Ha-Pardes (Orchard). In 1902, his essays were collected and published in two volumes by the Ahiasaf Society of Warsaw under the title Al Parashat Derakim (On the Crossroads).

Notwithstanding — perhaps because of — Ahad Ha-Am's opposition to Theodor Herzl's political Zionism, he participated in the first Zionist Congress of Basel in 1897. He argued his case for cultural Zionism. In the years prior to World War I, politics and diplomacy seemed hopeless options for many Jews, and Ahad Ha-Am's following was large, especially among the Jewish intelligentsia: His philosophy of Judaism seemed more logical than Herzl's; his teaching appeared rooted in reality. During World War I, Ahad Ha-Am, still opposing political Zionism, nevertheless served in 1917 as a consultant to the Zionist leaders in London negotiating the Balfour Declaration. Hayyim Weizmann, president of the World Zionist Organization at that time, considered himself a disciple of Ahad Ha-Am. In 1922, Ahad Ha-Am himself settled in Palestine; he died in Tel Aviv.

Ahad Ha-Am's interpretations of Jewish history, his deep insight into the life of his people, his insistence upon cultural and spiritual regeneration instead of politics, have won for him a high position among the Jewish thinkers of our time. Some of his more important essays have been translated into Russian, German, and English and have been widely read and commented upon. Here are five sample ideas from Ahad Ha-Am's essays:

> Any new idea, whether religious or moral, cannot be sustained in life unless there be a group of zealots willing and ready to dedicate their lives to it.

> When a land is destroyed but the people are alive, there comes Ezra or Nehemiah and rebuilds it. When a people is destroyed—who can come to help it?

> The two basic elements in man, the material and the spiritual, can live together, when the spiritual part uplifts the material. Instead of the spirit's descending to the level of

the material, the material should ascend to the level of the
spirit.

Convention is one of the most important factors in life.
There was a time when even philosophers thought that the
universal acceptance of an idea was a certain proof of its
truth. Philosophers now know that there is no lie, no piece
of folly, which cannot gain universal acceptance under suit-
able conditions.

Immorality places the "I" first and foremost, leaving
nothing for the next fellow. True justice places the "I"
and the "Thou" upon an equal basis.

AARON DAVID GORDON
(1856-1922)

Father of the idea of "labor as a religion" and a great idealist
who lived as he preached, Aaron David Gordon became the symbol of a people's regeneration through work. In Israel he became
the teacher of the working people, a writer who exerted an influence
by his idealistic work as well as by his pen.

He came to Israel at the age of forty-eight from a small Ukrainian town, and soon became a member of the oldest collective—
Daganiah. As a follower of Tolstoy, he considered honest labor
an integral part of life.

We lack the one thing needful—work. Not compulsory
work, but that kind of work with which such a being as
man is organically and naturally integrated and through
which, in turn, a people is integrated with its earth and
that culture which is rooted in the soil and in work.

In the Diaspora, taught Gordon, the Jewish people, being a
minority, can have no life of their own.

What we have in the Diaspora is a life which we have re-
fashioned according to the spirit of the time and land in
which we are living. In Israel where a new life is being
created it is necessary to rebuild national life from the bot-

tom up. A living culture, however, embraces the whole of life. Everything that life creates for life's necessities, that is culture—digging the earth, building houses and roads; such work, such labor, such activity is culture, or, rather, the basis and substance of culture. The order and manner and way according to which these things are done produce the form of a national culture. From this the highest culture—science, art, philosophy, poetry, ethics, religion—draws nourishment.

Gordon therefore opposed those who viewed national culture from the standpoint of art. "These high and sublimated aspects of culture are only the cream at the top of a national culture in the widest sense. But can one produce cream who has no milk? Or is it possible to skim one's own cream from a stranger's milk?"

SIMON DUBNOW
(1860-1941)

Russian-born Simon Dubnow wrote definitive treatises on the history of the Jews in Russia. He also produced a gifted three-volume study of Hasidism, a work based largely on original research and newly discovered documents. However, his magnum opus was his ten-volume history of the Jewish people, which of course demanded comparison with the work of Heinrich Graetz a generation earlier. Dubnow avoided many of the weaknesses of Graetz's history. His objectivity was considerably more in evidence. As might be expected, he gave full due to eastern European Judaism. He gave more emphasis than did Graetz to social and other factors, in an attempt to take account of greater complexity in history and interpretation.

MICAH JOSEPH BERDYCZEWSKI
(1865-1921)

A prominent Hebrew writer, an opponent of Ahad Ha-Am, Berdyczewski represented, to some extent, some of the ideas of Friedrich Nietzsche in Hebrew literature—something that sounded strange in the language of the prophets. Speaking in Hebrew of the Superman, of Power and Will, of the merciless Man for whose ambition masses of people might go to their doom was in opposition to everything Judaism had taught and preached. Even the lighter ideas of individualism which Berdyczewski defended so fiercely in his essays carried within them seeds of destruction.

Berdyczewski's assault upon the Talmudic sages for directing Jewish life towards the book and the Torah schools was rebellious to the extreme. "The sages," he wrote, "were more concerned about the school of Jamnia than about the saving of the citadel of Jerusalem." The despotic King Herod, the Edomite slave, as the Talmud calls him, was a superior type of man who was about to erect an Empire, except for the rabbis who thwarted his plans. This fiery critic even refused to acknowledge the historic role of such personalities as Ezra and Nehemiah.

Berdyczewski demanded, in the language of Nietzsche, a "transvaluation of values"; in the process of such basic changes, he cast doubts on everything which had been regarded as positive and certain in Judaism. Against all "certainties" he raised the axe of the doubting mind. To Berdyczewski the process of questioning and doubting seemed progressive, a "well of thought," whereas what was accepted as certain was static and represented "the extinction of thought." Illustrative of the new Jew who revolted against the ancient and time-hallowed traditions, he was constantly searching for a new departure.

Berdyczewski distinguished himself also as a novelist. He was among the first Hebrew writers who saw the collapse of the traditional Jewish family. Understanding the young because he himself rebelled against his faith and against his father, a pious and venerable rabbi, Berdyczewski wrote perceptively about these problems.

ISRAEL ZINBERG
(1873-1943)

Israel Zinberg is famous as the author of an eight-volume work in Yiddish on the history of Jewish literature—later translated into Hebrew. It is one of the most important works on Hebrew and Yiddish literature. Literary history was Zinberg's avocation. By profession he was a chemical engineer in Leningrad and perished in a Stalin purge in the Soviet Union.

JOSEPH KLAUSNER
(1874-1958)

Joseph Klausner was born in Lithuania and studied in Germany, where he took his doctorate at the University of Heidelberg. He returned to Russia and edited, for the next twenty-five years, the important journal Ha-Shiloah. In 1919 he settled in Israel and later became professor of modern Hebrew literature at Hebrew University in Jerusalem. In 1924 he received the Bialik Prize in Jewish Learning. He is noted as historian, editor, critic, essayist, and effective modernizer of the Hebrew language. Klausner was editor-in-chief of *Encyclopedia Hebraica*. He authored a five-volume history of the Second Commonwealth period and a six-volume history of modern Hebrew literature, which is a recognized classic. His books on Jesus and Paul (*Jesus of Nazareth* and *From Jesus to Paul*), tracing the growth of Christianity from a Jewish perspective, have been acclaimed by Christian and Jewish critics alike. He also produced a number of monographs on famous Jewish poets, for example, Leon Gordon, Hayyim N. Bialik, Saul Tchernihowsky.

LEO BAECK
(1875-1956)

Leo Baeck was one of the great rabbis and theologians of the 20th century. In 1939, when Jewish life in Germany became unbearable, Baeck was invited to come to America. Jews from many countries appealed to him to leave his country, but Baeck refused. He did not want to abandon his congregation in Berlin. He heroically stood up against the ruthless Nazi regime and was deported to Terezin in Czechoslovakia, where he was held for almost two years.

Baeck was a prolific writer. His book *The Essence of Judaism*, published in German and in English, is regarded as a standard work interpreting Judaism and Jewish history. The prophets, according to Baeck, were the true prototypes of Judaism. They were the ones to declare their faith in God, their faith in man, and their faith in mankind. Although Baeck does not oppose ritual and ceremonial traditions, he takes the stand that the moral law as expounded by the prophets, the Talmudic sages, and the codifiers is the essence of Judaism. The ceremonial customs are outward forms which are changeable. Baeck accepts these principles as basic: the divine in man (man created in the "image of God"), human life as a perpetual striving for moral perfection, the "priesthood of Israel." Israel's chosenness is not based on superiority, a level that other people cannot reach. What it does mean is greater responsibility, a stricter standard, and a willingness to suffer for an ideal. Israel is close to God only when she adheres to His laws. If, as it often happens, Israel abandons God's ways, then there is a separation between God and her. During mankind's recorded history, other nations have had an opportunity to lead the world to justice and love. They all failed. Israel, however, accepted the challenge of proclaiming God's name to the whole world and of realizing the moral law in life. The Jewish people are the only people in the world who, despite their failures and sinfulness, have been holding their own as "the people of the Covenant." For Baeck, religion is the only bond that can keep the Jewish people together. In his view, "Israel will either live as God has commanded, or it will not live at all." Baeck opposed political Zionism, though later in his life he changed his attitude toward the State of Israel considerably.

In 1927, Baeck's book *The Pharisees*, published first in German and later translated into English, made a furor in the Christian churches. In the New Testament, the Pharisees were portrayed as hypocrites, and by implication were blamed for the crucifixion of Jesus. Baeck proved that the Pharisees were the most progressive party at that time. Although it is true that he was not the first one to have taken this stand, he nevertheless succeeded in presenting such a good case, with his great learning and profound historic insight, that he was well heard in the scholarly world. It resulted in a lively international discussion that was halted only with the advent of Nazism. His last book,

Dieses Volk: Judische Existenz (This People: Jewish Existence), was composed while he was in the concentration camp.

Baeck died in London in 1956.

MARTIN BUBER
(1878-1965)

Martin Buber was recognized both by Jews and Christians as one of the most profound thinkers of our time, having distinguished himself in religious philosophy, in interpreting the Bible and Judaism, and in bringing to the attention of the world the inner meaning and significant role of Hasidism.

Buber possessed a broad Jewish and general education. From his grandfather, the well known scholar, Shloime Buber, in whose home he was reared during many years, he received his knowledge of the Bible and the Talmud. Later he studied in Vienna and in Berlin: philosophy, psychology, and sociology. After having received his doctoral degree, he devoted himself to journalistic work as a Zionist, first as editor of Theodor Herzl's journal, *Die Welt*. Disenchanted with political Zionism, Buber aligned himself for a while with the minority faction within the Zionist movement—the cultural Zionism of Ahad Ha-Am.

It was about this time that, as he later admitted, he found himself living "without the presence of the divine." Hasidism drew his attention. For years he studied Hasidic literature: miracle stories, interpretations replete with fervor and faith and joy, tales of devotion and profound moral teaching. From this, Buber produced *Tales of the Hasidim*, resurrecting for Judaism the richness of the Hasidic world, which was largely forgotten or unknown; and what was known was largely the objectionable features of the movement as represented by its opponents. As a result of Buber's collection, Hasidic tales became a part of both Jewish culture and European culture as well. Buber's *Tales* has been called "one of the great religious books of all time." In 1949, Herman Hesse, when he nominated Buber for the Nobel Prize in Literature, claimed that Buber was

"not only one of the few wise men living on earth," but also "he
has enriched world literature with a genuine treasure as has no
other living author—the *Tales of the Hasidim*."

As a matter of fact, Buber found himself through Hasidism. To
him, the Hasidic movement was nothing less than an attempt to establish a just community upon the basis of love of God and love
between man and man. Those two ideas became the axis upon
which Buber founded his own philosophy of life. Here we come to
Buber's two original ideas: the I-Thou idea and the I-It idea, set
forth in his famous book, *Ich und Du* (I and Thou), published in
1923. To grasp the difference between them means the same as entering into Buber's thought world. The remainder of this teaching
can be seen as an interpretation of these ideas. Both ideas express
relationships, but there is an abyss between the I-Thou relationship
and the I-It relationship. In the latter relationship, man relates
himself to another as to an "it," an object. When one looks at another as an "it," the latter is no more than a thing to be used; it
is a subject-object relationship. As a thing, an object to be used, it
remains closed. Just as a chair or anything else remains internally
closed, so there is no "closeness" between man and man in this
relationship. It is otherwise in the relation between man and man in
the I-Thou relationship. On this level one has to enter "the other
side," penetrating into the world of another. A dialogue between
them must be established. They must meet each other. This mutual
and two-sided experience Buber regards as the essence of friendship and love.

Buber thinks that man becomes Man, that is, really human, not
when he thinks of himself, but rather when he establishes relations
with another man on an "I-Thou" basis, neither for the sake of exploit-
ing or using him, nor for the sake of remaking him. The relationship must be between two personalities, each having his own right to
be what he is. Only then can there be a real dialogue between man
and man.

The same principle, the I-Thou principle, in a much wider and
deeper sense, must be applied to the relationship between man and
God. God, according to Buber, is the great Thou, in fact the greatest Thou that man can be related to. He is the eternal. He is the permanent Thou. His presence never fails. He is always on time and

in the right place. It is man that is absent, if the I-Thou dialogue does not take place. God is ever ready to accept man as His companion if only the latter opens his heart to him. But if the "I" is not there, the "Thou" has no one to talk to.

Buber holds that as long as man stays in the world of the "It" he cannot hope to find God. If one wants to find God he must transform himself into the world of the "Thou." Nay, more, in the "Thou" one finds God without seeking him. God actually waits there for man to come. Just as one who gives way to the world, dedicating himself to all its pleasures, cannot find God, so one who renounces the world, separating himself from it, cannot find God. The materialist reduces the world to the level of the "It," whereas the mystic tries to reduce himself to almost "nothing." Both fail in their efforts because God reveals himself only in a dialogue based upon the "Thou" in which the two, in this case God and man, confront each other on a relative equal footing. The purpose of the confrontation between God and man is to build a mutual relationship between man and man. Meeting God, according to Buber, does not mean that man is submerging himself in a supernatural world, to the exclusion of life as we know it, but rather confirms that life is meaningful. When this confirmation is realized, then man must return to the community in order to integrate his "I" in the "I" of the community.

Buber thinks that a community without God is impossible. True, people can put up false gods, but this would at best constitute a *collectivity*, in which the individual members are just mechanically and numerically "united." A *community* is distinguished by each member being related to a "living Center" and to each other; here there is communication between I's and Thou's, a dialogue.

Buber's philosophy of the I-Thou dialogue has exerted a profound influence upon the thinking of our age. It is a highly dynamic theory that can be applied in psychology, sociology, education, and other fields. His influence reaches far into the Christian world. Currently he is the one Jewish thinker in whom both Judaism and Christianity have met, not by virtue of a compromise on the part of Judaism, but in a dialogue secured by the I-Thou relationship.

Five quotations from Buber:

[The] most powerful expression in the primordial world is

the myth of the fall of man as it was incorporated in the book of Genesis. This myth establishes the elements of good and evil, the clearest and most telling of all the contents of man's inner duality, with consummate power and clearness. It represents man's task of being in the nature of a choice, and represents the whole future as dependent upon this decision.

The spiritual process of Judaism effectuates itself historically as the striving after an ever more perfect realization of three independent ideas: the Idea of Unity, the Idea of Action, the Idea of the Future. When I speak of ideas I do not, evidently, mean abstract concepts, but natural tendencies in the national character, which manifest themselves so powerfully and so enduringly as to produce that complex or web of spiritual works and values which may be fairly pronounced to be the absolute life of the people of Israel.

Open the great record of Jewish antiquity wherever you please; read in the historical books the tales of the apostasy from Yahveh or read in the prophetical books the call to the conquest of injustice or in Job the expression of insight into the necessity of inner dualism, which the pure will cannot master nor he who fights for his integrity escape, but only redemption can lead him forth from it; or hear in the Psalms the ever-returning cry for cleansing through God—and in all these passages you will find the experience of inner division and everywhere the striving after oneness in the soul of the individual; after oneness between faction and faction, between people and people, between humanity and all other living things, between God and the world.

It is the striving after unity that has rendered the Jew creative. Struggling out of the division of the "I" after oneness, he created the idea of *universal justice*; seeking to bring union out of the division of all living things, he created the idea of *universal love*; striving to unify a riven world, he created the *Messianic Ideal*, which a far later age, largely under the guidance of Jews, dwarfed and trivialized and called socialism.

We must not feel hopeless. If every man of goodwill will do what is in his power, then there is no dark fate.

FRANZ ROSENZWEIG
(1886-1929)

Franz Rosenzweig, born in Cassel, Germany, grew up in a Jewish home that was neither traditional nor assimilationist, in an atmosphere of indifference towards Judaism. He studied medicine but gave it up. Then he devoted some years to the study of history and philosophy, but after a time he started to doubt whether modern philosophy could adequately answer the questions of the individual. He felt a void in his soul that had to be filled with some content. He looked into religion; at first Christianity appeared to be a possible source of spiritual fulfilment, and he was about to accept Christianity, though his parents opposed it. But before embarking upon this course of action, he decided to visit once the synagogue and see what Judaism stood for. He came to an orthodox synagogue on Yom Kippur (the Day of Atonement) in the year 1913 and remained there the whole day. Rosenzweig suddenly discovered a community committed to God by the Covenant of Faith. He experienced something he had never felt before—a faith that was genuinely deep, a historic faith ingrained in the human soul for thousands of years, purified by self-sacrificing deeds and pervaded with Love of Man and Love of God. Rosenzweig, a man at the age of twenty-seven, had discovered that he was a Jew and there was absolutely no need of seeking other faiths. From then on Rosenzweig devoted all his intellectual powers to Judaism. Hermann Cohen's theories of Judaism swayed him tremendously, but his own mind was too dynamic to follow others. Rosenzweig found his own pathway.

In 1918, Rosenzweig started to write his book *Der Stern der*

Erlösung (The Star of Redemption). It was an expresion of the longing of an inspired man who stood face to face with God, a man who lived in his faith. Having visited Warsaw, he came in close contact with Hasidic Jews; observing their ways, he perceived the fervor of their faith. "Never have I heard such praying," he wrote about the Warsaw Jews. Rosenzweig poured his most profound sentiments into his work. He arrived at the conclusion that reason was not the whole of man; being was more than reason could capture or define. Rosenzweig, together with his friend and collaborator, Martin Buber, and the Russian philosopher, Lev Shestov (1866-1938), share history's podium as the three outstanding Jewish existentialists. As such, each expresses, in one way or another, existentialism's insistence about the limited power of reason and of objective truth. Truth must also be verified, Rosenzweig asserts, through an individual's decision, commitment, and risk. When Rosenzweig speaks of man, he means a concrete, existing, individual man, not an abstraction, not Man, not Mankind.

The Maggen David, the Shield of David, with its two triangles placed in reverse one upon the other, was employed by Rosenzweig as the symbol of Judaism, to illustrate Biblical affirmations. He saw God, man, and the world represented by the first three angles of the star; Creation, Revelation, and Redemption by the other three. Thus the Bible affirms the new combinations of God and Creation, man and Revelation, the world and Redemption.

Rosenzweig's collaboration with Buber was on their monumental task of translating the Hebrew Bible into German. As one commentator said: "Whereas Luther's translation had sought to make the Hebrew as German as possible, they sought to make the German as Hebrew as possible, rendering the very cadence and sound of the original." The result was a brilliant success. Though Rosenzweig died before the work was done, Buber finished the undertaking.

MORDECAI M. KAPLAN
(1881-   )

Dr. Mordecai M. Kaplan—scholar, philosopher, theologian—is a thinker in his own right, a profound writer on Judaism and the father of a religious movement known as Reconstructionism. Born in eastern Europe, he was raised in a strictly traditional Jewish home. From his early childhood he learned to cherish and observe the traditions of his people. Endowed with a keen understanding and a love of knowledge, he became an avid student of the Talmud and later Rabbinical literature. He also obtained an extensive general education, particularly in history, sociology, and philosophy. As with many other Jewish thinkers, there occurred in Kaplan's mind a clash between his religious beliefs and practices and modern conceptions nurtured by science.

Kaplan, in rethinking his Judaism as against modern life, reached the conclusion that Judaism is more than religion. Religion occupies an important, if not the most important, place in Judaism. In fact, religion colors everything in Judaism, imprinting its stamp upon every branch of Jewish activity. Yet Judaism covers a much wider and larger field than religion can ever aspire to cover. Judaism, according to Kaplan, is a civilization. Within this civilization called Judaism, which "embraces the entire cultural heritage of the Jews" and is the sum total of everything performed by the Jewish people and everything they are destined to perform, the Jewish religion represents the spiritual values and the consciousness of the people. The question arises then: How is the Jewish religion as it has come down to us to survive in a secular age when the Jew is confronted by the scientific concepts of our time?

Kaplan proposes not reform, as others did, but rather reconstruction, which, to him, means to retain those tenets of the Jewish faith that can be retained and relinquish those that cannot be retained. For instance, the concept of the Jews as "chosen people," which had been accepted since early times, cannot stand in the modern world because it does not agree with modern thinking. Hence there is no reason for retaining it. Also, the God-concept as traditionally presented by historic Judaism cannot be retained in its ancient form. Instead of the "God of miracles" and the "God of metaphysics," Kaplan proposes to substitute the "God of experience." If life itself demands a power which is God, there is no necessity for all the metaphysical and supernatural niceties which accompany the belief in God. If certain old concepts or practices stand in the way, they should be discarded. On the other hand, Reconstructionism exercises caution in making radical changes in Jewish traditions.

HEBREW WRITERS IN AMERICA

During the last two decades of the 19th century and the first two of the 20th, when mass immigration of Jews to America was at its height, literary activity in Hebrew in the United States was almost at a standstill or, at best, not substantial enough to be reckoned with. On the other hand, Yiddish literature showed spectacular growth during this same period, evidenced by the Yiddish press with a mass circulation of hundreds of thousands and the appearance of many periodicals and books, both original creations and translations from world literature, coupled with a living theater successfully maintained in the larger American cities. Hebrew seemed to have failed completely to strike roots in the American soil. The small circles of Lovers of Hebrew that existed here and there, especially in the larger cities, were not strong enough to make themselves felt meaningfully among the immigrants struggling for a living in their erstwhile adopted country. Jewish education generally, rooted as it was in the study of the Torah and of the Hebrew language, was then in a precarious situation. The Hebrew school was not being supported by the Jewish community at large. Indeed, Hebrew cultural life presented at that period a grim picture of failed attempts. Between 1880 and 1900, some fifteen to twenty periodicals in Hebrew were started, but due to lack of support most of them expired after a short life. Only a few survived more than two or three years. Ha-Ibri (The Hebrew), for instance, was published from 1892 to 1898; Ner Ha-Maarabi (Western Light) existed from 1895 to 1897; Ha-Pisgah (The Peak), started in 1890, continued under another name, Ha-Tehiyyah, until 1900. There were some poets and authors in America who were engaged in literary and research activities, writing in Hebrew. Such men were: Menahem Dolitzki (1858-1931), poet and novelist; Naphtali Herz Imber (1856-1909), famous today as author of Ha-Tikvah, the Jewish national anthem; Alexander Kohut (1848-1917), lexicographer and Hebrew scholar; Judah David Eisenstein (1856-1956), editor of the first Hebrew encyclopedia, Ha-Otzar (in ten volumes), and compiler of great anthologies from the literature of the early Middle Ages and the Midrashim. There were scores of other distinguished men of the pen. As we today look back on their work. we find their contributions significant, but at the time they made very little impact in the Jewish world.

A change for the better occurred at the end of World War I, when a new type of Jewish immigrant reached the shores of America. Whereas heretofore most of the Jewish immigrants had come from the lower strata of society in eastern Europe, now at around 1920 there appeared a larger percentage of more sophisticated and better educated Jews, who sought refuge in America from the ravages of war. At this time, we witness a successful attempt to establish a strong position for Hebrew culture in America. The Lovers of Hebrew had come of age. A powerful group of people organized themselves to found a daily Hebrew paper in New York. Owing to the shortage of funds and other difficulties that beset the project, it failed after six months; however, the daily Ha-Doar (The Post) was converted into a weekly which is still in existence today. Most of the young and old Hebrew writers in America enrolled as its contributors. Menahem Ribalov, a young critic and poet, was its editor for well over thirty years. It is now edited by the able writer, Itzhac Ivri.

During that post-World War I period, the Histadrut Ivrit, a society for the advancement of the Hebrew language, was organized. The Histadrut, with branches in many cities, founded a Hebrew publishing company under the name Oghen, whose task was to promote the publishing of Hebrew books, scholarly works and belles lettres. The Histadrut Ivrit has also undertaken during the years a program of lectures and seminars in Hebrew.

In 1939, another Hebrew periodical, a weekly, Bitzaron (Fortification), appeared under the editorship of Dr. Hayyim Chernowitz, the famous Talmudic scholar. It is now edited by a collegium. Further, strong Jewish community support revived the Hebrew schools, freeing them from neglect and from disadvantageous competition with the public schools.

We cannot give here a complete review of the Hebrew writers in America. Among the more significant writers the following richly deserve to be at least mentioned: Professor Simon Halkin (1898-), who was for years on the faculty of the College of Jewish Studies in Chicago and is presently teaching at the Hebrew University of Jerusalem; Dr. Meyer Waxman (1887-1970), author of a five-volume history of Jewish literature, in English, and other works in both English and Hebrew dealing with historical themes and Jewish life; S. L. Blank (1892-1962), a novelist of great talent, who distinguished himself in portraying Jewish village life in Bessarabia; Reuben Wallenrod (1899-), a novelist and critic both in Hebrew and English; A. Epstein (1880-1952), an able literary critic; Daniel Persky (1887-1962), feuilletonist and grammarian, known by his motto, "I'm a slave to Hebrew forever"; the poets A. A. Schwartz (1846-1931), Ephraim Lisitzky (1885-1962), Simon Ginzburg (1890-1944), and Daniel Preil (1911-), each of whom contributed greatly to Hebrew literature; N. Turoff (1877-1953) and Pinhos Churgin (1894-1957), educators and scholars; and many others who have dedicated themselves to Hebrew literature both as writers and teachers.

Appendix A

Important Dates in Jewish History

B.C.E.

c. 1800	Abraham, first Hebrew Patriarch
1300–1250	Moses and Exodus from Egypt
1200–1000	Conquest of Canaan; period of Judges
1013–973	Reign of King David over Judah and Israel
973–933	Reign of King Solomon over United Kingdom
933	Establishment of Kingdom of Israel by Jeroboam
c. 750	Amos and Hosea, prophets
621	Reformation of King Josiah
568	Destruction of Jerusalem and Solomon's Temple by Babylonians
538	King Cyrus proclamation; first return from Babylonia under Zerubbabel
458	Second return from Babylonia under Ezra the Scribe
445	Nehemiah, governor of Judah
332	Judah under the rule of Alexander the Great
c. 250	Septuagint
203	Judah under the rule of Seleucids of Syria
168	Attack on Judaism by Antiochus IV; edict forbidding practice of Judaism under the penalty of death; revolt of the Maccabees
165	Triumph of Maccabees over Syrians; liberation of Jerusalem and rededication of Temple
37	Rule of King Herod over Judea under the overlordship of Rome

A.C.E.

40	Synthesis of Greek and Jewish thought by Philo Judaeus
70	Destruction of Jerusalem by Titus; establishment of school at Jamnia by Johanan ben Zakkai

132–35	Bar Kochba revolt against Rome; death of Rabbi Akiba
200	Compilation of Mishnah by Judah the Prince
219	First Talmudic Academy by Rab (Abba Arika) at Sura, Babylonia
300	Completion of Jerusalem Talmud
499	Completion of Babylonian Talmud
535	Beginning of the Geonic period
740	Conversion of the Chazars
767	Karaite rift
928–942	Saadia, Gaon of Sura
950–970	Hasdai ibn Shaprut, leader of Spanish Jewry
960	Moses ben Enoch founds Talmudic academy in Cordova, Spain
1038	End of Geonic period; academies in Babylonia closed
1069	Death of Solomon ibn Gabirol
1105	Death of Rashi
1135	Maimonides born in Cordova
1144	First ritual charge against Jews in England
1190	Riots in England against Jews
1244	Talmud burned in Paris
1207	Nahmanides forced to leave Spain
1290	Jews expelled from England
1293	Death of Meir of Rothenburg
1300	Moses de Leon discovers the Zohar
1394	Jews expelled from France
1492	Ferdinand and Isabella expel Jews from Spain
1516	Ghetto introduced in Venice
1567	Joseph Caro completes the Code—Shulhan Aruch
1648	Massacres of Jews in Poland
1655	England readmits Jews
1665	Sabbatai Zevi proclaims himself the Messiah
1677	Death of Baruch Spinoza
1760	Death of Israel Baal Shem Tov
1786	Death of Moses Mendelssohn
1791	France grants Jews civil rights
1797	Death of Elijah, Gaon of Wilna
1840	Damascus blood accusation
1882	Massive immigration of Russian Jews to U.S.A.
1896	Theodor Herzl writes *Der Judenstaat* (Jewish State)
1897	First Zionist Congress at Basel
1903	Kishneff pogrom
1917	Balfour Declaration
1925	Hebrew University in Jerusalem dedicated
1948	Ben-Gurion proclaims the State of Israel

Appendix B

Other Hebrew Writers and Scholars

Space prohibited our discussing all Hebrew writers in the text of this book. The alphabetical list below of additional authors and scholars who have contributed significantly in various languages to Jewish culture and literature will, with the brief annotations, supplement the text and serve as a reference tool. Still, the list is partial; omissions and oversights must exist, for a complete roster of Hebrew writers and scholars cannot be made.

Alterman, Nathan (1910–   ). Popular Hebrew poet in Israel.
Anoikhi, Zalaman Isaac (Aronson) (1890–1948). Born White Russia, died Israel. Works: Reb Abba, *Between Heaven and Earth,* others.
An-ski, S. (Solomon Rapoport) (1863–1920). Yiddish essayist and folklorist. Author drama, *Dibbuk.*
Arieli, Levi Aryeh (1886–1943). Hebrew prose writer. Settled Israel 1909.
Arikha, Joseph (1906–1972). Hebrew novelist in Israel. Realist.
Avinoam, Reuben (Grossman) (1905–   ). Hebrew poet. Author Hebrew-English dictionary. Translated English poetry into Hebrew.

Baron, Deborah (1887–1956). Hebrew prose writer in Israel.
Baruch of Worms (early 13th century). Liturgical poet, commentator.
Beer-Hoffman, Richard (1860–1945). Austria. Author drama, *Jacob's Dream.*
Ben-Gurion, David (1886–   ). Statesman, essayist. Proclaimed State of Israel, 1948; first premier.

Ben-Z'vi, Itzhak (1884–1963). Second president of Israel. Born Poltava, Russia; died Israel. Scholar, essayist. Wrote about Samaritans and oriental Jewish communities.

Birnbaum, Nathan (1864–1937). Essayist. Leading Zionist. Participated in Czernowitz Conference (1908) for Yiddish. Turned to orthodoxy in old age.

Bistritzki, Nathan (1895–   ). Novelist. Described life in the Kibbutz.

Bovshover, Joseph (1872–1916). Yiddish poet in America. Poems of social protest.

Brainin, Reuben (1862–1939). Hebrew critic. Spokesman for Europeanization of literature and new literary forms.

Brod, Max (1884–1968). From Prague to Israel. Wrote in German. Outstanding novelist and dramatist.

Burla, Yehudah (1886–   ). Israeli novelist: about Sephardic and oriental Jews. Brought Eastern folklore into Hebrew literature.

Daniel ben Judah (late 14th century). Italy. Liturgical poet.

De Carrion, Santob (14th century). Spanish poet and proverb writer.

Der Nister (Phineas Kahanovich) (1884–1952). Yiddish writer in Soviet Russia. Perished in Stalin purge. Works: Mishpaha Mashber, other novels.

Dinezon, Jacob (1856–1919). Yiddish writer of sentimental novels. Works: Eben Negeff (Stumbling Block), Hanehovim We-Hanyimim (The Beloved and the Pleasant).

Edelstadt, David (1866–1892). One of first American Jewish poets. A workers' poet.

Feuchtwanger, Lion (1884–1958). Munich. One of most prominent Jewish writers in Germany. Works: *The Jew of Rome, Josephus, The Ugly Duchess,* others. Forced to flee Germany under Hitler.

Fleg, Edmond (1874–1963). Geneva. Critic, playwright, translator; one of most outstanding Jewish writers in France. Works: *The Life of Moses, Why I am a Jew, The Land of Promise.*

Glanz-Leyeles (1889–1968). Poland. Noted Yiddish poet in America.

Goldberg, Lea (1911–   ). Hebrew poetess. From Lithuania to Israel.

Güdeman, Moritz (1835–1918). Noted Austrian rabbi and scholar. Wrote extensively on historical themes, especially history of Jewish education and culture.

Günzburg, Mordecai Aaron (1795–1846). Prominent Hebrew writer and Maskil. Autobiography, *Abiezer,* very popular in early days of Haskalah in Russia.

Hameyeri, Avigdor (1886–1970). Hebrew novelist and poet. Born Carpato-Russ. Settled Israel 1921.

Katzenelson, Isaac (1886–1944). Hebrew poet. Perished in Auschwitz. Wrote there his famous poem about extermination of the Jewish people.
Klatzkin, Jacob (1882–1948). Hebrew scholar. Brilliant essayist, philosopher, critic. Editor of Eshkol, Hebrew encyclopedia.

Lazarus, Moritz (1824–1903). Author *Ethics of Judaism*. Founder of Science of Peoples' Psychology.
Leivick, H. (1888–1962). From Russia to New York. Foremost Yiddish poet, dramatist. Works: "Der Golem," "Di Gheulah Comedia."
Levi, David (1816–1898). Italian poet, dramatist. Wrote *Il Propheta* (The Prophet), taking Jeremiah as hero.
Lieberman, Aaron (1840–1880). Wilna. Founder first Hebrew socialist monthly, Ha-Emet. Died New York.
Lyessin, Abraham (1872–1948). Yiddish poet in America. Outstanding for his strong social and national sentiments.

Malbim, Meir Leibush (1809–1879). Russia. Noted Bible commentator. Wrote some poetry in Hebrew.
Mandelkern, Solomon (1846–1902). Ukraine. Poet, scholar. Author Hebrew concordance, Hekal Hakodesh.
Mani, Leib (Brahinsky) (1883–1953). Born Russia: died New York. Outstanding Yiddish lyric poet.
Meidanek, Elijah (1882–1904). Ukraine. Wrote short stories in Hebrew.
Mordecai ben Hillel Ha-Cohen (1856–1936). From Russia to Israel in 1907. Prose writer.
Moses ben Eliezer (1882–1949). Hebrew prose writer of stories and legends. From Wilna to Israel in 1925.

Noah, Mordecai Manuel (1785–1851). American journalist, playwright, philanthropist. Originated the plan of establishing a Jewish colony on Grand Island in New York state which he called Ararat. Works: *Travels, Gleanings from a Gathered Harvest, Discourse on the Restoration of the Jews*.
Nomberg, H. D. (1876–1927). Poland. Yiddish and Hebrew prose writer. Published two volumes of Hebrew stories.
Nordau, Max (Suedfeld) (1849–1923). Born Budapest; died Paris. Zionist leader. Prominent writer in French and Spanish. Works: *Conventional Lies, Degeneration*.

Opatoshu, Joseph (1887–1954). Born Poland; died New York. Noted Yiddish novelist. Wrote also Hebrew. Outstanding work: *Poilishe Velder.*

Pinsky, David (1872–1959). Russia. Yiddish dramatist, novelist. Lived in America; died in Israel. Some of his works rendered into English.

Puhachevsky, Nehama (1869–1934). Lithuania. Hebrew prose writer.

Reggio, Isaac Samuel (Yashar of Goritz) (1784–1855). Austro-Italian rabbi and scholar. Founder of famous rabbinic seminary at Padua, Italy. Works: Ha-Torah Weha-Pilusufiah (The Torah and the Philosophy), Behinat Ha-Kabalah (an edition of Leon de Modena's two treatises, Kol Sakal and Sha'agat Aryeh).

Reifman, Jacob (1818–1895). Russia/Poland. Scholarly works on the Bible and the Talmud: Minhat Zikkaron (one hundred Biblical passages critically explained), Peshar Davar (critical interpretations of Talmudic and Midrashic passages), others.

Reisen, Abraham (1870–1953). Born Russia; died New York. Prolific poet and prose writer; fourteen volumes of poetry published. Translated into many languages. Pen name: Ben Kalman.

Rosenfeld, Morris (1862–1923). Foremost Jewish poet in America. Songs of the ghetto, rendered into English.

Shazar, S. Z. (1890–   ). Russia. Third president of Israel. Hebrew critic, scholar.

Singer, Isaac Bashevis (1904–   ). Poland. Yiddish novelist, critic. Some works published in English.

Singer, I. J. (1893–1944). Poland. Foremost Yiddish novelist. Works: *Brothers Ashkenazi,* Yoshe Kalb, others.

Smilansky, Moses (1874–1953). Born Russia; one of first pioneers in Israel. Hebrew writer famous for stories of Arab life.

Sokolow, Nahum (1860–1936). Editor, Zionist leader, scholar, distinguished essayist.

Spector, Mordecai (1858–1925). Yiddish novelist in Russia. Works: Yiddisher Muzhik (Jewish Peasant), Aniyim We-Evyonim (Paupers).

Steinberg, Judah (1861–1908). Russia. Hebrew writer. Interpreter of Hasidism. Works: *In City and Country, In Those Days.* Translated into German and English.

Tavyov, Hayyim (1858–1921). Wrote stories and sketches from life. Prominent educator.

Tchernowitz, Hayyim (1871–1949). Talmudic scholar. Works: Toldot Ha-Halaka. Wrote Hebrew under pen name Rav Za'yir.

Warshavsky, Yakir (1885–1943). Hebrew prose writer. Perished in Warsaw ghetto.

Wasserman, Jacob (1873–1934). Famous German novelist. Works: *Dark Pilgrimage, World's Illusion, Maurizius Case,* others.

Yaari, Yehudah (1900–   ). Popular Hebrew writer; novels, stories, monographs of early pioneers.

Zangwill, Israel (1864–1924). English writer. Translated liturgical poems from Hebrew into English. Works: *Children of the Ghetto, King of Schnorrers, Dreamers of the Ghetto.*

Zarchi, Israel (1909–1947). Hebrew writer. Wrote about early pioneers and Yemenite life.

Zweifel, Eliezer Zebi (1815–1888). Russian scholar, commentator, defender of Hasidism. Also wrote poetry in Hebrew.

Zweig, Stephan (1881–1942). Vienna. Biographer, poet, dramatist.

Notes

Introduction

1. Arnold J. Toynbee, *A Study of History*, 135.

Chapter 1: Early Biblical Poetry and Traditions

1. Joseph H. Hertz, ed., *Daily Prayer Book*, 703.
2. Biblical Hebrew, the language employed in most of the books of the Jewish canonical scriptures, belongs to the Semitic family of languages. Those languages were indigenous to western Asia in the countries located between the eastern Mediterranean and the Euphrates and Tigris Rivers farther east, and between .Armenia and southern Arabia from north to south. This geographical range of the Semitic languages was not limited, however, to Asia; for in early times Arabic, for instance, spread over Abyssinia, and Phoenician (Punic) reached many islands and the northern seacoast of Africa, specifically Carthage and its colonies, possibly as far as present-day southern Spain.

   The designation Semitic languages is scientifically not exact. It is based on Genesis 10:21, where Shem, one of Noah's three sons, is represented as the progenitor of the Semites. However, the Canaanites, before the Israelites conquered the land, as well as the people of Tyre (Phoenicians), are traced back to Ham (Gen. 10:6-15), although their languages were definitely Semitic. Likewise, the Babylonians and Assyrians were long ago shown to be Semitic. Asshur (Assyria) is one of the descendants of Shem (Gen. 10:22). Some scholars suggest that the Semitic dialects originated from one primitive language.

Generally, the Semitic languages can be classified into four groups: a) *East Semitic*. This group includes the languages spoken in the northeastern part of the Mediterranean world. b) *Arabic*. This group includes classical Arabic, the southern Arabic of the Sabaean inscriptions, and Ethiopic or Ge'ez. c) *Aramaic*. This group includes Syriac, Samaritan, the language of the Nabataean inscriptions found in the Sinai peninsula, and Chaldee. The latter, an Aramaic dialect, is used in Daniel 2:4-7:28; Ezra 4:8-6:18, 7:12-26; in the Targums, and very often in the Talmud. d) *Canaanite*. This group includes Phoenician, Ugarit, Moabite, and probably other kindred tongues. Hebrew belonged to this group. It reached its Golden Age when the great prophets of Israel such as Amos, Hosea, and Isaiah appeared.

The rapid decline of Hebrew as the spoken language of the Jews began, of course, with the destruction and deportation of the Northern Kingdom, Israel, in the 8th century B.C.E. and culminated with the destruction and deportation of the Southern Kingdom, Judah, in the 6th century B.C.E. In the post-Biblical period, Hebrew was effectively dead as the spoken language of the Jewish people. For over 2,000 years then, Hebrew was only a prayer language and a religious-book language. But then in the late 19th century, a revival of Hebrew as the spoken language of a people occurred. Today Hebrew is the official language of the state of Israel. It is spoken by old and young, in the factory and the office, in the marketplace and the street, from the kindergarten to the universities. It is used in literature, art, and science. This miracle of language rebirth, one of the most remarkable phenomena in the history of world literature and world culture, is discussed in chapter 14, "Modern Hebrew Literature."

3. cf. Nathaniel Kravitz, *Genesis: A New Interpretation of the First Three Chapters.*

Chapter 2: The Prophetic Age

1. Julius A. Bewer, *The Literature of the Old Testament*, 90-91.
2. Ibid., 93.

Chapter 3: Poetic Works

1. Bewer, *Literature of the Old Testament*, 340-41, 347.
2. Herbert J. Muller, *The Uses of the Past.*

Chapter 5: Period of the Second Commonwealth

1. Paul Goodman, *History of the Jews*, 65.
2. Albert Schweitzer, *Paul and His Interpreters*, 51.
3. Israel Levi, *Ecclesiasticus.*

4. B. Halper, ed., *Post-Biblical Hebrew Literature*.
5. Philo, *The Embassy to Gaius*, XLIV.349-XLVI.370.
6. Josephus, *Against Apion*, Book I.
7. Christians have long searched for non-Christian literary or historical references to Jesus, contemporary or near-contemporary with his time, as confirmation of his life and work. Josephus' mention of Jesus has always been the major reference, but its authenticity was questionable; even Christians admitted that it was so pro-Christian it must be a later interpolation. Interest continues to focus on this problem. International headlines about this issue were made as recently as 1972, when a scholar announced that he had discovered what may be an uncorrupted version of the Josephus reference to Jesus (cf. New York *Times,* February 13, 1972, 1, 24).
8. *The Jewish Encyclopedia*, vol. VII, 279.
9. Josephus, *Antiquities of the Jews,* Introduction; *Against Apion,* Book I.
10. Josephus, *Against Apion,* Book I.
11. Ibid.
12. Ibid.
13. *Against Apion,* Book II.
14. Ibid.
15. Ibid.
16. Ibid.

Chapter 6: The Talmudic Period

1. Gustav Karpeles, *Jewish Literature and Other Essays*, 52-53.
2. From Romanzero series, Third Book, *Hebrew Melodies,* "Judah ben Halevi," section I.
3. *The Jewish Encyclopedia*, vol. X, 296.

Chapter 7: The Geonic Period

1. Kohen (Cohen): a descendant of Aaron Ha-Kohen, the High Priest at the time of Moses. The Kohanim (plural of Kohen) performed the sacrificial services in the Temple. Levi: a descendant of the tribe of Levi. The Levites did various works in the Temple, secondary to the Kohanim.
2. *The Jewish Encyclopedia*, vol. V, 292-93.
3. *The Jewish Encyclopedia*, vol. XI, 243.
4. Ibid., 244.
5. Isaac Hirsch Weiss, *Dor Dor We-Dorshow,* vol. III, 114.
6. Abraham Berliner, *Migdal Hananeel.*
7. Israel Zangwill, trans., in Morris Silverman, ed., *High Holiday Prayer Book,* 461.
8. Nina Davis, trans., in Nathan and Marynn Ausubel, eds., *A Treasury of Jewish Poetry,* 300-01.
9. Joel Müller [1827-1895], *Oevres Completes de Saadia ben*

Iosef Al-Fayyoumi, Introduction.
10. *The Jewish Encyclopedia,* vol. V, 90-91.
11. Flavius Josephus, *A History of the Jewish Wars,* Book VIII, chapter V.

Chapter 8: The Golden Age

1. Almost 200 years later we have a good example of changed travel opportunities: In the year 1160, Benjamin of Tudela went on a long trip from Saragossa in Spain through Catalonia, France, Italy, Greece, the islands of the Levant, Syria, Palestine, and Mesopotamia. Having reached Bagdad, Benjamin gathered information about the Jews in Persia and the countries beyond the Oxus. He sailed the Indian Ocean and visited Yemen and thence reached Egypt, where he stayed a long time. His trip took thirteen years. Benjamin was a good observer of life, seemingly interested in everything, not only concerning the Jews of his time, but other peoples as well. On returning to Spain, Benjamin composed a book in Hebrew titled Massa'ot shel Rabbi Binyamin (Travels of Rabbi Benjamin). In a printed form it appeared first in Constantinople (1543), and since then has been reprinted many times and translated into Latin, French, German, English, and Dutch.
2. Israel Abrahams, trans., in Ausubel, *Treasury of Jewish Poetry,* 380.
3. Heinrich Graetz, *History of the Jews,* vol. III.
4. Solomon Solis-Cohen, ed. and trans., *When Love Passed By and Other Verses,* 50.
5. Nina Davis, ed. and trans., *Songs of Exile,* 29. Adapted by N. Kravitz.
6. Karpeles, *Jewish Literature,* 200-01.
7. Abraham Cohen, trans., *Choice of Pearls.*
8. Ibn Yahya, *Shalshelet Ha-Kabbalah.*
9. Lewis Browne, ed., *The Wisdom of Israel,* 351.
10. Solis-Cohen, *When Love Passed By,* 59.
11. Ibid., 60.
12. S. Solis-Cohen, trans., in Ausubel, *Treasury of Jewish Poetry,* 158.
13. Emma Lazarus, trans., in Leo W. Schwarz, ed., *A Golden Treasury of Jewish Literature,* 573, 574. Only first, sixth, and tenth stanzas used here.
14. Ibid., 576.
15. Graetz, *History of the Jews,* vol. III, 188-89.
16. Halper, *Post-Biblical Hebrew Literature,* 106-07. Adapted by N. Kravitz.
17. Emma Lazarus, trans., in Schwarz, *Golden Treasury,* 577. Abridged by N. Kravitz.
18. Nina Davis, *Songs of Exile,* 55, 57.
19. Morris Silverman, ed., *Weekday Prayer Book,* 305.

20. Judah ben Samuel Halevi, *Ha-Kuzari,* part II, trans. Hartwig Hirschfeld.
21. Harry H. Fein, ed., *Gems of Hebrew Verse,* 95.
22. Philip Birnbaum, ed., *A Treasury of Judaism.*
23. Karpeles, *Jewish Literature,* 212-13.
24. J. Chotzner, trans., in Ausubel, *Treasury of Jewish Poetry,* 423-24.
25. Georg Depping, *Les juifs dans le moyen age* [1845], 98, as cited in Israel Zinberg, *Di geshichte fun der literatur bei yidn, eiropeishe tkufe,* vol. I, 266.
26. J. Chotzner, trans., in Ausubel, *Treasury of Jewish Poetry,* 426.
27. Karpeles, *Jewish Literature,* 222-23.
28. Halper, *Post-Biblical Hebrew Literature,* 221-24. Adapted by N. Kravitz.

Chapter 9: The Franco-German Lands

1. The polygamy prohibition came to be known as the "Ban of Rabbenu Gershom." What was the context of such a ban at the beginning of the 11th century in the Franco-German lands? With polygamy practiced by the patriarchs in the Pentateuch, Jews felt they could not use Torah Law to forbid it. However, practical considerations could dictate special regulations. Such was the case in 10th century France and Germany. Jews were so harassed by political and Church authorities that movement of individuals, families, and separated families from one locality to another was frequent. Husband and wife were often parted and second marriages consummated in a new town when in fact the first mate still lived—somewhere. Children of the two marriages might later meet and marry, never knowing they were step-children. Such experiential problems which these unstable times forced upon the Franco-German Jews led to the pragmatic "Ban of Rabbenu Gershom."
2. Israel Abrahams, *Ethical Wills,* vol. I. Adapted by N. Kravitz.
3. Davis, *Songs of Exile,* 83. "The Burning of the Law" is part of the Kinnah recited on the 9th of Ab, mourning the burning of the Talmud at Paris in the 13th century.
4. Halper, *Post-Biblical Hebrew Literature,* 183-84.

Chapter 10: Cabala

1. One example of the different methods used by the adherents of Cabala (variously spelled Cabbala, Kabalah, etc.) to divine their revealed or esoteric knowledge is gematria—the calculation of the numerical value of a word, using the numerical value which each letter of the Hebrew alphabet has. For instance, in Genesis 32:4, Jacob sends messengers to Esau, his brother, saying, "I have sojourned with Laban." The Hebrew word for "I have sojourned" is Garti. The four Hebrew letters of the word (Gim-

mel = 3, Resh = 200, Toff = 400, Yod = 10) add up to 613, the number of Pentateuchal commandments, the 613 laws of the Torah. Therefore, comments the Midrash, the full meaning of the phrase "I have sojourned" is to be read: "I have sojourned with Laban, but I observed the 613 commandments." This, then, is an exhortation to Jacob's descendents to be faithful to the Torah even when living among non-Jews.

2. A. Yellinek, *Treasures of Cabalistic Wisdom*, 16ff.
3. Samuel Caplan and Harold U. Ribalow, eds., *The Great Jewish Books and Their Influence on History*, 196-97.
4. Nina Davis Salaman, trans., in Schwarz, *Golden Treasury*, 594.

Chapter 11: Liturgical Poetry

1. Hertz, *Daily Prayer Book*, 263.
2. Silverman, *High Holiday Prayer Book*.
3. Ibid., 152.
4. Ibid., 353-54.
5. Nina Davis, trans., Ausubel, *Treasury of Jewish Poetry*, 330.
6. Silverman, *High Holiday Prayer Book*.
7. Ibid., 141-42.
8. Nina Davis, trans., Ausubel, *Treasury of Jewish Poetry*, 338-39.
9. Davis, *Songs of Exile*, 71.
10. Ibid.
11. Ibid., 93-97.
12. Silverman, *High Holiday Prayer Book*, 441.
13. Maurice H. Harris, *Hebraic Literature*, 369-71.
14. Silverman, *High Holiday Prayer Book*, iii.

Chapter 12: Period of Transition

1. Ausubel, *Treasury of Jewish Poetry*, 176.
2. Karpeles, *Jewish Literature*, 126, 127.
3. Birnbaum, *Treasury of Judaism*, 397-98.
4. Louis I. Newman and Samuel Spitz, eds., *The Hasidic Anthology*.
5. Louis Jacobs, *Seeker of Unity*.
6. Ibid.

Chapter 13: Period of Enlightenment and Emancipation

1. Franz Delitzsch, *Zur Geschichte der Judischen Poesie*, 88.
2. Nina Davis Salaman, trans., in Schwarz, *Golden Treasury*, 595.
3. Leopold Zunz, *Die Synagogale Poesie des Mitelalters*, 9.
4. Fein, *Gems of Hebrew Verse*, 89.
5. Abraham M. Klein, trans., in Ausubel, *Treasury of Jewish Poetry*, 428.
6. Fein, *Gems of Hebrew Verse*, 96.
7. Alice Lucas and Helena Frank, trans., in Ausubel, *Treasury of Jewish Poetry*, 96-97.

Chapter 14: Modern Hebrew Literature

1. *The Universal Jewish Encyclopedia*, vol. I, 50.
2. Mendele Mocher Seforim, *The Travels and Adventures of Benjamin the Third*, trans. from Yiddish by Mosche Spiegel, 15-19, 21-22.
3. A. A. Roback, *The Story of Yiddish Literature*, 139.
4. Joseph Leftwich, trans., in ibid., 111.
5. Curt Leviant, ed. and trans., *Stories and Satires by Sholem Aleichem*, 11, 12.
6. *The Universal Jewish Encyclopedia*, vol. IX, 516.
7. Leviant, *Stories and Satires by Aleichem*, 230-32.
8. Ibid., 156-59.
9. Abraham M. Klein, trans., in Caplan and Ribalow, *Great Jewish Books*, 333-34.
10. P. M. Raskin, trans., in Silverman, *High Holiday Prayer Book*, 388.
11. Reginald V. Feldman, trans., in Ausubel, *Treasury of Jewish Poetry*, 75.
12. I. M. Lask, trans., in ibid., 258.
13. Harry H. Fein, trans., in ibid., 334.
14. Joseph Klausner, *Historiah Shel Hasifruth Haivrith Hahadasha*.
15. From a short story, Ha-Nidach (The Banished).
16. Reuben Wallenrod, *Literature of Modern Israel*, 133.
17. Abraham M. Klein, trans., Ausubel, *Treasury of Jewish Poetry*, 107. Kinnereth is also known as the Sea of Chinnereth, the Sea of Galilee, or the Sea of Tiberias.
18. Ibid.

Chapter 15: Modern Sages

1. Even the great thinkers of the ancient world failed to grasp what Judaism was striving for. Aristotle classified the Jews among the Brahmins of India. Plutarch charged the Jews with being worshippers of the hog, probably because they abstained from eating it. Some of the Roman historians censured them as a people without religion, because they denied a plurality of gods. Florious called them Impia Gens, people with no faith. Appian, Justin and Strabo betrayed the same misconceptions. Tacitus viewed the Jews as worshippers of Bacchus, because Pompey found a golden vine among the ornaments of the Temple and because the Feast of Tabernacles fell at the same time as the celebrations of the orgies connected with Bacchus. All such misconceptions stemmed from the fact that the ancient world stood squarely upon the principle of a fragmented and static world in which the present predominated. With the idea of the Unity of God, the Jewish Messianic hope came into being and the present became no more than a transitory period leading towards the greater future beyond it.

Bibliography

The publishers' names and the copyright dates noted in this Bibliography reflect the acknowledgment information requested.

Abrahams, Israel. *By-Paths in Hebraic Bookland*. Philadelphia: The Jewish Publication Society of America, 1920.

———. *Chapters on Jewish Literature*. Philadelphia: The Jewish Publication Society of America, 1899.

———. *Ethical Wills*. Philadelphia: The Jewish Publication Society of America, 1926.

Aharoni, Yohanan and Michael Avi-Yonah. *The Macmillan Bible Atlas*. New York: The Macmillan Company, 1968.

Albright, William F. *Archaeology and the Religion of Israel*. Baltimore: The Johns Hopkins Press, 1942.

———. *From the Stone Age to Christianity: Monotheism and the Historical Process*, 2nd Edition. Garden City: Doubleday and Company (Anchor Books), 1957.

Alt, Albrecht. *Essays on Old Testament History and Religion*. Translated by R. A. Wilson. Garden City: Doubleday and Company (Anchor Books), 1957.

Ausubel, Nathan. *Pictorial History of the Jewish People from Bible Times to Our Own*. New York: Crown Publishing Company, 1953.

Ausubel, Nathan and Marynn, eds. *A Treasury of Jewish Poetry*. New York: Crown Publishing Company, 1957.

Bade, William Frederic. *The Old Testament in the Light of Today*. Boston: Houghton Mifflin, 1915.

Bader, Gershom. *Jewish Spiritual Heroes*. 3 vols. New York: Pardes Publishing Company, 1940.

Baron, Salo Wittmayer and Joseph L. Blau. *Judaism: Post-Biblical and Talmudic Period*. New York: Liberal Arts Press, 1954.

Beebe, H. Keith. *The Old Testament*. Belmont: Dickenson Publishing Company, 1970.

Bentzen, Aage. *Introduction to the Old Testament*. Copenhagen: G.E.C. Gadd, 1952.

Berliner, Abraham. *Migdal Hanaeel*. Leipzig, 1896.

Bertholet, Alfred. *Das Buch Hesekiel*. Leipzig, 1897.

Bewer, Julius A. *The Literature of the Old Testament*. New York: Columbia University Press, 1962.

Binns, L. Elliott. *The Jewish People and Their Faith*. Cambridge, England, 1929.

Birnbaum, Philip, ed. *A Treasury of Judaism*. New York: Hebrew Publishing Company, 1957.

Blackman, Philip, ed. and trans. *The Mishnah* (Hebrew and English). 7 vols. New York: Judaica Press, 1963.

Blau, Joseph L. *The Story of Jewish Philosophy*. New York: Random House, 1962.

Bloch, Joshua. *Modern Hebrew Literature*. (In Columbia University Course in Literature). New York: 1928.

Browne, Lewis, ed. *The Wisdom of Israel*. New York: Random House, 1945.

Burrows, Millar. *The Dead Sea Scrolls*. New York: Viking Press, 1955.

———. *An Outline of Biblical Theology*. Philadelphia: Westminster Press, 1946.

Caplan, Samuel and Harold U. Ribalow, eds. *The Great Jewish Books and Their Influence on History*. New York: Horizon Press, 1952.

Cassuto, Umberto. *Commentary on the Book of Genesis: Adam to Noah*. Translated by Israel Abrahams. Jerusalem: Magnes Press, Hebrew University, 1961.

———. *Commentary on the Book of Genesis: Noah to Abraham*. Translated by Israel Abrahams. Jerusalem: Magnes Press, Hebrew University, 1964.

Cohen, Abraham. *Everyman's Talmud*. London: J. M. Dent, 1932.

———. *Soncino Books of the Bible*. 14 vols. London: Soncino Press Ltd., 1967. 6th printing.

The Complete Babylonian Talmud in English. 18 vols. London: Soncino Press Ltd., 1948.

Cooke, George Albert. *The Book of Ezekiel*. 2 vols. New York: Charles Scribners and Sons, 1937.

Danby, Herbert. *Mishnah* (English). London: Oxford University Press, 1933-50.

Davis, Nina, ed. and trans. *Songs of Exile by Hebrew Poets*. Philadelphia: The Jewish Publication Society of America, 1901.

Davis (Salaman), Nina. *Selected Poems of Judah Halevi*. Philadelphia: The Jewish Publication Society of America, 1901.

Delitzsch, Franz. *Zur Geschichte der Judischen Poesie*. Leipzig: Karl Tauchnitz, 1836.

Deutsch, Emanuel. *The Talmud*. Philadelphia: The Jewish Publication Society of America, 1895.

Eichrodt, Walther. *Theology of the Old Testament.* Vols. I & II. Translated by J. A. Baker. Philadelphia: Westminster Press, 1961 & 1967.
Eissfeldt, Otto. *The Old Testament: An Introduction.* Translated by Peter R. Ackroyd. New York: Harper and Row, 1965.

Fein, Harry H., ed. *Gems of Hebrew Verse.* Boston: Bruce Humphries, 1940.
Ferrar, Dean. *The Bible and Its Supremacy.* 1895.
Finkelstein, Louis. *The Pharisees.* 2 vols. Philadelphia: The Jewish Publication Society of America, 1938.
Fowler, Henry Thatcher. *The Origin and Growth of the Hebrew Religion.* Chicago: University of Chicago Press, 1916.
Franck, Adolphe. *The Kabbalah.* New Hyde Park: University Books, 1967.
Freedman, Dr. H. and Maurice Simon, eds. *Midrash rabbah.* 10 vols. London: The Soncino Press Ltd., 1931 edition.

Gedaliah ibn Yahya. *Shalshelet Ha-Kabbalah.* Reprint of Venice edition. Jerusalem, 1962.
Geiger, Abraham. *Das Judenthum und Seine Geshichte.* Breslau,1910.
Ginzberg, Louis. *The Legends of the Jews.* 7 vols. Philadelphia: The Jewish Publication Society of America, 1968.
————. *Students, Scholars and Saints.* Philadelphia: The Jewish Publication Society of America, 1928.
Goldin, Judah, ed. *The Living Talmud: The Wisdom of the Fathers With Classical Commentaries.* New York: New American Library, 1957.
Goodman, Paul. *History of the Jews.* New York: E. P. Dutton, 1930.
Gordis, Robert. *Koheleth: The Man and His World.* 2nd augm. ed. New York: Bloch Publishing Company, 1955.
Gordon, Cyrus H. *Introduction to Old Testament Times.* Ventnor, New Jersey: Ventnor Publishing Incorporated, 1953.
Graetz, Heinrich. *Popular History of the Jews.* New York: Hebrew Publishing Company, 1930.
Guttmann, Julius. *Philosophies of Judaism.* First edition. Translated by David W. Silverman. New York: Holt, Rinehart and Winston, 1964.

Halevi, Judah ben Samuel. *Ha-Kuzari.* Translated by Hartwig Hirschfeld. New York: E. P. Dutton, 1905.
Halper, B., ed. *Post-Biblical Hebrew Literature.* Philadelphia: The Jewish Publication Society of America, 1921.
Harris, Maurice H. *Hebraic Literature.* New York: Tudor Publishing Company, 1939.
Hertz, Joseph H. *The Authorized Daily Prayer Book.* New York: Bloch Publishing Company, 1954.
————, ed. *The Pentateuch and Haftorahs.* 2nd edition. London: Soncino Press Ltd., 1970.
Hirsch, Samson Rephael, ed. *The Pentateuch.* New York: Judaica Press, 1969.

Husik, Isaac. *A History of Medieval Jewish Philosophy*. Philadelphia: The Jewish Publication Society of America, 1941.

Irwin, William A. *The Old Testament: Keystone of Human Culture*. New York: A. Schuman, 1952.

Jacobs, Louis. *Seeker of Unity*. New York: Basic Books, 1966.
Jastrow, Morris. *The Bible: Song of Songs and the Book of Job* (English). Philadelphia: J. B. Lippincott Company, 1920 and 1921.
Jellinek, A. *Ginze Hokhmat ha-kabalah*. Jerusalem: Makor, 1969.
The Jewish Encyclopedia. New York and London: Funk and Wagnalls, 1901-06.
Josephus, Flavius. *See* Whiston.

Kadushin, Max. *The Rabbinic Mind*. New York: Jewish Theological Seminary, 1952.
Kaplan, Mordecai Menahem. *Judaism as a Civilization*. New York: The Macmillan Company, 1934.
Karpeles, Gustav. *Jewish Literature and Other Essays*. Philadelphia: The Jewish Publication Society of America, 1895.
Kasher, Menachem Mendel. *Torah Shlemah* (Hebrew). Jerusalem, 1926.
Kautzsch, Emil. *Die Poesie und die poetischen Bücher des Alten Testaments*. Tubigen and Leipzig, 1902.
Klausner, Joseph. *Historiyah shel ha-sifrut ha-'ivrit ha-hadashah*. 7 vols. Jerusalem, 1930-50.
Köhler, Ludwig. *Old Testament Theology*. Philadelphia: Westminster Press, 1957.
Kravitz, Nathaniel. *Genesis: A New Interpretation of the First Three Chapters*. New York: Philosophical Library, 1967.
———. *Sayings of the Fathers*. Chicago: Ophir Publishers, 1957.
Kuenen, A. *The Religion of Israel to the Fall of the Jewish State*. 3 vols. London: Edinburgh, Williams and Norgate, 1874.

Leslie, Elmer A. *Old Testament Religion in the Light of Its Canaanite Background*. New York: Abingdon Press, 1936.
Lévi, Israel, ed. and trans. *L'Ecclésiastique*. 2 vols. Paris: 1898-1901.
Leviant, Curt, ed. and trans. *Stories and Satires by Sholem Aleichem*. New York: Thomas Yoseloff, 1959.
Lieberman, Saul. *Hellenism in Jewish Palestine*. New York: Jewish Theological Seminary, 1950.
Lods, Adolphe. *The Prophets and the Rise of Judaism*. New York: E. P. Dutton, 1937.

Malter, Henry. *Saadia Gaon, His Life and Work*. Philadelphia: The Jewish Publication Society of America, 1921.
May, Herbert G., ed. *Oxford Bible Atlas*. London: Oxford University Press, 1962.
Moore, George Foot. *Judaism in the First Century of the Christian Era.*

2 vols. Cambridge: Harvard University Press, 1927–30.

Moses ben Nahman. *Commentary on Genesis*. New York: Shiloh Press, 1970.

Muller, Herbert J. *The Uses of the Past*. Oxford: Oxford University Press, 1952.

Müller, Joel, ed. *Oeuvres Complètes de Saadia ben Josef al-Fayyoumi*. Vol. 9. Paris: E. Leroux, 1897.

Neumark, D. *The Philosophy of the Bible*. Cincinnati: Ark Publishing Company, 1918.

Newman, Louis I. and Samuel Spitz, eds. *The Hasidic Anthology*. New York: Schocken Books, 1963.

Noth, Martin. *The History of Israel*. 2nd edition. New York: Harper and Row, 1960.

Oesterley, William Oscar Emil ben Sira. *Jews and Judaism During the Greek Period*. New York: Macmillan Company, 1941.

Orlinsky, Harry Meyer. *Ancient Israel*. Ithaca, New York: Cornell University Press, 1954.

Pederson, Johs. *Israel: Its Life and Culture*. London: Oxford University Press, 1947.

Pheiffer, Robert H. *Introduction to the Old Testament*. New York: Harper Brothers, 1948.

———. *Religion in the Old Testament: The History of Spiritual Triumph*. Edited by Charles Conrad Forman. New York: Harper Brothers, 1961.

Philo. *The Embassy to Gaius*. Translated by F. H. Colson. Cambridge: Harvard University Press, 1962.

Radin, Max. *The Jews Among the Greeks and Romans*. Philadelphia: The Jewish Publication Society of America, 1915.

Renan, Ernest. *Histoire du Peuple d'Israel*. Paris: Calmann Lévy, 1887–1893.

Ringgren, Helmer. *Israelite Religion*. Translated by David E. Green. Philadelphia: Fortress Press, 1966.

Roback, A. A. *The Story of Yiddish Literature*. New York: Yiddish Scientific Institute, 1940.

Rosenbaum, Rev. M. and Dr. A. M. Silberman. *The Pentateuch*. Annotated. New York: The Hebrew Publishing Company, 1965.

Roth, Cecil. *Personalities and Events in Jewish History*. Philadelphia: The Jewish Publication Society of America, 1954.

Rowley, Harold H. *The Faith of Israel: Aspects of Old Testament Thought*. Philadelphia: Westminster Press, 1957.

———. *The Zodokite Fragments and the Dead Sea Scrolls*. Oxford: Blackwell, 1952.

Schecter, Solomon. *Some Aspects of Rabbinic Theology*. New York: Behrman House, 1936.

————. *Studies in Judaism.* Third Series. Philadelphia: The Jewish Publication Society of America, 1924.

Schwarz, Leo W., ed. *A Golden Treasury of Jewish Literature.* New York: Rinehart & Company, 1937.

————. *Great Ages and Ideas of the Jewish People.* New York: Random House, 1956.

Schweitzer, Albert. *Paul and His Interpreters.* New York: The Macmillan Company, 1950.

Seforim, Mendele Mocher. *The Travels and Adventures of Benjamin The Third.* Translated by Mosche Spiegel. New York: Schocken Books, 1949.

Sellin, Ernst. *Introduction to the Old Testament.* Revised by Georg Fohrer. Translated by David E. Green. New York: Abingdon Press, 1968.

Silverman, Morris, ed. *High Holiday Prayer Book.* Hartford: Prayer Book Press, 1951.

————. *Weekday Prayer Book.* Hartford: Prayer Book Press, 1942.

Slouschz, Nahum. *The Renascence of Hebrew Literature.* Philadelphia: The Jewish Publication Society of America, 1909.

Smith, William Robertson. *Prophets of Israel.* New York: D. Appleton and Company, 1882.

————. *The Religion of the Semites; the Fundamental Institutions.* New York: Meridan Books, 1956.

Solis-Cohen, Solomon. *Selected Poems of Moses ibn Ezra.* Philadelphia: The Jewish Publication Society of America, 1945.

————, ed. *When Love Passed By and Other Verses.* Philadelphia: The Rosenbach Company, 1929.

Solomon ibn Gabirol (Avicebron). *Choice of Pearls.* New York: Bloch Publishing Company, 1925.

Spiegel, Shalom. *Hebrew Reborn.* New York: World Publishing Company, 1962.

Stade, Bernard. *Geschichte des Volkes Israel.* 2 vols. Berlin: Grole, 1888.

Strack, Hermann Leberecht. *Introduction to the Talmud and Midrash.* Philadelphia: The Jewish Publication Society of America, 1931.

Thackeray, Henry St. John. *Josephus, the Man and the Historian.* New York: The Jewish Institute of Religion, 1924.

Toynbee, Arnold J. *A Study of History.* 1 vol. edition. Edited by D. C. Somervell. New York: Oxford University Press, 1947.

The Universal Jewish Encyclopedia. New York: The Universal Jewish Encyclopedia, Inc., 1939, 1943.

Vriezen, Theodorus C. *An Outline of Old Testament Theology.* Translated by S. Neuijen. Newton, Mass.: C. T. Branford Company, 1958.

Wallenrod, Reuben. *The Literature of Modern Israel.* New York: Abelard-Schuman, 1956.

Wallis, Louis. *The Bible and Modern Belief: A Constructive Approach to the*

Present Religious Upheaval. Durham, N.C.: Duke University Press, 1949.

Waxman, Meyer. *A Handbook of Judaism* 2nd edition. Chicago: L. M. Stein, 1953.

———. *A History of Jewish Literature.* 5 vols. New York: Bloch Publishing Company, 1938–1960.

Weiser, Artur. *The Old Testament: Its Formation and Development.* Translated by Dorthea M. Barton. New York: Association Press, 1961.

Weiss, Isaac Hirsch. *Dor Dor We-Dorshow.* Berlin and New York: 1924.

Wellhausen, Julius. *Prolegomena zur geschichte Israels.* Berlin: G. Reimer, 1886.

Whiston, William, ed. and trans. *The Works of Flavius Josephus.* Hartford: S. S. Scranton Company, 1912.

Wiener, Leo. *The History of Yiddish Literature in the 19th Century.* New York: Scribner's and Sons, 1899.

Wilson, Edmund. *Dead Sea Scrolls.* New York: Oxford University Press, 1969.

Wolfson, Harry A. *Philo: Foundations of Religious Philosophy in Judaism, Christianity, and Islam.* 2 vols. Cambridge: Harvard University Press, 1947.

Wortman, Moses. *Torat ha-beri'ah be-Yisrael.* Tel Aviv: 1932.

Wright, George E. and Floyd V. Filson, eds. *The Westminster Historical Atlas to the Bible.* Philadelphia: Westminster Press, 1945.

Zangwill, Israel. *Selected Religious Poems of Solomon ibn Gabirol.* Philadelphia: The Jewish Publication Society of America, 1923.

Zinberg, Israel. *Di geschichte fun der literatur bei Yidn.* Vilna: Tomor, 1929–1936.

The Zohar. 5 vols. Translated by Harry Sperling and Maurice Simon. London: The Soncino Press Ltd., 1949.

Zunz, Leopold. *Die Synagogale Poesie de Mittelalters.* Frankfurt: Kauffman, 1920.

Index

Italic numerals indicate page references to maps.

Aaron, 18, 38, 120
Aaron ben Elijah, 531
Aaron ben Moshe ben Asher, 226
Ab (month), 9th of, 49, 54, 55, 333, 381
Abba ben Zemina, 186
Abbahu, 154
Abba Mari ben Moses ha-Yarhi, 297–98
Abbt, Thomas, 435
Abd al-Hakim, 233
Abd al-Rahman, 232, 235
Abel, 5
Abiathar, 39
Abigdor ben Elijah Ha-Kohen, 325
Abimelech, 88, 89
Abraham (first patriarch), xiv, xv, 10, 14–15, 164, 178, 202, 214, 266, 355, 366
Abraham bar Hiyya Hanasi, 274–75
Abraham ben David of Posquieres, 279, 322–23, 343
Abraham ben Hasdai of Barcelona, 292
Abraham ben Meir ibn Ezra, 200, 212, 223, 239, 268–73, 297, 318, 320, 322, 406, 456
Abraham ibn Daud Halevi, 234, 275–76
Abramovich, Sholem Jacob, 429, 482, 484–90
Abravanel, Don Isaac, 304–06, 354
Abravanel, Judah (Leo Hebreus), 306,

393
Abulafia, Abraham ben Solomon, 347-49
Abulafia, Meir ben Todros, 279
Accentuation (Hebrew language), 225-27
Adah, 5, 6, 67
Adam, xv, 5, 10, 13, 86, 162
Adret, Solomon ben Abraham, 297–98, 332, 338, 348, 354
Aeschylus, 74
Aggada (Aggadic). See Haggadah
Agnon, Samuel Joseph, 520–22
Agobard, Bishop (of Lyons), 218
Agus, Jacob B., 353
Ahab, King, 19
Ahad Ha-Am (Asher Ginzberg), 535–38, 539, 543
Ahai of Shabha, 243
Ahriman (Persian god), 61
Akiba ben Joseph, xiv, 78, 124, 159–60, 164, 167, 181–82, 184, 214, 216, 372
Albalag, Isaac, 298–99
Albalia, Issac, 244
Albertus Magnus, 250
Albigenses, 205
Albo, Joseph, 304
Aleichem, Sholem, 479, 482, 492–503
Alexander the Great, xvi, 94, 96, 170, 224
Alexandria, 97, 104, 113, 122–25, 127–28. See also Philo

Alfasi, Isaac, 242–44, 296, 322–23, 334, 359
Alfonsi, Peter, 291
Al Hakim, 233
Ali ibn Ridwan, 294
Aliyah, xiv, 519–20
Al-Kalbi, 212
Alkabiz, Solomon, 356, 360–63
Alshech, Moses, 356, 360
Amaziah, King, 28
Am Ha-Aretz, 101
Amish sect, 103, 205
Amittai ben Shefatia, 376
Ammon (Ammonites), 25, 29, 45, 91
Amnon, Rabbi, 383–84
Amoraim, 153, 186, 189, 190
Amorites, 9
Amos, 21, 23, 24–6, 27, 28, 31, 37, 143, 561
Amoz, 28
Amran ben Sheshna (Gaon), 194, 370
Amsterdam, *388, 424*
Anan ben David, 205–06
Ananites. *See* Karaites
Anathoth, *20,* 39, 40
Anthropomorphism, 125, 218, 281–82
Antiochus Epiphanes, 65
Antoninus, 183
Apion. *See* Josephus
Apis, 23
Apocalyptic literature, 114–16
Apocrypha, 13, 111–12, 117
Apologetic literature, 116–17
Aquila, 124
Aquinas, Thomas, 250, 278
Ar, 7
Ari. *See* Luria
Arika, Abba (Rav), 149, 184, 201, 531
Ariosto, 397
Aristotle, 216, 233, 251, 264–65, 275, 280–01, 283–84, 297, 298, 302–03, 566
Armilus, 116
Arnon, River, 7, 9
Artaxerxes, King, 87, 99, 135
Ascarelli, Deborah, 399–40
Asch, Sholem, 518
Ashdod, 29
Asherah, 42
Asher ben Jehiel (Rosh), 242, 322, 332, 334–36
Ashi, Rab, 160, 195
Ashkenazim (Ashkenazic), xiv, xvii, 313–14, 323, 331–32, 334–35, 358, 370

Assumption of Moses, Book of the, 112, 115
Assyria, 21, 23, 24, 33, 45, 62, 86, 101, 108, 114, 223
Assyrian script, 96
Athanasius, Yeshue Samuel, 105
Athens, *2*
Augsburg, *388*
Averroes, 294
Avicebron, 250
Avila, 350
Azekah, *20, 49*
Azriel (Ezra), 344–46

Baal, 12, 23, 42, 44, 100
Baal Shem Tov. *See* Israel ben Eliezer
Baale Ha-Masoran, 226
Babel, Tower of, 14
Babylonia (Babylon, Babylonians), *2,* 19, 21, 24, 45–47, 51, 53, 55, 59, 60, 62, 63, 87, 95, 98, 125, 149, 189–99, 202, 207, 221, 225, 231–32, 234, 235
Babylonian Talmud, 149–50, 189
Back, S., 304
Baeck, Leo, 541–43
Baer of Meseritz, 414, 420, 421
Baer, S. I., 452
Banaa, R., 169
Bahaya ben Joseph ibn Pakuda, 252–55, 294
Barak, 9
Barash, Asher, 523
Barcelona, *188,* 194, *230*
Bar Kochba revolt, 148, 182, 396
Barleus, Caspar, 406
Baruch (scribe), 47, 112
Baruch ben Isaac, 325
Baruch ibn Albalia, 244
Baruch With the Epistle of Jeremiah, Book of, 112
Basnage, J. C., 220
Bassala, Moses, 356
Bath-sheba, 19, 90–91
Bedersi, Jedaiah ben Abraham, 337–39
Beeri, 27
Beer-sheba, *8, 20*
Behya ben Asher, 336–37
Bekor Shor, Joseph ben Isaac (of Orleans), 325, 326
Bel and the Dragon, Book of, 112
Belshazzar, King, 60
Ben Asher, Aaron ben Moshe, 226
Bene Mosheh, 222
Benjamin, Israel ben Joseph, 486

Benjamin of Tudela, 450, 486, 490, 563
Ben-Sira, Joshua. *See* Ecclesiasticus
Berab, Jacob, 390
Berdyczewski, Micah Joseph, 539–40
Berechiah of Natroni, 292
Berkowitz, Isaac Dov, 495, 519
Berlin, *388, 424,* 427, 429
Berliner, A., 452
Bershadski, I., 517
Bertinoro, Obadiah, 392
Beruriah, 173–74
Bethel, *20,* 23, 26, 42
Bethlehem, *8,* 86, 87, 317–18
Beziers, 279, *308,* 337
Bialik, Hayyim Nahman, 469, 504–09, 512, 514, 515, 541
Bitzaron, 551
Blank, S. L., 552
Bloomgarden, Solomon. *See* Yehoash
Boaz, 87
Bodelian Library, 254, 258, 392, 532
Bologna, *388*
Bomberg, Daniel, 394
Bonaparte, Napoleon, 54, 426
Bonifacio, Balthasar, 401
Book of the Righteous, 4
Book of the Wars of the Lord, 4, 7
Börne, Karl Ludwig, 450
Bostanai, 190
Brahe, Tycho, 408
Brandstadter, Mordecai David, 478
Braudes, Reuben Asher, 479–80
Brenner, Joseph Hayyim, 518
Brochart, Cunaeus, 406
Brody, *388, 424,* 428, 429, 441
Browning, Robert, 272–73
Bruno, Giordano, 250
Buber, Martin, xiv, 522, 535, 543–47, 548
Buber, Shloime, 543
Bucharest, *424*
Budapest, *388, 424*
Buddeus, 305
Bulan, King, 224

Cabala, xvii, 56, 214–16, 297, 299, 311–12, 326, 328, 335, 336–37, 340–68, 390–91, 407, 421–22, 472, 532
Cain, 5–6, 13, 162
Cairo, 106, *230,* 234, 287
Calabrese, Hayyim Vital, 356, 364, 366–67
Caligula, Emperor (Gaius Caesar), 97, 128–31
Canaan, xvi, 6, 7, 11, 14, 85, 317
Candia, 398–99
Caphtor, 25
Carchemish, *2,* 45
Caro, Joseph, xvii, 335, 354, 356, 358–60, 363, 396, 408
Carpzov, 305
Carthaginians, 94
Cassel, David, 452
Ceba, Ansaldo, 400–02
Cesena, *388*
Chaldeans, 49, 87, 136
Chazaria (Khazaria), 223, 224–25, 236, 237, 264, 450
Chebar, River, 51
Cheremon, 136
Chernowitz, Hayyim, 551
Christiani, Pablo, 295–96
Christianity (Christians), xv, 97, 104–05, 111, 117, 124–25, 127, 133, 205, 210, 224, 233, 234, 250, 264, 295, 304, 305, 309–12, 320, 321, 322, 330, 354, 383–84, 393, 407, 434, 445, 456, 472, 545, 562
Chronicles, Book of, 4, 86, 88
Churgin, Pinhos, 552
Clavius, 294
Clement VI, Pope, 301
Cohen, Hermann, 533–35, 547
Cohen (Kahan), Jacob Joseph, 385–86, 414, 512–14, 525
Cohen, Shalom, 432
Common Era, 172
Constance, *388,* 395
Copenhagen, *424*
Copernicus, 294
Cordova, *230,* 233, 234, 235, 236, 239, 276–77
Cordovero, Moses ben Jacob (Remak), 356, 361, 363–64, 367
Coucy, *308*
Covenanters, Dead Sea, 104
Cracow, 218, *388*
Crescas, Hasdai, 302–03, 407
Croesus, King, 60
Cromwell, Oliver, 405
Crusades, 310, 319, 321, 328, 347
Cush, 56
Cyrus the Great, 59, 60, 63, 87, 98, 148

da Costa, Uriel, 389, 402–04
da Gama, Vasco, 306
Damascus, *2, 8, 20,* 25, 366–67
Dan, *8, 20,* 23

Daniel, Book of, 22, 64–5, 114, 161
Dante Alighieri, 299–300, 399–400
David, King, 19, 21, 23, 39, 69, 85–86, 90–1, 102, 118
David ben Hagar, 239
David ben Meshulam, 371
David ben Saul, 279
David ben Zakkai, 207
Davidic dynasty (House of David), xvi, 23, 28, 39, 53, 87, 118, 149, 178, 190, 367
David Kimhi (Redak). *See* Kimhi family
Dead Sea, 104, 105
Dead Sea Scrolls, 104–10
de Barrios, Daniel, 406
Deborah, 9, 10, 67, 68
Decalogue. *See* Ten Commandments
de Coque, Paul, 479
dei Rossi, Azariah ben Moses, 133, 396–97
de Leon, Moses ben Shem Tov, 349–50
Delitzsch, Franz, 431, 452, 531
Delmedigo, Joseph Solomon, 390, 398–99
de-Lyra, Nicholas, 320
de Mirandola, Pico, 301, 354
de Modena, Leon, 390, 397–98, 399, 402
Descartes, René, 406
Dessau, *424*
de Trani, Isaiah, 325
Deutero-Isaiah (Isaiah II), 22, 57–61, 63
Deuteronomic Code, 84
Deuteronomy, Book of, 10, 11, 43, 156, 472
de Vidas, Elijah, 356
Diaspora, xvi, 98, 191, 207, 356, 390, 482, 511, 518, 520, 527, 538
Dick, Isaac Mayer, 429
di Lattes, Benet, 393
Dilaz, 207
di Lonzano, Menahem, 367
Dioscorides, 235
Dolitzki, Menahem M., 503, 551
Don Profiat Tibbon. *See* Jacob ibn Tibbon
Dubno, Solomon, 428, 434
Dubnow, Simon, 539
Dunash ben Labrat, 237–39, 322
Duns Scotus, 250–51
Dusseldorf, *424*

Ecclesiastes, Book of, 79, 81–83, 111,

456, 472
Ecclesiasticus, Book of, 112, 117–21
Edict of Tolerance, 426
Edom, 25, 54, 63, 108, 116
Edward I, King, 311
Egidius of Viterbo, 354, 393
Egypt, xvi, 10, 14, 16, 21, 23, 24, 25, 29, 38, 43, 45, 48, 49, 50, 59, 96, 97, 104, 108, 111, 115, 122–24, 136, 224, 267, 286, 366
Eichel, I., 428
Einstein, Albert, xiv, 528
Eisenstein, Judah David, 551
Eldad ben Mahli Ha-Dani, 221–23, 372, 490
Eleazar ben Arak, 160, 343
Eleazar ben Isaac ha-Gadol, 313
Eleazar ben Judah ben Kalonymos, 326, 328–30, 347
Eleazar Hakalir, 200–02, 217, 246
Elhanan ben Isaac, 325
Eli (high priest), 85
Eliezer (high priest), 122
Eliezer ben Azariah, 159–60, 169
Eliezer ben Hyrcanus, 181
Eliezer ben Joel Halevi, 325
Eliezer ben Nathan, 371
Eliezer ben Yehudah, 475, 482-83
Eliezer of Toques, 325
Elijah (prophet), 19, 21, 86, 100, 115, 164, 366
Elijah ben Solomon of Wilna, xiv, 354, 370, 414, 419–21, 427, 440
Elimelech of Lizianka, 414
Elisha, 19, 86
Elohim, 84
Enoch, Book of, 112, 115
En-Sof, 344–46, 354
Ephraim, 27
Ephraim ben Jacob of Bonn, 371
Epstein, A., 552
Erter, Isaac, 428, 443, 444–47
Esau, 15, 564
Esdras, Books of, 112, 116
Essenes, 101, 103–04, 107, 214, 472
Esther, 88
Esther, Book (Scroll) of, 156, 221
Ethiopia, 25, 59, 88, 221–22
Euclid, 294
Euphrates River, 14, 45, 51, 222, 560
Eve, 5, 13
Exilarch (Prince of Captivity), 190–92
Exodus, Book of, 10, 11, 156
Exodus journey, xvi, 9
Eybeschutz, Jonathon, 437

Ezekiel (prophet), 22, 51–57, 95, 114, 162, 218
Ezra (Azriel), 344-46
Ezra, Book of, 87
Ezra Synagogue of Fostat, 106
Ezra the Scribe, 64, 87, 94–96, 98–99, 101, 111, 143, 145, 148, 227, 276

Fagius, Paul, 395
Fayyum, 207
Feierberg, Mordecai Ze'eb, 517
Feldman, Aaron, 523
Ferdinand, King, 305
Fermo, *230*
Ferrara, *388*
Fez, *230,* 237, 242, 277
Fichman, Jacob, 524, 525
Finzi, Isaac, 396
Firkovich, Abraham, 459
First Commonwealth, xv
Flaccus, 127–28
Fostat, 106
Franck, Adolph, 214
Frank, Jacob (Frankists), 391
Frankel, Zacharias, 187, 452
Frederick the Great, 433, 435
Freud, Sigmund, xiv
Frishman, David, 504
Frug, Simeon Samuel, 504
Fuenn, Samuel Joseph, 428
Fürst, Julius, 452

Gad, 19
Gaius Ceasar. *See* Caligula
Galadoa, Elisha, 356
Galicia, *388, 424*
Galilee, 132
Galileo, Galilei, 132, 399
Gamzu, Nahum, 181
Gamaliel ben Simeon II, 148
Gans, David ben Solomon, 408–09
Ganz, Edward, 450
Gaon, 187, 189, 190, 197–99
Gath, *20,* 29, 35
Geiger, Abraham, 462–63
Gemara, 146, 149, 153
Geneva, *388, 424*
Genesis, Book of, xv, 4–6, 10, 12, 13, 298
Genoa, *388*
Genizah, 106
Gerizim, Mount, 101
Germanus, Moses, 410–11
Germany, 129
Gerona, *230*

Gerondi, Jonah, 279
Gershom ben Judah (Rabbenu; Ma'or Hagolah), 312, 313–314, 316, 322, 332, 371, 564
Gershon ben Eliezer ha-Levi, 224
Gersonides *See* Levi ben Gershon
Gibeon, *8,* 92
Gideon, 88, 89
Gilead, 25, 47
Ginsburg, Christian David, 100, 395
Ginzberg, Asher. *See* Ahad Ha-Am
Ginzburg, M. A., 428, 476
Ginzburg, Simon, 552
Glueckel of Hameln, 411–12
Gnessin, Uri Nissan, 517
Gnosticism, 214, 219
Goethe, J. W. von, xv, 87, 439, 511
Gog, 56–7, 116
Golem, 409–10
Gomer, 56
Goodman, Paul, xiii
Gordon, Aaron David, 538–39
Gordon, Leon (Judah Lob ben Asher), 467, 468–72, 505, 541
Gottlober, Abraham Baer, 465–66, 485
Graetz, Heinrich, 133, 219, 244, 259, 304, 452, 532–33, 539
Granada, *230,* 239
Great Assembly, Men of the, 96, 98–99
Greenberg, Uri Zevi, 526
Grimani, Domenico, 393
Grotius, Hugo, 406
Gumperz, Aaron Solomon, 433
Guttman, Julius, 444

Habad, 421–23
Ha-Bahir, Sefer, (Book of Brightness), 346–47, 351
Habakkuk (prophet), 22, 62, 106, 108
Habakkuk, Book of, 106, 108
Haberim, 101
Haburah, 101
Haftora, 395
Haggadah, 113, 154, 156, 222, 243, 316–17, 334, 336, 370, 396
Haggai (prophet), 22, 63
Hagiz, Joseph, 356
Hai Gaon, 196, 198–99, 216, 450
Halakha, 154, 213, 334
Halkin, Simon, 552
Ham, 560
Haman, 88
Hamburg, *388, 424*
Hameln, *388*
Hamitic tribes, 6

Hamlet, 74
Hamnuna the Elder, 353
Hananeel of Kairwan, 196-97,
243, 321
Hanania ben Teradyon, 181
Hanina, Rabbi, 186
Hannibal, 220
Hanukkah (Holiday of Lights), 113
Harkavy, A., 224
Hasandlor, Johanan, 186
Hasdai ibn Shaprut, 223, 225, 232, 234,
235-37, 264
Hasid. *See* Hasidism
Hasidism, xvii, 341, 391, 413-18, 420,
421, 427, 474, 532, 543-44, 548
Haskala, 427-28, 429, 465, 519, 531
Hasmonean. *See* Maccabees
Hasmoneans, Scroll of. *See* Scroll of
Antiochus
Hazaz, Hayyim, 523
Hazor, *8, 9*
Heber, 10
Hebraeus, Leon. *See* Levi ben Gershon
Hebreus, Leo. *See* Abravanel
Hebron, *8, 86*
Hegel, Georg Wilhelm Friedrich, xv
Heine, Heinrich, 156, 259, 447, 450,
453-55
Hekalot, 352
Hekalot Rabbati, Book of, 216-18
Hellas (Greece), 34, 122
Hellenism, xvi, 94, 96-7, 103, 117,
118, 122, 125, 132, 534. *See
also* Philo
Henry II, King, 393
Herod the Edomite, 179
Herodotus, 84
Hertz, Joseph, 372
Hertz, Marcus, 439
Herzfeld, L., 452
Herzl, Theodor, 475, 537, 543
Hess, Moses, 439, 529-30
Hesse, Herman, 543
Hezekiah, King, 24, 33, 42, 47, 62,
86, 366
Hibbat Zion (Love of Zion movement),
482
Hilkiah (high priest), 41-42
Hillel, 97, 102, 147, 148, 152, 163,
172-73, 176, 178-79, 182, 183, 276
Hirsch, Samson Rephael, 463-64
History of Susanna, Book of the, 112
Hiwi Al-Balkhi, 212
Hiya bar Abba, 154
Hoffman, David, 452

Holofernes, 114
Homberg, Herz, 435
Homer, 141, 511
Horowitz, Jacob, 524
Hosea (prophet), 22, 23, 27-28, 31,
37, 561
Hugo, Victor, 461
Huldah, 41-42
Huna, Mar, 185
Hushiel, 234
Hutterite sect, 103
Hymns of Solomon, Book of, 114

Ibn Hazin, 220
Ikkarim, Sefer (Book of First
Principles), 304
Imber, Naphtali Herz, 503, 551
Immanuel ben Solomon of Rome,
299-300
Innocent III, Pope, 310
Isaac (patriarch), 10, 15, 266
Isaac ben Asher Halevi, 325
Isaac ben Nathan, 236
Isaac ben Samuel, 381
Isaac ibn Ghayyut, 244
Isaac ibn Gikatilla, 239
Isaac ibn Yashush, 239
Isaac, Levi (of Berdychev), 414
Isaac Luria (Ari). *See* Luria
Isaac of Acro, 350
Isaac the Blind, 328, 343-44, 346
Isabella, Queen, 305
Isaiah (prophet), xiv, 22, 24, 28-35, 36,
37, 45, 62, 85, 106, 143, 161, 268,
282, 561
Isaiah II. *See* Deutero-Isaiah
Isaiah, Book of, 106, 108
Islam, xv, 208, 224, 233, 264, 304
Ishmael ben Elisha, 216
Isny, *388, 395*
Israel (Northern Kingdom), xvi, 23,
25-27, 28, 29, 30, 32-33, 45, 51, 86,
101, 223
Israel, State of, xiv, 483, 519
Israel ben Eliezer (Baal Shem Tov),
xvii, 413-18, 420, 421, 427, 439
Israeli, Isaac ben Suleiman, 207
Isserles, Moses, 354, 358-59, 408-09
Istanbul, *2*
Ivri, Itzhac, 551

Jabal, 5
Jacob (Israel), 15, 39, 317-18, 564
Jacob ben Asher, 334-35, 358, 359
Jacob ben Yakar, 313

Jacob ibn Tibbon (Don Profiat Tibbon; Profatias Judaeus), 294
Jacob of Chinon, 325
Jabin, King, 9
Jael, 10
Jamnia (Jabnah, Jabneel, Yabneh), 142, 143, 147–48, 180, 185, 540
Japheth, 6
Japhethite tribes, 6
Jaroslav, Aaron, 435
Jason of Cyrene, 113
Jehiel ben Joseph of Paris, 325, 331
Jehoiakim, King, 43, 45, 47
Jehu, King, 100
Jehudi ben Sheshet, 238
Jekuthiel ibn Hasan, 245
Jeremiah (prophet), 22, 24, 27, 28, 39–41, 45, 48–49, 50, 52, 86, 168, 200
Jericho, 8
Jeroboam, 23, 86
Jeroboam II, 26
Jerubbaal, 89
Jerusalem, xvi, 2, 8, 20, 22, 23, 24, 25, 28, 29, 31, 35, 36, 37, 39, 42, 45, 46, 47, 48, 49, 50, 51, 54, 55, 58, 60, 63, 78, 87, 95, 97, 99, 104, 106, 132, 147, 149, 281, 366, 390
Jesus Christ, 101, 104, 133, 205, 223, 321, 541, 542, 562
Job, Book of, 22, 74–77, 168
Joel (prophet), 22, 64
Joel Halevi, 371
Johanan ben Zakkai, 147, 160, 168, 169, 171, 179–81, 182, 184, 201, 343, 346
John of Giscala, 133
John the Baptist, 133
Jonadab, 100
Jonah, Book of, 22, 64–65
Jonah ibn Janah, 232–33, 239, 294
Jonah of Gerona, 279, 297
Jonathan, 19
Jonathan ben Uzziel, 124
Jordan, River, 11
Jose ben Jose Ha-Yathom, 161, 200
Joseph, xv, 10, 15, 317
Joseph, King, 225, 236, 264
Joseph II, Emperor, 426, 437
Joseph ben Jacob ibn Zaddik, 273–74
Joseph ben Mattathias. See Josephus
Joseph ben Shem-Tob, 281
Joseph Ha-Kohen, 133
Joseph ibn Migash, 244, 277
Joseph ibn Zabara, 291

Joseph Kimhi. See Kimhi family
Josephus, Flavius, 101, 103, 104, 122, 23, 132–40, 220, 223, 281, 562
Joshua (prophet), 98
Joshua, Book of, 85, 98, 101, 124
Joshua ben Hananiah, 124
Joshua ben Levi, 115
Joshua ben Nun, 221, 366
Josiah, King, 22, 24, 41, 42, 43, 62, 86
Josiah ben David, 205
Jost, Isaac Marcus, 49, 452, 532
Jotapata, 132
Jotham, 89
Jotham, King, 29, 35
Jubal, 5
Judah (Southern Kingdom), xvi, 23, 24–25, 28, 29, 30, 32–34, 40, 45, 50, 51, 60, 62, 64, 85, 86, 87, 94, 96, 98
Judah al-Harizi, 258, 268–69, 273, 287–91
Judah ben Asher, 334–36
Judah ben Meir HaKohen, 312, 313
Judah ben Nathan, 325
Judah ben Samuel Ha-Hasid, 326–27
Judah ben Samuel Halevi, 225, 231, 232, 255, 259–67, 333, 463, 504
Judah ben Saul ibn Tibbon, 294
Judah ha-Nasi (Judah the Prince), xiv, 94, 145, 182–84, 185, 276
Judah ibn Bal'am, 239
Judah ibn Daud Hayyuj, 232, 238–39
Judah ibn Ghiat, 255
Judah ibn Janah, 232
Judah ibn Sabbatai, 291, 338
Judah Lob ben Asher. See Gordon, Leon
Judah Lob ben Zeev, 428
Judah Löw ben Bezalel (Maaral of Prague), 409–10
Judaism, Science of, 450–52
Judges, Book of, 86
Judith, Book of, 112, 114
Justus of Tiberias, 133

Kabak, A. A., 518
Kadish, 192
Kahan. See Cohen
Kahira, Simon, 243
Kairwan, 188, 196, 230, 234
Kalir, See Eleazar HaKalir
Kallah, 194
Kalonymos ben Kalonymos, 293
Kant, Immanuel, 432, 439, 533
Kaplan, Mordecai M., 549–50

Karaites, 204–07, 208–09, 223, 231, 267, 398, 450, 472
Karpeles, Gustav, 146–47, 300
Kedusha, 341
Kepler, Johannes, 301, 408
Khayyam, Omar, 256
Khazaria. *See* Chazaria
Kidron, 42
Kiev, *424*
Kimhi, Dov, 523
Kimhi family: David (Redak), Joseph, Moses, 239, 294–95, 322, 463
Kings, Book of, 4, 86
Kir, 25
Kircher, Athanasius, 342
Kirsch, Abraham, 433
Kish, 86
Kittians, 108
Klausner, Joseph, 429, 515, 541
Kohelet, *See* Ecclesiastes
Kohut, Alexander, 551
Koran, 190, 233, 516–17
Krochmal, Nahman, 428, 441–42, 443, 445, 449, 531
Kuthim, 101

Laban, 564
Lachish, *20, 49*
Lamdan, Isaac, 527
Lamech, 5, 6, 66, 67
Lamentations, Book of, 49, 156
Landshuth, L., 452
Lavater, Johann Kaspar, 433–34
Law (Mosaic Law). *See* Torah
Lazarus, Emma, 454
Leah, 39, 201
Lebanon, 78, 119–20
Lebensohn, Abraham, 428, 444–45
Leibnitz, Gottfried W., 435
Leivick, H., 410
Lessing, Gotthold E., 426, 433
Letteris, Meir Halevi, 457–59
Letter of Aristeas, 122
Levi ben Gershon (Gersonides; Leon Hebraeus), 300–02, 407
Levi ben Jacob ibn Habib, 390
Levi, Israel, 118
Leviant, Curt, 495
Levin, Judah Loeb (Yehalel), 503
Levinsohn, Isaac Baer, 443–45, 465
Levita, Elijah, 227, 393–96, 456
Levites, 101, 107, 192, 221–22, 562
Leviticus, Book of, 10–11, 156
Levy, Jacob, 452
Leyden, 241

Library of Qumran. *See* Dead Sea Scrolls
Lichtenbaum, Joseph, 491
Lilienblum, Moses Lob, 476–77
Linetzki, Isaac Joel, 429
Lippstadt, *388*
Lisbon, *230*
Lisitzky, Ephraim, 552
Liturgical poetry, 369–86
Liverpool, *424*
Lo-ammi, 27
Locke, John, 433
London, *424*
Longfellow, Henry W., 511
Lo-ruhamah, 27
Lot, 14, 15
Lucena, *230,* 233, 239, 244
Lucian, 447
Lunel, *230,* 294
Luria, Isaac (Ari), 356, 364–65, 366, 367, 380
Luther, Martin, 112, 320, 342, 548
Luzzatto, Moses Hayyim, 429, 430–32, 437
Luzzatto, Samuel David, 449, 450, 455–57

Maaral of Prague. *See* Judah Löw ben Bezalel
Ma'aram of Rothenburg. *See* Meir ben Baruch
Maccabean revolt, 94, 96–7, 113–14, 132
Maccabees, Books of, 112, 113, 116–17
Magnus, Albertus, 250, 278
Magog, 56, 116
Mahzor (holiday prayer book), 200
Maimon, Solomon, 438–39
Maimonides (Moses ben Maimon), xiv, 127, 219, 232, 234, 242, 244, 273, 275, 276–87, 291, 294, 297, 301, 302–04, 322–23, 331, 334, 338, 342, 347, 349, 358, 359, 407, 456, 463, 531, 533
Makama, 288
Malachi (prophet), 22, 63–64
Malaga, *230,* 233, 245
Manasseh ben Israel, 404–06
Manasseh ben Joseph of Ilye, 439–40
Manasseh, King, 43
Manetho (Egyptian historian), 136
Manne, Mordecai Zevi, 503–04
Mantua, 220, *388*
Manual of Discipline, 106–07

Ma'or Hagolah. See Gershom ben
    Judah
Mapu, Abraham, 460–62, 476
Marduch, 12
Martini, Raymund (of Barcelona), 298
Martyrdom of Isaiah, Book of, 112
Masorah (Magna; Parva), 226
Masoretes (Masoretic text), xvi, 108,
    226–27, 313, 333, 452, 472–73
Mattathias the Hasmonean, 97,
    113, 132
Mayence, 308, 311, 313
Medes, 45, 59, 88
Megiddo, 43
Meir, Rabbi, 173–74, 184
Meir ben Baruch (Ma'aram of
    Rothenburg), 223, 325, 331–34
Meir ben Isaac of Orleans, 371
Meir ben Samuel 321, 325, 371
Melanchthon, Philipp, 342
Melo, David Abenator, 406
Menahem ben Saruk, 237, 322
Mendelssohn, Moses, xvii, 286, 426,
    428, 429, 432–38, 440, 450
Mendes, David Franco, 431
Mesech, 56
Meseritz, 388, 424, 439
Meshullum ben Kalonymos, 374
Messiah, 104, 108, 114, 115, 118,
    236, 274, 296, 312, 341, 356–57,
    361, 391, 556–57; ben David, 116;
    ben Joseph, 116, 367. See also Zevi
Messianic age, 118
Messianism, 534–35
Methushael, 5
Metz, 308, 313
Micah (prophet), 22, 35–39, 47, 106
Micah, Book of, 106
Midian, 16
Midrash, 96, 113, 117, 156, 223, 314,
    316, 319, 336, 421, 565
Miedzyboz, 388, 414
Mikrah (written Torah), 206
Milo, 89
Miriam, 7, 38
Mishnah, xvi, 94, 145–46, 149, 151–53,
    156–61, 183, 186, 214, 222, 277,
    359, 392. See also Judah ha-Nasi
Mitnaggedim, xvii, 420, 427, 522
Mitzvot, 145
Moab, 7, 9, 45, 87, 108
Modein, 97
Modena, 388
Mohammed, 190, 453
Moldavia, 388

Molierè, 511
Molko, Solomon, 357–58
Molo, Apollonius, 136
Moloch, 12, 43
Monotheism, 10–13, 17, 19, 22, 143–44
Montefiore, Moses, 445
Montpellier, 279, 308
Mordecai, 88
Moresheth (Moresha), 20, 35, 36
Morpurgo, Rahel Luzzatto, 448–49
Moscow, 388, 424
Moser, Moses, 450
Moses, xiv, xv, 7, 10–11, 16–18, 21, 28,
    33, 38, 43, 48, 67, 68, 69, 85, 98,
    106, 122, 126, 135, 136–37, 143, 145,
    163, 165, 182, 201, 211, 221, 233,
    276, 284–85, 454
Moses ben Enoch, 234
Moses ben Jacob of Coucy, 325,
    330-31
Moses ben Maimon. See Maimonides
Moses ben Meir of Ferrara, 295–97,
    325, 346
Moses ben Nahman (Nahmanides),
    295–97, 346
Moses ibn Ezra, 241, 250, 255–58, 263
Moses ibn Gikatilla, 239
Moses ibn Tibbon, 294
Moses Kimhi. See Kimhi family
Moses of Evreu, 325
Muhammed Abh-Dhib, 105–06
Muller, Herbert J., 83
Munk, Solomon, 251, 304
Munster, Sebastian, 286

Naamah, 5
Nahawend, 206
Nahawendi, Benjamin ben Moses, 206
Nahmanides. See Moses ben Nahman
Nahum (prophet), 22, 62
Nahum, Book of, 106
Nahum of Chernobyl, 414
Najara, Israel ben Moses, 356, 367–68
Naomi, 87
Narbonne, 230
Nasi (president of the Sanhedrin), 148
Nathan (prophet), 19, 21, 90–1
Nathan ben Isaac, 312
Nathan Hababli, 191
Nazi regime, 541
Nebozarhadden, 318
Nebuchadnezzar, King, 24, 45, 48, 49
Nehemiah, 64, 87, 94, 98–99, 111, 148
Nehemiah, Book of, 87
Nehunyah ben Hakanah, 346

Neto, David, 406
New Testament, 101–02, 116, 133,
205, 296, 312, 542
Nicholas III, Pope, 347
Nicholai, Friedrich, 433
Nietzsche, Friedrich, 540
Nineveh, 2, 45, 62, 114
Nissim, Rabbi, 243
Noah, 6, 10, 13–14, 560
Northern Kingdom. *See* Israel
(Northern Kingdom)
Numbers, Book of, 10, 11, 156
Nurenberg, *308*

Obadiah (prophet), 22, 63
Odessa, *424*
Omar (Calif), 190
Omri dynasty, 100
Orleans, *308*
Ormuzd, 61
Oshaya, Rabbi, 186
Otto the Great, King, 220, 236
Outside Works. *See* Apocrypha

Padua, *388, 424*
Palermo, 348
Pappa, Rab, 158–59
Pappenheim, Solomon, 428
Paris, 279, *308,* 331, 333, *388, 424*
Parousia, 116
Paul, 541
Payyetan, 200
Pentateuch 10–11, 43, 85, 100, 101,
143, 145, 156, 184, 205, 297, 335,
336, 393, 531, 564, 565
Peretz, Isaac Loeb, 490–92, 495, 518
Perez ben Elijah of Corbeil, 325
Perl, Joseph 428, 443, 445, 447
Persia, 21, 56, 59, 60, 61, 88, 96,
99, 149
Persky, Daniel, 552
Pesaro, *388*
Peshitta, 124
Pharaoh-Necho, 43, 45
Pharisees, 96, 101–02, 103, 542
Pharos, 123
Philistines (Philistia), 25, 29, 35, 86,
108
Philo Judaeus, xiv, 97, 104, 117, 122,
123, 125–31, 369
Phinehas ben Yayir, 195
Phoenicians, 136
Pinsker, Leo, 460, 477, 482
Pinsker, Simhah, 459–60
Pirke Aboth, 174–78

Piyyut, 200–02, 232, 258, 370
Plato, 34, 97, 125, 274, 533
Pliny the Elder, 104, 224
Plotinus, 251
Plutarch, 566
Polonnoye, *388*
Polygamy, 564
Polytheism, 13, 138
Porat, Joseph, 325
Posquieres, 279, *308*
Prague, *388*
Prayer of Manasses, Book of the, 112
Preil, Daniel, 552
Prince of Captivity (Resh Galutha),
149, 190. *See also* Exilarch
Profatias Judaeus. *See* Jacob ibn
Tibbon
Prometheus Bound, 74
Prophet of Redemption. *See* Deutero-
Isaiah
Provencal, Moses, 396
Proverbs, Book of, 68, 79–81, 111, 119
Psalms, Book of, 67, 68, 69, 74,
106, 108, 114, 268
Psalms of Solomon, Book of the, 112
Pseudepigrapha, 112–114
Ptolemies (Egyptian), 96, 113, 122
Ptolemy, 294, 300
Ptolemy Logos, 124
Ptolemy Philadelphus, 122–23
Pumbeditha, *142,* 143, 149, *188,* 189,
190, 191, 207
Purim, Feast of, 88
Put, 56

Qumran, 104–06, 108, 112; hymns of,
108

Ra-Amon, 12
Rabbenu Gershom. *See* Gershom ben
Judah
Rabbenu Tam. *See* Tam
Rabbi (title), 95, 183, 185–87
Rabinovitz, Sholem. *See* Aleichem
Rabina (Ravnayi), 158, 189
Rachel (poetess), 525–26
Rachel (wife of Jacob), 15, 39, 201,
317–18
Ramerupt, *308,* 320–21
Rapoport, Solomon, 443, 449–50
Rashbam. *See* Samuel ben Meir
Rashi (Solomon ben Isaac), 223, 237,
297, 313, 314–20, 322, 323–25, 332,
370, 392, 531
Rav. *See* Arika

Ravnayi. *See* Rabina
Ravnizki, I. H., 506
Rebbe, Bialer, 491
Rechabites, 100
Reconstructionism, 549
Redak. *See* Kimhi family
Red Sea, 7, 17, 68, 212
Regensburg, *308*
Rehoboam, King, 23
Reinhold, 294
Remak. *See* Cordovero
Rembrandt Van Rijn, 406
Resh Galutha. *See* Prince of Captivity
Responsa, 189, 193–97, 241, 243,
    297, 313
Rest of Esther, Book of the, 112
Re'ubeni, Aaron, 523
Re'ubeni, David, 357–58
Reuchlin, Johannes, 151, 215, 342,
    354, 393
Revelation of Rabbi Joshua ben Levi,
    Book of, 115
Ribalov, Menahem, 506, 551
Riblah, 49
Rieti, Moses, 399
Robock, A. A., 491
Romanelli, S. L., 432
Romano, Judah, 300
Rome, 94, 97, 104, 127, 132, 147–48,
    149, 165, *230*, *388*
Rosenzweig, Franz, 535, 547–78.
Rosh. *See* Asher ben Jehiel.
Rosh Hashanah, 174, 194, 370, 371,
    376, 499
Rothenburg, *308*
Rubaiyat, 256
Ruth, 87, 156

Saadia ben Joseph (Saadia Gaon), xiv,
    117, 127, 145, 197, 206, 207–13,
    214, 231, 232, 237, 275, 294, 347,
    370, 450, 531.
Saadia Gaon. *See* Saadia ben Joseph
Saboraim, 189
Sachs, Michael, 452
Sadducees, 101–03
Safed, 356–57, 390
Sahula, Abu Isaac, 292
St. Jerome, 81, 111, 117, 134
St. Paul, 116
St. Petersburg, *388*, *424*
Salamanca, *230*
Salvador, Joseph, 133, 425
Samaria (Shomron), *20*, 23, 33, 37
Samaritan Pentateuch, 124

Samaritans, 101
Sambation, River, 221, 223–24, 347,
    486
Samson of Sens, 325
Samuel (prophet), 18, 21, 85, 86, 89–90
Samuel ben Meir (Rashbam), 317,
    325, 326
Samuel ben Natronai, 325
Samuel ben Solomon of Falaise, 325
Samuel, Book of, 4, 18, 85, 86
Samuel ibn Nagdela, 239, 242
Samuel ibn Tibbon, 255, 286, 291, 294
Samuel of Evreu, 325
Sanhedrin, 132, 148, 194, 390
Saragossa, *230*, 233, 239
Sarah, 14, 15
Sargon, King, 23
Sar Shalom, Mar Rab, 195
Saruk, Israel, 356
Satanow, Isaac, 428
Saul, King, 19, 21, 86, 91
S. ben Zion, 417
Schaikewitz, Nahum Meir, 478–79
Schechter, Solomon, 106
Schiller, Johann, xv, 439, 473
Schnaiur, Zalman, 512, 514–16, 525
Schoffman, Gershon, 518
Schulman, Kalman, 428, 466
Schwartz, A. A., 552
Schweitzer, Albert, 116
Scroll of Antiochus (Scroll of the
    Hasmoneans), 113–14
Scroll of Esther. *See* Esther
Seba, 59
Second Commonwealth, xvi, 22,
    94–140, 219, 396, 442
Second Isaiah. *See* Deutero-Isaiah
Second Temple. *See* Temple
Seleucid dynasty, 96
Selihot, 371
Sennacherib, King, 86, 114
Sephardim (Sephardic), xiv, xvii, 313,
    323, 335, 370, 426, 523
Sephoris, *142*, 143
Septuagint, xvi, 111, 122–25
Seraphim, 28–29, 341
Seville, *230*, 233
Seynensis, Henricus, 150
Sforno, Obadiah, 392–93
Shaker sect, 103
Shakespeare, William, 74
Shami, Isaac, 523
Shamir, Moishe, 524
Shammai (Tanna), 152
Shaphan (scribe), 4

Shapira, M. W., 472
Shapiro, Constantin, 473
Shechem, *8, 89*
Shem, 6, 560
Shemariah ben Elhanan, 234
Sheol, 118
Shephatiah ben Amittai, 371
Sherira Gaon, 197–98, 219
Shestov, Lev, 548
Shiloh, 46, 85, 296
Shimoni. *See* Shimonowitz
Shimonowitz, David (Shimoni), 525
Shinar, 14
Shi'ur Komah, 218
Shlonski, Abraham, 527
Shomer. *See* Schaikewitz
Sibyl, 117
Sibylline Books, 112, 116–17
Siddur, 174, 208, 369, 370, 421
Silverman, Morris, 374
Simeon ben Gamaliel II, 182
Simhah ben Samuel of Speyer, 325
Simon (high priest), 113, 119
Simon ben Isaac, 371
Simon ben Yohai, 349–53, 372
Simon the Just, 96, 102, 174
Sin (Babylonian god), 12
Sinai, Mount, *2,* 10, 17, 98, 144, 145,
    153, 171, 211, 266, 534
Sisera, 9–10
Sixtus IV, Pope, 342
Slonimiski, Hayyim Selig, 464
Smilansky, Izhar. *See* Yizhar
Smolenskin, Peretz, 474–75
Solomon, King, 19, 22, 39, 77, 79, 81,
    91–93, 111, 281, 456. *See also*
    Temple of Solomon
Solomon ben Abraham, 279
Solomon ben Adret, 348
Solomon ben Isaac. *See* Rashi
Solomon ben Judah, 371
Solomon ben Judah Hababli, 371
Solomon ben Samuel, 381
Solomon ben Yeruham, 219
Solomon ibn Gabirol, 199, 214, 232,
    241, 245–52, 255, 259, 274, 275,
    294, 349
Song of Songs (Song of Solomon),
    Book of, 77–78, 111, 156, 472
Song of the Three Holy Children,
    Book of the, 112
Sopherim, 95, 96, 99, 153
Southern Kingdom. *See* Judah
Spaeth, Jonann Peter. *See* Germanus
Speyer, *308*

Spinoza, Baruch, 301, 364, 390,
    406–08, 456
Spivak, O. D., 517
Steinberg, Jacob, 525
Steinheim, Solomon Ludwig, 447–48
Steinman, Eliezer, 523
Steinschneider, Moritz, 452, 531–32
Strassburg, *308,* 311
Sue, Eugene, 461, 466
Sullam, Sara Copia, 400–02
Sura, *142,* 143, 149, *188,* 189, 190,
    191–92, 207, 237
Symmachus, 124
Synagogue, 95, 96
Syria, 25, 49, 96–97, 223
Syrian-Greek dynasty, 96
Syrians, xiii, 25, 45, 77, 97, 233

Taamirah, 105
Tabernacle, 10
Tahkemoni. *See* Makama
Talmud, xvi, 11, 28, 96, 98, 101, 102,
    114, 117, 122, 133, 141–88, 205–06,
    223, 242–44, 276, 292, 297, 310,
    314, 321, 323, 331, 333, 421, 531
Talmud Babli. *See* Babylonian Talmud
Tam, Jacob ben Meir (Rabbenu Tam),
    320, 322, 325, 326
Tanna (Tannaim), 115, 146, 153, 183,
    186, 190
Targum Onkelos, 124
Tarphon, R., 159–60
Tartarus, 139
Tchernihowsky, Saul, 469, 509–12,
    514, 515, 525, 541
Tekoa, *20,* 21, 25, 26
Temple (Second), xvi, 52, 63, 87, 94,
    95, 98, 103, 145, 147, 179
Temple of Solomon, 22, 23, 24, 36, 44,
    46, 49, 55, 86, 87, 93–4, 102,
    116, 147
Ten Commandments, 10, 17, 275
Ten Lost Tribes, 406, 486, 490
Ten Plagues, 17
Ten Sefirot, 352
Terezin, 541
Testaments of Twelve Patriarchs, 115
Theodoctes, 123
Theodotion, 124
Therapeutai sect, 104
Tibbon family, 294–95
Tiberia, xvi
Tiberias, *142,* 143, 226, 279, 287
Tigris River, 560
Tishbeh, *8,* 19

Tishre (month), 3rd of, 55
Titus, Emperor, 132, 147, 223
Tobias, 114
Tobit, Book of, 112, 114
Togarman, House of, 56
Toledo, 230, 233, 334
Tolstoy, Leo, 538
Torah, 10, 47, 56, 96, 97, 98, 99,
    102–03, 107, 117, 122, 123, 124,
    143–45, 153, 156, 162–63, 164, 175,
    176, 181, 192, 236, 350–51, 565
Tortosa, 237
Tosafists (Tosafot), 321, 323–25, 326,
    330, 334
Toynbee, Arnold, xiv
Trieste, 424
Troy, 2
Troyes, 308
Tubal, 56
Tubal-cain, 6
Twersky, Johanan, 523–24
Tyre, 2, 8, 20, 25

United Kingdom, 22, 86, See also
    Judah; Israel
Ur of the Chaldees, 2, 14
Uriah, 19, 21, 90–91
Usha 142, 143, 148
Uzziah, King, 28, 29, 35
Uzziel, Isaac. 406

Valerius, Demetrius, 122
Valladolid, 350
Venice, 217, 218, 227, 230, 388, 394
Vespasian, Emperor, 132, 147, 180
Vienna, 424
Vocalization (Hebrew language),
    225–27
von Rosenroth, Knorr Baron, 342
Vulgate, 117

Wailing Wall, 267
Waldenses, 205
Wallachia, 388
Wallenrod, Reuben, 524, 552
Wars of King Messiah, Book of, 116
Wars of the Lord. See Book of the
    Wars of the Lord
Warsaw, 388, 424
Waxman, Meyer, 552
Weigel, Valentin, 342
Weiss, Isaac Hirsch, 196, 531
Weizman, Hayyim, 537
Wessely, Naphtali Hirz, 428, 435, 437
Wilna, 388, 424, 428–29

Wisdom of Solomon, Book of the,
    112, 116–17
Wolff, Christian, 435, 438
Worms, 308, 328, 331

Xerxes, King, 135

Yahweh, 26
Yannai, 200, 202–04, 246
Yarhainai, Samuel, 149
Yehalel. See Levin
Yehoash (Solomon Bloomgarden), 516
Yehudai (Gaon), 243
Yellinek, A., 218, 348–49
Yemen, 113
Yetzirah, Sefer, 201, 213, 214–16,
    350, 421
Yizhar, S., 524
Yom Kippur, 370, 547
Yom Tov. See Zunz
Yose, Rabbi, 186
Yosippon, Book of, 219–21

Zacuto, Abraham ben Samuel, 306–07
Zaddik, 341, 414
Zadok (high priest), 102
Zalman, Shneor (of Liady), 370, 414,
    420, 421–23
Zamosz, Israel, 433
Zaslavl, 444
Zebadiah, 371
Zechariah (prophet), 22, 63, 68
Zechariah, Book of, 114
Zedekiah, King, 48, 50
Zemah (Gaon), 194, 197
Zemah ben Hayyim, 223
Zemah, Shloime, 522–23
Zephaniah (prophet), 22, 62
Zera, Rabbi, 184
Zerahiah, Halevi, 296
Zerubbabel, 148
Zevi, Sabbetai, 390–91, 414, 430, 463
Zillah, 5, 6, 67
Zion, 30, 37, 47, 54–5, 95, 463
Zionism, xvii, 429, 460, 474–75,
    479–80, 482, 512, 529–30, 535–37
    543
Zinberg, Israel, 540–41
Zohar, Sefer, 349, 350–56, 391,
    449, 456
Zunser, Eliakum, 503
Zunz, Leopold (Yom Tov), 218, 220,
    269, 327, 441, 450–53, 531, 532
Zurich, 221
Zutra, Mar, 171